SCIENCE FICTION IN PRINT: 1985

COLDHND - COLD HAND IN MINE, Robert Aickman, co SCB 1975
COLPMRG - COLLECTED POEMS OF ROBERT GRAVES, Robert Graves, co CAS 1975
COLSSMJ - COLLECTED SHORT STORIES OF M.R. JAMES, M.R. James, co 1924
COLSTWF - COLLECTED STORIES OF WILLIAM FAULKNER, William Faulkner, co 1930
COMBTSF - COMBAT SF, Gordon R. Dickson, an DBL 1975
COSMICO - COSMICOMICS, Italo Calvino, co HBW 1968
CPLSSSA - THE COMPLETE SHORT STORIES OF SAKI, Saki, co 1930
CRC - Creative Computing Magazine
CRMPR30 - CRIME PREVENTION IN THE 30th CENTURY, Hans Stefan Santesson, an WKR 1969
CRN - Crown Publishers, Inc.: New York
CRO - Thomas Y. Crowell
CRP - Crypt of Cthulhu
CRW - Crawdaddy
CRY - CHRYSALIS, Roy Torgeson, oa ZEB
cs - comic strip
CSM - Cosmos Science Fiction and Fantasy Magazine
CSMCKAL - COSMIC KALEIDOSCOPE, Bob Shaw, co GOL 1976
CSMCPRS - THE COSMIC PERSPECTIVE/CUSTER'S LAST STAND, Brian Stableford, oc DRM 1985
CSS - Cassell: London
CSSNDRA - CASSANDRA RISING, Alice Laurance, oa DBL 1978
ct - cartoon
CTCHDTH - CATCH YOUR DEATH AND OTHER GHOST STORIES, John Gordon, co 1984
CTM - CONTINUUM, Roger Elwood, oa
CTNYTLS - CAUTIONARY TALES, Chelsea Quinn Yarbro, co DBL 1978
CUP - College & University Press: New Haven, Conn.
CUTS - CUTS, Carter Scholz, oc DRM 1985
CVL - Cavalier
CYC - Crystal Crone
CYM - City Miner Magazine
DAMNTNS - DAMNATIONS, R.L. Leming, 1984 [Vincent McHardy]
DAWSFRD - THE DAW SCIENCE FICTION READER, Donald A. Wollheim, oa DAW 1976
DAY&NGT - DAY AND NIGHT STORIES, Algernon Blackwood, co CSS 1917
DAYSUNS - THE DAY THE SUN STOOD STILL, Robert Silverberg, oa NEL 1972
DBL - Doubleday & Co., Inc.: Garden City, N.Y.
DCH - The Daily Chronicle
DCM - The Diners Club Magazine
DCT - Delacorte Press: New York
DDL - Dandelion Magazine, Canada
DEADWIN - THE DEAD OF WINTER, Robert Lynn Asprin & Lynn Abbey, oa ACE 1985
DEATH - DEATH, Stuart David Schiff, oa PBP 1982
Dec - December
DEL - Dell Publishing Co., Inc.: New York
DFNS83C - Defense '83 Conference in Las Vegas
dg - digest size magazine
DGC - Darkover Grand Council Program Book
DGHTRGL - DAUGHTER OF REGALS AND OTHER TALES, Stephen R. Donaldson, co BAL 1984
DGM - Dragon Magazine
DHZ - Dark Horizons, British Fantasy Society
DKD - Dark Dreams, c/o Jeff Dempsey, 2 Looe Road, Croxteth, Liverpool L11 6LJ, England
DKH - Dark Harvest: Niles, IL
DMGALHR - THE DODD, MEAD GALLERY OF HORROR, Charles L. Grant, oa DOM 1983
DMM - Dime Mystery Magazine
DMNKIND - DEMON KIND, Roger Elwood, oa AVN 1973
DMR - Democratic Review
DNGRVIS - DANGEROUS VISIONS, Harlan Ellison, oa DBL 1967
DNN - The Donning Company/Publishers: Norfolk & Virginia Beach, VA
DNSTRRM - THE DOWNSTAIRS ROOM, Kate Wilhelm, co DBL 1968
DNT - J.M. Dent & Sons Ltd.: London
DOM - Dodd, Mead: New York
DON - The Donning Co.: Virginia Beach, VA
DR.OX - LE DOCTEUR OX, Jules Verne, co 1872
DRC - The San Francisco Dramatic Chronicle
DRCLGST - DRACULA'S GUEST, Bram Stoker, co 1914
DRD - Dreadnaught Co-operative
DREAMDY - DREAM DAYS, Kenneth Grahame, co 1899
DRF - Dragonfields
DRG - The Dragon
DRG&DRM - DRAGONS & DREAMS, Jane Yolen, Martin H. Greenberg & Charles G. Waugh, oa HPR 1986
DRGNDRK - DRAGONS OF DARKNESS, Orson Scott Card, oa ACE 1981
DRGNLGT - DRAGONS OF LIGHT, Orson Scott Card, oa ACE 1980
DRKCMPN - DARK COMPANIONS, Ramsey Campbell, co MAC 1982
DRKFRCS - DARK FORCES, Kirby McCauley, oa VIK 1980
DRKGODS - DARK GODS, T.E.D. Klein, co VIK 1985
DRKIMGN - DARK IMAGININGS, an DEL 1978
DRKMIND - DARK MIND, DARK HEART, August Derleth, oa ARK 1962
DRKMUSC - DARK MUSIC, Jack Snow, co HRL 1947
DRKOVRC - DARKOVER CONCORDANCE, Marion Zimmer Bradley, nf PNP 1979
DRM - Drumm Booklets, Chris Drumm: Polk City, IA
DRMWEVR - DREAM WEAVER, Jane Yolen, co CLN 1979
DSC - Descant
DSPCTHU - THE DISCIPLES OF CTHULHU, Edward P. Berglund, oa DAW 1976
DSPRFUT - THE DISAPPEARING FUTURE, George Hay, oa PTH 1970
DSPTCHS - DESPATCHES FROM THE FRONTIERS OF THE FEMALE MIND, Jen Green & Sarah Lefanu, oa WOP 1985
DST - DESTINIES, James Baen, oa ACE
DTHANGL - DEATH ANGEL'S SHADOW, Karl Edward Wagner, co WBK 1973
DTL - Detective Tales

DUT - E.P. Dutton & Co., Inc.: London
DYNGERT - THE DYING EARTH, Jack Vance, oc HIL 1950
DYSTVIS - DYSTOPIAN VISIONS, Roger Elwood, oa PRH 1975
EBN - Ebony Books: Melbourne
ECO - Ecco Press: New York
ed - editorial
EDGEVNG - THE EDGE OF EVENING, Nicholas Stuart Gray, co FAB 1976
EDGTMRW - THE EDGE OF TOMORROW, Isaac Asimov, co TOR 1985
EDT - Eldritch Tales
ELK - Elks Magazine
ELW - ELSEWHERE, Terri Winding & Mark Allan Arnold, oa ACE
EMB - Ed McBains Mystery Book
ENGNGHT - ENGINES OF THE NIGHT, Barry N. Malzberg, co 1982
EPO - Epoch
EPOCH - EPOCH, Roger Elwood & Robert Silverberg, oa BRK 1975
EQM - Ellery Queen's Mystery Magazine
ERC - Eerie Country
ERH&ELW - EARTH AND ELSEWHERE, Roger DeGaris, an MAC 1985
EROSORB - EROS IN ORBIT, Joseph Elder, oa TRI 1973
ESC - Escapade
ESP - Escape!
ETW - Etwas, Peggy Rae McKnight, ed.
EUR&ELW - EUROPE AND ELSEWHERE, Mark Twain, ed. Albert Bigelow Paine, co HPB 1923
EVTHBLV - EVERYTHING BUT LOVE, an MIR 1973
ex - extract
EYE - EYE, Frank Herbert, co BRK 1985
EYR - Eyre & Spottiswoode: London
F&T - Fantasy and Terror
fa - facetious article
FAB - Faber & Faber, Ltd.: London
FACECHS - THE FACE OF CHAOS, Robert Lynn Asprin & Lynn Abbey, oa ACE 1983
FACESFR - FACES OF FEAR, Douglas E. Winter, nf BRK 1985
FAD - Fantastic Adventures
FAERY! - FAERY!, Terri Windling, an ACE 1985
FAN - Fantastic
FARSIDE - THE FAR SIDE OF TIME, Roger Elwood, oa DOM 1974
FATMANI - THE FAT MAN IN HISTORY, Peter Carey, co 1974
FAW - Fawcett Crest Books
FBK - Fantasy Book [published by FPCI]
FBM - Fantasy Book magazine [published by Dennis Mallonee]
FBRBKMF - THE FABER BOOK OF MODERN FAIRY TALES, Sara & Stephen Corrin, an FAB 1985
FCR - Fantasy Crossroads
FEARS - FEARS, Charles L. Grant, oa BRK 1983
Feb - February
FEL - Fredrick Fell, Inc.
FFM - Famous Fantastic Mysteries magazine
FFR - FAR FRONTIERS, Jerry Pournelle & Jim Baen, oa BAE
FGM - Fawcett Gold Medal Books
FIENDIN - THE FIEND IN YOU, Charles Beaumont, an BAL 1962
FIG - Figaro, Paris
FIGHUMN - FIGURES OF THE HUMAN, David Ignatow, co WUP 1964
FIREBDI - FIREBIRD I, [Angela Carter]
FIREWTC - FIRE WATCH, Connie Willis, co BJB 1985
FKW - Funk & Wagnalls, Inc.: New York
FLGTNVR - FLIGHT FROM NEVERYON, Samuel R. Delanny, oc BAN 1985
Fll - Fall
FLLWSHP - FELLOWSHIP OF THE STARS, Terry Carr, oa SAS 1974
FLN - Flynn's Detective Fiction
FLS - FLASHING SWORDS, Lin Carter, oa DEL
FLTWYBA - FLEETWAY BOY'S ANNUAL
FMF - Famous Science Fiction
FMG - Fantasy Magazine
FNLSTGE - FINAL STAGE, Edward L. Ferman & Barry N. Malzberg, oa CHT 1974
FNTRWLD - FRONTIER WORLDS, Paul Collins, oa C&C 1983
FPL - Futura Publications Limited: London
FRAMZDK - FREE AMAZONS OF DARKOVER, Marion Zimmer Bradley and the Friends of Darkover, oa DAW 1985
FRG - Fantasy Readers Guide
FRGNBDY - FOREIGN BODIES, 1981 [Brian W. Aldiss]
FRIGHTS - FRIGHTS, Kirby McCauley, oa SMP 1976
FRM - The Forum
FRMOTO1 - FROM ZERO TO ONE, Robert Zend, SNN 1973
FRMHRTD - FROM THE HEART OF DARKNESS, David A. Drake, co TOR 1983
FRYLGND - FAIRY LEGENDS AND TRADITIONS OF THE SOUTH OF IRELAND, T. Crofton Croker, co 1825
FSB - Fantasy, British
FSF - The Magazine of Fantasy & Science Fiction
FSG - Farrar, Straus & Giroux, Inc.: New York
FSM - Fantastic Story Magazine
FSTRLGT - FASTER THAN LIGHT, George Zebrowski & Jack Dann, oa HPR 1976
FTL - Fantasy Tales
FUN - Fantastic Universe Science Fiction
FUT - Future Science Fiction magazine
FUTCITY - FUTURE CITY, Roger Elwood, oa TRI 1973
FUTPAST - FUTURE PASTIMES, Scott Edelstein, oa AUR 1977
fw - foreword
FWR - THE FUTURE AT WAR, Reginald Bretnor, an ACE
FYC - Fantasycon Programme Booklet
G&S - GHOSTS & SCHOLARS, Rosemary Pardoe, an
GAL - Galaxy
GCP - Golden Cockerell Press: Berkshire
GDY - Godey's Lady's Book
GEM - Gem
GENERTN - GENERATION, David Gerrold, oa DEL 1972
GHB - GHOST BOOK, Aidan Chambers/James Turner, an
GHOSTBK - THE GHOST-BOOK, Cynthia Asquith, an 1926
GHOSTS - GHOSTS, Edith Wharton, co APC 1937

GHOSTS2 - GHOSTS, Marvin Kaye, an DBL 1981
GHSTANT - GHOST STORIES OF AN ANTIQUARY, M.R. James, co 1904
GHSTLGT - THE GHOST LIGHT, Fritz Leiber, co BRK 1984
GHSTSHP - THE GHOST SHIP, Richard Middleton, co 1912
GHSTSHR - THE GHOST OF SHERLOCK HOLMES, [Leslie Halliwell]
GIRLWTH - THE GIRL WITH THE HUNGRY EYES, Donald A. Wollheim, oa
          AVN 1949
GLDNGTE - GOLDEN GATE AND OTHER STORIES, R.A. Lafferty, co CBR
          1982
GLG   - Graham's Lady's and Gentleman's Magazine
GLL   - Galileo Magazine
GLR   - Gallery Magazine
GLSTBSF - GOLLANCZ - SUNDAY TIMES BEST SF STORIES, oa GOL 1975
GML   - Greystoke Mobray Ltd.
GNC   - Gentleman's Companion
GNL   - W. Paul Ganley: Publisher: Buffalo, NY
gp   - group of related stories
gr   - game review
GRC   - The Grecourt Review
GRL   - Grils, Joyce Fisher, Sue Robinson, and Pam Janisch, eds.
GRLMKNS - GRIMALKIN'S TALES, Stella Whitelaw, Judy Gardiner & Mark
          Rosen, oa 1983
GRLWHOC - THE GIRL WHO CRIED FLOWERS, Jane Yolen, co CRO 1974
GRMLKNS - GRIMALKIN'S TALES, Stella Whitelaw, Judy Gardiner & Mark
          Ronson, oa SMP 1985
GRNGADV - THE GRAND ADVENTURE, Philip José Farmer, co BRK 1984
GRP   - The Graphic
GRUSMBK - THE GRUESOME BOOK, Ramsey Campbell, an PIC 1983
GRYSTBY - GREYSTONE BAY, Charles L. Grant, oa TOR 1985
GTEHELL - THE GATES OF HELL, C.J. Cherryh & Janet Morris, no BAE
          1986
GTH   - Gothism, Robert L. Chomorsky, ed.
GTNGEVN - GETTING EVEN, Woody Allen, co RDM 1971
H&I   - Hale & Ireminger Pty Ltd.: Sydney
HABITAT - HABITATS, Susan Shwartz, oa DAW 1984
HAW   - Hawthorn Books, Inc.
HBC   - Hayden Book Company: Hasbrouck Heights, NJ
HBJ   - Harcourt Brace Jovanovich Inc.: New York
HBW   - Harcourt Brace World Inc.: New York
hc   - hard cover
HECATES - HECATE'S CAULDRON, Susan M. Shwartz, oa DAW 1982
HEI   - William Heinemann Ltd.: London
HEROFAN - HEROIC FANTASY, Gerald W. Page & Hank Reinhardt, oa DAW
          1979
HEROVIS - HEROIC VISIONS, Jessica Amanda Salmonson, oa ACE 1983
HGT   - High Times
HHW   - Household Words
HIL   - Hillman
HKMRLSY - HENRT KUTTNER - A MEMORIAL SYMPOSIUM, Karen Anderson, nf
HLT   - Henry Holt
HLX   - Helix
HMF   - Houghton Mifflin Company: New York
HMS   - Hutchinson's Mystery Story Magazine
HNC   - Hartford Northeast Current
HNDFLDS - A HANDFUL OF DUST, Evelyn Waugh, co 1934
HNDSHLL - THE HOUNDS OF HELL, Michel Parry, an GOL 1974
HNL   - Haunted Library Publications
HNTDCST - HAUNTED CASTLES: THE COMPLETE GOTHIC TALES OF RAY
          RUSSELL, Ray Russell, co 1985
HORRTLS - HORROR TALES, Roger Elwood, oa RAN 1974
HPB   - Harper & Brothers: New York
HPR   - Harper & Row: New York
HRCMLDY - HERE COMES THE LADY, M. P. Shiel, co 1928
HRL   - Herald: New York
HRP   - Harper's Magazine
HRTSTND - HEART OF STONE, DEAR, R.A. Lafferty, co DRM 1984
HRV   - The Hudson Review: A Magazine of Literature and the Arts
HRW   - Holt, Rinehart and Winston: New York
HSCTHLU - THE HOUSE OF CTHULHU AND OTHER TALES OF THE PRIMAL LAND,
          Brian Lumley, co WBP 1984
HSH   - The Horror Show
HSMSHLD - THE HOUSE ON THE MARSHLANDS, Louise Gluck, co ECO 1975
HTS   - Haunts, Nightshade Publications, P.O. Box 3342,
          Providence, RI 02906
HTZ   - J. Hetzel: Paris
hu   - humor
HVNLYHT - HEAVENLY HOST, Isaac Asimov, na
IAA   - Isaac Asimov's SF Adventure Magazine
IAM   - ISAAC ASIMOV'S MAGICAL WORLDS OF FANTASY, Isaac Asimov,
          Martin H. Greenberg & Charles G. Waugh, an SIG
IAS   - Isaac Asimov's Science Fiction Magazine
ibc   - inside back cover
IDIOSYN - IDIOSYNCRACIES, ILP 1984
IDL   - The Idler
IDSTMRW - THE IDES OF TOMORROW, Terry Carr, oa LBR 1976
ifc   - inside front cover
IFS   - If/Worlds of If Science Fiction
IHOPEIS - I HOPE I SHALL ARRIVE SOON, Philip K. Dick, co DBL 1985
IKR   - Inside Karate
il   - illustration
ILP   - Illuminati Press
IMG   - Imagination
IMGNLND - IMAGINARY LANDS, Robin McKinley, oa ACE 1985
IMN   - Imagine
IMP   - (SF) Impulse, formerly Science Fantasy
in   - introduction
INAGLSS - IN A GLASS, DARKLY, Joseph Sheridan Le Fanu, co 1886
INALNFL - IN ALIEN FLESH, Gregory Benford, co TOR 1986
INF   - Infinity Science Fiction
INHBLKE - THE INHABITANT OF THE LAKE, Ramsey Campbell, co ARK 1964
INHSOWN - IN HIS OWN WRITE, John Lennon, co 1964
INMIDST - IN THE MIDST OF LIFE, Ambrose Bierce, co 1891

INR   - Indiana Review
ins   - insert
INTRFCS - INTERFACES, Ursula K. Le Guin & Virginia Kidd, oa ACE
          1980
INY   - INFINITY, Robert Hoskins, oa LAN
INZ   - Interzone
IRV   - The Iowa Review
IS   - Is, Tom Collins, ed.
ISBN   - international standard book number
ISTHATW - IS THAT WHAT PEOPLE DO?, Robert Sheckley, co HRW 1984
ITCAMEF - IT CAME FROM SCHENECTADY, Barry B. Longyear, co BJB 1984
ITM   - International Magazine
iv   - interview
ix   - index
IZA   - INTERZONE ANTHOLOGY, John Clute, Colin Greenland & David
          Pringle, an
Jan   - January
JBLJKNY - JUBILEE JACKANORY, BBC 1977
JDP   - Journal des Debats Politiques et Litteraires
JNK   - Herbert Jenkins: London
JNS   - Janus
Jul   - July
Jun   - June
JWC   - JOHN W. CAMPBELL MEMORIAL AWARDS, George R.R. Martin, oa
          BJB
JWLMOON - JEWEL OF THE MOON, William Kotzwinkle, oc PUT 1985
JWSHFYT - JEWISH FAIRY TALES AND STORIES, Gerald Friedlander, co
          1918
KHT   - Khatru, Jeffrey D. Smith, ed.
KINGYLW - THE KING IN YELLOW, Robert W. Chambers, co NLY 1895
KISSKIS - KISS KISS, Roald Dahl, co 1959
KITEWLD - KITEWORLD, Keith Roberts, no GOL 1985
KLK   - Kalki
KNB   - Knave (U.K. edition)
KNP   - Alfred A. Knopf, Inc.: New York
KPRSPRC - THE KEEPER'S PRICE, Marion Zimmer Bradley, oa DAW 1980
KPS   - Keepsake
KWAIDAN - KWAIDAN, Lafcadio Hearn, co 1904
LAN   - Lancer Books
LANDSCP - LANDSCAPE WITH LANDSCAPE, Gerald Murnane, oc NOR 1985
LAR   - Los Angeles Review
LAS   - Los Alamos Scientific Laboratory News
LAUGHTM - LAUGHING TIME, William Jay Smith, co DCT 1980
LBR   - Little, Brown and Co.
LDYBRGE - THE LADY OF THE BARGE, W.W. Jacobs, co HPR 1902
LGHSTCS - LEGENDS OF HASTUR AND CASSILDA, Marion Zimmer Bradley,
          co THP 1979
LGNDTLS - LEGENDS AND TALES OF THE OLD WEST, co 1962
LGTLNST - LIGHT FROM A LONE STAR, Jack Vance, co NSF 1985
LGTYR&D - LIGHT YEARS AND DARK, Michael Bishop, oa BRK 1984
LIAVEK - LIAVEK, Will Shetterly & Emma Bull, oa ACE 1985
LIP   - J.B. Lippincott Company
LNDLSTC - THE LAND OF LOST CONTENT, Robert Phillips, co 1970
LNDSNVR - LANDS OF NEVER, Maxim Jakubowski, oa A&U 1983
LNE   - John Lane: London
LOM   - London Magazine
lp   - large paperback - 8 1/2 x 11
LRB   - The London Review of Books
LSN   - Literary Storefront Newsletter
LSTBKWN - THE LAST BOOK OF WONDER, Lord Dunsany, co 1916
LTKNTED - LATE KNIGHT EDITION, Damon Knight, co NSF 1985
LTRSERT - LETTERS FROM THE EARTH, Mark Twain, ed. Bernard DeVoto,
          co HPR 1962
LUR   - T. Werner Laurie: London
LVLHMSP - L'VIEIL HOMME ET L'ESPACE, Daniel Sernine, co PRM 1981
LWV   - Last Wave, Scott Edelman, ed.
M&B   - Mills & Boon: London
MAC   - The Macmillan Publishing Co., Inc.: New York & London
MACPRBK - MIDAMERICON PROGRAM BOOK, 1976
MAD   - Mademoiselle
MAM   - Mystery Adventures Magazine
Mar   - March
MAR   - Marvel Science Fiction
May   - May
MCC   - McCalls
MCE   - Macmillan Educational Ltd.: Basingstoke & London
MCHSH10 - THE MACHINE IN SHAFT TEN, M. John Harrison, co PTH 1975
md   - mid, as in mid-December
MDNMASS - MIDNIGHT MASS, Paul Bowles, co BSP 1981
MDS   - Midnight Sun, Gary Hoppenstand, ed.
MDT   - Meredith Press
MENDEEP - MEN OF THE DEEP WATERS, William Hope Hodgson, co 1914
MENOWAR - MEN OF WAR, Jerry E. Pournelle, an TOR 1984
MER   - Magasin d'Education et de Recreation
MERYMEN - THE MERRY MEN AND OTHER TALES AND FABLES, Robert Louis
          Stevenson, co C&W 1887
MFL   - Mayflower Books: London
MFP   - Misfit Press: Dearborn, MI
mg   - magazine
MGB   - Magnum Books: London
MGE   - Mage, c/o The Colgate Science Fiction/Fantasy
          Association, Colgate University Student Association,
          Hamilton NY 13346
MGI   - MAGIC IN ITHCAR, Andre Norton & Robert Adams, oa TOR
          1985
MHT   - Manhunt
MIDNGHT - MIDNIGHT, Charles L. Grant, an TOR 1985
MINEOWN - MINE OWN PEOPLE, Rudyard Kipling, co 1891
MIR   - Mir Publishers: Moscow
MIS   - The Missouri Review
MJS   - Mother Jones
MLL   - McLelland and Stewart

MLNELPH - MELANCHOLY ELEPHANTS, Spider Robinson, co
MLNLWMN - MILLENNIAL WOMEN, Virginia Kidd, oa DCT 1978
MMM   - Malcolm's [Mystery Magazine]
MNE   - Maine Magazine
MNLYMNL - MAINLY IN MOONLIGHT, Nicholas Stuart Grey, co 1965
MNPOLMD - THE MODERN POLISH MIND, Maria Kuncewicz, an LBR 1962
MNSLDMN - THE MAN WHO SOLD THE MOON, Robert A. Heirlein, co SHS
           1950
MNSNGRF - MOONSINGER'S FRIENDS, Susan Shwartz, oa EJB 1985
MNSTRCL - THE MONSTER CLUB
MNWHBKX - THE MAN WHO BROKE OUT OF THE LETTER X, Robert Priest, co
           CHP 1984
MNYWRLD - THE MANY WORLDS OF SCIENCE FICTION, Ben Bova, oa DUT
           1971
MOH   - The Magazine of Horror
MPC   - Montcalm Publishing Corporation: New York
mr   - movie review
MRMAGIC - MORE MAGIC, Larry Niven, oa BRK 1984
MRP   - Moor Park, Miriam Dyches, ed.
MRTLSBW - MORE TALES OF THE BLACK WIDOWERS, Isaac Asimov, co DBL
           1976
MRWNDRN - MORE WANDERING STARS, Jack M. Dann, an DEL 1981
ms   - miscellaneous
MSH   - Manuscript House: New York
MSM   - Mike Shane Mystery Magazine
MSQ   - The Masquerade, Eton
MSRMAUR - MONSIEUR MAURICE, Amelia B. Edwards, co 1873
MSS   - MSS
MSTRFLY - THE MONSTER FLY, Charles A. Piddock, oc XEP 1974
MTFBLMN - MARK TWAIN'S FABLES OF MAN, ed. John S. Tuckey, co UCP
           1972
MTH   - Methuen: London
MTN   - MARK TWAIN'S NOTEBOOKS & JOURNALS, ed. Frederick
           Anderson, et al, co UCP
MTNTEBK - MARK TWAIN'S NOTEBOOK, ed. Albert Bigelow Paine, co HPB
           1935
MTQRHVN - MARK TWAIN'S QUARREL WITH HEAVEN: "CAPTAIN STORMFIELD'S
           VISIT TO HEAVEN" AND OTHER SKETCHES, ed. Ray B. Brown,
           co CUP 1970
MTWHDRM - MARK TWAIN'S WHICH WAS THE DREAM? AND OTHER SYMBOLIC
           WRITINGS OF THE LATER YEARS, ed. John S. Tuckey, co UCP
           1967
MUS   - Muse (Colorado arts newspaper)
MUT   - Mutual Book Co.: Boston
MVS   - Marvel Science Stories
MVT   - Marvel Tales
MYM   - Mystery Monthly Magazine
MYR   - Myrddin
MYSCURE - THE MYSTERIOUS CURE, J.O. Jeppson, co DBL 1985
MYSTHZN - MYSTERIES OF THE HORIZON, Lawrence Raab, co DBL 1972
n.   - novel
na   - novella
NAL   - New American Library: New York
NAR   - North American Review
NAS   - NEBULA AWARD STORIES, an
NCH   - New Classics House, Novel Books Inc.: Chicago
NCR   - Night Cry
NDB   - Nelson Doubleday, Inc.: Garden City, NY. Imprint of the
           Science Fiction Book Club.
NDM   - NEW DIMENSIONS, Robert Silverberg/Marta Randall, oa
NDP   - New Directions Publishing Corporation
NDT   - New Detective Magazine
NEA   - NEA Services, Inc.
NEB   - Nebula Science Fiction
NEDLFUL - THE NEEDLE ON FULL, Caroline Forbes, co CWP 1985
NEL   - Thomas Nelson, Inc.
NEM   - New England Magazine
NEW&SEL - NEW AND SELECTED POEMS, Ted Hughes, co HFR 1982
NEWMIND - THE NEW MIND, Roger Elwood, oa MAC 1973
nf   - non-fiction
NGTCHLS - NIGHT CHILLS, Kirby McCauley, an AVN 1975
NGTRIDE - NIGHT RIDE AND OTHER JOURNEYS, Charles Beaumont, co BAN
           1960
NGTSIDE - NIGHT-SIDE, Joyce Carol Oates, co 1977
NGV   - NIGHT VISIONS, Charles L. Grant, oa
NIE   - Niekas, fanzine published by Ed Meskys
NIVENSL - NIVEN'S LAWS, Larry Niven, co OLS 1984
NLB   - New English Library: London
NLR   - National Review
NLY   - F. Tennyson Neely: New York & Chicago
NOR   - Norstrilia Press: Melbourne, Australia
NOV   - NOVA, Harry Harrison, oa
Nov   - November
NPP   - North Point Press
NPT   - New Pathways into Science Fiction and Fantasy, MGA
           Services, P.O. Box 863994, Plano TX 75086-3994
NPTNRIS - NEPTUNE RISING, Jane Yolen, co PHM 1982
NRV   - New Review
NSA   - The New Satirist
NSF   - NESFA Press: Cambridge, MA
NSJ   - National Storyteller Journal
NSTRTBB - THE NOEL STREATFEILD BIRTHDAY BOOK
NTA   - The National Amateur
NTLCTHU - NEW TALES OF THE CTHULHU MYTHOS, Ramsey Campbell, oc ARK
           1980
NTLSPTM - NEW TALES OF SPACE AND TIME, Raymond J. Healy, oa HLT
           1951
NTLSTRR - NEW TALES OF TERROR, Hugh Lamb, oa MGB 1980
NTSSFWR - NOTES TO A SCIENCE FICTION WRITER, Ben Bova, co SCB 1975
NTVOICE - NIGHT VOICES, Robert Aickman, co GOL 1985
nv   - novelette
NVNSLWS - NIVEN'S LAWS, Larry Niven, co PHS 1984

NVP   - New Victoria Publishers, Inc.: Lebanon, NH
NWA   - New American Review
NWF   - NEW WORLDS OF FANTASY, Terry Carr, an ACE
NWISLND - NEW ISLANDS, Maria Luisa Bombal, co FSG 1982
NWQ   - NEW WORLDS QUARTERLY, Michael Moorcock, oa SPH & BKM
NWR   - NEW WRITINGS IN SF, oa
NWS   - New Worlds, British magazine
NWT   - NEW TERRORS, Ramsey Campbell, oa PAN 1980
NWTSPTM - NEW TALES OF SPACE AND TIME, Raymond J. Healey, oa HLT
           1951
NWV   - NEW VOICES IN SCIENCE FICTION, George R.R. Martin, oa
NXTEDIT - NEXT EDITIONS, 1980 [Angela Carter]
NYC   - Nyctalops
NYH   - The New York Herald
NYM   - New Yorker Magazine
NYR   - The New York Review of Books
oa   - original anthology
OBK   - THE OMNI BOOK OF SCIENCE FICTION, Ellen Datlow, an ZEB
oc   - original collection
Oct   - October
OCT   - Octopus Books Limited: London
ODP   - Odyssey Publications: Melrose Highlands, MA
OLDFIRE - OLD FIRES AND PROFITABLE GHOSTS, Sir Arthur
           Quiller-Couch, co SCB 1900
OLDMNBD - OLD MAN'S BEARD, H. Russell Wakefield, co BLS 1929
OLDTOWN - OLD TOWN FIRESIDE STORIES, Harriet Beecher Stowe, co OSG
           1871
OLS   - Owlswick Press: Philadelphia
om   - omnibus edition
OMEGA   - OMEGA, Roger Elwood, oa WKR 1973
OMN   - Omni
ONCEGNT - ONCE THERE WAS A GIANT, Keith Laumer, co TOR 1984
ORB   - ORBIT, Damon Knight, oa
ORI   - Oriental Stories
ORN   - Orion
OSF   - Orbit Science Fiction
OSG   - James R. Osgood: Boston
OTR   - Outre, J. Vernon Shea, ed.
OUI   - Oui
OUT   - Outworlds, William L. Bowers, ed.
OUTEVRY - OUT OF THE EVERYWHERE, AND OTHER EXTRAORDINARY VISIONS,
           James Tiptree, Jr., co BAL 1981
OUTOFHD - OUT OF MY HEAD, Robert Bloch, co NSF 1986
OUTOFTM - OUT OF TIME, Aidan Chambers, ca BDL 1984
OWF   - Owlflight
OWL   - OTHER WORLDS, Roy Torgesson, ca ZEB
OWLTIME - OWL TIME, M.A. Foster, oc DAW 1985
OWP   - Onlywomen Press: London
OWS   - Other Worlds
PALEAPE - THE PALE APE AND OTHER PULSES, M.P. Shiel, co LUR 1911
PAN   - Pan Books, Ltd.: London
PASTIME - PAST TIMES, Poul Anderson, co TOR 1984
pb   - paperback
PBK   - Paperback Library
PBM   - Potboiler Magazine
PBP   - Playboy Press: New York
PBY   - Playboy magazine
PCB   - Poetry Chapbook, Star/Sword Publications
PCM   - Popular Computing
PCTEXHB - PICTURES AT AN EXHIBITION, Ian Watson, oa GML 1981
PDD   - Pudding Magazine
PDN   - Philadelphia Dollar Newspaper
PEN   - Penguin Books: London
PFP   - Puffin Post
PGP   - Pangloss Papers
PHG   - Phantasmagoria
PHM   - Philomel Books
PHP   - Phantasia Press: West Bloomfield, MI
PHS   - The Philadelphia Science Fiction Society
PHT   - The Phantagraph
pi   - pictorial
PIC   - Piccolo Books, Pan Books Ltd.: London
PIG   - Pig Iron
PIN   - Pinnacle Books: New York
PIO   - The Pioneer
PIT   - Proceedings of the Institute for Twenty-First Century
           Studies
PLANETS - THE PLANETS, Byron Preiss, oa BAN 1985
PLE   - Plant Engineering
PLNTENG - PLAN[E]T ENGINEERING, Gene Wolfe, co NSF 1984
PLP   - Pulpsmith
PLS   - Planet Stories
pm   - poem
PMM   - Pall Mall Magazine
PMSNW&S - POEMS: NEW AND SELECTED (1957-1983), Robert Sward, co
           AYA 1983
PNP   - Pennyfarthing Press: San Francisco, CA
PNT   - Penthouse
POHLSTR - POHLSTARS, Frederik Pohl, co EAL 1984
POT   - Clarkson N. Potter, Publishers: New York
POW   - Powell Publications
pp   - number of pages
PPC   - Press Porcepic: Victoria, BC Canada
pr   - preface
PRB   - Parabola: Myth and the Quest for Meaning
PRH   - Prentice-Hall, Inc.
PRM   - Le Preambule: Longueuil, Quebec
PROTEUS - PROTEUS, Richard S. McEnroe, oa ACE 1981
PROTOST - PROTOSTARS, David Gerrold & Stephen Goldin, oa BAL 1971
PRPTLGT - PERPETUAL LIGHT, Alan Ryan, oa WBK 1982
PRS   - Pearson's Magazine

PRSDMAR - THE PRAESIDIUM OF ARCHIVE, Jefferson P. Swycaffer, oc
          AVN 1986
PSP   - Pierian Spring (Brandon, Manitoba)
PTH   - Panther Books Ltd.: London
PUL   - PULSAR, George Hay, oa PEN
PUN   - Punch
PUR   - Puritan Magazine
PUT   - G.P. Putnam's Sons: New York
PVL   - The Pavlat Report, Larry Shaw, ed.
PWRTIME - THE POWER OF TIME, Josephine Saxton, co C&W 1985
PYR   - Pyramid Books
pz   - puzzle
QDPHBIA - QUADRIPHOBIA, Alan Ryan, oc DBL 1986
qp   - quality paperback
QPB   - Quality Paperback Book Club
QRK   - QUARK, Samuel R. Delany & Marilyn Hacker, oa PBK
QRT   - Quartet Books Limited: London
QRY   - Quarry Magazine
RAN   - Rand, McNally & Company
RBK   - Redbook Magazine
RCR   - Red Clay Reader
RCS   - Rolling Stone College Papers
REACH   - THE REACH AND OTHER STORIES, Lilian Mohin & Sheila
          Shulman, an OWP 1984
REP   - Reporter
RHIALTO - RHIALTO THE MARVELLOUS, Jack Vance, n. Baen 1985 reprint
          contains the short story "Basileus" by C.J. Cherryh and
          Janet Moris, excerpted from a forthcoming original
          anthology HEROES IN HELL.
RIDDLE& - THE RIDDLE AND OTHER STORIES, Walter de la Mare, co S&B
          1923
RIG   - Rigel
RMINTWR - THE ROOM IN THE TOWER AND OTHER STORIES, E.F. Benson, co
          M&B 1912
RMSPRDS - ROOMS OF PARADISE, Lee Harding, oa 1978
RNDMACC - RABDOM ACCESS MESSAGES OF THE COMPUTER AGE, Thomas F.
          Monteleone, an HBC 1984
ROG   - Rogue Magazine
ROGUEBO - ROGUE BOLO, Keith Laumer, oc BAE 1986
RSC   - Rolling Stone College Papers
RST   - Rolling Stone
RTF&PPP - RETIEF AND THE PANGALACTIC PAGEANT OF PULCHRITUDE, Keith
          Laumer, co BAE 1986
RUNAMCK - RUNNING A MUCK, John Caldwell, co WDG 1978
S&B   - Selwyn and Blount: London
S&S   - SWORD AND SORCERESS, Marion Zimmer Bradley, oa DAW
S&T   - Space and Time
S*L   - Star*Line
S.F.B.C.- Science Fiction Book Club: Garden City, NY
S/P   - Scream/Press: Santa Cruz, CA
S83   - Science 83
S84   - Science 84
sa   - story adaptation of a play/screenplay
SADNSPM - SADNESS OF SPACEMEN, Robert Priest, co DRD 1980
SAO   - The South Australian Odd Fellows' Magazine
SAP   - Sorcerer's Apprentice
SAS   - Simon and Schuster, Inc.: New York
SAT   - Satellite Science Fiction
SBH   - STAR BOOK OF HORROR, Hugh Lamb, an STB
SCB   - Charles Scribner's Sons: New York
SCF   - Science Fantasy
SCHLRYM - THE SCHOLARLY MOUSE AND OTHER STORIES, 1957
SCIAGMN - SCIENCE AGAINST MAN, Anthony Cheetham, oa AVN 1970
SCK   - Schocken Books: New York
SCR   - Scribner's Magazine
SDA   - Stardate: The Multi-Media Science Fiction Magazine
SDW   - SHADOWS, Charles L. Grant, oa DBL
SEA   - The Seabury Press: New York
SELPMCS - SELECTED POEMS, Clark Ashton Smith, co ARK 1971
SELWRTC - SELECTED WRITINGS OF TRUMAN CAPOTE, Truman Capote, co
          1947
Sep   - September
SEP   - The Saturday Evening Post
SEV   - Seventeen
sf   - special feature
SF+   - Science Fiction Plus
SFA   - Science Fiction Adventures
SFB   - Science Fiction Adventures, British
SFC   - Scott, Foresman and Company: Glenview, IL
SFMRKTW - THE SCIENCE FICTION OF MARK TWAIN, ed. David Ketterer,
          co ACH 1984
SFQ   - Science Fiction Quarterly
SFS   - (The Original) Science Fiction Stories
SFTALES - SCIENCE FICTION TALES, Roger Elwood, oa RAN 1973
SFW   - SFWA Bulletin
SHDW3rd - THE SHADOWY THIRD AND OTHER STORIES, Ellen Glasgow, co
          DBL 1923
SHOWCSE - SHOWCASE, Roger Elwood, oa HPR 1973
SHPSHFT - SHAPE SHIFTERS, Jane Yolen, an SEA 1978
SHS   - Shasta Publishers
SHY   - Shayol
si   - section introduction
SIG   - Signet Books (NAL): New York
SIXTEEN - SIXTEEN, Donald Gallo, an DCT
SKTNCRW - SKELETON CREW, Stephen King, co PUT 1985
sl   - serial segment
SLIPPRY - SLIPPERY AND OTHER STORIES, R.A. Lafferty, oc DRM 1985
SLM   - Southern Literary Messenger
SLNCAMR - THE SILENCE OF AMOR, Fiona MacLeod, 1896
SLR   - The Seattle Review
SME   - Something Else
SMGSTST - SOME GHOST STORIES, A.M. Burrage, co 1927

SMI   - The Smith
SML   - SPACE MAIL, Isaac Asimov, Martin H. Greenberg, George
          R.R. Martin & Charles G. Waugh, an FAW
SMLPNCH - A SMALL PINCH OF WEATHER, Joan Aiken, co CAP 1974
SMM   - The Saint Mystery Magazine
SMNINRM - SOMEONE IN THE ROOM, Ex-Private X, co 1931
SMP   - St. Martin's Press: New York
SMTMNVR - SOMETIME, NEVER, Anonymous, oa EYR 1956
SMY   - Small Maynard, Publishers: Boston
sn   - short novel
SND   - The Strand Magazine, London
SNN   - Sono Nis: Victoria
SNR   - San Francisco Review
SNT&REL - SAINTS AND RELICS, Rosemary Pardoe
SNV   - SUPERNOVA, Philip Pollock, oa FAB
SOULCTY - SOUL OF THE CITY, Robert Lynn Asprin & Lynn Abbey, oa
          ACE 1986
sp   - speech
SPC   - SPACE, Richard Davis, oa ABS
SPECLTN - SPECULATIONS, Isaac Asimov & Alice Laurance, oa HMF 1982
SPECTER - SPECTER!, Bill Pronzini, an ARH 1982
SPH   - Sphere Books Limited: London
SPINOZA - THE SPINOZA OF MARKET STREET, Isaac Bashevis Singer, co
          FSG 1958
SPL   - The Spirit Lamp, Oxford
SPN   - Spinster
Spr   - Spring
SPS   - Space Stories
SRCRAPR - SORCERER'S APPRENTICE [Tanith Lee]
ss   - short story
SSF   - Space Science Fiction
SSP   - Shoe String Press: Hamden, CT
SSS   - Super Science Stories
SST   - Science Stories
STARSNO - STAR SHORT NOVELS, Frederik Pohl, oa BAL 1954
STB   - Star Books, W.H. Allen & Co. Ltd.: London
STL   - STELLAR, Judy-Lynn del Rey, oa BAL
STLSNOV - STELLAR SHORT NOVELS, Judy-Lynn del Rey, oa BAL 1976
STM   - Startling Mystery Stories
STO   - Story Magazine
STR   - STAR SCIENCE FICTION STORIES, Frederik Pohl, oa BAL
STRGATR - STRANGE ATTRACTIONS, Damien Broderick, oa H&I 1985
STRMSSN - STORM SEASON, Robert Lynn Asprin & Lynn Abbey, oa ACE
          1984
STRNGBD - STRANGE BEDFELLOWS, Thomas N. Scortia, an RDM 1972
STRNGTH - STRANGE THINGS HAPPEN, Robert Randolph Medcalf, Jr.,
          Quixsilver Press 1981
STRYQBC - STORIES FROM QUEBEC, Philip Stratford, an VNR 1974
STS   - Startling Stories
STT   - Strange Tales
STYNTRD - THE SATURDAY NIGHT READER, an [Angela Carter]
Sum   - Summer
SUN   - The Sun newspaper
SUP   - Super Science Fiction
SUPRHOR - SUPERHORROR, Ramsey Campbell, oa ALL 1976
SUPRNRD - THE SUPERNATURAL READER, Groff & Lucy Conklin, an LIP
          1953
SVNGWRL - SAVING WORLDS, Roger Elwood & Virginia Kidd, oa DBL 1973
SVT   - Survival Tomorrow
SVYDRMS - SAVOY DREAMS, 1983
SWC   - Sewickley Magazine
SWD   - SWORDS AGAINST DARKNESS, Andrew J. Offutt, oa ZEB
SWDAGTM - SWORDS AGAINST TOMORROW, Robert Hoskins, an SIG 1970
SWK   - Swank
SWO   - SPWAO Showcase
SYA   - Spicy-Adventure Stories
TABOO   - TABOO, Anonymous, oa NCH 1964
TAMASTR - TAMASTARA, Tanith Lee, DAW 1984
TDA   - Ten Detective Aces
TDW   - Today's Woman
TDY   - Today, The Philadelphia Inquirer Magazine
TERRORS - TERRORS, Charles L. Grant, oa PBP 1982
TESRCTS - TESSERACTS, Judith Merril, oa PPC 1985
THP   - Thendara House Publications: Berkeley, CA
THRUELG - THROUGH ELEGANT EYES, R.A. Lafferty, co CBR 1983
THSKIND - THIS KIND OF WAR, T.R. Fehrenbach, nf 1963
THVSWLD - THIEVES' WORLD, Robert Lynn Asprin, oa ACE 1979
TIG   - Tiger
TKG   - TK Graphics: Baltimore, MD
TLE   - The Leading Edge, 3163 JKHB, Provo UT 84602
TLSCTHU - TALES OF THE CTHULHU MYTHOS, August Derleth, an ARK 1969
TLSFRAM - TALES OF THE FREE AMAZONS, Marion Zimmer Bradley, an THP
          1980
TLSHRSY - TALES OF HEARSAY, Joseph Conrad, co DBL 1925
TLSTRVL - TALES OF A TRAVELLER, Washington Irving, co 1824
TLSWNDR - TALES OF WONDER, Jane Yolen, co SCK 1983
TMP   - Le Temps
TMPTRLM - TIME PATROLMAN, Poul Anderson, oc TOR 1983
TNGFIRE - TONGUES OF FIRE, Algernon Blackwood, co JNK 1924
TNGSCNS - TONGUES OF CONSCIENCE, Robert S. Hichens, co MTH 1900
TOCHPPL - TO THE CHAPEL PERILOUS, Naomi Mitchison, co A&U 1955
TOMOBED - TOM O'BEDLAM'S NIGHT OUT AND OTHER STRANGE EXCURSIONS,
          Darrell Schweitzer, co GNL 1985
TOR   - Tor Books, Tom Doherty Associates: New York
TRAFFIC - TRAFFICS AND DISCOVERIES, Rudyard Kipling, co MAC 1904
TRE   - The Virginia City Territorial Enterprise
TRI   - Trident Press
TRK   - Triskell Press
TRMNLBH - TERMINAL BEACH, J.G. Ballard, co GOL 1964
TRNGPTS - TURNING POINTS: ESSAYS ON THE ART OF SCIENCE FICTION,
          ed. Damon Knight, an 1977
TRNPLCE - THE TURNING PLACE, Jean A. Karl, oc DUT 1976

TRNSMUT - TRANSMUTATIONS, Rob Gerrand, oa NOR 1979
TRQ   - TriQuarterly
TRVLGRV - THE TRAVELLING GRAVE AND OTHER STORIES, L.P. Hartley, co
          ARK 1948
TSF   - Ten Story Fantasy
TSP   - TASP
TSTFRQT - A TASTE FOR QUIET, Judith Gorog, co PUT 1982
TTB   - The Thrill Book
TTL   - Terror Tales
TWK   - This Week
TWLGTZN - THE TWILIGHT ZONE: THE ORGINAL STORIES, Martin H.
          Greenberg, Richard Matheson & Charles G. Waugh, eds., an
          AVN 1985
TWOVIEW - TWO VIEWS OF WONDER, Thomas N. Scortia & Chelsea Quinn
          Yarbro, oa BAL 1973
TWRGLSS - THE TOWER OF GLASS, Ivan Angelo, oc 1979. English
          translation AVN 1986
TWS   - Thrilling Wonder Stories
TWT   - Twisted Tales
TXR   - The Texas Review
TZM   - Rod Serling's The Twilight Zone Magazine
U.K.   - United Kingdom
UBR   - Ubris
UCN   - Unicorn Books
UCP   - University of California Press: Berkeley CA
UNA   - The United Amateur
UNAUTHA - UNAUTHORIZED AUTOBIOGRAPHIES AND OTHER CURIOSITIES,
          Michael Resnic, co MFP 1984
UNCRNTD - THE UNICORN TRADE, Poul & Karen Anderson, co TOR 1984
UNE   - Unearth
UNI   - UNIVERSE, Terry Carr, oa
UNK   - Unknown/Unknown Worlds
UNSLNGT - UNSILENT NIGHT   [Tanith Lee]
UNVTGST - UNINVITED GHOSTS, Penelope Lively, co HEI 1984
UPCHMNY - UP THE DOWN CHIMNEY AND OTHER STORIES, Joan Aiken, oc
          1984
UPRBRTH - THE UPPER BERTH, F. Marion Crawford, co PUT 1894
UQG   - Unique Graphics: Oakland, CA
UQP   - University of Queensland Press
URBANFN - URBAN FANTASIES, David King & Russell Blackford, oa EBN
          1985
URN   - Uranus
USF   - Universe Science Fiction
UTPHNTR - UTOPIA HUNTERS, Somtow Sucharitkul, co BAN 1984
uw   - unfinished work
UWM   - Underwood-Miller: Columbia, PA
V   - Volume
VAN   - Vanguard Science Fiction
VCT   - Vector
VDP   - Void Publications: St. Kilda, Australia
VEL   - Velocities
vi   - vignette
VIK   - The Viking Press: New York
VIS&INV - VISIBLE AND INVISIBLE, E.F. Benson, co 1923
VIV   - Viva
VNC   - Vancouver Magazine
VNR   - Van Nostrand Reinhold, Ltd.: Toronto
VOD   - Void
VOG   - Vogue
VPG   - Vorpal Glass
VRCNMNT - VIRCONIUM NIGHTS, M. John Harrison, co ACE 1984, GOL
          1985
VSBLGHT - VISIBLE LIGHT, C.J. Cherryh, co PHP 1986
VSF   - Venture Science Fiction
VTR   - Ventura, Philip A. Harrell, ed.
VTX   - Vertex Magazine
WAR   - THERE WILL BE WAR, Jerry Pournelle, an TOR
WARLOCK - WARLOCK AT THE WHEEL AND OTHER STORIES, Diana Wynne
          Jones, co MAC 1984
WAY-OUT - SCIENCE FICTION ADVENTURES FROM WAY OUT, Roger Elwood,
          oa WHT 1974
WBK   - Warner Books: New York
WBO   - West by One and by One
WBP   - Weirdbook Press: Buffalo, NY
WBS   - Web Terror Stories
WBY   - Worlds Beyond
WCN   - Westercon Program Book
WDB   - Weirdbook magazine
WDG   - Writer's Digest Books
WDL   - WIND/Literary Journal
WDN   - What's Doing
WDP   - Weirdbook Press: Buffalo, NY
WEAREFR - WE ARE FOR THE DARK
WEB   - Charles L. Webster & Company
WER   - Whole Earth Review
WFC   - World Fantasy Convention Program Book
WHA   - WHISPERS, Stuart David Schiff, oa
WHITEHN - THE WHITEHORN WOOD AND OTHER MAGICKS, Jane Yolen, co TRK
          1984
WHS   - Whispers
WHT   - Whitman Books
Win   - Winter
WKR   - Walker and Company: New York
WLSHRBT - WELSH RAREBIT TALES, Harle Owen Cummins, co MUT 1902
WMJ   - Woman's Journal
WMNSPCE - WOMAN SPACE, Claudia Lamperti, oa NVP 1981
WNDROSE - THE WIND IN THE ROSE-BUSH AND OTHER STORIES OF THE
          SUPERNATURAL, Mary E. Wilkins Freeman, co DBL 1903
WNFRSUN - THE WIND FROM THE SUN, Arthur C. Clarke, co HBJ 1972
WNGSOMN - WINGS OF OMEN, Robert Lynn Asprin & Lyrn Abbey, oc ACE
          1984
WNTRNWS - WINTER NEWS, John Haines, co WUP 1966

WOF   - Worlds of Fantasy
WOP   - The Women's Press, Ltd.: London
WOT   - Worlds of Tomorrow
WPB   - The Washington Post Book World
WRI   - The Writer
WRLDCLP - A WORLD NAMED CLEOPATRA, Poul Anderson, oa PYR 1977
WRLDTLS - WORLD TALES, G. Randal Rau, oa WFC 1985
WRLKWHL - WARLOCK AT THE WHEEL, Diana Wynne Jones, co MAC 1984
WRNGCUR - A WARNING TO THE CURIOUS, M.R. James, co 1925
WRT   - Weird Tales
WRTRFUT - L. RON HUBBARD PRESENTS WRITERS OF THE FUTURE, Algis
          Budrys, oa BRG 1985
WSF   - Women's Studies International Forum
WSL   - The Weekly Sun Literary Supplement
WSTMDUG - THE WEST MIDLAND UNDERGROUND, 1975
WTB   - WEIRD TALES, Lin Carter, oa
WTCHBRD - WATCH THE BIRDIE, Ramsey Campbell, HNL 1984
WTD   - Weird Tales Ltd.: Oak Forest, IL
WTHFNGR - WITH A FINGER IN MY I, David Gerrold, co BAL 1972
WTS   - Witchcraft & Sorcery
WUP   - Wesleyan University Press
WVP   - Westview Press: Boulder, CO
WWR   - The White Wall Review
XEP   - Xerox Educational Publications: Middletown, CT
YAM   - Young American magazine
YBF   - THE YEAR'S BEST FANTASY STORIES, an DAW
YBH   - THE YEAR'S BEST HORROR STORIES, an DAW
YNGADLT - YOUNG ADULTS, Daniel M. Pinkwater, co Tor 1985
YNK   - Yankee magazine
YR2000 - THE YEAR 2000, Harry Harrison, oa DBL 1970
YRSCITY - THE YEARS OF THE CITY, Frederik Pohl, no SAS 1984
YRV   - Yale Review
YWT   - YOUNG WINTER'S TALES, oa MAC
ZEB   - Zebra Books, Kensington Publishing Corp.: New York
ZIE   - Mark V. Ziesing: Willimantic CT

SCIENCE FICTION IN PRINT: 1985

A Comprehensive Bibliography of
Books and Short Fiction Published
in the English Language

Charles N. Brown
William G. Contento

LOCUS PRESS
Oakland, California
1986

ISBN: 0-9616629-2-1

Printed in the United States.

SCIENCE FICTION IN PRINT—1985
CONTENTS

ORGANIZATION

The data in this book is based upon the monthly *Books Received* column in *Locus*, and includes books seen between December 1984 and December 1985. The information has been checked and corrected, some new comments have been added, and the contents of all new anthologies, collections, and magazines are listed. Appendicies contain a Book Summary, Cinema Summary, Magazine Report, Recommended Reading, and a small press publisher address directory.

The book contains six main sections in the following formats:

1. <u>Book Author List.</u> This section contains full publication information for each book printed in 1985, listed by book author. Notes about each book are included, as well as the contents for anthologies, collections and magazines first published in 1985.

format:

```
Edition Book Author   BOOK TITLE   (Publisher & ISBN, publication
date [date first seen], price, length, binding) Notes ..........
  Story Title.......... Author....... type, Publisher/date page
     Story Notes...................................
```

example:

```
*Asimov, Isaac & Martin H. Greenberg, eds.  ISAAC ASIMOV PRESENTS
THE GREAT SF STORIES: 14 (1952)  (DAW 0-88677-106-4, 01/86
[12/85], $3.50, 352pp, pb) Anthology of 19 stories from 1952.
Recommended. (CNB)
Contents:                                                     Page
1952 Introduction       Martin H. Greenberg           in     9
The Pedestrian          Ray Bradbury         ss REP Aug,51   13
                                                FSF Feb,52
The Moon is Green        Fritz Leiber        ss GAL May,52   19
```

2. <u>Book Title List.</u> A listing by title of all books entered in the Author Title List.

format:

```
Edition  BOOK TITLE........ Author....... type, Publisher/date
```

example:

```
*THE ALTERNATE ASIMOVS    Isaac Asimov          co Doubleday,86
*AMY'S EYES               Richard Kennedy     n  Harper & Row,85
 ANCIENT OF DAYS          Michael Bishop           n. SFBC,85
*BARBARIANS               Robert Adams, Martin H. Greenberg &
                          Charles G. Waugh, eds. an NAL/Signet,86
```

3. <u>1985 Original Publications.</u> This section lists by author all books and stories that first appeared in 1985. This includes some books and stories dated 1986 that were first seen in 1985.

format:

```
Author
  BOOK TITLE/Story Title................... type, Publisher/date
```

example:

```
Aiken, Joan
  UP THE CHIMNEY DOWN AND OTHER STORIES       oc Harper & Row,85

Arbur, Rosemarie
  MARION ZIMMER BRADLEY                          nf Starmont,85
```

4. <u>New Book Type List.</u> This section lists by type all books first published in 1985. Book Types include Science Fiction Novels, Fantasy Novels, Novelizations, Omnibus Volumes, Collections, Anthologies, Magazines, Reference, Art Books, Associational, and Miscellaneous books. A book may be listed under more than one type. For example, all Star Trek novels are listed under both Science Fiction Novels and Novelizations. For an accurate count of the types of books published see the Book Summary.

format:

```
Author
  BOOK TITLE.............................................. type
```

example:

```
-------------------- Science Fiction Novels --------------------

Burdekin, Katharine
  SWASTIKA NIGHT                                             n.

Callin, Grant
  SATURNALIA                                                 n.
```

5. <u>Story Author List.</u> This section lists by author all stories that are listed in the Book Author List. Included is information on the length and original source of the story, and a list of all 1985 books containing the story.

format:

```
Author
  Story Title.............................. type, Publisher/date
     Story Notes...............................
     BOOK CONTAINING STORY.................. Author........ type
```

example:

```
Benford, Gregory
  The Movement                                   ss FAN Oct,70
     TERRORISTS OF TOMORROW                   Poul Anderson+ an
  Reactionary Utopias                            ar FFR V 4,86
     FAR FRONTIERS VOL. IV/WINTER 1985   Jerry E. Pournelle+ oa
```

6. <u>Story Title List.</u> A listing by title of all stories entered in the Story Author List.

format:

```
Story Title............. Author............ type, Publisher/date
```

example:

```
The Adventure of the German Student
                        Washington Irving     ss TLSTRVL,1824
Afterword               Stephen King                       aw
The Age of the Warrior  Hank Reinhardt        ss HEROFAN,79
```

Abbreviations used in this book are listed on the end-papers in the following format:

```
Abbrev. - Description
```

example:

```
an    - anthology
AND   - ANDROMEDA, Peter Weston, oa FPL
ANGELS& - ANGELS AND SPACESHIPS, Fredric Brown, co DUT 1954
```

Special Considerations:

Sorting Rules: All data is sorted character by character in the following sequence:

1. Blank or space.
2. Special characters, except where they appear as the first characters of a title, in which case they are ignored.
3. Numbers.
4. Letters, upper and lower case are considered equal.

Edition: A one character code indicating the edition of the listed book. * = first edition, + = first U.S. edition. No code indicates a reprint or reissue.

Names: Prefixes to family names such as "de", "del", "Fitz", "van", etc. are listed according to the sorting rules with the position of spaces determined by the common spelling of the name. Therefore "de la Mare" appears before "deFord". Names beginning with "Mc" and "Mac" are sorted as other names. In the Story Author List the Book Author entry may be followed by a "+". This indicates that the book was a collaboration. Only the first author of a collaboration is listed.

Collaborations: All collaborators are listed for each book and story. The main entry for a book will be under the author listed first on the book. Collaborations are listed after solo appearances for each author in the Author sections. If one book lists a story as a collaboration, while another book lists the same story as by only one author, the story will have entries for each version.

Pseudonyms: Each book and story is listed under the author given in that book. As a result some books and stories may appear under the author's real name and under a pseudonym.

Story Titles: Each story title is the same as that given in the book containing the story, except for corrections made for minor punctuation or capitalization differences. If the original story title is different, or if the story also appears under a different title, that information is given in brackets after the story title. Other information that may appear after the story title includes pseudonym author used for the original publication of the story, author of the screenplay that the story is is based upon, notes about the story, or alternate source for the story.

Story Types: Story types are the same as that given the story when it was first published. When this is not given or not available the type is determined from the page length of the story according to the following formula:

```
        under 3 pages = vignette (vi)
          3-20 pages = short story (ss)
```

Organization

        21-50 pages = novelette (nv)
        51-100 pages = novella/short novel (na, sn)
        over 100 pages = novel (n.)

Story Publisher/date: The earliest found printing of the story.
This may additionally contain information on significant reprints
of the story.

examples:

    ASF Jan,85 -- *Analog*, January 1985
    DST V1 #4,79 -- DESTINIES, Volume 1 No. 4, 1979
    SEP Jun 17,67 -- *Saturday Evening Post*, June 17, 1967
    INZ # 3,82 -- *Interzone #3*, 1982
    PIO Jan,1843 -- *The Pioneer*, January 1843
    DEADWIN,85 -- THE DEAD OF WINTER, 1985

    IAS Dec md,83 -- *Asimov's*, mid-December 1983
    UNK Apr +1,39 -- *Unknown*, April and May 1939 (plus 1 issue)

In General:
    Book titles are listed in capitals, magazine titles are list-
ed in italics, movie titles are underlined.
    Novelizations are considered to be novels written from a play,
screenplay, teleplay or are based on a background developed by another author.

    William G. Contento is a Technical Support Engineer for CRAY
Research Inc. He has two previous publications in the science
fiction field; INDEX TO SCIENCE FICTION ANTHOLOGIES AND COLLEC-
TIONS (1978) and INDEX TO SCIENCE FICTION ANTHOLOGIES AND COLLEC-
TIONS 1977 - 1983 (1984), both published by G.K. Hall.

INTRODUCTION

1985, The SF Year in Review, by Charles N. Brown

First the good news: Science fiction had its best year ever
in commercial terms. More books were published, more books were
sold, authors' advances were up, sf books routinely made the
general bestseller lists, and sf was treated with respect by the
general media.

The bad news: Theodore Sturgeon died, Judy-Lynn del Rey did
not recover from a stroke, and, early in 1986, we lost Frank
Herbert. More on this in the obituary section.

Publishing

There were 1,332 sf or fantasy books published in 1985 -- up
13% from 1984 and higher than the previous 1979 record of 1,288.
They sold well too. Nearly all publishers of sf agreed it was the
best year yet. Science fiction did much better than general
publishing last year for at least two reasons. There were more
hardcovers than usual which were packaged, advertised, and sold
along with the paperbacks. The hardcover mass market book is
coming into its own in general publishing, but the sf field was
there first. The chain stores dramatically increased their sf
sales. Waldenbooks sf club had a year-end membership of 300,000
compared to 150,000 for romance and 60,000 for mystery.

As any science fiction reader should know, any advance brings
more problems and the seeds of its own destruction. Because sf
was selling so well, publishers overproduced both hardcovers and
paperbacks, and upped advances. Now there are too many books,
returns are way up, and prices are going higher. The average
paperback has gone from $2.95 to $3.50. The chains were also
forced into a price war with many top sf novels as loss leaders.
Unlike other areas where prices can vary tremendously and wholesale cost is much lower, books carry a retail price tag and cost
about 60% of that price wholesale. Bookstore overhead averages
20%, so any book sold for 20% or more under list price is probably
a money loser.

The sf field is dominated by seven publishers, although 122
companies did sf and fantasy books last year. The Berkley/Ace
combine did the most, had the most originals, and was second only
to Del Rey in the bestseller department. Science fiction editor-
in-chief Susan Allison was promoted to Vice President and given
more say in running the company. Del Rey was very strong in
fantasy and in general bestsellers. Executive editor Owen Lock
took over control in October. Tor expanded tremendously and more
than doubled their output; they actually passed Del Rey in total
number of books and were third in bestsellers. Beth Meacham was
promoted to science fiction editor-in-chief. The revitalized
program at Bantam, under publishing director Lou Aronica, did an
excellent job on all fronts. They hired Shawna McCarthy as senior
editor. DAW increased production slightly. Betsy Wollheim took
over the company when her father, Donald Wollheim, was felled by
serious illness. She hired Sheila Gilbert as her second in command. New companies Baen and Bluejay had excellent expansion
years. Warner/Popular Library launched a new line, Questar Books,
and Arbor House under editor David Hartwell expanded into original
publishing.

All was not completely well with publishers. Pinnacle Books
went bankrupt, tying up authors' properties for possibly years to
come. Pocket Books finished dismantling their Timescape program
in an orgy of self-destruction.

Books of the Year

The most popular novels of 1985 included ROBOTS AND EMPIRE by
Isaac Asimov (Doubleday), the latest item cementing together his
future history; THE CAT WHO WALKS THROUGH WALLS by Robert A.
Heinlein (Putnam), which reprises characters from a number of past
Heinlein books; CHAPTERHOUSE: DUNE by the late Frank Herbert
(Putnam), which brings the old saga to an end -- with room for new
beginnings which, alas, will now never be written; THE INVADERS
PLAN by L. Ron Hubbard (Bridge), the first part of a ten-volume
satire which the author finished before he died; FOOTFALL by Larry
Niven and Jerry Pournelle (Del Rey), where sf writers help save
the world; CONTACT by Carl Sagan (Simon & Schuster), a first novel
by the famed science writer; THE WISHSONG OF SHANNARA by Terry
Brooks (Del Rey), the conclusion of a simplified Tolkien-like
trilogy; THE VAMPIRE LESTAT by Anne Rice (Knopf), sequel to her
INTERVIEW WITH THE VAMPIRE; WITH A TANGLED SKEIN by Piers Anthony
(Del Rey), book three of the "fates personified" series; and
KILLASHANDRA by Anne McCaffrey (Del Rey), a blend of sf and romance.

The book that created the most controversy was ALWAYS COMING
HOME by Ursula K. Le Guin (Harper & Row), a utopian future history
told in poetry, prose, music (it comes with a cassette), sayings,
etc.

My personal favorites of the year were EON by Greg Bear (Bluejay) and BETWEEN THE STROKES OF NIGHT by Charles Sheffield (Baen),
two books with mind-boggling concepts; ARTIFACT by Gregory Benford
(Tor), a fine blend of thriller and sf; DINNER AT DEVIANT'S PALACE
by Tim Powers (Ace), for its rich imagery; HELLICONIA WINTER by
Brian Aldiss (Atheneum), a stunning conclusion to the trilogy;
LOVECRAFT'S BOOK by Richard A. Lupoff (Arkham House), an almost
believable alternate history; CUCKOO'S EGG by C.J. Cherryh (DAW),
for the best aliens of the year; and FIVE-TWELFTHS OF HEAVEN by
Melissa Scott (Baen), a unique brand of space opera and quasi-
magic.

Other excellent 1985 novels were BRIGHTNESS FALLS FROM THE AIR
by James Tiptree, Jr. (Tor), BLOOD MUSIC by Greg Bear (Arbor
House), THE SUMMER TREE by Guy Gavriel Kay (Arbor House), HUMAN
ERROR by Paul Preuss (Tor), TRUMPS OF DOOM by Roger Zelazny (Arbor
House), THE ENCHANTRESS by Han Suyin (Bantam), and LYONESSE II:
THE GREEN PEARL by Jack Vance (Underwood-Miller).

There were more good first novels in 1985 than we can possibly
list. Pay special attention to SARABAND OF LOST TIME by Richard
Grant (Avon), EMPRISE by Michael P. Kube-McDowell (Berkley), TER-
RARIUM by Scott Russell Sanders (Tor), THE TORCH OF HONOR by Roger
MacBride Allen (Baen), WALK THE MOONS ROAD by Jim Aikin (Del Rey),
SKIRMISH by Melisa C. Michaels (Tor), and TAILCHASER'S SONG by Tad
Williams (DAW).

There are also exciting stories by new authors in WRITERS OF
THE FUTURE edited by Algis Budrys (Bridge) and a whole course in
sf writing in MEDEA: HARLAN'S WORLD edited by Harlan Ellison
(Bantam).

Small Press

The small press publishers, most of whom have specialized in
high-priced limited signed editions in the past decade, are doing
more original fiction and hardcover library editions of books only
available in paperback.

The high-priced limited edition is still there -- especially
for Stephen King collectors. Special signed editions of THE
TALISMAN (Donald Grant) and SKELETON CREW (Scream/Press) were
selling for hundreds of dollars just days after their publication.
THE EYES OF THE DRAGON (Philtrum Press), a King original and the
most lavishly produced book of the year, is worth at least six
times its published price of $125.00 already.

Small press books should usually be ordered directly from the
publisher -- especially for limited signed editions. Write them
for availability of past books and for advance notice of future
works. Phantasia Press was outstanding for straight science fiction in 1985, with special editions of CUCKOO'S EGG and THE KIF
STRIKE BACK by C.J. Cherryh, MEDEA edited by Harlan Ellison, a
revised hardcover of the Hugo and Nebula winner David Brin's
STARTIDE RISING, as well as others. Donald M. Grant did a lavishly illustrated version of THE TALISMAN by King and Straub which is
still available, as well as THE BOOK OF KANE by Karl Edward Wagner
and a new special edition of KULL by Robert E. Howard. And don't
miss the wonderfully macabre illustrated poem A MONSTER AT CHRIST-
MAS by Thomas Canty. Underwood-Miller specializes in Jack Vance.
They did the first edition of LYONESSE II: THE GREEN PEARL as well
as some fantasy work. They also did limited editions of Zelazny's
TRUMPS OF DOOM, Silverberg's SAILING TO BYZANTIUM, etc. Scream/
Press specializes in horror books chillingly illustrated by J.K.
Potter and Harry O. Morris. Their 1985 offerings included the
lavish SKELETON CREW by King, COLD PRINT by Ramsey Campbell, the
BOOKS OF BLOOD by Clive Barker, and TOPLIN by Michael McDowell.
Mark V. Ziesing does excellent sf collections such as BEASTMARKS
by A.A. Attanasio and THE BOOK OF IAN WATSON. Corroboree Press
publishes editions of R.A. Lafferty. They also did Philip K.
Dick's screenplay for his novel UBIK. NESFA Press produces short
story collections honoring guests of honor at conventions. LATE
KNIGHT EDITION by Damon Knight and LIGHT FROM A LONE STAR by Jack
Vance were their 1985 books. Dark Harvest did a collection of
original horror stories, NIGHT VISIONS 2, edited by Charles L.
Grant, for the World Fantasy Convention. Dragon Press produced a
non-sf original by Philip K. Dick, IN MILTON LUMKY TERRITORY.
There were many others, some of which I'll try to cover if they
still exist next year.

Obituaries

Theodore Sturgeon, 67, died May 8, 1985, of fibrosis compli-
cated by pneumonia. Sturgeon was unquestionably one of the greats
of science fiction. He started writing in the thirties and pro-

duced a handful of good to excellent stories between 1939 and 1940 including "It", "Microcosmic God", "Shottle Bop", and "Bianca's Hands" -- which was rejected many times before appearing as a prize-winning story in England half a decade later. It was his most important early work and explored his main themes of love and empathy for strange characters. In the late forties and fifties he developed these themes brilliantly in "The World Well Lost", "The Wages of Synergy", "Saucer of Loneliness", "To Here and the Easel", and the classic MORE THAN HUMAN (1953), arguably one of the ten best novels ever written. It won the 1954 International Fantasy Award. Sturgeon never attained that height again at novel length, but continued to turn out excellent shorter work. There are successful and unsuccessful stories, but few bad ones. Sturgeon's stories always had something to say but were rarely didactic, and his command of imagery and language was awesome. His first novel THE DREAMING JEWELS (1950) is still a reading experience, as is THE COSMIC RAPE (1958) and VENUS PLUS X (1960). Sturgeon's best work is in the short story collections A WAY HOME (1955), CAVIAR (1955), E PLURIBUS UNICORN (1953), and A TOUCH OF STRANGE (1958). His 1970 story "Slow Sculpture" won both Hugo and Nebula Awards. Sturgeon wrote few stories after 1962, turning more to reviewing, teaching, and lecturing. Both his writing and teaching left a lasting impression on most who came in contact with them.

Frank Herbert, 65, author of DUNE, died February 11, 1986 of complications following cancer surgery. Although he wrote over two dozen books and numerous short stories, his reputation rests on DUNE (1965), probably the best selling sf novel of all time. The series has an estimated 25 million copies in print. Herbert's first novel, THE DRAGON IN THE SEA (1956) aka UNDER PRESSURE, was a fully mature work exploring his lifelong preoccupations with man and his environment. DUNE was rejected by over a dozen publishers because of its length and complexity. It was finally printed in a small edition by Chilton, a non-fiction publisher, to satisfy their editor, sf writer Sterling Lanier. It won both Hugo and Nebula, achieved cult status over the next decade, and earned author and publisher millions of dollars. It usually heads lists of the top sf novels of all time. The third book in the series, CHILDREN OF DUNE (1976), was the first genuine science fiction bestseller -- 75,000 copies in hardcover. Herbert became one of the earliest sf authors able to command a million-dollar advance. He was an excellent didactic writer whose books are filled with ideas and concepts frequently tinged with mysticism. In many ways, he was the opposite of Sturgeon, whose stories are about humanism and understanding. Herbert's best work is at novel length. Outside the "Dune" series, I would particularly recommend WHIPPING STAR (1964), THE DOSADI EXPERIMENT (1977), and the non-sf novel SOUL CATCHER (1972).

Judy-Lynn del Rey, 43, publisher of Del Rey Books, suffered a massive brain hemorrhage on October 16, 1985. She died four months later, on February 20, 1986, without ever regaining consciousness. Judy-Lynn Benjamin began her editorial career in 1965 at *Galaxy* magazine, where she became managing editor in 1969, replacing Lester del Rey, whom she married in 1971. She was hired by Betty Ballantine in 1973 and became Ballantine sf editor in 1974 when the Ballantines suddenly left the company. She had an unerring eye for commercial fiction and was a genius at promotion and at conveying her enthusiasms to the sales force. She hired her husband in 1975 as fantasy editor and, between them, they produced the most successful sf and fantasy publishing list of all time. In 1977 she was given her own imprint, Del Rey Books. Her first two efforts were STAR WARS, which she bought a year before the movie appeared (it sold nearly 4 million copies), and THE SWORD OF SHANNARA by Terry Brooks, the first fantasy trade paperback to make the *New York Times* bestseller list. It wasn't a fluke. Del Rey Books did the same with Anne McCaffrey, Stephen R. Donaldson, Piers Anthony, David Eddings, Larry Niven, Marion Zimmer Bradley, and many others. She was particularly proud of being the publisher of Heinlein, Asimov, and Clarke. One industry insider described her as "the E.F. Hutton of publishing. When she talks, everybody listens."

L. Ron Hubbard, 74, Golden Age science fiction author, founder of Dianetics and Scientology, and, most recently, a bestselling science fiction writer, died of a stroke on January 24, 1986. Hubbard was a prodigious pulp writer in the thirties and forties, famed for being able to write saleable first draft fiction very quickly. He wrote for *Astounding* and *Unknown* from 1939 to 1950, when he announced Dianetics, the Science of Mental Health, in some *Astounding* articles and in the bestselling book DIANETICS (1950). Many sf writers were early converts, but dropped out when Dianetics blossomed into Scientology and the Church of Scientology. In 1982, he returned to science fiction with the bestselling BATTLEFIELD EARTH. He also finished a ten-part novel, MISSION EARTH; the first two volumes have appeared, and the rest are scheduled. He also sponsored the "Writers of the Future" contest, awards, and publications. His early magazine fiction was republished in book form. The best ones are FINAL BLACKOUT (1948), SLAVES OF SLEEP (1948), FEAR AND TYPEWRITER IN THE SKY (1951), and OLE DOC METHUSELAH (1970).

Jack Gaughan, 54, died July 21, 1985, of cancer. He was a four-time Hugo winner and the field's most popular artist in the late sixties.

Larry T. Shaw, 60, a well-known editor, died April 1, 1985 of cancer. He edited *Infinity* magazine in the fifties, and was a book editor at Regency, Lancer, and Dell in the sixties. Harlan Ellison described him as "the single most important editor in my life." Shaw also developed the "Conan" properties for Lancer. He was a moving tribute in his last public appearance at the 1984 world convention.

Robert P. Mills, 65, two-time Hugo-winning editor of *The Magazine of Fantasy & Science Fiction* (1958-1962) and well-known literary agent, was found dead of a heart attack on February 8, 1986.

Other 1985 deaths included Italo Calvino, 62, famed Italian writer and winner of the World Fantasy Award; Leo R. Summers, 59,

a major artist for *Astounding/Analog*; Robert Nathan, 91, author of PORTRAIT OF JENNIE (1940); T.L. Sherred, 69, author of "E for Effort" (1947); Douglass Wallop, 65, who wrote THE YEAR THE YANKEES LOST THE PENNANT (1954); Bernard Wolfe, 70, author of LIMBO (1952); Walter B. Gibson, 88, author of "The Shadow" series; Rene Barjavel, 74, well-known French sf author; and Robert Graves, 90, whose heretical views on mythology and history affected several generations of fantasy writers.

Magazines

The specialty magazines published some excellent fiction this year. *Asimov's* and *Analog* did especially well, but it didn't help circulation. *Asimov's* dropped 20% while *Analog's* was flat. *Fantasy & Science Fiction* and *Twilight Zone* lost circulation, while *Amazing* went up slightly. Only *Omni* did well.

Three new magazines appeared. *Far Frontiers*, a hybrid anthology/magazine in paperback form, edited by Jerry Pournelle and Jim Baen, published four issues. *Night Cry*, a *Twilight Zone* spinoff edited by Alan Rodgers and specializing in pure horror, also published four issues. *Stardate*, a former games/media magazine now edited by David Bischoff, added one-third fiction; it published two issues. The long-awaited L. Ron Hubbard's *To the Stars* did not appear. *Weird Tales* and *The Last Wave* disappeared. *If* and *Aboriginal SF* have been announced for 1986.

Michael Blaine replaced T.E.D. Klein as editor of *The Twilight Zone* and plans to move the fiction away from pure horror to "more human-centered fantasy." Gardner Dozois replaced Shawna McCarthy at *Asimov's*. Patrick L. Price replaced George Scithers at *Amazing* early in 1986.

There were 58 issues of specialty magazines plus 26 original anthologies plus lots of stories in *Omni* and other general magazines -- about 840 stories all told -- up more than 20% from last year.

Movies

1985 wasn't a good year for sf movies. <u>Back to the Future</u> and <u>Cocoon</u> did well enough. <u>Mad Max: Beyond Thunderdome</u> did ok. <u>The Black Cauldron</u>, <u>D.A.R.Y.L.</u>, <u>My Science Project</u>, <u>Silver Bullet</u>, <u>Ladyhawke</u>, and <u>Return to Oz</u> were all failures. <u>Enemy Mine</u> failed commercially but got good reviews within the sf field.

The three new television anthology shows, <u>Amazing Stories</u>, <u>Twilight Zone</u>, and <u>Alfred Hitchcock</u>, all had middle ratings and might or might not last. <u>Twilight Zone</u> got the best critical reception.

Science fiction and fantasy do very well on videotape and video disk. The release of <u>Star Trek</u> episodes helped sales tremendously. 1985 also saw the expansion of the sf audio market. You can now listen to dramatized tape versions of Clarke's CHILDHOOD'S END, Heinlein's THE GREEN HILLS OF EARTH, Asimov's THE GODS THEMSELVES, Le Guin's THE LEFT HAND OF DARKNESS, Farmer's TO YOUR SCATTERED BODIES GO, etc.

1986, with <u>Aliens</u> and <u>Star Trek IV</u>, should be a much better year for movies.

Headliners

Stephen King continued to be a whole industry unto himself. When it was revealed he was also Richard Bachman, the latest Bachman novel, THINNER, zoomed to the top of the bestseller list, as did an omnibus reissue of the four earlier Bachman novels. SKELETON CREW and THE TALISMAN also were up there on the lists, as was PET SEMATARY. King set a new advance record with $5 million per book on a two-book contract with NAL. His TALISMAN co-author, Peter Straub, got a mere $1 million per book on a three-book contract. Between September 1986 and November 1987, a new King novel is set to appear every 3 1/2 months. Perhaps a separate Stephen King bestseller list?

Robert A. Heinlein sold THE CAT WHO WALKS THROUGH WALLS for a multi-million-dollar advance, celebrated his 78th birthday, and started a new novel.

Arthur C. Clarke turned in THE SONGS OF DISTANT EARTH for Spring 1986 publication.

Isaac Asimov turned in FOUNDATION AND EARTH for Fall 1986 publication.

Harlan Ellison did not turn in THE LAST DANGEROUS VISIONS.

Martin H. Greenberg edited eight of the thirty-eight reprint anthologies and became the consulting editor of *Amazing Stories*.

Awards

Robin McKinley won the Newbery Award, presented annually for the outstanding juvenile book of the year, with her fantasy THE HERO AND THE CROWN.

William Gibson won the Philip K. Dick Memorial Award for best original paperback of 1984 with NEUROMANCER.

The John W. Campbell Memorial Award for best novel of 1984 went to Frederik Pohl for THE YEARS OF THE CITY.

The 1984 Nebula Awards were presented at an overcrowded banquet at the Warwick Hotel in New York City on May 4th, 1985. Winners were: Best Novel, NEUROMANCER by William Gibson; Best Novella, "PRESS ENTER ■" by John Varley; Best Novelette, "Bloodchild" by Octavia E. Butler; Best Short Story, "Morning Child" by Gardner Dozois. A special award was given to Ian and Betty Ballantine for their pioneering contributions in publishing science fiction and fantasy. The Nebula Awards are nominated and voted on by members of the Science Fiction Writers of America.

The 1985 *Locus* awards were announced on May 23rd, 1985, in Oakland California. Winners were: Best SF Novel, THE INTEGRAL TREES by Larry Niven; Best Fantasy Novel, JOB: A COMEDY OF JUSTICE by Robert A. Heinlein; Best First Novel, THE WILD SHORE by Kim Stanley Robinson; Best Novella, "PRESS ENTER ■" by John Varley; Best Novelette, "Bloodchild" by Octavia E. Butler; Best Short Story, "Salvador" by Lucius Shepard; Best Anthology, LIGHT YEARS

AND DARK edited by Michael Bishop; Best Single Author Collection, THE GHOST LIGHT by Fritz Leiber; Best Related Non-Fiction Book, SLEEPLESS NIGHTS IN THE PROCRUSTEAN BED by Harlan Ellison; Best Artist, Michael Whelan; Best Magazine, *Locus*; Best Publisher, Ballantine/Del Rey. The *Locus* Awards are chosen by subscribers to *Locus* magazine.

The 1985 Hugo Awards were presented in Melbourne, Australia on August 25th. Winners were: Best Novel, NEUROMANCER by William Gibson; Best Novella, "PRESS ENTER ■" by John Varley; Best Novelette, "Bloodchild" by Octavia E. Butler; Best Short Story, "The Crystal Spheres" by David Brin; Best Non-Fiction Book, WONDER'S CHILD: MY LIFE IN SCIENCE FICTION by Jack Williamson; Best Dramatic Presentation, <u>2010</u>; Best Professional Editor, Terry Carr; Best Professional Artist, Michael Whelan; Best Semi-Prozine, *Locus*, edited by Charles N. Brown; Best Fanzine, *File 770*, edited by Mike Glyer; Best Fan Writer, Dave Langford; Best Fan Artist, Alexis Gilliland. The John W. Campbell Award for best new writer went to Lucius Shepard. Nominations and voting for the Hugo Awards and the Campbell Award are open to any member of the World Science Fiction Convention in the year of presentation.

The 1985 World Fantasy Awards were presented at the World Fantasy Convention in Tucson, Arizona on November 3rd. Winners were: Life Achievement, Theodore Sturgeon; Best Novel (tie) MYTHAGO WOOD by Robert Holdstock, BRIDGE OF BIRDS by Barry Hughart; Best Novella, "The Unconquered Country" by Geoff Ryman; Best Short Fiction (tie), "Still Life With Scorpion" by Scott Baker, "The Bones Wizard" by Alan Ryan; Best Anthology/Collection, CLIVE BARKER'S BOOKS OF BLOOD, Vols. 1-3 by Clive Barker; Best Artist, Edward Gorey; Special Award (Professional), Chris Van Allsburg for THE MYSTERIES OF HARRIS BURDICK; Special Award (Non-Professional), Stuart David Schiff for *Whispers* and Whispers Press; Special Convention Award, Evangeline Walton. The awards are chosen by a panel of judges.

<u>Conventions</u>

The 43rd World Science Fiction Convention, Aussiecon Two, was held in Melbourne, Australia August 22 to 26, 1985, with Gene Wolfe and Ted White as guests of honor and Bob Shaw as toastmaster. The total attendance was 1,600, making it the smallest worldcon since Aussiecon One ten years ago. There were between 300 and 400 Americans and about 100 other foreigners present, and we had a ball despite a somewhat poorly organized committee. The flavor of the yearly party was somewhat different -- and that was all to the good. The point driven home time after time was that Australia is BIG, bigger than the United States but with a population smaller than California. Many Australian fans could not make the convention because the distance was too much and internal air costs are high. Those that did showed us a different, friendly culture which was not quasi-American despite a similar language. What held us together was science fiction -- a truly international language. At the end of the convention, while others were continuing their tours or sightseeing, a hundred of the hardiest (or craziest) souls, including this reporter, packed their bags and headed for the American national convention in Texas.

The North American Science Fiction Convention, held whenever the world convention is outside the United States, took place in Austin TX August 29 to September 2, 1985. It was appropriately called The First Occasional Lone Star Science Fiction Convention and Chili Cook-off, and was certainly different from the world convention. The shock of going from an Australian winter to a hot Texas summer was -- different. The chili cookoff was spicier, the attendance of 2,700 was higher, but the convention was spread out on both sides of a river, and it seemed smaller and less crowded. The guests of honor, Jack Vance, Richard Powers, Joanne Burger, and Chad Oliver, were friendly and approachable, and Orson Scott Card's Secular Humanism Revival was most popular. A good time was had by most -- even those who complained the loudest.

--Charles N. Brown

AUTHOR LIST, BOOKS

AARON, CHESTER

ALDISS, BRIAN W.

*Aaron, Chester OUT OF SIGHT, OUT OF MIND (Lippincott 0-397-32100-7, 09/85 [09/85], $11.50, 184pp, hc) Juvenile fantasy novel of twin telepathic teenagers working for world peace.

Abbey, Lynn THE BLACK FLAME (Ace 0-441-06587-2, 07/85 [06/85], $3.50, 376pp, pb) Reissue (Ace 1980) fantasy novel, sequel to DAUGHTER OF THE BRIGHT MOON. Third printing.

Abbey, Lynn DAUGHTER OF THE BRIGHT MOON (Ace 0-441-13873-X, 05/85 [04/85], $3.50, 410pp, pb) Reissue (Ace 1979) fantasy novel. Fifth printing.

*Abbey, Lynn & Robert Lynn Asprin, eds. CROSS-CURRENTS Main listing under Robert Lynn Asprin.

Abbey, Lynn & Robert Lynn Asprin, eds. THE FACE OF CHAOS Main listing under Robert Lynn Asprin.

Abbey, Lynn & Robert Lynn Asprin, eds. TALES FROM THE VULGAR UNICORN Main listing under Robert Lynn Asprin.

*Abbey, Lynn & Robert Lynn Asprin, eds. THIEVES' WORLD, BOOK 7: THE DEAD OF WINTER Main listing under Robert Lynn Asprin.

*Abbey, Lynn & Robert Lynn Asprin, eds. THIEVES' WORLD, BOOK 8: SOUL OF THE CITY Main listing under Robert Lynn Asprin.

Abbey, Lynn & Robert Lynn Asprin, eds. WINGS OF OMEN Main listing under Robert Lynn Asprin.

*Abrams, R. Vaughan PARA (Seven Suns 0-931783-00-4, 01/86 [12/85], $17.95, 372pp, hc) Mystical fantasy novel, first of a series, with illustrations by Lyn Durham Abrams. Not available in bookstores.

+Adams, Douglas THE ORIGINAL HITCHHIKER RADIO SCRIPTS (Crown/Harmony 0-517-55950-1, 12/85 [11/85], $9.95, 248pp, pb) Reprint (Pan 1985), first American edition of a compendium of scripts, with a new introduction by the author plus comments and some material not broadcast.

Adams, Douglas SO LONG, AND THANKS FOR ALL THE FISH (SFBC #4082, 08/85 [07/85], $4.98, 152pp, hc) Reprint (Pan 1984) sf novel, fourth in the "Hitchhiker" trilogy.

Adams, Douglas SO LONG, AND THANKS FOR ALL THE FISH (Pocket 0-671-52580-8, 11/85 [10/85], $3.95, 204pp, pb) Reprint (Pan 1984) humorous sf novel, #4 in the "Hitchhiker" trilogy.

*Adams, Richard MAIA (Viking U.K. 0-670-80033-3, 1984 [12/84], -L12.95, 1056pp, hc) Fantasy novel. This is fast-paced adventure, despite the length, and set in the same Beklan Empire as SHARDIK. Recommended. (FCM)

+Adams, Richard MAIA (Knopf 0-394-52857-3, 02/85 [01/85], $19.95, 1062pp, hc) Reprint (Viking U.K. 1984) fantasy novel, first U.S. edition.

Adams, Richard MAIA (SFBC #6246, 09/85 [10/85], $7.98, 891pp, hc) Reprint (Viking U.K. 1984) fantasy novel.

Adams, Richard WATERSHIP DOWN (Avon 0-380-00293-0, 01/86 [12/85], $4.50, 478pp, pb) Reissue (Macmillan 1974) fantasy novel of talking rabbits.

Adams, Robert CASTAWAYS IN TIME (NAL/Signet 0-451-12664-5, 01/85 [12/84], $2.75, 234pp, pb) Reissue (Starblaze 1980) sf novel.

Adams, Robert THE HORSECLANS 1: THE COMING OF THE HORSECLANS (Macdonald 0-356-10666-7, 04/85 [03/85], £8.95, 199pp, hc) Reprint (Pinnacle 1975) sf novel, first of the series. This is the first hardcover edition.

*Adams, Robert HORSES OF THE NORTH (NAL/Signet 0-451-13626-8, 06/85 [05/85], $3.50, 253pp, pb) Sf novel, "Horseclans" #13.

*Adams, Robert THE SEVEN MAGICAL JEWELS OF IRELAND (NAL/Signet 0-451-13340-4, 01/85 [12/84], $2.95, 254pp, pb) Sf novel, sequel to CASTAWAYS IN TIME.

*Adams, Robert TALES OF THE HORSECLANS (NAL/Plume 0-452-25726-3, 11/85 [10/85], $8.95, 578pp, pb) Omnibus edition of the first three novels in the "Horseclans" sf series.
Contents: Page
THE COMING OF THE HORSECLANS
                          Robert Adams   n. PIN 1975
SWORDS OF THE HORSECLANS Robert Adams   n. PIN 1977
REVENGE OF THE HORSECLANS
                          Robert Adams   n. PIN 1977

*Adams, Robert, Martin H. Greenberg & Charles G. Waugh, eds. BARBARIANS (NAL/Signet 0-451-14054-0, 01/86 [12/85], $3.95, 368pp, pb) Anthology of 13 stories.
Contents: Page
Introduction   Robert Adams   in   7
Scylla's Daughter   Fritz Leiber   na FAN May,61   10
Stone Man   Fred Saberhagen   nv WOT May,67   65
Sand Sister   Andre Norton   na HEROFAN,79   96
Swordsman of Lost Terra Poul Anderson   nv PLS Nov,51 140
The Were-Wolf   Clemence Housman   nv ATA 1896   184
Swords Against the Marluk
                      Katherine Kurtz   nv FLS # 4,77 217

Not Long Before the End Larry Niven   ss FSF Apr,69 242
Maureen Birnbaum, Barbarian Swordsperson
                      George Alec Effinger ss FSF Jan,82 253
Thurigon Agonistes   Ardath Mayhar   ss 1983   261
Vault of Silence   Lin Carter   nv SWDAGTM,70   270
The Other One   Karl Edward Wagner ss ESP # 1,77 297
The Age of the Warrior Hank Reinhardt   ss HEROFAN,79 305
Beyond the Black River Robert E. Howard nv WRT May,35 318

*Adams, Robert & Andre Norton, eds. MAGIC IN ITHKAR Main listing under Andre Norton.

*Adams, Robert & Andre Norton, eds. MAGIC IN ITHKAR 2 Main listing under Andre Norton.

*Ahern, Jerry THE SURVIVALIST #12: THE REBELLION (Zebra 0-8217-1676-X, 10/85 [09/85], $2.50, 252pp, pb) Sf novel in a post-holocaust adventure series.

*Aickman, Robert NIGHT VOICES: STRANGE STORIES (Gollancz 0-575-03648-6, 11/85 [11/85], £8.95, 185pp, hc) Collection of horror stories, with a foreword by Barry Humphries.
Contents: Page
Foreword   Barry Humphries   fw   9
The Stains   Robert Aickman   na NWT # 1,80   13
Just a Song at Twilight Robert Aickman   ss GHB # 4   71
Laura   Robert Aickman   ss CLDFEAR,77   87
Rosamund's Bower   Robert Aickman   nv NTVOICE,85   97
The Trains   Robert Aickman   nv WEAREFR   123
Mark Ingestre: The Customer's Tale
                      Robert Aickman   ss DRKFRCS,80 165

*Aigner, Kurt W. ALLISTAR: JOURNEY THROUGH A MIND (Vantage 0-533-06159-8, 04/85 [03/85], $8.95, 101pp, hc) Fantasy novel, published by a vanity press.

Aiken, Joan MIDNIGHT IS A PLACE (Dell/Yearling 0-440-45634-7, 1985 [11/85], $3.50, 287pp, pb) Reprint (Cape 1974) juvenile novel set in Aiken's alternate-world Britain.

+Aiken, Joan UP THE CHIMNEY DOWN AND OTHER STORIES (Harper & Row 0-06-020036-7, 11/85 [12/85], $11.95, 248pp, hc) Reprint (UK 1984), first U.S. edition. Collection of fantasy stories. Also available in a library edition, 0-06-020037-5, $11.89.
Contents: Page
The Last Chimney Cuckoo Joan Aiken   nv UPCHMNY,84   1
Miss Hooting's Legacy Joan Aiken   nv UPCHMNY,84   27
The Gift Giving   Joan Aiken   ss SIXTEEN   50
The Dog on the Roof   Joan Aiken   nv UPCHMNY,84   66
The Missing Heir   Joan Aiken   nv UPCHMNY,84   96
Up the Chimney Down   Joan Aiken   nv UPCHMNY,84 118
Christmas at Troy   Joan Aiken   nv UPCHMNY,84 149
The Midnight Rose   Joan Aiken   ss UPCHMNY,84 171
The Happiest Sheep in London
                      Joan Aiken   nv UPCHMNY,84 191
The Fire Dogs   Joan Aiken   ss UPCHMNY,84 212
Potter's Gray   Joan Aiken   ss UPCHMNY,84 228

*Aikin, Jim WALK THE MOONS ROAD (Ballantine/Del Rey 0-345-32169-3, 06/85 [05/85], $2.95, 340pp, pb) Sf novel, a first novel. Excellent adventure, with well-done aliens. Recommended. (DLN)

Akers, Alan Burt KROZAIR OF KREGEN (DAW 0-88677-037-8, 04/85 [03/85], $2.75, 223pp, pb) Reissue (DAW 1977) fantasy novel, 3rd printing. "The Krozair Cycle" #3. Illustrations by Josh Kirby.

Akers, Alan Burt RENEGADE OF KREGEN (DAW 0-88677-035-1, 04/85 [03/85], $2.75, 192pp, pb) Reissue (DAW 1976) fantasy novel, 3rd printing. "The Krozair Cycle" #2. Illustrations by Jack Gaughan.

Akers, Alan Burt THE TIDES OF KREGEN (DAW 0-88677-034-3, 04/85 [03/85], $2.75, 208pp, pb) Reissue (DAW 1976) fantasy novel. "The Krozair Cycle" #1, 3rd DAW printing. Cover and illustrations by Michael Whelan. For some reason, DAW has brought back the Akers name even though the later books are as by Dray Prescot. In either case, the actual author of these Burroughs pastiches is Ken Bulmer. All three reprints have covers by Michael Whelan with his name almost as big as that of the author.

Aldiss, Brian W. GALAXIES LIKE GRAINS OF SAND (NAL/Signet 0-451-13416-8, 02/85 [01/85], $2.75, 189pp, pb) Reissue (NAL/Signet 1960) quasi-novel. 6th Signet printing. U.S. version of the British collection THE CANOPY OF TIME (Faber 1959) with connecting material. The American version is much better. Recommended. (CNB)

*Aldiss, Brian W. THE HELLICONIA TRILOGY (Atheneum 0-689-11566-0, 05/85 [04/85], $50.00, 3 vols., hc) Signed, boxed set of HELLICONIA SPRING, HELLICONIA SUMMER, and HELLICONIA WINTER. The three volumes are copies of earlier listed books. Only the box, ISBN number, autograph, and price are new.

*Aldiss, Brian W. HELLICONIA WINTER (Atheneum 0-689-11541-5, 04/85 [03/85], $17.95, 281pp, hc) Sf novel, conclusion of the "Helliconia" trilogy. Highly recommended. (FCM)

*Aldiss, Brian W. HELLICONIA WINTER (Jonathan Cape 0-224-01847-7, 04/85 [05/85], £8.95, 281pp, hc) Sf novel, conclusion of the "Helliconia" trilogy. Simultaneous with the U.S. edition.

Aldiss, Brian W. <u>HELLICONIA WINTER</u> (SFBC #4733, 09/85 [10/85], $5.98, 301pp, hc) Reprint (Atheneum 1985) sf novel, conclusion of the "Helliconia" trilogy.

*Aldiss, Brian W. <u>THE HORATIO STUBBS SAGA</u> (Granada/Panther 0-586-06031-6, 1985 [10/85], £3.50, 670pp, pb) Non-sf/fantasy, associational. An omnibus edition of three semi-autobiographical novels chronicling the bawdy (mis)adventures of Stubbs: THE HAND-REARED BOY (Weidenfeld & Nicolson 1970), A SOLDIER ERECT (Weidenfeld & Nicolson 1971), and A RUDE AWAKENING (Weidenfeld & Nicolson 1978).

Aldiss, Brian W. <u>THE MALACIA TAPESTRY</u> (Berkley 0-425-08079-X, 09/85 [08/85], $3.50, 402pp, pb) Reprint (Cape 1976) sf novel of an alternate, fantastical world.

*Aldiss, Brian W. <u>THE PALE SHADOW OF SCIENCE</u> (Serconia no ISBN, 04/85 [03/85], $10.00; limited to 500 copies, 128pp, hc) Non-fiction, collection of essays ranging from autobiography to sf criticism.

Aldiss, Brian W. <u>STARSWARM</u> (Baen 0-671-55999-0, 12/85 [11/85], $2.95, 246pp, pb) Reprint (Signet 1964) collection. This is labeled "first complete U.S. edition." It adds one story "Intangibles, Inc." to the earlier collection and drops all earlier copyright mention.
Contents:

				Page
A Kind of Artistry	Brian W. Aldiss	nv FSF Oct,62	1
Hearts and Engines [Soldiers Running]	Brian W. Aldiss	ss NWS Jun,60	31
The Underprivileged	Brian W. Aldiss	ss NWS May,63	46
The Game of God [Segregation]	Brian W. Aldiss	na NWS Jul,58	66
Shards	Brian W. Aldiss	ss FSF Apr,62	115
Legends of Smith's Burst	Brian W. Aldiss	nv NEB Jun,59	127
O Moon of My Delight [Moon of Delight]	Brian W. Aldiss	nv NWS Mar,61	168
Intangibles Inc.	Brian W. Aldiss	nv SCF Feb,59	202
Old Hundredth	Brian W. Aldiss	ss NWS Nov,60	231

*Aldridge, Alexandra <u>THE SCIENTIFIC WORLD VIEW IN DYSTOPIA</u> (UMI 0-9357-1572-8, 1984 [05/85], $24.95 + postage, 97pp, hc) Non-fiction, literary criticism. This revision of a doctoral thesis appeared in 1984, but we did not see it until 1985.

Alexander, Lloyd <u>THE BEGGAR QUEEN</u> (Dell/Laurel Leaf 0-440-90548-6, 10/85 [09/85], $2.95, 237pp, pb) Reprint (Dutton 1984) young-adult fantasy novel. Conclusion of the "Westmark" trilogy, a Graustarkian adventure series.

Alexander, Lloyd <u>TIME CAT</u> (Dell/Yearling 0-440-48677-7, 09/85 [08/85], $3.25, 191pp, pb) Reprint (Holt 1963) juvenile fantasy novel.

*Allen, Roger Macbride <u>THE TORCH OF HONOR</u> (Baen 0-671-55938-9, 03/85 [02/85], $2.95, 339pp, pb) Sf novel, a first novel. Strong Heinleinian characters and tone. (DLN)

*Allison, Susan, ed. <u>THE FANTASY SAMPLER</u> (Berkley/Ace no ISBN, 10/85 [11/85], free to members of the 1985 World Fantasy Convention, unpaginated, pa) Excerpts from upcoming Ace and Berkley books. Available only in galley form.
Contents:

			Page
Dear Reader	Susan Allison	pr	
Brokedown Palace	Steven Brust	ex ACE Jan,86	
Wizard of the Pigeons	Megan Lindholm	ex ACE Jan,86	
The Princess of Flames	Ru Emerson	ex ACE Jan,86	
Tain	Gregory Frost	ex ACE 1986	
A Malady of Magicks	Craig Shaw Gardner	ex ACE Feb,86	
The Book of Blood	Clive Barker	ss CBB # 1,84	

Alvarado, Manuel & John Tulloch <u>DOCTOR WHO: THE UNFOLDING TEXT</u> Main listing under John Tulloch.

*<u>Amazing Science Fiction Stories</u> [v.58 #5, January 1985] George H. Scithers, ed. (TSR, 01/85 [11/84], $1.75, 162pp, pb)
Contents:

			Page
Opinion	Robert Silverberg	ar AMZ	4
Cartoon, Cartoon	William Rotsler & Alexis Gilliland	ct AMZ	7
Book Reviews	Frank Catalano	br AMZ	9
Book Reviews	Robert Coulson	br AMZ	14
Dragons and Dudgeons	Beverly Grant	pm AMZ Jan,85	19
The Cave of Shadows	John Devin	pm AMZ Jan,85	25
Gaby	Andrew M. Greeley	nv AMZ Jan,85	26
Screen Reviews	Baird Searles	mr AMZ	58
On Springfield Mountain	Rand B. Lee	nv AMZ Jan,85	62
Tourist in Escherland	Susan Palwick	pm AMZ Jan,85	92
After the Guillotine	Tanith Lee	ss AMZ Jan,85	96
Lover as Vampire	Wendy McElroy	pm AMZ Jan,85	109
Buccaneer Treasure	Robert E. Howard	pm AMZ Jan,85	110
The Observatory	George H. Scithers	ed AMZ	115
Mars Child	Robert F. Young	ss AMZ Jan,85	116
The Traveler	Gene Wolfe	pm AMZ Jan,85	135
To Melville	Gene Wolfe	pm AMZ Jan,85	136
MS. Found in a Cruet Set	Sharon N. Farber	ss AMZ Jan,85	137
The Servant of Saibel	Diana L. Paxson	ss AMZ Jan,85	142
Lady Who Rode the Central Line	Tina Rath	ss AMZ Jan,85	153
SF Cliches III: Time Machines	John M. Ford	pm AMZ Jan,85	162

*<u>Amazing Science Fiction Stories</u> [v.58 #6, March 1985] George H. Scithers, ed. (TSR, 03/85 [01/85], $1.75, 162pp, pb)
Contents:

			Page
Opinion	Robert Silverberg	ar AMZ	4
Book Reviews	Frank Catalano	br AMZ	9
Book Reviews	Robert Coulson	br AMZ	14
Book Reviews	Patrick L. Price & Roger Raupp	br AMZ	21
Hellflower	Eluki bes Shahar	nv AMZ Mar,85	32
The Scientific Literature	Stephen L. Gillett, Ph.D.	ar AMZ Mar,85	53
Upon the Shoal of Time	Lillian Stewart Carl	ss AMZ Mar,85	60
Improbable Bestiary-- The Faun	F. Gwynplaine MacIntyre	pm AMZ Mar,85	73
Improbable Bestiary-- The Ogre	F. Gwynplaine MacIntyre	pm AMZ Mar,85	74
The Perfect Day	James Turpin	ss AMZ Mar,85	76
On the Dream Channel Panel	Ian Watson	ss AMZ Mar,85	92
Screen Reviews	Baird Searles	mr AMZ	107
Plot Template	Wil Creveling	pm AMZ	111
The Blind Minotaur	Michael Swanwick	ss AMZ Mar,85	112
The Mittens of Ulysses	Thomas M. Disch	pm AMZ Mar,85	127
What Happened on Cranberry Road	Grania Davis	nv AMZ Mar,85	128
The Observatory	George H. Scithers	ed AMZ	162

*<u>Amazing Science Fiction Stories</u> [v.59 #1, May 1985] George H. Scithers, ed. (TSR, 05/85 [03/85], $1.75, 162pp, pb)
Contents:

			Page
Opinion	Robert Silverberg	ar AMZ	4
Book Reviews	Robert Coulson	br AMZ	8
Book Reviews	Frank Catalano	br AMZ	14
Cartoon, Cartoon	William Rotsler & Alexis Gilliland	ct AMZ	19
Offerings at Medusa	Joel Henry Sherman	ss AMZ May,85	26
Field Guide	John Devin	pm AMZ May,85	37
The Werebear and the Rainbow	J.P. Boyd	ss AMZ May,85	38
O Lyric Love	Charles L. Harness	ss AMZ May,85	52
The Cambrian Explosion	Stephen L. Gillett, Ph.D.	ar AMZ May,85	66
Through Time & Space with Ferdinand Feghoot Q	Grendel Briarton	vi AMZ May,85	79
Night on the Interchange	James Haralson	ss AMZ May,85	80
The Expedition	Frederick Turner	pm AMZ May,85	99
Kitecadet	Keith Roberts	ss AMZ May,85	102
For Those Who Love Danger	John Devin	pm AMZ May,85	119
Screen Reviews	Baird Searles	mr AMZ	120
Duke Pasquale's Ring	Avram Davidson	nv AMZ May,85	124
The Observatory	George H. Scithers & Darrell Schweitzer	ed AMZ May,85	162

*<u>Amazing Science Fiction Stories</u> [v.59 #2, July 1985] George H. Scithers, ed. (TSR, 07/85 [05/85], $1.75, 162pp, pb)
Contents:

			Page
Opinion	Robert Silverberg	ar AMZ	4
Book Reviews	Robert Coulson	br AMZ	9
Book Reviews	Frank Catalano	br AMZ	15
Cartoon, Cartoon	William Rotsler & Alexis Gilliland	ct AMZ	22
Catacombs	Jayge Carr	nv AMZ Jul,85	30
Magazine Section	R.A. Lafferty	ss AMZ Jul,85	55
Space Weapons	Ben Bova	ar AMZ Jul,85	65
The Last of the Shadow Titans	Darrell Schweitzer	ss AMZ Jul,85	74
Memo to an Asteroid Miner	John Gregory Betancourt	pm AMZ Jul,85	91
Mental Blocks	Steven Gould	ss AMZ Jul,85	92
Look at It This Way	David Langford	pm AMZ Jul,85	102
Screen Reviews	Baird Searles	mr AMZ	103
The Neighbor's Wife	Susan Palwick	pm AMZ Jul,85	107
Lyric for the Darkness	Richard Grant	ss AMZ Jul,85	108
Dialogue With a Spider	Thomas M. Disch	pm AMZ Jul,85	119
Katzenjammer	Dian Girard	ss AMZ Jul,85	120
The Observatory	George H. Scithers	ed AMZ	128
Bet	Wil Creveling	ss AMZ Jul,85	129
Unholy Trinity	Eric G. Iverson	nv AMZ Jul,85	134
S' Magic	Lorna Crowe	pm AMZ Jul,85	162

*<u>Amazing Science Fiction Stories</u> [v.59 #3, September 1985] George H. Scithers, ed. (TSR, 09/85 [07/85], $1.75, 162pp, pb)
Contents:

			Page
Opinion	Robert Silverberg	ar AMZ	4
Book Reviews	Robert Coulson	br AMZ	8
Book Reviews	Frank Catalano	br AMZ	16
The Amulet of the Firegod	J.O. Jeppson	ss AMZ Sep,85	30
Batrachian	Alan Dean Foster	ss AMZ Sep,85	45
Rolls Rex, King of Cars	Sharon N. Farber	ss AMZ Sep,85	54
Interview with David Gerrold	Darrell Schweitzer	iv AMZ Sep,85	69
A Friendly Game of Crola	Esther M. Friesner	ss AMZ Sep,85	79
The Ultimate Diagnostic	Christopher Gilbert	ss AMZ Sep,85	83
Skydiver	Thomas M. Disch	pm AMZ Sep,85	95
Finalities Besides the Grave	John Barnes	ss AMZ Sep,85	96

AMAZING SCIENCE FICTION STORIES

Ames, Mildred   ANNA TO THE INFINITE POWER (Scholastic/Point 0-590-33732-7, 1985 [09/85], $2.25, 202pp, pb) Reprint (Scribner's 1981) young-adult sf novel.

*Anderson, Craig SCIENCE FICTION FILMS OF THE SEVENTIES (McFar-
land 0-89950-086-2, 09/85 [08/85], $15.95 + $1.00 postage, 261pp,
pb) Historical and critical survey, with numerous photographs.

Anderson, Poul   AGENT OF THE TERRAN EMPIRE (Ace 0-441-01070-9,
03/85 [02/85], $2.95, 282pp, pb) Reissue (Chilton 1965) collec-
tion of 4 stories of Dominic Flandry. "Flandry" #3, fifth printing.

Anderson, Poul   BRAIN WAVE (Ballantine/Del Rey 0-345-32521-4,
09/85 [08/85], $2.50, 166pp, pb) Reissue (Ballantine 1954) sf
novel. 8th printing.

Anderson, Poul   THE DEVIL'S GAME (Baen 0-671-55995-8, 11/85
[10/85], $2.95, 251pp, pb) Reprint (Pocket 1980) occult fantasy
novel.

*Anderson, Poul   DIALOGUE WITH DARKNESS (Tor 0-812-53083-7, 02/85
[01/85], $2.95, 320pp, pb) Collection of sf stories.
Contents: Page
A Chapter of Revelation   Poul Anderson   na DAYSUNS,72   7
Sister Planet   Poul Anderson   na SAT May,59   81
The Life of Your Time   [as Michael Karageorge]
                          Poul Anderson   nv ASF Sep,65   137
Time Heals   Poul Anderson   nv ASF Oct,49   165
SOS   Poul Anderson   nv IFS Mar,70   193
Conversation in Arcady   Poul Anderson   ss ASF Dec,63   223
Dialogue   Poul Anderson   nv FSTRLGT,76   235
The Communicators   Poul Anderson   na INY # 1,70   269

Anderson, Poul   ENSIGN FLANDRY (Ace 0-441-20729-4, 01/85 [12/84],
$2.95, 277pp, pb) Reissue (Chilton 1966) sf novel. 8th Ace
printing. This is the first in the "Flandry" series.

Anderson, Poul   FLANDRY OF TERRA (Ace 0-441-24074-7, 02/85
[01/85], $2.95, 291pp, pb) Reissue (Chilton 1965) collection of
three novellas. 7th Ace printing. Book 2 in the 'Flandry" series.

*Anderson, Poul   THE GAME OF EMPIRE (Baen 0-671-55959-1, 05/85
[04/85], $3.50, 278pp, pb) Sf novel featuring Diana, daughter of
Dominic Flandry.

Anderson, Poul   THE GAME OF EMPIRE (SFBC #06320, 10/85 [11/85],
$4.98, 182pp, hc) Reprint (Baen 1985) sf novel, first hardcover
edition. Features Dominic Flandry's daughter.

Anderson, Poul   A MIDSUMMER TEMPEST (Tor 0-812-53079-9, 12/85
[11/85], $2.95, 318pp, pb) Reissue (Doubleday 1974) fantasy
novel. 2nd Tor printing.

Anderson, Poul   A STONE IN HEAVEN (Ace 0-441-78658-8, 04/85
[03/85], $2.95, 255pp, pb) Reissue (Ace 1979) sf novel, #4 in
the "Dominic Flandry" series. Fifth Ace printing.

Anderson, Poul & Gordon R. Dickson   EARTHMAN'S BURDEN (Avon 0-
380-47993-1, 09/85 [08/85], $2.95, 189pp, pb) Reissue (Gnome
1957) collection of humorous sf stories about the Hokas. Third
Avon printing. The Cartier illustrations have become blobs on
this cheap pulp paper.

*Anderson, Poul, Martin H. Greenberg & Charles G. Waugh, eds.
MERCENARIES OF TOMORROW (Critic's Choice 0-931773-41-5, 11/85
[10/85], $2.95, 372pp, pb) Sf anthology. Anderson is listed as
"Creator", which could either mean editor or "you can put my name
on the cover and I'll write an introduction." We don't know
which.
Contents: Page
Introduction to Mercenaries of Tomorrow
                          Poul Anderson   in   ix
The Soldier From the Stars
                          Poul Anderson   nv FUN Jun,55   1
Brothers   Gordon R. Dickson na ASTNDNG,73   27
But Loyal to His Own   David A. Drake   nv GAL Oct,75   80
That Share of Glory   C.M. Kornbluth   nv ASF Jan,52   104
Priest of the Baraboo   Barry B. Longyear nv IAS Jul,79   135
Blacksword   Andrew J. Offutt   nv GAL Dec,59   171
The Quest   Kit Reed   nv FUN Jan,60   202
Mercenary   Mack Reynolds   na ASF Apr,62   227
Recruiting Station   A.E. van Vogt   na ASF Mar,42   284
Straw   Gene Wolfe   ss GAL Jan,75   365

*Anderson, Poul, Martin H. Greenberg & Charles G. Waugh, eds.
TERRORISTS OF TOMORROW (Critic's Choice 0-931773-54-7, 01/86
[12/85], $3.50, 376pp, pb) Sf anthology. According to the jack-
et, Anderson "created" it and Greenberg and Waugh edited it.
Contents: Page
Introduction   Poul Anderson   in   1
The Oracle   Robert Bloch   ss PNT May,71   5
Pacifist   Mack Reynolds   ss FSF Jan,64   11
A Time of the Fourth Horseman
                          Chelsea Quinn Yarbro nv INY # 3,72   29
Truck Driver   Robert Chilson   ss ASF Jan,72   54
Satan's Shrine   Daniel F. Galouye nv GAL Sep,54   74
The Missing Man   Katherine MacLean nv ASF Mar,71   101
The Movement   Gregory Benford   ss FAN Oct,70   150
The Wind from a Burning Woman
                          Greg Bear   nv ASF Oct,78   166
How It Was When the Past Went Away
                          Robert Silverberg na 3FRTMRW,69   195
Sam Hall   Poul Anderson   nv ASF Aug,53   256
Waterclap   Isaac Asimov   nv IFS Apr,70   289
Very Proper Charlies   Dean Ing   na DST V1 #1,78 322

*Angelo, Ivan   THE TOWER OF GLASS (Avon/Bard 0-380-89607-9, 01/86
[12/85], $3.95, 195pp, pb) Collection of five interlocking sto-
ries with elements of dystopian sf, translated (from a 1979
Brazilian edition) by Ellen Watson.
Contents: Page
Conquest   Ivan Angelo   nv TWRGLSS,86   1
Friday Night/Saturday Morning
                          Ivan Angelo   nv TWRGLSS,86   35
The Real True Son of the Bitch
                          Ivan Angelo   nv TWRGLSS,86   71
The Tower of Glass   Ivan Angelo   nv TWRGLSS,86   119
Lost & Found   Ivan Angelo   nv TWRGLSS,86   157

*Anonymous   THE 1985 RHYSLING ANTHOLOGY (Science Fiction Poetry
Association no ISBN, 1985 [12/85], $1.00, 20pp, pb) Anthology of
sf poems, finalists for the 1985 Rhysling awards.
Contents: Page
Preface   Anonymous   pr   2
The Twenty-Fifth   Hope Athearn   pm IAS Jul,84   3
Independence Day Forever Michael Bishop   pm FSF Jul,84   4
For Spacers Snarled in the Hair of Comets
                          Bruce Boston   pm IAS Apr,84   5
Launcelot in Winter   Anne Braude   pm NIE #27,84   6
A Letter from Caroline Herschel
                          Siv Cedering   pm S84 Jun,84   7
For Alfred, Lord Tennyson
                          Helen Ehrlich   pm S*L V7 #2,84   9
Audible Lithography   Bill Hotchkiss   pm PDD #11,84   10
Hominid Voices   Andrew Joron & Robert Frazier
                                             pm URN # 4,84   12
How It All Began   Suzanne Lummis   pm IDIOSYN,84   15
The Still Point   David Lunde   pm IAS Apr,84   16
The Man Who Left Us Behind
                          Chuck Oliveros   pm VEL # 3,84   19
The Problem of Pain   Jonathan V. Post   pm PCB # 1,84   20
Rhysling Awards--history [Misc. Material]   bi   21

*Anonymous   ANALOG: THE BEST OF SCIENCE FICTION (A&W/Galahad 0-
88365-637-X, 07/85 [06/85], $12.95, 621pp, hc) Anthology of 32
stories, published as an "instant remainder."
Contents: Page
The Day Is Done   Lester del Rey   ss ASF May,39   11
Adam and No Eve   Alfred Bester   ss ASF Sep,41   22
Ogre   Clifford D. Simak nv ASF Jan,44   32
Invariant   John Pierce   ss ASF Apr,44   66
Desertion   Clifford D. Simak ss ASF Nov,44   70
Rescue Party   Arthur C. Clarke   nv ASF May,46   80
The Chronokinesis of Jonathan Hull
                          Anthony Boucher   ss ASF Jun,46   100
Police Operation   H. Beam Piper   nv ASF Jul,48   113
Tiger Ride   James Blish & Damon Knight
                                             ss ASF Oct,48   136
Over the Top   Lester del Rey   ss ASF Nov,49   146
Incommunicado   Katherine MacLean nv ASF Jun,50   156
The Little Black Bag   C.M. Kornbluth   nv ASF Jul,50   178
Berom   John Berryman   nv ASF Jan,51   199
The Waiting Game   Randall Garrett   nv ASF Jan,51   214
Protected Species   H.B. Fyfe   ss ASF Mar,51   233
"The Years Draw Nigh"   Lester del Rey   ss ASF Oct,51   242
Thinking Machine   H.B. Fyfe   nv ASF Oct,51   252
Implode and Peddle   H.B. Fyfe   nv ASF Nov,51   269
Belief   Isaac Asimov   nv ASF Oct,53   292
Minor Ingredient   Eric Frank Russell ss ASF Mar,56   317
Barnacle Bull   Winston P. Sanders ss ASF Sep,60   330
Monument   Lloyd Biggle, Jr. nv ASF Jun,61   343
Blind Man's Lantern   Allen Lang   nv ASF Dec,62   377
Thin Edge   Jonathan Blake MacKenzie
                                             ss ASF Dec,63   400
The Permanent Implosion   Dean McLaughlin   nv ASF Feb,64   420
A Case of Identity   Randall Garrett   nv ASF Sep,64   445
Balanced Ecology   James H. Schmitz   ss ASF Mar,65   492
The Easy Way Out   Lee Correy   ss ASF Apr,66   506
The Last Command   Keith Laumer   ss ASF Jan,67   515
The Powers of Observation
                          Harry Harrison   ss ASF Sep,68   529
The Gold at the Starbow's End
                          Frederik Pohl   nv ASF Mar,72   540
Hero   Joe W. Haldeman   nv ASF Jun,72   579

*Anthony, Piers   ANTHONOLOGY (Tor 0-312-93027-5, 04/85 [03/85],
$14.95, 381pp, hc) Collection with both reprint stories and
originals, introduced by the author with lots of material between
each story about Anthony and his trials and tribulations in the
sf field.
Contents: Page
Possible to Rue   Piers Anthony   ss FAN Apr,63   9
The Toaster   Piers Anthony   ss ANTHNGY,85   15
Quinquepedalian   Piers Anthony   ss AMZ Nov,63   22
Encounter   Piers Anthony   ss FAN Oct,64   42
Phog   Piers Anthony   ss FAN Jun,65   50
The Ghost Galaxies   Piers Anthony   nv IFS Sep,66   64
Within the Cloud   Piers Anthony   ss GAL Apr,67   93
The Life of the Stripe   Piers Anthony   ss FAN Feb,69   98
In the Jaws of Danger   Piers Anthony   nv IFS Nov,67   103
Beak by Beak   Piers Anthony   ss ASF Dec,67   122
Getting Through University
                          Piers Anthony   nv IFS Aug,68   133
In the Barn   Piers Anthony   nv AGNDNGR,72   172
Up Schist Crick   Piers Anthony   nv GENERTN,72   208
The Whole Truth   Piers Anthony   ss NOV # 1,70   230
The Bridge   Piers Anthony   ss WOT #24,70   245
On the Uses of Torture   Piers Anthony   nv BKS V 3,81   262

Small Mouth, Bad Taste	Piers Anthony	ss SCIAGMN,70	288
Wood You?	Piers Anthony	ss FSF Oct,70	307
Hard Sell	Piers Anthony	ss IFS Aug,72	319
Hurdle	Piers Anthony	nv IFS Dec,72	338
Gone to the Dogs	Piers Anthony	ss ANTHNGY,85	371

Anthony, Piers BEARING AN HOURGLASS (SFBC #1917, 03/85 [02/85], $5.98, 311pp, hc) Reprint (Ballantine/Del Rey 1984) fantasy novel, "Incarnations of Immortality" #2.

Anthony, Piers BEARING AN HOURGLASS (Ballantine/Del Rey 0-345-31315-1, 10/85 [09/85], $3.95, 372pp, pb) Reprint (Del Rey 1984) fantasy novel, "Incarnations of Immortality" #2.

Anthony, Piers BIO OF A SPACE TYRANT, VOL. I: REFUGEE (Gregg 0-8398-2900-0, 12/85 [12/85], $13.95, 312pp, hc) Reprint (Avon 1983) sf novel, first in the series. First hardcover edition, offset from the original paperback.

Anthony, Piers BIO OF A SPACE TYRANT, VOL. II: MERCENARY (Gregg 0-8398-2901-9, 12/85 [12/85], $13.95, 373pp, hc) Reprint (Avon 1984) sf novel, first hardcover edition.

*Anthony, Piers BIO OF A SPACE TYRANT, VOL. III: POLITICIAN (Avon 0-380-89685-0, 05/85 [04/85], $2.95, 345pp, pb) Sf novel.

Anthony, Piers BIO OF A SPACE TYRANT, VOL. III: POLITICIAN (Gregg 0-8398-2902-7, 12/85 [12/85], $13.95, 345pp, hc) Reprint (Avon 1985) sf novel, first hardcover edition.

*Anthony, Piers BIO OF A SPACE TYRANT, VOL. IV: EXECUTIVE (Avon 0-380-89834-9, 12/85 [11/85], $3.50, 330pp, pb) Sf novel.

Anthony, Piers CHAINING THE LADY (Avon 0-380-01779-2, 03/85 [02/85], $2.95, 342pp, pb) Reissue (Avon 1978) sf novel, #2 in the "Cluster" series.

Anthony, Piers CLUSTER (Avon 0-380-01755-5, 03/85 [02/85], $2.95, 254pp, pb) Reissue (Avon 1977) sf novel, #1 in the "Cluster" series.

*Anthony, Piers CREWEL LYE (Ballantine/Del Rey 0-345-31309-7, 01/85 [12/84], $3.50, 309pp, pb) Fantasy novel in the humorous "Xanth" series.

Anthony, Piers CREWEL LYE (SFBC #1694, 08/85 [07/85], $5.98, 273pp, hc) Reprint (Del Rey 1984) fantasy novel in the "Xanth" series. First hardcover edition.

Anthony, Piers HASAN (Tor 0-812-53112-4, 01/86 [12/85], $2.95, 242pp, pb) Reprint (Borgo 1969) Arabian Nights fantasy novel, with a new author's note about the history of the book.

Anthony, Piers KIRLIAN QUEST (Avon 0-380-01778-4, 03/85 [02/85], $2.95, 313pp, pb) Reissue (Avon 1978) sf novel, #3 in the "Cluster" series.

Anthony, Piers MACROSCOPE (Gregg 0-8398-2899-3, 12/85 [12/85], $14.95, 480pp, hc) Reprint (Avon 1969) sf novel. This first hardcover is offset from the paperback original.

Anthony, Piers OMNIVORE (Avon 0-380-00262-0, 11/85 [10/85], $2.95, 221pp, pb) Reissue (Ballantine 1968) sf novel, first in a trilogy. 10th Avon printing in seven years.

Anthony, Piers ORN (Avon 0-380-00266-3, 11/85 [10/85], $2.95, 256pp, pb) Reissue (SFBC 1971) sf novel, second in the "Omnivore" trilogy. 14th printing.

Anthony, Piers OX (Avon 0-380-00461-5, 11/85 [10/85], $2.95, 256pp, pb) Reissue (SFBC 1976) sf novel, conclusion of the "Omnivore" trilogy. 11th printing.

Anthony, Piers RACE AGAINST TIME (Tor 0-812-53110-8, 09/85 [08/85], $2.95, 224pp, pb) Reprint (Hawthorne 1973) sf novel. There's also a 22 page excerpt from Anthony's HASAN included.

+Anthony, Piers STEPPE (Tor 0-312-93748-2, 09/85 [08/85], $13.95, 252pp, hc) Reprint (Millington 1976) sf novel. First U.S. edition. There is a new author's note explaining the publishing background.

Anthony, Piers THOUSANDSTAR (Avon 0-380-75556-4, 06/85 [05/85], $2.95, 294pp, pb) Reissue (Avon 1980) sf novel, #4 in the "Cluster" series.

Anthony, Piers VISCOUS CIRCLE (Avon 0-380-79897-2, 06/85 [05/85], $2.95, 266pp, pb) Reissue (Avon 1982) sf novel, #5 in the "Cluster" series.

*Anthony, Piers WITH A TANGLED SKEIN (Ballantine/Del Rey 0-345-31884-6, 10/85 [09/85], $14.95, 280pp, hc) Fantasy novel, Book Three of "Incarnations of Immortality".

Anthony, Piers & Frances Hall PRETENDER (Tor 0-812-53108-6, 06/85 [05/85], $3.50, 254pp, pb) Reprint (Borgo 1979) sf novel. There is also a 30-page excerpt of STEPPE included.

*Arbur, Rosemarie MARION ZIMMER BRADLEY (Starmont 0-916732-95-9, 12/85 [12/85], $8.95, 138pp, pb) Non-fiction, critical study, including annotated primary and secondary bibliographies.

*Aronica, Lou, ed. THE BANTAM SPECTRA SAMPLER (Bantam Spectra 0-553-17925-X, 06/85 [05/85], no price given, 93pp, pb) Special promotional book, distributed free at the ABA and various bookstores, with excerpts from 8 upcoming Spectra books.
Contents:

			Page
Dear Reader	Lou Aronica	in	1
West of Eden	Harry Harrison	ex BAN 1984	5
The Christening Quest	Elizabeth Scarborough	ex BAN Aug,85	13
The Last Rainbow	Parke Godwin	ex BAN Jul,85	21
Polar Fleet	Warren Norwood	ex BAN Jun,85	31
The Book of Kells	R.A. MacAvoy	ex BAN Aug,85	39
The Dream Years	Lisa Goldstein	ex BAN Aug,85	49
The Darkling Wind	Somtow Sucharitkul	ex BAN Jul,85	63
Child of Fortune	Norman Spinrad	ex BAN Jul,85	73

*Arscott, David & David Marl A FLIGHT OF BRIGHT BIRDS (Allen & Unwin 0-04-823270-X, 1985 [12/85], £8.95, 229pp, hc) Fantasy novel set in an imaginary Victorian-type city. Sort of a cross between M. John Harrison and Tim Powers (with less humor). (FCM)

*Ashe, Geoffrey THE DISCOVERY OF KING ARTHUR (Doubleday/Anchor 0-385-19032-8, 06/85 [05/85], $18.95, 226pp, hc) Non-fiction; associational. Written in association with the Arthurian Committee of Debrett's Peerage, this study includes discussion of Arthurian literature and fantasies over the centuries, plus historical research.

*Ashley, Mike & Frank H. Parnell MONTHLY TERRORS: AN INDEX TO THE WEIRD FANTASY MAGAZINES PUBLISHED IN THE UNITED STATES AND GREAT BRITAIN Main listing under Frank H. Parnell.

*Ashley, Steven LOVE OUT OF TIME (Berkley 0-425-07967-8, 07/85 [06/85], $3.95, 263pp, pb) Sf/romance novel. Wild Bill Hickock gets caught up in a time machine experiment and ends up in the present, where he falls in love and has some gunfights.

*Asimov, Isaac THE ALTERNATE ASIMOVS (Doubleday 0-385-19784-5, 01/86 [12/85], $16.95, 272pp, hc) Collection of three early unpublished drafts for "Pebble in the Sky", "The End of Eternity", and "Belief", plus historical comment by Asimov.
Contents:

			Page
Introduction	Isaac Asimov	in	ix
GROW OLD ALONG WITH ME [written in summer of 1947]			
	Isaac Asimov	n. ALTASMV,86	1
original version of the novel PEBBLE IN THE SKY			
THE END OF ETERNITY [written in winter of 1953-1954]			
	Isaac Asimov	n. ALTASMV,86	137
original version of the novel THE END OF ETERNITY			
Belief [first version]	Isaac Asimov	nv ALTASMV,86	215
Belief [ending of the published version]			
	Isaac Asimov	ex ASF Oct,53	255
Final Word	Isaac Asimov	aw	271

Asimov, Isaac THE BICENTENNIAL MAN...AND OTHER STORIES (Ballantine/Del Rey 0-345-32071-9, 02/85 [01/85], $2.95, 222pp, pb) Reprint (Doubleday 1976) collection of 12 stories.

*Asimov, Isaac THE EDGE OF TOMORROW (Tor 0-312-93200-6, 06/85 [05/85], $15.95, 462pp, hc) Collection, a combination of sf and non-fiction, dealing with "scientists past and future." Most of the stories have appeared in other collections. The non-fiction is all from Asimov's F&SF columns.
Contents:

			Page
Foreword	Ben Bova	fw	xi
Introduction	Isaac Asimov	in	1
Unique Is Where You Find It			
	Isaac Asimov	ss EDGTMRW,85	4
The Eureka Phenomenon	Isaac Asimov	ar FSF Jun,71	20
The Feeling of Power	Isaac Asimov	ss IFS Feb,58	33
The Comet That Wasn't	Isaac Asimov	ar FSF Nov,76	44
Found!	Isaac Asimov	ss OMN Oct,78	57
Twinkle, Twinkle, Microwaves			
	Isaac Asimov	ar FSF May,77	73
Pate de Foie Gras	Isaac Asimov	ss ASF Sep,56	85
The Bridge of the Gods	Isaac Asimov	ar FSF Mar,75	104
Belief	Isaac Asimov	nv ASF Oct,53	116
Euclid's Fifth	Isaac Asimov	ar FSF Mar,71	150
The Plane Truth	Isaac Asimov	ar FSF Apr,71	162
The Billiard Ball	Isaac Asimov	ss IFS Mar,67	174
The Winds of Change	Isaac Asimov	ss SPECLTN,82	194
The Figure of the Fastest			
	Isaac Asimov	ar FSF Nov,73	210
The Dead Past	Isaac Asimov	nv ASF Apr,56	222
The Fateful Lightning	Isaac Asimov	ar FSF Jun,69	272
"Breeds There a Man--?"	Isaac Asimov	nv ASF Jun,51	284
The Man Who Massed the Earth			
	Isaac Asimov	ar FSF Sep,69	322
Nightfall	Isaac Asimov	nv ASF Sep,41	334
The Planet That Wasn't	Isaac Asimov	ar FSF May,75	371
The Ugly Little Boy [Lastborn]			
	Isaac Asimov	na GAL Sep,58	383
The Three Who Died Too Soon			
	Isaac Asimov	ar FSF Jul,82	425
The Last Question	Isaac Asimov	ss SFQ Nov,56	437
The Nobel Prize That Wasn't			
	Isaac Asimov	ar FSF Apr,70	451

Asimov, Isaac THE MARTIAN WAY (Ballantine/Del Rey 0-345-32587-7, 10/85 [09/85], $2.95, 217pp, pb) Reprint (Doubleday 1955) collection of 4 novellas. The title story is one of Asimov's best. (CNB)

ASIMOV, ISAAC

Asimov, Isaac NINE TOMORROWS (Ballantine/Del Rey 0-345-32072-7, 02/85 [01/85], $2.95, 224pp, pb) Reprint (Doubleday 1959) collection.

*Asimov, Isaac OPUS 300 (Houghton Mifflin 0-395-36108-7, 01/85 [12/84], $18.95, 377pp, hc) Non-fiction, associational, with material from Asimov's third set of 100 books, plus the new essay "The Forever Foundation".

*Asimov, Isaac ROBOTS AND EMPIRE (Doubleday 0-385-19092-1, 09/85 [08/85], $16.95, 383pp, hc) Sf novel. This edition is simultaneous with the limited edition from Phantasia.

*Asimov, Isaac ROBOTS AND EMPIRE (Phantasia 0-932096-37-9, 09/85 [08/85], $50.00, 349pp, hc) This signed, boxed, limited edition (of 650 copies) of Asimov's sf novel appeared simultaneously with the trade edition.

Asimov, Isaac ROBOTS AND EMPIRE (SFBC #1937, 11/85 [11/85], $5.98, 383pp, hc) Reprint (Doubleday 1985) sf novel. This is the connecting novel between the Robot series and the pre-Foundation books.

Asimov, Isaac THE UNION CLUB MYSTERIES (Fawcett/Crest 0-449-20525-8, 03/85 [02/85], $2.95, 210pp, pb) Reprint (Doubleday 1983) collection of mysteries; non-sf, associational.

*Asimov, Isaac, ed. THE HUGO WINNERS, VOLUME 4: 1976-1979 (Doubleday 0-385-18934-6, 04/85 [03/85], $18.95, 561pp, hc) Anthology of the award-winning stories from four conventions, plus introductions to each by Asimov.
Contents:

				Page
Introduction: What Again?	Isaac Asimov		in	xi
Home Is the Hangman	Roger Zelazny	na ASF Nov,75		1
The Borderland of Sol	Larry Niven	nv ASF Jan,75		70
Catch That Zeppelin!	Fritz Leiber	ss FSF Mar,75		116
By Any Other Name	Spider Robinson	na ASF Nov,76		141
Houston, Houston, Do You Read?	James Tiptree, Jr.	na AURORA ,76		200
The Bicentennial Man	Isaac Asimov	nv STL # 2,76		259
Tricentennial	Joe W. Haldeman	ss ASF Jul,76		302
Stardance	Spider Robinson & Jeanne Robinson	na ASF Mar,77		327
Eyes of Amber	Joan D. Vinge	nv ASF Jun,77		391
Jeffty Is Five	Harlan Ellison	ss FSF Jul,77		432
Persistence of Vision	John Varley	na FSF Mar,78		459
Hunter's Moon	Poul Anderson	nv ASF Nov,78		510
Cassandra	C.J. Cherryh	ss FSF Oct,78		553

Asimov, Isaac, ed. THE HUGO WINNERS, VOLUME 4: 1976-1979 (SFBC #5647, 11/85 [11/85], $6.98, 495pp, hc) Reprint (Doubleday 1985) anthology. The jacket misspellings have been corrected from the trade edition.

Asimov, Isaac, Terry Carr & Martin H. Greenberg, eds. 100 GREAT FANTASY SHORT STORIES (Avon 0-380-69917-6, 08/85 [07/85], $2.95, 395pp, pb) Reprint (Doubleday 1984) anthology.

*Asimov, Isaac & Karen A. Frenkel ROBOTS: MACHINES IN MAN'S IMAGE (Crown/Harmony 0-517-55110-1, 06/85 [05/85], $19.95, 246pp, hc) Non-fiction; associational. The book emphasizes industrial and scientific development of robots, with numerous color and b&w photos. Some sf film stills and illustrations also appear.

*Asimov, Isaac & Martin H. Greenberg, eds. AMAZING STORIES: 60 YEARS OF THE BEST SCIENCE FICTION (TSR 0-88038-216-3, 07/85 [08/85], $7.95, 255pp, pb) Anthology of 20 stories which originally appeared in *Amazing*, with a section of color illustrations showing magazine covers.
Contents:

				Page
Amazing Stories and I	Isaac Asimov		in	5
The Revolt of the Pedestrians	David H. Keller, M.D.	ss AMZ Feb,28		9
The Gostak and the Doshes	Miles J. Breuer	ss AMZ Mar,30		29
Pilgrimage [The Priestess Who Rebelled]	Nelson Bond	ss AMZ Oct,39		43
I, Robot	Eando Binder	ss AMZ Jan,39		57
The Strange Flight of Richard Clayton	Robert Bloch	ss AMZ Mar,39		67
The Perfect Woman	Robert Sheckley	ss AMZ Jan,54		75
Momento Homo [Death of a Spaceman]	Walter M. Miller, Jr.	ss AMZ Mar,54		79
What is This Thing Called Love? [Playboy and the Slime God]	Isaac Asimov	ss AMZ Mar,61		93
Requiem	Edmond Hamilton	ss AMZ Apr,62		103
Hang Head, Vandal!	Mark Clifton	ss AMZ Apr,62		115
Drunkboat	Cordwainer Smith	nv AMZ Oct,63		125
60 Years of Amazing Stories' Covers	[Misc. Material]		il	ins.
The Days of Perky Pat	Philip K. Dick	nv AMZ Dec,63		147
Semley's Necklace [The Dowry of Angyar]	Ursula K. Le Guin	ss AMZ Sep,64		165
Calling Dr. Clockwork	Ron Goulart	ss AMZ Mar,65		179
There's No Vinism Like Chauvinism	John Jakes	nv AMZ Apr,65		187
The Oogenesis of Bird City	Philip José Farmer	ss AMZ Sep,70		215
The Man Who Walked Home	James Tiptree, Jr.	ss AMZ May,72		225
Manikins	John Varley	ss AMZ Jan,76		237
In the Islands	Pat Murphy	ss AMZ Mar,83		247

ASIMOV, ISAAC, MARTIN H. GREENBERG & CHARLES G. WAUGH, eds.

*Asimov, Isaac & Martin H. Greenberg, eds. ISAAC ASIMOV PRESENTS THE GREAT SF STORIES: 13 (1951) (DAW 0-88677-058-0, 07/85 [06/85], $3.50, 337pp, pb) Anthology of the best of 1951 plus an introduction about the year in the world and in sf. An excellent anthology. The whole series is highly recommended. (CNB)
Contents:

				Page
Introduction	Martin H. Greenberg		in	ix
Null-P	William Tenn	ss WBY Jan,51		1
The Sentinel [The Sentinel of Eternity]	Arthur C. Clarke	ss TSF Spr,51		15
The Fire Balloons [In This Sign]	Ray Bradbury	ss IMG Apr,51		27
The Marching Morons	C.M. Kornbluth	nv GAL Apr,51		48
The Weapon	Fredric Brown	ss ASF Apr,51		83
Angel's Egg	Edgar Pangborn	nv GAL Jun,51		88
"Breeds There a Man--?"	Isaac Asimov	nv ASF Jun,51		130
Pictures Don't Lie	Katherine MacLean	ss GAL Aug,51		171
Superiority	Arthur C. Clarke	ss FSF Aug,51		193
I'm Scared	Jack Finney	ss COL Sep 15,51		206
The Quest for St. Aquin	Anthony Boucher	ss NWTSPTM,51		222
Tiger by the Tail	Alan E. Nourse	ss GAL Nov,51		244
With These Hands	C.M. Kornbluth	nv GAL Dec,51		253
A Pail of Air	Fritz Leiber	ss GAL Dec,51		274
Dune Roller	Julian May	nv ASF Dec,51		291

*Asimov, Isaac & Martin H. Greenberg, eds. ISAAC ASIMOV PRESENTS THE GREAT SF STORIES: 14 (1952) (DAW 0-88677-106-4, 01/86 [12/85], $3.50, 352pp, pb) Anthology of stories from 1952. Recommended. (CNB)
Contents:

				Page
1952 Introduction	Martin H. Greenberg		in	9
The Pedestrian	Ray Bradbury	ss REP Aug,51 FSF Feb,52		13
The Moon is Green	Fritz Leiber	ss GAL May,52		19
Lost Memory	Peter Phillips	ss GAL May,52		35
What Have I Done?	Mark Clifton	ss ASF May,52		48
Fast Falls the Eventide	Eric Frank Russell	ss ASF May,52		67
The Business, as Usual	Mack Reynolds	ss FSF Jun,52		85
A Sound of Thunder	Ray Bradbury	ss COL Jun 28,52		90
Hobson's Choice	Alfred Bester	ss FSF Aug,52		103
Yesterday House	Fritz Leiber	nv GAL Aug,52		119
The Snowball Effect	Katherine MacLean	ss GAL Sep,52		146
Delay in Transit	F.L. Wallace	nv GAL Sep,52		160
Game for Blondes	John D. MacDonald	ss GAL Oct,52		206
The Altar at Midnight	C.M. Kornbluth	ss GAL Nov,52		217
Command Performance	Walter M. Miller, Jr.	ss GAL Nov,52		225
The Martian Way	Isaac Asimov	nv GAL Nov,52		243
The Impacted Man	Robert Sheckley	ss ASF Dec,52		289
What's It Like Out There?	Edmond Hamilton	nv TWS Dec,52		308
Sail On! Sail On!	Philip José Farmer	ss STS Dec,52		331
Cost of Living	Robert Sheckley	ss GAL Dec,52		342

*Asimov, Isaac, Martin H. Greenberg & Charles G. Waugh, eds. BAKER'S DOZEN: 13 SHORT SCIENCE FICTION NOVELS (Bonanza 0-517-47646-0, 1985 [10/85], $7.98, 574pp, hc) Anthology of novellas, with an introduction by Asimov. An "instant remainder" book.
Contents:

				Page
Introduction: Novellas	Isaac Asimov		in	vii
Profession	Isaac Asimov	na ASF Jul,57		1
Who Goes There? [as Don A. Stuart]	John W. Campbell, Jr.	na ASF Aug,38		49
For I Am a Jealous People!	Lester del Rey	na STARSNO,54		97
The Mortal and the Monster	Gordon R. Dickson	na STLSNOV,76		133
Time Safari	David A. Drake	na DST V3 #2,81		177
In the Western Tradition	Phyllis Eisenstein	na FSF Mar,81		227
The Alley Man	Philip José Farmer	na FSF Jun,59		269
The Sellers of the Dream	John Jakes	na GAL Jun,63		305
The Moon Goddess and the Son	Donald Kingsbury	na ASF Dec,79		337
Enemy Mine	Barry B. Longyear	na IAS Sep,79		385
Flash Crowd	Larry Niven	na 3TRPSTM,73		439
In the Problem Pit	Frederik Pohl	na FSF Sep,73		485
The Desert of Stolen Dreams	Robert Silverberg	na FSF Jun,81		531

*Asimov, Isaac, Martin H. Greenberg & Charles G. Waugh, eds. GREAT SCIENCE FICTION BY THE WORLD'S GREAT SCIENTISTS (Fine 0-917657-26-8, 07/18/85 [06/85], $17.95, 400pp, hc) Sf anthology. Some of the writers are scientists; most are teachers; only one could be called a great scientist, and he's a lousy writer.
Contents:

				Page
Introduction	Isaac Asimov		in	vii
White Creatures	Gregory Benford	ss NDM # 5,75		1
The Singing Diamond	Robert L. Forward	ss OMN Feb,79		19
Publish and Perish	Paul J. Nahin	ss ASF Apr,78		29
Skystalk	Charles Sheffield	nv DST V1 #4,79		41
The Universal Library	Kurd Lasswitz	ss 1901		63
Translated by Willy Ley				
Long Shot	Vernor Vinge	ss ASF Aug,72		73
Blackmail	Fred Hoyle	ss FSF Feb,67		89
Jeannette's Hands	Philip Latham	nv FSF Jan,73		95
The Warm Space	David Brin	ss FFR V 1,85		119
The Wind from the Sun [Sunjammer]	Arthur C. Clarke	nv BLF Mar,64		137
Industrial Accident	Lee Correy	nv ASF Mar,69		159
Choice	J.R. Pierce	ss GAL Mar,71		183
The Winnowing	Isaac Asimov	ss ASF Feb,76		199
Dr. Snow Maiden	Larry Eisenberg	ss FSF Aug,75		209
On the Fourth Planet	J.F. Bone	ss GAL Apr,63		219

ASIMOV, ISAAC, MARTIN H. GREENBERG & CHARLES G. WAUGH, eds.

Learning Theory   James V. McConnell   ss IFS Dec,57   239
Love Is the Plan the Plan Is Death
                         James Tiptree, Jr.   ss ALNCNDT,73   255
Transfusion   Chad Oliver   nv ASF Jun,59   275
In the Beginning   Morton Klass   ss ASF Jul,54   319
Modulation in All Things Suzette Haden Elgin   ss 1980   337
The Bones of Charlemagne Mario A. Pei   nv 1958   355

*Asimov, Isaac, Martin H. Greenberg & Charles G. Waugh, eds.
ISAAC ASIMOV'S MAGICAL WORLDS OF FANTASY #3: COSMIC KNIGHTS
(NAL/Signet 0-451-13342-0, 01/85 [12/84], $3.95, 339pp, pb)
Anthology of fantasy stories.
Contents: Page
Introduction   Isaac Asimov   in   1
Crusader Damosel   Vera Chapman   ss 1978   7
Divers Hands   Darrell Schweitzer   nv YBH # 7,79 21
The Reluctant Dragon   Kenneth Grahame   nv DREAMDY,1899 49
The Immortal Game   Poul Anderson   ss FSF Feb,54 71
The Stainless-Steel Knight [as John Rackham]
                         John T. Phillifent   nv IFS Jul,61 85
Diplomat-at-Arms   Keith Laumer   v FAN Jan,60   117
Dream Damsel   Evan Hunter   ss FUN Oct,54 165
The Last Defender of Camelot
                         Roger Zelazny   nv IAA Sum,79 177
A Knyght Ther Was   Robert F. Young   nv ASF Jul,63 201
Divide and Rule   L. Sprague de Camp   na UNK Apr +1,39 251

*Asimov, Isaac, Martin H. Greenberg & Charles G. Waugh, eds.
ISAAC ASIMOV'S MAGICAL WORLDS OF FANTASY #4: SPELLS (NAL/Signet
0-451-13578-4, 05/85 [04/85], $3.95, 350pp, pb) Anthology of
fantasy stories.
Contents: Page
Curses!   Isaac Asimov   in   7
The Candidate   Henry Slesar   ss ROG 1961   10
The Christmas Shadrach   Frank R. Stockton   ss CNY Dec,1891 18
The Snow Woman   Fritz Leiber   na FAN Apr,70 37
Invisible Boy   Ray Bradbury   ss MAD Nov,45 106
The Hero Who Returned   Gerald W. Page   nv HEROFAN,79 116
Toads of Grimmerdale   Andre Norton   nv FLS # 2,74 140
A Literary Death   Martin H. Greenberg   ss 1985   188
Satan and Sam Shay   Robert Arthur   ss ELK Aug,42 191
Lot No. 249   Arthur Conan Doyle   nv HRP Sep,1892 206
The Witch Is Dead   Edward D. Hoch   ss 1956   239
I Know What You Need   Stephen King   nv CMP Sep,76 259
The Miracle Workers   Jack Vance   na ASF Jul,58 282

*Asimov, Isaac, Martin H. Greenberg & Charles G. Waugh, eds.
ISAAC ASIMOV'S MAGICAL WORLDS OF FANTASY #5: GIANTS (NAL/Signet
0-451-13922-4, 11/85 [10/85], $3.95, 351pp, pb) Anthology of
fantasy stories.
Contents: Page
Introduction: Giants in the Earth
                         Isaac Asimov   in   7
The Riddle of Ragnarok   Theodore Sturgeon   nv FUN Jun,55 11
Straggler from Atlantis Manly Wade Wellman   nv SWD # 1,77 31
He Who Shrank   Henry Hasse   na AMZ Aug,36 57
From the Dark Waters   David A. Drake   ss 1976   123
Small Lords   Frederik Pohl   nv SFQ Feb,57 139
The Mad Planet   Murray Leinster   na ARG Jun 12,20 161
Dreamworld   Isaac Asimov   vi FSF Nov,55 220
The Thirty and One   David H. Keller, M.D.   ss MAR Nov,38 222
The Law-Twister Shorty   Gordon R. Dickson   nv MNYWRLD,71 235
In the Lower Passage   Harle Owen Cummins   ss WLSHRBT,02 279
Cabin Boy   Damon Knight   nv GAL Sep,51 284
The Colossus of Ylourgne Clark Ashton Smith   nv WRT Jun,34 312

*Asimov, Isaac, Martin H. Greenberg & Charles G. Waugh, eds.
ISAAC ASIMOV'S MAGICAL WORLDS OF FANTASY: WITCHES & WIZARDS
(Bonanza 0-517-47669-X, 1985 [10/85], $6.98, 649pp, hc) Omnibus
edition of reprint anthologies ISAAC ASIMOV'S MAGICAL WORLDS OF
FANTASY #1: WIZARDS (NAL/Signet 1983) and #2: WITCHES (NAL/Signet
1984).
Contents: Page
WITCHES [ISAAC ASIMOV'S MAGICAL WORLDS OF FANTASY #2:
 WITCHES]   Isaac Asimov, Martin H. Greenberg &
                           Charles G. Waugh, eds.
                                                 an SIG Apr pa,84   7
Introduction: Witches   Isaac Asimov   in   9
My Mother Was a Witch   William Tenn   ss 1966   12
A Message from Charity   William M. Lee   ss FSF Nov,67 18
The Witch   A.E. van Vogt   nv UNK Feb,43 37
The Witches of Karres   James H. Schmitz   nv ASF Dec,49 58
Spree   Barry N. Malzberg   ss IAM # 2,84 99
Devil's Henchman [as Will F. Jenkins]
                         Murray Leinster   ss ARG May,52 107
Malice in Wonderland   Rufus King   nv EQM Oct,57 121
Operation Salamander   Poul Anderson   nv FSF Jan,57 140
Wizard's World   Andre Norton   na IFS Jun,67 166
Sweets to the Sweet   Robert Bloch   ss WRT Mar,47 212
Poor Little Saturday   Madeleine L'Engle   nv FUN Oct,56 221
Squeakie's First Case   Margaret Manners   nv EQM May,43 236
The Ipswich Phial   Randall Garrett   nv ASF Dec,76 258
Black Heart and White Heart
                         H. Rider Haggard   na 1896   303
WIZARDS [ISAAC ASIMOV'S MAGICAL WORLDS OF FANTASY #1:
 WIZARDS]   Isaac Asimov, Martin H. Greenberg &
                           Charles G. Waugh, eds.
                                                 an SIG Oct pa,83 351
Introduction: Wizards   Isaac Asimov   in   353
Mazirian the Magician   Jack Vance   ss DYNGERT,50 357
Please Stand By   Ron Goulart   nv FSF Jan,62 373

What Good is a Glass Dagger?
                         Larry Niven   nv FSF Sep,72 395
The Eye of Tandyla   L. Sprague de Camp   nv FAD May,51 430
The White Horse Child   Greg Bear   ss UNI # 9,79 453
Semley's Necklace [The Dowry of Angyar]
                         Ursula K. Le Guin   ss AMZ Sep,64 472
And the Monsters Walk   John Jakes   nv FAD Jul,52 491
The Seeker in the Fortress
                         Manly Wade Wellman   nv HEROFAN,79 528
The Wall Around the World
                         Theodore R. Cogswell   nv BEY Sep,53 550
The People of the Black Circle
                         Robert E. Howard   na WRT Sep,34 576

Asimov, Isaac, Martin H. Greenberg & Charles G. Waugh, eds. THE
LAST MAN ON EARTH (Fawcett Crest 0-449-20990-3, 10/85 [09/85],
$3.50, 352pp, pb) Reissue (Ballantine 1982) anthology of 14
stories. 4th printing.

*Asimov, Isaac, Martin H. Greenberg & Charles G. Waugh, eds.
YOUNG GHOSTS (Harper & Row 0-06-020171-1, 09/25/85 [09/85],
$11.95, 210pp, hc) Young-adult anthology.
Contents: Page
Ghosts   Isaac Asimov   in   ix
Lost Hearts   M.R. James   ss GHSTANT,04 1
On the Brighton Road   Richard Middleton   ss GHSTSHP,12 17
Poor Little Saturday   Madeleine L'Engle   nv FUN Oct,56 23
The Lake   Ray Bradbury   ss WRT May,44 48
A Pair of Hands   Sir Arthur Quiller-Couch
                                                 ss OLDFIRE,00 58
Old Haunts   Richard Matheson   ss FSF Oct,57 77
An Uncommon Sort of Spectre
                         Edward Page Mitchell
                                                 ss SUN Mar,1879 93
The House of the Nightmare
                         Edward Lucas White   ss TTB Sep,19 107
The Shadowy Third   Ellen Glasgow   nv SHDW3rd,23 122
The Twilight Road   H.F. Brinsmead   ss 1968   160
The Voices of El Dorado [as Ward Smith]
                         Howard Goldsmith   ss HORRTLS,74 169
The Changing of the Guard [by Rod Serling]
                         Anne Serling-Sutton   sa TZM Feb,85 186

*Asimov, Isaac, Martin H. Greenberg & Charles G. Waugh, eds.
YOUNG MONSTERS (Harper & Row 0-06-020170-3, 04/85 [06/85],
$11.89, 213pp, hc) Anthology aimed at younger readers. This
edition in library binding.
Contents: Page
Introduction   Isaac Asimov   in
Homecoming   Ray Bradbury   ss MAD Oct,46 7
Good-by, Miss Paterson   Phyllis MacLennan   ss FSF Jan,72 27
Disturb Not My Slumbering Fair
                         Chelsea Quinn Yarbro   ss CTNYTLS,78 32
The Wheelbarrow Boy   Richard Parker   ss FSF Mar,53 51
The Cabbage Patch   Theodore R. Cogswell   ss FSF Dec,57 58
The Thing Waiting Outside
                         Barbara Williamson   ss   65
Red as Blood   Tanith Lee   ss FSF Jul,79 74
Gabriel-Ernest   Saki   ss CPLSSSA,30 90
Fritzchen   Charles Beaumont   ss OSF # 1,53 101
The Young One   Jerome Bixby   nv FAN May,54 118
Optical Illusion   Mack Reynolds   ss SST Dec,53 160
Idiot's Crusade   Clifford D. Simak   ss GAL Oct,54 166
One for the Road   Stephen King   ss MNE Mar,77 190
Angelica   Jane Yolen   ss FSF Dec,79 216

*Asimov, Isaac, Martin H. Greenberg & Charles G. Waugh, eds.
YOUNG MONSTERS (Harper & Row 0-06-020169-X, 04/85 [06/85], $7.95,
213pp, pb) Paperback edition of the above.

Asprin, Robert Lynn HIT OR MYTH (Ace 0-441-33850-X, 09/85
[08/85], $2.95, 170pp, pb) Reprint (Donning 1983) humorous fan-
tasy novel, book 4 in the "Myth" series.

*Asprin, Robert Lynn LITTLE MYTH MARKER (Donning/Starblaze 0-
89865-413-0, 10/85 [11/85], $7.95, 172pp, pb) Humorous fantasy
novel, book 6 in the "Myth" series. Illustrations by Phil Foglio.
The copyright page lists both a limited signed and regular hardcover edition.

Asprin, Robert Lynn MYTH CONCEPTIONS (Ace 0-441-55519-5, 02/85
[01/85], $2.95, 217pp, pb) Reprint (Donning 1980) humorous fan-
tasy novel, book 2 in the "Myth" series.

Asprin, Robert Lynn MYTH DIRECTIONS (Ace 0-441-55525-X, 06/85
[05/85], $2.95, 202pp, pb) Reprint (Donning/Starblaze 1982)
humorous fantasy novel, book 3 in the "Myth" series.

*Asprin, Robert Lynn MYTH-ING PERSONS (Donning/Starblaze 0-89865-
379-7, 01/85 [12/84], $6.95, 170pp, pb) humorous fantasy novel,
book 5 in the "Myth" series.

Asprin, Robert Lynn TAMBU (Ace 0-441-79744-X, 08/85 [07/85],
$2.75, 195pp, pb) Reissue (Ace 1979) sf novel, second mass-
market printing.

Asprin, Robert Lynn, ed. SHADOWS OF SANCTUARY (Ace 0-441-80586-
8, 07/85 [10/85], $2.95, 338pp, pb) Reissue (Ace 1981) original
anthology, "Thieves' World" #3, 12th printing.

Asprin, Robert Lynn, ed. STORM SEASON (Ace 0-441-78713-4, 07/85 [10/85], $2.95, 305pp, pb) Reissue (Ace 1982) original anthology, "Thieves' World" #4; 9th printing.

Asprin, Robert Lynn, ed. TALES FROM THE VULGAR UNICORN (Ace 0-441-80585-X, 07/85 [10/85], $2.95, 299pp, pb) Reissue (Ace 1980) original anthology, "Thieves' World" #2.

Asprin, Robert Lynn, ed. THIEVES' WORLD (Ace 0-441-80584-1, 07/85 [10/85], $2.95, 308pp, pb) Reissue (Ace 1979) original anthology, The first "Thieves' World" book. 17th Ace printing.

Asprin, Robert Lynn, ed. THIEVES' WORLD (Ace 0-441-80583-3, 12/85 [11/85], $2.95, 308pp, pb) Reissue (Ace 1979) original anthology. "Thieves' World" #1. The cover credits both Asprin and Lynn Abbey as editors, but Abbey became co-editor later on. 18th printing. This is the first printing with the new packaging.

*****Asprin, Robert Lynn & Lynn Abbey, eds.** CROSS-CURRENTS (SFBC #1934, 12/84 [01/85], $7.50, 628pp, hc) Omnibus edition of three "Thieves' World" anthologies.
Contents:

			Page
STORM SEASON	Robert Lynn Asprin, ed.		
		oa ACE Oct,82	
Editor's Note	Robert Lynn Asprin	pr	
Storm Season Introduction			
	Robert Lynn Asprin	in	
Exercise in Pain	Robert Lynn Asprin	nv STRMSSN,82	
Downwind	C.J. Cherryh	nv STRMSSN,82	
A Fugitive Art	Diana L. Paxson	nv STRMSSN,82	
Steel	Lynn Abbey	na STRMSSN,82	
Wizard Weather	Janet Morris	na STRMSSN,82	
Godson	Andrew J. Offutt	nv STRMSSN,82	
Epilog	Robert Lynn Asprin	aw STRMSSN,82	
THE FACE OF CHAOS	Robert Lynn Asprin & Lynn Abbey, eds.		
		oa ACE Oct,83	
Introduction	Robert Lynn Asprin	in	
High Moon	Janet Morris	na FACECHS,83	
Necromant	C.J. Cherryh	nv FACECHS,83	
The Art of Alliance	Robert Lynn Asprin	ss FACECHS,83	
The Corners of Memory	Lynn Abbey	nv FACECHS,83	
Votary	David A. Drake	nv FACECHS,83	
Mirror Image	Diana L. Paxson	nv FACECHS,83	
WINGS OF OMEN	Robert Lynn Asprin & Lynn Abbey, eds.		
		oa ACE Nov,84	
Introduction	Robert Lynn Asprin	in	
What Women Do Best	Chris Morris & Janet Morris		
		nv WNGSOMN,84	
Daughter of the Sun	Robin W. Bailey	nv WNGSOMN,84	
A Breath of Power	Diana L. Paxson	nv WNGSOMN,84	
The Hand That Feeds You	Diane Duane	nv WNGSOMN,84	
Witching Hour	C.J. Cherryh	nv WNGSOMN,84	
Rebels aren't Born in Palaces			
	Andrew J. Offutt	nv WNGSOMN,84	
Gyskouras	Lynn Abbey	nv WNGSOMN,84	
A Fish Without Feathers Is Out of His Depth			
	Robert Lynn Asprin	ss WNGSOMN,84	
A Special Note from the Editors			
	Robert Lynn Asprin & Lynn Abbey		
		aw WNGSOMN,84	

Asprin, Robert Lynn & Lynn Abbey, eds. THE FACE OF CHAOS (Ace 0-441-80587-6, 07/85 [10/85], $2.95, 242pp, pb) Reissue (Ace 1983) original anthology, "Thieves' World" #5; 8th printing -- it says "July 1984" inside, but it should be 1985.

Asprin, Robert Lynn & Lynn Abbey, eds. TALES FROM THE VULGAR UNICORN (Ace 0-441-79580-3, 01/86 [12/85], $2.95, 299pp, pb) Reissue (Ace 1980) original anthology, "Thieves' World" #2. 14th printing. The earlier printings listed Asprin alone as editor.

*****Asprin, Robert Lynn & Lynn Abbey, eds.** THIEVES' WORLD, BOOK 7: THE DEAD OF WINTER (Ace 0-441-14089-0, 11/85 [10/85], $2.95, 273pp, pb) Original fantasy anthology in the series set in Sanctuary. This has the new packaging for the series.
Contents:

			Page
Dramatis Personae	Lynn Abbey	pr	x
Introduction	Robert Lynn Asprin	in	1
Hell to Pay	Janet Morris	nv DEADWIN,85	9
The Veiled Lady, or A Look at the Normal Folk			
	Andrew J. Offutt	nv DEADWIN,85	39
The God-Chosen	Lynn Abbey	nv DEADWIN,85	75
Keeping Promises	Robin W. Bailey	nv DEADWIN,85	102
Armies of the Night	C.J. Cherryh	nv DEADWIN,85	134
Down by the Riverside	Diane Duane	nv DEADWIN,85	176
When the Spirit Moves You			
	Robert Lynn Asprin	ss DEADWIN,85	225
The Color of Magic	Diana L. Paxson	nv DEADWIN,85	240
Afterword	Andrew J. Offutt	aw DEADWIN,85	266

*****Asprin, Robert Lynn & Lynn Abbey, eds.** THIEVES' WORLD, BOOK 8: SOUL OF THE CITY (Ace 0-441-77581-0, 01/86 [12/85], $2.95, 242pp, pb) Original anthology/braided novel of 6 stories by 3 authors -- Abbey, Cherryh, and Morris -- set in the world of Sanctuary.
Contents:

			Page
Dramatis Personae	Lynn Abbey	pr	x
Power Play	Janet Morris	nv SOULCTY,86	1
Dagger in the Mind	C.J. Cherryh	nv SOULCTY,86	40
Children of All Ages	Lynn Abbey	nv SOULCTY,86	85
Death in the Meadow	C.J. Cherryh	nv SOULCTY,86	128
The Small Powers that Endure			
	Lynn Abbey	nv SOULCTY,86	173
Pillar of Fire	Janet Morris	nv SOULCTY,86	213

Asprin, Robert Lynn & Lynn Abbey, eds. WINGS OF OMEN (Ace 0-441-80588-4, 07/85 [10/85], $2.95, 277pp, pb) Reissue (Ace 1984) original anthology, "Thieves' World" #6; 4th printing.

*****Asprin, Robert Lynn & Phil Foglio** MYTH ADVENTURES ONE (Donning/Starblaze 0-89865-414-9, 10/85 [10/85], $12.95, 107pp, pb) Fantasy "graphic novel" with art by Phil Foglio, a collected and colored version of the Warp b&w comic "Myth Adventures".

Asprin, Robert Lynn & George Takei MIRROR FRIEND, MIRROR FOE (Ace 0-441-53380-9, 12/85 [11/85], $2.75, 223pp, pb) Reprint (Playboy 1979) sf novel. Ninjas in space.

*****Attanasio, A.A.** BEASTMARKS (Ziesing 0-9612970-2-6, 01/85 [01/85], $25.00 signed edition; $13.95 trade, 120pp, hc) Collection of 7 stories, apparently all originals. The illustrations are by Rich Schindler. The book is copyright 1984, but did not appear until January 1985. Recommended. (FCM)
Contents:

			Page
Nuclear Tan	A.A. Attanasio	ss BEASTMK,85	1
Over the Rainbow	A.A. Attanasio	ss BEASTMK,85	5
The Last Dragon Master	A.A. Attanasio	ss BEASTMK,85	13
Monkey Puzzle	A.A. Attanasio	ss BEASTMK,85	33
Sherlock Holmes and Basho			
	A.A. Attanasio	ss BEASTMK,85	47
Matter Mutter Mother	A.A. Attanasio	ss BEASTMK,85	55
The Answerer of Dreams	A.A. Attanasio	nv BEASTMK,85	75

Attanasio, A.A. RADIX (Bantam Spectra 0-553-25406-5, 10/85 [09/85], $3.95, 466pp, pb) Reprint (Morrow 1981) literary sf novel. This was an impressive first novel which created quite a stir, both positive and negative. It was a Nebula finalist.

Auel, Jean CLAN OF THE CAVE BEAR (Bantam 0-553-25042-6, 08/85 [07/85], $4.95, 495pp, pb) Reissue (Crown 1980) novel of prehistoric times, Volume One of "Earth's Children". 19th Bantam printing.

*****Auel, Jean** THE MAMMOTH HUNTERS (Crown 0-517-55627-8, 12/85 [11/85], $19.95, 645pp, hc) Prehistoric sf novel, third in the "Earth's Children" series. The first printing of over 1 million copies set a new record.

*****Austin, Richard** THE GUARDIANS (Jove 0-515-07980-4, 02/85 [01/85], $2.75, 230pp, pb) Sf/survivalist novel of a "four-man elite survival team."

*****Austin, Richard** THE GUARDIANS #2: TRIAL BY FIRE (Jove 0-515-08184-1, 05/85 [04/85], $2.75, 231pp, pb) Second in a post-holocaust action/adventure series.

*****Austin, Richard** THE GUARDIANS: NIGHT OF THE PHOENIX (Jove 0-515-08392-5, 1985 [10/85], $2.75, 216pp, pb) Post-holocaust sf adventure novel, fourth in a series.

*****Austin, Richard** THE GUARDIANS: THUNDER OF HELL (Jove 0-515-08327-5, 08/85 [07/85], $2.75, 217pp, pb) Sf novel, third in a survivalist series; post-holocaust adventure.

*****Avi** BRIGHT SHADOW (Bradbury Press 0-02-707750-0, 10/85 [11/85], $11.95, 167pp, hc) Young-adult fantasy novel. A 12-year-old girl is the repository for the last wishes left in the kingdom.

Bachman, Richard THINNER (NAL/Signet 0-451-13796-5, 09/85 [08/85], $4.50, 318pp, pb) Reprint (NAL 1984) horror novel. Bachman is a pseudonym for Stephen King.

Bachman, Richard THINNER (Large Print Book Club #1359, 11/85 [11/85], price unknown, 504pp, hc) Reprint (NAL 1984) horror novel.

Bachman, Richard THINNER (SFBC #6494, 1985 [12/85], $4.98, 282pp, hc) Reprint (NAL 1984) horror novel. The author is Stephen King.

*****Baen, Jim, John F. Carr & Jerry E. Pournelle, eds.** THE SCIENCE FICTION YEARBOOK Main listing under Jerry E. Pournelle.

*****Baen, Jim & Jerry E. Pournelle, eds.** FAR FRONTIERS Main listing under Jerry E. Pournelle.

*****Baen, Jim & Jerry E. Pournelle, eds.** FAR FRONTIERS VOL. II/SUMMER 1985 Main listing under Jerry E. Pournelle.

*****Baen, Jim & Jerry E. Pournelle, eds.** FAR FRONTIERS VOL. III/FALL 1985 Main listing under Jerry E. Pournelle.

*****Baen, Jim & Jerry E. Pournelle, eds.** FAR FRONTIERS VOL. IV/WINTER 1985 Main listing under Jerry E. Pournelle.

Bailey, Dennis R. & David F. Bischoff TIN WOODMAN Main listing under David F. Bischoff.

*****Bailey, Robin W.** SKULL GATE (Tor 0-812-53139-6, 10/85 [09/85], $2.95, 288pp, pb) Fantasy novel, sequel to FROST.

*****Baldwin, Merl** THE HELMSMAN (Popular Library/Questar 0-445-20027-8, 06/85 [05/85], $2.95, 311pp, pb) Sf novel, a first novel. Also listed inside as by Bill Baldwin.

Ballard, J.G. THE BEST SHORT STORIES OF J.G. BALLARD (Pocket/ Washington Square Press 0-671-61451-7, 12/85 [12/85], $4.95, 358pp, pb) Reprint (Holt, Rinehart & Winston 1978) collection of 19 stories.

Ballard, J.G. CONCRETE ISLAND (Vintage 0-394-74107-2, 09/85 [09/85], $3.95, 176pp, pb) Reprint (Jonathan Cape 1973) quasi-fantasy novel. Thematic sequel to CRASH.

Ballard, J.G. CRASH (Vintage 0-394-74109-9, 09/85 [09/85], $3.95, 224pp, pb) Reprint (Jonathan Cape 1973) auto-erotic fantasy novel.

Ballard, J.G. EMPIRE OF THE SUN (Washington Square Press 0-671-53053-4, 10/85 [09/85], $4.50, 375pp, pb) Reprint (Gollancz 1984) autobiographical novel; non-sf, associational.

Ballard, J.G. EMPIRE OF THE SUN (QPB/Simon & Schuster no ISBN, 12/85 [12/85], $7.95, 279pp, pb) Reprint (Gollancz 1984) associational item, a non-sf/fantasy novel by a renowned sf author. Identical to the Simon & Schuster edition, with the jacket printed as the paperback cover.

Ballard, J.G. THE TERMINAL BEACH (Gollancz 0-575-03514-5, 02/85 [01/85], £8.95, 221pp, hc) Reissue (Gollancz 1964) collection. This differs from the earlier American paperback TERMINAL BEACH (Berkley 1964).

Ballard, J.G. THE UNLIMITED DREAM COMPANY (Washington Square Press 0-671-60537-3, 11/85 [10/85], $4.50, 254pp, pb) Reprint (Jonathan Cape 1979) surrealistic fantasy novel.

Ballard, J.G. THE VOICES OF TIME (Gollancz 0-575-03515-3, 02/85 [01/85], £8.95, 197pp, hc) Reissue (Gollancz 1974 as THE FOUR-DIMENSIONAL NIGHTMARE) collection. It differs from the earlier version, THE FOUR-DIMENSIONAL NIGHTMARE (Gollancz 1963) by two stories and also differs from THE VOICES OF TIME AND OTHER STORIES (Berkley 1962).

*Barker, Clive BOOKS OF BLOOD (Scream/Press 0-910489-14-9, 11/85 [11/85], $50.00 special boxed edition, $30.00 trade edition, 455pp, hc) Omnibus edition of CLIVE BARKER'S BOOKS OF BLOOD, VOL.S 1, 2, & 3 (all Sphere 1984). First omnibus, and first American edition of an original collection which was split into three volumes for its first appearance. All 3 have corrected texts and some slight rewriting here. World Fantasy Award winner Barker is one of the hottest new talents, and the book is fittingly illustrated with gruesome artwork by J.K. Potter and Harry O. Morris. Recommended--but not for the easily offended or the faint of heart. (FCM)
Contents: Page
CLIVE BARKER'S BOOKS OF BLOOD, VOLUME 1
                              Clive Barker   oc SPH 1984
Introduction   Ramsey Campbell   in   xi
The Book of Blood   Clive Barker   ss CBB # 1,84   1
The Midnight Meat Train   Clive Barker   nv CBB # 1,84   13
The Yattering and Jack   Clive Barker   ss CBB # 1,84   39
Pig Blood Blues   Clive Barker   nv CBB # 1,84   59
Sex, Death and Starshine   Clive Barker   nv CBB # 1,84   87
In the Hills, the Cities   Clive Barker   nv CBB # 1,84 121
CLIVE BARKER'S BOOKS OF BLOOD, VOLUME 2
                              Clive Barker   oc SPH 1984
Dread   Clive Barker   nv CBB # 2,84 149
Hell's Event   Clive Barker   nv CBB # 2,84 183
Jacqueline Ess: Her Will and Testament
                              Clive Barker   nv CBB # 2,84 205
The Skins of the Fathers   Clive Barker   nv CBB # 2,84 237
New Murders in the Rue Morgue
                              Clive Barker   nv CBB # 2,84 267
CLIVE BARKER'S BOOKS OF BLOOD, VOLUME 3
                              Clive Barker   oc SPH 1984
Son of Celluloid   Clive Barker   nv CBB # 3,84 293
Rawhead Rex   Clive Barker   nv CBB # 3,84 325
Confession of a (Pornographer's) Shroud
                              Clive Barker   nv CBB # 3,84 365
Scapegoats   Clive Barker   nv CBB # 3,84 395
Human Remains   Clive Barker   nv CBB # 3,84 419

Barker, Clive CLIVE BARKER'S BOOKS OF BLOOD, VOL.S ONE, TWO & THREE (Weidenfeld & Nicolson 0-297-78788-8, 1985 [12/85], £75, 149 + 150 + 182pp, hc) Reprint (Sphere 1984) boxed set, original collection in three volumes, signed and with cover art by the author. Limited to 200 boxed sets. There is also an unboxed, unsigned edition of 800 copies available.

*Barker, Clive CLIVE BARKER'S BOOKS OF BLOOD, VOLUME 4 (Sphere 0-7221-1373-0, 07/85 [06/85], £1.50, 151pp, pb) Original collection of five tales, part of the new set of three "Books of Blood" issued simultaneously.
Contents: Page
The Body Politic   Clive Barker   nv CBB V 4,85   1
The Inhuman Condition   Clive Barker   nv CBB V 4,85   34
Revelations   Clive Barker   nv CBB V 4,85   68
Down, Satan!   Clive Barker   ss CBB V 4,85 108
The Age of Desire   Clive Barker   nv CBB V 4,85 113

*Barker, Clive CLIVE BARKER'S BOOKS OF BLOOD, VOLUME 5 (Sphere 0-7221-1374-9, 07/85 [06/85], £1.50, 149pp, pb) Original collection of four dark tales.
Contents: Page
The Forbidden   Clive Barker   nv CBB V 5,85   1
The Madonna   Clive Barker   nv CBB V 5,85   38
Babel's Children   Clive Barker   nv CBB V 5,85   76
In the Flesh   Clive Barker   nv CBB V 5,85 103

*Barker, Clive CLIVE BARKER'S BOOKS OF BLOOD, VOLUME 6 (Sphere 0-7221-1375-7, 07/85 [06/85], £1.50, 152pp, pb) Original collection of four stories and a "postscript."
Contents: Page
The Life of Death   Clive Barker   nv CBB V 6,85   1
How Spoilers Bleed   Clive Barker   nv CBB V 6,85   35
Twilight at the Towers   Clive Barker   nv CBB V 6,85   66
The Last Illusion   Clive Barker   na CBB V 6,85   97
The Book of Blood (a postscript) On Jerusalem Street
                              Clive Barker   aw CBB V 6,85 149

*Barker, Clive THE DAMNATION GAME (Weidenfeld & Nicolson 0-297-78720-9, 09/85 [08/85], £8.95, 374pp, hc) Horror novel; Barker's first novel.

*Barker, M.A.R. FLAMESONG (DAW 0-88677-076-9, 09/85 [08/85], $3.50, 412pp, pb) Fantasy novel, a new adventure set on Tekumel. Based on the author's board game, "Empire of the Petal Throne."

Barker, M.A.R. THE MAN OF GOLD (DAW 0-88677-082-3, 09/85 [08/85], $3.95, 367pp, pb) Reissue (DAW 1984) fantasy novel; 4th printing.

*Barrie, Monica QUEEN OF KNIGHTS (Pocket 0-671-46973-8, 03/85 [02/85], $3.95, 372pp, pb) Historical fantasy novel; "Monica Barrie" is a pseudonym for David Wind. Wind, in a private letter, insists the book (despite its romance packaging) is a straight historical fantasy with Robin Hood, Richard the Lion-Heart, and Celtic mythology.

*Bartholomew, Barbara CHILD OF TOMORROW (NAL/Signet 0-451-13781-7, 08/85 [07/85], $2.50, 192pp, pb) Young-adult sf novel, Book 2 of the "Time Keeper" trilogy.

*Bartholomew, Barbara THE TIME KEEPER (NAL/Signet Vista 0-451-13629-2, 06/85 [05/85], $2.50, 191pp, pb) Sf novel, first of a young-adult series.

*Bartholomew, Barbara WHEN DREAMERS CEASE TO DREAM (NAL/Signet/Vista 0-451-13869-4, 10/85 [09/85], $2.50, 190pp, pb) Young-adult sf novel, Book 3 of "The Time Keeper" trilogy.

Barton, S.W. & Michael Kurland THE LAST PRESIDENT Main listing under Michael Kurland.

*Baskin, Hosie & Leonard Baskin A BOOK OF DRAGONS (Knopf 0-394-86298-8, 10/85 [09/85], $12.95, unpaginated, hc) An art book with illustrations by Leonard and text by his son Hosie. Monsters not usually thought of as dragons are included, and the artwork often creates a mood of dark horror. Recommended for anyone liking non-traditional fantasy art. (FCM)

*Baskin, Leonard & Hosie Baskin A BOOK OF DRAGONS Main listing under Hosie Baskin.

*Bates, Cary, Gene Colan & Neal McPheeters NIGHTWINGS (DC Comics 0-930289-06-04, 12/85 [12/85], $5.95, unpaginated, pb) "Graphic novel" adaptation of a novelette by Robert Silverberg (*Galaxy*, Sep. 1968). It's an 8.5" x 11" paperback.

Bauer, Steven SATYRDAY (Berkley 0-425-07964-3, 07/85 [06/85], $2.75, 223pp, pb) Reprint (Berkley-Putnam 1980) fantasy novel.

Baum, L. Frank THE EMERALD CITY OF OZ (Ballantine/Del Rey 0-345-32028-X, 06/85 [05/85], $2.50, 299pp, pb) Reissue (Reilly & Britton 1910) juvenile fantasy novel, "Oz" #6. 3rd Del Rey printing.

Baum, L. Frank LITTLE WIZARD STORIES OF OZ (Schocken 0-8052-4005-5, 10/85 [09/85], $14.95, 145pp, hc) Reprint (Reilly & Britton 1914) collection of 6 short "Oz" stories for younger readers, with 42 color illustrations by John R. Neill and an introduction by Michael Patrick Hearn.

Baum, L. Frank THE MARVELOUS LAND OF OZ (Morrow/Books of Wonder 0-688-05439-0, 08/85 [09/85], $15.00, 289pp, hc) Reprint (Reilly & Britton 1904) juvenile fantasy novel, facsimile of the first edition, with b&w and color illustrations by John R. Neill.

Baum, L. Frank THE WIZARD OF OZ (Unicorn 0-88101-018-9, 12/85 [12/85], $14.95, 191pp, hc) Reprint (Hill 1900 as THE WONDERFUL WIZARD OF OZ) fantasy novel, illustrated by Greg Hildebrandt.

Baxter, Lorna THE EGGCHILD (Ace 0-441-19258-0, 12/85 [11/85], $2.75, 161pp, pb) Reprint (Dutton 1979) juvenile fantasy novel, with new illustrations by Charles Vess.

*Bayley, Barrington J. THE FOREST OF PELDAIN (DAW 0-88677-068-8, 08/85 [07/85], $2.75, 223pp, pb) Fantasy novel.

*Bayley, Barrington J. THE ROD OF LIGHT (Methuen 0-413-58160-8, 10/85 [10/85], £2.50, 193pp, pb) Sf novel, sequel to THE SOUL OF THE ROBOT. "Beneath a fake landscape in a wild bare desert, the impossible is happening. Robots are trying to make souls."

*Bear, Greg BLOOD MUSIC (Arbor House 0-87795-720-7, 05/85 [04/85], $14.95, 262pp, hc) Sf novel based on the award-winning story of the same name. Recommended. (FCM)

Bear, Greg BLOOD MUSIC (SFBC #2354, 11/85 [11/85], $4.98, 215pp, hc) Reprint (Arbor House 1985) sf novel.

*Bear, Greg EON (Bluejay 0-312-94144-7, 08/85 [07/85], $16.95, 504pp, hc) Sf novel of wild universe spanning conflicts. Highly recommended. (CNB)

Bear, Greg STRENGTH OF STONES (Ace 0-441-79066-6, 01/86 [12/85], $2.75, 237pp, pb) Reissue (Ace 1981) sf novel formed from related novelettes. 2nd Ace printing.

*Beattie, Ann SPECTACLES (Workman/Ariel 0-89480-924-5, 10/31/85 [11/85], $10.95, 37pp, hc) Juvenile fantasy short story, illustrated by Winslow Pels.

*Beere, Peter TRAUMA 2020 #3: SILENT SLAUGHTER (Arrow 0-09-943480-6, 1985 [10/85], £1.95, 202pp, pb) 21st-century action thriller, third novel in a series.

Bellairs, John THE MUMMY, THE WILL, AND THE CRYPT (Bantam/Skylark 0-553-15323-4, 03/85 [02/85], $2.50, 168pp, pb) Reprint (Dial 1983) juvenile fantasy novel, second in the "Johnny Dixon" series.

*Bellairs, John THE REVENGE OF THE WIZARD'S GHOST (Dial 0-8037-0170-5, 11/85 [10/85], $11.95, 147pp, hc) Young-adult fantasy novel in the series featuring Johnny Dixon. Also announced in a library edition, -0177-2, $11.89.

Bellairs, John THE SPELL OF THE SORCERER'S SKULL (Bantam/Skylark 0-553-15357-9, 11/85 [10/85], $2.50, 170pp, pb) Reprint (Dial 1984) young-adult fantasy novel.

Bellairs, John THE TREASURE OF ALPHEUS WINTERBORN (Bantam/Skylark 0-553-15095-2, 12/85 [11/85], $2.50, 180pp, pb) Reissue (Harcourt 1978) young-adult fantasy novel. Illustrations by Judith Gwyn Brown. Second printing.

*Bendixen, Alfred, ed. HAUNTED WOMEN: THE BEST SUPERNATURAL TALES BY AMERICAN WOMEN WRITERS (Ungar 0-8044-2052-1, 10/31/85 [11/85], $14.95, 276pp, hc) Anthology of 13 stories, mostly written in the last century.
Contents:

			Page
Introduction	Alfred Bendixen	in	
The Amber Gods	Harriet Prescott Spofford	na	13
The True Story of Guenever			
	Elizabeth Stuart Phelps	ss	66
The Ghost in the Cap'n Brown House			
	Harriet Beecher Stowe		
		ss OLDTOWN,1871	80
The Yellow Wallpaper	Charlotte Perkins Gilman		
		ss NEM 1892	92
The Story of a Day	Grace King	ss	110
The Little Room	Madelene Yale Wynne	ss	119
Her Letters	Kate Chopin	ss	133
The Foreigner	Sarah Orne Jewett	nv	143
Luella Miller	Mary E. Wilkins Freeman		
		ss WNDROSE,03	171
The Lost Ghost	Mary E. Wilkins Freeman		
		ss WNDROSE,03	186
The Bell in the Fog	Gertrude Atherton	nv BELLFOG,05	205
The Fullness of Life	Edith Wharton	ss	231
Pomegranate Seed	Edith Wharton	nv GHOSTS ,37	243

Benford, Gregory ACROSS THE SEA OF SUNS (SFBC #1814, 03/85 [02/85], $7.98, 342pp, hc) Reprint (Timescape 1984) sf novel, sequel to IN THE OCEAN OF NIGHT. Highly recommended. (CNB)

*Benford, Gregory ARTIFACT (Tor 0-312-93048-8, 06/85 [05/85], $16.95, 533pp, hc) Sf novel, a complex entertaining story with bestseller thriller elements. Recommended. (FCM)

Benford, Gregory & William Rotsler SHIVA DESCENDING (Tor 0-812-53183-3, 11/85 [10/85], $3.95, 394pp, pb) Reprint (Avon 1980) sf novel.

*Benni, Stefano TERRA! (Pantheon 0-394-74064-5, 10/85 [10/85], $6.95, 360pp, pb) Satiric sf novel of a decadent post-holocaust world of "madcap adventure." A first novel, published in Italy in 1983; translation by Annapaola Cancogni.

*Benoit, Hendra PSI PATROL: HENDRA'S BOOK (Scholastic/Point 0-590-33202-3, 1985 [09/85], $2.25, 137pp, pb) Young-adult fantasy novel, part of a series about kids who "touched a piece of satellite that dropped through the roof of the mall" and developed psychic powers. Authorship is credited to the heroine, although it's written in the third person.

*Benson, Michael VINTAGE SCIENCE FICTION FILMS, 1896-1949 (McFarland 0-89950-085-4, 04/85 [03/85], $18.95, 219pp, hc) Chronological filmography of about 375 films, with annotations and indexes. There is light-hearted and very readable commentary throughout, plus lots of behind-the-scenes information. A book to read as well as keep for reference. Recommended. (CNB)

Bickham, Jack M. ARIEL (Tor 0-812-58086-9, 10/85 [09/85], $3.95, 348pp, pb) Reprint (St. Martin's 1984) sf novel of a sentient computer.

*Biggle, Lloyd, Jr. & T.L. Sherred ALIEN MAIN (Doubleday 0-385-19358-0, 07/85 [06/85], $12.95, 182pp, hc) Sf novel, a sequel to Sherred's ALIEN ISLAND (1970) completed by Biggle.

*Bischoff, David F. THE DESTINY DICE (NAL/Signet 0-451-13489-3, 03/85 [02/85], $2.95, 238pp, pb) Fantasy novel, Book One of "The Gaming Magi".

*Bischoff, David F. GALACTIC WARRIORS (Ace 0-441-27256-8, 09/85 [08/85], $2.75, 188pp, pb) Sf novel, "StarHounds" #2.

*Bischoff, David F. STAR HOUNDS, BOOK ONE: THE INFINITE BATTLE (Ace 0-441-37018-7, 04/85 [03/85], $2.75, 171pp, pb) Sf novel, "Starhounds" #1.

*Bischoff, David F. WRAITH BOARD (NAL/Signet 0-451-13669-1, 07/85 [06/85], $2.95, 238pp, pb) Gaming fantasy novel, "The Gaming Magi" #2.

Bischoff, David F. & Dennis R. Bailey TIN WOODMAN (Ace 0-441-81293-7, 12/85 [11/85], $2.75, 182pp, pb) Reissue (Doubleday 1979) sf novel. 2nd Ace printing.

*Bischoff, David F., Rich Brown & Linda Richardson A PERSONAL DEMON (NAL/Signet 0-451-13814-7, 09/85 [08/85], $2.95, 253pp, pb) Fantasy novel. Portions appeared previously as stories by "Michael F.X. Milhaus."
Contents:

				Page
A Personal Demon	Michael F.X. Milhaus	nv	FAN Feb,76	
In a Pig's Eye	Michael F.X. Milhaus	nv	FAN May,76	
With Good Intentions	Michael F.X. Milhaus	ss	FAN Sep,77	
A Trick of the Tail	Michael F.X. Milhaus	nv	FAN Dec,77	
Where Angels Fear to Tread				
	Michael F.X. Milhaus	nv	FAN Apr,78	

*Bischoff, David F. & Thomas F. Monteleone NIGHT OF THE DRAGONSTAR (Berkley 0-425-07963-5, 07/85 [06/85], $2.95, 264pp, pb) Sf novel, sequel to DAY OF THE DRAGONSTAR, described in the publicity as "lizards from outer space." It isn't a "V" novel.

Bischoff, David F. & Ted White FORBIDDEN WORLD Main listing under Ted White.

*Bishop, Michael ANCIENT OF DAYS (Arbor House 0-87795-724-8, 08/85 [07/85], $16.95, 354pp, hc) Sf novel, an expansion of "Her Habiline Husband". Highly recommended. (DLN)

Bishop, Michael ANCIENT OF DAYS (SFBC #1604, 11/85 [12/85], $7.98, 337pp, hc) Reprint (Arbor House 1985) sf novel of a *homo habilis* alive in modern America. The original novella covered the ground completely. (CNB)

*Bittner, James APPROACHES TO THE FICTION OF URSULA K. LE GUIN (UMI 0-8357-1573-6, 1984 [05/85], $24.95 + postage, 161pp, hc) Non-fiction, literary criticism. This revision of a doctoral thesis appeared in 1984, but we didn't see it until 1985.

*Blackford, Jenny, Russell Blackford, Lucy Sussex & Norman Talbot, eds. CONTRARY MODES (Ebony Books 0-9590655-2-0, 08/85 [09/85], A$4.95, 155pp, pb) Non-fiction; critical studies. The Proceedings of the 1985 worldcon's academic track, 10 essays by George Turner, Russell Blackford, and others. Available by surface mail for US$6.00/£3.50, by air mail for US$11.00/£5.50.

*Blackford, Russell, Jenny Blackford, Lucy Sussex & Norman Talbot, eds. CONTRARY MODES Main listing under Jenny Blackford.

*Blackford, Russell & David King, eds. URBAN FANTASIES Main listing under David King.

*Blakeney, Jay D. THE CHILDREN OF ANTHI (Ace 0-441-10399-5, 07/85 [06/85], $2.75, 251pp, pb) Sf novel; probably a first novel.

Blamires, Harry COLD WAR IN HELL (Nelson 0-8407-5930-4, 02/85 [01/85], $4.95, 195pp, pb) Reprint (Longmans 1955) fantasy novel, second in a trilogy.

Blamires, Harry THE DEVIL'S HUNTING GROUNDS (Nelson 0-8407-5932-0, 02/85 [01/85], $4.95, 172pp, pb) Reprint (Longmans 1954) satiric Christian fantasy novel, first in a trilogy.

Blamires, Harry HIGHWAY TO HEAVEN (Nelson 0-8407-5928-2, 02/85 [01/85], $4.95, 192pp, pb) Reprint (Longmans 1955) fantasy novel, conclusion of a trilogy.

*Bleich, David UTOPIA: THE PSYCHOLOGY OF A CULTURAL FANTASY (UMI 0-8357-1574-4, 1984 [05/85], $24.95 + postage, 154pp, hc) Non-fiction; literary criticism. This first book version of a dissertation appeared in 1984, but we didn't see it until 1985.

*Bleiler, E.F., ed. SUPERNATURAL FICTION WRITERS: FANTASY & HORROR, 2 VOLS. (Scribners 0-684-17808-7, 11/85 [11/85], $135.00, 1169pp, hc) A major reference work in two volumes with critical essays on fantasy authors. The book is done chronologically and is excellent on earlier work but fairly sketchy on the current crop (22 post-1940 writers are discussed). It has excellent coverage of the early 20th Century. Recommended, especially for libraries. Not Available in bookstores. Must be ordered direct. (CNB)

Blish, James SPOCK MUST DIE! (Bantam 0-553-24634-8, 04/85 [03/85], $2.95, 118pp, pb) Reissue (Bantam 1970) Star Trek novel. 17th printing.

Blish, James & J.A. Lawrence STAR TREK 12 (Bantam Spectra 0-553-25252-6, 11/85 [09/85], $2.95, 177pp, pb) Reissue (Bantam 1977) collection of adaptations of stories from the original Star Trek tv series. It was announced under the new title THE CORBOMITE MANEUVER but kept its original title after all.

*Bloch, Robert HELL ON EARTH See listing under Keith Giffen & Robert Loren Fleming.

*Bonanno, Margaret Wander DWELLERS IN THE CRUCIBLE (Pocket 0-671-60373-6, 09/85 [08/85], $3.50, 308pp, pb) Star Trek novel, Star Trek #25.

*Border Land [v.1 #2] R.S. Hadji, ed. (Artimus Publications, 1985 [11/85], C$3.00, 40pp, pb)
Contents: Page
Fearful Pleasures   Various Hands   br BLD   2
Midnight Matinees   Don Hutchison   mr BLD   4
Of Time and Space   Hugh B. Cave   ss BLD V1 #2,85   8
The Oviparous Tailor   Thomas Lovell Beddoes
                                                pm BLD V1 #2,85   12
Dead Men's Fingers   Phillip C. Heath   nv BLD V1 #2,85   13
The Brother in the Lake   Randolph Cirilo   ss BLD V1 #2,85   24
The Revenge of the Past: Part 2
                           David Aylward   ar BLD V1 #2,85   29
The Other Side   Count Eric Stenbock
                                                ss SPL Jun 6,1893   34
Winter Walk in Deep December
                           Joseph Payne Brennan
                                                pm BLD V1 #2,85   40

*Border Land [v.1 #3] R.S. Hadji, ed. (Artimus Publications, 1985 [11/85], C$3.00, 40pp, pb)
Contents: Page
Fearful Pleasures   Various Hands   br BLD   2
Midnight Matinees   Don Hutchison   mr BLD   5
Christobel   Janet Fox   ss BLD V1 #3,85   8
The Demon of the Gibbet   Fitz-James O'Brien   pm   14
Deadlights   Charles Wagner   ss TWT # 9,84   15
The Spirit of Things   John M. Skipp   ss BLD V1 #3,85   19
The Children Open Their Green Flesh
                           Penny Gracey   pm BLD V1 #3,85   22
The King Under the Water   Lillian Stewart Carl
                                                ss BLD V1 #3,85   24
The Dig   Ardath Mayhar   ss BLD V1 #3,85   32
Azucena   Nancy Etchemendy   vi BLD V1 #3,85   35
The Sumach   Ulric Daubeny   ss   36

*Borges, Jorge Luis ATLAS (Dutton 0-525-24334-5, 11/85 [11/85], $14.95, 95pp, hc) A "scrapbook" of prose, poems, travel notes, and photographs, assembled in collaboration with Maria Kodama and translated by Anthony Kerrigan. It originally appeared in Argentina, under the same title, from Editoria Sudamerica S.A. (1984).

Bova, Ben AS ON A DARKLING PLAIN (Tor 0-812-53200-7, 06/85 [05/85], $2.95, 287pp, pb) Reprint (Walker 1972) sf novel.

*Bova, Ben THE ASTRAL MIRROR (Tor 0-812-53217-1, 10/85 [09/85], $2.95, 274pp, pb) Collection, with both stories and non-fiction essays on a variety of topics.
Contents: Page
The Astral Mirror   Ben Bova   in   ix
Starflight   Ben Bova   ar 1973   1
Free Enterprise   Ben Bova   ss ASF Feb,84   15
Robot Welfare   Ben Bova   ar 1985   35
The Angel's Gift [as Oxford Williams]
                           Ben Bova   ss OBK # 1,83   54
The Secret Life of Henry K.
                           Ben Bova   ss GLR May,73   62
Science Fiction   Ben Bova   ar 1985   77
Love Calls [as Oxford Williams]
                           Ben Bova   ss BOM # 4,82   93
Amorality Tale   Ben Bova   ss 1985   107
Out of Time   Ben Bova   ss OMN Nov,84   117
Science Fiction and Reality
                           Ben Bova   ar WRI 1979   134
To Be or Not   Ben Bova   ss DST V1 #2,79   143
The Man Who Saw "Gunga Din" Thirty Times
                           Ben Bova   ss SHOWCSE,73   154
The System   Ben Bova   vi ASF Jan,68   160
Cement   Ben Bova   fa ASF Jan,84   162
Building a Real World   Ben Bova   ar RIG F11,81   166
It's Right Over Your Nose
                           Ben Bova   ar ASF Jun,68   177
The Perfect Warrior [The Dueling Machine]
                           Ben Bova   na ASF May,63   186
The Future of Science: Prometheus, Apollo, Athena
                           Ben Bova   ar NAS # 9,74   259

Bova, Ben ORION (Tor 0-812-53215-5, 04/85 [03/85], $2.95, 432pp, pb) Reprint (Simon & Schuster 1984) sf novel.

Bova, Ben ORION (Severn House 0-7278-1235-1, 10/85 [10/85], £9.95, 432pp, hc) Reprint (S&S/Fireside 1984) sf novel, first British publication and first hardcover edition.

*Bova, Ben PRIVATEERS (Tor 0-312-93604-4, 09/85 [08/85], $15.95, 383pp, hc) Sf novel. Near future political novel featuring privateering in space.

Bova, Ben VOYAGERS (Bantam 0-553-21702-X, 04/85 [03/85], $2.25, 382pp, pb) Reissue (Doubleday 1981) sf novel. 2nd printing.

Bowker, Richard FORBIDDEN SANCTUARY (Ballantine/Del Rey 0-345-32784-4, 11/85 [10/85], $2.95, 203pp, pb) Reissue (Del Rey 1982) sf novel; 2nd printing.

*Boyajian, Jerry & Kenneth R. Johnson INDEX TO THE SCIENCE FICTION MAGAZINES 1984 (Twaci Press no ISBN, 03/85 [02/85], $4.75 postpaid, 31pp, pb) Bibliography. Indexes the 1984 issues of Amazing, Analog, Asimov's, F&SF, and Twilight Zone only, plus selected stories from general magazines.

Boye, Karin KALLOCAIN (Fromm Int'l 0-88064-050-2, 10/85 [10/85], $7.95, 193pp, pb) Reprint (Univ. of Wisconsin 1966) dystopian sf novel, first published in Sweden in 1940.

Brackett, Leigh THE LONG TOMORROW (Ballantine/Del Rey 0-345-32926-0, 01/86 [12/85], $2.95, 262pp, pb) Reissue (Doubleday 1955) sf novel. Fourth printing. The paperback is now the same price as the original hardcover.

*Bradbury, Ray DEATH IS A LONELY BUSINESS (Knopf 0-394-54702-0, 10/85 [10/85], $15.95, 278pp, hc) Non-sf/fantasy; associational. Bradbury's first novel in 23 years is billed as a nostalgic hard-boiled detective novel.

*Bradbury, Ray FROST AND FIRE See listing under Klaus Janson.

*Bradley, Marion Zimmer THE BEST OF MARION ZIMMER BRADLEY (Academy Chicago 0-89733-166-4, 1985 [11/85], $4.95, 367pp, pb) Collection of 16 stories arranged chronologically. Edited by Martin H. Greenberg. A hardcover was announced, but did not appear until 1986.
Contents: Page
Centaurus Changeling   Marion Zimmer Bradley nv FSF Apr,54
The Climbing Wave   Marion Zimmer Bradley na FSF Feb,55   50
Exiles of Tomorrow   Marion Zimmer Bradley ss FUN Mar,55   121
Death Between the Stars   Marion Zimmer Bradley ss FUN Mar,56   128
Bird of Prey   Marion Zimmer Bradley nv VSF May,57   146
The Wind People   Marion Zimmer Bradley ss IFS Feb,59   181
The Wild One   Marion Zimmer Bradley ss BKW # 1,60   199
Treason of the Blood   Marion Zimmer Bradley ss WBS Aug,62   215
The Jewel of Arwen   Marion Zimmer Bradley   ss TKG 1973   231
The Day of the Butterflies
                           Marion Zimmer Bradley ss DAWSFRD,76   241
Hero's Moon   Marion Zimmer Bradley nv FSF Oct,76   253
The Engine   Marion Zimmer Bradley ss VIV Mar,77   277
The Secret of the Blue Star
                           Marion Zimmer Bradley ss THVSWLD,79   283
To Keep the Oath   Marion Zimmer Bradley nv BLDYSUN,79   303
Elbow Room   Marion Zimmer Bradley ss STL # 5,80   331
Blood Will Tell   Marion Zimmer Bradley ss KPRSPRC,80   349

Bradley, Marion Zimmer THE BLOODY SUN (Ace 0-441-06858-8, 06/85 [05/85], $3.50, 408pp, pb) Reissue (Ace 1979), 7th printing. Part of the "Darkover" sf series. This contains the revised text of THE BLOODY SUN (Ace 1964) plus the short story "To Keep the Oath" (1979).

Bradley, Marion Zimmer CITY OF SORCERY (SFBC #1493, 03/85 [02/85], $3.98, 305pp, hc) Reprint (DAW 1984) "Darkover" novel, first hardcover edition.

Bradley, Marion Zimmer THE HERITAGE OF HASTUR (DAW 0-88677-079-3, 09/85 [08/85], $3.95, 381pp, pb) Reissue (DAW 1975) sf novel in the "Darkover" series.

*Bradley, Marion Zimmer NIGHT'S DAUGHTER (Ballantine/Del Rey 0-345-30920-0, 02/85 [01/85], $2.95, 249pp, pb) Fantasy novel based on Mozart's opera "The Magic Flute".

Bradley, Marion Zimmer THE PLANET SAVERS & THE SWORD OF ALDONES (Ace 0-441-67026-1, 08/85 [07/85], $3.50, 359pp, pb) Reissue (Ace 1980) omnibus with THE PLANET SAVERS (Ace 1962) and THE SWORD OF ALDONES (Ace 1962), plus a 1980 "Darkover Retrospective" by Bradley and a 1976 short story. Sixth Ace printing.

Bradley, Marion Zimmer SHARRA'S EXILE (DAW 0-88677-988-7, 09/85 [08/85], $3.95, 365pp, pb) Reissue (DAW 1981) sf novel in the "Darkover" series.

Bradley, Marion Zimmer STAR OF DANGER (Ace 0-441-77956-5, 02/85 [01/85], $2.75, 213pp, pb) Reissue (Ace 1965) sf novel, part of the "Darkover" series. 8th printing.

Bradley, Marion Zimmer STORMQUEEN! (DAW 0-88677-092-0, 09/85 [08/85], $3.95, 364pp, pb) Reissue (DAW 1978) sf novel; 9th printing. Part of the "Darkover" series.

*Bradley, Marion Zimmer WARRIOR WOMAN (DAW 0-88677-075-0, 09/85 [08/85], $2.95, 205pp, pb) Fantasy novel. Very minor Bradley. (CNB) Written as a response to John Norman's "Gor" series and unfortunately more like Norman than like other Bradley. (DLN)

*Bradley, Marion Zimmer WEB OF DARKNESS (Richard Drew 0-86267-092-6, 1985 [10/85], £9.95, 369pp, hc) Omnibus edition of WEB OF LIGHT (Timescape 1983) and WEB OF DARKNESS (Donning 1983), an Atlantean fantasy saga. This is the first hardcover edition as well as the first one-volume edition. The book was written as such but split in the U.S. for various profitable reasons.
Contents: Page
WEB OF LIGHT   Marion Zimmer Bradley n. PKT 1983
WEB OF DARKNESS   Marion Zimmer Bradley n. DON 1983

Bradley, Marion Zimmer THE WINDS OF DARKOVER (Ace 0-441-89256-6, 04/85 [03/85], $2.75, 185pp, pb) Reissue (Ace 1970) sf novel, 5th Ace printing.

Bradley, Marion Zimmer THE WORLD WRECKERS (Ace 0-441-91177-3, 10/85 [09/85], $2.95, 215pp, pb) Reissue (Ace 1971) sf novel in the "Darkover" series. 7th Ace printing.

*Bradley, Marion Zimmer, ed. SWORD AND SORCERESS II (DAW 0-88677-041-6, 05/85 [04/85], $2.95, 287pp, pb) Anthology of 15 original stories.

Contents:

				Page
Introduction	Marion Zimmer Bradley		in	7
A Night at Two Inns	Phyllis Ann Karr	nv	S&S # 2,85	11
The Red Guild	Rachel Pollack	nv	S&S # 2,85	34
Shadow Wood	Diana L. Paxson	nv	S&S # 2,85	64
Unicorn's Blood	Bruce D. Arthurs	nv	S&S # 2,85	86
The Unshadowed Land	C.J. Cherryh	ss	S&S # 2,85	109
Shimenege's Mask	Charles R. Saunders	ss	S&S # 2,85	119
The Black Tower	Stephen L. Burns	ss	S&S # 2,85	137
The Lady and the Tiger	Jennifer Roberson	ss	S&S # 2,85	155
Fireweb	Deborah Wheeler	nv	S&S # 2,85	172
Cold Blows the Wind	Charles de Lint	ss	S&S # 2,85	200
Sword of the Mother	Dana Kramer Rolls	ss	S&S # 2,85	215
Hunger	Russ Garrison	ss	S&S # 2,85	227
On First Looking into Bradley's Guidelines, or Stories I Don't Want to Read Either				
	Elizabeth Thompson	pm	S&S # 2,85	236
The Chosen Maiden	Raul Reyes	ss	S&S # 2,85	239
Red Pearls	Richard Corwin	ss	S&S # 2,85	251
Wound on the Moon	Vera Nazarian	nv	S&S # 2,85	266

*Bradley, Marion Zimmer & The Friends of Darkover FREE AMAZONS OF DARKOVER (DAW 0-88677-096-3, 12/85 [11/85], $3.50, 304pp, pb) Original anthology of 18 stories about the Free Amazons. Many of these appeared in earlier Darkover fanzines but have not been published professionally. There are two stories by Bradley plus an introduction and notes on each story.

Contents:

				Page
Introduction: About Amazons				
	Marion Zimmer Bradley		in	7
The Oath of the Free Amazons				
	Walter Breen	ms	DRKOVRC,79	15
The Legend of Lady Bruna	Marion Zimmer Bradley	ss	LGHSTCS,79	23
Cast Off Your Chains	Margaret Silvestri	ss	FRAMZDK,85	33
The Banshee	Sherry Kramer	ss	TLSFRAM,80	50
On the Trail	Barbara Armistead	ss	FRAMZDK,85	66
To Open a Door	P. Alexandra Riggs	ss	FRAMZDK,85	77
The Meeting [revised]	Nina Boal	ss	TLSFRAM,80	96
The Mother Quest	Diana L. Paxson	nv	FRAMZDK,85	110
Child of the Heart	Elisabeth Waters	ss	FRAMZDK,85	133
Midwife	Deborah Wheeler	ss	FRAMZDK,85	141
Recruits	Maureen Shannon	ss	FRAMZDK,85	153
A Different Kind of Courage				
	Mercedes Lackey	ss	FRAMZDK,85	171
Knives	Marion Zimmer Bradley	ss	FRAMZDK,85	190
Tactics	Jane M.H. Bigelow	ss	FRAMZDK,85	208
This One Time	Joan Marie Verba	ss	FRAMZDK,85	227
Her Own Blood	Margaret Carter	ss	FRAMZDK,85	240
The Camel's Nose	Susan Holtzer	ss	FRAMZDK,85	258
Girls Will Be Girls	Patricia Shaw-Mathews	ss	FRAMZDK,85	274
Growing Pains	Susan M. Shwartz	ss	FRAMZDK,85	286
Oath of the Free Amazons: Terran, Techno Period				
	Jaida n'ha Sandra	ms	FRAMZDK,85	302

+Brandao, Ignacio deLoyola AND STILL THE EARTH Main listing under deLoyola Brandao, Ignacio.

*Brandner, Gary THE HOWLING III (Fawcett/Gold Medal 0-449-12834-2, 10/85 [12/85], $3.50, 252pp, pb) Dark fantasy/horror novel about werewolves. This precedes any movie of the same name; THE HOWLING II is currently in production.

*Brennan, Joseph Payne SIXTY SELECTED POEMS (New Establishment Press 0-932445-10-1, 02/85 [01/85], $5.00, 75pp, pb; also announced in hc for $14.00) A collection of "mainstream" poetry, but with overtones of dark fantasy, from the *Weird Tales* author. The book contains some excellent work, and readers with an interest in poetry as well as fantasy should give it a try. Recommended. (FCM)

*Brigg, Peter J.G. BALLARD (Starmont 0-916732-83-5, 12/85 [12/85], $6.95, 138pp, pb) Non-fiction, critical study with a bibliography of Ballard's works.

*Brin, David THE POSTMAN (Bantam Spectra 0-553-05107-5, 11/85 [09/85], $14.95, 294pp, hc) Sf novel set in Oregon after a limited war and a slide towards anarchy.

Brin, David STARTIDE RISING (Phantasia Press 0-932096-38-7, 11/85 [11/85], $45.00 signed, 375 limited edition, $18.00 1125 copy trade edition, 392pp, hc) Reprint (Bantam 1983) sf novel. The text has been corrected, and there are some minor revisions in this version.

Brin, David SUNDIVER (Bantam U.K. 0-553-17162-3, 07/85 [06/85], £1.95, 340pp, pb) Reprint (Bantam 1980) sf novel. First British edition.

*Brindel, June Rachny PHAEDRA (St. Martin's 0-312-60399-1, 08/85 [07/85], $14.95, 227pp, hc) Historical fantasy novel, a reinterpretation of the Greek legend of Phaedra, Theseus, etc., "from a feminine perspective."

*Broderick, Damien, ed. STRANGE ATTRACTORS (Hale & Iremonger 0-86806-208-1, 08/85 [09/85], A$19.95, 237pp, hc) Original anthology.

Contents:

				Page
Introduction	Damien Broderick		in	7
The Lipton Village Society				
	Lucy Sussex	ss	STRGATR,85	14
Time and Flowers	Anthony Peacey	ss	STRGATR,85	29
A Step in Any Direction	Timothy Dell	ss	STRGATR,85	43
The Way She Smiles, the Things She Says				
	Greg Egan	ss	STRGATR,85	51
Mr. Lockwood's Narrative	Yvonne Rousseau	ss	STRGATR,85	62
Glass Reptile Breakout	Russell Blackford	ss	STRGATR,85	75
After the Beowulf Expedition				
	Norman Talbot	ss	STRGATR,85	92
Precious Bane	Gerald Murnane	ss	STRGATR,85	103
The Ballad of Hilo Hill	Cherry Wilder	ss	STRGATR,85	112
The Elixir Operon	David Foster	ss	STRGATR,85	132
The Sanctuary Tree	John Playford	ss	STRGATR,85	151
On the Nursery Floor	George Turner	nv	STRGATR,85	164
Cave Amantem	Carmel Bird	ss	STRGATR,85	193
Jagging	Anthony Peacey	nv	STRGATR,85	198
The Interior	Damien Broderick	ss	STRGATR,85	226
Notes on Contributors	[Misc. Material]		bg	235

*Broderick, Damien, ed. STRANGE ATTRACTORS (Hale & Iremonger 0-86806-209-X, 08/85 [09/85], A$9.95, 237pp, pb) Paperback edition of the above.

*Brooks, Terry THE WISHSONG OF SHANNARA (Ballantine/Del Rey 0-345-31823-4, 05/85 [04/85], $18.95, 498pp, hc) Fantasy novel, conclusion of the trilogy.

*Brooks, Terry THE WISHSONG OF SHANNARA (Ballantine/Del Rey 0-345-30833-6, 05/85 [04/85], $8.95, 498pp, pb) Trade paperback of the above.

Brooks, Terry THE WISHSONG OF SHANNARA (SFBC #01600, 11/85 [12/85], $8.50, 469pp, hc) Reprint (Ballantine/Del Rey 1985) fantasy novel, conclusion of a "Tolkienesque" trilogy.

Brown, Fredric HOMICIDE SANITARIUM: FREDRIC BROWN IN THE DETECTIVE PULPS, VOL. 1 (Dennis McMillan 0-9609986-2-4, 11/85 [11/85], $5.95, 194pp, pb) Reprint (Dennis McMillan 1984) associational, non-sf collection. Listed for Brown collectors. This is the first trade edition after a limited first hc. Contains seven pulp mysteries plus an introduction by Bill Pronzini.

*Brown, Jerry Earl DARKHOLD (Ace 0-441-13784-9, 11/85 [10/85], $2.95, 342pp, pb) Sf novel -- the hero "created a space-age paradise and then cloned five lovers." Trouble ensues.

*Brown, Ken NOTES FROM THE NERVOUS BREAKDOWN LANE (Perennial Library 0-06-096014-0, 11/85 [11/85], $7.95, unpaginated, pb) Book of cartoons, many of which originally appeared as postcards. The style and surrealism closely resemble the works of Briton Glen Baxter, but Brown's wacked-out world is all-American. It's weird, wonderful, and frequently hilarious. Recommended. (FCM)

*Brown, Rich, David F. Bischoff & Linda Richardson A PERSONAL DEMON Main listing under David F. Bischoff.

Brown, Rosel George & Keith Laumer EARTHBLOOD Main listing under Keith Laumer.

Brunner, John AGE OF MIRACLES (DAW 0-88677-024-6, 03/85 [02/85], $2.95, 238pp, pb) Reprint (Ace 1973) sf novel.

Brunner, John THE TIDES OF TIME (SFBC #6241, 06/85 [05/85], $4.98, 182pp, hc) Reprint (Del Rey 1984) sf novel, first hardcover edition.

*Brust, Steven BROKEDOWN PALACE (Ace 0-441-07181-3, 01/86 [12/85], $2.95, 270pp, pb) Fantasy novel set in a country very much like Hungary.

Brust, Steven TO REIGN IN HELL (Ace 0-441-81496-4, 05/85 [04/85], $2.95, 269pp, pb) Reprint (Steel-Dragon 1984) fantasy novel. First mass-market edition.

*Buckley, William F., Jr. THE TEMPTATION OF WILFRED MALACHEY (Workman/Ariel 0-89480-923-7, 10/31/85 [11/85], $10.95, 45pp, hc) Juvenile fantasy short story, illustrated by John Gurney.

*Budrys, Algis BENCHMARKS: GALAXY BOOKSHELF (S. Illinois Univ. Press 0-8093-1187-9, 05/85 [04/85], $19.95, 349pp, hc) Nonfiction, reviews which originally appeared in *Galaxy*; contains all 54 columns, plus an "evaluation" by Catherine L. McClenahan and an introduction by Frederik Pohl. Prime, incisive critical material from one of sf's most exciting periods. Recommended. (DLN)

*Budrys, Algis, ed. L. RON HUBBARD PRESENTS WRITERS OF THE FUTURE (Bridge 0-88404-170-0, 03/85 [02/85], $3.95, 354pp, pb) Original anthology of 15 stories by winners and runners-up in Hubbard's New Writers contest, plus essays by some of the judges.

BUDRYS, ALGIS, ed.

Contents:			Page
About L. Ron Hubbard	Algis Budrys	bg WRTRFUT,85	ix
Introduction	L. Ron Hubbard	in	xiii
On Shaping Creativity	Algis Budrys	ar WRTRFUT,85	xv
Tyson's Turn	Michael D. Miller	nv WRTRFUT,85	1
A Step Into Darkness	Nina Kiriki Hoffman	nv WRTRFUT,85	25
Tiger Hunt	Jor Jennings	nv WRTRFUT,85	49
A Writer's Beginnings	Robert Silverberg	ar WRTRFUT,85	83
In the Garden	A.J. Mayhew	ss WRTRFUT,85	89
Arcadus Arcane	Dennis J. Pimple	ss WRTRFUT,85	105
Recalling Cinderella	Karen Joy Fowler	nv WRTRFUT,85	125
The Ebbing	Leonard Carpenter	nv WRTRFUT,85	147
What Are You Doing Here?	Theodore Sturgeon	ar WRTRFUT,85	185
The Land of the Leaves	Norma Hutman	ss WRTRFUT,85	189
Anthony's Wives	Randell Crump	ss WRTRFUT,85	203
The Thing from the Old Seaman's Mouth			
	Victor L. Rosemund	ss WRTRFUT,85	219
Without Wings	L.E. Carroll	ss WRTRFUT,85	229
On Science Fiction	Jack Williamson	ar WRTRFUT,85	245
Shanidar	David Zindell	nv WRTRFUT,85	251
One Last Dance	Dean Wesley Smith	ss WRTRFUT,85	283
Measuring the Light	Michael Green	nv WRTRFUT,85	299
A Way Out	Mary Frances Zambreno	ss WRTRFUT,85	333
The Writer's Life and Uniqueness			
	Roger Zelazny	ar WRTRFUT,85	349
About the Artists	[Misc. Material]	bg WRTRFUT,85	355
About the Contest	[Misc. Material]	ms WRTRFUT,85	357

*Bull, Emma & Will Shetterly, eds. LIAVEK Main listing under Will Shetterly.

*Bunch, Chris & Allan Cole COURT OF A THOUSAND SUNS Main listing under Allan Cole.

+Burdekin, Katharine SWASTIKA NIGHT (Feminist Press 0-935312-56-0, 1985 [12/85], $8.95, 196pp, pb) Reprint (Gollancz 1937) Nazi dystopian sf novel, originally published under the pseudonym Murray Constantine. There is a new introduction by Daphne Patai. This is the first American edition.

*Burgess, Michael & Jeffrey M. Elliot THE WORK OF R. REGINALD: AN ANNOTATED BIBLIOGRAPHY AND GUIDE (Borgo 0-89370-484-9, 03/85 [02/85], $9.95, 48pp, pb) Non-fiction, guide to Reginald's work in sf and other areas. Also available in hardcover, $19.95. I presume it's accurate since Burgess and Reginald are the same person.

Burroughs, Edgar Rice AT THE EARTH'S CORE (Ace 0-441-03328-8, 01/85 [12/84], $2.75, 210pp, pb) Reissue (McClurg 1922) sf novel.

Burroughs, Edgar Rice BACK TO THE STONE AGE (Ace 0-441-04638-X, 05/85 [04/85], $2.75, 251pp, pb) Reissue (Burroughs 1937) sf novel, fifth in the Pellucidar septology. 13th Ace printing.

Burroughs, Edgar Rice I AM A BARBARIAN (Ace 0-441-35807-1, 10/85 [09/85], $2.75, 287pp, pb) Reissue (ERB Inc. 1967) historical adventure novel.

Burroughs, Edgar Rice LAND OF TERROR (Ace 0-441-47002-5, 06/85 [05/85], $2.75, 176pp, pb) Reissue (Burroughs 1944) sf novel. 7th Ace printing. Book 5 in the "Pellucidar" septology.

Burroughs, Edgar Rice THE MOON MAID (Ace 0-441-53707-3, 08/85 [07/85], $2.75, 187pp, pb) Reissue (McClurg 1926) of part 1 of the original novel. Part 2, THE MOON MEN, was part of the 1926 edition. 12th Ace printing.

Burroughs, Edgar Rice THE MOON MEN (Ace 0-441-53757-X, 09/85 [08/85], $2.75, 246pp, pb) Reissue (Ace 1962) sf novel based on the 1925 magazine series which was later revised as part of THE MOON MAID (McClurg 1926); the latter was reissued by Canaveral in 1962 as THE MOON MEN, to complicate things further. 11th Ace printing.

Burroughs, Edgar Rice PELLUCIDAR (Ace 0-441-65857-1, 02/85 [01/85], $2.75, 191pp, pb) Reissue (McClurg 1923) novel. 9th Ace printing. Book 2 in the series.

Burroughs, Edgar Rice SAVAGE PELLUCIDAR (Ace 0-441-75137-7, 07/85 [06/85], $2.75, 255pp, pb) Reissue (Canaveral 1963) sf novel. The seventh and concluding volume in the series. 12th Ace printing.

Burroughs, Edgar Rice TANAR OF PELLUCIDAR (Ace 0-441-79798-9, 03/85 [02/85], $2.75, 254pp, pb) Reissue (Metro 1930) sf novel. "Pellucidar" #3.

Burroughs, Edgar Rice TARZAN AT THE EARTH'S CORE (Ace 0-441-79858-6, 04/85 [03/85], $2.75, 256pp, pb) Reissue (Metropolitan 1930) sf novel, 4th in the "Pellucidar" series and 13th in the "Tarzan" series. 10th Ace printing.

Burroughs, William S. EXTERMINATOR! (Penguin 0-14-005003-5, 11/85 [10/85], $4.95, 168pp, pb) Reprint (Viking 1973) experimental novel which includes "science-fantasy war," conspiracies, and Dr. Fu Manchu.

Busby, F.M. ALL THESE EARTHS (Bantam Spectra 0-553-25413-8, 12/85 [11/85], $2.95, 215pp, pb) Reprint (Berkley 1978) sf novel.

*Busby, F.M. REBEL'S QUEST (Bantam 0-553-24727-1, 01/85 [12/84], $2.75, 243pp, pb) Sf novel, sequel to STAR REBEL. An excellent space opera. Recommended. (CNB)

Butler, Octavia E. CLAY'S ARK (Ace 0-441-11089-4, 06/85 [05/85], $2.75, 201pp, pb) Reprint (St. Martin's 1984) sf novel.

*Byers, Edward A. THE LONG FORGETTING (Baen 0-671-55980-X, 09/85 [08/85], $2.95, 283pp, pb) Sf novel, a first novel.

*Caidin, Martin KILLER STATION (Baen 0-671-55996-6, 12/85 [11/85], $3.50, 370pp, pb) Sf novel. Watch out for the falling space station. The 1984 copyright is apparently a mistake. It's an original.

*Callin, Grant SATURNALIA (Baen 0-671-65546-9, 01/86 [12/85], $2.95, 278pp, pb) Sf novel.

*Campbell, Ramsey COLD PRINT (Scream/Press 0-910489-13-0, 03/85 [04/85], $37.50 signed/boxed edition of 250; $17.50 trade edition, 219pp, hc) Collection of 15 "Cthulhu Mythos" stories, plus two essays, with illustrations by J.K. Potter.

Contents:			Page
Introduction	Ramsey Campbell	in	xv
The Church in High Street			
	Ramsey Campbell	ss DRKMIND,62	1
The Room in the Castle	Ramsey Campbell	ss INHBLKE,64	11
The Horror from the Bridge			
	Ramsey Campbell	ss INHBLKE,64	25
The Insects from Shaggai	Ramsey Campbell	ss INHBLKE,64	43
The Render of the Veils	Ramsey Campbell	ss INHBLKE,64	61
The Inhabitant of the Lake			
	Ramsey Campbell	nv INHBLKE,64	69
The Will of Stanley Brooke			
	Ramsey Campbell	ss INHBLKE,64	93
The Moon-Lens	Ramsey Campbell	ss INHBLKE,64	99
Before the Storm	Ramsey Campbell	ss FRG Mar,80	111
Cold Print	Ramsey Campbell	ss TLSCTHU,69	119
Among the pictures are these:			
	Ramsey Campbell	ss NYC Mar,81	131
The Tugging	Ramsey Campbell	nv DSPCTHU,76	137
The Faces at Pine Dunes	Ramsey Campbell	nv NTLCTHU,80	159
Blacked Out	Ramsey Campbell	ss CLDPRNT,85	183
Voice of the Beach	Ramsey Campbell	nv FTL Sum,82	195

Campbell, Ramsey THE DOLL WHO ATE HIS MOTHER (Tor 0-812-51654-0, 08/85 [07/85], $3.50, 284pp, pb) Reprint (Bobbs-Merrill 1976) horror novel.

Campbell, Ramsey THE FACE THAT MUST DIE (Tor 0-812-51658-3, 11/85 [10/85], $3.95, 351pp, pb) Reprint (Scream/Press 1983) horror novel. Revised text of the 1979 British edition. This has the 1983 foreword.

Campbell, Ramsey THE NAMELESS (Tor 0-812-58125-3, 02/85 [01/85], $3.50, 312pp, pb) Reprint (Macmillan 1981) horror-fantasy novel.

*Campbell, Ramsey OBSESSION (Macmillan 0-02-521130-7, 03/85 [02/85], $16.95, 247pp, hc) Dark fantasy/horror novel.

*Canty, Thomas A MONSTER AT CHRISTMAS (Donald M. Grant 0-937986-67-4, 10/85 [10/85], $30.00, 44pp, hc) Fantasy/horror poem with text by Canty, color illustrations by Phil Hale, a jauntily gruesome production à la Gremlins, guaranteed to give nightmares to sensitive tots. (FCM) Oversized volume in limited edition signed by author and artist.

Capek, Karel WAR WITH THE NEWTS (Northwestern Univ. Press 0-8101-0663-9, 05/85 [04/85], $8.95, 348pp, pb) Reprint (Allen & Unwin 1937) classic satiric sf novel translated by M & R Weatherall from the Czeck VALKA S MLOKY (1936), with a new introduction by Czech dissident writer Ivan Klima. A hardcover edition (0-8101-0700-7, $24.95) has also been announced, but we haven't seen it and it isn't on their order sheet.

*Capek, Karel WAR WITH THE NEWTS (Allen & Unwin/Unicorn 0-04-823308-0, 1985 [12/85], £2.95, 241pp, pb) This is a new translation, by Ewald Osers, of the satiric Czech sf novel VALKA S MLOKY (Prague 1936); an earlier English version appeared from Allen & Unwin in 1937.

*Card, Orson Scott ENDER'S GAME (Tor 0-812-53252-X, 1984 [01/85], $13.95, 357pp, hc) Sf novel set mostly at a space academy. Expansion of a novella that first appeared in *Analog*, August 1977. Recommended. (FCM)

Card, Orson Scott ENDER'S GAME (Tor 0-812-53253-8, 01/86 [12/85], $3.50, 357pp, pb) Reprint (Tor 1984) sf novel. A Nebula nominee.

+Carey, Peter ILLYWHACKER (Harper & Row 0-06-015425-X, 08/85 [07/85], $18.95, 600pp, hc) Reprint (UQP 1984) wacky mainstream novel with elements of fantasy. First American edition. A Booker Prize nominee.

*Carl, Lillian Stewart SABAZEL (Ace 0-441-74522-9, 03/85 [02/85], $2.75, 251pp, pb) Fantasy novel of barbarians and amazons; a first novel.

Carlyon, Richard THE DARK LORD OF PENGERSICK (Ace 0-441-13786-5, 10/85 [09/85], $2.75, 168pp, pb) Reprint (U.K. 1976) juvenile fantasy novel.

*Carpenter, Humphrey SECRET GARDENS: THE GOLDEN AGE OF CHILDREN'S LITERATURE (Houghton Mifflin 0-395-35293-2, 07/85 [06/85], $16.95, 235pp, hc) Non-fiction, examination of children's literature from Carroll to Milne; the so-called golden age of children's fantasy. There may be an earlier British edition.

*Carr, Jayge THE TREASURE IN THE HEART OF THE MAZE (Doubleday 0-385-18831-5, 09/85 [09/85], $12.95, 183pp, hc) Sf novel, sequel to NAVIGATOR'S SINDROME.

*Carr, John F., Jim Baen & Jerry E. Pournelle, eds. THE SCIENCE FICTION YEARBOOK Main listing under Jerry E. Pournelle.

*Carr, John F. & Roland Green GREAT KING'S WAR Main listing under Roland Green.

Carr, John F. & Jerry E. Pournelle, eds. THE ENDLESS FRONTIER, VOL. II Main listing under Jerry E. Pournelle.

Carr, Terry, ed. BEST SF OF THE YEAR #14 (Gollancz 0-575-03714-8, 10/85 [10/85], £9.95, 376pp, hc) Reprint (Tor 1985, as TERRY CARR'S BEST SCIENCE FICTION OF THE YEAR) anthology. Charles N. Brown's report on the Year in SF, 1984, was omitted from this edition.

Carr, Terry, ed. BEST SF OF THE YEAR #14 (Gollancz 0-575-03747-4, 10/85 [10/85], £4.95, 376pp, pb) Trade paperback edition of the above.

*Carr, Terry, ed. TERRY CARR'S BEST SCIENCE FICTION OF THE YEAR #14 (Tor 0-812-53273-2, 07/85 [06/85], $3.50, 384pp, pb) Anthology, one of the four year's bests. Recommended. (CNB)
Contents:

			Page
Introduction	Terry Carr	in	9
PRESS ENTER ■	John Varley	na IAS May,84	11
Blued Moon	Connie Willis	nv IAS Jan,84	73
Summer Solstice	Charles L. Harness	nv ASF Jun,84	108
Morning Child	Gardner Dozois	ss OMN Jan,84	153
The Aliens Who Knew, I Mean, Everything			
	George Alec Effinger	ss FSF Oct,84	160
A Day in the Skin (or, The Century We Were Out of Them)			
	Tanith Lee	ss HABITAT,84	176
Instructions	Bob Leman	ss FSF Sep,84	194
The Lucky Strike	Kim Stanley Robinson	nv UNI #14,84	203
Green Hearts	Lee Montgomerie	ss INZ #10,84	240
Bloodchild	Octavia E. Butler	nv IAS Jun,84	258
Trojan Horse	Michael Swanwick	nv OMN Dec,84	278
Fears	Pamela Sargent	ss LGTYR&D,84	312
Trinity	Nancy Kress	na IAS Oct,84	325
1984, the SF Year in Review			
	Charles N. Brown	ar 1985	375
Recommended Reading	Terry Carr	bi	383

Carr, Terry, ed. UNIVERSE 13 (Tor 0-812-53269-4, 03/85 [02/85], $2.95, 253pp, pb) Reprint (Doubleday 1983) original anthology.

*Carr, Terry, ed. UNIVERSE 15 (Doubleday 0-385-19890-6, 08/16/85 [08/85], $12.95, 179pp, hc) Original anthology. On the whole, a disappointing offering this time, with good writers not at their best. The standout is "The Slovo Stove" by Avram Davidson, typically quirky but haunting (and funny). (FCM)
Contents:

			Page
Mercurial	Kim Stanley Robinson	nv UNI #15,85	1
Paladin of the Lost Hour	Harlan Ellison	nv UNI #15,85	31
Giraffe Tuesday	Juleen Brantingham	ss UNI #15,85	53
Evergreen	Arthur Jean Cox	nv UNI #15,85	62
Mengele	Lucius Shepard	ss UNI #15,85	88
Originals	Pamela Sargent	nv UNI #15,85	101
Johann Sebastian Brahms	Barry N. Malzberg	ss UNI #15,85	122
Encounter on the Ladder	Mona A. Clee	ss UNI #15,85	129
Tidal Effects	Jack McDevitt	ss UNI #15,85	149
The Slovo Stove	Avram Davidson	nv UNI #15,85	155

Carr, Terry, Isaac Asimov & Martin H. Greenberg, eds. 100 GREAT FANTASY SHORT STORIES Main listing under Isaac Asimov.

*Carson, David, Daryl Lane & William Vernon THE SOUND OF WONDER: INTERVIEWS FROM "THE SCIENCE FICTION RADIO SHOW" Main listing under Daryl Lane.

*Carson, David, Daryl Lane & William Vernon THE SOUND OF WONDER: INTERVIEWS FROM "THE SCIENCE FICTION RADIO SHOW", VOL. 2 Main listing under Daryl Lane.

*Carter, Angela BLACK VENUS (Chatto & Windus/Hogarth Press 0-7011-3964-1, 10/85 [10/85], £8.95, 121pp, hc) Collection of 8 stories, first book publication.
Contents:

			Page
Black Venus	Angela Carter	ss NXTEDIT,80	7
The Kiss	Angela Carter	ss HRP 1977	25
Our Lady of the Massacre [new title]			
	Angela Carter	ss STYNTRD,79	31
The Cabinet of Edgar Allan Poe			
	Angela Carter	ss INZ # 1,82	49
Overture and Incidental Music for "A Midsummer Night's Dream"	Angela Carter	ss INZ # 3,82	63
Peter and the Wolf	Angela Carter	ss FIREBDI,82	77
The Kitchen Child	Angela Carter	ss VOG 1979	89
The Fall River Axe Murders [new title]			
	Angela Carter	ss LRB 1981	101

+Carter, Angela NIGHTS AT THE CIRCUS (Viking 0-670-80375-8, 03/85 [02/85], $15.95, 195pp, hc) Reprint (Chatto & Windus 1984) fantasy novel, first U.S. edition. The extravagant, astonishing tale of a winged blonde Cockney at the turn of the century -- highly recommended. (FCM)

*Carter, Lin FOUND WANTING (DAW 0-88677-050-5, 06/85 [05/85], $2.75, 220pp, pb) Fantasy novel.

Carter, Lin, L. Sprague de Camp & Robert E. Howard CONAN Main listing under Robert E. Howard.

Carter, Lin, L. Sprague de Camp & Robert E. Howard CONAN OF CIMMERIA Main listing under Robert E. Howard.

Carter, Lin, L. Sprague de Camp & Robert E. Howard CONAN THE WANDERER Main listing under Robert E. Howard.

Carver, Jeffrey A. THE INFINITY LINK (SFBC #5965, 06/85 [05/85], $6.98, 498pp, hc) Reprint (Bluejay 1984) sf novel.

Carver, Jeffrey A. THE INFINITY LINK (Tor 0-812-53300-3, 10/85 [09/85], $3.95, 540pp, pb) Reprint (Bluejay 1984) sf novel.

Cassidy, Sylvia BEHIND THE ATTIC WALL (Avon/Camelot 0-380-69843-9, 03/85 [02/85], $2.95, 315pp, pb) Reprint (Crowell 1983) juvenile fantasy novel.

*Chalker, Jack L. DOWNTIMING THE NIGHT SIDE (Tor 0-812-53288-0, 05/85 [04/85], $2.95, 384pp, pb) Sf novel.

Chalker, Jack L. THE IDENTITY MATRIX (Baen 0-671-65547-7, 01/86 [12/85], $2.95, 309pp, pb) Reprint (Timescape 1982) sf novel.

*Chalker, Jack L. THE MESSIAH CHOICE (Bluejay 0-312-94301-6, 07/85 [06/85], $16.95, 380pp, hc) Near-future sf adventure novel with elements of fantasy. Computers and ancient evil.

*Chalker, Jack L. SOUL RIDER, BOOK FOUR: THE BIRTH OF FLUX & ANCHOR (Tor 0-812-53284-8, 12/85 [11/85], $3.50, 374pp, pb) Fourth in the sf series, but a prequel to the others.

*Chalker, Jack L. SOUL RIDER, BOOK THREE: MASTERS OF FLUX & ANCHOR (Tor 0-812-53281-3, 01/85 [12/84], $2.95, 429pp, pb) Sf novel, third in the series.

*Chalker, Jack L. VENGEANCE OF THE DANCING GODS (Ballantine/Del Rey 0-345-31549-9, 07/85 [06/85], $3.50, 303pp, pb) Fantasy novel, #3 in the series.

+Chambers, Aidan, ed. OUT OF TIME (Harper & Row 0-06-021201-2, 09/85 [09/85], $11.95, 186pp, hc) Young-adult sf original anthology. First U.S. edition.
Contents:

			Page
Extinction Is Forever	Louise Lawrence	ss OUTOFTM,84	1
Rigel Light	Louise Lawrence	nv OUTOFTM,84	17
Captain Courage and the Rose Street Gang			
	Jan Mark	nv OUTOFTM,84	40
Urn Burial	Robert Westall	ss OUTOFTM,84	66
In a Ship Called Darkness			
	Christopher Leach	ss OUTOFTM,84	84
The Blades	Joan Aiken	nv OUTOFTM,84	101
Zone of Silence	Monica Hughes	ss OUTOFTM,84	122
Pied Piper	Ann Ruffell	ss OUTOFTM,84	136
Hally's Paradise	Douglas Hill	ss OUTOFTM,84	155
Program Loop	Jill Paton Walsh	ss OUTOFTM,84	173

+Chandler, A. Bertram KELLY COUNTRY (DAW 0-88677-065-3, 08/85 [07/85], $3.50, 348pp, pb) Reprint (Penguin Australia 1983) parallel-world sf novel; first U.S. edition.

+Chandler, A. Bertram THE WILD ONES (DAW 0-88677-031-9, 04/85 [03/85], $2.95, 253pp, pb) Reprint (Cory & Collins 1984), first U.S. edition of the last novel in the "Grimes" sf adventure series written by Chandler. This edition does not acknowledge the original Australian copyright.

Chant, Joy THE HIGH KINGS (Bantam Spectra 0-553-24306-3, 11/85 [09/85], $3.50, 245pp, pb) Reprint (Bantam 1983) non-fiction study of Arthurian legends. This could almost be called a new book, since it contains only the text of what had originally been a wonderfully illustrated art book.

*Chapman, Edgar L. THE MAGIC LABYRINTH OF PHILIP JOSÉ FARMER (Borgo 0-83970-258-7, 03/85 [02/85], $4.95, 96pp, pb) Non-fiction, critical study. Also announced in hardcover, $11.95.

+Charles, Robert THE COMET (Tor 0-812-50141-1, 03/85 [02/85], $3.50, 351pp, pb) Reprint (Corgi 1984, as NIGHTWORLD). First U.S. edition. Near-future disaster novel -- Halley's Comet is disrupted by scientific probes and surrounds Earth; "civilization begins to crumble."

*Charnas, Suzy McKee THE BRONZE KING (Houghton Mifflin 0-395-38394-3, 10/85 [09/85], $12.95, 195pp, hc) Young-adult fantasy novel set in modern New York.

*Cherryh, C.J. ANGEL WITH THE SWORD (DAW 0-8099-0001-7, 09/85 [09/85], $15.95, 293pp, hc) Sf adventure novel.

Cherryh, C.J. CHANUR'S VENTURE (DAW 0-87997-989-5, 01/85 [12/84], $2.95, 312pp, pb) Reprint (Phantasia 1984) sf novel, second in the "Chanur" series. First mass market paperback.

Cherryh, C.J. CHANUR'S VENTURE (SFBC #3885, 04/85 [03/85], $3.98, 182pp, hc) Reprint (Phantasia 1984) sf novel, sequel to THE PRIDE OF CHANUR.

*Cherryh, C.J. CUCKOO'S EGG (Phantasia 0-932096-34-4, 05/85 [04/85], $40.00 signed/boxed/numbered edition of 350; $17.00 trade edition, 206pp, hc) Sf novel about a human raised by aliens. Recommended. (CNB)

Cherryh, C.J. CUCKOO'S EGG (DAW 0-88677-083-1, 10/85 [09/85], $3.50, 319pp, pb) Reprint (Phantasia 1985) sf novel, first mass-market edition.

Cherryh, C.J. CUCKOO'S EGG (SFBC #6318, 10/85 [11/85], $4.98, 186pp, hc) Reprint (Phantasia 1985) sf novel.

*Cherryh, C.J. THE KIF STRIKE BACK (Phantasia 0-932096-35-2, 05/85 [05/85], $40.00 350-copy signed, numbered special edition, $17.00 2,000-copy trade edition, 294pp, hc) Sf novel, third in the "Chanur" series.

Cherryh, C.J. THE KIF STRIKE BACK (DAW 0-88677-104-8, 01/86 [12/85], $3.50, 301pp, pb) Reprint (Phantasia 1985), sf novel, third in the "Chanur" series.

Cherryh, C.J. SERPENT'S REACH (DAW 0-88677-088-2, 10/85 [09/85], $3.50, 287pp, pb) Reissue (DAW 1980) sf novel.

Cherryh, C.J. VOYAGER IN NIGHT (DAW 0-88677-107-2, 01/86 [12/85], $2.95, 221pp, pb) Reissue (DAW 1984) sf novel. Third printing.

*Chesbro, George C. THE BEASTS OF VALHALLA (Atheneum 0-689-11516-4, 06/85 [05/85], $15.95, 329pp, hc) Sf/mystery novel, #4 in the series featuring Mungo the dwarf. This one crosses Mungo with LORD OF THE RINGS and is the only fantasy in the series.

*Chetwin, Grace OUT OF THE DARK WORLD (Morrow/Lothrop, Lee & Shepard 0-688-04272-4, 11/85 [11/85], $10.25, 154pp, hc) Young-adult fantasy involving enchantresses and computers.

*Child, Lincoln, ed. DARK BANQUET: A FEAST OF 12 GREAT GHOST STORIES (St. Martin's 0-312-18233-3, 10/85 [11/85], $15.95, 255pp, hc) Anthology of 12 tales of the supernatural.
Contents:

			Page
A Note on the Selections	Lincoln Child	pr	ix
Introduction to the Banquet			
	Lincoln Child	in	xi
The Signalman [from "Mugby Junction"]			
	Charles Dickens	ss AYR Chr,1866	1
Thrawn Janet	Robert Louis Stevenson		
		ss MERYMEN,1887	15
The Upper Berth	F. Marion Crawford	nv UPRBRTH,1894	26
The Horror of the Heights			
	Arthur Conan Doyle	ss SND Nov,13	48
How Love Came to Professor Guildea			
	Robert Hichens	nv TNGSCNS,00	65
The Yellow Sign	Robert W. Chambers	nv KINGYLW,1895	111
They	Rudyard Kipling	nv TRAFFIC,04	131
The House of Sounds	M.P. Shiel	nv PALEAPE,11	154
The Inexperienced Ghost [The Story of the Inexperienced Ghost]			
	H.G. Wells	ss SND Mar,02	184
The Man Who Went Too Far	E.F. Benson	nv RMINTWR,12	198
Seaton's Aunt	Walter de la Mare	nv RIDDLE&,23	220
Blind Man's Buff	H. Russell Wakefield	ss OLDMNBD,29	251

Clarke, Arthur C. 2010: ODYSSEY TWO (Quality Paperback Book Club/Del Rey no ISBN, 1985 [10/85], no price given, 291pp, pb) Reprint (Del Rey 1982) sf novel, sequel to 2001. Hardcover printing bound as a trade paperback; available only to club members. This and other QPB editions listed here may not all be '85 publications, but were first seen in 1985.

Clarke, Arthur C. INTERPLANETARY FLIGHT (Berkley 0-425-06448-4, 02/85 [01/85], $2.95, 164pp, pb) Reprint (Harper & Row 1950) of Clarke's first published book. Non-sf, associational. There's a new introduction for this edition. This is an outdated semi-technical book which is being reprinted only because of Clarke's name.

Clarke, Arthur C. THE OTHER SIDE OF THE SKY (NAL/Signet 0-451-14018-4, 12/85 [11/85], $2.95, 256pp, pb) Reissue (Harcourt Brace 1958) collection. Twelfth printing.

Clarke, Arthur C. PROFILES OF THE FUTURE (Warner 0-446-32107-9, 04/85 [03/85], $3.50, 282pp, pb) Reprint (Holt, Rinehart & Winston 1984); non-fiction, associational. A revised version of a 1963 collection of future possibilities. A primer for sf authors. Recommended. (CNB)

Clarke, Arthur C. THE PROMISE OF SPACE (Berkley 0-425-07565-6, 01/85 [12/84], $3.50, 316pp, pb) Reprint (Harper & Row 1968). Non-fiction, associational.

Clarke, Arthur C. REPORT ON PLANET THREE AND OTHER SPECULATIONS (Berkley 0-425-07592-3, 03/85 [02/85], $3.50, 245pp, pb) Reprint (Harper 1972). Non-fiction, associational. Essays on possible futures.

*Clarke, Arthur C. & Peter Hyams THE ODYSSEY FILE (Ballantine/Del Rey 0-345-32108-1, 01/85 [12/84], $3.95, 133pp, pb) Non-fiction, associational, a record of the computer communications between the author and the director for 2010. Illustrated with color stills from the film.

*Clarke, Boden THE WORK OF JEFFREY M. ELLIOT: AN ANNOTATED BIBLIOGRAPHY AND GUIDE (Borgo 0-89370-481-4, 03/85 [02/85], $9.95, 50pp, pb) Non-fiction, reference book covering the work of sf scholar/interviewer Elliot. Also available in hardcover, $19.95.

*Clayton, Jo A BAIT OF DREAMS (DAW 0-88677-001-7, 02/85 [01/85], $3.50, 404pp, pb) Fantasy novel composed of fairly similar short stories, hence rather choppy, but entertaining. (DLN)
Contents:

			Page
A Bait of Dreams	Jo Clayton	nv IAS Feb,79	7
Interlude Among the Shaborn			
	Jo Clayton	vi BAITDRM,85	50
A Thirst For Broken Water			
	Jo Clayton	na IAS Jun,79	52
Southwind My Mother	Jo Clayton	na IAS Apr,80	109
Companioning	Jo Clayton	na IAS Dec,80	167
Currents	Jo Clayton	na BAITDRM,85	229
Old Acquaintances and New			
	Jo Clayton	na BAITDRM,85	309

*Clayton, Jo CHANGER'S MOON (DAW 0-88677-065-3, 08/85 [07/85], $3.50, 352pp, pb) Fantasy novel, conclusion of the "Duel of Sorcery" trilogy.

Clayton, Jo MOONGATHER (DAW 0-88677-072-6, 08/85 [07/85], $3.50, 240pp, pb) Reissue (DAW 1982) fantasy novel, "Duel of Sorcery" #1. 4th printing.

Clayton, Jo MOONSCATTER (DAW 0-88677-071-8, 08/85 [07/85], $3.50, 304pp, pb) "Duel of Sorcery" #2. 4th printing.

*Cleve, John SPACEWAYS #19: KING OF THE SLAVERS (Berkley 0-425-07134-0, 01/85 [12/84], $2.95, 227pp, pb) Sf novel, conclusion of the soft-core porn series.

*Clough, B.W. THE DRAGON OF MISHBIL (DAW 0-88677-078-8, 09/85 [08/85], $2.95, 190pp, pb) Fantasy novel, sequel to THE CRYSTAL CROWN.

*Clute, John, Colin Greenland & David Pringle, eds. INTERZONE: THE 1ST ANTHOLOGY (Dent/Everyman 0-460-02294-6, 03/85 [02/85], £3.95, 206pp, pb) Anthology of 13 stories, 12 from Interzone and one an original. One of the year's best anthologies. (FCM)
Contents:

			Page
Introduction	John Clute, Colin Greenland & David Pringle	in	vii
O Happy Day!	Geoff Ryman	nv IZA # 1,85	1
The Cabinet of Edgar Allan Poe			
	Angela Carter	ss INZ # 1,82	36
The Flash! Kid	Scott Bradfield	ss INZ # 5,83	48
After-Images	Malcolm Edwards	ss INZ # 4,82	60
Kitemaster	Keith Roberts	ss INZ # 1,82	73
The Monroe Doctrine	Neil Ferguson	ss INZ # 6,83	89
Angel Baby	Rachel Pollack	nv INZ # 2,82	107
On the Deck of the Flying Bomb			
	David Redd	ss INZ # 4,82	129
What Cindy Saw	John Shirley	ss INZ # 5,83	134
Object of the Attack	J.G. Ballard	ss INZ # 9,84	146
Something Coming Through	Cherry Wilder	ss INZ # 6,83	161
Dreamers	Kim Newman	ss INZ # 8,84	176
Tissue Ablation and Variant Regeneration			
	Michael Blumlein	ss INZ # 7,84	188
Notes on the Authors	[Misc. Material]	bg	203
Acknowledgements	[Misc. Material]	bi	205

*Coffey, Frank NIGHT PRAYERS (Jove 0-515-08453-0, 01/86 [12/85], $3.50, 249pp, pb) Erotic horror novel.

*Cohen, Daniel THE ENCYCLOPEDIA OF THE STRANGE (Dodd, Mead 0-396-08656-X, 12/85 [12/85], $16.95, 291pp, hc) Non-fiction, associational; reference book. A surprisingly middle-of-the-road discussion of various strange beliefs, cults, etc. Very useful for writers who want quick information on the Hope Diamond, Bermuda Triangle, and lots of Fortean phenomena. (CNB)

*Colan, Gene, Cary Bates & Neal McPheeters NIGHTWINGS Main listing under Cary Bates.

*Cole, Allan & Chris Bunch COURT OF A THOUSAND SUNS (Ballantine/Del Rey 0-345-31681-9, 01/86 [12/85], $2.95, 275pp, pb) Sf adventure novel, third in the "Sten" series.

*Collings, Michael R. STEPHEN KING AS RICHARD BACHMAN (Starmont 0-930261-00-3, 09/85 [08/85], $9.95, 168pp, pb) Non-fiction, critical study of the King-as-Bachman novels. Written and published in near-record time. This was also announced in hardcover, -01-1, $17.95.

*Collings, Michael R. & David Engebretson THE SHORTER WORKS OF STEPHEN KING (Starmont 0-930261-02-X, 09/85 [09/85], $9.95, 202pp, pb) Critical study, examining both the uncollected stories and the various collections. A hardcover is also listed as available at $17.95.

COLLINS, ROBERT A. & HOWARD D. PEARCE, eds.

DANN, JACK & GARDNER DOZOIS, eds.

*Collins, Robert A. & Howard D. Pearce, eds. THE SCOPE OF THE FANTASTIC: CULTURE, BIOGRAPHY, THEMES, CHILDREN'S LITERATURE (Greenwood 0-313-23448-5, 11/85 [12/85], $35.00, xii + 284pp, hc) Non-fiction, critical studies; second volume of selected essays from the First International Conference on the Fantastic in Literature and Film.

*Collins, Robert A. & Howard D. Pearce, eds. THE SCOPE OF THE FANTASTIC: THEORY, TECHNIQUE, MAJOR AUTHORS (Greenwood 0-313-23447-7, 06/85 [05/85], $35.00, xii + 295pp, hc) Non-fiction, critical works. Selected essays from the First International Conference on the Fantastic.

+Como, James T., ed. C.S. LEWIS AT THE BREAKFAST TABLE, AND OTHER REMINISCENCES (Collier 0-02-049700-8, 08/85 [09/85], $8.95, 299pp, pb) Reprint (Macmillan U.K. 1984) non-fiction, biographical. Reminiscences by Lewis' friends, plus an introduction by the editor and a bibliography by Lewis' literary executor. First U.S. edition.

Compton, D.G. ASCENDANCIES (Ace 0-441-03088-2, 01/85 [12/84], $2.75, 224pp, pb) Reprint (Gollancz 1980) sf novel.

Coney, Michael GODS OF THE GREATAWAY (SFBC #2084, 02/85 [01/85], $3.98, 243pp, hc) Reprint (Houghton Mifflin 1984) sf novel, sequel to THE CELESTIAL STEAM LOCOMOTIVE.

*Cook, Fred & Sheldon Jaffery THE COLLECTOR'S INDEX TO WEIRD TALES Main listing under Sheldon Jaffery.

*Cook, Glen DARKWAR TRILOGY 1: DOOMSTALKER (Popular Library/Questar 0-445-20062-6, 08/85 [07/85], $2.95, 264pp, pb) Fantasy novel, first in the "Darkwar" trilogy.

*Cook, Glen A MATTER OF TIME (Ace 0-441-52213-0, 04/85 [03/85], $2.95, 268pp, pb) Sf novel.

*Cook, Glen PASSAGE AT ARMS (Popular Library/Questar 0-445-20006-5, 04/85 [03/85], $2.95, 265pp, pb) Taut, convincingly gritty sf novel narrated by a war correspondent in the future. Recommended. (FCM)

*Cook, Glen WARLOCK (Popular Library/Questar 0-445-20062-6, 11/85 [10/85], $2.95, 268pp, pb) Fantasy novel, "Darkwar Trilogy" #2.

*Cook, Glen THE WHITE ROSE (Tor 0-812-53374-7, 04/85 [03/85], $2.95, 317pp, pb) Fantasy novel, the "Third Chronicle of the Black Company."

*Cook, Glen WITH MERCY TOWARD NONE (Baen 0-671-55925-7, 03/85 [02/85], $2.95, 336pp, pb) Fantasy novel, sequel to THE FIRE IN HIS HANDS.

*Cook, Paul DUENDE MEADOW (Bantam Spectra 0-553-25374-3, 11/85 [09/85], $2.95, 227pp, pb) Sf novel. Paranoid post-holocaust underground civilization emerges to find friendly Russian farmers on former U.S. territory.

Cook, Paul TINTAGEL (Ace 0-441-81298-8, 07/85 [06/85], $2.75, 210pp, pb) Reprint (Berkley 1981) sf novel.

*Cooke, Catherine MASK OF THE WIZARD (Tor 0-812-53384-4, 03/85 [02/85], $2.95, 384pp, pb) Fantasy novel.

Coontz, Otto ISLE OF THE SHAPESHIFTERS (Bantam/Starfire 0-553-24801-4, 03/85 [02/85], $2.50, 210pp, pb) Reprint (Houghton Mifflin 1983) juvenile fantasy novel.

*Cooper, Clare EARTHCHANGE (Hodder & Stoughton 0-340-35167-5, 06/85 [05/85], £5.95, 96pp, hc) Young-adult short sf novel about Earth after a catastrophe.

*Cooper, Louise THE INITIATE (Tor 0-812-53392-5, 12/85 [11/85], $2.95, 278pp, pb) Fantasy novel, Book 1 in the "Time Master" trilogy.

Correy, Lee SHUTTLE DOWN (Ballantine/Del Rey 0-345-33179-6, 01/86 [12/85], $2.95, 216pp, pb) Reissue (Del Rey 1981) sf novel of the space shuttle making an emergency landing on Easter Island, with ensuing political complications. Second printing.

Correy, Lee SPACE DOCTOR (Ballantine/Del Rey 0-345-32486-2, 06/85 [05/85], $2.95, 245pp, pb) Reissue (Del Rey 1981) sf novel. 5th printing.

*Couper, Heather & David Pelham UNIVERSE (Random House 0-394-54691-1, 09/85 [09/85], $19.95, unpaginated, hc) Spectacular pop-up book of cosmic history, perhaps the most elaborate work of paper engineering yet. James Diaz, David Carter, and David Pelham did the engineering. There's a (probably simultaneous) edition from Century Hutchinson in Britain.

+Cowley, Stewart SPACEBASE 2000 (St. Martin's 0-312-74940-6, 04/85 [03/85], $14.95, 192pp, pb) Reprint (Hamlyn 1984), first U.S. edition. "A full-color, large-format history of the 21st century," featuring pictures of spaceships, space battles, etc. Part of it is co-authored by Charles Herridge. Artists include Jim Burns, Tony Roberts, Colin Hay, and Angus McKie.

Crispin, A.C. V (Gregg 0-8398-840-3, 01/85 [12/84], $13.95, 402pp, hc) Reprint (Pinnacle 1984) sf novelization based on the tv series. First hard-cover edition.

*Crispin, A.C. & Deborah A. Marshall V: DEATH TIDE (Pinnacle 0-523-42469-8, 07/85 [06/85], $2.95, 207pp, pb) Media tie-in sf novel.

Crispin, A.C. & Andre Norton GRYPHON'S EYRIE Main listing under Andre Norton.

Crispin, A.C. & Howard Weinstein V: EAST COAST CRISIS Main listing under Howard Weinstein.

+Crossley-Holland, Kevin & Gwyn Thomas, trans. TALES FROM THE MABINOGION (Overlook 0-87951-987-8, 03/85 [02/85], $14.95, 8.5" x 11" 88pp, hc) Reprint (U.K. 1984) Four mythic tales from the MABINOGION in a new juvenile translation, with color illustrations by Margaret Jones. First American edition.

Cuddon, J.A., ed. THE PENGUIN BOOK OF GHOST STORIES (Penguin 0-14-006800-7, 1985 [10/85], £4.95/$6.95, 512pp, pb) Reissue (Penguin 1984) anthology of classic supernatural fantasy tales.

Cuddon, J.A., ed. THE PENGUIN BOOK OF HORROR STORIES (Viking U.K. 0-670-81034-7, 1985 [10/85], £10.95, 607pp, hc) Reprint (Penguin 1984) anthology of dark tales from authors including Henry James, Poe, Kafka, William Hope Hodgson, Ray Bradbury, and other major authors.

Culbreath, Myrna & Sondra Marshak THE FATE OF THE PHOENIX Main listing under Sondra Marshak.

Culbreath, Myrna & Sondra Marshak THE PRICE OF THE PHOENIX Main listing under Sondra Marshak.

Culbreath, Myrna & Sondra Marshak, eds. STAR TREK: THE NEW VOYAGES Main listing under Sondra Marshak.

Culbreath, Myrna & Sondra Marshak, eds. STAR TREK: THE NEW VOYAGES 2 Main listing under Sondra Marshak.

*Cunningham, Jere LOVE OBJECT (Dream/Press 0-919489-03-3, 11/85 [11/85], $12.50, 164pp, hc) A "gothic fantasy" of a woman who builds her own dream lover.

Daley, Brian THE DOOMFARERS OF CORAMONDE (Ballantine/Del Rey 0-345-32379-3, 05/85 [04/85], $2.95, 344pp, pb) Reissue (Del Rey 1977) fantasy novel. Seventh printing.

*Daley, Brian JINX ON A TERRAN INHERITANCE (Ballantine/Del Rey 0-345-31488-3, 12/85 [11/85], $3.50, 403pp, pb) Sf novel, sequel to REQUIEM FOR A RULER OF WORLDS.

*Daley, Brian REQUIEM FOR A RULER OF WORLDS (Ballantine/Del Rey 0-345-31487-5, 05/85 [04/85], $3.50, 290pp, pb) Sf novel of intergalactic adventurer Alacrity Fitzhugh.

*Dalmas, John FANGLITH (Baen 0-671-55988-5, 10/85 [09/85], $2.95, 245pp, pb) Sf novel. Spaceships vs armored 11th-century knights.

*Dalmas, John THE SCROLL OF MAN (Tor 0-812-53425-5, 01/85 [12/84], $2.95, 255pp, pb) Sf novel.

*Dann, Jack THE MAN WHO MELTED (Bluejay 0-312-94293-1, 1984 [12/84], $14.95, 280pp, hc) Sf novel of a decadent future. A Nebula Award finalist.

Dann, Jack THE MAN WHO MELTED (Bantam Spectra 0-553-25562-2, 01/86 [12/85], $3.50, 258pp, pb) Reprint (Bluejay 1984) sf novel.

*Dann, Jack & Gardner Dozois, eds. BESTIARY! (Ace 0-441-05506-0, 10/85 [09/85], $2.95, 304pp, pb) Anthology of fantasy stories about dragons, unicorns, centaurs, etc.
Contents:

				Page
Preface	Jack Dann & Gardner Dozois		pr	xv
The Man Who Painted the Dragon Griaule	Lucius Shepard	nv	FSF Dec,84	4
Draco, Draco	Tanith Lee	nv	BYNDLND,84	35
The Rule of Names	Ursula K. Le Guin	ss	FAN Apr,64	58
The Black Horn	Jack Dann	nv	FSF Nov,84	71
Walk Like a Mountain	Manly Wade Wellman	ss	FSF Jun,55	95
Treaty in Tartessos	Karen Anderson	ss	FSF May,63	115
The Woman Who Loved the Centaur Pholus	Gene Wolfe	ss	IAS Dec,79	121
The Sleep of Trees	Jane Yolen	ss	FSF Sep,80	135
The Hardwood Pile	L. Sprague de Camp	nv	UNK Sep,40	147
The Blind Minotaur	Michael Swanwick	ss	AMZ Mar,85	177
Landscape With Sphinxes	Karen Anderson	ss	FSF Nov,62	197
Simpson's Lesser Sphynx	Esther M. Friesner	ss	ELW # 3,84	201
God's Hooks	Howard Waldrop	ss	UNI #12,82	209
A Leg Full of Rubies	Joan Aiken	ss	SMLPNCH,74	231
The Valor of Cappen Varra	Poul Anderson	ss	FUN Jan,57	243
The Troll	T.H. White	ss	DRKIMGN,78	258
Return of the Griffins	A.E. Sandeling	ss	STO 1948	272
The Last of His Breed	Robert Chilson	ss	BYNDLND,84	290

*Dann, Jack & Gardner Dozois, eds. MERMAIDS! (Ace 0-441-52567-9, 01/86 [12/85], $2.95, 260pp, pb) Anthology of 17 fantasy tales featuring mermaids, plus an original essay on the subject by Avram Davidson.
Contents:

			Page
The Prevalence of Mermaids	Avram Davidson	ar	1986	1

DANN, JACK & GARDNER DOZOIS, eds.

***Datlow, Ellen, ed.** THE FOURTH OMNI BOOK OF SCIENCE FICTION (Zebra 0-8217-1630-1, 07/85 [06/85], $3.95, 397pp, pb) Anthology of 19 stories, most from *Omni*. There are 1 2/3 originals -- the fraction's part of a Gene Wolfe triptych.

Contents:

***Datlow, Ellen, ed.** THE THIRD OMNI BOOK OF SCIENCE FICTION (Zebra 0-8217-1575-5, 04/85 [03/85], $3.95, 479pp, pb) Anthology of 19 stories including one original.

Contents:

Davidson, Lionel UNDER PLUM LAKE (Bantam Spectra 0-553-25372-7, 10/85 [09/85], $2.50, 152pp, pb) Reissue (Cape 1980) young-adult fantasy novel set in an underwater realm near Cornwall.

Davies, Robertson THE DEPTFORD TRILOGY (King Penguin 0-14-006500-8, 11/85 [12/85], $8.95, 864pp, pb) Reissue (Penguin 1983) omnibus edition of FIFTH BUSINESS (Macmillan Canada 1970), THE MANTICORE (Viking 1972), and WORLD OF WONDERS (Macmillan Canada 1975), novels combining mainstream with archetypes, illusionism, and wonders.

+Davies, Robertson WHAT'S BRED IN THE BONE (Viking 0-670-80916-0, 11/85 [11/85], $17.95, 436pp, hc) The tale of a hero who's artist, forger, and spy, this novel includes supernatural beings, Tintagel Castle, and other unusual elements. Says "first American edition", so there probably was an earlier Canadian one (not seen). Fantasy mainly by courtesy, but very enjoyable anyway. (FCM)

***Davis, Frederick C.** THE NIGHT NEMESIS: THE COMPLETE ADVENTURES OF THE MOON MAN--VOL. ONE (Purple Prose Press 0-931801-1, 08/85 [07/85], $30.00, 469pp, hc) Edited by Garyn G. Roberts & Gary Hoppenstand. 1,000-copy edition signed by the editors. Pulp mystery/fantasy adventure offset from the original *Ten Detective Aces*, 1933-1934.

Contents:

Day, David A TOLKIEN BESTIARY (Harbour no ISBN, 02/85 [01/85], $18.95, 287pp, pb) Canadian reprint (Ballantine 1979) of an illustrated reference book.

de Camp, L. Sprague CONAN: THE TREASURE OF TRANICOS See listing under Robert E. Howard.

***de Camp, L. Sprague** THE RELUCTANT KING (SFBC #1820, 02/85 [02/85], $8.98, 533pp, hc) Omnibus edition of the three "Jorian" fantasy novels.

Contents:

de Camp, L. Sprague ROGUE QUEEN (Bluejay 0-312-94396-2, 06/85 [05/85], $7.95, 165pp, pb) Reprint (Doubleday 1951) sf novel, with uninspired illustrations by Philip Hagopian. Part of the "Viagens" series.

de Camp, L. Sprague, Lin Carter & Robert E. Howard CONAN Main listing under Robert E. Howard.

de Camp, L. Sprague, Lin Carter & Robert E. Howard CONAN OF CIMMERIA Main listing under Robert E. Howard.

de Camp, L. Sprague, Lin Carter & Robert E. Howard CONAN THE WANDERER Main listing under Robert E. Howard.

de Camp, L. Sprague & Robert E. Howard CONAN THE FREEBOOTER Main listing under Robert E. Howard.

de Camp, L. Sprague & Robert E. Howard CONAN: THE FLAME KNIFE Main listing under Robert E. Howard.

de Camp, L. Sprague & Fletcher Pratt THE LAND OF UNREASON (Bluejay 0-312-94278-8, 03/85 [02/85], $7.95, 197pp, pb) Reprint (Holt 1942) fantasy novel, with illustrations by Tim Kirk. One of the classics of the genre. Recommended. For once, the illustrations actually belong and add to the text. (CNB)

***de Lint, Charles** THE HARP OF THE GREY ROSE (Donning/Starblaze 0-89865-374-6, 08/85 [07/85], $7.95, 207pp, pb) Fantasy novel, first of a projected series. Illustrations by George Barr.

***de Lint, Charles** MULENGRO (Ace 0-441-54484-3, 10/85 [09/85], $3.50, 351pp, pb) Fantasy novel of ghosts and Gypsy magic, set in contemporary Ottawa.

+Dean, Martyn, ed. THE GUIDE TO FANTASY ART TECHNIQUES (Arco 0-668-06233-9, 03/85 [02/85], $19.95, 111pp, hc) Non-fiction, collection of articles on artists and their work (reproduced in full color), and how they work (based on interviews). Included are Burns, Woodroffe, Vallejo, Foss, and others. Published in England by Paper Tiger/Dragon's Dream (1984). Highly recommended. (CNB)

+Dean, Martyn & Roger Dean MAGNETIC STORM Main listing under Roger Dean.

*Dean, Pamela THE SECRET COUNTRY (Ace 0-441-75739-1, 05/85 [04/85], $2.95, 293pp, pb) Fantasy novel of gaming turned real, a first novel.

+Dean, Roger & Martyn Dean MAGNETIC STORM (Harmony 0-517-55626-X, 04/85 [03/85], $12.95, 155pp, pb) Reprint (Dragon's World 1984), first U.S. edition. Non-fiction, art. This successor to VIEWS tells and shows what the Dean brothers have been doing in publishing, the rock world, architecture, movies, etc., these last ten years. It's marvelous stuff and a prime sampler of the Deans' talents. Highly recommended. (CNB)

*DeGaris, Roger, ed. EARTH AND ELSEWHERE (Macmillan 0-02-518240-4, 02/86 [12/85], $22.95 FPT, 315pp, hc) Anthology of five sf tales from Soviet authors including Kir Bulychev (the only "author" name listed on the cover), the Strugatskys, and Sever Gansovsky.
Contents:

		Page
The Way to Amalteia	Arkady Strugatsky & Boris Strugatsky	na ERH&ELW,85 1
A Part of the World	Sever Gansovski	na ERH&ELW,85 60
Another's Memory	Kir Bulychev	na ERH&ELW,85 135
A Tale of Kings	Olga Larionova	na ERH&ELW,85 216
Tower of Birds	Oleg Korabelnikov	na ERH&ELW,85 275

*Delaney, Joseph H. IN THE FACE OF MY ENEMY (Baen 0-671-55993-1, 11/85 [10/85], $2.95, 349pp, pb) Sf novel based on Delaney's Hugo-nominated story of the same name.

*Delany, Samuel R. FLIGHT FROM NEVERYON (Bantam 0-553-24856-1, 05/85 [04/85], $3.95, 385pp, pb) Fantasy novel -- or collection of related pieces; conclusion of the "Neveryon" trilogy. Sometimes difficult and literary, but fascinating. Read the appendices too. Recommended. (FCM)
Contents:

		Page
The Tale of Fog and Granite	Samuel R. Delany	na FLGTNVR,85 1
The Mummer's Tale	Samuel R. Delany	nv FLGTNVR,85 127
Appendix A: The Tale of Plagues and Carnivals, or, Some Informal Remarks toward the Modular Calculus, Part Five	Samuel R. Delany	na FLGTNVR,85 173
Appendix B: Closures and Openings	Samuel R. Delany	nv FLGTNVR,85 355

Delany, Samuel R. NOVA (Bantam Spectra 0-553-23621-0, 01/86 [12/85], $2.95, 215pp, pb) Reissue (Doubleday 1968) sf novel. 13th Bantam printing.

Delany, Samuel R. STARS IN MY POCKET LIKE GRAINS OF SAND (Bantam Spectra 0-553-25149-X, 09/85 [08/85], $3.95, 375pp, pb) Reprint (Bantam 1984) sf novel, first of a "diptych." Recommended -- for the adventurous. A literary sf extravaganza. (FCM)

Delany, Samuel R. STARS IN MY POCKET LIKE GRAINS OF SAND (QPB/Bantam no ISBN, 11/85 [11/85], $8.95, 368pp, pb) Reprint (Bantam 1984) sf novel, first of a "dilogy". This edition is identical to the Bantam hardcover with the jacket printed on the paperback cover.

Delany, Samuel R. TRITON (Bantam Spectra 0-553-22979-6, 01/86 [12/85], $3.95, 369pp, pb) Reissue (Bantam 1976) sf novel, 11th printing.

+deLoyola Brandao, Ignacio AND STILL THE EARTH (Avon/Bard 0-380-89874-8, 08/85 [07/85], $4.95, 374pp, pb) Dystopian sf novel, the first English version of NAO VERAS PAIS NENHUM (Brazil 1982), translated by Ellen Watson.

*DeVore, Howard & Donald Franson A HISTORY OF THE HUGO, NEBULA, AND INTERNATIONAL FANTASY AWARDS, Updated Edition Main listing under Donald Franson.

*DeWeese, Gene BLACK SUITS FROM OUTER SPACE (Putnam 0-399-21261-2, 09/85 [10/85], $12.95, 144pp, hc) Young-adult comic sf novel.

Dexter, Susan THE RING OF ALLAIRE (Ballantine/Del Rey 0-345-31121-3, 03/85 [02/85], $2.75, 231pp, pb) Reissue (Ballantine/Del Rey 1981) fantasy novel.

*Dexter, Susan THE SWORD OF CALANDRA (Ballantine/Del Rey 0-345-29717-2, 03/85 [02/85], $2.95, 341pp, pb) Fantasy novel, sequel to THE RING OF ALLAIRE.

*Diamond, Graham CINNABAR (Fawcett Gold Medal 0-345-12463-0, 04/85 [03/85], $2.95, 291pp, pb) Oriental fantasy novel, starring Aladdin.

Dick, Philip K. DR. BLOODMONEY (Bluejay 0-312-94105-6, 05/85 [04/85], $7.95, 314pp, pb) Reprint (Ace 1965) sf novel. Afterwords by Philip K. Dick (from the 1980 Dell edition) and James Frenkel (new).

*Dick, Philip K. I HOPE I SHALL ARRIVE SOON (Doubleday 0-385-19567-2, 07/85 [06/85], $12.95, 179pp, hc) Collection with 10 stories and a previously unpublished speech. Edited by Mark Hurst and Paul Williams.
Contents:

		Page
How to Build a Universe That Doesn't Fall Apart Two Days Later	Philip K. Dick	sp IHOPEIS,85 1
The Short Happy Life of the Brown Oxford	Philip K. Dick	ss FSF Jan,54 24
Explorers We	Philip K. Dick	ss FSF Jan,59 35
Holy Quarrel	Philip K. Dick	nv WOT May,66 46
What'll We Do with Ragland Park?	Philip K. Dick	nv AMZ Nov,63 73
Strange Memories of Death	Philip K. Dick	ss IHOPEIS,85 97
The Alien Mind	Philip K. Dick	ss FSF Oct,81 104
The Exit Door Leads In	Philip K. Dick	nv RCS Fll,79 107
Chains of Air, Web of Aether	Philip K. Dick	nv STL # 5,80 128
Rautavaara's Case	Philip K. Dick	ss OMN Oct,80 151
I Hope I Shall Arrive Soon [Frozen Journey]	Philip K. Dick	ss PBY Dec,80 161

*Dick, Philip K. IN MILTON LUMKY TERRITORY (Dragon Press 0-911499-09-1, 06/85 [05/85], $29.95, 213pp, hc) Non-sf/fantasy, associational; this is the first edition of a mainstream novel written by Dick in 1958.

*Dick, Philip K. PUTTERING ABOUT IN A SMALL LAND (Academy Chicago 0-89733-149-4, 10/85 [10/85], $16.95, 291pp, hc) Non-sf/fantasy; associational. The first publication of a mainstream novel set in Los Angeles in the early fifties. Very enjoyable, focusing on the lives and times of "unimportant" people. (DLN)

*Dick, Philip K. RADIO FREE ALBEMUTH (Arbor House 0-87795-762-2, 12/85 [11/85], $14.95, 214pp, hc) Dick's "last" sf novel, actually an early and substantially different version of VALIS.

*Dick, Philip K. UBIK: THE SCREENPLAY (Corroboree 0-911169-06-7, 08/85 [07/85], $23.00 plus $1.50/book postage, 154pp, hc) Dick's own adaptation of UBIK, with illustrations by Ron Lindahn, Val Lakey-Lindahn, and Doug Rice. There is an excellent historical introduction by Paul Williams and another piece by Tim Powers. The script, written in 1974, shows that Dick really could write movie material. It's a pity the movie was never made. (CNB) There is also a 50-copy deluxe edition signed by the artists, Powers, Williams, and Dick (signatures from checks), for $180.00.

Dick, Philip K. VALIS (Bantam Spectra 0-553-25370-0, 11/85 [09/85], $2.95, 227pp, pb) Reissue (Bantam 1981) sf novel.

Dick, Philip K. THE ZAP GUN (Bluejay 0-312-94488-8, 05/85 [04/85], $7.95, 258pp, pb) Reprint (Pyramid 1967) sf novel. There is a new afterword by Maxim Jakubowski.

*Dickinson, Peter A BOX OF NOTHING (Gollancz 0-575-03530-7, 05/85 [04/85], £5.95, 128pp, hc) Juvenile fantasy adventure novel, with illustrations by Ian Newsham.

*Dickinson, Peter THE CHANGES TRILOGY (Puffin 0-14-031846-1, 1985 [10/85], £2.95, 348pp, pb) Omnibus edition of three young-adult fantasy novels. An excellent group of related books about England under an anti-technological magic spell. Recommended. (FCM)
Contents:

		Page
THE DEVIL'S CHILDREN	Peter Dickinson	n. GOL 1970 9
HEARTSEASE	Peter Dickinson	n. GOL 1969 105
THE WEATHERMONGER	Peter Dickinson	n. GOL 1969 237

+Dickinson, Peter THE HEALER (Delacorte 0-385-29372-0, 04/85 [03/85], $14.95, 184pp, hc) Reprint (Gollancz 1983) young-adult sf novel. First American edition. Recommended. (FCM)

*Dickson, Gordon R. BEYOND THE DAR AL-HARB (Tor 0-812-53550-2, 11/85 [10/85], $2.95, 253pp, pb) Collection of 3 stories, packaged as a novel. The title story seems to be an original novella, featuring Red Jamie in an Arabian fantasy land. Not mentioned on the cover are two other stories with entirely different settings, at least one of them sf.
Contents:

		Page
Beyond the Dar al-Harb	Gordon R. Dickson	na BYNDDAR,85 7
On Messenger Mountain	Gordon R. Dickson	na WOT Jun,64 95
Things Which Are Caesar's	Gordon R. Dickson	na DAYSUNS,72 165

Dickson, Gordon R. THE FINAL ENCYCLOPEDIA (Ace 0-441-23776-2, 10/85 [09/85], $4.95, 696pp, pb) Reprint (Tor 1984) sf novel in the "Childe Cycle." The print has been shot down from the hardcover and is microscopic.

Dickson, Gordon R. THE FINAL ENCYCLOPEDIA (SFBC #03853, 12/85 [12/85], $10.98, 696pp, hc) Reprint (Tor 1984) sf novel, part of the "Childe Cycle."

*Dickson, Gordon R. FORWARD! (Baen 0-671-55971-0, 07/85 [06/85], $2.95, 242pp, pb) Collection of 11 stories, mostly from the fifties, edited and with an introduction by Sandra Miesel.
Contents:

		Page
Editor's Introduction	Sandra Miesel	in 1
Building on the Line	Gordon R. Dickson	nv GAL Nov,68 3
Babes in the Woods	Gordon R. Dickson	ss OWS May,53 47
Napoleon's Skullcap	Gordon R. Dickson	nv FSF May,62 66
Rescue Mission	Gordon R. Dickson	ss FSF Jan,57 88
Robots are Nice?	Gordon R. Dickson	ss GAL Oct,57 110
The Dreamsman	Gordon R. Dickson	ss STR # 6,59 126
The R of A	Gordon R. Dickson	ss FSF Jan,59 135
One on Trial	Gordon R. Dickson	ss FSF Jan,60 151
The Queer Critter	Gordon R. Dickson	ss OSF Dec,54 163
Twig	Gordon R. Dickson	nv STL # 1,74 167
The Game of Five	Gordon R. Dickson	nv FSF Apr,60 205

Guided Tour	Gordon R. Dickson	pm FSF Oct,59	241

*Dickson, Gordon R. INVADERS! (Baen 0-671-55994-X, 11/85 [10/85], $2.95, 253pp, pb) Collection of 8 stories (mostly from the '50s), with an introduction by Sandra Miesel.
Contents:

			Page
Introduction	Sandra Miesel	in	7
The Error of Their Ways	Gordon R. Dickson	ss ASF Jul,51	9
Itco's Strong Right Arm	Gordon R. Dickson	nv CSM Jul,54	27
Fellow of the Bees	Gordon R. Dickson	nv OSF # 3,54	51
Richochet on Miza	Gordon R. Dickson	ss PLS Mar,52	77
The Law-Twister Shorty	Gordon R. Dickson	nv MNYWRLD,71	87
An Ounce of Emotion	Gordon R. Dickson	nv IFS Oct,65	137
Roofs of Silver	Gordon R. Dickson	nv FSF Dec,62	165
The Invaders	Gordon R. Dickson	na SPS Oct,52	197

Dickson, Gordon R. THE OUTPOSTER (Tor 0-812-53564-2, 10/85 [09/85], $2.95, 251pp, pb) Reissue (Lippincott 1972) sf novel, 2nd Tor printing.

Dickson, Gordon R. SLEEPWALKER'S WORLD (Tor 0-812-53556-1, 09/85 [08/85], $2.95, 255pp, pb) Reissue (Lippincott 1971) sf novel.

Dickson, Gordon R. SPACE WINNERS (Tor 0-812-53558-8, 01/86 [12/85], $2.95, 250pp, pb) Reprint (Holt, Rinehart & Winston 1965) young adult sf novel.

Dickson, Gordon R. STEEL BROTHER (Tor 0-812-53552-9, 12/85 [11/85], $2.95, 236pp, pb) Reprint (NESFA 1984 as DICKSON!) collection. This new version does not acknowledge the 1984 book. It adds one story, "The Man in the Mailbag", plus an interview. The Sandra Miesel story introductions are used, but not credited.
Contents:

			Page
Introduction	Poul Anderson	in	ix
Out of the Darkness	Gordon R. Dickson	ss EQM Feb,61	1
The Man in the Mailbag	Gordon R. Dickson	nv GAL Apr,59	14
The Hard Way	Gordon R. Dickson	nv ASF Jan,63	52
Perfectly Adjusted	Gordon R. Dickson	na SFS Jul,55	99
Steel Brother	Gordon R. Dickson	nv ASF Feb,52	166
The Childe Cycle Status Report [updated]			
	Gordon R. Dickson	ar SFW F11,79	195
A Conversation With Gordon R. Dickson			
	Sandra Miesel	iv AGL Spr,78	214

Dickson, Gordon R. TIME-STORM (Bantam 0-553-25146-5, 04/85 [03/85], $3.50, 420pp, pb) Reissue (St. Martin's 1977) sf novel. 5th printing.

Dickson, Gordon R. WOLFLING (Baen 0-671-55962-1, 05/85 [04/85], $2.95, 245pp, pb) Reprint (Dell 1969) sf novel.

Dickson, Gordon R. & Poul Anderson EARTHMAN'S BURDEN Main listing under Poul Anderson.

Dickson, Gordon R. & Harry Harrison THE LIFESHIP (Baen 0-671-55981-8, 09/85 [08/85], $2.95, 251pp, pb) Reprint (Harper & Row 1976) sf novel.

*Dikty, Thaddeus, & R. Reginald THE WORK OF JULIAN MAY: AN ANNO-TATED BIBLIOGRAPHY & GUIDE (Borgo 0-89370-482-2, 08/85 [07/85], $9.95, 66pp, pb) Non-fiction; the bibliography includes everything from school study-guides to audio cassettes, non-fiction and fiction material. A hardcover version is also available for $19.95.

*Dillard, J.M. STAR TREK #27: MINDSHADOW (Pocket 0-671-60756-1, 01/86 [12/85], $3.50, 252pp, pb) Sf novel in the Star Trek series.

Disch, Thomas M. ON WINGS OF SONG (Bantam 0-553-25076-0, 05/85 [04/85], $3.50, 359pp, pb) Reissue (St. Martin's 1979) literary sf novel. A Nebula and Hugo nominee and winner of the John W. Campbell Memorial Award. It finally has a cover that fits the book.

Donaldson, Stephen R. DAUGHTER OF REGALS AND OTHER TALES (Ballantine/Del Rey 0-345-31443-3, 04/85 [03/85], $3.95, 366pp, pb) Reprint (Del Rey 1984) collection.

*Douglas, Carole Nelson PROBE (Tor 0-812-53585-5, 07/85 [06/85], $6.95, 383pp, pb) Sf novel of a mysterious amnesia victim "Jane Doe" and the psychologist who becomes obsessed with her. Though the writing is often awkward, it's a strong, enjoyable story which would make an excellent film. (FCM)

*Dozois, Gardner, ed. THE YEAR'S BEST SCIENCE FICTION, SECOND ANNUAL COLLECTION (Bluejay 0-312-94484-5, 04/85 [05/85], $19.95, 573pp, hc) Sf anthology.
Contents:

			Page
Summation: 1984	Gardner Dozois	in	9
Salvador	Lucius Shepard	nv FSF Apr,84	27
Promises to Keep	Jack McDevitt	ss IAS Dec,84	45
Bloodchild	Octavia E. Butler	nv IAS Jun,84	63
Blued Moon	Connie Willis	nv IAS Jan,84	82
A Message to the King of Brobdingnag			
	Richard Cowper	nv FSF May,84	113
The Affair	Robert Silverberg	ss PBY Jun,84	135
PRESS ENTER ■	John Varley	na IAS May,84	153
New Rose Hotel	William Gibson	ss OMN Jul,84	207
The Map	Gene Wolfe	ss LGTYR&D,84	219
Interlocking Pieces	Molly Gloss	ss UNI #14,84	232
Trojan Horse	Michael Swanwick	nv OMN Dec,84	239

Bad Medicine	Jack Dann	nv IAS Oct,84	269
At the Embassy Club	Elizabeth A. Lynn	ss OMN Jun,84	291
Pursuit of Excellence	Rena Yount	ss CLRAWDS,84	301
The Kindly Isle	Frederik Pohl	nv IAS Nov,84	319
Rock On	Pat Cadigan	ss LGTYR&D,84	341
Sunken Gardens	Bruce Sterling	ss OMN Jun,84	350
Trinity	Nancy Kress	na IAS Oct,84	365
The Trouble with the Cotton People			
	Ursula K. Le Guin	ss MIS V7 #2,84	409
Twilight Time	Lewis Shiner	ss IAS Apr,84	420
Black Coral	Lucius Shepard	nv UNI #14,84	440
Friend	James Patrick Kelley & John Kessel		
		ss FSF Jan,84	466
Foreign Skins	Tanith Lee	nv TAMASTR,84	484
Company in the Wings	R.A. Lafferty	ss HRTSTND,84	511
A Cabin on the Coast	Gene Wolfe	ss FSF Feb,84	524
The Lucky Strike	Kim Stanley Robinson	nv UNI #14,84	536
Honorable Mentions: 1984	Gardner Dozois	bi	569

*Dozois, Gardner, ed. THE YEAR'S BEST SCIENCE FICTION, SECOND ANNUAL COLLECTION (Bluejay 0-312-94485-3, 04/85 [05/85], $10.95, 573pp, pb) Trade paperback of the above.

*Dozois, Gardner & Jack Dann, eds. BESTIARY! Main listing under Jack Dann.

*Dozois, Gardner & Jack Dann, eds. MERMAIDS! Main listing under Jack Dann.

*Drake, Asa WARRIOR WITCH OF HEL (Popular Library/Questar 0-445-20039-1, 09/85 [08/85], $2.95, 218pp, pb) Fantasy novel, first in a series.

*Drake, David A. AT ANY PRICE (Baen 0-671-55978-8, 09/85 [08/85], $3.50, 288pp, pb) Sf novel in the "Hammer's Slammers" military adventure series.

Drake, David A. BIRDS OF PREY (Tor 0-812-53612-6, 08/85 [07/85], $2.95, 348pp, pb) Reprint (Baen 1984) time travel sf novel set in ancient Rome.

*Drake, David A. & Janet Morris ACTIVE MEASURES Main listing under Janet Morris.

*Drake, David A. & Karl Edward Wagner KILLER (Baen 0-671-55931-1, 01/85 [12/84], $2.95, 270pp, pb) Sf novel of an alien loose in ancient Rome.

Drew, Wayland DRAGONSLAYER (Ballantine/Del Rey 0-345-32306-8, 06/85 [05/85], $2.95, 218pp, pb) Reissue (Del Rey 1981) 4th printing. Based on the screenplay for the movie of the same name, this fantasy novel stands on its own -- well-written and enjoyable. (FCM)

*Drew, Wayland THE GAIAN EXPEDIENT (Ballantine/Del Rey 0-345-30888-3, 06/85 [05/85], $2.95, 259pp, pb) Sf novel, Part Two of "The Erthring Cycle."

*Drumm, D.B. TRAVELER #5: ROAD WAR (Dell 0-440-17471-6, 02/85 [01/85], $2.25, 158pp, pb) Post-catastrophe adventure series in the vein of MAD MAX. Apparently written by sf author John Shirley.

*Drumm, D.B. TRAVELER #6: BORDER WAR (Dell 0-440-10767-8, 06/85 [05/85], $2.50, 172pp, pb) Post-catastrophe survivalist novel, part of an endless series. John Shirley is the author of at least some of these.

*Drumm, D.B. TRAVELER #7: THE ROAD GHOST (Dell 0-440-17469-4, 10/85 [09/85], $2.50, 172pp, pb) Sf novel in a post-holocaust adventure series.

*Drury, Nevill DICTIONARY OF MYSTICISM AND THE OCCULT (Harper & Row 0-06-062093-5, 05/85 [04/85], $24.95, 281pp, hc) Non-fiction, reference book whose entries range from the MABINOGION to Arthur Machen, from modern psychics to ancient gods. Fascinating browsing, and useful for writers in search of brief introductions to matters occult. (FCM)

*Drury, Nevill DICTIONARY OF MYSTICISM AND THE OCCULT (Harper & Row 0-06-062094-3, 05/85 [04/85], $12.95, 281pp, pb) Paperback version of the above.

*Duane, Diane DEEP WIZARDRY (Delacorte 0-385-29373-9, 04/85 [03/85], $15.95, 272pp, hc) Young-adult fantasy novel, sequel to SO YOU WANT TO BE A WIZARD. Well-crafted and exciting, including that fantasy rarity, a real surprise ending. Recommended. (DLN)

Duane, Diane THE DOOR INTO FIRE (Bluejay 0-312-94107-2, 01/85 [12/84], $7.95, 290pp, pb) Reprint (Dell 1979) fantasy novel, first of a series.

Duane, Diane THE DOOR INTO FIRE (Tor 0-812-53671-1, 08/85 [07/85], $2.95, 290pp, pb) Reprint (Dell 1979) fantasy novel, first in a series.

Duane, Diane THE DOOR INTO SHADOW (Tor 0-812-53673-8, 06/85 [05/85], $2.95, 298pp, pb) Reprint (Bluejay 1984) fantasy novel, sequel to THE DOOR INTO FIRE.

Duane, Diane <u>MY ENEMY, MY ALLY</u> (SFBC #2590, 02/85 [01/85], $4.98, 210pp, hc) Reprint (Pocket 1984) Star Trek novel. First hardcover edition.

Eager, Edward <u>HALF MAGIC</u> (Harcourt Brace Jovanovich 0-15-637990-2, 07/85 [06/85], $4.95, 217pp, pb) Reprint (Harcourt Brace 1954) juvenile fantasy novel, with illustrations by N.M. Bodecker. 8th paperback printing. A wonderful ode to E. Nesbit. Recommended. (CNB)

Eager, Edward <u>KNIGHT'S CASTLE</u> (Harcourt Brace Jovanovich 0-15-647350-X, 07/85 [06/85], $4.95, 183pp, pb) Reprint (Harcourt Brace 1956) juvenile fantasy novel illustrated by N.M. Bodecker. A parody of IVANHOE. 6th paperback printing.

Eager, Edward <u>MAGIC OR NOT?</u> (Harcourt Brace Jovanovich 0-15-655121-7, 07/85 [06/85], $4.95, 190pp, pb) Reissue (Harcourt Brace 1959) juvenile fantasy novel, illustrated by N.M. Bodecker. 2nd paperback printing.

Eager, Edward <u>THE TIME GARDEN</u> (HBJ/Voyager 0-15-288190-5, 11/85 [12/85], $4.95, 188pp, pb) Reissue (Harcourt Brace 1958) juvenile fantasy.

Eager, Edward <u>THE WELL-WISHERS</u> (HBJ/Voyager 0-15-294992-5, 11/85 [12/85], $4.95, 191pp, pb) Reissue (Harcourt Brace 1960) juvenile fantasy novel.

*Easton, M. Coleman <u>MASTERS OF GLASS</u> (Popular Library/Questar 0-445-20064-2, 07/85 [06/85], $2.95, 245pp, pb) Fantasy novel, a first novel. Well done, with an interesting twist on magic. Recommended. (FCM)

Eddings, David <u>THE BELGARIAD 1</u> (Century 0-7126-0879-6, 1985 [12/85], £12.95, 691pp, hc) Reprint (SFBC 1985) omnibus edition of the first three books in the fantasy series, PAWN OF PROPHECY (Del Rey 1982), QUEEN OF SORCERY (Del Rey 1982), and MAGICIAN'S GAMBIT (Del Rey 1983). First British omnibus edition.

Eddings, David <u>THE BELGARIAD 2</u> (Century 0-7126-0951-2, 1985 [12/85], £12.95, 548pp, hc) Reprint (SFBC 1985) omnibus edition of the concluding two books of the fantasy saga, THE CASTLE OF WIZARDRY (Del Rey 1984) and ENCHANTER'S END GAME (Del Rey 1984). First British omnibus edition.

*Eddings, David <u>THE BELGARIAD: PART ONE</u> (SFBC #4654, 08/85 [07/85], $9.98, 759pp, hc) Omnibus edition of the first three novels in the "Belgariad" series.

Contents:

			Page
PAWN OF PROPHECY	David Eddings	n. BAL 1983	
QUEEN OF SORCERY	David Eddings	n. BAL 1982	
MAGICIAN'S GAMBIT	David Eddings	n. BAL 1983	

*Eddings, David <u>THE BELGARIAD: PART TWO</u> (SFBC #3973, 08/85 [07/85], $7.98, 626pp, hc) Omnibus edition of the fourth and fifth novels in the "Belgariad" series.

Contents:

			Page
CASTLE OF WIZARDRY	David Eddings	n. BAL 1984	1
ENCHANTERS' END GAME	David Eddings	n. BAL 1984	317

Eddings, David <u>ENCHANTERS' END GAME</u> (Century 0-7126-0865-6, 04/85 [03/85], £9.95, 372pp, hc) Reprint (Del Rey 1984) fantasy novel, conclusion of the "Belgariad" series. First U.K. edition, and the first hardcover.

+Edwards, Malcolm & Robert Holdstock, eds. <u>LOST REALMS</u> Main listing under Robert Holdstock.

*Effinger, George Alec <u>THE NICK OF TIME</u> (Doubleday 0-385-19230-0, 07/85 [06/85], $12.95, 180pp, hc) Sf absurdist novel about time travel. A sequel is planned.

Eklund, Gordon <u>DEVIL WORLD</u> (Bantam 0-553-24677-1, 01/85 [12/84], $2.95, 153pp, pb) Reissue (Bantam 1979) Star Trek novel.

*<u>Eldritch Tales No. 11</u> [v.3 #2] Crispin Burnham, ed. (Yith Press, 1985 [07/85], $6.00, 130pp, pb)

Contents:

				Page
The Haters of Innocence	Carol Ann Cupitt	pm	EDT #11,85	ii
Eldritch Lair	Crispin Burnham	ed	EDT #11,85	1
Eldritch Lair - Dungeon Level	Charles L. Baker	ed	EDT #11,85	6
Andrew Patterson	Charles L. Grant	ss	EDT #11,85	8
Looking Backwards	Lawrence Harding	pm	EDT #11,85	14
Snarker's Son	Brian Lumley	ss	NTLSTRR,80	15
Swamp Parasite	Edward Darton	pm	EDT #11,85	20
Snail Ghost	Will Murray	ss	EDT #11,85	21
Whispers	Scott Green	pm	EDT #11,85	25
Pulled Down to Sleep	Steve Rasnic Tem	ss	EDT #11,85	27
Innocents	Will Johnson	pm	EDT #11,85	30
Shadow of the Immortal (1 of 3)	Charles L. Baker	sl	EDT #11,85	31
The Gospel According to...	Charles L. Baker	bi	EDT #11,85	39
The Spectracycle Cop	Robert Randolf Medcalf, Jr.	pm	EDT #11,85	41
Taking Care of Bertie	Janet Fox	ss	EDT #11,85	43
The Abominations of Yoni	Frederick J. Mayer	pm	EDT #11,85	47
The Adventures of the Red Leech	Fraser Sherman	ss	EDT #11,85	49
Night Bus	Donald R. Burleson	vi	EDT #11,85	58
Bardicide	Steve Eng	pm	EDT #11,85	60
Book Reviews	Christina Kiplinger	br	EDT #11,85	63
Book Reviews	Thomas M. Egan	br	EDT #11,85	64
Book Reviews	Crispin Burnham	br	EDT #11,85	66
The Devil in the Deep	Klaus Dieter Yurk	ss	EDT #11,85	69
Dead in the West (2 of 4)	Joe R. Lansdale	sl	EDT #11,85	80
Night-Scape: A Painter's Tale	Morgan Griffith	pm	EDT #11,85	96
The Lingering Chill	Claudia Peck	ss	EDT #11,85	98
The Dismal Dismissal	Mark Calcamuggio	pm	EDT #11,85	101
The Chess Set	Jean Sullivan	ss	EDT #11,85	103
The Dead Sleep	Stephen Studach	pm	EDT #11,85	108
City of Anapais	Donald R. Broyles	vi	EDT #11,85	109
The Eldritch Eye	Gary A. Braunbeck	mr	EDT #11,85	110
Stillness	Mark Calcamuggio	pm	EDT #11,85	121
Writhings	Stephen Gresham	ss	EDT #11,85	123
Contributors	[Misc. Material]		bg	128

*Elgin, Don D. <u>THE COMEDY OF THE FANTASTIC: ECOLOGICAL PERSPECTIVES ON THE FANTASY NOVEL</u> (Greenwood 0-313-23283-0, 02/85 [08/85], $29.95, 204pp, hc) Non-fiction, critical study, with chapters on Tolkien, Lewis, Charles Williams, Frank Herbert, and Joy Chant.

*Elliot, Jeffrey M. & Michael Burgess <u>THE WORK OF R. REGINALD: AN ANNOTATED BIBLIOGRAPHY AND GUIDE</u> Main listing under Michael Burgess.

*Elliott, Richard <u>THE BURNT LANDS</u> (Fawcett/Gold Medal 0-449-12771-0, 10/85 [09/85], $3.50, 263pp, pb) Near-future disaster novel of Earth "ravaged by a solar flare which erupts when a star wars weapon misfires and hits the sun." The authors are Elton P. Elliott and Richard E. Geis.

*Ellis, A.C. <u>WORLDMAKER</u> (Ace 0-441-91102-1, 09/85 [08/85], $2.95, 233pp, pb) Sf novel.

Ellison, Harlan <u>APPROACHING OBLIVION</u> (Bluejay 0-312-94018-1, 05/85 [04/85], $7.95, 213pp, pb) Reprint (Walker 1974) collection. There is a new "introduction to the introduction" dated 1984.

*Ellison, Harlan <u>AN EDGE IN MY VOICE</u> (Donning 0-89865-341-X, 08/85 [07/85], $9.95, 548pp, pb) Non-fiction, associational. Ellison's columns for the L.A. Weekly, in the polemic mode. There is also a regular hardcover and a limited-edition hardcover.

*Ellison, Harlan, ed. <u>MEDEA: HARLAN'S WORLD</u> (Phantasia 0-932096-36-0, 06/85 [05/85], $50.00 signed numbered 475-copy special edition; $20.00 725-copy trade edition, 532pp, hc) This small-press version is simultaneous with the one from Bantam Spectra and is the only hardcover. The special edition is sold out. It's a fine job of bookbinding and should be a highly prized collector's item. (CNB)

Contents:

			Page
Cosmic Hod-Carriers	Harlan Ellison	in	1
Introduction	Harlan Ellison	in	9
Basic Concepts: Astrophysics, Geology	Hal Clement	ar	11
Geology, Meteorology, Oceanography, Geology, Nomenclature, Biology	Poul Anderson	ar	14
Biology, Ecology, Xenology	Larry Niven	ar	28
Xenology, Sociology, Politics, Theology, Mathematics	Frederik Pohl	ar	34
The Concept Seminar	Thomas M. Disch, Frank Herbert, Robert Silverberg, Theodore Sturgeon & Harlan Ellison	ms	45
The Extrapolations, the Questions	Thomas M. Disch, Frank Herbert, Robert Silverberg, Theodore Sturgeon & Harlan Ellison	ms	121
Second Thoughts	Poul Anderson, Thomas M. Disch, Hal Clement, Larry Niven & Frederik Pohl	ms	171
Farside Station	Jack Williamson	nv IAS Nov,78	187
Flare Time	Larry Niven	nv AND # 3,78	217
With Virgil Oddum at the East Pole	Harlan Ellison	ss OMN Jan,85	253
Swanilda's Song	Frederik Pohl	nv IAS Oct,78	269
Seasoning	Hal Clement	nv IAS Sep,78	295
Concepts	Thomas M. Disch	nv FSF Dec,78	321
Songs of a Sentient Flute	Frank Herbert	nv ASF Feb,79	357
Hunter's Moon	Poul Anderson	nv ASF Nov,78	401
The Promise [The Mind of Medea]	Kate Wilhelm	nv OMN Jan,83	433
Why Dolphins Don't Bite	Theodore Sturgeon	nv OMN Feb +2,80	461
Waiting for the Earthquake	Robert Silverberg	ss BOM # 2,81	509
The Contributors	[Misc. Material]	bg	529

*Ellison, Harlan, ed. <u>MEDEA: HARLAN'S WORLD</u> (Bantam 0-553-34170-7, 06/85 [05/85], $10.95, 532pp, pb) Anthology of 11 stories set on a planet conceived by Harlan Ellison. Authors include Poul Anderson, Frank Herbert, and Larry Niven. Illustrations by Kelly Freas.

*Emerson, Ru <u>THE PRINCESS OF FLAMES</u> (Ace 0-441-67919-6, 01/86 [12/85], $2.95, 327pp, pb) Quasi-medieval fantasy novel.

ENDE, MICHAEL

FARMER, PHILIP JOSÉ

+Ende, Michael MOMO (Doubleday 0-385-19093-X, 02/85 [01/85], $14.95, 227pp, hc) This is a new English translation of a fanta- sy novel which previously appeared as THE GREY GENTLEMAN (Burke 1974).   J. Maxwell Brownjohn did the new translation. The book is printed in sepia.

Ende, Michael   MOMO (Quality Paperback Book Club/Doubleday no ISBN, 1985 [10/85], no price given, 227pp, pb) Reprint (Double- day 1985) fantasy novel; the hardcover printing in trade paper- back binding; available only to book club members.

*Engebretson, David & Michael R. Collings THE SHORTER WORKS OF STEPHEN KING Main listing under Michael R. Collings.

*Erickson, Steve DAYS BETWEEN STATIONS (Poseidon/Simon & Schuster 0-671-53275-8, 08/85 [07/85], $15.95, 253pp, hc) Literary sf novel of the future, billed as "darkly romantic, tinged with the surreal."

*Estes, Rose CHILDREN OF THE DRAGON (Random House 0-394-86433-6, 05/85 [04/85], $2.95, 205pp, pb) Juvenile fantasy novel, with black and white illustrations by Carl Lundgren.

*Estes, Rose CHILDREN OF THE DRAGON (Random House 0-394-96433-0, 05/85 [04/85], $5.99, 205pp, hc) The above in a library binding.

*Etchemendy, Nancy THE CRYSTAL CITY (Avon/Camelot 0-380-89699-0, 09/85 [09/85], $2.50, 173pp, pb) Young-adult sf novel, sequel to THE WATCHERS OF SPACE.

Etchemendy, Nancy   THE WATCHERS OF SPACE (Avon/Camelot 0-380- 75374-X, 09/85 [09/85], $2.50, 124pp, pb) Reissue (Avon/Camelot 1980) young-adult sf novel; 3rd printing.

*Etherington, Norman RIDER HAGGARD (Twayne 0-6869-6, 1984 [12/85], $15.95, 138pp, hc) Non-fiction, critical study -- most- ly a Freudian analysis of the early novels. This has a 1984 copyright date, but we did not see it until 1985.

+Eyles, Allen THE WORLD OF OZ: A FANTASTIC EXPEDITION OVER THE RAINBOW (HP Books 0-89586-415-0, 11/85 [11/85], $9.95, 8" x 10",96pp, pb) An affectionate look at the Land of Oz in book & film. The highlight of the book is the reprinting of numerous color illustrations and stills on slick paper--the reprints, in many cases, are better than the originals.

+Fairley, John & Simon Welfare ARTHUR C. CLARKE'S WORLD OF STRANGE POWERS (Putnam 0-399-13066-7, 09/85 [08/85], $19.95, 248pp, hc) Reprint (U.K. 1984), first U.S. edition. Non-fiction, book version of a tv series on strange phenomena, etc. Clarke wrote the foreword and epilogue. Listed for Clarke completists.

*Fantasy Book [v.4 #1, March 1985] Dennis Mallonee & Nick Smith, eds. (Fantasy Book Enterprises, 03/85 [01/85], $3.95, 64pp, pb) Contents: Page
The Dungeons of Ravan   Stephen Goldin   nv FBM Mar,85   2
The Elf Queen   Janice Law   nv FBM Mar,85   10
The Rune-Sword of Jotunheim
                        Glenn Rahman & Richard L. Tierney
                                           nv FBM Mar,85   17
Indistinguishable from Magic
                        Susan L. Fox-Davis vi FBM Mar,85   24
Ballad of the Rails   S.R. Daugherty   nv FBM Mar,85   26
Grandma's House   John Edward Damon pm FBM Mar,85   31
The Jester's Tale   Esther M. Friesner ss FBM Mar,85   32
Baikal   Mary Elizabeth Counselman
                                           pm FBM Mar,85   35
Small Red Cap   D.B. Rahtjen   ss FBM Mar,85   36
Windfall   Kristine K. Thompson nv FBM Mar,85 40
Harry Tales   Lee Nordling & Cheri Lane
                                           cs FBM Mar,85   46
Credibility Problem   Greg Cox   ss FBM Mar,85   47
Cartoons   Harry Nelson   ct FBM Mar,85   49
You Ain't Just Whistlin' Dixie
                        Scott Edelman   nv FBM Mar,85   50
Fantasy Game Reviews   Andrew M. Robinson   gr FBM   56
Fantasy Book Index, Volume 3
                        [Misc. Material]   ix FBM Mar,85   58
The Golden Fleece   Edouard Rene Lefebvre de Laboulaye
                                           nv HRP Apr,1868 59
     Translated by Mary L. Booth, introduction by Jessica
     Amanda Salmonson.

*Fantasy Book [v.4 #2, June 1985] Dennis Mallonee & Nick Smith, eds. (Fantasy Book Enterprises, 06/85 [04/85], $3.95, 64pp, pb) Contents: Page
The Sorceress of the Silvered Wood
                        Michael R. Collings pm FBM Jun,85 2
Black Eons   Robert E. Howard & Robert M. Price
                                           nv FBM Jun,85   3
The Seventh Dragon   Sheila Finch-Rayner ss FBM Jun,85 10
M'butu's God   Tom Smith   nv FBM Jun,85   14
Cartoon   Groginski   ct FBM Jun,85   23
Thunder Pigeon   Bruce J. Balfour   ss FBM Jun,85   24
Coming of Age in the City of the Goddess
                        Darrell Schweitzer nv FBM Jun,85   26
Fantasy Game Reviews   Barry Wilson   gr FBM   31
Burning Brand   Jefferson P. Swycaffer
                                           nv FBM Jun,85   32
A Kind of Death, With Wings
                        Ardath Mayhar   pm FBM Jun,85   39

The Planet   Anonymous   ss KNB Jul,1853 42
     Introduction by Darrell Schweitzer.
A Story Whose Name Is Forgot
                        Mark Baker   nv FBM Jun,85   46
The Monk's Tale   Esther M. Friesner ss FBM Jun,85   50
The Running Back from Yuggoth
                        William R. Trotter nv FBM Jun,85   53
The Death of Nimue   Esther M. Friesner ss FBM Jun,85   59
The Black Dwarf   Gerald Friedlander nv JWSHFYT,18   61
     Introduction by Jessica Amanda Salmonson.

*Fantasy Book [v.4 #3, September 1985] Dennis Mallonee & Nick Smith, eds. (Fantasy Book Enterprises, 09/85 [07/85], $3.95, 64pp, pb)
Contents: Page
Satan's Hook   Jefferson P. Swycaffer
                                           nv FBM Sep,85   2
The Weird of Mazal   John Gregory Betancourt
                                           ss FBM Sep,85   13
The Castle of the Sparrowhawk
                        Harry Turtledove   ss FBM Sep,85   16
The Dark at the End of the Tunnel
                        Richard Mueller   nv FBM Sep,85   20
Changes   Josepha Sherman   nv FBM Sep,85   26
The Vixen   Lee Adkins   pm FBM Sep,85   32
Requiem   Kristine K. Thompson nv FBM Sep,85 34
Wolf Song   Lee Barwood   nv FBM Sep,85   40
Chivalry   Esther M. Friesner pm FBM Sep,85   48
Turnabout   Mercedes Lackey   nv FBM Sep,85   50
Editorial   Dennis Mallonee   ed FBM Sep,85   58
In the Frozen Zoo for Extinct Beasts
                        Robert Frazier   pm FBM Sep,85   58
Fantasy Game Reviews   Nick Smith   gr FBM   59
Inside Man   Horace L. Gold   ss GAL Oct,65   61

*Fantasy Book [v.4 #4, December 1985] Dennis Mallonee & Nick Smith, eds. (Fantasy Book Enterprises, 12/85 [11/85], $3.95, 64pp, pb)
Contents: Page
Billingsgate Molly   Esther M. Friesner nv FBM Dec,85   2
Editorial   Nick Smith   ed FBM Dec,85   7
A Spell in Time   Sansoucy Kathenor nv FBM Dec,85   8
Incantation   Jim Neal   pm FBM Dec,85   18
Like Shytt!   Jefferson P. Swycaffer
                                           ss FBM Dec,85   20
The Shaper of Butterflies
                        Diana L. Paxson   nv FBM Dec,85   22
Three Centaur Tales   Richard A. Lupoff ss FBM Dec,85   29
The Mermaid Barnacle   Robert Frazier   pm FBM Dec,85   31
The Rape   Terri E. Pinckard vi FBM Dec,85   32
The Sad Wizard   John T. Aquino   nv FBM Dec,85   34
The Bride   Denise Dumars   ss FBM Dec,85   40
Fantasy Game Reviews   Andrew M. Robinson   gr FBM   43
Biofeedbach   Charles L. Harness ss FBM Dec,85   46
Faramigon's Eye   John Gregory Betancourt
                                           nv FBM Dec,85   50
Wings   Mary Elizabeth Counselman
                                           ss FBM Dec,85   55
A Haunted Tale of Justice
                        Jessica Amanda Salmonson
                                           ss FBM Dec,85   58
The Vampire of Gretna Green
                        Esther M. Friesner pm FBM Dec,85   61
The Nasty Naughty Nazi Ninja Nudnik Elves
                        Joshua Quagmire   cs FBM Dec,85   62

*Fantasy Tales [v.7 #14, Summer 1985] Stephen Jones, ed. (Steph- en Jones, 07/85 [07/85], 90p + 18p p&p, 56pp, pb)
Contents: Page
The Sneering   Ramsey Campbell   ss FTL Sum,85   2
The Pushover   Ardath Mayhar   ss FTL Sum,85   12
Yuggoth   David Cowperthwaite pm FTL Sum,85 17
The Castle at World's End
                        Chris Naylor   ss FTL Sum,85   18
House of Ill Repute   Jeffrey Goddin   ss FTL Sum,85   24
The Forbidden   Clive Barker   nv CBB V 5,85   28
Other Side   C. Bruce Hunter   vi MSM Nov,82   52

*Farmer, Philip José DAYWORLD (Putnam 0-399-12967-7, 02/85 [01/85], $16.95, 320pp, hc) Sf novel, start of a new series. This is set in the same universe as "The Sliced Crosswise Only on Tuesday World" but is not otherwise connected. It's Farmer's best book in years. Recommended. (CNB)

Farmer, Philip José DAYWORLD (SFBC #2548, 09/85 [08/85], $6.98, 248pp, hc) Reprint (Putnam 1985) sf novel.

Farmer, Philip José GODS OF RIVERWORLD (Berkley 0-425-07322-X, 01/85 [12/84], $3.50, 331pp, pb) Reprint (Putnam 1983) sf novel, in the "Riverworld" series.

Farmer, Philip José IMAGE OF THE BEAST (Berkley 0-425-07708-X, 06/85 [05/85], $3.50, 336pp, pb) Reprint (Playboy 1979) erotic fantasy novel. Omnibus edition of IMAGE OF THE BEAST (Essex House 1968) and BLOWN (Essex House 1969) run together as one novel. The original Sturgeon afterword has become a foreword.

Farmer, Philip José KEEPERS OF THE SECRETS (Severn House 0-7278- 1140-1, 1985 [10/85], £7.95, 152pp, hc) Reprint (Ace 1970 as THE MAD GOBLIN) sf novel of James Caliban, MD, battling The Nine; sequel to THE LORD OF THE TREES. First hardcover edition.

FARMER, PHILIP JOSÉ

Farmer, Philip José THE LAVALITE WORLD (Berkley 0-425-07515-X, 02/85 [01/85], $2.75, 282pp, pb) Reprint (Ace 1977) sf novel. "World of Tiers" #5.

Farmer, Philip José TIME'S LAST GIFT (Tor 0-812-53764-5, 03/85 [02/85], $2.95, 352pp, pb) Reprint (Ballantine 1972; revised ed. Ballantine 1977) sf novel. This edition follows the 1977 revised text.

Farmer, Philip José TRAITOR TO THE LIVING (Tor 0-812-53766-1, 01/85 [12/84], $2.95, 286pp, pb) Reprint (Ballantine 1973) sf novel.

Farmer, Philip José TWO HAWKS FROM EARTH (Berkley 0-425-08092-7, 07/85 [06/85], $2.95, 311pp, pb) Reprint (Ace 1979) sf novel. A rewritten and expanded version of THE GATE OF TIME (Belmont 1966). A modern man on a primitive parallel earth.

+Farren, Mick PROTECTORATE (Ace 0-441-68680-X, 01/85 [12/84], $2.75, 250pp, pb) Reprint (U.K. 1984) sf novel. First U.S. edition.

Farris, John THE FURY (Tor 0-812-58262-4, 12/85 [11/85], $3.50, 349pp, pb) Reprint (Dell 1976) horror novel. A movie was made from the book.

Feist, Raymond E. MAGICIAN: APPRENTICE (Bantam Spectra 0-553-25575-4, 01/86 [12/85], $3.50, 323pp, pb) Reprint (Doubleday 1982, as MAGICIAN) fantasy novel. This is only the first half of the Doubleday book, which is being split in two. There are also two sequels to come.

*Feist, Raymond E. SILVERTHORN (Doubleday 0-385-19210-X, 06/85 [05/85], $15.95, 352pp, hc) Fantasy novel, sequel to MAGICIAN; second in the "Riftwar" trilogy.

Feist, Raymond E. SILVERTHORN (SFBC #04727, 09/85 [08/85], $6.98, 309pp, hc) Reprint (Doubleday 1985) fantasy novel, sequel to MAGICIAN.

*Felice, Cynthia DOWNTIME (Bluejay 0-312-94115-3, 08/85 [07/85], $15.95, 246pp, hc) Sf novel.

*Ferrell, Keith GEORGE ORWELL: THE POLITICAL PEN (Evans 0-87131-444-4, 04/85 [03/85], $11.95, 180pp, hc) Biography written "for young readers," covering Orwell's life and works, with an epilogue on 1984 and 1984.

*Finch, Sheila INFINITY'S WEB (Bantam Spectra 0-553-25251-8, 09/85 [08/85], $2.95, 230pp, pb) Sf novel, a first novel.

+Findley, Timothy NOT WANTED ON THE VOYAGE (Delacorte 0-385-29415-8, 09/85 [08/85], $17.95, 352pp, hc) Reprint (Penguin Books--Canada 1984), first U.S. edition. Fantasy novel of Noah and the Flood. Funny, poignant, eccentric. Recommended. (FCM)

Finney, Jack TIME AND AGAIN (S&S/Fireside 0-671-24295-4, 01/86 [12/85], $9.95, 397pp, pb) Reissue (Simon & Schuster 1970) fantasy novel.

Fisher, Paul R. MONT CANT GOLD (Ace/Tempo 0-441-53602-6, 02/85 [01/85], $2.25, 209pp, pb) Reprint (Atheneum 1981) young-adult fantasy novel.

*Fitzpatrick, Jim ERINSAGA: THE MYTHOLOGICAL PAINTINGS OF JIM FITZPATRICK (De Danann 0-904745-04-X, 11/85 [11/85], £9.95, 111pp, pb) Art book with an introduction by Andrew M. Greeley, featuring Fitzpatrick's unique blend of Celtic, Art Nouveau, and comic-book graphics. Available from the exclusive American distributor, Bud Plant, Inc. The release with the book does not give a U.S. price.

*Fleming, Robert Loren & Keith Giffen HELL ON EARTH Main listing under Keith Giffen.

*Fletcher, Jo & Stephen Jones, eds. Fantasycon X Programme Booklet Main listing under Stephen Jones.

*Flint, Kenneth C. MASTER OF THE SIDHE (Bantam Spectra 0-553-25261-5, 09/85 [08/85], $2.95, 248pp, pb) Fantasy novel, conclusion of a trilogy.

Flint, Kenneth C. A STORM UPON ULSTER (Bantam 0-553-24710-7, 03/85 [02/85], $3.50, 309pp, pb) Reissue (Bantam 1981) fantasy novel.

*Flynn, John L. FUTURE THREADS: COSTUME DESIGN FOR THE SCIENCE FICTION WORLD (New Media no ISBN, 07/85 [06/85], $9.95, 80pp, pb) Media-oriented book for costumers; mostly STAR TREK. There is also supposed to be a hardcover edition for $19.95, but we have not seen it.

*Foglio, Phil & Robert Lynn Asprin MYTH ADVENTURES ONE Main listing under Robert Lynn Asprin.

Fonstad, Karen Wynn THE ATLAS OF PERN (SFBC #3911, 04/85 [03/85], $9.98, 169pp, hc) Reprint (Ballantine 1984); non-fiction; reference book with maps and descriptions from Anne McCaffrey's "Pern" series.

*Fonstad, Karen Wynn THE ATLAS OF THE LAND (Ballantine 0-345-31431-X, 10/85 [10/85], $19.95, 201pp, hc) Non-fiction; reference book with maps and descriptions of The Land, setting of Stephen R. Donaldson's "Covenant" novels.

*Fonstad, Karen Wynn THE ATLAS OF THE LAND (Ballantine/Del Rey 0-345-31433-6, 10/85 [10/85], $9.95, 201pp, pb) Trade paperback of the above.

*Forbes, Caroline THE NEEDLE ON FULL: LESBIAN FEMINIST SCIENCE FICTION (Onlywomen 0-906500-19-2, 1985 [09/85], £3.95/$7.95, 267pp, pb) Collection of 9 stories from a "radical feminist and lesbian" publisher. The U.S. distributor is Inland Book Co.
Contents:

			Page
The Needle on Full	Caroline Forbes	nv CYC 1980	9
Snake	Caroline Forbes	ss SPN V1 #2,80	38
Marianna and the Graduation			
	Caroline Forbes	ss REACH ,84	45
The Visitors	Caroline Forbes	ss NEDLFUL,85	64
Transplant	Caroline Forbes	vi CYC 1980	76
London Fields	Caroline Forbes	na NEDLFUL,85	78
Equal Rights	Caroline Forbes	ss NEDLFUL,85	152
Night Life	Caroline Forbes	ss NEDLFUL,85	155
The Comet's Tail	Caroline Forbes	na NEDLFUL,85	168

Ford, John M. THE DRAGON WAITING (Avon 0-380-69887-0, 03/85 [02/85], $3.50, 383pp, pb) Reprint (Timescape 1983) alternate-world fantasy novel. It won the 1984 World Fantasy Award. Recommended. (CNB)

*Forrester, John BESTIARY MOUNTAIN (Bradbury Press 0-02-735530-6, 10/85 [11/85], $11.95, 140pp, hc) Young-adult sf novel, first in the "Bestiary Trilogy"; a first novel. Four teenagers from the moon return to a ravaged Earth.

*Forstchen, William R. A DARKNESS UPON THE ICE (Ballantine/Del Rey 0-345-31682-7, 03/85 [02/85], $2.95, 275pp, pb) Sf novel, conclusion of the "Ice Prophet" trilogy.

Forstchen, William R. THE FLAME UPON THE ICE (Ballantine/Del Rey 0-345-31137-X, 03/85 [02/85], $2.95, 279pp, pb) Reissue (Ballantine/Del Rey 1984) sf novel, second in the "Ice Prophet" trilogy.

Forward, Robert L. THE FLIGHT OF THE DRAGONFLY (Baen 0-671-55937-0, 03/85 [02/85], $3.50, 376pp, pb) Reprint (Timescape 1984) sf novel.

*Forward, Robert L. STARQUAKE (Ballantine/Del Rey 0-345-31232-5, 10/85 [09/85], $14.95, 326pp, hc) Sf novel, a sequel to DRAGON'S EGG.

Foster, Alan Dean THE MAN WHO USED THE UNIVERSE (Warner 0-446-32819-7, 07/85 [06/85], $2.95, 316pp, pb) Reissue (SFBC 1983) sf novel.

Foster, Alan Dean THE MOMENT OF THE MAGICIAN (Warner 0-446-32326-8, 03/85 [02/85], $2.95, 312pp, pb) Reprint (Phantasia 1984) fantasy novel, #4 in the "Spellsinger" series (or #3, going by the hardcovers).

*Foster, Alan Dean THE PATHS OF THE PERAMBULATOR (Phantasia 0-932096-39-5, 11/85 [11/85], $40.00 signed, boxed limited edition of 300, $17.00 for 1200 copy trade edition, 204pp) Humorous fantasy novel, "Spellsinger" #5 (or #4 if you're going by the hardcovers, where the first two books appeared in one volume).

*Foster, Alan Dean SEASON OF THE SPELLSONG (SFBC #01827, 11/85 [12/85], $8.50, 730pp, hc) Omnibus edition of the first books in the "Spellsinger" series.
Contents:

			Page
SPELLSINGER	Alan Dean Foster	n. WBK 1983	
THE HOUR OF THE GATE	Alan Dean Foster	n. WBK 1984	
THE DAY OF THE DISSONANCE			
	Alan Dean Foster	n. WBK 1984	

*Foster, Alan Dean SENTENCED TO PRISM (Ballantine/Del Rey 0-345-31980-X, 09/85 [08/85], $3.50, 273pp, pb) Sf novel, part of the "Commonwealth" series.

Foster, Alan Dean STARMAN (Corgi 0-552-12688-8, 07/85 [06/85], £1.95, 192pp, pb) Reprint (Warner 1984) sf novel, a novelization of the film script by Bruce A. Evans & Raynold Gideon. First British edition.

Foster, M.A. THE DAY OF THE KLESH (DAW 0-88677-016-5, 01/85 [12/84], $2.95, 271pp, pb) Reissue (DAW 1978) sf novel, conclusion of the trilogy. 3rd printing.

Foster, M.A. THE GAMEPLAYERS OF ZAN (DAW 0-87997-993-3, 01/85 [12/84], $3.95, 445pp, pb) Reissue (DAW 1977) sf novel, part of a loosely connected trilogy which started with THE WARRIORS OF DAWN. Recommended! (FCM) 8th printing.

Foster, M.A. THE MORPHODITE (DAW 0-88677-017-3, 01/85 [12/84], $2.95, 255pp, pb) Reissue (DAW 1981) sf novel, first in a series. 3rd printing.

*Foster, M.A. OWL TIME (DAW 0-87797-992-5, 01/85 [12/84], $2.95, 251pp, pb) Collection of four novellas written in four different styles.
Contents:

			Page
Preface	M.A. Foster	pr	9

The Man Who Loved Owls	M.A. Foster		na	OWLTIME,85	11
Leanne	M.A. Foster		na	OWLTIME,85	59
The Conversation	M.A. Foster		na	OWLTIME,85	95
Entertainment	M.A. Foster		na	NWV # 4,81	151

*Foster, M.A. PRESERVER (DAW 0-88677-095-5, 11/85 [10/85], $2.95, 253pp, pb) Sf novel, conclusion of the "Morphodite" trilogy.

Foster, M.A. THE WARRIORS OF DAWN (DAW 0-87997-994-1, 1984 [12/84], $3.25, 303pp, pb) Reissue (DAW 1975) sf novel, first in a fine trilogy. (FCM) 8th printing.

*Fowles, John A MAGGOT (Little, Brown 0-316-28994-9, 09/85 [09/85], $19.95, length not known, hc) This novel is billed as "part detective story, part science fiction, part gothic horror tale"; it takes place in the 18th century. A limited special edition is available for $100.00, 0-316-29115-3; there's also a simultaneous British edition from Cape.

*Frakes, Randal & Bill Wisher THE TERMINATOR (Bantam 0-553-25317-4, 11/85 [09/85], $2.95, 240pp, pb) Novelization of the sf movie, based on the screenplay by James Cameron and Gale Anne Hurd. The British novelization, by another author, is completely different.

*Franson, Donald & Howard DeVore A HISTORY OF THE HUGO, NEBULA, AND INTERNATIONAL FANTASY AWARDS, Updated Edition (Misfit no ISBN, 01/85 [12/84], $6.00 postpaid, 185pp, pb) This edition, which covers 1984 and earlier awards, has a 1985 copyright on the inside cover, a 1981 copyright on the title page, but is actually a 1984 book.

*Frazetta, Frank FRANK FRAZETTA: BOOK FIVE (Bantam 0-553-34175-8, 06/85 [05/85], $12.95, 95pp, pb) Art book with color and black and white work.

*Freddi, Cris THE ELDER (Knopf 0-394-53914-1, 09/85 [08/85], $16.95, 323pp, hc) Novel set in a world where the Elders have absolute power over the young; the hero rebels. A first novel.

*Frenkel, Karen A. & Isaac Asimov ROBOTS: MACHINES IN MAN'S IMAGE Main listing under Isaac Asimov.

*Friedman, Michael Jan THE HAMMER AND THE HORN (Popular Library/Questar 0-445-20028-6, 06/85 [05/85], $2.95, 297pp, pb) Fantasy novel, a first novel. Entertaining retellings and embellishments of Norse mythology. (DLN)

*Friedman, Michael Jan THE SEEKERS AND THE SWORD (Popular Library/Questar 0-445-20139-8, 12/85 [11/85], $2.95, 263pp, pb) Fantasy novel starring Vidar Jawbreaker, son of Odin.

*Friends of Darkover, The & Marion Zimmer Bradley FREE AMAZONS OF DARKOVER Main listing under Marion Zimmer Bradley.

*Friesner, Esther M. MUSTAPHA AND HIS WISE DOG (Avon 0-380-89676-1, 07/85 [06/85], $2.95, 175pp, pb) Fantasy novel, a first novel.

Frith, Nigel KRISHNA (Allen & Unwin/Unicorn 0-04-823283-1, 05/85 [04/85], £2.95, 238pp, pb) Reprint (Sheldon 1975 as THE LEGEND OF KRISHNA) fantasy novel.

*Frost, Jason THE WARLORD #5: TERMINAL ISLAND (Zebra 0-8217-1697-2, 11/85 [11/85], $2.50, 235pp, pb) Sf adventure novel in a post-holocaust series.

*Gaiman, Neil & Kim Newman GHASTLY BEYOND BELIEF (Arrow 0-09-936830-7, 06/85 [05/85], £2.50, 344pp, pb) Non-fiction; both a reference and a humor book. This is a compilation of awful excerpts, hilarious blunders, rare moments of intentional humor, and quotes by and about sf authors, filmmakers, etc. Enough to reduce the sternest reader to helpless laughter, this is a comic gem. Highly recommended. (FCM)

*Gallagher, Edward J. THE ANNOTATED GUIDE TO FANTASTIC ADVENTURES (Starmont 0-916732-70-3, 05/85 [04/85], $9.95, 170pp, pb) Non-fiction, reference. Has a chronological listing of each of the 843 stories published in the pulp *Fantastic Adventures* (1939 to 1953) with a summary of each plus the usual indexes, etc.

*Gallun, Raymond Z. BIOBLAST (Berkley 0-425-08185-0, 10/85 [09/85], $2.95, 236pp, pb) Sf novel. "Was he superman or super-monster?"

+Gardiner, Judy, Mark Ronson & Stella Whitelaw GRIMALKIN'S TALES Main listing under Stella Whitelaw.

Gardner, John GRENDEL (Vintage 0-394-74056-4, 10/85 [09/85], $3.95, 152pp, pb) Reprint (Knopf 1971) fantasy novel, retelling BEOWULF from the monster's point of view. Recommended. (FCM)

Gardner, John MIKKELSSON'S GHOSTS (Vintage 0-394-72938-2, 05/85 [04/85], $6.95, 590pp, pb) Reprint (Knopf 1982) fantasy novel.

+Garner, Alan ALAN GARNER'S BOOK OF BRITISH FAIRY TALES (Delacorte 0-385-29425-5, 10/85 [10/85], $16.95, 160pp, hc) Reprint (Collins 1984), first U.S. edition. Garner's retelling of 21 fairy tales, with woodcut illustrations by Derek Collard.

*Garrett, Randall & Vicki Ann Heydron RETURN TO EDDARTA (Bantam 0-553-24709-3, 03/85 [02/85], $2.75, 150pp, pb) Fantasy novel, #6 in the "Gandalara" series. Although Garrett outlined the beginning of the series, it's now written entirely by his wife.

Gaskell, Jane ATLAN (DAW 0-88677-049-1, 06/85 [05/85], $3.50, 334pp, pb) Reprint (Hodder 1965) fantasy novel, #3 in the "Atlan Saga".

Gaskell, Jane THE CITY (DAW 0-88677-085-8, 10/85 [09/85], $3.50, 276pp, pb) Reprint (Hodder & Stoughton 1966) fantasy novel, "Atlan" #4.

Gaskell, Jane THE DRAGON (DAW 0-88677-021-1, 03/85 [02/85], $2.95, 240pp, pb) Reprint (St. Martin's 1977) of the second half of THE SERPENT (Hodder 1963), now the second book in the "Atlan" fantasy saga.

Gaskell, Jane THE SERPENT (DAW 0-87997-990-9, 01/85 [12/84], $2.95, 320pp, pb) Reprint (St. Martins 1977) fantasy novel, the first half of THE SERPENT (Hodder 1963), now the first book in the "Atlan" saga.

Gearhart, Sally Miller THE WANDERGROUND (Women's Press 0-7043-3947-1, 06/85 [05/85], £1.95, 212pp, pb) Reprint (Persephone 1980) feminist sf novel.

*Gemmell, David THE KING BEYOND THE GATE (Century 0-7126-0871-0, 08/85 [10/85], £9.95, 309pp, hc) Heroic fantasy novel, set in the same world as LEGEND.

Gentle, Mary GOLDEN WITCHBREED (SFBC #1763, 03/85 [02/85], $5.98, 429pp, hc) Reprint (Gollancz 1983) sf novel.

Gentle, Mary GOLDEN WITCHBREED (NAL/Signet 0-451-13606-3, 06/85 [05/85], $3.95, 495pp, pb) Reprint (Gollancz 1983) sf novel.

+Gentle, Mary A HAWK IN SILVER (Morrow/Lothrop Lee & Shepard 0-688-04213-9, 05/85 [04/85], $10.95 FPT, 237pp, hc) Reprint (Gollancz 1977), first U.S. edition of a young-adult fantasy novel written when Mary Gentle was 18.

Gerrold, David A DAY FOR DAMNATION: VOLUME 2 OF THE WAR AGAINST THE CHTORR (Pocket 0-671-45121-9, 03/85 [02/85], $3.95, 382pp, pb) Reprint (Timescape 1984) sf novel.

*Gerrold, David & Barry B. Longyear ENEMY MINE Main listing under Barry B. Longyear.

Gibson, William NEUROMANCER (Ace 0-441-56958-7, 08/85 [10/85], $2.95, 271pp, pb) Reissue (Ace 1984) award-winning sf novel; 4th printing. This won the Hugo, Nebula, and Philip K. Dick awards for best novel of 1984.

*Giffen, Keith & Robert Loren Fleming HELL ON EARTH (DC Comics 0-9320289-05-6, 09/85 [09/85], $5.95, 48pp, pb) Graphic story adaptation of a Robert Bloch story from the March 1942 issue of *Weird Tales*.

*Gilliland, Alexis WHO SAYS PARANOIA ISN'T "IN" ANY MORE? (Loompanics Unlimited 0-915179-21-0, 03/85 [02/85], $5.95, unpaginated, pb) Gilliland's second collection of cartoons.

Gilman, Robert Cham THE REBEL OF RHADA (Ace 0-441-71068-9, 01/86 [12/85], $2.95, 184pp, pb) Reissue (Harcourt Brace World 1968) sf novel, #2 in the "Rhada" series; it used to be #1. Gilman is a pen name for Alfred Coppel.

*Gilman, Robert Cham THE WARLOCK OF RHADA (Ace 0-441-87310-3, 10/85 [09/85], $2.75, 172pp, pb) This seems to be an unpublished prequel to the "Rhada" trilogy, a space adventure series written by Alfred Coppel before he became a Big-Time author. The other three were published 1968-1970. This one reads about the same and is probably an older Coppel manuscript.

*Gilmour, William THE UNDYING LAND (Donald M. Grant 0-937986-62-3, 10/85 [10/85], $20.00, 208pp, hc) Novel of fantastic adventure, with a pulp-style swashbuckler in a lost kingdom somewhere in Africa. It's new, but written as if it were from a 1920's *Adventure* magazine. llustrations by Kevin Johnson.

*Gipe, George BACK TO THE FUTURE (Berkley 0-425-08205-9, 07/85 [06/85], $2.95, 248pp, pb) Novelization of the Spielberg movie, from a screenplay by Robert Zemeckis & Bob Gale.

*Giroux, Leo, Jr. THE RISHI (Evans 0-87131-463-0, 09/85 [09/85], $16.95, 355pp, hc) Fantasy/horror adventure novel of the revival of the Indian cult of Thuggee, and the acts of dark gods. A first novel.

Godwin, Parke BELOVED EXILE (Bantam Spectra 0-553-24924-X, 06/85 [05/85], $3.95, 437pp, pb) Reprint (Bantam 1984) Arthurian novel, sequel to FIRELORD.

Godwin, Parke FIRELORD (Bantam Spectra 0-553-25269-0, 06/85 [05/85], $3.95, 369pp, pb) Reissue (Doubleday 1970) realistic Arthurian novel. 3rd printing.

*Godwin, Parke THE LAST RAINBOW (Bantam 0-553-34142-1, 07/85 [06/85], $7.95, 358pp, pb) Fantasy historical novel featuring St. Patrick and a woman of Faerie.

GODWIN, PARKE & MARVIN KAYE

Godwin, Parke & Marvin Kaye THE MASTERS OF SOLITUDE Main listing under Marvin Kaye.

*Goldin, Stephen & E.E. "Doc" Smith REVOLT OF THE GALAXY Main listing under E.E. "Doc" Smith.

Goldman, William THE SILENT GONDOLIERS: A FABLE BY S. MORGENSTERN (Ballantine/Del Rey 0-345-32583-4, 12/85 [11/85], $3.50, 110pp, pb) Reprint (Del Rey 1983) fantasy fable with illustrations by Paul Giovanopoulos. This is the first time Goldman's name has appeared on the jacket.

*Goldstein, Lisa THE DREAM YEARS (Bantam Spectra 0-553-05090-7, 08/85 [07/85], $13.95, 181pp, hc) Fantasy novel of time travel, the Surrealist movement, and revolution. Beautifully crafted, superbly structured. One of the best novels of 1985. (DLN)

*Goodwin, Michael & Robert Teague A GUIDE TO THE COMMONWEALTH: THE OFFICIAL GUIDE TO ALAN DEAN FOSTER'S HUMANX COMMONWEALTH UNIVERSE Main listing under Robert Teague.

Gotlieb, Phyllis EMPEROR, SWORDS, PENTACLES (Ace 0-441-20547-X, 05/85 [04/85], $2.95, 299pp, pb) Reissue (Ace 1982) sf novel in the "Khreng and Prandra" series. Third Ace printing.

Gotlieb, Phyllis A JUDGEMENT OF DRAGONS (Ace 0-441-42032-X, 03/85 [02/85], $2.95, 263pp, pb) Reprint (Berkley 1980) collection of four stories starring sentient cats. First book in a trilogy.

*Gotlieb, Phyllis THE KINGDOM OF CATS (Ace 0-441-44453-9, 07/85 [06/85], $2.95, 284pp, pb) Sf novel, third in the "Ungruwarkh" trilogy. This tour-de-force underscores Gotlieb's much-underestimated talent - a complex, demanding and rewarding book. Not to be missed. (DLN)

Goulart, Ron AFTER THINGS FELL APART (Berkley 0-425-07647-4, 04/85 [03/85], $2.75, 189pp, pb) Reprint (Ace 1977) satiric sf novel.

*Goulart, Ron BRAINZ, INC. (DAW 0-88677-042-4, 05/85 [04/85], $2.75, 205pp, pb) Sf novel. Part of the "Odd Jobs, Inc." series.

*Goulart, Ron SUICIDE, INC. (Berkley 0-425-07586-9, 03/85 [02/85], $2.75, 156pp, pb) Sf novel.

*Grant, Charles L. THE TEA PARTY (Pocket 0-671-50522-X, 05/85 [04/85], $3.50, 312pp, pb) Horror novel.

*Grant, Charles L., ed. GREYSTONE BAY (Tor 0-812-51852-7, 10/85 [09/85], $2.95, 271pp, pb) Original anthology of connected stories, all set in "the city horror calls its own." This book is The First Chronicles.
Contents:

			Page
Prologue	Charles L. Grant	pr GRYSTBY,85	1
Croome House	Reginald Bretnor	nv GRYSTBY,85	8
Used Books	Robert E. Vardeman	ss GRYSTBY,85	29
Street Life	Douglas E. Winter	ss GRYSTBY,85	40
Something in a Song	Galad Elflandsson	ss GRYSTBY,85	55
Hiding From the Sun	Nina Kiriki Hoffman	ss GRYSTBY,85	67
Memory and Desire	Alan Ryan	nv GRYSTBY,85	74
The Red House	Robert R. McCammon	nv GRYSTBY,85	117
Night Catch	Chelsea Quinn Yarbro	nv GRYSTBY,85	140
Nocturne	Robert Bloch	ss GRYSTBY,85	165
A Heritage Upheld	Joseph Payne Brennan	nv GRYSTBY,85	173
The Only	Al Sarrantonio	ss GRYSTBY,85	212
The Disintegration of Alan			
	Melissa Mia Hall	ss GRYSTBY,85	227
In a Guest House	Steve Rasnic Tem	ss GRYSTBY,85	233
Power	Kathryn Ptacek	nv GRYSTBY,85	247
Chroniclers	[Misc. Material]	bg	272

*Grant, Charles L., ed. MIDNIGHT (Tor 0-812-51850-0, 02/85 [01/85], $2.95, 284pp, pb) Anthology of dark fantasy. Many of the stories are originals.
Contents:

			Page
Introduction	Charles L. Grant	in	7
Old Cloths	Ramsey Campbell	ss MIDNGHT,85	9
Road to Granville	Joseph Payne Brennan	ss MIDNGHT,85	23
The Visitor	Leanne Frahm	ss MIDNGHT,85	40
Sweets to the Sweet	Robert Bloch	ss WRT Mar,47	47
Masks	Douglas E. Winter	ss MIDNGHT,85	59
The Fly-by-Night	R. Chetwynd-Hayes	nv MNSTRCL,75	75
The Extension	Thomas Sullivan	ss MIDNGHT,85	99
The Sacrifice	Julie Stevens	ss MIDNGHT,85	108
The Spot	Dennis Etchison & Mark Johnson		
		ss NWT # 1,80	116
Overnight Guest	Craig Shaw Gardner	ss MIDNGHT,85	135
Intimately, With Rain	Janet Fox	ss CLG Nov,78	148
Spring Fever	Susan Casper	ss MIDNGHT,85	157
Pictures of a Woman Gone	Leslie Ann Horvitz	nv MIDNGHT,85	169
The Green Man	Kelvin Jones	ss FTL V7 #12,83	201
Ceremony	William F. Nolan	nv MIDNGHT,85	214
Of Memories Dying	Michael Bracken	ss MIDNGHT,85	237
A Tapestry of Little Murders			
	Michael Bishop	ss FSF Jun,71	244
No Other Gods	Reginald Bretnor	nv MIDNGHT,85	261

*Grant, Charles L., ed. NIGHT VISIONS 2 (Dark Harvest 0-913165-06-9, 10/85 [10/85], $45.00 signed, boxed numbered edition of 300; $18.00 trade edition, 327pp, hc) Original anthology of work by David Morrell, Joseph Payne Brennan, and Karl Edward Wagner,

with illustrations by Robert W. Lavoie.
Contents:

			Page
Introduction	Charles L. Grant	in	11
Black and White and Red All Over			
	David Morrell	nv NGV # 2,85	19
Mumbo Jumbo	David Morrell	nv NGV # 2,85	41
Dead Image	David Morrell	nv NGV # 2,85	79
Wanderson's Waste	Joseph Payne Brennan	nv NGV # 2,85	119
Pick-Up	Joseph Payne Brennan	ss NGV # 2,85	139
Canavan Calling	Joseph Payne Brennan	ss NGV # 2,85	145
Oasis of Abomination	Joseph Payne Brennan	nv NGV # 2,85	161
Starlock Street	Joseph Payne Brennan	ss NGV # 2,85	187
The Haunting at Juniper Hill			
	Joseph Payne Brennan	nv NGV # 2,85	201
Shrapnel	Karl Edward Wagner	ss NGV # 2,85	233
Old Loves	Karl Edward Wagner	ss NGV # 2,85	245
Blue Lady, Come Back	Karl Edward Wagner	na NGV # 2,85	263

Grant, Charles L., ed. SHADOWS 3 (Berkley 0-425-07453-6, 01/85 [12/84], $2.95, 211pp, pb) Reprint (Doubleday 1980) original anthology of dark fantasy.

Grant, Charles L., ed. SHADOWS 4 (Berkley 0-425-07650-4, 04/85 [03/85], $2.95, 216pp, pb) Reprint (Doubleday 1981) original horror anthology.

*Grant, Charles L., ed. SHADOWS 8 (Doubleday 0-385-19823-X, 10/85 [10/85], $12.95, 191pp, hc) Original anthology with 17 tales of dark fantasy and horror.
Contents:

			Page
Introduction	Charles L. Grant	in	7
Everything's Going to Bee All Right			
	Gene DeWeese	ss SDW # 8,85	13
Cycles	Kim Antieau	ss SDW # 8,85	21
The Tuckahoe	Nancy Etchemendy	ss SDW # 8,85	27
Between the Windows of the Sea			
	Jack Dann	ss SDW # 8,85	37
The Battering	Steve Rasnic Tem	ss SDW # 8,85	51
The Shadow of a Hawk	Nina Kiriki Hoffman	ss SDW # 8,85	63
Toy	Bill Pronzini	ss SDW # 8,85	67
The Pooka	Peter Tremayre	ss SDW # 8,85	73
The Man Who Loved Water	Craig Shaw Gardner	ss SDW # 8,85	91
Blood Gothic	Nancy Jones Holder	ss SDW # 8,85	99
Sand	Alan Ryan	ss SDW # 8,85	105
The Blue Man	Terry L. Parkinson	ss SDW # 8,85	119
A Demon in Rosewood	Sharon Webb	ss SDW # 8,85	127
Wish	Al Sarrantonio	ss SDW # 8,85	137
The Blind Man	Jessica Amanda Salmonson		
		ss SDW # 8,85	145
A Night at the Head of a Grave			
	Thomas Sullivan	ss SDW # 8,85	149
Do I Dare to Eat a Peach?			
	Chelsea Quinn Yarbro	nv SDW # 8,85	159

*Grant, Richard SARABAND OF LOST TIME (Avon 0-380-89533-1, 02/85 [01/85], $2.95, 327pp, pb) Far-future sf novel. A first novel. Very promising despite some flaws. Recommended. (FCM)

*Gray, Alasdair THE FALL OF KEVIN WALKER (Canongate 0-86241-072-X, 09/85 [08/85], £7.95, 144pp, hc) Gray's new novel (or novella) is mainstream, not sf or fantasy, and we list it for his fans. It's an enjoyable fable of an eccentric young Scotsman storming London in the sixties -- more straightforward than previous Gray, but with a sharp satiric bite and fine characterization. (FCM).

Gray, Alasdair LANARK: A LIFE IN 4 BOOKS (Braziller 0-8076-1108-5, 04/85 [03/85], $20.00, 561pp, hc) Reprint (Canongate 1981), the first hardcover edition to appear in the U.S. An excellent novel blending fantasy with mainstream -- this won a British award. Recommended. (FCM)

Gray, Alasdair LANARK: A LIFE IN 4 BOOKS (Canongate 0-903937-74-3, 06/85 [05/85], £15.00, 561pp, hc) Reprint (Canongate 1981) literary/allegorical fantasy novel; this is billed as the "definitive" edition, and is numbered and signed by the author.

Greeley, Andrew M. THE MAGIC CUP (Warner 0-446-32438-8, 01/85 [12/84], $3.50, 296pp, pb) Reprint (McGraw Hill 1979) fantasy novel of medieval Ireland.

*Green, Jen & Sarah Lefanu, eds. DESPATCHES FROM THE FRONTIERS OF THE FEMALE MIND (Women's Press 0-7043-3973-0, 09/85 [10/85], £2.50, 248pp, pb) Original anthology with sf stories by Tanith Lee, Raccoona Sheldon, Mary Gentle, Josephine Saxton, and others.
Contents:

			Page
Introduction	Jen Green & Sarah Lefanu	in	1
Big Operation on Altair Three			
	Josephine Saxton	ss DSPTCHS,85	9
Spinning the Green	Margaret Elphinstone	ss DSPTCHS,85	15
The Cliches from Outer Space			
	Joanna Russ	ar WSF V7 #2,84	27
The Intersection	Gwyneth Jones	ss DSPTCHS,85	35
Long Shift	Beverley Ireland	ss DSPTCHS,85	48
Love Alters	Tanith Lee	ss DSPTCHS,85	60
Cyclops	Lannah Battley	ss DSPTCHS,85	74
Instructions for Exiting This Building in Case of Fire			
	Pamela Zoline	ss INZ #12,85	93
A Sun in the Attic	Mary Gentle	ss DSPTCHS,85	111
Atlantis 2045: no love between planets			
	Frances Gapper	ss DSPTCHS,85	129
From a Sinking Ship	Lisa Tuttle	ss DSPTCHS,85	136

GREEN, JEN & SARAH LEFANU, eds.

The Awakening	Pearlie McNeill	ss DSPTCHS,85	150
Words	Naomi Mitchison	ss DSPTCHS,85	164
Relics	Zoe Fairbairns	ss DSPTCHS,85	175
Mab	Penny Casdagli	ss DSPTCHS,85	190
Morality Meat	Raccoona Sheldon	nv DSPTCHS,85	209
Apples in Winter	Sue Thomason	ss DSPTCHS,85	235

*Green, Roland PEACE COMPANY (Ace 0-441-65740-0, 10/85 [09/85], $2.75, 210pp, pb) Sf novel, first of a military sf series.

*Green, Roland & John F. Carr GREAT KING'S WAR (Ace 0-441-30200-9, 03/85 [02/85], $2.95, 357pp, pb) Sf novel, sequel to H. Beam Piper's stories of Lord Kalvan of Paratime.

*Green, Roland & Frieda Murray THE THRONE OF SHERRAN, VOL. I: THE BOOK OF KANTELA (Bluejay 0-312-94035-1, 08/85 [07/85], $8.95, 340pp, pb) Fantasy novel, first in a trilogy. The authors are a husband-wife team.

*Green, Sharon GATEWAY TO XANADU (DAW 0-88677-089-0, 12/85 [11/85], $3.95, 413pp, pb) Sf novel, second in the "Diana Santee, Spaceways Agent" series.

*Green, Sharon THE WILL OF THE GODS (DAW 0-88677-03904, 05/85 [04/85], $3.50, 383pp, pb) Fantasy novel. The fourth adventure of Jalav, Amazon warrior.

*Greenberg, Martin H., Robert Adams & Charles G. Waugh, eds. BARBARIANS Main listing under Robert Adams.

*Greenberg, Martin H., Poul Anderson & Charles G. Waugh, eds. MERCENARIES OF TOMORROW Main listing under Poul Anderson.

*Greenberg, Martin H., Poul Anderson & Charles G. Waugh, eds. TERRORISTS OF TOMORROW Main listing under Poul Anderson.

*Greenberg, Martin H. & Isaac Asimov, eds. AMAZING STORIES: 60 YEARS OF THE BEST SCIENCE FICTION Main listing under Isaac Asimov.

*Greenberg, Martin H. & Isaac Asimov, eds. ISAAC ASIMOV PRESENTS THE GREAT SF STORIES: 13 (1951) Main listing under Isaac Asimov.

*Greenberg, Martin H. & Isaac Asimov, eds. ISAAC ASIMOV PRESENTS THE GREAT SF STORIES: 14 (1952) Main listing under Isaac Asimov.

Greenberg, Martin H., Isaac Asimov & Terry Carr, eds. 100 GREAT FANTASY SHORT STORIES Main listing under Isaac Asimov.

*Greenberg, Martin H., Isaac Asimov & Charles G. Waugh, eds. BAKER'S DOZEN: 13 SHORT SCIENCE FICTION NOVELS Main listing under Isaac Asimov.

*Greenberg, Martin H., Isaac Asimov & Charles G. Waugh, eds. GREAT SCIENCE FICTION BY THE WORLD'S GREAT SCIENTISTS Main listing under Isaac Asimov.

*Greenberg, Martin H., Isaac Asimov & Charles G. Waugh, eds. ISAAC ASIMOV'S MAGICAL WORLDS OF FANTASY #3: COSMIC KNIGHTS Main listing under Isaac Asimov.

*Greenberg, Martin H., Isaac Asimov & Charles G. Waugh, eds. ISAAC ASIMOV'S MAGICAL WORLDS OF FANTASY #4: SPELLS Main listing under Isaac Asimov.

*Greenberg, Martin H., Isaac Asimov & Charles G. Waugh, eds. ISAAC ASIMOV'S MAGICAL WORLDS OF FANTASY #5: GIANTS Main listing under Isaac Asimov.

*Greenberg, Martin H., Isaac Asimov & Charles G. Waugh, eds. ISAAC ASIMOV'S MAGICAL WORLDS OF FANTASY: WITCHES & WIZARDS Main listing under Isaac Asimov.

*Greenberg, Martin H., Isaac Asimov & Charles G. Waugh, eds. THE LAST MAN ON EARTH Main listing under Isaac Asimov.

*Greenberg, Martin H., Isaac Asimov & Charles G. Waugh, eds. YOUNG GHOSTS Main listing under Isaac Asimov.

*Greenberg, Martin H., Isaac Asimov & Charles G. Waugh, eds. YOUNG MONSTERS Main listing under Isaac Asimov.

*Greenberg, Martin H., Richard Matheson & Charles G. Waugh, eds. THE TWILIGHT ZONE: THE ORIGINAL STORIES (Avon 0-380-89601-X, 07/85 [06/85], $8.95, 550pp, pb) Anthology of nearly all the stories which Rod Serling bought for the original Twilight Zone tv series, plus story adaptations of two of his own scripts.
Contents:

			Page
Preface	Carol Serling	pr	1
Introduction	Richard Matheson	in	3
One for the Angels [by Rod Serling]			
	Anne Serling-Sutton	sa TWLGTZN,85	9
Perchance to Dream	Charles Beaumont	ss PBY Oct,58	27
Disappearing Act	Richard Matheson	ss FSF Mar,53	37
Time Enough to Last	Lynn A. Venable	ss IFS Jan,53	54
What You Need	Lewis Padgett	ss ASF Oct,45	61
Third from the Sun	Richard Matheson	ss GAL Oct,50	79
Elegy	Charles Beaumont	ss IMG Feb,53	88
Brothers Beyond the Void	Paul Fairman	ss FAD Mar,52	98
The Howling Man [as C.B. Lovehill]			
	Charles Beaumont	ss ROG Nov,59	107
It's a Good Life	Jerome Bixby	ss STR # 2,53	125

The Valley Was Still	Manly Wade Wellman	ss WRT Aug,39	146
The Jungle	Charles Beaumont	nv IFS Dec,54	163
To Serve Man	Damon Knight	ss GAL Nov,50	189
Little Girl Lost	Richard Matheson	ss AMZ Nov,53	199
Four O'Clock	Price Day	ss 1958	213
I Sing the Body Electric! [The Beautiful One is Here]			
	Ray Bradbury	nv MCC Aug,69	218
The Changing of the Guard [by Rod Serling]			
	Anne Serling-Sutton	sa TZM Feb,85	258
In His Image [The Man Who Made Himself]			
	Charles Beaumont	nv IMG Feb,57	273
Mute	Richard Matheson	nv FIENDIN,62	300
Death Ship	Richard Matheson	nv FSM Mar,53	332
The Devil, You Say?	Charles Beaumont	nv AMZ Jan,51	356
Blind Alley	Malcolm Jameson	nv UNK Jun,43	384
Song for a Lady	Charles Beaumont	ss NGTRIDE,60	423
Steel	Richard Matheson	nv FSF May,56	441
Nightmare at 20,000 Feet	Richard Matheson	ss ALONEBY,62	468
The Old Man	Henry Slesar	ss DCM 1962	488
The Self-Improvement of Salvadore Ross			
	Henry Slesar	ss FSF May,61	493
The Beautiful People	Charles Beaumont	ss IFS Sep,52	506
Long Distance Call [Sorry, Right Number]			
	Richard Matheson	ss BEY Nov,53	526
An Occurrence at Owl Creek Bridge			
	Ambrose Bierce	ss INMIDST,1891	540

*Greenberg, Martin H. & Walter M. Miller, Jr., eds. BEYOND ARMAGEDDON Main listing under Walter M. Miller, Jr..

*Greenberg, Martin H. & Robert Silverberg, eds. THE TIME TRAVELERS: A SCIENCE FICTION QUARTET Main listing under Robert Silverberg.

*Greenland, Colin, John Clute & David Pringle, eds. INTERZONE: THE 1ST ANTHOLOGY Main listing under John Clute.

*Griffin, Russell M. THE TIME-SERVERS (Avon 0-380-89525-0, 02/85 [01/85], $3.50, 238pp, pb) Satiric sf novel of bureaucrats on a wretched boondocks planet. This is black humor of the deepest dye. You may wince with every laugh. (FCM)

*Guigonnat, Henri DAEMON IN LITHUANIA (New Directions 0-8112-0930-X, 05/85 [04/85], $14.00, 136pp, hc) "Neo-gothic" fantasy novel, winner of the first Prix de l'Insolite in France. It resembles an Edward Gorey book put into lyrical prose á la Francais -- short on plot, but long on demented charm. Translated by Barbara Wright. (FCM)

*Guigonnat, Henri DAEMON IN LITHUANIA (New Directions 0-8112-0939-3, 05/85 [04/85], $7.95, 136pp, pb) Paperback edition of the above.

Gunn, James E. THE LISTENERS (Ballantine/Del Rey 0-345-30036-X, 05/85 [04/85], $2.95, 226pp, pb) Reprint (Scribners 1972) sf novel. A classic of realistic first contact. Recommended. (CNB)

Haggard, H. Rider KING SOLOMON'S MINES (Tor 0-812-58356-6, 12/85 [12/85], $3.50, 286pp, pb) Reprint (Cassell 1885) lost race adventure novel, movie tie-in edition. The text, however, seems to be the original and the only tie-in, thank god, is the cover. One of the classics of adventure literature and still exciting on its 100th birthday. Recommended. (CNB)

*Haiblum, Isidore THE HAND OF GANZ (NAL/Signet 0-451-13341-2, 01/85 [12/84], $2.75, 238pp, pb) Sf novel.

*Hailey, Johanna ENCHANTED PARADISE (Zebra 0-8217-1672-3, 10/85 [09/85], $3.95, 525pp, pb) Elvish romance novel. (Not about Adam and Eve, as the cover art and blurb -- "they risked everything for a night of passion!" -- might suggest.) The authors are "Marcia Yvonne Howl" and Sharon Jarvis.

*Haldeman, Jack C., II THE FALL OF WINTER (Baen 0-671-55947-8, 03/85 [02/85], $2.95, 284pp, pb) Sf novel.

*Haldeman, Joe W. DEALING IN FUTURES (Viking 0-670-80635-8, 09/85 [08/85], $16.95, 277pp, hc) Collection of 11 stories and 3 poems, with an introduction and afterword. There are also afterwords to each story, blending into the introductions of the next one. Recommended. (CNB)
Contents:

			Page
Introduction	Joe W. Haldeman	in	1
Seasons	Joe W. Haldeman	na ALIENST,85	2
A !Tangled Web	Joe W. Haldeman	nv ASF Sep 14,81	86
Manifest Destiny	Joe W. Haldeman	nv FSF Oct,83	122
Blood Sisters	Joe W. Haldeman	nv PBY Jul,79	148
Blood Brothers	Joe W. Haldeman	ss THVSWLD,79	173
You Can Never Go Back	Joe W. Haldeman	na AMZ Nov,75	188
More Than the Sum of His Parts			
	Joe W. Haldeman	nv PBY May,85	293
Seven and the Stars	Joe W. Haldeman	ss TZM May,81	323
Lindsay and the Red City Blues			
	Joe W. Haldeman	ss DRKFRCS,80	332
No Future in It	Joe W. Haldeman	ss OMN Apr,79	349
The Pilot	Joe W. Haldeman	ss DST V1 #3,79	361
The Big Bang Theory Explained			
	Joe W. Haldeman	pm PLP	369
The Gift	Joe W. Haldeman	pm	375
Saul's Death: Two Sestinas			
	Joe W. Haldeman	pm WAR V 1,83	377
Postscript	Joe W. Haldeman	aw	382

Haldeman, Joe W. WORLD WITHOUT END (Bantam 0-553-24174-5, 01/85 [12/84], $2.95, 150pp, pb) Reissue (Bantam 1979) Star Trek novel.

Haldeman, Joe W., ed. NEBULA AWARD STORIES 17 (Ace 0-441-56797-5, 06/85 [05/85], $3.50, 291pp, pb) Reprint (Holt 1983) anthology. Contains the 1981 winners and runners-up.

Hall, Frances & Piers Anthony PRETENDER Main listing under Piers Anthony.

*Hambly, Barbara DRAGONSBANE (Ballantine/Del Rey 0-345-31572-3, 01/86 [12/85], $3.50, 341pp, pb) Fantasy novel. A new slant on the dragon-slayer tale. Recommended. (FCM)

*Hambly, Barbara ISHMAEL (Pocket 0-671-55427-1, 05/85 [04/85], $3.50, 255pp, pb) Star Trek novel.

*Hamilton, Virginia THE PEOPLE COULD FLY: AMERICAN BLACK FOLK-TALES (Knopf 0-394-86925-7, 10/85 [11/85], $12.95, 178pp, hc) (Also available in library binding, 0-394-96925-1, $13.99). Hamilton's retelling of 24 folktales, with b&w illustrations by Leo and Diane Dillon.

*Hancock, Niel THE FIRES OF WINDAMEIR (Warner 0-446-32369-1, 02/85 [01/85], $2.95, 407pp, pb) Fantasy novel, first of a new series.

Handley, Max MEANWHILE (Popular Library/Questar 0-445-20068-5, 08/85 [07/85], $3.50, 314pp, pb) Reprint (Arlington 1977) humorous sf novel.

*Hansen, Karl DREAM GAMES (Ace 0-441-16691-1, 05/85 [04/85], $2.95, 252pp, pb) Sf novel, Book 1 in the "Hybrid" series.

*Harding, Richard THE OUTRIDER #5: BUILT TO KILL (Pinnacle 0-523-42216-4, 08/85 [07/85], $2.95, 181pp, pb) Latest in a post-holocaust sf series; adventure novel.

+Hardy, Phil, ed. SCIENCE FICTION: THE COMPLETE FILM SOURCEBOOK (Morrow 0-688-00842-9, 01/85 [12/84], $25.00, 400pp, hc) Reprint (Aurum 1984 as THE AURUM FILM ENCYCLOPEDIA: SCIENCE FICTION), first U.S. edition. Non-fiction, reference book with plot summaries, critical commentaries, black & white and color illustrations, etc.

+Harpur, Patrick THE SERPENT'S CIRCLE (St. Martin's 0-312-71314-2, 03/85 [02/85], $12.95, 232pp, hc) Reprint (Macmillan U.K. 1985) "theological thriller" with fantasy elements. First U.S. edition.

Harrison, Harry ONE STEP FROM EARTH (Tor 0-812-53972-9, 09/85 [08/85], $2.95, 253pp, pb) Reprint (Macmillan 1970) collection of 9 stories plus an introduction, masquerading as a novel. There is a 1985 copyright date which may indicate some rewriting. The original publications of the stories are not acknowledged.

Harrison, Harry SKYFALL (Ace 0-441-76945-4, 11/85 [10/85], $3.50, 281pp, pb) Reissue (Faber & Faber 1976) sf novel of a potentially disastrous space experiment. 3rd Ace printing.

*Harrison, Harry A STAINLESS STEEL RAT IS BORN (Bantam Spectra 0-553-24708-5, 10/85 [09/85], $2.95, 219pp, pb) Sf novel, prequel to the rest of the series.

Harrison, Harry THE TECHNICOLOR TIME MACHINE (Tor 0-812-53970-2, 05/85 [04/85], $2.95, 250pp, pb) Reissue (Doubleday 1967) sf novel. Second Tor printing.

Harrison, Harry WEST OF EDEN (SFBC #5263, 01/85 [12/84], $5.98, 461pp, hc) Reprint (Bantam 1984) sf novel.

Harrison, Harry WEST OF EDEN (Bantam Spectra 0-553-24935-5, 07/85 [06/85], $3.95, 508pp, pb) Reprint (Bantam 1984) sf novel set in an alternate prehistoric past. Collectors should note that the step-back cover is available in either blue or maroon.

Harrison, Harry & Gordon R. Dickson THE LIFESHIP Main listing under Gordon R. Dickson.

Harrison, M. John THE CENTAURI DEVICE (Bantam 0-553-23646-6, 04/85 [03/85], $2.95, 212pp, pb) Reissue (Doubleday 1974) sf novel. 2nd printing.

*Harrison, M. John VIRICONIUM NIGHTS (Gollancz 0-575-03662-1, 11/85 [11/85], £8.95, 158pp, hc) Collection of 7 stories. This shares only the title and a couple of stories with VIRICONIUM NIGHTS (Ace 1984). There are original works and rewritten stories in the new version.

Contents:

			Page
The Luck in the Head	M. John Harrison	nv VRCNMNT,84	11
The Lamia & Lord Cromis	M. John Harrison	nv NWQ # 1,71	37
Strange Great Sins	M. John Harrison	ss INZ # 5,83	61
Viriconium Knights	M. John Harrison	nv ELW # 1,81	77
The Dancer from the Dance	M. John Harrison	nv VRCNMNT,85	99
The Lords of Misrule	M. John Harrison	ss SVYDRMS,83	123
A Young Man's Journey to Viriconium	M. John Harrison	nv INZ #12,85	137

*Hartmann, William K., Pamela Lee & Ron Miller OUT OF THE CRADLE: EXPLORING THE FRONTIERS BEYOND EARTH (Workman 0-89480-770-6, 1984 [02/85], $11.95, 190pp, pb) Text and artwork combine science with hard sf, envisioning mankind's movement into the solar system. A hardcover edition has also been announced, but we have not seen it. This was apparently a 1984 book.

*Hartwell, David AGE OF WONDERS: EXPLORING THE WORLD OF SCIENCE FICTION (Walker 0-8027-0808-0, 1984 [12/84], $15.95, 205pp, hc) Non-fiction, general book about sf and fandom, mainly for the non-sf reader.

Hartwell, David AGE OF WONDERS: EXPLORING THE WORLD OF SCIENCE FICTION (McGraw-Hill 0-07-026963-7, 11/85 [11/85], $3.95, 224pp, pb) Reprint (Walker 1984); non-fiction, criticism and history of the field. This edition includes material not in the hardcover, notably a selection of 101 "best" sf novels and two suggested syllabi for academic sf courses.

*Hassler, Donald M., ed. PATTERNS OF THE FANTASTIC II (Starmont 0-916732-87-8, 05/85 [04/85], $8.95, 91pp, pb) Non-fiction, criticism; selected papers presented in the scholars' program track at ConStellation (Worldcon 1983).

*Hassler, Donald M. & Carl B. Yoke, eds. DEATH AND THE SERPENT: IMMORTALITY IN SCIENCE FICTION Main listing under Carl B. Yoke.

+Hawdon, Robin A RUSTLE IN THE GRASS (Dodd Mead 0-396-08522-9, 04/85 [03/85], $13.95, 244pp, hc) Reprint (Arrow 1984) fantasy novel, first U.S. edition. "An anthropomorphic extravaganza of life among the ants," featuring a hero named Dreamer. A first novel.

*Hawke, Simon THE NAUTILUS SANCTION (Ace 0-441-56566-2, 12/85 [11/85], @2.95, 196pp, pb) Sf novel, "Time Wars" #5. Hawke is a pen name for Nicholas Yermekov.

*Hawke, Simon TIMEWARS #4: THE ZENDA VENDETTA (Ace 0-441-95915-6, 05/85 [04/85], $2.75, 206pp, pb) Sf novel in a time travel series. Simon Hawke is a pseudonym for Nicholas Yermakov.

*Hawkins, Ward RED FLAME BURNING (Ballantine/Del Rey 0-345-32121-9, 08/85 [07/85], $2.95, 280pp, pb) Sf novel, start of a new adventure series. A first novel. Hawkins wrote a couple of stories for the pulps forty years ago, and this has a true pulp sensibility of the worst sort. (DLN)

*Hawkins, Ward SWORD OF FIRE (Ballantine/Del Rey 0-345-32348-3, 10/85 [09/85], $2.95, 297pp, pb) Humorous sf novel, sequel to RED FLAME BURNING.

Haynes, Mary WORDCHANGER (Dell/Laurel Leaf 0-440-99671-6, 06/85 [05/85], $2.75, 252pp, pb) Reprint (Lothrop, Lee & Shepard 1983) young-adult sf novel.

*Hazel, Paul WINTERKING (Atlantic Monthly 0-87113-026-2, 10/85 [11/85], $18.95FPT, 297pp, hc) Fantasy novel, conclusion of the "Finnbranch Trilogy". This one is set in an alternate world modern age.

*Heinlein, Robert A. THE CAT WHO WALKS THROUGH WALLS: A COMEDY OF MANNERS (Putnam 0-399-13103-5, 11/85 [10/85], $17.95, 382pp, hc) Sf novel whose characters include Lazarus Long, Adam Selene, and others from previous Heinlein novels. Collectors note: There is a loose errata slip with the first printing.

Heinlein, Robert A. THE CAT WHO WALKS THROUGH WALLS: A COMEDY OF MANNERS (Putnam 0-399-13116-7, 11/85 [11/85], $75.00, 382pp, hc) Reprint (Putnam 1985) sf novel; signed, limited, boxed edition of 350 copies. This edition does not have the errata card from the first issue--the line has been corrected.

Heinlein, Robert A. THE DOOR INTO SUMMER (Gollancz 0-575-03698-2, 09/85 [09/85], £8.95, 190pp, hc) Reissue (Doubleday 1957) sf novel; 5th Gollancz edition.

Heinlein, Robert A. FRIDAY (Ballantine/Del Rey 0-345-30988-X, 11/85 [10/85], $3.95, 357pp, pb) Reissue (Del Rey 1982) sf novel.

Heinlein, Robert A. JOB: A COMEDY OF JUSTICE (SFBC #5620, 08/85 [07/85], $5.98, 311pp, hc) Reprint (Ballantine/Del Rey 1984) fantasy novel.

Heinlein, Robert A. JOB: A COMEDY OF JUSTICE (Ballantine/Del Rey 0-345-31650-9, 11/85 [10/85], $4.50, 439pp, pb) Reprint (Del Rey 1984) fantasy novel.

Heinlein, Robert A. TIME FOR THE STARS (Gollancz 0-575-03697-4, 09/85 [09/85], £8.95, 244pp, hc) Reissue (Scribner's 1956) sf novel; 6th Gollancz edition.

*Herbert, Brian THE GARBAGE CHRONICLES (Berkley 0-425-07450-1, 01/85 [12/84], $2.95, 298pp, pb) Sf novel.

*Herbert, Brian SUDANNA, SUDANNA (Arbor House 0-87795-657-X, 04/85 [03/85], $15.95, 251pp, hc) Sf novel.

*Herbert, Frank CHAPTER HOUSE DUNE (Gollancz 0-575-03576-5, 03/85 [02/85], £8.95, 379pp, hc) Sf novel. This is the first edition of the latest "Dune" book; the American one will follow.

+Herbert, Frank CHAPTERHOUSE: DUNE (Putnam 0-399-13027-6, 05/85 [04/85], $17.95, 464pp, hc) Reprint (Gollancz 1985) sf novel, latest in the "Dune" series. First American edition. Please note: the British first edition is CHAPTER HOUSE DUNE.

Herbert, Frank DIRECT DESCENT (Berkley 0-425-08186-9, 10/85 [09/85], $2.95, 188pp, pb) Reprint (Ace 1980) short sf novel in a heavily illustrated edition.

*Herbert, Frank EYE (Berkley 0-425-08398-5, 11/85 [10/85], $7.95, 328pp, pb) Collection of stories, excerpts, and articles, with illustrations by Jim Burns.
Contents:

			Page
Introduction	Frank Herbert	in	9
Rat Race	Frank Herbert	nv ASF Jul,55	15
Dragon in the Sea [Under Pressure]			
	Frank Herbert	ex ASF Nov,55	43
Cease Fire	Frank Herbert	nv ASF Jan,58	79
A Matter of Traces	Frank Herbert	ss FUN Nov,58	101
Try to Remember	Frank Herbert	nv AMZ Oct,61	117
The Tactful Saboteur	Frank Herbert	nv GAL Oct,64	159
The Road to Dune	Jim Burns	pi EYE ,85	191
By the Book	Frank Herbert	nv ASF Aug,66	211
Seed Stock	Frank Herbert	ss ASF Apr,70	239
Murder Will In	Frank Herbert	nv FSF May,70	255
Passage for Piano	Frank Herbert	nv BKHRBRT,73	289
Death of a City	Frank Herbert	ss FUTCITY,73	313
Frogs and Scientists	Frank Herbert	vi DST V1 #4,79	325

Herbert, Frank EYE (Berkley 0-425-08399-3, 1985 [12/85], $100.00, 328pp, hc) Reprint (Berkley 1985) collection; signed, boxed limited edition of 200 copies, 175 for sale.

Herbert, Frank THE GREEN BRAIN (Berkley 0-425-07676-8, 05/85 [04/85], $2.95, 215pp, pb) Reprint (Ace 1966) sf novel.

Herbert, Frank HERETICS OF DUNE (Berkley 0-425-07669-5, 03/85 [02/85], $7.95, 480pp, pb) Reprint (Putnam 1984) "Dune" sf novel, first trade paperback edition.

Herbert, Frank THE SANTAROGA BARRIER (Berkley 0-425-08468-X, 08/85 [07/85], $2.95, 255pp, pb) Reissue (Berkley 1968) sf novel. 19th printing.

+Herbert, James DOMAIN (NAL/Signet 0-451-13471-0, 04/85 [03/85], $3.50, 350pp, pb) Reprint (U.K. 1984) sf horror novel, first U.S. edition. Bloodthirsty rats run wild after the Holocaust.

*Herron, Don THE LITERARY WORLD OF SAN FRANCISCO & ITS ENVIRONS (City Lights 0-87286-157-0, 06/85 [05/85], $9.95, 247pp, pb) A fascinating guidebook organized by neighborhoods, streets, etc., with entries for places associated with writers, scenes in books and stories, and various literary movements. The handy index will allow you to track down the numerous sf writers mentioned in the book; *Locus* is there too. Recommended. (FCM)

*Heydron, Vicki Ann & Randall Garrett RETURN TO EDDARTA Main listing under Randall Garrett.

*Hickman, Tracy & Margaret Weis DRAGONLANCE CHRONICLES, VOL. 2: DRAGONS OF WINTER NIGHT Main listing under Margaret Weis.

*Hickman, Tracy & Margaret Weis DRAGONLANCE CHRONICLES, VOL. 3: DRAGONS OF SPRING DAWNING Main listing under Margaret Weis.

High, Philip E. SOLD - FOR A SPACESHIP (Hamlyn/Venture 0-09-942780-X, 09/85 [10/85], £1.75, 175pp, pb) Reprint (Hale 1973) sf adventure novel. Volume 7 in a series of space opera reprints.

*Hildebrandt, Rita & Tim Hildebrandt MERLIN AND THE DRAGONS OF ATLANTIS (Bobbs-Merrill 0-672-52704-9, 01/85 [12/84], $16.95, 199pp, hc) Allegorical fantasy of "mysticism and techno-warfare" by Rita, with illustrations (black & white) by Tim.

*Hildebrandt, Tim & Rita Hildebrandt MERLIN AND THE DRAGONS OF ATLANTIS Main listing under Rita Hildebrandt.

*Hill, Carol THE ELEVEN MILLION MILE HIGH DANCER (Holt Rinehart & Winston 0-03-070699-8, 04/85 [03/85], $16.95, 447pp, hc) Sf novel of a female astronaut's intergalactic adventures. There are elements of "Wonderwoman" and Buckaroo Banzai, plus darker strains, in this serio-comic extravaganza, which eventually collapses under its weight of unlikely plot elements -- but not without some fun along the way. Schrodinger the narcoleptic cat is almost worth the price of admission. (FCM)

+Hill, Douglas THE CAVES OF KLYDOR (Atheneum/Argo 0-689-50320-2, 03/85 [02/85], $9.95, 118pp, hc) Reprint (Gollancz 1984) young-adult sf novel, sequel to EXILES OF COLSEC. First U.S. edition.

*Hill, Douglas COLSEC REBELLION (Gollancz 0-575-03610-9, 06/85 [05/85], £5.50, 121pp, hc) Young-adult sf novel, conclusion of the "Colsec" trilogy.

+Hill, Douglas COLSEC REBELLION (Atheneum/Argo 0-689-50360-1, 10/85 [12/85], $9.95, 121pp, hc) Reprint (Gollancz 1985) young-adult sf novel, conclusion of the "Colsec" trilogy. First U.S. publication.

Hoban, Russell PILGERMANN (Pocket 0-671-61893-8, 01/86 [12/85], $2.95, 240pp, pb) Reprint (Jonathan Cape 1983) fantasy novel.

*Hodgell, P.C. DARK OF THE MOON (Atheneum/Argo 0-689-31171-0, 10/85 [10/85], $15.95, 386pp, hc) Young-adult fantasy novel, sequel to GODSTALK. It comes with a loose map by "P.C. Hodgell - 1984." Follows both Jame and her brother Tori in adventures as wild and wondrous as those in GODSTALK. Recommended. (DLN)

*Hogan, James P. THE PROTEUS OPERATION (Bantam Spectra 0-553-05095-8, 09/85 [08/85], $16.95, 403pp, hc) Sf time travel novel centered around World War II.

+Holdstock, Robert MYTHAGO WOOD (Arbor House 0-87795-761-4, 10/85 [10/85], $14.95, 252pp, hc) Reprint (Gollancz 1984) fantasy novel, first U.S. edition. Winner of the World Fantasy Award -- a haunting, superb book. (FCM)

Holdstock, Robert MYTHAGO WOOD (SFBC #04000, 12/85 [12/85], $4.98, 215pp, hc) Reprint (Gollancz 1984) fantasy novel, winner of the British Fantasy Award and the World Fantasy Award.

+Holdstock, Robert & Malcolm Edwards, eds. LOST REALMS (Salem House 0-88162-075-0, 03/85 [02/85], $14.95, unpaginated, pb) First U.S. edition (Dragon's World 1984). Non-fiction, collection of illustrated fantasy legends done in full-color. Available from Merrimack Publishers' Circle.

*Holland, Cecilia PILLAR OF THE SKY (Knopf 0-53538-3, 06/85 [05/85], $17.95, 534pp, hc) Associational; historical novel about the builder of Stonehenge. There is some mysticism, but no fantasy. Recommended. (FCM)

Hoover, H.M. CHILDREN OF MORROW (Puffin 0-14-031873-9, 05/85 [04/85], $3.95, 229pp, pb) Reprint (Four Winds 1973) young-adult sf novel.

Hoover, H.M. THIS TIME OF DARKNESS (Puffin 0-14-031872-0, 05/85 [04/85], $3.95, 161pp, pb) Reprint (Viking Penguin 1980) young-adult sf novel.

*Hopkins, Mariane S., ed. FANDOM DIRECTORY #7, 1985-1986 EDITION (Hopkins no ISBN, 05/85 [04/85], $9.95, 416pp, pb) Indexes of fan publications, conventions, fan clubs, selected research libraries, stores, and (state by state) fans, plus artwork, advertisements, etc.

*Hoppe, Stephanie T. THE WINDRIDER (DAW 0-88677-020-3, 03/85 [02/85], $2.95, 253pp, pb) Fantasy novel.

Horowitz, Anthony THE DEVIL'S DOOR-BELL (Putnam/Pacer 0-399-21140-3, 05/85 [04/85], $2.25, 159pp, pb) Reprint (U.K. 1983) young-adult fantasy novel.

+Horowitz, Anthony THE NIGHT OF THE SCORPION (Putnam/Pacer 0-488-47751-3, 05/85 [04/85], $12.95, 160pp, hc) Reprint (Hardy 1984), first U.S. edition. Young-adult fantasy/horror novel, sequel to THE DEVIL'S DOOR-BELL.

Horowitz, Anthony THE NIGHT OF THE SCORPION (Berkley/Pacer 0-425-08447-7, 01/86 [12/85], $2.50, 159pp, pb) Reprint (Patrick Hardy 1984) young-adult fantasy/horror novel. Sequel to THE DEVIL'S DOOR-BELL.

Howard, Robert E. CONAN: THE TREASURE OF TRANICOS (Ace 0-441-82246-0, 07/85 [06/85], $2.75, 191pp, pb) Reissue (Ace 1980) short fantasy novel, illustrated by Esteban Maroto. 4th printing. Although de Camp's name doesn't appear on the cover, this is actually a posthumous collaboration of de Camp and Howard with two other stories by de Camp.

Howard, Robert E. KULL (Donald M. Grant 0-937986-75-5, 11/85 [11/85], $50.00 deluxe boxed edition, $25.00 trade edition, 247pp, hc) Reprint (Lancer 1967 as KING KULL by R.E. Howard & Lin Carter) collection. This edition follows the revised text (Bantam 1978 as KULL) without the introduction. First hc edition. There are color illustrations by Ned Dameron.

Howard, Robert E., Lin Carter & L. Sprague de Camp CONAN (Ace 0-441-11584-5, 11/85 [11/85], $2.95, 221pp, pb) Reissue (Lancer 1981) collection. "Conan" #1.

Howard, Robert E., Lin Carter & L. Sprague de Camp CONAN OF CIMMERIA (Ace 0-441-11453-9, 12/85 [11/85], $2.95, 189pp, pb) Reissue (Lancer 1969) collection. "Conan" #2. 15th Ace printing.

Howard, Robert E., Lin Carter & L. Sprague de Camp CONAN THE WANDERER (Ace 0-441-11597-7, 01/86 [12/85], $2.95, 222pp, pb) Reissue (Lancer 1968) collection. "Conan" #4.

Howard, Robert E. & L. Sprague de Camp CONAN THE FREEBOOTER (Ace 0-441-11700-1, 01/86 [12/85], $2.95, 223pp, pb) Reissue (Lancer 1968) collection. "Conan" #3. 18th Ace printing.

Howard, Robert E. & L. Sprague de Camp CONAN: THE FLAME KNIFE (Ace 0-441-11665-5, 09/85 [08/85], $2.95, 159pp, pb) Reissue (Ace 1981) of a Howard novella rewritten by de Camp into a Conan novel; illustrations by Esteban Maroto. It first appeared in a collection TALES OF CONAN (Gnome 1955). 6th Ace printing.

Hoyle, Sir Fred OCTOBER THE FIRST IS TOO LATE (Baen 0-671-55943-5, 03/85 [02/85], $2.95, 281pp, pb) Reprint (Heinemann 1966) sf novel.

Hoyle, Trevor THE LAST GASP (Zebra 0-8217-1508-9, 03/85 [02/85], $3.95, 590pp, pb) Reprint (Crown 1983) near-future sf novel.

*Hoyle, Trevor VAIL (Riverrun/John Calder 0-7145-4055-2, 1984 [12/85], £4.95/$7.95, 188pp, pb) Near-future sf novel. This was announced as a 1985 US release, but this edition seems to be a simultaneous UK/US first edition with a 1984 copyright date. We have not listed it before. It is distributed by Flatiron Distributors.

Hruska, Alan BORROWED TIME (Baen 0-671-55973-7, 08/85 [07/85], $2.95, 277pp, pb) Reprint (Dial 1984) sf novel of crossed alternate worlds.

*Hubbard, L. Ron MISSION EARTH, VOL. I: THE INVADERS PLAN (Bridge 0-88404-194-8, 10/85 [09/85], $18.95, 559pp, hc) Sf novel, first book of a projected ten-volume "science fiction satire."

Hughart, Barry BRIDGE OF BIRDS (Ballantine/Del Rey 0-345-32138-3, 05/85 [04/85], $2.95, 278pp, pb) Reprint (St. Martin's 1984) fantasy novel. This is an excellent first novel set in ancient China. Winner, World Fantasy Award. Recommended! (FCM)

*Hughes, Edward P. THE LONG MYND (Baen 0-671-55992-3, 11/85 [10/85], $2.95, 318pp, pb) Sf novel. A post-holocaust world caused by psi powers. A first novel.

+Hughes, Monica DEVIL ON MY BACK (Atheneum/Argo 0-689-31095-1, 03/85 [02/85], $9.95, 170pp, hc) Reprint (U.K. 1984) young-adult sf novel. First U.S. edition.

*Hughes, Robert Don THE POWER AND THE PROPHET (Ballantine/Del Rey 0-345-30353-9, 04/85 [03/85], $2.95, 339pp, pb) Fantasy novel, Book Three of "Pelmen the Powershaper."

Hughes, Robert Don THE PROPHET OF LAMATH (Ballantine/Del Rey 0-345-32544-3, 04/85 [03/85], $2.95, 357pp, pb) Reissue (Ballantine/Del Rey 1979) fantasy novel, Book One of the "Pelmen" series. 3rd printing.

Hull, E. Mayne & A.E. van Vogt THE WINGED MAN Main listing under A.E. van Vogt.

*Hurley, Maxwell PSI PATROL #3: MAX'S BOOK (Scholastic/Point 0-590-33203-1, 10/85 [12/85], $2.25, 151pp, pb) Young-adult fantasy novel -- psionic teenagers make and solve problems. It's credited as being written by the hero.

*Hyams, Peter & Arthur C. Clarke THE ODYSSEY FILE Main listing under Arthur C. Clarke.

*Ing, Dean WILD COUNTRY (Tor 0-812-54102-2, 11/85 [10/85], $2.95, 317pp, pb) Sf novel; sequel to SINGLE COMBAT and SYSTEMIC SHOCK. Post-holocaust adventure.

*Ing, Dean & Mack Reynolds TROJAN ORBIT Main listing under Mack Reynolds.

*Irwin, Walter & G.B. Love, eds. THE BEST OF TREK #8 (NAL/Signet 0-451-13488-5, 03/85 [02/85], $2.95, 221pp, pb) Non-fiction, anthology of articles on Star Trek.

*Irwin, Walter & G.B. Love, eds. THE BEST OF TREK #9 (NAL/Signet 0-451-13816-3, 09/85 [08/85], $2.95, 207pp, pb) Anthology of non-fiction material from *Trek*, the Star Trek magazine.

Mooney's Module   Gerry Mooney   ct IAS   179
On Books: Books into Movies
                             Norman Spinrad   br IAS Nov,85 180
SF Conventional Calendar Erwin S. Strauss   ms IAS   192

*Isaac Asimov's Science Fiction Magazine [v. 9 #12, December 1985] Shawna McCarthy, ed. (Davis, 12/85 [10/85], $2.00, 192pp, pb)
Contents: Page
Civil War   Isaac Asimov   ed IAS Dec,85   3
Gaming   Dana Lombardy   gr IAS   20
Bull's Eyes and Pratfalls
                             Martin Gardner   pz IAS Dec,85   24
Toward Artificial Intelligence
                             Marvin Minsky   ar IAS Dec,85   28
Mooney's Module   Gerry Mooney   ct IAS   53
Empire Dreams   Ian McDonald   nv IAS Dec,85   54
Perception Barriers   Robert Frazier   pm IAS Dec,85   79
The War of the Roses   Karen Joy Fowler   nv IAS Dec,85   80
O Little Town of Bethlehem II
                             Robert F. Young   ss IAS Dec,85   106
"...How My Heart Breaks When I Sing This Song..."
                             Lucius Shepard   ss IAS Dec,85   116
The Nebraskan and the Nereid
                             Gene Wolfe   ss IAS Dec,85   132
Presuppositional Ghostbusting
                             Suzette Haden Elgin   pm IAS Dec,85   140
Cartoon   John Caldwell   ct RUNAMCK,78   141
Boulevard Life   Robert Charles Wilson   ss IAS Dec,85   142
Meadows of Light   Sydney J. Van Scyoc   nv IAS Dec,85   158
On Books   Baird Searles   br IAS   183
SF Conventional Calendar Erwin S. Strauss   ms IAS   192

*Isaac Asimov's Science Fiction Magazine [v. 9 #13, Mid-December 1985] Shawna McCarthy, ed. (Davis, 12/85 [11/85], $2.00, 192pp, pb)
Contents: Page
Up Front   Shawna McCarthy   ms IAS Dec md,85   4
Irritations   Isaac Asimov   ed IAS Dec md,85   5
Gaming   Dana Lombardy   gr IAS   24
Flarp Flips Another Fiver
                             Martin Gardner   pz IAS Dec md,85 28
All This and Heaven Too   James Tiptree, Jr.   nv IAS Dec md,85   30
Aftermath   Bill Bickel   ss IAS Dec md,85 66
Ways to Get Home   Susan Palwick   ss IAS Dec md,85 80
Lord Kelvin's Machine   James P. Blaylock   nv IAS Dec md,85   92
Mooney's Module   Gerry Mooney   ct IAS   125
The Wire Around the War   Ian Watson   ss IAS Dec md,85   126
Send No Money   Susan Casper & Gardner Dozois
                                                      ss IAS Dec md,85 134
Storming the Cosmos   Rudy Rucker & Bruce Sterling
                                                      na IAS Dec md,85 144
On Books   Baird Searles   br IAS   183
SF Conventional Calendar Erwin S. Strauss   ms IAS   192

*Isaac Asimov's Science Fiction Magazine [v.10 # 1, January 1986] Gardner Dozois, ed. (Davis, 01/86 [12/85], $2.0C, 192pp, pb)
Contents: Page
Old Hundredth   Isaac Asimov   ed IAS Jan,86   4
Blues in the Night   Martin Gardner   pz IAS Jan,86   18
Harmony of the Spheres at Spion Kop
                             Roger Meador   pm IAS Jan,86   19
Gaming   Dana Lombardy   gr IAS   20
Theodore Sturgeon: 1918-1985
                             Harlan Ellison   bg IAS Jan,86   24
Theodore Sturgeon: 1918-1985
                             Damon Knight   bg IAS Jan,86   28
Theodore Sturgeon: 1918-1985
                             Isaac Asimov   bg IAS Jan,86   28
Theodore Sturgeon: 1918-1985
                             Brian W. Aldiss   bg BSG 166,85   29
Theodore Sturgeon: 1918-1985
                             Stephen King   bg WPB 1985   33
Theodore Sturgeon: 1918-1985
                             Somtow Sucharitkul   bg IAS Jan,86   34
A Quotella for Ted Sturgeon
                             Robert Frazier   pm IAS Jan,86   37
Pretty Boy Crossover   Pat Cadigan   ss IAS Jan,86   38
Reduction   Gregory Frost & John Kessel
                                                      ss IAS Jan,86   52
Special Education   Tim Sullivan   ss IAS Jan,86   66
Jeff Beck   Lewis Shiner   ss IAS Jan,86   83
Interstellar Dust   Peter Payack   pm IAS Jan,86   93
The Eye of the Beholder   Isaac Asimov   ss IAS Jan,86   94
A Trivial Matter   Peter Payack   pm IAS Jan,86   104
Count Zero [Part 1 of 3]
                             William Gibson   sl IAS Jan,86   106
Moonburn   Peter Payack   pm IAS Jan,86   177
On Books: Must There Be War?
                             Norman Spinrad   br IAS Jan,86   178
Why There Is Now (and Most Probably Always Will Be) a
  Shortage of Subatomic Physicists
                             Peter Payack   ms IAS Jan,86   186
Index to 1985   [Misc. Material]   ix IAS Jan,86   187
Mooney's Module   Gerry Mooney   ct IAS   191
SF Conventional Calendar Erwin S. Strauss   ms IAS   192

*Jaffery, Sheldon R., ed. SENSUOUS SCIENCE FICTION FROM THE WEIRD AND SPICY PULPS (Bowling Green Popular Press 0-87972-305-X, 01/85 [12/84], $19.95, 164pp, hc) Anthology of reproductions (complete with ads) from the pulps, plus introduction and supplementary material. The editor keeps apologizing about how bad they are.

Contents: Page
Introduction   Sheldon R. Jaffery   in   1
Test-Tube Frankenstein   Wayne Robbins   ss TTL May,40   5
Zenith Rand, Planet Vigilante
                             Richard Tooker   nv MAM Jun,36 24
The Angel From Hell   Nils O. Sonderlund   nv MVT Dec,39 47
World Without Sex   Robert Wentworth, [Edmond Hamilton]
                                                      ss MVT May,40 98
The Robot Awakes   Lew Merrill   ss SYA Oct,40 114
Shawm of the Stars   Hugh Speer   ss SYA Sep,40 132
Planet of Peril   Henri St. Maur   ss SYA Sep,40 150

*Jaffery, Sheldon R., ed. SENSUOUS SCIENCE FICTION FROM THE WEIRD AND SPICY PULPS (Bowling Green Popular Press 0-87972-306-8, 01/85 [12/84], $8.95, 164pp, pb) Paperback edition of the above.

*Jaffery, Sheldon R. & Fred Cook THE COLLECTOR'S INDEX TO WEIRD TALES (Bowling Green Popular Press 0-87972-283-5, 10/85 [10/85], $20.95, 162pp, hc) Non-fiction; bibliography. An index to *Weird Tales*, plus a separate one to *Magic Carpet* and *Oriental Tales*, including the revivals. It has issue by issue, authors index, poetry index, and cover artist index.

*Jaffery, Sheldon R. & Fred Cook THE COLLECTOR'S INDEX TO WEIRD TALES (Bowling Green Popular Press 0-87972-284-3, 10/85 [10/85], $10.95, 162pp, pb) Paperback edition of the above; 8.5" x 11".

*Janos, Leo & General Chuck Yeager YEAGER: AN AUTOBIOGRAPHY Main listing under General Chuck Yeager.

*Janson, Klaus FROST AND FIRE (DC Comics 0-930289-07-2, 12/85 [12/85], $5.95, unpaginated, pb) Pictorial version of a novelette by Ray Bradbury (original title "The Creatures That Time Forgot", *Planet Stories*, Fall 1946).

*Jeppson, J.O. THE MYSTERIOUS CURE AND OTHER STORIES OF PSHRINKS ANONYMOUS (Doubleday 0-385-19085-9, 04/19/85 [03/85], $11.95, 180pp, hc) Collection of 13 stories plus an intro by the author's husband.
Contents: Page
Introduction   Isaac Asimov   in   vii
The Mysterious Cure   J.O. Jeppson   ss IAS Dec md,82 1
The Hotter Flash   J.O. Jeppson   ss IAS Apr,81   17
A Million Shades of Green
                             J.O. Jeppson   nv IAS Jul,81   31
August Angst   J.O. Jeppson   ss MYSCURE,85   53
Seasonal Special   J.O. Jeppson   ss AMZ Jul,84   62
The Beanstalk Analysis   J.O. Jeppson   ss IAS Dec,80   72
The Horn of Elfland   J.O. Jeppson   ss IAS Mar,83   81
A Pestilence of Psychoanalysts
                             J.O. Jeppson   ss IAS Sep,80   96
Consternation and Empire J.O. Jeppson   ss IAS Sep,81   105
The Noodge Factor   J.O. Jeppson   ss MYSCURE,85   120
The Ultimate Biofeedback Device
                             J.O. Jeppson   ss IAS May,83   129
The Curious Consultation J.O. Jeppson   ss IAS May,82   147
The Time-Warp Trauma   J.O. Jeppson   ss IAS Dec,81   165

*Jeter, K.W. THE GLASS HAMMER (Bluejay 0-312-94173-0, 08/85 [07/85], $8.95, 248pp, pb) Punk sf rovel.

*Joels, Kerry Mark THE MARS ONE CREW MANUAL (Ballantine/Del Rey 0-345-32747-0, 11/85 [11/85], $24.95, unpaginated, hc) Illustrated guide to an as-yet fictional mission to Mars.

Joels, Kerry Mark THE MARS ONE CREW MANUAL (Ballantine 0-345-31881-1, 11/85 [11/85], $12.95, unpaginated, pb) Trade paperback edition of the above.

*Johnson, Anabelle & Edgar Johnson PRISONERS OF PSI (Atheneum/Argo 0-689-31132-X, 09/85 [10/85], $12.95, 149pp, hc) Young-adult sf novel about a teenage psychic kidnapped by Libyan terrorists. The book is set in 2000 AD.

*Johnson, Crockett BARNABY #1: WANTED: A FAIRY GODFATHER (Ballantine/Del Rey 0-345-32673-3, 11/85 [10/85], $2.95, 213pp, pb) First book publication of a humorous fantasy cartoon strip which originally appeared in the '40s and '50s. These long-awaited editions contain strips never before available in book form. Few fantasy lovers of any age will be able to resist the matter-of-fact Barnaby and his totally self-important fairy-godfather. (DLN)

*Johnson, Crockett BARNABY #2: MR. O'MALLEY AND THE HAUNTED HOUSE (Ballantine/Del Rey 0-345-32674-1, 11/85 [10/85], $2.95, 218pp, pb) Second in the series of comics; first time in book form.

*Johnson, Crockett BARNABY #3: JACKEEN J.O. O'MALLEY FOR CONGRESS (Ballantine/Del Rey 0-345-32981-3, 01/86 [12/85], $2.95, 218pp, pb) Art/humor. The third volume of "Barnaby" daily comic strips.

*Johnson, Denis FISKADORO (Knopf 0-394-53839-0, 06/85 [05/85], $14.95, 221pp, hc) Literary sf novel of post-holocaust America, haunting and very well written. (FCM)

*Johnson, Edgar & Anabelle Johnson PRISONERS OF PSI Main listing under Anabelle Johnson.

*Johnson, Kenneth R. & Jerry Boyajian INDEX TO THE SCIENCE FICTION MAGAZINES 1984 Main listing under Jerry Boyajian.

*Johnstone, William W. ALONE IN THE ASHES (Zebra 0-8217-1721-9, 12/85 [11/85], $3.50, 350pp, pb) Sf survivalist novel; after the nuclear war one guy tries to rebuild the world. Fifth in the series.

*Johnstone, William W. BLOOD IN THE ASHES (Zebra 0-8217-1537-2, 02/85 [01/85], $3.50, 396pp, pb) Post-holocaust survivalist novel. Fourth in the series.

Jones, D.F. COLOSSUS (Berkley 0-425-07648-2, 04/85 [03/85], $2.75, 223pp, pb) Reissue (Rupert Hart-Davis 1966) sf novel, first of a trilogy. This was filmed as THE FORBIN PROJECT.

Jones, Diana Wynne FIRE AND HEMLOCK (Methuen 0-416-50960-6, 1985 [12/85], £8.95, 341pp, hc) Reprint (Greenwillow 1984) fantasy novel, a fine modern retelling of the "Tam Lin" tale. (FCM) First British edition.

Jones, Diana Wynne THE HOMEWARD BOUNDERS (Ace 0-441-34266-3, 01/86 [12/85], $2.95, 224pp, pb) Reprint (Macmillan UK 1981) fantasy novel -- the "real game" theme given odd and fascinating twists by an excellent author. Recommended. (FCM)

+Jones, Diana Wynne WARLOCK AT THE WHEEL AND OTHER STORIES (Greenwillow 0-688-04305-4, 06/85 [05/85], $10.95, 156pp, hc) Reprint (Macmillan U.K. 1984) collection of young-adult fantasy stories.
Contents:

			Page
Warlock at the Wheel	Diana Wynne Jones	ss WARLOCK,84	7
The Plague of Peacocks	Diana Wynne Jones	ss WARLOCK,84	23
The Fluffy Pink Toadstool	Diana Wynne Jones	ss PFP V13 #4,79	35
Auntie Bea's Day Out	Diana Wynne Jones	ss CATFLAP,79	43
Carruthers	Diana Wynne Jones	nv YWT # 8,78	54
No One	Diana Wynne Jones	nv WARLOCK,84	75
Dragon Reserve, Home Eight	Diana Wynne Jones	nv WARLOCK,84	100
The Sage of Theare	Diana Wynne Jones	nv HECATES,82	129

*Jones, Stephen & Jo Fletcher, eds. Fantasycon X Programme Booklet (Fantasycon X no ISBN, 09/85 [09/85], free with membership, else £2.50/$5.00, 92pp, pb) Program booklet containing stories, articles and artwork for Fantasycon X held in Birmingham, U.K.
Contents:

			Page
Introduction	Stephen Jones & Jo Fletcher	in	5
Robert Holdstock- Man, Myth or Magic?	Chris Evans	bg FYC #10,85	9
The Other Place	Robert Holdstock	ss FYC #10,85	12
Quiet Fear: Charles L. Grant	Douglas E. Winter	bg FYC #10,85	27
Penny Daye	Charles L. Grant	ss FYC #10,85	32
The Magic of Diana Wynne Jones	Lisa Tuttle	bg FYC #10,85	38
No One	Diana Wynne Jones	nv WARLOCK,84	42
Incarnate [deleted chapter from the novel "Incarnate"]	Ramsey Campbell	ex WFC 1983	60
Guest Notes	[Misc. Material]	bg FYC #10,85	78
Film Notes	Kim Newman	mr FYC #10,85	85
British Fantasy Awards-1984 [nominees]	[Misc. Material]	ms FYC #10,85	90

Jordan, Robert CONAN THE TRIUMPHANT (Tor 0-812-54242-8, 04/85 [03/85], $2.95, 314pp, pb) Reprint (Tor 1983) "Conan" novel, first mass-market edition.

Jordan, Robert CONAN THE VICTORIOUS (Tor 0-812-54246-0, 12/85 [11/85], $2.95, 280pp, pb) Reprint (Tor 1984) fantasy novel, in the series based on the Robert E. Howard character.

*Kagan, Janet UHURA'S SONG (Pocket 0-671-54730-5, 01/85 [12/84], $3.95, 373pp, pb) Star Trek novel.

Kahn, James TIME'S DARK LAUGHTER (Ballantine/Del Rey 0-345-32701-2, 11/85 [10/85], $3.50, 318pp, pb) Reissue (Del Rey 1982) sf novel, sequel to WORLD ENOUGH AND TIME. 2nd printing.

Kahn, James WORLD ENOUGH AND TIME (Ballantine/Del Rey 0-345-32700-4, 11/85 [10/85], $3.50, 340pp, pb) Reissue (Del Rey 1980) sf novel. 2nd printing.

*Karl, Jean E. STRANGE TOMORROW (Dutton 0-525-44162-X, 05/85 [04/85], $12.95, 135pp, hc) Juvenile sf novel, related to her earlier book THE TURNING PLACE.

Karr, Phyllis Ann FROSTFLOWER AND THORN (Berkley 0-425-07588-5, 03/85 [02/85], $2.95, 275pp, pb) Reissue (Berkley 1980) fantasy novel.

Karr, Phyllis Ann FROSTFLOWER AND WINDBOURNE (Berkley 0-425-07677-6, 05/85 [04/85], $2.95, 234pp, pb) Reissue (Berkley 1982) fantasy novel. Second printing.

Karr, Phyllis Ann THE IDYLLS OF THE QUEEN (Berkley 0-425-08080-3, 09/85 [08/85], $2.95, 341pp, pb) Reprint (Ace 1982) Arthurian fantasy/mystery novel.

Karr, Phyllis Ann WILDRAITH'S LAST BATTLE (Berkley 0-425-08026-9, 08/85 [07/85], $2.95, 282pp, pb) Reprint (Ace 1982) fantasy novel. Sword & sorcery.

Kavan, Anna ICE (Norton 0-393-02273-0, 10/85 [12/85], $14.95, 158pp, hc) Reprint (P. Owen 1967) surreal sf novel.

Kavan, Anna ICE (Norton 0-393-30256-3, 10/85 [12/85], $5.95, 158pp, pb) Paperback edition of the above.

*Kay, Guy Gavriel THE SUMMER TREE (McClelland & Stewart 0-7710-4472-0, 1984 [05/85], C$19.95, 323pp, hc) This Canadian first edition of the first in a fantasy trilogy (also a first novel) appeared in 1984, but didn't reach us until 1985. Book One of "The Fionavar Tapestry". Highly recommended. (FCM)

+Kay, Guy Gavriel THE SUMMER TREE (Arbor House 0-87795-760-6, 09/85 [09/85], $15.95, 323pp, hc) Reprint (McClellan & Stewart 1984) fantasy novel in the Tolkien tradition; first U.S. edition.

*Kaye, Marvin, ed. MASTERPIECES OF TERROR AND THE SUPERNATURAL (SFBC #5144, 05/85 [04/85], $6.98, 623pp, hc) Anthology of 53 stories and poems by writers ranging from Bram Stoker and Poe to Walt Whitman and Tennessee Williams, with more recent authors represented as well.
Contents:

			Page
Introduction: In Search of Masterpieces	Marvin Kaye	in	xiii
Dracula's Guest	Bram Stoker	ss DRCLGST,14	3
The Professor's Teddy Bear	Theodore Sturgeon	ss WRT Mar,48	14
Bubnoff and the Devil	Ivan Turgenev	ss	24
English adaption by Marvin Kaye			
The Quest for Blank Claveringi [revised from The Snails]	Patricia Highsmith	ss SEP Jun 17,67	31
The Erl-King	Johann Wolfgang Von Goethe	pm	44
English adaption by Marvin Kaye			
The Bottle Imp	Robert Louis Stevenson	nv BAW Mar,1891	46
A Malady of Magicks	Craig Shaw Gardner	ss FAN Oct,78	71
Lan Lung [expanded from Dragon...Ghost]	M. Lucie Chin	nv AES Mar,80	86
The Dragon Over Hackensack	Richard L. Wexelblat	pm 1985	106
The Transformation	Mary W. Shelley	ss KPS 1831	107
The Faceless Thing	Edward D. Hoch	ss MOH Nov,63	122
The Anchor	Jack Snow	ss DRKMUSC,47	129
When the Clock Strikes	Tanith Lee	ss WTB # 1,81	134
Oshidori	Lafcadio Hearn	vi KWAIDAN,04	149
Carmilla	Joseph Sheridan Le Fanu	na INAGLSS,1886	151
Eumenides in the Fourth Floor Lavatory	Orson Scott Card	nv CRY # 4,79	214
Lenore	Gottfried August Burger	pm Jun,1844	229
English adaption by Dante Gabriel Rossetti			
The Black Wedding	Isaac Bashevis Singer	ss SPINOZA,58	237
translated by Martha Glicklich			
Hop-Frog	Edgar Allan Poe	ss SLM Apr,1836	245
Sardonicus	Ray Russell	nv PBY Jan,61	254
Graveyard Shift [The Faces]	Richard Matheson	ss EMB # 1,60	286
Wake Not the Dead	Johann Ludwig Tieck	nv	291
Night and Silence	Maurice Level	ss WRT Feb,32	314
Flies	Isaac Asimov	ss FSF Jun,53	321
The Night Wire	H.F. Arnold	ss WRT Sep,26	328
Last Respects	Dick Baldwin	ss 1975	335
The Pool of the Stone God	A. Merritt	ss AWK Sep 23,23	340
A Tale of the Thirteenth Floor	Ogden Nash	pm FSF Jul,55	344
The Tree	Dylan Thomas	ss ADVSKIN,55	348
Stroke of Mercy	Parke Godwin	ss TZM Sep,81	355
Lazarus	Leonid Andreyev	ss	374
The Waxwork [as Ex-Private X]	A.M. Burrage	ss SMNINRM,31	393
The Silent Couple	Pierre Courtois	ss FIG 1826	404
translated and adapted by Faith Lancereau and Marvin Kaye			
Moon-Face	Jack London	ss	408
Death in the School-Room	Walt Whitman	ss 1841	413
The Upturned Face	Stephen Crane	ss	419
One Summer Night	Ambrose Bierce	vi	423
The Easter Egg	H.H. Munro	ss	425
The House in Goblin Wood [as Carter Dickson]	John Dickson Carr	ss EQM Nov,47	429
The Vengeance of Nitocris	Tennessee Williams	ss WRT Aug,28	448
The Informal Execution of Soupbone Pew	Damon Runyon	ss	459
His Unconquerable Enemy	W.C. Morrow	ss	472
Rizpah	Alfred Lord Tennyson	pm	481
The Question [The Question My Son Asked]	Stanley Ellin	ss EQM Nov,62	486
The Flayed Hand	Guy de Maupassant	ss	497
The Hospice	Robert Aickman	nv COLDHND,75	502
The Christmas Banquet	Nathaniel Hawthorne	ss	533
The Hungry House	Robert Bloch	nv IMG Apr,51	549
The Demon of the Gibbet	Fitz-James O'Brien	pm	566
The Owl	Anatole Le Braz	ss	568
translated by Faith Lancereau			
No. 252 Rue M. Le Prince	Ralph Adams Cram	ss BLKSPRT,1895	575
The Music of Erich Zann	H.P. Lovecraft	ss NTA Mar,22 WRT May,25	588
Riddles in the Dark (Original Version) [Chapter 5 of "The Hobbit"]	J.R.R. Tolkien	ex HMF 1938	596
Afterword: Is Terror a Dying Art?	Marvin Kaye	aw	609
Miscellaneous Notes	Marvin Kaye	bi	615
Selected Bibliography	Marvin Kaye	bi	619

Kaye, Marvin, ed. <u>MASTERPIECES OF TERROR AND THE SUPERNATURAL: A TREASURY OF SPELLBINDING TALES OLD & NEW</u> (Doubleday 0-385-18549-9, 06/85 [05/85], $15.95, 623pp, hc) Reprint (SFBC 1985), first trade edition of this anthology which appeared first from the book club.

Kaye, Marvin & Parke Godwin <u>THE MASTERS OF SOLITUDE</u> (Bantam 0-553-24726-3, 01/85 [12/84], $3.50, 401pp, pb) Reprint (Doubleday 1978) sf novel, first of a projected trilogy. Recommended. (FCM)

*Kelleher, Victor <u>THE BEAST OF HEAVEN</u> (Univ. of Queensland Press 0-7022-1795-6, 1984 [06/85], $10.00, 205pp, hc) Published in Australia in 1984, this post-holocaust sf novel is now available through Queensland University Press. There doesn't seem to be a separate U.S. edition, just a sticker on the Australian one.

Kelly, James Patrick <u>PLANET OF WHISPERS</u> (Tor 0-812-54291-6, 07/85 [06/85], pb) Reprint (Bluejay 1984) sf novel, Volume 1 of "The Messenger Chronicles".

*Kelly, James Patrick & John Kessel <u>FREEDOM BEACH</u> (Bluejay 0-312-94167-6, 11/85 [12/85], $15.95, 259pp, hc) Sf novel rewritten from novelettes.
Contents: Page
Freedom Beach   James Patrick Kelley & John Kessel
                                               nv FSF Aug,84   1
Sea Change   James Patrick Kelley   pm AMZ Sep,82   24
The Big Dream   John Kessel   nv IAS Apr,84   124
The Empty World   James Patrick Kelley   nv IAS Dec,84   183

*Kelly, James Patrick & John Kessel <u>FREEDOM BEACH</u> (Bluejay 0-312-94168-4, 11/85 [12/85], $8.95, 259pp, pb) Paperback edition of the above.

*Kendall, Gordon <u>WHITE WING</u> (Tor 0-812-54297-5, 07/85 [06/85], $2.95, 319pp, pb) Sf novel; better than average military space opera. (FCM) This is actually a collaboration by Susan Shwartz and Shariann Lewitt.

*Kennealy, Patricia <u>THE COPPER CROWN</u> (Bluejay 0-312-94062-9, 02/85 [01/85], $15.95, 329pp, hc) Fantasy novel of a "Keltic" empire in space, first of a nine-book series. A first novel.

*Kennedy, Richard <u>AMY'S EYES</u> (Harper & Row 0-06-023219-6, 1985 [12/85], $13.50, 437pp, hc) Young-adult fantasy novel sea epic, illustrated by Richard Egielski.

*Kessel, John & James Patrick Kelly <u>FREEDOM BEACH</u> Main listing under James Patrick Kelly.

*Kidd, Ronald <u>THE GLITCH</u> (Dutton/Lodestar 0-525-67160-9, 10/85 [11/85], $11.95, 117pp, hc) Juvenile sf novel of a sixth-grader trapped in the Computer Kingdom.

*Kilian, Crawford <u>BROTHER JONATHAN</u> (Ace 0-441-08227-0, 06/85 [05/85], $2.75, 183pp, pb) Sf novel.

Kilian, Crawford <u>THE EMPIRE OF TIME</u> (Ballantine/Del Rey 0-345-32528-1, 09/85 [08/85], $2.50, 182pp, pb) Reissue (Del Rey 1978) sf novel. 3rd printing.

Kilian, Crawford <u>EYAS</u> (Bantam Spectra 0-553-25371-9, 09/85 [08/85], $3.50, 254pp, pb) Reissue (Bantam 1982) sf novel, an ambitious and impressive tale of far-future Earth. (FCM) 2nd printing.

*Killough, Lee <u>LIBERTY'S WORLD</u> (DAW 0-88677-023-8, 03/85 [02/85], $2.95, 238pp, pb) Sf novel.

*Killus, James <u>SUNSMOKE</u> (Ace 0-441-79083-6, 03/85 [02/85], $2.75, 182pp, pb) Sf/horror novel beginning when "a crazed meteorologist injects a computer programmed ancient Japanese devil" into Los Angeles smog.

Kilworth, Garry <u>SPLIT SECOND</u> (Popular Library/Questar 0-445-20114-2, 12/85 [11/85], $2.95, 230pp, pb) Reprint (Faber 1979) sf novel of a journey back to Cro-Magnon times.

*King, Bernard <u>STARKADDER</u> (New English Library 0-450-06100-0, 06/85 [05/85], £8.95, 244pp, hc) Nordic fantasy novel, possibly a first novel.

*King, David & Russell Blackford, eds. <u>URBAN FANTASIES</u> (Ebony Books 0-9590655-1-2, 08/85 [09/85], A$4.95, 177pp, pb) Original anthology of 13 stories, both sf and fantasy.
Contents: Page
Introduction   David King & Russell Blackford in   vii
Du   David Brooks   ss URBANFN,85   1
A Tooth for Every Child Damien Broderick   ss URBANFN,85   7
Confusion Day   Philippa C. Maddern   ss URBANFN,85   27
The Other Side of the Other Side of the Street
                         Norman Talbot   ss URBANFN,85   35
Down from Demolition   John Baxter   ss URBANFN,85   53
Outlines for Urban Fantasies
                         Michael Wilding   ss URBANFN,85   63
Flags   David King   ss URBANFN,85   71
Tangled Up   Greg Egan   ss URBANFN,85   75
The Government in Exile Paul Collins   vi URBANFN,85   93
Montage   Lucy Sussex   ss URBANFN,85   93
The Fittest   George Turner   nv URBANFN,85 105
The Bullet that Grows in the Gun
                         Terry Dowling   ss URBANFN,85 133

The Twist of Fate   David Grigg   nv URBANFN,85 151
Authors and Editors   [Misc. Material]   bg   179

*King, Stephen <u>THE BACHMAN BOOKS: FOUR EARLY NOVELS BY STEPHEN KING</u> (NAL 0-453-00507-1, 10/85 [09/85], $19.95, 692pp, hc) Omnibus edition of the books King published under the pseudonym "Richard Bachman". There's a new foreword by King.
Contents: Page
Why I Was Bachman   Stephen King   fw   v
RAGE   Richard Bachman   n. SIG 1977   1
THE LONG WALK   Richard Bachman   n. SIG 1979   161
ROADWORK   Richard Bachman   n. SIG 1981   323
THE RUNNING MAN   Richard Bachman   n. SIG 1982   531

*King, Stephen <u>THE BACHMAN BOOKS: FOUR EARLY NOVELS BY STEPHEN KING</u> (NAL/Plume 0-452-25774-3, 10/85 [09/85], $9.95, 692pp, pb) Paperback edition of the above.

King, Stephen <u>CYCLE OF THE WEREWOLF</u> (NAL/Signet 0-451-82111-4, 05/85 [04/85], $8.95, 128pp, pb) Reprint (Land of Enchantment 1983) horror tale with illustrations by Berni Wrightson. First trade edition.

King, Stephen <u>CYCLE OF THE WEREWOLF</u> (NAL/Signet 0-451-82111-4, 10/85 [09/85], $8.95, 128pp, pb) Reissue (Land of Enchantment 1983) werewolf novella with illustrations by Berni Wrightson. Third printing.

*King, Stephen <u>THE EYES OF THE DRAGON</u> (Philtrum no ISBN, 02/85 [01/85], $120.00, 314pp, hc) Juvenile fantasy novel, in a signed, boxed, numbered edition of 1250 copies, with illustrations by Kenneth R. Linkhauser. A special giant-size (8.5" x 13", 4.5 lb) first edition on fine paper with linen slipcase and binding.

*King, Stephen <u>SILVER BULLET</u> (NAL/Signet Special 0-451-82128-9, 11/85 [12/85], $9.95, 255pp, pb) Movie tie-in edition including CYCLE OF THE WEREWOLF (basis of the film), the <u>Silver Bullet</u> screenplay, an introduction and afterword by King, and 8 pages of movie stills.
Contents: Page
Introduction   Stephen King   in
CYCLE OF THE WEREWOLF   Stephen King   n.
Silver Bullet   Stephen King   pl
Afterword   Stephen King   aw

*King, Stephen <u>SKELETON CREW</u> (Putnam 0-399-13039-X, 06/21/85 [05/85], $18.95, 512pp, hc) Collection, which includes a reprint of "The Mist" plus a number of fine stories in their first book appearance. Recommended. (FCM)
Contents: Page
Introduction   Stephen King   in   13
The Mist   Stephen King   na DRKFRCS,80   21
Here There Be Tygers   Stephen King   ss UBR Spr,68 135
The Monkey   Stephen King   nv GLR Nov,80 141
Cain Rose Up   Stephen King   ss UBR Spr,68 175
Mrs. Todd's Shortcut   Stephen King   nv RBK May,84 181
The Jaunt   Stephen King   nv TZM Jun,81 203
The Wedding Gig   Stephen King   ss EQM Dec 1,80 227
Paranoid: A Chant   Stephen King   ss SKTNCRW,85 241
The Raft   Stephen King   nv GLR Nov,82 245
Word Processor of the Gods [The Word Processor]
                         Stephen King   ss PBY Jan,83 271
The Man Who Would Not Shake Hands
                         Stephen King   ss SDW # 4,81 289
Beachworld   Stephen King   ss WRT 1985   305
The Reaper's Image   Stephen King   ss STM Spr,69 321
Nona   Stephen King   nv SDW # 1,78 329
For Owen   Stephen King   ss SKTNCRW,85 359
Survivor Type   Stephen King   ss TERRORS,82 361
Uncle Otto's Truck   Stephen King   ss YNK Oct,83 379
Morning Deliveries (Milkman #1)
                         Stephen King   ss SKTNCRW,85 395
Big Wheels: A Tale of the Laundry Game (Milkman #2)
                         Stephen King   ss NWT # 2,80 401
Gramma   Stephen King   nv WDB 1984   415
The Ballad of the Flexible Bullet
                         Stephen King   nv FSF Jun,84 443
The Reach [Do the Dead Sing?]
                         Stephen King   ss YNK Nov,81 487
Notes   Stephen King   bi   507

King, Stephen <u>SKELETON CREW</u> [special edition] (Scream/Press 0-910489-12-2, 10/85 [10/85], $75.00, boxed signed & numbered limited edition, 545pp, hc) Reprint (Putnam 1985) collection, with a preface and afterword by the author, and illustrations by J.K. Potter. This special edition has one extra story, "Becka Paulson", not found in the trade edition. There is also a foldout full-color poster/illustration and a color illo. on the box. Sold out in advance of publication.
Contents: Page
Introduction   Stephen King   in
The Mist   Stephen King   na DRKFRCS,80
Here There Be Tygers   Stephen King   ss UBR Spr,68
The Monkey   Stephen King   nv GLR Nov,80
Cain Rose Up   Stephen King   ss UBR Spr,68
Mrs. Todd's Shortcut   Stephen King   nv RBK May,84
The Jaunt   Stephen King   nv TZM Jun,81
The Wedding Gig   Stephen King   ss EQM Dec 1,80
Paranoid: A Chant   Stephen King   ss SKTNCRW,85
The Raft   Stephen King   nv GLR Nov,82

Word Processor of the Gods [The Word Processor]
                        Stephen King   ss PBY Jan,83
The Man Who Would Not Shake Hands
                        Stephen King   ss SDW # 4,81
Beachworld   Stephen King   ss WRT 1985
The Reaper's Image   Stephen King   ss STM Spr,69
Nona   Stephen King   nv SDW # 1,78
For Owen   Stephen King   ss SKTNCRW,85
Survivor Type   Stephen King   ss TERRORS,82
Uncle Otto's Truck   Stephen King   ss YNK Oct,83
Morning Deliveries (Milkman #1)
                        Stephen King   ss SKTNCRW,85
Big Wheels: A Tale of the Laundry Game (Milkman #2)
                        Stephen King   ss NWT # 2,80
Gramma   Stephen King   nv WDB 1984
The Ballad of the Flexible Bullet
                        Stephen King   nv FSF Jun,84
The Reach [Do the Dead Sing?]
                        Stephen King   ss YNK Nov,81
Becka Paulson [The Revelations of 'Becka Paulson]
                        Stephen King   ss RST Jul 19,84
Notes   Stephen King   bi

King, Stephen <u>STEPHEN KING'S DANSE MACABRE</u> (Berkley 0-425-07984-8, 04/85 [03/85], $4.50, 437pp, pb) Reissue (Everest House 1981); non-fiction, King's personal views on horror in books and films.

King, Stephen <u>STEPHEN KING'S DANSE MACABRE</u> (Berkley 0-425-08842-1, 11/85 [10/85], $4.50, 437pp, pb) Reissue (Everest House 1981) book of non-fiction. 15th printing.

King, Stephen & Peter Straub <u>THE TALISMAN</u> (Grant 0-937986-65-8, 02/85 [01/85], $120 signed/boxed/numbered edition of 1200 copies; $65 boxed trade edition; 2 vols., 464 + 336pp, hc) Reprint (Viking 1984) fantasy novel, with illustrations by ten artists, including Rowena, Maitz, and Wrightson, in full color. As usual, Grant has produced a fine piece of bookmaking and an excellent collector's edition. The so-called "trade" edition is not signed or as intricately designed, but is still eye-popping and still available. (CNB)

King, Stephen & Peter Straub <u>THE TALISMAN</u> (Berkley 0-425-08181-8, 11/85 [10/85], $4.95, 770pp, pb) Reprint (Viking 1984) fantasy novel.

*****King, Tappan & Viido Polikarpus** <u>DOWNTOWN</u> (Arbor House 0-87795-673-1, 06/85 [05/85], $16.95, 293pp, hc) Fantasy novel, printed in sepia; Polikarpus is also the illustrator. Modern urban fantasy with a young-adult protagonist. A first novel.

Klein, T.E.D. <u>THE CEREMONIES</u> (Bantam 0-553-25055-8, 07/85 [06/85], $3.95, 555pp, pb) Reprint (Viking 1984) dark fantasy novel.

*****Klein, T.E.D.** <u>DARK GODS</u> (Viking 0-670-80590-4, 08/85 [07/85], $15.95, 259pp, hc) Collection of fantasy/horror tales. Three of them were previously published "in slightly different form"; "Nadelman's God" seems to be new.
Contents: Page
Children of the Kingdom T.E.D. Klein   na DRKFRCS,80   1
Petey   T.E.D. Klein   na SDW # 2,79   73
Black Man with a Horn   T.E.D. Klein   nv NTLCTHU,80 129
Nadelman's God   T.E.D. Klein   na DRKGODS,85 175

*****Knight, Damon** <u>CV</u> (Tor 0-312-93513-7, 05/85 [04/85], $13.95, 285pp, hc) Sf novel.

*****Knight, Damon** <u>LATE KNIGHT EDITION</u> (NESFA Press 0-915368-85-4, 03/85 [02/85], 200 copy signed/boxed/numbered edition $25.00; 600 copy regular edition $13.00 + $1.00 postage per order, 150pp, hc) Collection of 6 stories (one an original) and two essays, published in conjunction with Knight's appearance as Guest of Honor at Boskone XXII. The boxed, signed edition sold out at the convention.
Contents: Page
Introduction   Kate Wilhelm   in   v
What Is Science Fiction? Damon Knight   ar TRNGPTS,77   3
The Third Little Green Man
                        Damon Knight   nv PLS Sum,48   15
Who Is Damon Knight?   Damon Knight   ar PLS Sum,48   39
Definition   Damon Knight   ss STS Feb,53   41
I See You   Damon Knight   ss FSF Nov,76   61
Tarcan of the Hoboes   Damon Knight   nv FSF Oct,82   79
La Ronde   Damon Knight   ss FSF Oct,83 101
The Cage   Damon Knight   nv LTKNTED,85 119
Good-bye, Henry J. Kostkos, Good-bye
                        Damon Knight   ar CLR # 2,72 143

Knight, Damon <u>THE MAN IN THE TREE</u> (Gollancz 0-575-03595-1, 05/85 [04/85], £8.95, 246pp, hc) Reprint (Berkley 1984) sf novel, first U.K. edition and the first hardcover.

*****Koontz, Dean R.** <u>TWILIGHT EYES</u> (Land of Enchantment 0-9603828-4-4, 12/85 [12/85], $32.00, 263pp, hc) Novel of dark fantasy, 8.5" x 11", with numerous illustrations by Phil Parks in both color and black & white. Also available in a signed, limited edition, price unknown.

*****Kornbluth, C.M. & Frederik Pohl** <u>SEARCH THE SKY</u> Main listing under Frederik Pohl.

Kornbluth, C.M. & Frederik Pohl <u>THE SPACE MERCHANTS</u> Main listing under Frederik Pohl.

*****Kornbluth, C.M. & Frederik Pohl** <u>VENUS, INC.</u> Main listing under Frederik Pohl.

*****Kotani, Eric & John Maddox Roberts** <u>ACT OF GOD</u> (Baen 0-671-55979-6, 09/85 [08/85], $2.95, 282pp, pb) Near-future war novel. Russians hatch a plot to bomb the U.S. with comet fragments. Kotani is supposedly the pseudonym for a "world-class space scientist."

Kotzwinkle, William <u>E.T. THE EXTRA-TERRESTRIAL</u> (Berkley 0-425-08168-0, 07/85 [06/85], $3.50, 246pp, pb) Reissue (Putnam 1982) novelization of the cutesy film. 26th Berkley printing.

*****Kotzwinkle, William** <u>E.T.: THE BOOK OF THE GREEN PLANET</u> (Berkley 0-425-07642-3, 03/85 [02/85], $3.50, 245pp, pb) This sequel to the <u>E.T.</u> novelization is based on a story by Stephen Spielberg. This is not the story of the next movie, but the bridge to that movie. You will have to read it to understand what will be going on.

*****Kotzwinkle, William** <u>E.T.: THE BOOK OF THE GREEN PLANET</u> (Berkley 0-425-08001-3, 03/85 [02/85], $2.95, 89pp, pb) This edition is the "illustrated novel for young readers" with pictures by David Wiesner, a simple version of the above.

*****Kotzwinkle, William** <u>E.T.: THE STORYBOOK OF THE GREEN PLANET</u> (Putnam 0-399-21257-4, 09/85 [08/85], $8.95, 78pp, hc) Juvenile story with illustrations by David Wiesner, based on a story by Steven Spielberg. Its relationship to the previously published BOOK OF THE GREEN PLANET by Kotzwinkle isn't made clear.

*****Kotzwinkle, William** <u>JEWEL OF THE MOON</u> (Putnam 0-399-13113-2, 12/85 [11/85], $14.95, 160pp, hc) Collection of 15 stories, only two of them previously published. Most are very short fantasies.
Contents: Page
The Day Stokowski Saved the World
                        William Kotzwinkle   ss JWLMOON,85   9
The Curio Shop   William Kotzwinkle   ss OMN Sep,80   15
Jewel of the Moon   William Kotzwinkle   ss JWLMOON,85   21
Postcard Found in a Trunk
                        William Kotzwinkle   ss JWLMOON,85   41
Sun, Moon, and Storm   William Kotzwinkle   ss JWLMOON,85   49
Tell Her You Love Her with a Ring from DAVE'S HOUSE OF
DIAMONDS   William Kotzwinkle   ss JWLMOON,85   65
Disturbance Reported on a Pipeline
                        William Kotzwinkle   ss JWLMOON,85   69
Mr. Jones's Convention William Kotzwinkle   ss JWLMOON,85   77
Fading Tatoo   William Kotzwinkle   ss JWLMOON,85   87
Victory at North Antor William Kotzwinkle   ss JWLMOON,85   93
A Man Who Knew His Birds William Kotzwinkle   ss OMN Feb,85 113
Letter to a Swan   William Kotzwinkle   ss JWLMOON,85 123
Star Cruisers, Welcome William Kotzwinkle   ss JWLMOON,85 133
That Winter When Prince Borisov Was Everybody's Favorite
                        William Kotzwinkle   ss JWLMOON,85 141
Fana   William Kotzwinkle   ss JWLMOON,85 151

Kress, Nancy <u>THE GOLDEN GROVE</u> (Berkley 0-425-08476-0, 01/86 [12/85], $2.95, 246pp, pb) Reprint (Bluejay 1984) fantasy novel.

*****Kress, Nancy** <u>TRINITY AND OTHER STORIES</u> (Bluejay 0-312-94438-1, 08/85 [08/85], $15.95, 279pp, hc) Collection of 11 stories, plus an introduction by Gene Wolfe.
Contents: Page
Explaining Nancy Kress Gene Wolfe   in   1
With the Original Cast Nancy Kress   nv OMN May,82   6
Casey's Empire   Nancy Kress   ss FSF Nov,81   36
Talp Hunt   Nancy Kress   ss UNI #12,82   56
Against a Crooked Stile Nancy Kress   nv IAS May,79   76
Explanations, Inc.   Nancy Kress   ss FSF Jul,84   98
Shadows on the Cave Wall Nancy Kress   nv UNI #11,81 116
Ten Thousand Pictures, One Word
                        Nancy Kress   ss TZM Aug,84 146
Night Win   Nancy Kress   nv IAS Sep,83 162
Borovsky's Hollow Woman Nancy Kress & Jeff Duntemann
                                         nv OMN Oct,83 186
Out of All Them Bright Stars
                        Nancy Kress   ss FSF Mar,85 218
Trinity   Nancy Kress   na IAS Oct,84 228

*****Kress, Nancy** <u>THE WHITE PIPES</u> (Bluejay 0-312-94451-9, 03/85 [02/85], $14.95, 218pp, hc) Fantasy novel.

*****Kube-McDowell, Michael P.** <u>EMPRISE</u> (Berkley 0-425-07763-2, 06/85 [05/85], $2.95, 304pp, pb) Sf novel, Book One of "the Trigon Disunity". An excellent first novel. (FCM)

Kunetka, James & Whitley Streiber <u>WAR DAY</u> Main listing under Whitley Streiber.

Kurland, Michael & S.W. Barton <u>THE LAST PRESIDENT</u> (Critic's Choice 0-931773-09-1, 1985 [10/85], $3.50, 357pp, pb) Reprint (Morrow 1980) futuristic political novel.

Kurtz, Katherine <u>THE BISHOP'S HEIR</u> (SFBC #6401, 05/85 [04/85], $5.98, 304pp, hc) Reprint (Ballantine/Del Rey 1984) fantasy novel, Book 1 in the "Histories of King Kelson" trilogy, part of the "Deryni" series.

Kurtz, Katherine THE BISHOP'S HEIR (Ballantine/Del Rey 0-345-3009997-1, 08/85 [07/85], $3.50, 361pp, pb) Reprint (Del Rey 1984) fantasy novel, Vol. I of "The Histories of King Kelson" trilogy, and Book 7 in the "Deryni" series.

*Kurtz, Katherine THE CHRONICLES OF THE DERYNI (SFBC #6411, 05/85 [04/85], $9.98, 753pp, hc) Omnibus edition of three "Deryni" fantasy novels.
Contents:

			Page
DERYNI RISING	Katherine Kurtz	n. BAL 1970	1
DERYNI CHECKMATE	Katherine Kurtz	n. BAL 1972	197
HIGH DERYNI	Katherine Kurtz	n. BAL 1973	417
Appendix I Index of Characters			
	[Misc. Material]	ix	737
Appendix II Index to Place Names			
	[Misc. Material]	ix	744
Appendix III Time Line for History of the Eleven Kingdoms			
	[Misc. Material]	ix	748
Appendix IV The Genetic Basis for Deryni Inheritance			
	[Misc. Material]	ix	750

*Kurtz, Katherine THE KING'S JUSTICE (Ballantine/Del Rey 0-345-31825-0, 11/85 [11/85], $16.95FPT, 337pp, hc) Fantasy novel, Vol. II of "The Histories of King Kelson" and eighth in the ongoing "Deryni" series.

L'Engle, Madeleine A HOUSE LIKE A LOTUS (Dell/Laurel Leaf 0-440-93685-3, 1985 [11/85], $3.50, 308pp, pb) Reprint (Farrar Straus Giroux 1984) associational novel. Not sf or fantasy, but a companion book to THE ARM OF THE STARFISH and DRAGONS IN THE WATERS.

Lafferty, R.A. THE FLAME IS GREEN (Corroboree 0-911169-04-0, 05/85 [04/85], $25.00, 237pp, hc) Reprint (Walker 1971) historical fantasy novel, Book One of the "Coscuin Chronicles". There are new illustrations by David Brian Erickson (some in color).

Lafferty, R.A. THE FLAME IS GREEN (Corroboree 0-911169-05-9, 05/85 [04/85], $35.00, 237pp, hc) 250 copy signed, numbered edition of the above.

*Lafferty, R.A. SLIPPERY AND OTHER STORIES (Drumm no ISBN, 02/85 [02/85], $5.00, 40pp, pb) Collection of four new stories. This is the limited edition version, 176 signed/numbered copies with a stiff cover and a Lafferty sonnet on the back. The regular edition price is $2.00. Drumm Booklet #19.
Contents:

			Page
Slippery	R.A. Lafferty	ss SLIPPRY,85	3
All Hollow Though You Be	R.A. Lafferty	ss SLIPPRY,85	11
Ewe Lamb	R.A. Lafferty	ss SLIPPRY,85	20
John Salt	R.A. Lafferty	ss SLIPPRY,85	33
Sonnet for limited version of SLIPPERY AND OTHER STORIES			
	R.A. Lafferty	pm SLIPPRY,85	40

Lainez, Manuel Mujica THE WANDERING UNICORN See listing under Mujica Lainez, Manuel.

*Lance, Kathryn PANDORA'S GENES (Popular Library/Questar 0-445-20004-9, 04/85 [03/85], $2.95, 279pp, pb) Sf novel; a first novel. Competent post-holocaust novel with an overly romantic ending. (DLN)

*Lane, Daryl, David Carson & William Vernon THE SOUND OF WONDER: INTERVIEWS FROM "THE SCIENCE FICTION RADIO SHOW" (Oryx Press 0-89774-175-7, 11/85 [11/85], $18.50, 203pp, pb) Non-fiction biographical. Has transcriptions of interviews with 9 authors and artists: Donaldson, Cherryh, Clement, Harness, Sturgeon, Waldrop, Williamson, Rucker, and Whelan.

*Lane, Daryl, David Carson & William Vernon THE SOUND OF WONDER: INTERVIEWS FROM "THE SCIENCE FICTION RADIO SHOW", VOL. 2 (Oryx Press 0-89774-233-8, 12/85 [11/85], $18.50, 201pp, pb) Non-fiction biographical. Has transcripts of interviews with Anthony, Bryant, Farmer, Wollheim, Hogan, Bradley, Ebert, Wolfe, Dickson, and Martin.

Langford, David THE LEAKY ESTABLISHMENT (Sphere 0-7221-5378-3, 11/85 [11/85], £2.25, 197pp, pb) Reprint (Muller 1984) humorous novel; non-sf, associational. Life in a scientific establishment.

+Langford, David & Brian Stableford THE THIRD MILLENNIUM: A HISTORY OF THE WORLD: AD 2000-3000 Main listing under Brian Stableford.

*Larson, Glen S. & Robert Thurston BATTLESTAR GALACTICA 11: THE NIGHTMARE MACHINE (Berkley 0-425-08618-6, 12/85 [11/85], $2.95, 216pp, pb) Sf novel based on the tv series.

*Larson, Majliss STAR TREK #26: PAWNS AND SYMBOLS (Pocket 0-671-55425-5, 11/85 [10/85], $3.50, 277pp, pb) Star Trek novel.

*Laumer, Keith END AS A HERO (Ace 0-441-20656-5, 08/85 [07/85], $2.95, 150pp, pb) Sf novel.

Laumer, Keith THE LONG TWILIGHT (Ace 0-441-48928-1, 01/86 [12/85], $2.95, 222pp, pb) Reprint (Putnam 1969) sf novel.

Laumer, Keith THE OTHER SKY/THE HOUSE IN NOVEMBER (Tor 0-812-54377-7, 11/85 [10/85], $2.95, 249pp, pb) Reprint (Tor 1981) omnibus "Tor Double" with back-to-back sf novels.

Laumer, Keith A PLAGUE OF DEMONS (Baen 0-671-55982-6, 09/85 [08/85], $2.75, 218pp, pb) Reprint (Berkley 1965) sf novel.

Laumer, Keith RETIEF AT LARGE (Ace 0-441-71507-9, 05/85 [04/85], $3.50, 440pp, pb) Reissue (Ace 1978) collection, 6th Ace printing. The stories are culled from earlier Retief collections.

Laumer, Keith RETIEF OF THE CDT (Baen 0-671-55990-7, 10/85 [09/85], $2.95, 220pp, pb) Reprint (Doubleday 1971) collection of stories featuring Retief.

Laumer, Keith RETIEF UNBOUND (Ace 0-441-71254-1, 03/85 [02/85], $2.95, 343pp, pb) Reissue (Ace 1979) of an omnibus volume which collects 5 of the 6 stories from ENVOY TO NEW WORLDS (Ace 1963) plus the novel RETIEF'S RANSOM (Putnam 1971).

Laumer, Keith RETIEF'S WAR (Baen 0-671-55976-1, 08/85 [07/85], $2.95, 218pp, pb) Reprint (Doubleday 1966) sf novel.

Laumer, Keith THE RETURN OF RETIEF (Baen 0-671-55902-8, 12/85 [11/85], $2.95, 221pp, pb) Reissue (Baen 1984) sf novel. Second printing.

*Laumer, Keith ROGUE BOLO (Baen 0-671-65545-0, 01/86 [12/85], $2.95, 233pp, pb) Collection of two connected short novels, apparently new, plus a reprint of "A Short History of the Bolo Fighting Machines".
Contents:

			Page
Rogue Bolo	Keith Laumer	na ROGUEBO,86	3
Final Mission	Keith Laumer	na ROGUEBO,86	149
A Short History of the Bolo Fighting Machines			
	Keith Laumer	ar BOLO ,76	

Laumer, Keith WORLDS OF THE IMPERIUM (Tor 0-812-54379-3, 01/86 [12/85], $2.95, 288pp, pb) Reissue (Tor 1982) collection of the title novel (Ace 1962) plus two novelettes. Third Tor printing in this form.

Laumer, Keith & Rosel George Brown EARTHBLOOD (Bluejay 0-312-94125-0, 02/85 [01/85], $7.95, 318pp, pb) Reprint (Doubleday 1966) sf adventure novel. New illustrations by Alan Gutierrez.

Lawhead, Stephen DREAM THIEF (Crossway 0-89107-266-7, 1985 [09/85], $7.95, 410pp, pb) Reissue (Crossway 1983) Christian-oriented sf novel.

*Lawhead, Stephen EMPHYRION: THE SEARCH FOR FIERRA (Crossway 0-89107-358-2, 1985 [09/85], $7.95, 436pp, pb) Christian-oriented sf novel.

Lawhead, Stephen IN THE HALL OF THE DRAGON KING (Crossway 0-89107-257-8, 1985 [09/85], $7.95, 351pp, pb) Reissue (Crossway 1982) fantasy novel, first in a trilogy. 4th printing.

Lawhead, Stephen THE SWORD AND THE FLAME (Crossway 0-89107-310-8, 1985 [09/85], $7.95, 313pp, pb) Reissue (Crossway 1984) fantasy novel, conclusion of the "Dragon King" trilogy. The three books are available as a boxed set.

Lawhead, Stephen THE WARLORDS OF NIN (Crossway 0-89107-278-0, 1985 [09/85], $7.95, 367pp, pb) Reissue (Crossway 1983) fantasy novel, second in the "Dragon King" trilogy. 4th printing.

Lawrence, J.A. MUDD'S ANGELS (Bantam 0-553-24666-6, 02/85 [01/85], $2.95, 177pp, pb) Reissue (Bantam 1978) Star Trek book, adaptation of two episodes from the tv show. 2nd printing.

Lawrence, J.A. & James Blish STAR TREK 12 Main listing under James Blish.

*Lawrence, Louise CHILDREN OF THE DUST (Harper & Row 0-06-023738-4, 09/85 [09/85], $12.50, 183pp, hc) Young-adult sf novel about mutants after a nuclear holocaust. There may be be an earlier or simultaneous British edition.

+Laws, Stephen GHOST TRAIN (Beaufort 0-8253-0315-X, 08/85 [09/85], $15.95, 314pp, hc) Reprint (U.K. 1985), first U.S. edition of a dark fantasy/horror novel; a first novel.

*Le Guin, Ursula K. ALWAYS COMING HOME (Harper & Row 0-06-015456-X, 10/09/85 [09/85], $25.00, 525pp, pb) An unusual combination of sf "novel" by Le Guin, line drawings by Margaret Chodos, and a cassette of music by Todd Barton (plus readings by Le Guin), depicting a far-future California society. One of the most complex and exciting future cultures ever created, including everything from plays to recipes. A major book. (DLN)
Contents:

			Page
A First Note	Ursula K. Le Guin	fw ALWCMHM,85	xi
The Quail Song	Ursula K. Le Guin	pm ALWCMHM,85	1
Towards an Archeology of the Future			
	Ursula K. Le Guin	in ALWCMHM,85	3
Stone Telling, Part One	Ursula K. Le Guin	nv ALWCMHM,85	7
The Serpentine Codex	Ursula K. Le Guin	ss ALWCMHM,85	43
Chart of the Nine Houses	Ursula K. Le Guin	ms ALWCMHM,85	46
Where It Is	Ursula K. Le Guin	ss ALWCMHM,85	50
Pandora Worries About What She Is Doing: The Pattern			
	Ursula K. Le Guin	vi ALWCMHM,85	53
Some Stories Told Aloud One Evening in the Dry Season at a Summer Place Above Sinshan			
	Ursula K. Le Guin	ss ALWCMHM,85	54
Shahugoten	Ursula K. Le Guin	ss ALWCMHM,85	57
The Keeper	Ursula K. Le Guin	ss ALWCMHM,85	60
Dried Mice	Ursula K. Le Guin	vi ALWCMHM,85	63
Dira	Ursula K. Le Guin	ss PRB Win,84	64

*Le Guin, Ursula K. <u>ALWAYS COMING HOME</u> (Harper & Row 0-06-015545-0, 10/09/85 [11/85], $50.00 boxed with cassette, $34.60 without cassette, 525pp, hc) Hardcover versions of the above.

Le Guin, Ursula K.   THE DISPOSSESSED (Avon 0-380-00382-1, 11/85
[10/85], $3.25, 311pp, pb) Reissue (Harper & Row 1974) sf novel
of political/philosophical speculation. 16th Avon printing.

*Le Guin, Ursula K.   FIVE COMPLETE NOVELS (Avenel 0-517-48010-7,
11/85 [11/85], $7.98, 579pp, hc) Omnibus edition. "Instant re-
mainder" book published by Bonanza and distributed by Crown, for
sale mainly in discount stores. The text of the 3 earlier books
is the slightly corrected one from the Harper & Row reprints.
Contents: Page
ROCANNON'S WORLD   Ursula K. Le Guin   n. ACE 1966   5
PLANET OF EXILE   Ursula K. Le Guin   n. ACE 1966   99
CITY OF ILLUSIONS   Ursula K. Le Guin   n. ACE 1967   181
THE LEFT HAND OF DARKNESS
                          Ursula K. Le Guin   n. ACE 1969   311
THE WORD FOR WORLD IS FOREST
                          Ursula K. Le Guin   n. BRK 1976   493

*Le Guin, Ursula K.   KING DOG: A SCREENPLAY (Capra 0-88496-236-9,
10/85 [11/85], $9.50, 125pp, pb) This screenplay by Le Guin
(inspired by Hindu mythology) is bound back-to-back with DOSTOY-
EVSKY: A SCREENPLAY, mainstream by Raymond Carver & Tess Gallagher (an additional 111pp). A signed limited edition has also
been announced for $25.00.

Le Guin, Ursula K.   THE LANGUAGE OF THE NIGHT: ESSAYS ON FANTASY
AND SCIENCE FICTION (Berkley 0-425-07668-1, 03/85 [02/85], $5.95,
270pp, pb)   Reissue (Putnam 1979) collection of non-fiction essays on fantasy and sf. Edited by Susan Wood.

Le Guin, Ursula K.   MALAFRENA (Berkley 0-425-08477-9, 01/86
[12/85], $3.50, 343pp, pb) Reissue (Berkley-Putnam 1979) quasi-
historical novel set in an imaginary country in an era of revolu-
tion. 3rd Berkley printing.

*Lee, Pamela, William K. Hartmann & Ron Miller   OUT OF THE CRADLE:
EXPLORING THE FRONTIERS BEYOND EARTH Main listing under William
K. Hartmann.

Lee, Tanith   THE BIRTHGRAVE (DAW 0-88677-127-7, 01/86 [12/85],
$3.95, 408pp, pb) Reissue (DAW 1975) fantasy novel; 7th print-
ing.

*Lee, Tanith   DAYS OF GRASS (DAW 0-88677-094-7, 11/85 [10/85],
$3.50, 250pp, pb) Sf novel set 137 years after an alien invasion
of Earth.

Lee, Tanith   DEATH'S MASTER (Highland 0-916261-01-8, 02/85
[01/85], $45.00 signed boxed edition of 500, 327pp, hc) Reprint
(DAW 1979) fantasy. This first hardcover of the second "Demon
Princes" novel (winner of the British Fantasy Award) has a superb
color cover by Michael Whelan and less impressive b&w illustrations by Randy Broecker. It's an excellently made small press
limited edition at a bargain price. (CNB)

Lee, Tanith   EAST OF MIDNIGHT (Ace/Tempo 0-441-18191-0, 03/85
[02/85], $2.25, 175pp, pb) Reprint (Macmillan U.K. 1977) young-
adult fantasy novel.

*Lee, Tanith   THE GORGON AND OTHER BEASTLY TALES (DAW 0-88677-003-
3, 02/85 [01/85], $2.95, 288pp, pb) Collection of 11 stories.
Though only 8 are credited in the acknowledgements, these may all
be reprints.
Contents: Page
The Gorgon   Tanith Lee   nv SDW # 5,82   7
Anna Medea   Tanith Lee   ss AMZ Jan,83   34
Meow   Tanith Lee   ss SDW # 4,81   53
The Hunting of Death: The Unicorn
                          Tanith Lee   na   68
Magritte's Secret Agent   Tanith Lee   nv TZM May,81   121
Monkey's Stagger   Tanith Lee   ss SRCRAPR,79   168
Sirriamnis   Tanith Lee   nv UNSLNGT,81   185
Because Our Skins Are Finer
                          Tanith Lee   ss TZM Nov,81   222
Quatt-Sup   Tanith Lee   ss   241
Draco, Draco   Tanith Lee   nv BYNDLND,84   247
La Reine Blanche   Tanith Lee   ss IAS Jul,83   276

Lee, Tanith   THE GORGON AND OTHER BEASTLY TALES (SFBC #6088,
06/85 [05/85], $4.98, 184pp, hc) Reprint (DAW 1985) collection,
first hardcover edition.

Lee, Tanith   THE SILVER METAL LOVER (DAW 0-8099-5000-6, 09/85
[09/85], $6.95, 240pp, pb) Reprint (DAW 1981) sf novel, the
first trade paperback edition.

*Lee, Tanith   THE SILVER METAL LOVER See listing under Trina
Robbins.

*Lefanu, Sarah & Jen Green, eds.   DESPATCHES FROM THE FRONTIERS OF
THE FEMALE MIND Main listing under Jen Green.

Leiber, Fritz   THE SINFUL ONES (Baen 0-671-65549-3, 01/86
[12/85], $2.95, 250pp, pb) Reprint (Universal 1953) fantasy
novel. This edition follows the slightly revised 1980 Pocket text
and has the 1980 afterword. The condensed version was published
as YOU ARE ALL ALONE (Ace 1972).

Leiber, Fritz   SWORDS AGAINST DEATH (Ace 0-441-79193-X, 01/86
[12/85], $2.95, 251pp, pb) Reissue (Ace 1970) collection of 10
stories, "Fafhrd and the Gray Mouser" #2. 13th printing.

Leiber, Fritz   SWORDS AND DEVILTRY (Ace 0-441-79193-3, 11/85
[10/85], $2.95, 254pp, pb) Reissue (Ace 1970) collection of 3
tales featuring "Fafhrd and the Gray Mouser." 16th Ace printing.
Chronologically, this is the first book in the classic fantasy
series.

*Leiber, Justin   THE SWORD AND THE EYE (Tor 0-812-54429-3, 05/85
[04/85], $2.95, 252pp, pb) Fantasy novel, Book One of "The Saga
of the House of Eigin".

*Leiber, Justin   THE SWORD AND THE TOWER (Tor 0-812-54431-5, 01/86
[12/85], $2.95, 216pp, pb) Fantasy novel, sequel to THE SWORD
AND THE EYE.

Lem, Stanislaw   THE CYBERIAD: FABLES FOR THE CYBERNETIC AGE
(HBJ/Harvest 0-15-623550-1, 08/85 [07/85], $4.95, 295pp, pb)
Reprint (Seabury/Continuum 1974) collection, the English version
of CYBERIADA (Warzawa 1967, 1972).

Lem, Stanislaw   THE FUTUROLOGICAL CONGRESS (HBJ/Harvest 0-15-
634040-2, 10/85 [10/85], $3.95, 149pp, pb) Reprint (Continuum
1974) sf novel, translated by Michael Kandel. Originally published as ZE WSPOMNIEN IJONA TICHEGO: KONGRES FUTUROLOGICZNY
(Krakow 1971).

Lem, Stanislaw   IMAGINARY MAGNITUDE (HBJ/Harvest 0-15-644180-2,
10/85 [10/85], $3.95, 248pp, pb) Reprint (Harcourt Brace Jovano-
vich 1984) sf satire -- introductions to various 21st-century
books, plus a preface on prefaces. Translation by Marc E. Heine
of WIELKOSC UROJONA (Warsaw 1973) plus two other pieces which
first appeared in GOLEM XIV (Kracow 1981).

*Lem, Stanislaw   MICROWORLDS: WRITINGS ON SCIENCE FICTION (Har-
court Brace Jovanovich 0-15-159480-5, 02/85 [01/85], $14.95,
285pp, hc)   Non-fiction, collection of ten critical essays.
Edited by Franz Rottensteiner. Very patronizing and superior, but
thought-provoking. (DLN)

Lem, Stanislaw   THE STAR DIARIES (HBJ/Harvest 0-15-684905-4,
08/85 [07/85], $4.95, 275pp, pb) Reprint (Seabury/Continuum
1976) sf novel, English version of DZIENNIKI GWIAZDOWE (Warzawa
1971).

*Lerner, Frederick Andrew   MODERN SCIENCE FICTION AND THE AMERICAN
LITERARY COMMUNITY (Scarecrow 0-8108-1794-2, 08/85 [07/85],
$26.00, 325pp, hc) Non-fiction, study of the response to sf in
the U.S., with a history of sf conventions, etc. It's a doctoral
thesis and is aimed at dumb professors. (CNB)

*Leroe, Ellen W.   ROBOT ROMANCE (Harper & Row 0-06-023746-5, 07/85
[06/85], $7.95, 179pp, pb; $11.89 hc -- library binding) Young-
adult sf novel of a robot-run high school.

*Levin, Ira   THREE BY IRA LEVIN: ROSEMARY'S BABY, THIS PERFECT
DAY, THE STEPFORD WIVES (Random House 0-394-54512-5, 08/85
[07/85], $12.95, 485pp, hc) Omnibus of three horror/sf/dark
fantasy novels.
Contents: Page
ROSEMARY'S BABY   Ira Levin   n. RDM 1967
THIS PERFECT DAY   Ira Levin   n. RDM 1970
THE STEPFORD WIVES   Ira Levin   n. RDM 1972

Levin, Jeremy   CREATOR (Pocket 0-671-54205-2, 04/85 [03/85],
$3.95, 581pp, pb) Reissue (Coward, McCann 1980) sf clone novel.
Movie tie-in edition.

+Lewis, C.S.   BOXEN: THE IMAGINARY WORLD OF THE YOUNG C.S. LEWIS
(Harcourt Brace Jovanovich 0-15-11360-0, 10/85 [11/85], $13.95,
206pp, hc) Fantasy collection and miscellania. Stories and draw-
ings set in the imaginary world of Boxen and featuring "assorted
animals and gentlemen"; these were done when Lewis was a boy.
First American edition. The British one appeared several months
earlier.
Contents: Page
Introduction   Walter Hooper   in   7
The Boxen Manuscripts   Walter Hooper   ar 1985   21
The King's Ring   C.S. Lewis   pl BOXEN ,85   25
Manx Against Manx   C.S. Lewis   vi BOXEN ,85   35
The Relief of Murry   C.S. Lewis   vi BOXEN ,85   37
History of Mouse-Land from Stone-Age to Bublish I
                          C.S. Lewis   vi BOXEN ,85   39
History of Animal-Land   C.S. Lewis   ss BOXEN ,85   43
The Chess Monograph   C.S. Lewis   ss BOXEN ,85   50
The Geography of Animal-Land
                          C.S. Lewis   vi BOXEN ,85   55
Boxen: or Scenes from Boxonian City Life
                          C.S. Lewis   ss BOXEN ,85   61
The Locked Door   C.S. Lewis   nv BOXEN ,85   91
Than-Kyu   C.S. Lewis   ss BOXEN ,85   145
The Sailor   C.S. Lewis   nv BOXEN ,85   153
Encyclopedia Boxoniana   C.S. Lewis   ms BOXEN ,85   195

*Lewis, C.S.   LETTERS TO CHILDREN (Macmillan 0-02-570830-9, 07/85
[06/85], $9.95, 120pp, hc) Non-fiction; biographical. A collec-
tion of letters Lewis wrote to young readers of his "Narnia"
fantasies, plus a discussion of Lewis' own childhood, and a
"Narnia" bibliography including calendars, maps, and films as
well as the books. Edited by Lyle W. Dorset & Marjorie Lamp Mead.
There may be an earlier British edition.

*Lichtenberg, Jacqueline   CITY OF A MILLION LEGENDS (Berkley 0-425-07513-3, 02/85 [01/85], $2.75, 227pp, pb) Sf novel. Sequel to MOLT BROTHER.

*Lichtenberg, Jacqueline   DUSHAU (Popular Library/Questar 0-445-20015-4, 05/85 [04/85], $2.95, 238pp, pb) Sf novel, #1 in the "Dushau Trilogy".

*Lichtenberg, Jacqueline   FARFETCH (Popular Library/Questar 0-445-20106-1, 09/85 [08/85], $2.95, 238pp, pb) Sf novel, #2 in the "Dushau Trilogy".

Lichtenberg, Jacqueline   HOUSE OF ZEOR (Berkley 0-425-07745-4, 06/85 [05/85], $2.75, 224pp, pb) Reprint (Doubleday 1974) sf novel, the first "Sime/Gen" book. Has the intro and minor corrections from the 1976 Pocket edition.

Lichtenberg, Jacqueline   MOLT BROTHER (Berkley 0-425-07452-8, 01/85 [12/84], $2.75, 254pp, pb) Reprint (Playboy 1982) sf novel.

*Lichtenberg, Jacqueline   OUTREACH (Popular Library/Questar 0-445-20140-1, 01/86 [12/85], $3.50, 237pp, pb) Sf novel, conclusion of the "Dushau Trilogy".

Lichtenberg, Jacqueline   UNTO ZEOR FOREVER (Berkley 0-425-08187-7, 10/85 [09/85], $2.95, 318pp, pb) Reprint (Doubleday 1978) sf novel.

*Lindholm, Megan   WIZARD OF THE PIGEONS (Ace 0-441-89467-4, 01/86 [12/85], $2.95, 214pp, pb) Fantasy novel set in modern Seattle and featuring a Vietnam vet/streetperson/wizard. Recommended. (FCM)

Lindsay, David   A VOYAGE TO ARCTURUS (Citadel 0-8065-0944-9, 08/85 [07/85], $5.95, 248pp, pb) Reprint (Methuen 1920) allegorical sf novel, with an introduction by Galad Elflandsson which has a good summary of Lindsay's life and works.

*Linzner, Gordon   THE SPY WHO DRANK BLOOD (Space & Time 0-917053-01-X, 02/85 [01/85], $5.95, 127pp, pb) The first novel-length tale of the vampire agent whose adventures appeared in *Space & Time* magazine, this fantasy includes terrorists, lawmen, and a "swamp creature."

*Liquori, Sal   PSI PATROL: SAL'S BOOK (Scholastic/Point 0-590-33201-5, 1985 [09/85], $2.25, 148pp, pb) Young-adult fantasy novel, part of a series. Authorship is credited to the hero, although it's written in the third person.

+Lively, Penelope   UNINVITED GHOSTS (Dutton 0-525-44165-4, 05/85 [04/85], $10.95, 120pp, hc) Reprint (Heinemann 1984) collection of eight juvenile fantasy stories. First U.S. edition.

Contents:			Page
A Martian Comes to Stay	Penelope Lively	ss UNVTGST,84	9
The Disastrous Dog	Penelope Lively	ss UNVTGST,84	29
Uninvited Ghosts	Penelope Lively	ss BIGDIPR,81	40
The Dragon Tunnel	Penelope Lively	ss ALT # 6,74	50
Time Trouble	Penelope Lively	ss UNVTGST,84	64
Princess by Mistake	Penelope Lively	ss JBLJKNY,77	75
A Flock of Gryphons	Penelope Lively	ss UNVTGST,84	90
The Great Mushroom Mistake			
	Penelope Lively	ss UNVTGST,84	108

Llewellyn, Edward   BRIGHT COMPANION (DAW 0-88677-007-6, 02/85 [01/85], $2.50, 176pp, pb) Reissue (DAW 1980) sf novel. 3rd printing.

Llewellyn, Edward   THE DOUGLAS CONVOLUTION (DAW 0-88677-006-8, 02/85 [01/85], $2.50, 190pp, pb) Reissue (DAW 1979) sf novel. 3rd printing.

*Llewellyn, Edward   FUGITIVE IN TRANSIT (DAW 0-88677-002-5, 02/85 [01/85], $2.95, 302pp, pb) Sf novel.

Llewellyn, Edward   PRELUDE TO CHAOS (DAW 0-88677-008-4, 02/85 [01/85], $2.95, 256pp, pb) Reissue (DAW 1983) sf novel. 3rd printing.

Llewellyn, Edward   SALVAGE AND DESTROY (DAW 0-88677-009-2, 02/85 [01/85], $2.95, 256pp, pb) Reissue (DAW 1984) sf novel. 3rd printing.

*Longyear, Barry B.   IT CAME FROM SCHENECTADY (Bluejay 0-312-94239-7, 12/84 [12/84], $15.95, 346pp, hc) Sf collection of 12 stories.

Contents:			Page
Forepiece	Barry B. Longyear	fw	11
Collector's Item	Barry B. Longyear	ss ASF Apr,81	19
Dreams	Barry B. Longyear	nv IAS Aug,79	39
The House of If	Barry B. Longyear	nv IAS Apr,81	65
The Initiation [as Mark Ringdahl]			
	Barry B. Longyear	ss IAS Jul,79	109
The Portrait of Baron Negay			
	Barry B. Longyear	nv IAS Jun,81	115
SHAWNA, Ltd. [as Frederick Longbeard]			
	Barry B. Longyear	ss IAS Sep,79	147
A Time for Terror [as Frederick Longbeard]			
	Barry B. Longyear	nv IAS Mar,79	159
The Homecoming	Barry B. Longyear	nv IAS Oct,79	187
Twist Ending	Barry B. Longyear	ss IAS Nov,79	237
Catch the Sun	Barry B. Longyear	na IAS Nov,80	245

Adagio	Barry B. Longyear	nv ITCAMEF,84	309
Where Do You Get Your Ideas? [as Mark Ringdahl]			
	Barry B. Longyear	vi IAA Fll,79	343

*Longyear, Barry B. & David Gerrold   ENEMY MINE (Ace/Charter 0-441-20672-7, 12/85 [11/85], $2.95, 218pp, pb) Novelization of the screenplay by Edward Khmara, based on the story by Longyear.

Lorrah, Jean   THE VULCAN ACADEMY MURDERS (SFBC #6412, 05/85 [04/85], $4.98, 214pp, hc) Reprint (Pocket 1984) Star Trek novel. First hardcover edition.

*Love, G.B. & Walter Irwin, eds.   THE BEST OF TREK #8 Main listing under Walter Irwin.

*Love, G.B. & Walter Irwin, eds.   THE BEST OF TREK #9 Main listing under Walter Irwin.

Lovecraft, H.P.   AT THE MOUNTAINS OF MADNESS (Arkham House 0-87054-038-6, 12/85 [11/85], $16.95, 458pp, hc) Reissue (Arkham House 1964) collection. The Derleth introduction has been dropped, but there is a new introduction by James Turner and a note on the texts by S.T. Joshi. This is a corrected "definitive" version, second in what will be a three-volume set.

Lovecraft, H.P.   THE DUNWICH HORROR AND OTHERS (Arkham House 0-87054-037-8, 02/85 [01/85], $15.95, 433pp, hc) Reissue (Arkham House 1963), "corrected 6th printing" of this Lovecraft collection, the first in a projected three-volume critical edition based on the author's original texts. S.T. Joshi edited it, and there's a new introduction by Robert Bloch, reprinted from the 1982 Ballantine collection BLOOD CURDLING TALES OF SUPERNATURAL HORROR: THE BEST OF H.P. LOVECRAFT. There are thousands of minor changes from the 1963 edition.

*Lovejoy, Jack   A VISION OF BEASTS 3: THE BROTHERHOOD OF DIABLO (Tor 0-812-54504-4, 05/85 [04/85], $2.95, 285pp, pb) Sf novel, third in a series.

*Lumley, Brian   THE HOUSE OF CTHULHU AND OTHER TALES OF THE PRIMAL LAND (Weirdbook 0-932445-08-X, 1984 [12/84], $7.50 + $1 postage, 94pp, pb) Collection of 11 stories. There is also an announced hardcover edition for $20.00.

Contents:			Page
Introduction	Brian Lumley	in 1984	9
The Sorcerer's Book	Brian Lumley	ss HSCTHLU,84	15
How Kank Thad Returned to Bhur-Esh			
	Brian Lumley	nv FAN Jun,77	23
The House of Cthulhu	Brian Lumley	ss WHS V1 #1,73	31
Tharquest and the Lamia Orbiquita			
	Brian Lumley	nv FAN Nov,76	36
Mylakhrion the Immortal	Brian Lumley	ss FTL Sum,77	40
Isles of the Suhm-Yi	Brian Lumley	ss HSCTHLU,84	44
Lords of the Morass	Brian Lumley	ss HSCTHLU,84	54
Curse of the Golden Guardians			
	Brian Lumley	ss HSCTHLU,84	66
Cryptically Yours	Brian Lumley	ss ESP 1977	79
		SWD # 4,79	
The Wine of the Wizard	Brian Lumley	ss HSCTHLU,84	84
The Sorcerer's Dream	Brian Lumley	ss WHS V1 #1,79	93

*Lumley, Brian   PSYCHAMOK (Granada/Panther 0-586-06409-5, 1985 [10/85], £2.50, 445pp, pb) Sf/horror novel of ESP, immortality, and an evil machine; sequel to PSYCHOMECH and PSYCHOSPHERE. "Now is the balance flung back in favour of grossest evil. Now is a hideous curse visited on the next generation. Now is the time of the Gibbering!"

Lupoff, Richard A. CIRCUMPOLAR! (Berkley 0-425-08193-1, 08/85 [07/85], $2.95, 295pp, pb) Reprint (Timescape 1984) humorous sf hollow earth/alternate world adventure novel.

*Lupoff, Richard A. LOVECRAFT'S BOOK (Arkham House 0-87054-151-X, 06/85 [05/85], $15.95, 260pp, hc) Quasi-historical adventure novel. A delightful alternate-history romp through pre-World War II politics, based on a great deal of research. Pulp adventure at its very best! Lovecraft is the hero. (DLN)

Lynn, Elizabeth A.   THE SARDONYX NET (Berkley 0-425-08635-6, 12/85 [11/85], $3.50, 423pp, pb) Reissue (Berkley-Putnam 1981) sf novel. 4th Berkley printing.

*Macaulay, David   BAAA (Houghton Mifflin 0-395-38948-8, 09/85 [08/85], $12.95, 63pp, hc--library edition) Satiric fantasy written and illustrated by Macaulay; sheep take over the world and don't do much better than the people had.

*Macaulay, David   BAAA (Houghton Mifflin 0-395-39588-7, 09/85 [08/85], $4.95, 63pp, pb) Paperback edition of the above.

*MacAvoy, R.A.   THE BOOK OF KELLS (Bantam Spectra 0-553-25260-7, 08/85 [07/85], $3.50, 340pp, pb) Fantasy novel set in 10th century Ireland, with modern time travelers.

MacAvoy, R.A.   DAMIANO (Bantam U.K. 0-553-17154-2, 04/85 [03/85], £1.95, 243pp, pb) Reprint (Bantam U.S. 1983) fantasy novel, first in the "Damiano" trilogy. First U.K. edition.

*MacAvoy, R.A.   A TRIO FOR LUTE (SFBC #3842, 04/85 [03/85], $7.98, 632pp, hc) Omnibus edition of a fantasy trilogy.

Contents:			Page
DAMIANO	R.A. MacAvoy	n. BAN 1983	

MACAVOY, R.A.

DAMIANO's LUTE   R.A. MacAvoy   n. BAN 1984
RAPHAEL   R.A. MacAvoy   n. BAN 1984

+**Mace, David** <u>DEMON-4</u> (Ace 0-441-14257-5, 01/86 [12/85], $2.75, 184pp, pb) Reprint (Panther 1984), first U.S. edition of a remarkably lyrical sf novel of advanced military technology. (FCM)

***Mace, David** <u>NIGHTRIDER</u> (Granada 0-586-06206-8, 04/85 [03/85], £1.95, 304pp, pb) Sf novel.

***MacLeod, Charlotte** <u>THE CURSE OF THE GIANT HOGWEED</u> (Doubleday 0-385-19609-1, 02/85 [01/85], $11.95, 184pp, hc) Though issued in the Crime Club series, this is basically a comic fantasy novel somewhat like Pratt and de Camp's "Enchanter" stories, though even sillier. Good, lightweight entertainment. Its part of a series of humerous mysteries; the rest aren't fantasies. (FCM)

*<u>The Magazine of Fantasy & Science Fiction</u> [v.68 #1, January 1985] Edward L. Ferman, ed. (Mercury Press, 01/85 [12/84], $1.75, 162pp, pb)
Contents:

				Page
Revenge of the Cat-Lady	Avram Davidson	ss FSF	Jan,85	8
Books	Algis Budrys	br FSF		14
A Matter of Sensitivity	Chet Williamson	ss FSF	Jan,85	22
Feeny's Trials	David Wiltse	ss FSF	Jan,85	33
Final Performance	Kevin J. Anderson	ss FSF	Jan,85	40
Harlan Ellison's Watching	Harlan Ellison	mr FSF		56
Cartoon	Henry Martin	ct FSF		59
My Old Car	Thomas Wylde	ss FSF	Jan,85	60
The Milk of Paradise	Rivka Jacobs	ss FSF	Jan,85	70
Science: Far, Far Below	Isaac Asimov	ar FSF	Jan,85	82
CV (1st of 3 parts)	Damon Knight	sl FSF	Jan,85	93
F&SF Competition: Report on Competition 36	[Misc. Material]	ms FSF	Jan,85	158

*<u>The Magazine of Fantasy & Science Fiction</u> [v.68 #2, February 1985] Edward L. Ferman, ed. (Mercury Press, 02/85 [01/85], $1.75, 162pp, pb)
Contents:

				Page
With Friends Like These	Connie Willis	nv FSF	Feb,85	8
Cartoon	Joseph Farris	ct FSF		35
Cartoon	R. Chast	ct NYM	1984	36
Books	Algis Budrys	br FSF		38
The Face in the Cloth	Jane Yolen	ss FSF	Feb,85	46
Cartoon	Nurit Karlin	ct FSF		54
My Life in the Jungle	Jim Aikin	ss FSF	Feb,85	55
Harlan Ellison's Watching	Harlan Ellison	mr FSF		67
White Socks	Ian Watson	nv FSF	Feb,85	76
1984	Barry N. Malzberg	vi FSF	Feb,85	97
CV (2nd of 3 parts)	Damon Knight	sl FSF	Feb,85	98
Science: Salt and Battery	Isaac Asimov	ar FSF	Feb,85	130
Cartoon	Alexis Gilliland	ct FSF		140
The Boy Who Talked to Animals	Stephen Gallagher	ss FSF	Feb,85	141

*<u>The Magazine of Fantasy & Science Fiction</u> [v.68 #3, March 1985] Edward L. Ferman, ed. (Mercury Press, 03/85 [02/85], $1.75, 162pp, pb)
Contents:

				Page
Out of All Them Bright Stars	Nancy Kress	ss FSF	Mar,85	8
Books	Algis Budrys	br FSF		16
Vestibular Man	Felix C. Gotschalk	nv FSF	Mar,85	24
Legacy	Terence M. Green	ss FSF	Mar,85	50
Roimata	Daphne de Jong	nv FSF	Mar,85	54
Cartoon	Rex May	ct FSF		74
Some Work of Noble Note	John Morressy	ss FSF	Mar,85	75
Harlan Ellison's Watching	Harlan Ellison	mr FSF		83
CV (3rd of 3 parts)	Damon Knight	sl FSF	Mar,85	92
The Shadow of the Mountain	Gene O'Neill	ss FSF	Mar,85	122
Science: Current Affairs	Isaac Asimov	ar FSF	Mar,85	136
Top of the Charts	Bradley Denton	ss FSF	Mar,85	146

*<u>The Magazine of Fantasy & Science Fiction</u> [v.68 #4, April 1985] Edward L. Ferman, ed. (Mercury Press, 04/85 [03/85], $1.75, 162pp, pb)
Contents:

				Page
Send Me a Kiss By Wire	Hilbert Schenck	ss FSF	Apr,85	6
Books	Algis Budrys	br FSF		25
The SF Book of Lists	Larry Tritten	ss FSF	Apr,85	34
The Snail out of Space	Phyllis Eisenstein	ss FSF	Apr,85	39
Cartoon	Henry Martin	ct FSF		50
Collectible	Alan Dean Foster	ss FSF	Apr,85	51
Harlan Ellison's Watching	Harlan Ellison	mr FSF		61
The Shadow of the Starlight	Gael Baudino	nv FSF	Apr,85	66
Rift	Robert Grossbach	ss FSF	Apr,85	96
Cartoon	Nurit Karlin	ct FSF		105
Science: Forcing the Lines	Isaac Asimov	ar FSF	Apr,85	106
To the Storming Gulf	Gregory Benford	na FSF	Apr,85	117
Acrostic Puzzle	Rachel Cosgrove Payes	pz FSF		158

*<u>The Magazine of Fantasy & Science Fiction</u> [v.68 #5, May 1985] Edward L. Ferman, ed. (Mercury Press, 05/85 [04/85], $1.75, 162pp, pb)
Contents:

				Page
The Jaguar Hunter	Lucius Shepard	nv FSF	May,85	8
Rats in Space	Jack C. Haldeman, II	ss FSF	May,85	32
Books	Algis Budrys	br FSF		38
Cartoon	Joseph Farris	ct FSF		46
Turnabout	Steven Hardesty	ss FSF	May,85	48
The Nifty Murder Case	Richard Mueller	ss FSF	May,85	57
No Regrets	Lisa Tuttle	ss FSF	May,85	73
The Haunting of Goodhope	Juleen Brantingham	ss FSF	May,85	93
Science: Arise, Fair Sun!	Isaac Asimov	ar FSF	May,85	109
The Tensor of Desire	Wayne Wightman	nv FSF	May,85	120

*<u>The Magazine of Fantasy & Science Fiction</u> [v.68 #6, June 1985] Edward L. Ferman, ed. (Mercury Press, 06/85 [05/85], $1.75, 162pp, pb)
Contents:

				Page
The Embezzled Blessing	Robert M. Green, Jr.	nv FSF	Jun,85	6
Cartoon	Henry Martin	ct FSF		44
Books	Algis Budrys	br FSF		48
Two Fables	John Morressy	ss FSF	Jun,85	57
The Poplar Street Study	Karen Joy Fowler	ss FSF	Jun,85	60
The Man Who Made the Fur Fly	John Brunner	nv FSF	Jun,85	74
Cartoon	Joseph Farris	ct FSF		92
Harlan Ellison's Watching	Harlan Ellison	mr FSF		93
Side Effects	Walter Jon Williams	nv FSF	Jun,85	101
The Last	James Patrick Kelley	ss FSF	Jun,85	128
Science: The Rule of Numerous Small	Isaac Asimov	ar FSF	Jun,85	143
The Woman Who Went Out	Gene Wolfe	ss FSF	Jun,85	153
F&SF Competition: Report on Competition 37	[Misc. Material]	ms FSF	Jun,85	158
Index to Volume 68	[Misc. Material]	ix FSF	Jun,85	162

*<u>The Magazine of Fantasy & Science Fiction</u> [v.69 #1, July 1985] Edward L. Ferman, ed. (Mercury Press, 07/85 [06/85], $1.75, 162pp, pb)
Contents:

				Page
The God Machine	Damon Knight	ss FSF	Jul,85	8
The Proud Foot of the Conqueror	Reginald Bretnor	ss WAR	V 4,85	21
Cartoon	Sidney Harris	ct FSF		38
The Blue Gularis	Robert Charles Wilson	ss FSF	Jul,85	39
Books	Algis Budrys	br FSF		12
Skin Day, and After	Ian Watson	ss FSF	Jul,85	51
Neighbors	Rolaine Hochstein	ss FSF	Jul,85	61
The White Quetzal	Gene O'Neill	ss FSF	Jul,85	68
Science: Poison in the Negative	Isaac Asimov	ar FSF	Jul,85	81
Cartoon	Rex May	ct FSF		91
When Winter Ends	Michael P. Kube-McDowell	na FSF	Jul,85	92

*<u>The Magazine of Fantasy & Science Fiction</u> [v.69 #2, August 1985] Edward L. Ferman, ed. (Mercury Press, 08/85 [07/85], $1.75, 162pp, pb)
Contents:

				Page
Pira	Brad Strickland	ss FSF	Aug,85	6
Cartoon	Nurit Karlin	ct FSF		22
Books	Algis Budrys	br FSF		24
My First Game as an Immortal	George Alec Effinger	pm FSF	Aug,85	32
Man of Parts	James Gunn	ss FSF	Aug,85	34
Cartoon	Joseph Farris	ct FSF		41
The Lights	Robert Onopa	ss FSF	Aug,85	42
The Summer We Saw Diana	Bradley Denton	nv FSF	Aug,85	51
Harlan Ellison's Watching	Harlan Ellison	mr FSF		69
Three-Mile Syndrome	Robert F. Young	ss FSF	Aug,85	80
Cartoon	Sidney Harris	ct FSF		88
The Ladies of Wahloon Lake	Nancy Etchemendy	ss FSF	Aug,85	89
Furgussen's Wrath	Mike Conner	nv FSF	Aug,85	105
Science: Tracing the Traces	Isaac Asimov	ar FSF	Aug,85	129
Stone Lives	Paul DiFilippo	nv FSF	Aug,85	141

*<u>The Magazine of Fantasy & Science Fiction</u> [v.69 #3, September 1985] Edward L. Ferman, ed. (Mercury Press, 09/85 [08/85], $1.75, 162pp, pb)
Contents:

				Page
In Hector's Grave	Russell M. Griffin	ss FSF	Sep,85	8
Books	Algis Budrys	br FSF		24
No Life For Me Without You, Vodyanoi	Stephen Gallagher	nv FSF	Sep,85	32
Cartoon	Nurit Karlin	ct FSF		53
The Great Wall	Wayne Wightman	ss FSF	Sep,85	54
The Armistead House	W.S. Doxey	ss FSF	Sep,85	70
Cartoon	Sidney Harris	ct FSF		86
Harlan Ellison's Watching	Harlan Ellison	mr FSF		87
Cartoon	Henry Martin	ct FSF		90
The Dragon's Boy	Jane Yolen	nv FSF	Sep,85	91
Little Friends	Richard Mueller	ss FSF	Sep,85	107
Pain Killer	Haskell Barkin	ss FSF	Sep,85	116
Science: The Goblin Element	Isaac Asimov	ar FSF	Sep,85	126

Richenda	Keith Roberts	nv FSF Sep,85	137

__The Magazine of Fantasy & Science Fiction__ [v.69 #4, October 1985] Edward L. Ferman, ed. (Mercury Press, 10/85 [09/85], $1.75, 162pp, pb)
Contents: Page

The Only Neat Thing to Do			
	James Tiptree, Jr.	na FSF Oct,85	8
Books	Algis Budrys	br FSF	54
That Wonderful Summer	Ron Goulart	ss FSF Oct,85	61
Cartoon	Joseph Farris	ct FSF	72
The Children, They Laugh So Sweetly			
	Charles L. Grant	ss FSF Oct,85	73
Sea Wrack	Marion Zimmer Bradley	nv MNSNGRF,85	82
Harlan Ellison's Watching			
	Harlan Ellison	mr FSF	103
As Duly Authorized	Fred Saberhagen	ss FSF Oct,85	112
Hard to Credit	John Brunner	ss FSF Oct,85	122
Science: A Little Leaven	Isaac Asimov	ar FSF Oct,85	129
The Fringe	Orson Scott Card	nv FSF Oct,85	140
Cartoon	Henry Martin	ct FSF	160

__The Magazine of Fantasy & Science Fiction__ [v.69 #5, November 1985] Edward L. Ferman, ed. (Mercury Press, 11/85 [10/85], $1.75, 162pp, pb)
Contents: Page

The Green Tent	Ellen Gilchrist	ss FSF Nov,85	6
Books	Algis Budrys	br FSF	12
You Never Asked My Name	Brian W. Aldiss	ss FSF Nov,85	20
The Black and Tan Man	Cooper McLaughlin	nv FSF Nov,85	34
Cartoon	Joseph Farris	ct FSF	67
Six of Swords	Gregor Hartmann	ss FSF Nov,85	68
Cartoon	Alexis Gilliland	ct FSF	75
Sport of Kings	Edward F. Shaver	nv FSF Nov,85	76
Harlan Ellison's Watching			
	Harlan Ellison	mr FSF	95
See Me Safely Home	Richard Wilson	ss FSF Nov,85	101
The High Purpose	Barry N. Malzberg & Carter Scholz		
		ss FSF Nov,85	113
Science: The Biochemical Knife Blade			
	Isaac Asimov	ar FSF Nov,85	129
The Persistence of Memory			
	Gael Baudino	ss FSF Nov,85	140
F&SF Competition: Report on Competition 38			
	[Misc. Material]	ms FSF Nov,85	158

__The Magazine of Fantasy & Science Fiction__ [v.69 #6, December 1985] Edward L. Ferman, ed. (Mercury Press, 12/85 [11/85], $1.75, 162pp, pb)
Contents: Page

A Spanish Lesson	Lucius Shepard	nv FSF Dec,85	6
Books	Algis Budrys	br FSF	36
Cartoon	Sidney Harris	ct FSF	46
A Matter of No Great Significance			
	Richard Cowper	ss FSF Dec,85	47
Fear of Flying	Hal Hill	ss FSF Dec,85	54
Our Extraterrestrial Visitors			
	Stan Dryer	nv FSF Dec,85	62
The Sword and the Stone	Jane Yolen	nv FSF Dec,85	87
Magic Cookies	Thomas Wylde	ss FSF Dec,85	105
Cartoon	Rex May	ct FSF	117
Savant	Joe L. Hensley	ss FSF Dec,85	118
Science: The Discovery of the Void			
	Isaac Asimov	ar FSF Dec,85	128
The Bird of Time Bears Bitter Fruit			
	George Alec Effinger	nv FSF Dec,85	139
Index to Volume 69	[Misc. Material]	ix FSF Dec,85	162

__The Magazine of Fantasy & Science Fiction__ [v.70 #1, January 1986] Edward L. Ferman, ed. (Mercury Press, 01/86 [12/85], $1.75, 162pp, pb)
Contents: Page

State of the Art	Robert Charles Wilson	ss FSF Jan,86	6
Books	Algis Budrys	br FSF	16
To Dance By the Light of the Moon			
	Stephen Gallagher	nv FSF Jan,86	24
The Christmas Tree	Ken Wisman	ss FSF Jan,86	48
The Rise and Fall of Father Alex			
	Amyas Naegele	ss FSF Jan,86	54
Outsider	Robert J. Tilley	ss FSF Jan,86	73
Cartoon	Joseph Farris	ct FSF	83
Harlan Ellison's Watching			
	Harlan Ellison	mr FSF	84
Seymourlama	Harvey Jacobs	ss FSF Jan,86	94
A Creature of Water	Richard Mueller	ss FSF Jan,86	104
Science: Chemistry of the Void			
	Isaac Asimov	ar FSF Jan,86	117
Newton Sleep	Gregory Benford	nv FSF Jan,86	127
Cartoon	Sidney Harris	ct FSF	159

*Maglio, Mitchell __THE OFFICIAL STAR TREK QUIZ BOOK__ (Pocket/Wallaby 0-671-55652-5, 05/85 [04/85], $6.95, 256pp, pb) Non-fiction, quiz book for Trekkies.

Mahy, Margaret __THE CHANGEOVER: A SUPERNATURAL ROMANCE__ (Scholastic/Point 0-590-33798-X, 09/85 [08/85], $2.25, 263pp, pb) Reprint (U.K. 1984), an excellent young-adult fantasy novel, winner of the Carnegie Medal. Recommended! (FCM)

Malzberg, Barry N. __THE ENGINES OF THE NIGHT__ (Bluejay 0-312-94141-2, 01/85 [12/84], $6.95, 199pp, pb) Reprint (Doubleday 1982). Mostly non-fiction, a collection of essays on sf. The book won the Locus Award for best non-fiction of 1982. Recommended. (CNB)

*Malzberg, Barry N. __THE REMAKING OF SIGMUND FREUD__ (Ballantine/Del Rey 0-345-31861-7, 07/85 [06/85], $2.95, 275pp, pb) Sf novel cobbled together from some shorter works.

*Marl, David & David Arscott __A FLIGHT OF BRIGHT BIRDS__ Main listing under David Arscott.

Marquez, Gabriel Garcia __COLLECTED STORIES__ (Perennial Library 0-06-091306-1, 10/85 [10/85], $6.95, 311pp, pb) Reprint (Harper & Row 1984) collection of 26 stories which first appeared in 3 collections: LEAF STORM AND OTHER STORIES (1972), NO ONE WRITES TO THE COLONEL AND OTHER STORIES (1968), and INNOCENT ERENDIRA AND OTHER STORIES (1978).

Marshak, Sondra & Myrna Culbreath __THE FATE OF THE PHOENIX__ (Bantam 0-553-24638-0, 04/85 [03/85], $2.95, 262pp, pb) Reissue (Bantam 1979) Star Trek novel. 5th printing.

Marshak, Sondra & Myrna Culbreath __THE PRICE OF THE PHOENIX__ (Bantam 0-553-24635-6, 03/85 [02/85], $2.95, 182pp, pb) Reissue (Bantam 1977) Star Trek novel. Fifth printing.

Marshak, Sondra & Myrna Culbreath, eds. __STAR TREK: THE NEW VOYAGES__ (Bantam Spectra 0-553-25073-6, 08/85 [07/85], $2.95, 237pp, pb) Reissue (Bantam 1976) Star Trek anthology. 12th printing.

Marshak, Sondra & Myrna Culbreath, eds. __STAR TREK: THE NEW VOYAGES 2__ (Bantam Spectra 0-553-23756-X, 09/85 [08/85], $2.95, 252pp, pb) Reissue (Bantam 1978) Star Trek anthology. 9th printing.

*Marshall, Deborah A. & A.C. Crispin __V: DEATH TIDE__ Main listing under A.C. Crispin.

Martin, George R.R. __THE ARMAGEDDON RAG__ (Pocket 0-671-53253-7, 01/85 [12/84], $3.95, 399pp, pb) Reprint (Simon & Schuster/Poseidon 1983) fantasy/horror/60s/rock'n'roll novel. Highly recommended. (CNB)

*Martin, George R.R. __NIGHTFLYERS__ (Bluejay 0-312-94332-6, 12/85 [12/85], $8.95, 295pp, pb) Collection of 6 stories.
Contents: Page

Nightflyers [expanded from ASF Apr,80]			
	George R.R. Martin	na BST # 5,81	1
Override	George R.R. Martin	nv ASF Sep,73	104
Weekend in a War Zone	George R.R. Martin	nv FUTPAST,77	136
And Seven Times Never Kill Man			
	George R.R. Martin	nv ASF Jul,75	157
Nor the Many-Colored Fires of a Star Ring			
	George R.R. Martin	nv FSTRLGT,76	199
Song for Lya	George R.R. Martin	na ASF Jun,74	225

Martin, George R.R. __SONGS THE DEAD MEN SING__ (Gollancz 0-575-03566-8, 11/85 [11/85], £8.95, 224pp, hc) Reprint (Dark Harvest 1983) collection. This edition has only 7 of the 9 stories in the original and also omits the Budrys introduction.
Contents: Page

The Monkey Treatment	George R.R. Martin	nv FSF Jul,83	7
...for a single yesterday			
	George R.R. Martin	nv EPOCH ,75	31
The Needle Men	George R.R. Martin	ss FSF Oct,81	52
Meathouse Man	George R.R. Martin	nv ORB #18,76	69
Sandkings	George R.R. Martin	nv OMN Aug,79	94
Nightflyers [expanded from ASF Apr,80]			
	George R.R. Martin	na BST # 5,81	131
Remembering Melody	George R.R. Martin	ss TZM Apr,81	209

Martin, George R.R. & Lisa Tuttle __WINDHAVEN__ (Pocket 0-671-49616-6, 11/85 [10/85], $3.95, 324pp, pb) Reissue (Timescape 1981) sf novel.

Martin, Graham Dunstan __THE SOUL MASTER__ (Allen & Unwin/Unicorn 0-04-823301-3, 11/85 [10/85], £2.95, 293pp, pb) Reprint (Allen & Unwin 1984) "sf-fantasy" novel -- "in Tethesta, the laws of the universe no longer operate...and the souls of men are controlled by a single consciousness."

*Martin, Les __THE BRIDE: A TALE OF LOVE AND DOOM__ (Random House 0-394-87370-X, 07/85 [06/85], $3.95, 93pp, pb) Brief novelization of the remake of THE BRIDE OF FRANKENSTEIN, with color stills from the movie.

Masefield, John __THE MIDNIGHT FOLK__ (Dell/Yearling 0-440-45631-2, 1985 [10/85], $4.95, 224pp, pb) Reprint (Heineman 1927) juvenile fantasy novel about a boy who meets witches. An early 20th century fantasy classic; one of Edward Eager's inspirations. Recommended despite its rather dated style. There's a new afterword by Madeleine L'Engle. (DLN)

Matheson, Richard __HELL HOUSE__ (Warner 0-446-32624-0, 06/85 [05/85], $2.95, 247pp, pb) Reprint (Viking 1971) fantasy novel; one of the famous haunted house stories.

*Matheson, Richard, Martin H. Greenberg & Charles G. Waugh, eds. THE TWILIGHT ZONE: THE ORIGINAL STORIES Main listing under Martin H. Greenberg.

*Matthews, Rodney IN SEARCH OF FOREVER (Paper Tiger/Dragon's World 1-85028-004-5, 09/85 [10/85], £12.95, 142pp, hc) Book of artwork with text by Nigel Suckling, Rodney Matthews, and Michael Moorcock. Sf and fantasy art, including reproductions of book covers, posters, and album jackets. A well-designed compendium which will be a must for all Matthews fans. Recommended. (FCM)

*Matthews, Rodney IN SEARCH OF FOREVER (Paper Tiger/Dragon's World 1-85028-003-7, 09/85 [10/85], £7.95, 142pp, pb) Paperback edition of the above.

May, Julian THE ADVERSARY (Ballantine/Del Rey 0-345-31422-0, 03/85 [02/85], $3.50, 472pp, pb) Reprint (Houghton Mifflin 1984) sf novel, Vol. IV (and conclusion--for now) of the "Saga of Pliocene Exile."

May, Julian THE GOLDEN TORC (Ballantine/Del Rey 0-345-32419-6, 03/85 [02/85], $3.50, 387pp, pb) Reissue (Houghton Mifflin 1982) sf novel, "Pliocene Exile" #2; fourth printing.

May, Julian A PLIOCENE COMPANION: A GUIDE TO THE SAGA OF PLIO- CENE EXILE (SFBC #1898, 03/85 [02/85], $5.98, 209pp, hc) Reprint (Houghton Mifflin 1984) non-fiction companion-piece to the sf series.

May, Julian A PLIOCENE COMPANION: A GUIDE TO THE SAGA OF PLIO- CENE EXILE (Ballantine/Del Rey 0-345-32290-8, 05/85 [04/85], $3.50, 290pp, pb) Reprint (Houghton Mifflin 1984) non-fiction guide to the world of the "Pliocene Exile" books.

*Mayhar, Ardath THE SAGA OF GRITTEL SUNDOTHA (Atheneum/Argo 0-689-31097-8, 04/85 [03/85], $12.95, 196pp, hc) Young-adult fan- tasy novel.

*Mayhar, Ardath THE WORLD ENDS IN HICKORY HOLLOW (Doubleday 0-384-18753-X, 03/85 [02/85], $11.95, 182pp, hc) Post-holocaust sf novel.

McCaffrey, Anne CRYSTAL SINGER (Ballantine/Del Rey 0-345-32786- 1, 12/85 [11/85], $3.95, 311pp, pb) Reissue (Severn House 1982) sf novel, first in the series featuring Killashandra Ree. 8th Del Rey printing.

*McCaffrey, Anne THE IRETA ADVENTURE (SFBC #04743, 09/85 [08/85], $7.50, 376pp, hc) Omnibus edition of a sf series.
Contents: Page
DINOSAUR PLANET   Anne McCaffrey   n. FPL 1978
DINOSAUR PLANET SURVIVORS
                               Anne McCaffrey   n. BAL 1984

*McCaffrey, Anne KILLASHANDRA (Ballantine/Del Rey 0-345-31599-5, 12/85 [11/85], $16.95, 303pp, hc) Sf novel, sequel to CRYSTAL SINGER.

McCaffrey, Anne THE KILTERNAN LEGACY (Underwood-Miller/Brandy- wyne 0-88733-050-9, 02/85 [01/85], $25.00 signed; $13.95 trade, 269pp, hc) Reprint (Dell 1975) romantic novel set in Ireland. Non-sf/fantasy, of associational interest.

McCaffrey, Anne THE MARK OF MERLIN (Underwood-Miller/Brandywyne 0-88733-049-5, 02/85 [01/85], $25.00 signed; $13.95 trade, 180pp, hc) Reprint (Dell 1971) Gothic romance set in New England in the forties, of associational interest.

McCaffrey, Anne RING OF FEAR (Underwood-Miller/Brandywyne 0-88733-051-7, 02/85 [01/85], $25.00 signed edition; $13.95 trade edition, 252pp, hc) Reprint (Dell 1971) romantic novel of sus- pense; of associational interest.

McCaffrey, Anne STITCH IN SNOW (Tor 0-312-93753-9, 05/85 [04/85], $14.95, 254pp, hc) Reprint (Brandywyne 1984) non-sf/ fantasy, romance novel; listed for McCaffrey fans.

McCammon, Robert USHER'S PASSING (Ballantine 0-345-32407-2, 10/85 [09/85], $3.95, 407pp, pb) Reprint (Holt, Rinehart & Winston 1984) dark fantasy/horror novel featuring the further adventures of Poe's Usher family.

*McCarthy, Shawna, ed. ISAAC ASIMOV'S FANTASY (Dial 0-385-23017- 6, 04/19/85 [03/85], $12.95, 348pp, hc) Anthology of 19 stories from *Asimov's*.
Contents: Page
The Storming of Annie Kinsale
                    Lucius Shepard   ss IAS Sep,84   10
Greek   Leigh Kennedy   ss IAS Oct,83   29
A Surfeit of Melancholic Humours
                    Sharon N. Farber   ss IAS Mar,84   42
Still Life with Scorpion Scott Baker   ss IAS May,84   62
Close of Night   Daphne Castell   ss IAS May,84   77
Street Magic   Ron Goulart   ss IAS Mar,84   92
What Seen but the Wolf Gregg Keizer   nv IAS Feb,84   106
Galatea   Kristi Olesen   ss IAS Mar,84   136
How F. Scott Fitzgerald Became Beloved in Springfield
                    George Alec Effinger ss IAS Aug,84   148
The Leopard's Daughter Lee Killough   ss IAS Feb,84   168
Chand Veda   Tanith Lee   ss IAS Oct,83   187
The Fire at Sarah Siddons
                    Robert Thurston   ss IAS Aug,84   199

The Rim of the Wheel   Lillian Stewart Carl   ss IAS Feb,84   214
The Laughter of Elves   Juleen Brantingham   ss IAS Jan,84   234
The Power of the Press Richard Kearns   nv IAS Dec md,83 246
The Closing Time   George R.R. Martin   ss IAS Nov,82   268
And Who Would Pity a Swan?
                        Connie Willis   ss IAS Jan,85   279
Son of the Morning   Ian McDowell   ss IAS Dec,83   292
The Big Dream   John Kessel   nv IAS Apr,84   314

*McCollum, Michael PROCYON'S PROMISE (Ballantine/Del Rey 0-345- 30097-1, 08/85 [07/85], $3.50, 283pp, pb) Sf novel, sequel to LIFE PROBE.

*McCullough, Colleen A CREED FOR THE THIRD MILLENNIUM (Harper & Row 0-06-015301-6, 06/85 [05/85], $17.95, 346pp, hc) Sf novel set in 2032, by the author of THE THORNBIRDS. This one, about the Second Coming, has gotten mostly negative reviews.

*McDowell, Michael JACK AND SUSAN IN 1953 (Ballantine 0-345- 32366-1, 08/85 [07/85], $3.50, 280pp, pb) First in a new series featuring a couple that remains "forever young" through various adventures that will eventually span the 20th century. There isn't any other fantasy content.

*McDowell, Michael TOPLIN (Scream/Press 0-910489-11-4, 11/85 [11/85], $20.00, 172pp, hc) Horror novel. Illustrations by Harry O. Morris.

*McEnroe, Richard S. SKINNER (Bantam Spectra 0-553-24597-X, 06/85 [05/85], $2.95, 198pp, pb) Sf adventure novel. Third book set in "The Shattered Stars" universe.

*McEvoy, Seth NOT QUITE HUMAN #1: BATTERIES NOT INCLUDED (Pocket/ Archway 0-671-60081-8, 1985 [10/85], $2.25, 147pp, pb) Young- adult sf novel, first in a series about an android boy in junior high. A one-joke series, but the one joke is enough for most junior high school students, or at least it was when I was that age. (DLN)

*McEvoy, Seth NOT QUITE HUMAN #2: ALL GEARED UP (Pocket/Archway 0-671-60082-6, 1985 [10/85], $2.25, 149pp, pb) Young-adult nov- el, second in the series featuring an android schoolboy; this time he joins a rock band.

*McEvoy, Seth NOT QUITE HUMAN #3: A BUG IN THE SYSTEM (Pocket/ Archway 0-671-60083-4, 11/85 [11/85], $2.25, 148pp, pb) Sf nov- el, third in the series about a robot high schooler.

*McEvoy, Seth SAMUEL R. DELANY (Ungar 0-8044-6462-6, 03/85 [03/85], $6.95, 142pp, pb) Non-fiction, critical study with some biographical information. This just appeared despite the 1984 copyright date.

*McEvoy, Seth SAMUEL R. DELANY (Ungar 0-8044-2669-4, 05/85 [04/85], $12.95, x + 142pp, hc) This is the hardcover edition of the non-fiction critical study listed above. Publication may have been simultaneous.

*McGuire, Patrick L. RED STARS: POLITICAL ASPECTS OF SOVIET SCIENCE FICTION (UMI 0-8357-1579-5, 06/85 [05/85], $24.95 + post- age, 152pp, hc) Non-fiction, critical study of Russian sf and its content. Recommended. (CNB)

McIntyre, Vonda N. THE EXILE WAITING (Tor 0-812-54552-4, 12/85 [11/85], $2.95, 248pp, pb) Reprint (SFBC 1975) sf novel.

McIntyre, Vonda N. STAR TREK III: THE SEARCH FOR SPOCK (Gregg 0-8398-2839-X, 01/85 [12/84], $12.95, 297pp, hc) Reprint (Pocket 1984) novelization of the third Star Trek film.

McKiernan, Dennis L. THE DARK TIDE (NAL/Signet 0-451-13668-3, 08/85 [07/85], $2.95, 303pp, pb) Reprint (Doubleday 1984) fan- tasy novel, Book One of the "Iron Tower" trilogy.

McKiernan, Dennis L. THE DARKEST DAY (NAL/Signet 0-451-13865-1, 10/85 [09/85], $2.95, 302pp, pb) Reprint (Doubleday 1984) fan- tasy novel, conclusion of the "Iron Tower" trilogy.

McKiernan, Dennis L. SHADOWS OF DOOM (NAL/Signet 0-451-13815-5, 09/85 [08/85], $2.95, 300pp, pb) Reprint (Doubleday 1984) fan- tasy novel, Book 2 of the "Iron Tower Trilogy."

*McKillip, Patricia A. THE MOON AND THE FACE (Atheneum/Argo 0-689-31158-3, 09/85 [09/85], $10.95, 146pp, hc) Young-adult sf novel, sequel to MOON-FLASH.

McKillip, Patricia A. MOON-FLASH (Berkley 0-425-08457-4, 10/85 [09/85], $2.75, 150pp, pb) Reprint (Atheneum 1984) young-adult sf novel.

McKinley, Robin BEAUTY (Harper & Row 0-06-024149-7, 1985 [12/85], $11.95FPT, 247pp, hc) Reissue (Harper & Row 1978) fantasy novel, a retelling of "Beauty and the Beast". There is no indication on this edition that it's a reprint, except for the missing first edition slug on the copyright page. The only date inside is the original 1978 one. There's also a Harpercrest library edition, 0-06-024150-0, $10.89.

McKinley, Robin THE HERO AND THE CROWN (SFBC #3927, 04/85 [03/85], $5.98, 224pp, hc) Reprint (Greenwillow 1984) fantasy novel. Winner of the Newbery prize as best juvenile of the year. A fine prequl to THE BLUE SWORD, even better than its predecessor. (DLN)

*McKinley, Robin, ed. IMAGINARY LANDS (Ace 0441-36694-5, 12/85 [11/85], $2.95, 230pp, PB) Original anthology of nine fantasy stories. Recommended. (FCM)
Contents:

			Page
Paper Dragons	James P. Blaylock	nv IMGNLND,85	1
The Old Woman and the Storm			
	Patricia A. McKillip	ss IMGNLND,85	23
The Big Rock Candy Mountain			
	Robert Westall	nv IMGNLND,85	35
Flight	Peter Dickinson	nv IMGNLND,85	59
Evian Steel	Jane Yolen	nv IMGNLND,85	91
Stranger Blood	P.C. Hodgell	nv IMGNLND,85	125
The Curse of Igamor	Michael de Larrabeiti	ss IMGNLND,85	155
Tam Lin	Joan D. Vinge	nv IMGNLND,85	169
The Stone Fey	Robin McKinley	nv IMGNLND,85	199

McNelly, Dr. Willis E., ed. THE DUNE ENCYCLOPEDIA (Corgi 0-552-99131-7, 01/85 [12/84], £5.95, 526pp, pb) Reprint (Berkley 1984) reference book which treats "Dune" as a historical series.

*McPheeters, Neal, Cary Bates & Gene Colan NIGHTWINGS Main listing under Cary Bates.

McQuay, Mike ESCAPE FROM NEW YORK (Bantam Spectra 0-553-25375-1, 12/85 [11/85], $2.95, 181pp, pb) Reissue (Bantam 1981) novelization of the sf movie.

McQuay, Mike LIFE-KEEPER (Bantam 0-553-25075-2, 04/85 [03/85], $2.95, 260pp, pb) Reprint (Avon 1980) sf novel.

*McQuay, Mike MOTHER EARTH (Bantam Spectra 0-553-25123-6, 08/85 [07/85], $3.50, 371pp, pb) Sf novel, sequel to PURE BLOOD.

*McQuay, Mike MY SCIENCE PROJECT (Bantam 0-553-25378-6, 09/85 [08/85], $2.95, 169pp, pb) Novelization of the sf movie, based on a screenplay by Jonathan Betuel.

*McQuay, Mike PURE BLOOD (Bantam 0-553-24668-2, 02/85 [01/85], $2.95, 281pp, pb) Sf novel, first of at least two parts.

*Meaney, Dee Morrison ISEULT (Ace 0-441-37387-9, 08/85 [07/85], $2.95, 229pp, pb) Arthurian fantasy novel.

*Meluch, R.M. JERUSALEM FIRE (NAL/Signet 0-451-13923-2, 11/85 [10/85], $3.50, 331pp, pb) Sf novel of Arabs in space.

Meluch, R.M. SOVEREIGN (NAL/Signet 0-451-13924-0, 11/85 [11/85], $2.95, 230pp, pb) Reissue (NAL/Signet 1979) sf novel. Fourth printing.

Meluch, R.M. WIND DANCERS (NAL/Signet 0-451-14056-7, 01/86 [12/85], $2.50, 166pp, pb) Reissue (NAL 1981) sf novel, 3rd printing.

*Menville, Douglas & R. Reginald FUTURE VISIONS: THE GOLDEN AGE OF THE SCIENCE FICTION FILM (Newcastle/Greenbriar 0-87877-081-X, 11/85 [11/85], $12.95, 192pp, pb) 8 1/2 x 11 reference book on sf films, it concentrates on 1977-1985 and has many stills. Mary A. Burgess is also credited as a contributor, but not on the cover. The book is apparently also available as a library hc, 0-89370-681-X, $24.95. The pb is available from Newcastle Publishing Co., the hc reprint is produced and distributed by The Borgo Press.

*Merril, Judith, ed. TESSERACTS (Press Porcepic 0-88878-242-X, 11/85 [11/85], C$9.95, 292pp, pb) Original and reprint anthology of Canadian sf. Distributed by Beaverbooks. For information, write Press Porcepic.
Contents:

			Page
Foreword	Judith Merril	fw	1
Home by the Sea	Elisabeth Vonarburg	ss TESRCTS,85	4
translated by Jane Brierley			
Chronos' Christmas	Rhea Rose	ss TESRCTS,85	21
A Strange Visitor	Robert Zend	pm TESRCTS,85	39
The Byrds	Michael G. Coney	ss CHANGES,83	40
Report on the Earth-Air Addicts			
	Robert Priest	pm MNWHBKX,84	54
Johnny Appleseed and the New World			
	Candas Jane Dorsey	ss TESRCTS,85	55
Letter from Mars-Dome #1	Eileen Kernaghan	pm LSN Oct,78	62
Hinterlands	William Gibson	ss OMN Oct,81	64
Points in Time	Christopher Dewdney	pm TESRCTS,85	83
Stardust Boulevard	Daniel Sernine	ss LVLHMSP,81	84
translated by Jane Brierley		TESRCTS,85	
The Last Will and Testament of the Unknown Earthman Lost in the Second Vegan Campaign			
	D.M. Price	pm TESRCTS,85	101
The Woman Who is the Midnight Wind			
	Terence M. Green	ss TESRCTS,85	103
Instinct	Dorothy Corbett Gentleman		
		pm PSP Spr,80	115
Cee	Gerry Truscott	ss TESRCTS,85	116
On the Planet Grafool	Benjamin Freedman	ss TESRCTS,85	125
Tauf Aleph	Phyllis Gotlieb	nv MRWNDRN,81	129
Anthropology 101	Gary Eikenberry	ss BBL # 9,83	151

The Train	Marc Sevigny	ss AURBRL1,83	157
translated by Frances Morgan		TESRCTS,85	
Countdown	John Robert Colombo	pm TESRCTS,85	172
Questionnaire	John Robert Colombo	pm TESRCTS,85	172
Sophie, 1990	Marian Engel	ss 1980	173
Future City	D.M. Price	pm TESRCTS,85	177
Totem	Margaret McBride	ss TESRCTS,85	179
An Adventure in Miracle-Land			
	Robert Zend	pm TESRCTS,85	187
2DWORLD [from "The Planiverse"]			
	A.K. Dewdney	ex MLL 1984	188
Variation	Robert Zend	pm FRMOTO1,73	206
The Man Doll [revised]	Susan Swan	ss DSC F11,82	207
The Early Education of the Num-Nums			
	Robert Priest	pm SADNSPM,80	217
The Loneliness of the Long-Distance Writer			
	Lesley Choyce	ss ORN V1 #2,82	218
Report from the Front	Robert Sward	pm PMSNW&S,83	226
God is an Iron	Spider Robinson	nv OMN May,79	227
The Effect of Terminal Cancer on Potential Astronauts			
	David Kirkpatrick	pm TESRCTS,85	247
Afterword: We Have Met the Alien (And It Is Us)			
	Judith Merril	aw	274
The Contributors	[Misc. Material]	bg	285

Meyers, Richard S. DOOMSTAR (Popular Library/Questar 0-445-20051-0, 07/85 [06/85], $2.95, 296pp, pb) Reissue (Carlyle Books 1978) sf novel featuring ship's commander Larry, cat-woman Napoleon, and Harlan "the invincible human weapon." This is apparently revised from the original appearance.

*Meyers, Richard S. RETURN TO DOOMSTAR (Popular Library/Questar 0-445-20125-8, 10/85 [09/85], $2.95, 295pp, pb) Sf adventure novel featuring the Light Orbit Space Theater and hitchhikers the catwoman Napoleon and 9' tall Harlan. Sequel to DOOMSTAR. This is a rewrite of DOOMSTAR II (Carlyle 1979). The earlier work is not acknowledged.

*Michaels, Melisa C. FIRST BATTLE (Tor 0-812-54568-0, 11/85 [10/85], $2.95, 253pp, pb) Sf novel, second in the "Skyrider" series, although not packaged as such. Military space opera.

*Michaels, Melisa C. SKYRIDER I: SKIRMISH (Tor 0-812-54566-4, 03/85 [02/85], $2.95, 252pp, pb) Sf adventure novel about a female spaceship pilot. A first novel.

*Miklowitz, Gloria D. AFTER THE BOMB (Scholastic/Point 0-590-33287-2, 06/85 [09/85], $2.25, 156pp, pb) Young-adult post-holocaust sf novel.

*Milan, Victor THE CYBERNETIC SAMURAI (Arbor House 0-87795-642-1, 08/85 [07/85], $15.95, 300pp, hc) Sf novel. Complex, careful treatment of both Japanese and computer themes doesn't save this novel from the problems of predictability and unsuccessful characterization. (DLN)

Milan, Victor & Robert E. Vardeman THE CITY IN THE GLACIER Main listing under Robert E. Vardeman.

Milan, Victor & Robert E. Vardeman THE DESTINY STONE Main listing under Robert E. Vardeman.

Milan, Victor & Robert E. Vardeman THE FALLEN ONES Main listing under Robert E. Vardeman.

Milan, Victor & Robert E. Vardeman THE SUNDERED REALM Main listing under Robert E. Vardeman.

Miller, Chuck & Tim Underwood, eds. FEAR ITSELF: THE HORROR FICTION OF STEPHEN KING Main listing under Tim Underwood.

Miller, J.P. THE SKOOK (Warner 0-446-32861-8, 08/85 [07/85], $3.95, 307pp, pb) Reprint (Warner 1984) allegorical fantasy novel.

Miller, Phyllis & Andre Norton HOUSE OF SHADOWS Main listing under Andre Norton.

*Miller, Phyllis & Andre Norton RIDE THE GREEN DRAGON Main listing under Andre Norton.

Miller, Richard SNAIL (Holt/Owl 0-03-063309-5, 10/85 [11/85], $7.95, 294pp, pb) Reprint (Holt, Rinehart & Winston 1984) allegorical fantasy novel (one of whose characters is Kilgore Trout).

*Miller, Ron, William K. Hartmann & Pamela Lee OUT OF THE CRADLE: EXPLORING THE FRONTIERS BEYOND EARTH Main listing under William K. Hartmann.

*Miller, Walter M., Jr. & Martin H. Greenberg, eds. BEYOND ARMAGEDDON (Donald I Fine 0-917657-55-1, 10/85 [10/85], $18.95, 387pp, hc) Anthology of 21 post-holocaust sf stories, with an introduction by Miller.
Contents:

			Page
Alibi	Walter M. Miller, Jr.	pm	viii
Forewarning (an Introduction)			
	Walter M. Miller, Jr.	in	1
Salvador	Lucius Shepard	nv FSF Apr,84	13
The Store of the Worlds	[The World of Heart's Desire]		
	Robert Sheckley	ss PBY Sep,59	31
The Big Flash	Norman Spinrad	nv ORB # 5,69	39
Lot	Ward Moore	nv FSF May,53	61

MILLER, WALTER M., JR. & MARTIN H. GREENBERG, eds.

A Day at the Beach	Carol Emshwiller	ss FSF Aug,59	85
The Wheel	John Wyndham	ss STS Jan,52	95
Jody After the War	Edward Bryant	ss ORB #10,72	103
The Terminal Beach	J.G. Ballard	ss NWS Mar,64	111
Tomorrow's Children	Poul Anderson	nv ASF Mar,47	131
Heirs Apparent	Robert Abernathy	nv FSF Jun,54	157
A Master of Babylon	[The Music Master of Babylon]		
	Edgar Pangborn	nv GAL Nov,54	177
Game Preserve	Rog Phillips	ss IFS Oct,57	201
By the Waters of Babylon	[The Place of the Gods]		
	Stephen Vincent Benet	ss SEP Jul,37	215
There Will Come Soft Rains			
	Ray Bradbury	ss COL May 6,50	227
To the Chicago Abyss	Ray Bradbury	ss FSF May,63	235
Lucifer	Roger Zelazny	ss WOT Jun,64	245
Eastward Ho!	William Tenn	ss FSF Oct,58	251
The Feast of Saint Janis	Michael Swanwick	nv NDM #11,80	267
"If I Forget Thee, Oh Earth..."			
	Arthur C. Clarke	ss FUT Sep,51	295
A Boy and His Dog	Harlan Ellison	nv NWS Apr,69	301
My Life in the Jungle	Jim Aikin	ss FSF Feb,85	337

*Millhiser, Marlys THE THRESHOLD (Putnam 0-399-13012-8, 01/85 [12/84], $16.95, 334pp, hc) Novel of time travel and the supernatural, mixed with Colorado history.

*Minsky, Marvin, ed. ROBOTICS (Doubleday/Anchor 0-385-19414-5, 06/85 [05/85], $19.95, 317pp, hc) Non-fiction, a group of essays on robots in fact and fiction; it includes an essay by Robert Sheckley. I opened the book to an essay by T.A. Heppenheimer and found several wrong details in his citing of Asimov stories -- either poor scholarship or sloppy proofreading. (CNB)

*Mitchell, Elizabeth, ed. AFTER THE FLAMES (Baen 0-671-55998-2, 12/85 [11/85], $2.95, 277pp, pb) Anthology of three novellas set after the Holocaust. Each is in "slightly different form" than as originally published. "Alien Stars" Vol. II.
Contents:

			Page
The Election	Robert Silverberg	na ASF Mar,83	3
World War Last	Norman Spinrad	na IAS Aug,85	73
When Winter Ends	Michael P. Kube-McDowell		
		na FSF Jul,85	171

*Mitchell, Elizabeth, ed. ALIEN STARS (Baen 0-671-55934-6, 01/85 [12/84], $2.95, 254pp, pb) Anthology of three original novellas.
Contents:

			Page
The Scapegoat	C.J. Cherryh	na ALIENST,85	7
Seasons	Joe W. Haldeman	na ALIENST,85	75
Cordon Sanitaire	Timothy Zahn	na ALIENST,85	153

Mitchison, Naomi TRAVEL LIGHT (Virago Modern Classics 0-86068-562-4, 08/85 [07/85], $7.95/L2.95, 147pp, pb) Reprint (Faber & Faber 1952) historical fantasy novel, available in the U.S. as an import.

*Modesitt, L.E., Jr. THE HAMMER OF DARKNESS (Avon 0-380-89798-9, 08/85 [07/85], $2.95, 343pp, pb) Sf novel.

*Monaco, Richard BLOOD AND DREAMS (Berkley 0-425-08024-2, 08/85 [07/85], $2.95, 230pp, pb) Fantasy novel, fourth in the "Parsival" series; a surreal retelling of the legends.

*Monaco, Richard BROKEN STONE (Ace 0-441-08134-7, 01/85 [12/84], $2.95, 230pp, pb) Fantasy novel, the sequel to RUNES.

*Monaco, Richard JOURNEY TO THE FLAME (Bantam Spectra 0-553-25373-5, 12/85 [11/85], $3.50, 260pp, pb) Fantasy adventure novel, a sort of sequel to SHE with Haggard and Kipling as minor characters.

*Monteleone, Thomas F. & David F. Bischoff NIGHT OF THE DRAGON-STAR Main listing under David F. Bischoff.

Moorcock, Michael THE CHAMPION OF GARATHORM (Berkley 0-425-07646-6, 04/85 [03/85], $2.75, 159pp, pb) Reprint (Mayflower 1973) fantasy novel. "Chronicles of Count Brass" II.

*Moorcock, Michael THE CHRONICLES OF CASTLE BRASS (Granada 0-246-12714-7, 09/85 [07/85], £9.95, 150+138+144pp, hc) Omnibus edition of three fantasy novels of Dorian Hawkmoon, sequel to "The History of the Runestaff".
Contents:

			Page
COUNT BRASS	Michael Moorcock	n. MFL 1973	7
THE CHAMPION OF GARATHORM			
	Michael Moorcock	n. MFL 1973	151
THE QUEST FOR TANELORN	Michael Moorcock	n. MFL 1975	289

Moorcock, Michael COUNT BRASS (Berkley 0-425-07514-1, 02/85 [01/85], $2.75, 147pp, pb) Reprint (Mayflower 1973) fantasy novel. "The First Book of the Chronicles of Count Brass" and also Book 5 in the "Dorian Hawkmoon" series.

Moorcock, Michael ELRIC AT THE END OF TIME (DAW 0-88677-040-8, 05/85 [04/85], $2.95, 221pp, pb) Reprint (NEL 1984) collection of odds and ends including three "Elric" pieces. Not "the seventh Elric novel", despite the cover copy.

Moorcock, Michael THE ICE SCHOONER (Harrap 0-245-54284-1, 1985 [10/85], £8.95, 237pp, hc) Reprint (Sphere 1969) sf novel, a re-revision of the revised 1977 Harper & Row edition. It becomes the definitive edition until the next revision.

Moorcock, Michael THE JEWEL IN THE SKULL (DAW 0-88677-043-2, 05/85 [04/85], $2.75, 176pp, pb) Reissue (DAW 1977) revised fantasy novel, "Runestaff" #1. First published by Lancer in 1968. 7th DAW printing.

+Moorcock, Michael THE LAUGHTER OF CARTHAGE (Random House 0-394-52997-9, 02/85 [01/85], $17.95 FPT, 561pp, hc) Reprint (Secker & Warburg 1984), first U.S. edition. A picaresque mainstream novel, sequel to BYZANTIUM ENDURES. Some of Moorcock's sf characters show up in this one too. The text varies somewhat from the British edition.

Moorcock, Michael THE MAD GOD'S AMULET (DAW 0-88677-044-0, 05/85 [04/85], $2.75, 160pp, pb) Reissue (DAW 1977) fantasy novel, "Runestaff" #2. Revised from SORCERER'S AMULET (Lancer 1968). 5th DAW printing.

Moorcock, Michael THE QUEST FOR TANELORN (Berkley 0-425-07707-1, 06/85 [05/85], $2.75, 155pp, pb) Reprint (Mayflower 1975) fantasy novel, "Chronicles of Castle Brass" III; also part of the "Dorian Hawkmoon" and "Erekose" groups.

Moorcock, Michael THE RUNESTAFF (DAW 0-88677-046-7, 05/85 [04/85], $2.75, 158pp, pb) Reissue (DAW 1977) fantasy novel, "Runestaff" #4 (conclusion of the series). Revised from THE SECRET OF THE RUNESTAFF (Lancer 1969). 6th DAW printing.

Moorcock, Michael THE SILVER WARRIORS (Berkley 0-425-08078-1, 09/85 [08/85], $2.95, 220pp, pb) Reprint (Mayflower 1970 as PHOENIX IN OBSIDIAN) fantasy novel of The Eternal Champion.

Moorcock, Michael THE SWORD OF THE DAWN (DAW 0-88677-045-9, 05/85 [04/85], $2.75, 173pp, pb) Reissue (DAW 1977) fantasy novel, "Runestaff" #3. Revised from the 1968 Lancer edition. 6th DAW printing.

Moorcock, Michael THE WAR HOUND AND THE WORLD'S PAIN (Pocket 0-671-60409-0, 08/85 [07/85], $2.95, 207pp, pb) Reissue (Simon & Schuster/Timescape 1981) fantasy novel. Second printing. Highly recommended. (CNB)

Moore, Ward GREENER THAN YOU THINK (Crown 0-517-55866-1, 10/85 [09/85], $9.95, 322pp, hc) Reprint (Sloane 1947) sf novel, with a new introduction by George Zebrowski.

Morressy, John KINGSBANE (Ace 0-441-44575-6, 01/85 [12/84], $2.75, 255pp, pb) Reprint (Playboy 1982) fantasy novel, "The Iron Angel" #3.

*Morressy, John THE TIME OF THE ANNIHILATOR (Ace 0-441-81191-4, 08/85 [07/85], $2.95, 217pp, pb) Fantasy novel, fourth in the IRONBRAND trilogy.

Morris, Chris & Janet Morris THE 40-MINUTE WAR Main listing under Janet Morris.

*Morris, Janet BEYOND SANCTUARY (Baen 0-671-55957-5, 06/85 [05/85], $15.95, 312pp, hc) Fantasy novel set in the "Thieves' World" universe.

Morris, Janet BEYOND SANCTUARY (SFBC #03843, 12/85 [12/85], $5.50, 247pp, hc) Reprint (Baen 1985) fantasy novel set in the "Thieves' World" universe.

*Morris, Janet BEYOND THE VEIL (Baen 0-671-55984-2, 01/86 [12/85], $15.95, 314pp, hc) Fantasy novel, second in the trilogy featuring Tempus, Morris' character from "Thieves' World".

Morris, Janet THE CARNELIAN THRONE (Baen 0-671-55936-2, 03/85 [02/85], $2.95, 310pp, pb) Reprint (Bantam 1979) sf novel. "Silistra" #4.

Morris, Janet WIND FROM THE ABYSS (Baen 0-671-55932-X, 01/85 [12/84], $2.95, 369pp, pb) Reprint (Bantam 1978) sf novel, Book 3 of the "Silistra" series.

*Morris, Janet, ed. AFTERWAR (Baen 0-671-55967-2, 06/85 [06/85], $2.95, 284pp, pb) Original anthology of 12 stories set after a nuclear holocaust.
Contents:

			Page
Introduction	Janet Morris	in	7
Hero's Welcome	Janet Morris	ss AFTRWAR,85	14
Going After Arviq	Michael Armstrong	nv AFTRWAR,85	26
To the Storming Gulf	Gregory Benford	na FSF Apr,85	47
Flamestones	Stephen Leigh	nv AFTRWAR,85	107
The Phoenix Garden	Diana L. Paxson	nv AFTRWAR,85	132
Primary	Esther M. Friesner	ss AFTRWAR,85	171
When Idaho Dived	Ian Watson	ss AFTRWAR,85	191
Bar and Grill	Craig Shaw Gardner	ss AFTRWAR,85	199
Pots	C.J. Cherryh	nv AFTRWAR,85	214
Notes for a Newer Testament			
	David Langford	ss AFTRWAR,85	251
The Guardroom	David A. Drake	nv AFTRWAR,85	261

*Morris, Janet & David A. Drake ACTIVE MEASURES (Baen 0-671-55945-1, 04/85 [03/85], $3.95, 365pp, pb) Near-future spy adventure novel. There's a $10,000 prize offered for the best answer to 7 questions. Unfortunately, you have to pay 50 cents to enter and have to use the official form only, which is part of the book....

Morris, Janet & Chris Morris THE 40-MINUTE WAR (Baen 0-671-55986-9, 10/85 [09/85], $3.50, 281pp, pb) Reprint (Baen 1984) near-future sf novel. Washington is destroyed by a nuclear terrorist attack.

*Morris, Winifred WITH MAGICAL HORSES TO RIDE (Atheneum 0-689-31108-7, 03/85 [02/85], $11.95, 152pp, hc) Juvenile fantasy novel.

Morrow, James THE CONTINENT OF LIES (Gollancz 0-575-03659-1, 06/85 [05/85], £9.95, 274pp, hc) Reprint (Holt, Rinehart 1984) sf novel. First British edition.

Morrow, James THE CONTINENT OF LIES (Baen 0-671-55969-9, 07/85 [06/85], $2.95, 281pp, pb) Reprint (Holt, Rinehart 1984) sf novel.

*Moskowitz, Sam, ed. A. MERRITT: REFLECTIONS IN THE MOON POOL (Oswald Train no ISBN, 07/85 [06/85], $20.00, 399pp, hc) Collection of Merritt marginalia. Includes poems, letters, stories, and fragments, plus a long biographical introduction by Moskowitz and 16 pages of photos.

Contents:			Page
The Life, Work and Times of A. Merritt			
	Sam Moskowitz	bg	11
Pilgrimage, or, Obi Giese			
	A. Merritt	ss	167
The Pool of the Stone God			
	A. Merritt	ss AWK Sep 23,23	187
Bootleg and Witches. A Fragment			
	A. Merritt	ms	191
The Devil in the Heart. An Outline			
	A. Merritt	ms	197
The Challenge from Beyond [Part 2]			
	A. Merritt	vi FMG Sep,35	200
An Unpublished Ending for Dwellers in the Mirage			
	A. Merritt	ms	203
The Poems of A. Merritt	A. Merritt	pm	207
Poems in Praise of A. Merritt			
	Various Hands	pm	255
Letters and Correspondence			
	A. Merritt	ms	261
The Autobiography of A. Merritt			
	A. Merritt	bg	329
	Edited by Walter Wentz		
A. Merritt--His Life and Times			
	A. Merritt & Jack Chapman Miske	bg	342
Man and the Universe	A. Merritt	ar	352
Interview of A. Merritt	Julius Schwartz	iv	356
What Is Fantasy?	A. Merritt	ar	361
Background of Dwellers in the Mirage			
	A. Merritt	ar	364
Background of Burn, Witch, Burn!			
	A. Merritt	ar	367
Background of Creep, Shadow!			
	A. Merritt	ar	370
A. Merritt's Own Selected Credoes			
	A. Merritt	ar	373
A Newsman's Notebook	Gilbert Brown	ar	377
Index	[Misc. Material]	ix	383

*Mueller, Richard GHOSTBUSTERS: THE SUPERNATURAL SPECTACULAR (Tor 0-812-58598-4, 08/85 [07/85], $2.95, 251pp, pb) Novelization based on the movie screenplay by Dan Aykroyd and Harold Ramis.

Mujica Lainez, Manuel THE WANDERING UNICORN (SFBC #3734, 01/85 [12/84], $7.98, 322pp, hc) Reprint (Lester & Orpen Dennys 1982) fantasy novel. World Fantasy Award finalist.

Mujica Lainez, Manuel THE WANDERING UNICORN (Berkley 0-425-08386-1, 12/85 [11/85], $2.95, 320pp, pb) Reprint (Lester & Orpen Dennys 1982) fantasy novel. Translated from the Spanish by Mary Fitton. A 1965 Argentinian book with an introduction by Jorge Luis Borges. It was a nominee for the World Fantasy Award.

Mundy, Talbot KING, OF THE KHYBER RIFLES (Carroll & Graf 0-88184-169-2, 07/85 [06/85], $3.95, 395pp, pb) Reprint (Bobbs-Merrill 1916) fantasy adventure novel. The most famous of Mundy's novels. Highly recommended. (CNB) The awful cover, left over from The Charge of the Light Brigade, has nothing to do with the book.

Mundy, Talbot KING, OF THE KHYBER RIFLES (Critic's Choice 0-931773-14-8, 1985 [10/85], $2.95, 395pp, pb) Reprint (Bobbs-Merrill 1916) fantasy novel. This is the mass market edition of the Carroll & Graff edition issued earlier. It's identical except for the publisher, ISBN and price.

*Murnane, Gerald LANDSCAPE WITH LANDSCAPE (Norstrilia 0-909106-15-0, 1985 [09/85], A$17.00, 267pp, hc) Collection of six loosely connected stories, some with elements of surreal fantasy.

Contents:			Page
Landscape with Freckled Woman			
	Gerald Murnane	nv LANDSCP,85	1
Sipping the Essence	Gerald Murnane	nv LANDSCP,85	27
The Battle of Acosta Nu	Gerald Murnane	na HLX	71
A Quieter Place than Clun			
	Gerald Murnane	nv LANDSCP,85	123
Charlie Alcock's Cock	Gerald Murnane	nv LANDSCP,85	171
Landscape with Artist	Gerald Murnane	na LANDSCP,85	217

+Murnane, Gerald THE PLAINS (Braziller 0-8076-1123-9, 08/85 [09/85], $12.95, 126pp, hc) Reprint (Norstrilia 1982) short novel of an alternate Australia; first U.S. edition.

*Murphy, Shirley Rousseau NIGHTPOOL (Harper & Row 0-06-024360-0, 09/85 [09/85], $11.95, 250pp, hc) Young-adult fantasy novel, first in a trilogy.

*Murray, Frieda & Roland Green THE THRONE OF SHERRAN, VOL. I: THE BOOK OF KANTELA Main listing under Roland Green.

Myers, John Myers THE HARP AND THE BLADE (Ace 0-441-31750-2, 02/85 [01/85], $2.75, 230pp, pb) Reprint (Dutton 1941) quasi-fantasy novel. There's a druid and a curse, but basically this is a fine Celtic historical novel set in the 10th century. Recommended. (CNB)

Myers, John Myers SILVERLOCK (Ace 0-441-76674-9, 12/85 [11/85], $3.95, 516pp, pb) Reissue (Dutton 1949) fantasy novel. 9th Ace printing. One of the classics of modern fantasy literature. Highly recommended. (CNB)

*Nelson, Ray Faraday TIMEQUEST (Tor 0-812-54650-4, 11/85 [10/85], $2.95, 286pp, pb) Sf novel, extensively rewritten version of BLAKE'S PROGRESS (Laser 1975), featuring the adventures of William Blake and his wife Catherine in strange times and dimensions.

*NESFA Press THE N.E.S.F.A. INDEX TO THE SCIENCE FICTION MAGAZINES AND ORIGINAL ANTHOLOGIES 1983 (NESFA Press 0-915368-23-4, 03/85 [02/85], $5.00, 68pp, pb) Non-fiction, bibliography of the 1983 short fiction field. It's a year later than the Twaci version but covers more. Although it covers British anthologies, for some reason it does not list *Interzone*. Still useful for the anthology listings.

*Newman, Kim & Neil Gaiman GHASTLY BEYOND BELIEF Main listing under Neil Gaiman.

*Newman, Sharan GUINEVERE EVERMORE (St. Martin's 0-312-35322-7, 05/85 [04/85], $15.95, 277pp, hc) Arthurian fantasy novel, conclusion of the "Guinevere" trilogy.

+Nicholls, Peter THE WORLD OF FANTASTIC FILMS: AN ILLUSTRATED SURVEY (Dodd Mead 0-396-08381-1, 01/85 [12/84], $22.95, 224pp, hc) Reprint (D.S. Colour 1983), first U.S. edition. Illustrated study of sf/fantasy films, with emphasis on movies made from 1968 to the 80s. Illustrated in color and black & white.

+Nicholls, Peter THE WORLD OF FANTASTIC FILMS: AN ILLUSTRATED SURVEY (Dodd Mead 0-396-08382-X, 01/85 [12/84], $14.95, 224pp, pb) Paperback edition of the above.

*Night Cry [v.1 #2, Summer 1985] T.E.D. Klein, ed. (TZ Publications, 02/85 [02/85], $2.95, 194pp, pb)

Contents:			Page
From the Editor	T.E.D. Klein	in	6
Scenicruiser and the Silver Lady			
	Peter S. Alterman	nv TZM Jun,81	8
The Death Runner	Thomas Sullivan	ss TZM Apr,81	27
Worms from Mars	Augustine Funnell	nv NCR V1 #2,85	32
Food, Gas, Lodging	Craig W. Anderson	ss TZM Jul,82	53
The Ash-Tree	M.R. James	ss GHSTANT,04	61
Zombies	Dolly Ogawa	ss TZM Jun,82	75
Hell Is Murkey	John Alfred Taylor	nv TZM Nov,82	80
Cruising	Donald Tyson	ss TZM Sep,82	100
The Thing from the Slush	George Alec Effinger	ss TZM Apr,82	103
The Dark	Benjamin Gleisser	ss NCR V1 #2,85	119
Bugs	Larry Tritten	ss NCR V1 #2,85	132
W.S.	L.P. Hartley	ss GHB # 2,52	136
New Man	Barbara Owens	ss TZM Mar,82	147
Four Days Before the Snow			
	A.R. Morlan	nv NCR V1 #2,85	161

*Night Cry [v.1 #3, Fall 1985] T.E.D. Klein, ed. (TZ Publications, 05/85 [05/85], $2.95, 194pp, pb)

Contents:			Page
Terror in the Back Seat	Alan Rodgers	in	5
Bagman	William R. Trotter	ss NCR V1 #3,85	6
The Man Who Couldn't Remember			
	David Curtis	ss TZM Aug,81	19
Fright Night	Vincent McHardy	ss NCR V1 #3,85	28
The Bite	Elizabeth Morton	ss TZM Mar,82	43
The Spook Man	Al Sarrantonio	ss TZM Nov,82	47
The Woman's Version	David J. Schow	ss NCR V1 #3,85	57
Jockeying for Time	David Shifren	ss TZM Dec,82	70
Profile: Henry James	David Morrell	bg NCR V1 #3,85	86
Friends of the Friends	Henry James	nv 1896	92
Vastation	David Morrell	ss NCR V1 #3,85	118
The Lighthouse	Edgar Allan Poe & Robert Bloch		
		ss FAN Jan,53	122
In the Sunken Museum	Gregory Frost	ss TZM May,81	138
Luna	G.W. Perriwills	ss TZM Jul,81	156
Children of the Hydra	Dale Hammell	nv NCR V1 #3,85	164

*Night Cry [v.1 #4, Winter 1985] Alan Rodgers, ed. (TZ Publications, 09/85 [09/85], $2.95, 194pp, pb)

Contents:			Page
Warning:	Alan Rodgers	in NCR V1 #4,85	6
Bargain Cinema	Jay Sheckley	ss NCR V1 #4,85	12
A Thousand Paces Along the Via Dolorosa			
	Robert Silverberg	nv TZM Jul,81	19

My Old Man	George Alec Effinger	nv TZM Feb,82	43
The Dog That Ate the Baby	Peter A. Bobley	vi NCR V1 #4,85	61
Heimlich's Curse	Evan Eisenberg	ss TZM Nov,81	64
Bunny Didn't Tell Us	David J. Schow	ss NCR V1 #4,85	73
The Long Ride	John M. Skipp	ss TZM Sep,82	84
Occupational Hazard	G.L. Raisor	vi NCR V1 #4,85	96
Monarch of the Glen	Jon Wynne-Tyson	ss NCR V1 #4,85	98
Arcade	Thomas Wylde	ss NCR V1 #4,85	105
Profile: A.E. Coppard	Thomas E. Sanders (Nippawanock)	bg NCR V1 #4,85	110
Adam and Eve and Pinch Me	A.E. Coppard	ss ADM&EVE,21	116
An Exciting New Technology Comes to Pickerington, Ohio	Linda Haught	vi NCR V1 #4,85	127
Midtown Bodies	John Robert Bensink	ss TZM Aug,82	130
Going Native	Andrew Weiner	ss NCR V1 #4,85	137
A Haunted House	Susan Sheppard	pm NCR V1 #4,85	152
Scrap When Empty	A.R. Morlan	ss NCR V1 #4,85	159
An Appreciation: Theodore Sturgeon	Samuel R. Delany	bg NCR V1 #4,85	165
Bright Segment	Theodore Sturgeon	nv CAVIAR ,55	170

			Page
Welcome to the Magazine of Terror	Alan Rodgers	in NCR V1 #5,86	5
Special Delivery	Anita Kranitz Schlank	ss NCR V1 #5,86	12
Hellcatcher	Steven Popkes	ss NCR V1 #5,86	20
The Yougoslaves	Robert Bloch	nv NCR V1 #5,86	30
Coming of Age at Apple Creek	Thomas E. Sanders (Nippawanock)	ss NCR V1 #5,86	51
The Light at the End	John M. Skipp & Craig Spector	ex BAN 1986	60
Profile: Bram Stoker	Thomas E. Sanders (Nippawanock)	bg NCR V1 #5,86	72
The Squaw	Bram Stoker	ss	80
American Dream	V.K. Gibson	ss NCR V1 #5,86	93
Brass, Part I of II	David J. Schow	sl NCR V1 #5,86	101
Leaving	Darrell Schweitzer	ss NCR V1 #5,86	128
Mayaland	Paul Witcover	ss NCR V1 #5,86	139
The Holiday House	A.R. Morlan	ss NCR V1 #5,86	150
Three Poems: The Shaman	Ronald Terry	pm NCR V1 #5,86	161
Still-Life	Julie Yobst	ss	163
The Promise	Frank Meyer	vi NCR V1 #5,86	170
The Book of Webster's	J.N. Williamson	nv NCR V1 #5,86	173

Niven, Larry THE INTEGRAL TREES (Ballantine/Del Rey 0-345-32065-4, 02/85 [01/85], $3.50, 272pp, pb) Reprint (Ballantine/Del Rey 1984) sf novel, first paperback edition. A probable Hugo contender.

***Niven, Larry** LIMITS (Ballantine/Del Rey 0-345-32142-1, 02/85 [01/85], $2.95, 240pp, pb) Collection of 12 stories, including several collaborations.
Contents:

			Page
Introduction	Larry Niven	in	vii
The Lion in His Attic	Larry Niven	nv FSF Jul,82	1
Spirals	Larry Niven & Jerry E. Pournelle	na DST V1 #3,79	23
Talisman	Larry Niven & Dian Girard	ss FSF Nov,81	66
The Locusts	Larry Niven & Steve Barnes	nv ASF Jun,79	78
Yet Another Modest Proposal: The Roentgen Standard	Larry Niven	fa OMN Jul,80	114
Folk Tale	Larry Niven	ss NVNSLWS,84	157
The Green Marauder	Larry Niven	ss DST V2 #1,80	200
War Movie	Larry Niven	ss STL # 7,81	205
The Real Thing	Larry Niven	ss IAS Nov,82	221
Limits	Larry Niven	ss IAS Sep 28,81	226

Niven, Larry LIMITS (SFBC #1818, 03/85 [02/85], $3.98, 205pp, hc) Reprint (Ballantine/Del Rey 1985) collection, first hardcover edition.

Niven, Larry THE MAGIC GOES AWAY (Ace 0-441-51554-1, 10/85 [09/85], $2.95, 212pp, pb) Reissue (Ace 1978) short fantasy novella, with illustrations by Esteban Maroto. This is the 9th Ace printing.

***Niven, Larry & Jerry E. Pournelle** FOOTFALL (Ballantine/Del Rey 0-345-32347-5, 06/85 [05/85], $17.95, 495pp, pb) Sf novel of aliens invading Earth. Sf writers help save the world.

Niven, Larry & Jerry E. Pournelle FOOTFALL (Gollancz 0-575-03690-7, 09/85 [08/85], £9.95, 495pp, hc) Reprint (Del Rey 1985) sf novel, first British edition. The U.S. edition said it was "perhaps the finest novel of alien invasion," while the British one proclaims it "the ultimate."

Niven, Larry & Jerry E. Pournelle FOOTFALL (SFBC #03475, 12/85 [12/85], $6.98, 575pp, hc) Reprint (Del Rey 1985) sf novel.

Niven, Larry & Jerry E. Pournelle INFERNO (Pocket 0-671-49766-9, 08/85 [07/85], $3.50, 237pp, pb) Reissue (Pocket 1976) fantasy novel. 13th printing.

***Nolan, William F.** LOOK OUT FOR SPACE (Int'l Polygonics 0-930330-20-X, 06/85 [05/85], $4.95, 188pp, pb) The new "Sam Space" novel, sequel to SPACE FOR HIRE.

Nolan, William F. SPACE FOR HIRE (Int'l Polygonics 0-930330-19-6, 06/85 [05/85], $4.95, 174pp, pb) Reprint (Lancer 1971) humorous sf/private eye novel, with a new introduction by the author.

Norman, John BEASTS OF GOR (DAW 0-88677-028-9, 03/85 [02/85], $3.95, 444pp, pb) Reissue (DAW 1978), "Gor" #12. 10th printing.

***Norman, John** DANCER OF GOR (DAW 0-88677-100-5, 11/85 [10/85], $3.95, 479pp, pb) Sf novel, "Gor" #22.

Norman, John HUNTERS OF GOR (DAW 0-88677-010-6, 03/85 [02/85], $2.95, 320pp, pb) Reissue (DAW 1974) sf novel, "Gor" #8. 19th printing.

Norman, John MARAUDERS OF GOR (DAW 0-88677-025-4, 03/85 [02/85], $3.50, 296pp, pb) Reissue (DAW 1975), "Gor" #9. 17th printing.

***Norman, John** MERCENARIES OF GOR (DAW 0-88677-018-1, 03/85 [02/85], $3.95, 446pp, pb) Sf novel, #21 in the "Tarl Cabot Saga".

Norman, John SLAVE GIRL OF GOR (DAW 0-88677-027-0, 03/85 [02/85], $3.95, 446pp, pb) Reissue (DAW 1977), "Gor" #11. 13th printing.

Norman, John TRIBESMEN OF GOR (DAW 0-88677-026-2, 03/85 [02/85], $3.50, 364pp, pb) Reissue (DAW 1976), "Gor" #10. 15th printing.

Norton, Andre BREED TO COME (Ace 0-441-07900-8, 07/85 [06/85], $2.50, 288pp, pb) Reissue (Viking 1972) sf novel. 9th Ace printing.

Norton, Andre THE CROSSROADS OF TIME (Ace 0-441-12316-3, 08/85 [07/85], $2.50, 242pp, pb) Reissue (Ace 1956) sf novel. 8th Ace printing since 1974, plus god knows how many before. This is early Norton, but still one of her outstanding books. (CNB)

Norton, Andre THE CRYSTAL GRYPHON (Tor 0-812-54738-1, 07/85 [06/85], $2.95, 255pp, pb) Reprint (Atheneum 1982) fantasy novel. Part of the "Witch World" series and book 1 of the "Gryphon" trilogy.

Norton, Andre DRAGON MAGIC (Ace 0-441-16654-7, 10/85 [09/85], $2.50, 192pp, pb) Reissue (Crowell 1972) juvenile fantasy novel. 5th Ace printing.

***Norton, Andre** FORERUNNER: THE SECOND VENTURE (Tor 0-312-93256-1, 08/85 [07/85], $13.95, 254pp, hc) Sf novel, sequel to FORERUNNER.

Norton, Andre FORERUNNER: THE SECOND VENTURE (SFBC #2413 #2413, 11/85 [11/85], $6.98, 181pp, hc) Reprint (Tor 1985) sf novel. Sequel to FORERUNNER.

Norton, Andre GARAN THE ETERNAL (DAW 0-88677-055-6, 06/85 [05/85], $2.95, 206pp, pb) Reissue (FPCI 1972) quasi-novel of fantasy, made up of 5 shorts. 6th DAW printing.

Norton, Andre HERE ABIDE MONSTERS (Tor 0-812-54732-2, 12/85 [11/85], $2.95, 252pp, pb) Reprint (Atheneum 1973) fantasy novel.

Norton, Andre HORN CROWN (DAW 0-88677-051-3, 06/85 [05/85], $2.95, 255pp, pb) Reissue (DAW 1981) fantasy novel. This is chronologically the first of the "Witch World" books. 6th printing.

Norton, Andre LAVENDER-GREEN MAGIC (Ace 0-441-47443-8, 01/86 [12/85], $2.75, 241pp, pb) Reissue (Crowell 1974) juvenile fantasy novel. 6th Ace printing.

Norton, Andre MERLIN'S MIRROR (DAW 0-88677-052-1, 06/85 [05/85], $2.95, 205pp, pb) Reissue (DAW 1975) sf novel about Merlin. 8th printing.

Norton, Andre MOON OF THREE RINGS (Ace 0-441-53899-1, 04/85 [03/85], $2.50, 294pp, pb) Reissue (Viking 1966) sf novel, 12th Ace printing.

Norton, Andre NIGHT OF MASKS (Ballantine/Del Rey 0-345-32070-0, 02/85 [01/85], $2.25, 191pp, pb) Reprint (Harcourt Brace & World 1964) sf novel.

Norton, Andre NO NIGHT WITHOUT STARS (Ballantine/Del Rey 0-345-32520-6, 09/85 [08/85], $2.95, 223pp, pb) Reprint (Atheneum 1975) sf novel.

Norton, Andre OPERATION TIME SEARCH (Ballantine/Del Rey 0-345-32586-9, 12/85 [11/85], $2.95, 223pp, pb) Reprint (Harcourt Brace 1967) sf novel.

Norton, Andre ORDEAL IN OTHERWHERE (Ace 0-441-63819-8, 02/85 [01/85], $2.50, 203pp, pb) Reissue (World 1964) sf novel. "Forerunner" #2. 4th Ace printing.

Norton, Andre PLAGUE SHIP (Ace 0-441-66837-2, 06/85 [05/85], $2.50, 204pp, pb) Reissue (Gnome 1956, as by Andrew North) sf novel, Book 2 in the "Solar Queen" series. 7th Ace printing.

Norton, Andre <u>POSTMARKED THE STARS</u> (Ballantine/Del Rey 0-345-32069-7, 01/85 [12/84], $2.50, 192pp, pb) Reprint (Harcourt 1959) sf novel, fourth in the "Solar Queen" series.

Norton, Andre <u>QUEST CROSSTIME</u> (Ace 0-441-69685-6, 03/85 [02/85], $2.50, 250pp, pb) Reissue (Viking 1965) sf novel. 5th printing.

Norton, Andre <u>RED HART MAGIC</u> (Ace 0-441-71098-0, 11/85 [10/85], $2.50, 179pp, pb) Reissue (Crowell 1976) young adult time warp fantasy novel, illustrated by Donna Diamond. 3rd Ace printing.

Norton, Andre <u>SARGASSO OF SPACE</u> (Ace 0-441-74987-9, 09/85 [08/85], $2.50, 248pp, pb) Reissue (Gnome 1955, as by Andrew North) sf novel, Book 1 in the "Solar Queen" series. 7th Ace printing.

Norton, Andre <u>SECRET OF THE LOST RACE</u> (Ace 0-441-75836-3, 05/85 [04/85], $2.50, 179pp, pb) Reissue (Ace 1959) sf novel. 11th printing.

Norton, Andre <u>STAR MAN'S SON</u> (Ballantine/Del Rey 0-345-32588-5, 10/85 [09/85], $2.95, 224pp, pb) Reprint (Harcourt Brace 1952 as STAR MAN'S SON 2250 A.D.) sf novel.

Norton, Andre <u>STAR RANGERS</u> (Ballantine/Del Rey 0-345-32308-4, 08/85 [07/85], $2.50, 223pp, pb) Reprint (Harcourt Brace 1953) sf novel.

Norton, Andre <u>STORM OVER WARLOCK</u> (Ace 0-441-78747-9, 01/85 [12/84], $2.50, 201pp, pb) Reissue (World 1960) sf novel, first in the "Forerunner" series. 7th Ace printing.

Norton, Andre <u>WITCH WORLD</u> (Ace 0-441-89708-8, 01/86 [12/85], $2.75, 282pp, pb) Reissue (Ace 1963) fantasy novel, first in the series. 11th printing.

Norton, Andre <u>YURTH BURDEN</u> (DAW 0-88677-054-8, 06/85 [05/85], $2.95, 206pp, pb) Reissue (DAW 1978) sf novel. 5th printing.

Norton, Andre <u>THE ZERO STONE</u> (Ace 0-441-95966-0, 12/85 [11/85], $2.75, 221pp, pb) Reissue (Viking 1968) sf novel. 6th Ace printing.

*Norton, Andre & Robert Adams, eds. <u>MAGIC IN ITHKAR</u> (Tor 0-812-54740-3, 05/85 [04/85], $6.95, 317pp, pb) Anthology of original fantasy stories, all set in the same fantasy world.
Contents:

				Page
Prologue	Robert Adams		pr	11
The Goblinry of Ais	Lin Carter	ss	MGI # 1,85	21
To Take a Thief	C.J. Cherryh	nv	MGI # 1,85	29
Jezeri and Her Beast Go to the Fair and Find More Excitement Than They Want	Jo Clayton	nv	MGI # 1,85	63
Fletcher Found	Morgan Llywelyn	ss	MGI # 1,85	93
Well Met in Ithkar	Patricia Mathews	nv	MGI # 1,85	113
Esmene's Eyes	Ardath Mayhar	ss	MGI # 1,85	139
Swamp Dweller	Andre Norton	nv	MGI # 1,85	157
Qazia and a Ferret-Fetch	Judith Sampson	ss	MGI # 1,85	189
For Lovers Only	Roger C. Schlobin	nv	MGI # 1,85	205
Dragon's Horn	J.W. Schutz	nv	MGI # 1,85	231
Homecoming	Susan M. Shwartz	nv	MGI # 1,85	259
The Prince Out of the Past	Nancy Springer	ss	MGI # 1,85	285
Cold Spell	Elisabeth Waters	ss	MGI # 1,85	297
Biographical Notes	[Misc. Material]	bg		313

*Norton, Andre & Robert Adams, eds. <u>MAGIC IN ITHKAR 2</u> (Tor 0-812-54745-4, 12/85 [11/85], $6.95, 306pp, pb) Original anthology of 14 fantasy stories all set in mythical Ithkar.
Contents:

				Page
Prologue	Robert Adams		pr	1
Flux of Fortune	Mildred Downey Broxon	nv	MGI # 2,85	10
Geydelle's Protective	Lin Carter	ss	MGI # 2,85	35
If There Be Magic	Marylois Dunn	nv	MGI # 2,85	42
Babes on Bawd Way	George Alec Effinger	nv	MGI # 2,85	71
Sardofa's Horseshoes	Gregory Frost	nv	MGI # 2,85	97
The Ruby Wand of Asrazel	Joseph Green	nv	MGI # 2,85	120
Bird of Paradise	Linda Haldeman	nv	MGI # 2,85	144
Flaming-Arrow	R.A. Lafferty	nv	MGI # 2,85	169
The Shaman Flute	Shariann Lewitt	nv	MGI # 2,85	190
Shadow Quest	Brad Linaweaver	nv	MGI # 2,85	212
Kissmeowt and the Healing Friar	A.R. Major	ss	MGI # 2,85	235
The Cards of Eldrianza	Mary H. Schaub	nv	MGI # 2,85	253
The Marbled Horn	Lynn Ward	nv	MGI # 2,85	280
Biographical Notes	[Misc. Material]	bg		303

Norton, Andre & A.C. Crispin <u>GRYPHON'S EYRIE</u> (Tor 0-812-54736-5, 03/85 [02/85], $2.95, 248pp, pb) Reprint (Tor 1984) fantasy novel, conclusion of the "Gryphon" trilogy. First paperback edition.

Norton, Andre & A.C. Crispin <u>GRYPHON'S EYRIE</u> (SFBC #1594, 08/85 [07/85], $4.98, 220pp, hc) Reprint (Tor 1984) fantasy novel, third in the "Gryphon" series.

Norton, Andre & Phyllis Miller <u>HOUSE OF SHADOWS</u> (Tor 0-812-54743-8, 10/85 [09/85], $2.95, 250pp, pb) Reprint (Atheneum 1984) young-adult fantasy novel of a haunted house.

*Norton, Andre & Phyllis Miller <u>RIDE THE GREEN DRAGON</u> (Atheneum 0-689-50331-8, 09/85 [10/85], $12.95, 231pp, hc) Young adult mystery/adventure novel; it may not have fantasy elements, but is listed for Norton fans.

Norton, Mary <u>THE BORROWERS AVENGED</u> (HBJ/Voyager 0-15-210531-X, 01/85 [12/84], $6.95, 298pp, pb) Reprint (Harcourt 1982) juvenile fantasy novel, fifth in the "Borrowers" series. Illustrated by Beth & Joe Krush.

*Norwood, Warren <u>POLAR FLEET</u> (Bantam Spectra 0-553-24877-4, 06/85 [05/85], $2.95, 234pp, pb) Sf novel, sequel to MIDWAY BETWEEN.

Nourse, Alan E. <u>THE FOURTH HORSEMAN</u> (Pinnacle 0-523-42432-9, 02/85 [01/85], $3.50, 405pp, pb) Reprint (Harper & Row 1983) sf novel of plague in the near future.

O'Neill, Joseph <u>LAND UNDER ENGLAND</u> (Overlook 0-87951-218-0, 09/85 [10/85], $7.95, 296pp, pb) Reprint (Gollancz 1935) sf novel.

*O'Riordan, Robert <u>CADRE ONE</u> (Ace 0-441-09022-2, 01/86 [12/85], $2.95, 263pp, pb) Sf novel of an "intergalactic super-police force," a first novel.

*Okrand, Marc <u>STAR TREK: THE KLINGON DICTIONARY</u> (Pocket 0-671-54349-0, 12/85 [11/85], $3.95, 172pp, pb) Star Trek tie-in. English-Klingon/Klingon-English "lexicon of familiar expressions with a complete grammar handbook and pronunciation key."

Oliver, Chad <u>SHADOWS IN THE SUN</u> (Crown 0-517-55867-X, 10/85 [09/85], $8.95, 207pp, hc) Reprint (Ballantine 1954) sf novel, with a new introduction by George Zebrowski. There is also a new afterword by the author.

*Orr, A. <u>A WORLD IN AMBER</u> (Bluejay 0-312-94459-4, 09/85 [08/85], $14.95, 214pp, hc) Fantasy novel, a first novel.

*Pachter, Josh, ed. <u>TOP FANTASY</u> (Dent 0-460-04659-4, 06/85 [05/85], £9.50, 311pp, hc) "Author's choice" anthology, plus comments by the authors on why each story is their personal favorite. An excellent anthology and well worth the trouble of ordering it from an English dealer. (CNB)
Contents:

				Page
Introduction	Josh Pachter	in		vii
The Man Who Walked On Air	Michael Avallone	ss	WRT Sep,53	1
Report on an Unidentified Space Station	J.G. Ballard	ss	LNDSNVR,82	12
The Ship of Disaster	Barrington J. Bayley	ss	NWS Jun,65	18
Collaborating	Michael Bishop	ss	RMSPRDS,78	33
The Man Who Collected Poe	Robert Bloch	ss	FFM Oct,51	51
The Fog Horn [The Beast from 20,000 Fathoms]	Ray Bradbury	ss	SEP Jun 23,51	65
The Day of the Butterflies	Marion Zimmer Bradley	ss	DAWSFRD,76	73
The Depths	Ramsey Campbell	ss	DRKCMPN,82	84
Touchstone	Terry Carr	ss	FSF May,64	104
Let Us Quickly Hasten to the Gate of Ivory	Thomas M. Disch	ss	QRK # 1,70	117
Trouble with Water	Horace L. Gold	ss	UNK Mar,39	134
Harpist	Joe L. Hensley	ss	SPECLTN,82	154
Blue Vase of Ghosts	Tanith Lee	ss	DRF # 4,83	168
The Wife's Story	Ursula K. Le Guin	ss	CMPSRSE,82	188
The House of Cthulhu	Brian Lumley	ss	WHS V1 #1,73	193
The Real Shape of the Coast	John Lutz	ss	EQM Jun,71	206
The Smallest Dragonboy	Anne McCaffrey	ss	SFTALES,73	217
Caves in Cliffs	Josh Pachter	ss	1984	230
The Broken Hoop	Pamela Sargent	ss	TZM Jun,82	239
Dancers in the Time-Flux	Robert Silverberg	ss	HEROVIS,83	253
Amends, A Tale of the Sun Kings	Nancy Springer	ss	FSF May,83	270
Sing a Last Song of Valdese	Karl Edward Wagner	nv	CHA # 1,76	281
The Father of the Bride	Connie Willis	ss	TZM May,82	293
Kevin Malone	Gene Wolfe	ss	NWT # 1,80	301

*Pachter, Josh, ed. <u>TOP SCIENCE FICTION</u> (Dent 0-460-04647-0, 1984 [02/85], £8.95, 340pp, hc) Anthology of 25 "author's choice" stories with brief forewords by the authors. An excellent selection, and the various forewords are fascinating. (CNB)
Contents:

				Page
Introduction	Josh Pachter	in		vii
All the World's Tears	Brian W. Aldiss	ss	NEB May,57	1
The Last Question	Isaac Asimov	ss	SFQ Nov,56	12
The Men Who Murdered Mohammed	Alfred Bester	ss	FSF Oct,58	25
A Small Kindness	Ben Bova	ss	ASF Apr,83	38
There Will Come Soft Rains	Ray Bradbury	ss	COL May 6,50	52
The Totally Rich	John Brunner	nv	WOT Jun,63	59
Internal Combustion	L. Sprague de Camp	ss	INF Feb,56	83
Hop-Friend	Terry Carr	ss	FSF Nov,62	99
Transit of Earth	Arthur C. Clarke	ss	PBY Jan,71	111
Going Under	Jack Dann	nv	OMN Sep,81	124
Why Johnny Can't Speed	Alan Dean Foster	ss	GAL Sep,71	143
Rescue Operation	Harry Harrison	ss	ASF Dec,64	155
Mazes	Ursula K. Le Guin	ss	EPOCH ,75	169
Endfray of the Ofay	Fritz Leiber	ss	IFS Mar,69	174
A Galaxy Called Rome	Barry N. Malzberg	nv	FSF Jul,75	189

The Ship Who Sang	Anne McCaffrey	ss FSF Apr,61	208
The Green Marauder	Larry Niven	ss DST V2 #1,80	226
A Typical Day	Doris Piserchia	ss GAL Mar,74	231
Day Million	Frederik Pohl	ss ROG Feb,66	242
Capricorn Games	Robert Silverberg	ss FARSIDE,74	248
The Engineer and the Executioner			
	Brian Stableford	nv AMZ May,75	266
Film Library	A.E. van Vogt	ss ASF Jul,46	281
The Cosmic Express	Jack Williamson	ss AMZ Nov,30	301
Daisy, in the Sun	Connie Willis	nv GLL Nov,79	309
In Looking-Glass Castle	Gene Wolfe	ss TRQ #49,80	327

Pachter, Josh, ed. TOP SCIENCE FICTION (Dent 0-460-02425-6, 09/85 [08/85], £2.95, 340pp, pb) Reprint (Dent 1984) anthology.

*Palmer, David R. THRESHOLD (Bantam Spectra 0-553-24878-2, 12/85 [11/85], $2.95, 274pp, pb) Sf adventure novel.

*Palmer, Jane THE PLANET DWELLER (Women's Press 0-7043-3948-X, 06/85 [05/85], £1.95, 147pp, pb) Humorous sf novel, a first novel.

Pangborn, Edgar A MIRROR FOR OBSERVERS (SFBC #2299, 05/85 [04/85], $4.98, 182pp, hc) Reprint (Doubleday 1954) sf novel. One of the classics of science fiction. Highly recommended. (CNB)

*Parker, Helen N. BIOLOGICAL THEMES IN MODERN SCIENCE FICTION (UMI 0-8357-1577-9, 1984 [05/85], $24.95 + postage, 109pp, hc) Non-fiction, literary criticism. This revision of a doctoral thesis appeared in 1984, but we did not see it until 1985.

*Parnell, Frank H. & Mike Ashley MONTHLY TERRORS: AN INDEX TO THE WEIRD FANTASY MAGAZINES PUBLISHED IN THE UNITED STATES AND GREAT BRITAIN (Greenwood 0-313-23989-4, 05/85 [04/85], $65.00, xvii + 602pp, hc) Non-fiction, reference book which covers semi-pro magazines as well as professional magazines never before indexed. It also goes up to 1983. Important for major libraries and those with major magazine collections, despite the price. (CNB)

Parrinder, Patrick, ed. H.G. WELLS: THE CRITICAL HERITAGE (Routledge & Kegan Paul 0-7102-0515-5, 09/85 [09/85], $15.00, 351pp, pb) Reprint (Routledge & Kegan Paul 1972) non-fiction book, selection of reviews contemporaneous with Wells' works, plus some retrospective and obituary notices.

Parry, Michel, ed. SANTA 2000 (Granada/Dragon 0-583-30750-7, 1985 [10/85], £1.50, 86pp, pb) Reprint (Granada 1984) young-adult anthology of 6 sf stories about Santa Claus.
Contents:

			Page
Introduction	Michel Parry	in	1
Santa Rides a Saucer	Donald A. Wollheim	ss 2DZDRGN,69	3
Christmas Treason	James White	nv FSF Jan,62	8
Sanity Clause	Edward Wellen	ss FSF Jan,75	33
The Santa Claus Planet	Frank M. Robinson	nv BSFS:51,51	38
Christmas on Ganymede	Isaac Asimov	ss STS Jan,42	64
The Santa Claus Compromise			
	Thomas M. Disch	ss CRW Dec,74	82

*Parvin, Brian THE SINGING TREE (Hale 0-7090-2159-3, 1985 [10/85], £8.95, 185pp, hc) Post-holocaust animal fable of a fox's quest, with numerous b&w illustrations by an uncredited artist.

+Pattrick, William, ed. MYSTERIOUS SEA STORIES (Salem House 0-88162-046-7, 07/85 [06/85], $14.95, 247pp, hc) Anthology of 14 sea fantasies. There is a simultaneous British edition from W.H. Allen.
Contents:

			Page
Introduction	William Pattrick	in	1
MS. Found in a Bottle	Edgar Allan Poe	ss BSV Oct 12,1833	5
The Legend of the Bell Rock			
	Captain Frederick Marryat	ss	19
Hoods Isle and the Hermit Oberlus			
	Herman Melville	ss	31
A Bewitched Ship	W. Clark Russell	ss	43
J. Habakuk Jephson's Statement			
	Arthur Conan Doyle	nv CNH Jan,1884	57
The Benevolent Ghost and Captain Lowrie			
	Richard Sale	nv 1940	91
Make Westing	Jack London	ss	113
The Black Mate	Joseph Conrad	nv TLSHRSY,25	123
A Matter of Fact	Rudyard Kipling	ss 1935	153
The Findings of the Graiken			
	William Hope Hodgson	nv	169
Davy Jones' Gift	John Masefield	ss 1907	193
In the Abyss	H.G. Wells	ss PRS Aug,1896	199
Undersea Guardians	Ray Bradbury	ss AMZ Dec,44	217
The Turn of the Tide	C.S. Forester	ss 1934	235

*Pearce, Howard D. & Robert A. Collins, eds. THE SCOPE OF THE FANTASTIC: CULTURE, BIOGRAPHY, THEMES, CHILDREN'S LITERATURE Main listing under Robert A. Collins.

*Pearce, Howard D. & Robert A. Collins, eds. THE SCOPE OF THE FANTASTIC: THEORY, TECHNIQUE, MAJOR AUTHORS Main listing under Robert A. Collins.

*Pelham, David & Heather Couper UNIVERSE Main listing under Heather Couper.

*Perret, Patti THE FACES OF SCIENCE FICTION (Bluejay 0-312-94147-1, 1984 [12/84], $11.95, 163pp, pb) Non-fiction, associational. Book of photographs of sf and fantasy authors, including Asimov, Bradley, Disch, Pohl, and Simak. Includes a brief "statement" by each of the subjects. This is a fine book, marvelous to take to a convention for autographs. (FCM)

Perret, Patti THE FACES OF SCIENCE FICTION (Bluejay 0-312-94148-X, 03/85 [02/85], $35.00, unpaginated, hc) Reprint (Bluejay 1984) non-fiction, collection of photos of sf authors. This is the hardcover library edition.

*Perry, Steve THE MAN WHO NEVER MISSED (Ace 0-441-51916-4, 08/85 [07/85], $2.95, 195pp, pb) Sf novel, a one-man guerrilla army against an oppressive empire. Above-average martial-arts sf. (PJH)

*Phillips, Ann THE OAK KING & THE ASH QUEEN (Oxford Univ. Press 0-19-271495-3, 1984 [05/85], £6.95; U.S. import $12.95. 171pp, hc) This young-adult fantasy novel appeared in England in 1984, but we didn't see it until 1985. The U.S. distributor is Merrimack Publishers Circle.

Pierce, Meredith Ann A GATHERING OF GARGOYLES (Tor 0-812-54902-3, 07/85 [06/85], $2.95, 263pp, pb) Reprint (Atlantic Monthly 1984) fantasy novel, second in the "Darkangel" trilogy. Recommended. (FCM)

*Pierce, Meredith Ann THE WOMAN WHO LOVED REINDEER (Atlantic Monthly 0-87113-042-4, 10/85 [10/85], $13.95, 242pp, hc) Young-adult fantasy novel set in a Lapp-like world with were-reindeer.

Pinkwater, Daniel M. THE SNARKOUT BOYS & THE BACONBURG HORROR (NAL/Signet Vista 0-451-13581-4, 06/85 [05/85], $2.50, 175pp, pb) Reprint (Lothrop, Lee & Shepard 1984) humorous young-adult fantasy novel.

*Pinkwater, Daniel M. YOUNG ADULTS (Tor 0-812-58710-3, 11/85 [10/85], $5.95, 224pp, pb) Collection of two short novels, YOUNG ADULT NOVEL (1982) and its previously unpublished sequel DEAD END DADA, plus a chapter of a third novel in progress, and an assortment of Pinkwater "things." Lunatic fun. Recommended for people who are already unstable. (DLN)
Contents:

			Page
Young Adult Novel	Daniel M. Pinkwater	na 1982	9
W.A. Mozart, Superhero I	Daniel M. Pinkwater	cs YNGADLT,85	59
Dead End Dada	Daniel M. Pinkwater	nv YNGADLT,85	77
The Buttonaid (Buttons Through the Ages)			
	Daniel M. Pinkwater	cs YNGADLT,85	115
W.A. Mozart, Superhero II			
	Daniel M. Pinkwater	cs YNGADLT,85	125
The Dada Boys in Collitch (The First Chapter)			
	Daniel M. Pinkwater	ex YNGADLT,85	143
Pigamorphosis	Daniel M. Pinkwater	cs YNGADLT,85	169
Confessions of Pinkwater by Ken Kelman			
	Daniel M. Pinkwater	ss YNGADLT,85	205

Pohl, Frederik BEYOND THE BLUE EVENT HORIZON (Ballantine/Del Rey 0-345-32067-0, 04/85 [03/85], $2.95, 309pp, pb) Reissue (Del Rey 1980) sf novel. Book Two of the "Heechee Saga". 5th printing.

*Pohl, Frederik BLACK STAR RISING (Ballantine/Del Rey 0-345-31903-6, 05/85 [04/85], $15.95, 282pp, hc) Sf novel.

Pohl, Frederik BLACK STAR RISING (SFBC #01730, 11/85 [12/85], $4.98, 214pp, hc) Reprint (Ballantine/Del Rey 1985) sf novel of aliens visiting a politically messy Earth.

Pohl, Frederik HEECHEE RENDEZVOUS (SFBC #3827, 01/85 [12/84], $3.98, 274pp, hc) Reprint (Ballantine/Del Rey 1984) sf novel, third in the "Heechee" trilogy.

Pohl, Frederik HEECHEE RENDEZVOUS (Ballantine/Del Rey 0-345-30055-6, 04/85 [03/85], $3.50, 331pp, pb) Reprint (Ballantine/Del Rey 1984) sf novel, third in the "Heechee" series. First paperback edition.

Pohl, Frederik JEM (Bantam 0-553-25144-9, 04/85 [03/85], $2.95, 312pp, pb) Reissue (St. Martin's 1979) sf novel, 5th printing. A fine, down-beat tale of the end of humanity. A Hugo and Nebula nominee and a winner of the American Book Award. Recommended. (CNB)

Pohl, Frederik MAN PLUS (Bantam 0-553-24809-X, 04/85 [03/85], $2.95, 246pp, pb) Reissue (Random House 1976) sf novel. 6th printing. A Nebula Award winner and one of Pohl's best. Highly recommended. (CNB)

Pohl, Frederik THE MERCHANTS' WAR (Gollancz 0-575-03691-5, 08/85 [07/85], £8.95, 209pp, hc) Reprint (St. Martin's 1984) sf novel. First British edition. Sequel to THE SPACE MERCHANTS.

Pohl, Frederik THE YEARS OF THE CITY (Pocket 0-671-46047-1, 08/85 [07/85], $3.95, 375pp, pb) Reprint (Timescape 1984) novel or sf collection of linked novelettes, depending on who you talk to. Recommended. (CNB)

*Pohl, Frederik & C.M. Kornbluth SEARCH THE SKY (Baen 0-671-55989-3, 10/85 [09/85], $2.95, 245pp, pb) Sf novel, "substantially" rewritten from the 1954 Ballantine version.

Pohl, Frederik & C.M. Kornbluth THE SPACE MERCHANTS (St. Martin's 0-312-74952-X, 09/85 [08/85], $5.95, 169pp, pb) Reprint (Ballantine 1953) sf novel. One of the famous sf satirical novels of the '50s. There is a recent sequel. Ignore the various copyright notices inside. The text is unchanged. (CNB)

*Pohl, Frederik & C.M. Kornbluth VENUS, INC. (SFBC #1272, 06/85 [07/85], $4.98, 346pp, hc) Omnibus edition of THE SPACE MERCHANTS and Pohl's sequel.
Contents:

		Page
THE SPACE MERCHANTS	Frederik Pohl & C.M. Kornbluth	
	n. BAL 1953	1
THE MERCHANT'S WAR	Frederik Pohl	
	n. SMP 1984	159

*Polikarpus, Viido & Tappan King DOWNTOWN Main listing under Tappan King.

Pope, Elizabeth Marie THE SHERWOOD RING (Ace/Tempo 0-441-76111-9, 04/85 [03/85], $2.25, 180pp, pb) Reprint (Houghton Mifflin 1958) young-adult fantasy novel. Recommended. (DLN)

*Potter, J.K. THE ART OF SKELETON CREW (Scream/Press no ISBN, 11/85 [11/85], $15.00, unpaginated, pb) Art book. Limited edition of 500 signed copies of a portfolio featuring most of Potter's illustrations for the book by Stephen King. Potter is the best horror artist working today. Recommended. (CNB)

Pournelle, Jerry E. RED DRAGON (Ace/Charter 0-441-71092-1, 12/85 [11/85], $2.95, 201pp, pb) Reprint (Berkley Medallion 1971, as by Wade Curtis) non sf/fantasy; associational. Spy thriller, a sequel to RED HEROIN.

Pournelle, Jerry E. RED HEROIN (Charter 0-441-71089-1, 11/85 [10/85], $2.95, 156pp, pb) Reprint (Berkley Medallion 1969 as by "Wade Curtis") novel, non-sf/fantasy; associational. First of a series of three espionage adventure novels. Listed for Pournelle fans. There is a Heinlein quote on the cover.

Pournelle, Jerry E., ed. THE ENDLESS FRONTIER (Ace 0-441-02669-7, 06/85 [05/85], $3.50, 376pp, pb) Reissue (Ace 1979) anthology of stories and non-fiction. 3rd Ace printing.

*Pournelle, Jerry E., ed. THERE WILL BE WAR, VOL. IV: DAY OF THE TYRANT (Tor 0-812-54957-0, 05/85 [04/85], $2.95, 370pp, pb) Anthology of 21 stories and articles about war, with five of the stories and most of the non-fiction appearing for the first time.
Contents:

			Page
Introduction: Sic Semper Tyrannis			
	Jerry E. Pournelle	in	ix
MacDonough's Song [from As Easy as A.B.C.]			
	Rudyard Kipling	pm LOM Apr,12	1
The Cloak and the Staff	Gordon R. Dickson	nv ASF Aug,80	4
Winter Snow	Eric Vinicoff & Marcia Martin		
		ss ASF Nov,84	41
A Way Out Maybe...or a Dead End for Sure			
	John Brunner	ar WAR V 4,85	55
Editor's Afterword to: John Brunner's "A Way Out Maybe."			
	Jerry E. Pournelle	aw WAR V 4,85	69
A Letter from the Soviet Union			
	Alexander Shatravka	ar 1984	76
Emergency Rations	Theodore R. Cogswell	ss IMG Sep,53	81
The Proud Foot of the Conqueror			
	Reginald Bretnor	ss WAR V 4,85	88
Lepanto	Gilbert Keith Chesterton	pm	112
A Cure for Croup	Edward P. Hughes	nv FFR V 2,85	120
Comment and Discussion on "Elevation of the U.S. Fleet" by Captain Richard B. Laning, USN (Ret.)			
	Kenneth Roy, P.E.	ar WAR V 4,85	143
Battle at Kahlkhopolis	Robert Adams	nv WAR V 4,85	148
The Conqueror of Vectis	Keith Taylor	nv WAR V 4,85	169
Pretty Baby [Operation Kill-Quota]			
	Ray Peekner	ss SWK 1978	195
The Man in the Gray Weapons Suit			
	Paul J. Nahin	ss FWR V 1,79	207
Reagan vs. the Scientists			
	Robert Jastrow	ar CMM Jan,84	220
Joined the Space Force to Wear My Blues			
	John Maddox Roberts	ss WAR V 4,85	247
Psyops	Stefan T. Possony	sp DFNS83C,83	254
Three Soldiers	D.C. Poyer	nv GLL May,78	265
Interim Justice	William F. Wu	ss WAR V 4,85	288
No Truce With Kings	Poul Anderson	na FSF Jun,63	302

*Pournelle, Jerry E. & Jim Baen, eds. FAR FRONTIERS (Baen 0-671-55935-4, 01/85 [12/84], $2.95, 315pp, pb) Original anthology or first issue of a pocket-size magazine; take your pick. Since it has no date or frequency on it, we'll consider it an anthology. Recommended. (CNB)
Contents:

			Page
Editors Introduction to: A Step Further Out			
	Jerry E. Pournelle	in FFR V 1,85	7
A Step Further Out: "The Association for the Abolition of Science"			
	Jerry E. Pournelle	ar FFR V 1,85	11
The Warm Space	David Brin	ss FFR V 1,85	25
The Jefferson Orbit	Ben Bova	ar FFR V 1,85	52
The Boys from the Moon	Rivka Jacobs	nv FFR V 1,85	69
Brain Salad	Norman Spinrad	ss FFR V 1,85	123
Goodbye, Dr. Ralston	Damon Knight	ss FFR V 1,85	141
Future Scenarios for Space Development			
	G. Harry Stine	ar FFR V 1,85	150
Lost in Translation	Dean Ing	ss FFR V 1,85	176
Through Road No Whither	Greg Bear	ss FFR V 1,85	210

			Page
The Paradox of Interstellar Transport			
	Robert L. Forward	ar FFR V 1,85	222
Pride	Poul Anderson	nv FFR V 1,85	242
Table Manners	Larry Niven	ss FFR V 1,85	280
The Leading Edge	Richard E. Geis	br FFR	305

*Pournelle, Jerry E. & Jim Baen, eds. FAR FRONTIERS VOL. II/SUMMER 1985 (Baen 0-671-55954-0, 04/85 [03/85], $2.95, 319pp, pb) Original anthology/magazine.
Contents:

			Page
A Step Further Out: "A Few Good Books..."			
	Jerry E. Pournelle	ar FFR V 2,85	5
Nuclear Autumn	Ben Bova	ss FFR V 2,85	23
Talion	John Brunner	na FFR V 2,85	31
Petrogypsies	Rory Harper	nv FFR V 2,85	91
IRAS, Vega, and Intelligent Life in the Universe			
	Dr. Robert W. Bussard	ar FFR V 2,85	118
A Cure for Croup	Edward P. Hughes	nv FFR V 2,85	131
Evileye	Dean Ing	ss FFR V 2,85	160
The Software Plague	John Park	nv FFR V 2,85	177
Cheap Shots	G. Harry Stine	ar FFR V 2,85	205
Avenging Angel	Eric L. Davin	ss FFR V 2,85	222
House of Weapons	Gordon R. Dickson	na FFR V 2,85	239
The Leading Edge	Richard E. Geis	br FFR	309

*Pournelle, Jerry E. & Jim Baen, eds. FAR FRONTIERS VOL. III/FALL 1985 (Baen 0-671-55975-3, 08/85 [07/85], $2.95, 319pp, pb) Original anthology/magazine.
Contents:

			Page
Preface	Jerry E. Pournelle	pr	6
The Ungoverned	Vernor Vinge	nv FFR V 3,85	10
The Ultimate Whodunit	Charles R. Pellegrino	ar FFR V 3,85	70
Morning on Venus	Rivka Jacobs	nv FFR V 3,85	86
Right-Angle Realities	Dr. John Gribbin	ar FFR V 3,85	152
A Wink in the Eye of the Wolf			
	Alexander Jablokov	nv FFR V 3,85	164
The Bond	David A. Drake	ss FFR V 3,85	205
Space Talking	Charles Sheffield	ar FFR V 3,85	213
A Step Further Out	Jerry E. Pournelle	ar FFR V 3,85	236
Space Shuttle Crashes!	Thomas Wylde	ss FFR V 3,85	259
The Leading Edge	Roland J. Green	br FFR	267
Out of the North a Giant	John Dalmas	nv FFR V 3,85	280

*Pournelle, Jerry E. & Jim Baen, eds. FAR FRONTIERS VOL. IV/WINTER 1985 (Baen 0-671-65548-5, 01/86 [12/85], $2.95, 278pp, pb) Original anthology or paperback magazine, with stories, articles, and reviews. There is also an excerpt from HEROES IN HELL which appears to be the first publication of a C.J. Cherryh story.
Contents:

			Page
Dydeetown Girl	F. Paul Wilson	na FFR V 4,86	7
Opening Move on Egil's World			
	John Dalmas	nv FFR V 4,86	70
The Leading Edge	Roland J. Green	br FFR	111
Shark Destiny	Terry Rich Hartley	ss FFR V 4,86	122
Golden Dawn	Ronald Anthony Cross	nv FFR V 4,86	137
Cops and Robbers	S.M. Stirling	ss FFR V 4,86	180
Star Wars is Not MAD	James Benford	ar FFR V 4,86	192
Reactionary Utopias	Gregory Benford	ar FFR V 4,86	214
The Prince	C.J. Cherryh	nv FFR V 4,86	230

*Pournelle, Jerry E., Jim Baen & John F. Carr, eds. THE SCIENCE FICTION YEARBOOK (Baen 0-671-55983-4, 09/85 [09/85], $15.95, 344pp, hc) Anthology of selected stories from 1984, plus non-fiction essays. A new entry in the "Best of the Year" sweepstakes.
Contents:

			Page
Preface	Jerry E. Pournelle	pr	1
1984, Nineteen Eighty-Four, and Other SF Novels, Signs, and Portents	Algis Budrys	ar 1985	4
New Rose Hotel	William Gibson	ss OMN Jul,84	21
Me and My Shadow	Michael Resnick	ss UNAUTHA,84	35
Hard Science in the Real World			
	Gregory Benford	ar 1984	52
Me/Days	Gregory Benford	ss UNI #14,84	73
Silicon Muse	Hilbert Schenck	nv ASF Sep,84	85
The Dominus Demonstration			
	Charles Sheffield	nv ASF Apr,84	109
The Crystal Spheres	David Brin	nv ASF Jan,84	134
The Strange Journey: 1984			
	James Gunn	ar 1985	156
A Day in the Life of a Classics Professor			
	Stan Dryer	nv FSF Dec,84	166
The Picture Man	John Dalmas	nv FSF Aug,84	188
The Weigher	Eric Vinicoff & Marcia Martin		
		na ASF Oct,84	210
Demon Lover	M. Sargent Mackay	nv FSF Jun,84	261
Tourist Trade	Robert Silverberg	nv PBY Dec,84	302
1984: The Fifty-Candle Blowout			
	Michael Glyer	ar 1985	328

Pournelle, Jerry E. & John F. Carr, eds. THE ENDLESS FRONTIER, VOL. II (Ace 0-441-20671-9, 09/85 [08/85], $3.50, 429pp, pb) Reissue (Ace 1982) anthology of stories and articles about space. 2nd printing.

*Pournelle, Jerry E. & Larry Niven FOOTFALL Main listing under Larry Niven.

Pournelle, Jerry E. & Larry Niven INFERNO Main listing under Larry Niven.

Powers, Tim THE ANUBIS GATES (Ace 0-441-02382-7, 01/85 [12/84], $3.50, 387pp, pb) Reissue (Ace 1983), 4th Ace printing of this fantasy novel, winner of the Philip K. Dick Memorial Award. Highly recommended. (FCM)

Powers, Tim THE ANUBIS GATES (Chatto & Windus 0-7011-2929-8, 04/85 [03/85], £9.95, 387pp, hc; also available in pb; 0-7011-2930-1) Reprint (Ace 1983) fantasy novel, winner of the Philip K. Dick Memorial Award. First British edition, and first hardcover.

*Powers, Tim DINNER AT DEVIANT'S PALACE (Ace 0-441-14879-4, 1984 [12/84], $2.95, 294pp, pb) Sf novel.

Powers, Tim DINNER AT DEVIANT'S PALACE (SFBC #02540, 09/85 [08/85], $4.98, 219pp, hc) Reprint (Ace 1984) sf novel, first hardcover edition. Recommended. (CNB)

*Powys, John Cowper THREE FANTASIES (Carcanet 0-85635-544-5, 08/85 [07/85], $14.95, 186pp, hc) Collection of 3 novellas with an afterword by Glen Cavaliero. It's described as "space fantasy" and surreal. This is an import of a British book.
Contents: Page
Topsy Turvey   John Cowper Powys   na 1959
Abertacle   John Cowper Powys   na 1960
Cataclysm   John Cowper Powys   na 1960
Afterword   Glen Cavaliero   aw

Pratchett, Terry THE COLOUR OF MAGIC (Corgi 0-552-12475-3, 03/85 [02/85], £1.75, 238pp, pb) Reprint (Colin Smythe 1983) satiric fantasy novel. Pratchett zeroes in on everything from heroic duos to dragonriders, and the result is very funny. Recommended. (FCM)

Pratchett, Terry THE COLOUR OF MAGIC (NAL/Signet 0-451-13577-6, 05/85 [04/85], $2.95, 253pp, pb) Reprint (Colin Smythe 1983) fantasy novel.

Pratt, Fletcher & L. Sprague de Camp THE LAND OF UNREASON Main listing under L. Sprague de Camp.

*Preiss, Byron, ed. THE PLANETS (Bantam 0-553-05109-1, 12/85 [10/85], $24.95, 336pp, hc) Original anthology of non-fiction and fiction. A guide to the solar system, featuring original stories by well-known sf writers plus essays by scientists and work by sf/astronomy artists.
Contents: Page
Diversity   Byron Preiss   in   7
The Solar System: An Introduction
                          Andrew Fraknoi   in   11
Illustration   Isaac Kerlow   il PLANETS,85 13
Writing of Two Sorts   Isaac Asimov   ar PLANETS,85 18
Illustration   Moebius   il PLANETS,85 19
Space Flight: Imagination and Reality
                          Arthur C. Clarke   ar PLANETS,85 22
Illustration   Robert McCall   il PLANETS,85 25
Illustration   Robert McCall   il PLANETS,85 29
Earth: The Water Planet   Ursula B. Marvin   ar PLANETS,85 36
After the Storm   Harry Harrison   ss PLANETS,85 49
Illustration   Bill Sanderson   il PLANETS,85 53
Earth's Moon: Doorway to the Solar System
                          G. Jeffrey Taylor   ar PLANETS,85 64
Illustration   Alan Bean   il PLANETS,85 67
Illustration   Alan Bean   il PLANETS,85 73
Handprints on the Moon   William K. Hartmann   ss PLANETS,85 77
Illustration   Lebbeus Woods   il PLANETS,85 79
Mars: The Red Planet   Michael H. Carr   ar PLANETS,85 92
The Love Affair   Ray Bradbury   ss PLANETS,85 104
Illustration   Wayne Barlowe   il PLANETS,85 109
Jupiter's World: A Colossal Realm
                          Joseph Veverka   ar PLANETS,85 114
The Future of the Jovian System
                          Gregory Benford   ss PLANETS,85 129
Illustration   James Gurney   il PLANETS,85 135
Saturn: A Ringed World   David Morrison   ar PLANETS,85 144
Dreadsong   Roger Zelazny   ss PLANETS,85 155
Illustration   John Harris   il PLANETS,85 159
Uranus: Distant Giant   Dale P. Cruikshank   ar PLANETS,85 166
Uranus or UFO Versus IRS Philip José Farmer   ss PLANETS,85 174
Illustration   Richard Courtney   il PLANETS,85 177
Dies Irae   Charles Sheffield   ss PLANETS,85 187
Illustration   Pat Ortega   il PLANETS,85 195
Neptune: Farthest Giant   Dale P. Cruikshank   ar PLANETS,85 204
At the Human Limit   Jack Williamson   ss PLANETS,85 212
Illustration   Ralph McQuarrie   il PLANETS,85 213
Illustration   Ralph McQuarrie   il PLANETS,85 223
Pluto: Outermost   Robert Silverberg   ar PLANETS,85 228
Sunrise on Pluto   Robert Silverberg   ss PLANETS,85 236
Illustration   Joel Hagan   il PLANETS,85 241
Mercury: The Sun's Closest Companion
                          Clark R. Chapman   ar PLANETS,85 248
Transcript: Mercury Program
                          Frank Herbert   ss PLANETS,85 259
Illustration   Kikuo Hayashi   il PLANETS,85 261
Venus: The Veiled Planet Lawrence Colin   ar PLANETS,85 274
Big Dome   Marta Randall   ss PLANETS,85 286
Illustration   Bob Eggleton   il PLANETS,85 287
The Billion Other Planets: Asteroids and Comets
                          William K. Hartmann   ar PLANETS,85 304
Halley's Comet   William K. Hartmann   ar PLANETS,85 316
Small Bodies   Paul Preuss   ss PLANETS,85 318
Illustration   Roger Ressmeyer   il PLANETS,85 319
The Contributors   [Misc. Material]   bg   332

Selected Reading   Andrew Fraknoi   bi 335

*Prescot, Dray OMENS OF KREGEN (DAW 0-88677-090-4, 12/85 [11/85], $2.95, 222pp, pb) Fantasy novel, "Dray Prescot" #36.

*Prescot, Dray STORM OVER VALHALLA (DAW 0-88677-069-6, 08/85 [07/85], $2.95, 254pp, pb) Fantasy novel, "Dray Prescot" #35.

*Prescot, Dray WEREWOLVES OF KREGEN (DAW 0-87997-991-7, 01/85 [12/84], $2.50, 220pp, pb) Fantasy novel. "Dray Prescot" #33. The author is Ken Bulmer on all the Prescot series.

*Prescot, Dray WITCHES OF KREGEN (DAW 0-88677-032-7, 04/85 [03/85], $2.75, 223pp, pb) Fantasy novel, "Dray Prescot" #34.

*Preuss, Paul HUMAN ERROR (Tor 0-312-93332-0, 10/85 [10/85], $14.95, 351pp, hc) Sf novel about organic computers infecting the world and changing the human race. Recommended. (CNB)

*Price, E. Hoffmann OPERATION EXILE (Ballantine/Del Rey 0-345-32599-0, 01/86 [12/85], $2.95, 281pp, pb) Sf novel, third in a series.

+Priest, Christopher THE GLAMOUR (Doubleday 0-385-19761-6, 05/85 [04/85], $15.95, 302pp, hc) Reprint (Jonathan Cape 1984), first U.S. edition. Fantasy novel of ambiguous relationships and invisibility. It's mysterious and suspenseful as a thriller, though it's also a story of modern love. Recommended! (FCM) This is slightly different from the British edition.

Priest, Christopher THE GLAMOUR (SFBC #1011, 09/85 [10/85], $5.98, 246pp, hc) Reprint (Doubleday 1985) sf novel. The British edition (Jonathan Cape 1984) is somewhat different.

*Pringle, David SCIENCE FICTION: THE 100 BEST NOVELS (Xanadu 0-947761-11-X, 10/85 [10/85], £9.95, 224pp, hc) Non-fiction, critical study with essays on Pringle's choice of novels, from 1984 to NEUROMANCER. Foreword by Michael Moorcock.

*Pringle, David SCIENCE FICTION: THE 100 BEST NOVELS (Xanadu 0-947761-10-1, 10/85 [10/85], £3.95, 224pp, pb) Paperback edition of the above.

*Pringle, David, John Clute & Colin Greenland, eds. INTERZONE: THE 1ST ANTHOLOGY Main listing under John Clute.

*Proctor, George W. V: THE CHICAGO CONVERSION (Pinnacle 0-523-42429-9, 01/85 [12/84], $2.95, 184pp, pb) Sf novel associated with the tv series.

*Proctor, George W. V: THE TEXAS RUN (Pinnacle 0-523-42470-1, 09/85 [08/85], $2.95, 183pp, pb) Media tie-in sf novel in a series of novelizations by various authors.

*Proctor, George W. & Robert E. Vardeman BLOOD FOUNTAIN Main listing under Robert E. Vardeman.

*Proctor, George W. & Robert E. Vardeman TO DEMONS BOUND Main listing under Robert E. Vardeman.

*Proctor, George W. & Robert E. Vardeman A YOKE OF MAGIC Main listing under Robert E. Vardeman.

*Ptacek, Kathryn BLOOD AUTUMN (Tor 0-812-52447-0, 01/85 [12/84], $3.50, 349pp, pb) Horror/dark fantasy novel.

*Purtill, Richard L. J.R.R. TOLKIEN: MYTH, MORALITY, AND RELIGION (Harper & Row 0-06-066712-5, 03/85 [02/85], $12.95, 154pp, hc) Non-fiction, a study of myth and religion in Tolkien's fantasies. The author is both a professor of philosophy and a fantasy writer.

Pyle, Howard THE STORY OF SIR LANCELOT AND HIS COMPANIONS (Scribner's 0-684-18313-7, 05/85 [04/85], $14.95, 340pp, hc) Reissue (Scribners 1907), the third of the four-part Arthurian saga written and illustrated by Pyle -- poorly reproduced, with the color plates omitted. There's also no copyright date, past or present. (CNB)

*Rabkin, Eric S. & George E. Slusser, eds. SHADOWS OF THE MAGIC LAMP: FANTASY AND SCIENCE FICTION IN FILM Main listing under George E. Slusser.

Ramsay, Jay NIGHT OF THE CLAW (Tor 0-812-52500-0, 04/85 [03/85], $3.95, 367pp, pb) Reprint (St. Martin's 1983) fantasy horror novel by Ramsey Campbell.

Randall, Marta THE SWORD OF WINTER (Pocket 0-671-55456-6, 04/85 [03/85], $3.50, 271pp, pb) Reprint (Timescape 1983) fantasy novel.

*Rau, G. Randal, ed. WORLD TALES (1985 World Fantasy Convention no ISBN, 11/85 [11/85], $15.00 [free to convention members], 88pp, pb) Original anthology of stories and articles published as the souvenir book for the Tucson World Fantasy Convention, in the format of the old Weird Tales. It's a beautiful job down to the pre-yellowed paper. There is original fiction by Donaldson, Walton, and Yarbro plus bibliography, biography, poetry, art, etc.
Contents: Page
Stephen R. Donaldson: Six Appreciations
                          Stephanie Donaldson   in WRLDTLS,85   3

Stephen R. Donaldson: An Appreciation			
	Suzy McKee Charnas	bg WRLDTLS,85	4
Stephen R. Donaldson: An Appreciation			
	Robert E. Vardeman	bg WRLDTLS,85	5
Stephen R. Donaldson: An Appreciation			
	Nancy Kress	bg WRLDTLS,85	5
Stephen R. Donaldson: An Appreciation			
	David Cherry	bg WRLDTLS,85	6
Stephen R. Donaldson: An Appreciation			
	Muff Musgrave & Real Musgrave		
		bg WRLDTLS,85	6
Stephen R. Donaldson: An Appreciation			
	Fred Saberhagen	bg WRLDTLS,85	6
The Resume of Stephen R. Donaldson			
	Stephen R. Donaldson	bg WRLDTLS,85	11
The Djinn Who Watches Over the Accursed			
	Stephen R. Donaldson	ss WRLDTLS,85	12
Chelsea Quinn Yarbro: Truth and Fiction			
	Whitley Streiber	bg WRLDTLS,85	31
Chelsea Quinn Yarbro Bibliography			
	Chelsea Quinn Yarbro	bi WRLDTLS,85	35
Such Nice Neighbors	Chelsea Quinn Yarbro	ss WRLDTLS,85	39
Terror at London Bridge	William F. Nolan	ar WRLDTLS,85	57
City of the Titans [written 1915]			
	Clark Ashton Smith	pm SELPMCS,71	62
Victoria Poyser: An Appreciation			
	Michael Whelan	bg WRLDTLS,85	65
The Works of Victoria Poyser			
	Victoria Poyser	bi WRLDTLS,85	67
Evangeline Walton Ensley: An Appreciation			
	Kenneth Zahorski	bg WRLDTLS,85	71
The Books of Evangeline Walton			
	Evangeline Walton	bi WRLDTLS,85	72
The Forest That Would Not Be Cut Down			
	Evangeline Walton	ss WRLDTLS,85	75
The Crow's Nest	Donald D. Markstein	ms WRLDTLS,85	81
Production Notes	Donald D. Markstein	ms WRLDTLS,85	88

Reaves, Michael THE SHATTERED WORLD (SFBC #2418, 02/85 [01/85], $7.98, 307pp, hc) Reprint (Timescape 1984) fantasy novel.

Reaves, Michael THE SHATTERED WORLD (Baen 0-671-55951-6, 03/85 [02/85], $3.50, 413pp, pb) Reprint (Timescape 1984) fantasy novel.

*****Reed, Kit** FORT PRIVILEGE (Doubleday 0-385-19405-6, 04/85 [03/85], $11.95, 186pp, hc) Sf novel. No new ideas, but a well-executed novel of urban deterioration. (DLN)

*****Reeder, Dan** THE SIMPLE SCREAMER (Falcon 0-87905-163-9, 02/85 [01/85], $14.95, 80pp, pb) A step-by-step guide to the art of making papier mâché and cloth monsters, with both black and white and color illustrations featuring Reeder's delightful and humorous beasties. Whether you plan to make your own or just admire his work, this is a pleasure to have. (FCM)

*****Reginald, R. & Douglas Menville** FUTURE VISIONS: THE GOLDEN AGE OF THE SCIENCE FICTION FILM Main listing under Douglas Menville.

*****Reilly, Robert, ed.** THE TRANSCENDENT ADVENTURE: STUDIES OF RELIGION IN SCIENCE FICTION/FANTASY (Greenwood 0-313-23062-5, 03/85 [02/85], $35.00, x + 266pp, hc) Non-fiction, 17 scholarly essays by critics.

Reinius, Trish THE PLANET OF TEARS (Iris 0-932987-00-1, 09/85 [08/85], $8.00, 157pp, pb) Reprint (Dawne-Leigh 1979) fantasy novel. Distributed by Strawberry Hill Press.

*****Reinius, Trish** POWER OF THE WHITE WOLF (Iris 0-932987-01-X, 09/85 [08/85], $8.00, 160pp, pb) Fantasy novel, sequel to THE PLANET OF TEARS. Order from Strawberry Hill Press.

*****Resnick, Mike** ADVENTURES (NAL/Signet 0-451-13867-8, 85/10 [09/85], $2.95, 239pp, pb) Humorous quasi-fantasy novel featuring adventurer Dr. Lucifer Jones.

Resnick, Mike EROS AT ZENITH (NAL/Signet 0-451-13667-5, 07/85 [06/85], $2.95, 255pp, pb) Reprint (Phantasia 1984) sf novel, "Tales of the Velvet Comet" #2. Murder mystery set in a pleasure dome in space.

*****Resnick, Mike** TALES OF THE VELVET COMET #3: EROS DESCENDING (NAL/Signet 0-451-14017-6, 12/85 [11/85], $2.95, 250pp, pb) Sf novel, third in a series about an interstellar whorehouse. The earlier 2 volumes had hardcover editions, but this one is an original.

*****Reynolds, Alfred** KITEMAN OF KARANGA (Knopf 0-394-86347-X, 10/85 [10/85], $11.95, 217pp, hc) Young-adult sf novel of a young flyer vs. an evil empire. A first novel. Also available in a library binding (-96347-4, $11.99).

*****Reynolds, Mack & Dean Ing** TROJAN ORBIT (Baen 0-671-55942-7, 03/85 [02/85], $2.95, 374pp, pb) Sf novel set in an L-5 colony. Reynolds wrote the first draft, Ing the final.

*****Rice, Anne** THE VAMPIRE LESTAT (Knopf 0-394-53443-3, 10/85 [10/85], $17.95, 481pp, hc) Fantasy novel, sequel to INTERVIEW WITH THE VAMPIRE. A richly inventive tale with some splendid characters. A third book in the series is promised. Recommended. (FCM)

*****Richardson, Linda, David F. Bischoff & Rich Brown** A PERSONAL DEMON Main listing under David F. Bischoff.

*****Rickman, Gregg** PHILIP K. DICK: THE LAST TESTAMENT (Fragments West 0-916063-02-X, 04/85 [03/85], $9.95, 240pp, pb) Non-fiction (maybe). These are interviews with Dick plus letters, etc., on his 1974 religious conversion and what came after. It's philosophical, religious, or paranoid ravings, depending on your point of view. Introduction by Robert Silverberg.

Robbins, Tom JITTERBUG PERFUME (Bantam 0-553-25148-1, 11/85 [09/85], $4.50, 388pp, pb) Reprint (Bantam 1984) fantasy novel.

*****Robbins, Trina** THE SILVER METAL LOVER (Crown/Harmony 0-517-55853-X, 11/85 [11/85], $6.95, 57pp, pb) This "graphic novel" is a comic-book adaptation of the sf novel by Tanith Lee.

*****Roberson, Jennifer** THE SONG OF HOMANA (DAW 0-88677-057-2, 07/85 [06/85], $3.50, 352pp, pb) Fantasy novel, second in the "Chronicles of the Cheysuli".

*****Roberts, John Maddox** THE CINGULUM (Tor 0-812-55200-8, 02/85 [01/85], $2.95, 285pp, pb) Sf novel.

*****Roberts, John Maddox** CLOAK OF ILLUSION (Tor 0-812-55202-4, 08/85 [07/85], $2.95, 287pp, pb) Sf novel, sequel to THE CINGULUM.

*****Roberts, John Maddox** CONAN THE VALOROUS (Tor 0-812-54244-4, 09/85 [08/85], $6.95, 280pp, pb) Fantasy novel in the continuing series based on the Robert E. Howard character.

*****Roberts, John Maddox & Eric Kotani** ACT OF GOD Main listing under Eric Kotani.

*****Roberts, Keith** KITEWORLD (Gollancz 0-575-03604-4, 06/85 [05/85], £8.95, 288pp, hc) Episodic sf novel of a strange post-holocaust culture. Parts of it previously appeared as three novelettes.
Contents:

			Page
Kitemaster	Keith Roberts	ss INZ # 1,82	7
Kitecadet	Keith Roberts	ss AMZ May,85	23
Kitemistress	Keith Roberts	nv INZ #11,85	43
Kitecaptain	Keith Roberts	na KITEWLD,85	71
Kiteservant	Keith Roberts	nv KITEWLD,85	135
Kitewaif	Keith Roberts	na KITEWLD,85	173
Kitemariner	Keith Roberts	nv KITEWLD,85	231
Kitekillers	Keith Roberts	ss KITEWLD,85	267

*****Robinson, Kim Stanley** THE MEMORY OF WHITENESS (Tor 0-312-93467-X, 09/85 [08/85], $15.95, 351pp, hc) Sf novel. Robinson's finest effort to date, an exquisitely structured musical tour of the solar system from the perspective of the musician who plays an entire orchestra. One of the year's finest novels. (DLN)

*****Robinson, Kim Stanley** THE NOVELS OF PHILIP K. DICK (UMI 0-8357-1589-2, 1984 [02/85], $24.95 + postage, 150pp, hc) Non-fiction, critical study. This is a revision of a thesis Robinson did in 1982. The book came out in 1984, but we missed it.

*****Robinson, Spider** MELANCHOLY ELEPHANTS [Canadian edition] (Penguin [Canada] 0-14-007427-9, 1984 [05/85], C$6.95, 239pp, pb) Collection of 12 stories. Published in a 1984 Canadian trade edition only. This is the first we've seen of it. Completists, take note.
Contents:

			Page
Introduction	Spider Robinson	in	xi
Melancholy Elephants	Spider Robinson	ss ASF Jun,82	1
Antinomy	Spider Robinson	nv DST V1 #1,78	21
Half an Oaf	Spider Robinson	nv ANLGANL,76	55
Satan's Children	Spider Robinson	na NWV # 2,79	83
No Renewal	Spider Robinson	ss GAL Mar,77	123
In the Olden Days	Spider Robinson	ss MLNELPH,84	131
Not Fade Away	Spider Robinson	ss IAS Aug,82	141
True Minds	Spider Robinson	nv MLNELPH,84	153
Chronic Offender	Spider Robinson	nv TZM May,81	175
It's a Sunny Day	Spider Robinson	ss GAL Jan,76	199
High Infidelity	Spider Robinson	ss OUI Apr,83	217
Rubber Soul	Spider Robinson	ss BOM # 4,82	231

+**Robinson, Spider** MELANCHOLY ELEPHANTS [U.S. edition] (Tor 0-812-55231-8, 06/85 [05/85], $2.95, 244pp, pb) Collection of 13 stories plus an introduction explaining the special 1984 Canadian trade edition. This edition drops one story and adds two stories plus a "concordiat" to another story.
Contents:

			Page
Introductory Note	Spider Robinson	in	ix
Melancholy Elephants	Spider Robinson	ss ASF Jun,82	1
Half an Oaf	Spider Robinson	nv ANLGANL,76	21
High Infidelity	Spider Robinson	ss OUI Apr,83	51
Antinomy	Spider Robinson	nv DST V1 #1,78	65
In the Olden Days	Spider Robinson	ss MLNELPH,84	101
Chronic Offender	Spider Robinson	nv TZM May,81	109
No Renewal	Spider Robinson	ss GAL Mar,77	135
Common Sense	Spider Robinson	ss MLNELPH,85	141
Rubber Soul	Spider Robinson	ss BOM # 4,82	149
Concordiat to "Rubber Soul"			
	Spider Robinson	aw	157
Father Paradox	Spider Robinson	ss MLNELPH,85	165
True Minds	Spider Robinson	nv MLNELPH,84	169
Satan's Children	Spider Robinson	na NWV # 2,79	191
Not Fade Away	Spider Robinson	ss IAS Aug,82	235

*Robinson, Spider NIGHT OF POWER (Baen 0-671-55944-3, 05/85 [04/85], $13.95, 287pp, hc) Near-future sf novel about a black uprising in Manhattan.

Robinson, Spider NIGHT OF POWER (Berkley 0-425-08475-2, 01/86 [12/85], $2.95, 287pp, pb) Reprint (Baen 1985) near-future sf novel of race war in New York.

*Rod Serling's The Twilight Zone Magazine [v.4 #6, January/February 1985] T.E.D. Klein, ed. (TZ Publications, 02/85 [12/84], $3.00, 106pp, pb)
Contents:

				Page
The Story Hour	T.E.D. Klein	ed	TZM Feb,85	6
Books	Thomas M. Disch	br	TZM	8
Screen	Gahan Wilson	mr	TZM	12
Nostalgia: Old Dark House for Rent				
	Ron Goulart	ar	TZM Feb,85	16
Movie Teaser Quiz	William D. Munster	pz	TZM Feb,85	22
Etc.; The Man Who Killed Santa Claus				
	Bruce J. Balfour	ar	TZM Feb,85	23
TZ Profile: Helen Slater: 'Supergirl' with Smarts				
	James Verniere	iv	TZM Feb,85	24
The Changing of the Guard [by Rod Serling]				
	Anne Serling-Sutton	sa	TZM Feb,85	26
Family Obligations	Lori Allen	ss	TZM Feb,85	32
The Time Wife	Thomas Tolnay	ss	TZM Feb,85	35
In Late December, Before the Storm				
	Paul M. Sammon	ss	TZM Feb,85	39
David Lynch: From Art School to Arrakis				
	Randy Lofficier & Jean-Marc Lofficier	iv	TZM Feb,85	44
Twisted Shadow	Roger F. Dunkley	ss		46
TZ Screen Preview: '2010': Hollywood Reprises a Classic				
	James Verniere	ar	TZM Feb,85	51
1985 TZ Calendar Special	Gahan Wilson	il	TZM Feb,85	53
John Lithgow: No Fear of Flying				
	James Verniere	bg	TZM Feb,85	61
Stephen King, Peter Straub, & the Quest for 'The Talisman'				
	Douglas E. Winter	iv	TZM Feb,85	62
Lonesome Coyote Blues	Oliver Lowenbruck	ss	TZM Feb,85	69
Laughs! Thrills! Romance!				
	Ron Wolfe	vi	TZM Feb,85	78
Legacy	Leigh Essex	ss	TZM Feb,85	81
The Weight of Zero	John Alfred Taylor	ss	TZM Feb,85	85
Nightmare	Larry Brown	vi	TZM Feb,85	91
Beyond the Zone...	Feggo	ct	TZM	94
TZ Theater: Shelf Life	Jim Ryan	cs	TZM Feb,85	96
The Outer Limits	David J. Schow	ar	TZM Feb,85	98
The Outer Limits Show-by-Show Guide, Part 7				
	David J. Schow & Jeffrey Frentzen	bi	TZM Feb,85	101

*Rod Serling's The Twilight Zone Magazine [v.5 #1, March/April 1985] T.E.D. Klein, ed. (TZ Publications, 04/85 [02/85], $2.50, 102pp, pb)
Contents:

				Page
A Word from the Publisher				
	Carol Serling	fw	TZM Apr,85	6
Fair Warnings	T.E.D. Klein	ed	TZM Apr,85	8
Books	D.W. "Doc" Kennedy	br	TZM	10
Screen	Gahan Wilson	mr	TZM	14
My Darkest Fantasy: Hell Through a Windshield				
	Joe R. Lansdale	ms	TZM Apr,85	18
Wiley's Hunger	David B. Schock	ss	TZM Apr,85	20
Short story contest 1st place winner.				
In the Shadow of the Castle				
	Randolph Cirilo	ss	TZM Apr,85	25
Short story contest 2nd place winner.				
Does It Make a Sound?	Joseph Calabro	ss	TZM Apr,85	29
Short story contest 3rd place winner.				
Airmail	Ken McCormack	vi	TZM Apr,85	33
Cartoon	M. Flinn	ct	TZM Apr,85	37
Cartoon	Leslie Sternbergh	ct	TZM Apr,85	38
TZ Profile: Kenneth McMillan: Never Out of Characters				
	Lorenzo Carcaterra	iv	TZM Apr,85	38
Bloodfall	T. Coraghessan Boyle	ss	EPO	40
Rod Serling Viewed from Beyond 'The Twilight Zone'				
	Andrew Sarris	bg	TZM Apr,85	45
Beyond the Zone...	Feggo	ct	TZM	50
TZ Screen Preview: 'Brazil'				
	James Verniere	ar	TZM Apr,85	52
Rod Serling's 'Night Gallery' [Part 1]				
	Kathryn M. Drennan & J. Michael Straczynski	ar	TZM Apr,85	54
A Show-by-Show Guide to Rod Serling's 'Night Gallery', Part 1				
	Kathryn M. Drennan & J. Michael Straczynski	bi	TZM Apr,85	57
Aliens in Hollywood	Victor Steinbach	ar	TZM Apr,85	61
Pattern for Survival	Richard Matheson	vi	FSF May,55	65
The Big Bang Theory of Creation				
	Vahan Shirvanian	ct	TZM Apr,85	69
Ben at the Window	Jon Cohen	ss	TZM Apr,85	71
Barter	Lois McMaster Bujold	ss	TZM Apr,85	74
The Magistrate's Pillow	Gordon Linzner	ss	TZM Apr,85	78
Quiz: Celebrity Autograph Hunt				
	Herman M. Darvick	pz	TZM Apr,85	83
Special Report: 'The Twilight Zone' Returns				
	Jefferson Graham	ar	TZM Apr,85	84
TZ Theater: A Brief Encounter of the Third Kind				
	Jim Ryan	cs	TZM Apr,85	88
Where Is Everybody?	Rod Serling	pl	CBS Oct 2,59	90

*Rod Serling's The Twilight Zone Magazine [v.5 #2, May/June 1985] T.E.D. Klein, ed. (TZ Publications, 06/85 [04/85], $2.50, 102pp, pb)
Contents:

				Page
Inspirations	T.E.D. Klein	ed	TZM Jun,85	6
Cartoon	Baum	ct	TZM Jun,85	8
Cartoon	Mason	ct	TZM Jun,85	10
Books	D.W. "Doc" Kennedy	br	TZM	12
Screen	Gahan Wilson	mr	TZM	16
Viewpoint: Broccoli, Oranges, and Science Fiction				
	Stanley Schmidt	ar	TZM Jun,85	20
Cartoon	Cheney	ct	TZM Jun,85	21
TZ Profile: John Hurt: Man of the Year				
	James Verniere	iv	TZM Jun,85	22
TZ Profile: Charles Martin Smith: Lighting Up 'Starman'				
	Lorenzo Carcaterra	iv	TZM Jun,85	24
Quiz: Fantasy Film Refresher Course				
	William Fulwiler	pz	TZM Jun,85	25
Flying to Byzantium	Lisa Tuttle	ss	TZM Jun,85	26
Through the Safety Net	Charles Baxter	ss	TZM Jun,85	38
Dayblood	Roger Zelazny	ss	TZM Jun,85	42
The Screening	Michael Blaine	ss	TZM Jun,85	45
Oz Revisited	James Verniere	ar	TZM Jun,85	49
Algernon Blackwood: The Ghostly Tale's Great Visionary				
	Mike Ashley	iv	TZM Jun,85	56
"Posthumous interview" based on Blackwood's letters and other writings.				
The Occupant of the Room	Algernon Blackwood	ss	DAY&NGT,17	64
Little Beggar	Algernon Blackwood	ss	TNGFIRE,24	68
Rescuing Andy	Paul DiFilippo	ss	TZM Jun,85	72
Jungle Eyes	Darrell Schweitzer	ss	TZM Jun,85	80
Rod Serling's 'Night Gallery' [Part 2]				
	J. Michael Straczynski & Kathryn M. Drennan	ar	TZM Jun,85	83
A Show-by-Show Guide to Rod Serling's 'Night Gallery', Part 2				
	J. Michael Straczynski & Kathryn M. Drennan	bi	TZM Jun,85	86
TZ Theater: The Hook	Jim Ryan	cs	TZM Jun,85	90
And When the Sky Was Opened				
	Rod Serling	pl	CBS Dec 11,59	94
Based on the story 'Disappearing Act' by Richard Matheson, ss FSF Mar,53.				

*Rod Serling's The Twilight Zone Magazine [v.5 #3, July/August 1985] T.E.D. Klein, ed. (TZ Publications, 08/85 [06/85], $2.50, 102pp, pb)
Contents:

				Page
Bye!	T.E.D. Klein	ed	TZM Aug,85	6
Books	D.W. "Doc" Kennedy	br	TZM	10
TZ Profile: Tanya Roberts: Putting Her Stock in Bond				
	James Verniere	iv	TZM Aug,85	14
Swamp Cypress	Mary Elizabeth Counselman	pm		16
Quiz: Break a Leg!	Ben P. Indick	pz	TZM Aug,85	17
My Darkest Fantasy: Terror from the Postal Zone				
	Larry Tritten	ms	TZM Aug,85	18
Screen	Gahan Wilson	mr	TZM	22
I Hear You Callin' CTHULHU				
	Gahan Wilson	gr	TZM Aug,85	26
Tip of the Scorpion	Steven Popkes	ss	TZM Aug,85	36
Ah, Whoreson Caterpillars! Bacon-Fed Knaves!				
	John Shea	ss	TZM Aug,85	41
A Foot in the Door	Bruce Jay Friedman	ss	PBY Oct,60	44
TZ Screen Preview: 'Lifeforce'				
	James Verniere	ar	TZM Aug,85	49
TZ Screen Preview: 'Mad Max: Beyond Thunderdome'				
	Robert Martin	ar	TZM Aug,85	55
This article is listed in the contents, but the listed page actually contains material duplicated from another article.				
The Bookshop	Nelson Bond	ss	BBM Oct,41	56
Mother's Day	Stephen F. Wilcox	ss	TZM Aug,85	60
Image in a Dark Glass	Garry Kilworth	ss	TZM Aug,85	64
And the Dutchman Docked at Rotterdam				
	Richard H. Fawcett	vi		69
The Malice of Inanimate Objects				
	M.R. James	ss	MSQ Jun,33	70
Snow Blind	Peter Heyrman	ss	TZM Aug,85	73
Side Tracked	Roger F. Dunkley	ss	TZM Aug,85	76
Rod Serling's 'Night Gallery' [Part 3]				
	Kathryn M. Drennan & J. Michael Straczynski	ar	TZM Aug,85	78
A Show-by-Show Guide to Rod Serling's 'Night Gallery', Part 3				
	Kathryn M. Drennan & J. Michael Straczynski	bi	TZM Aug,85	81
TZ Screen Preview: 'Cocoon'				
	Paul M. Sammon	mr	TZM Aug,85	86
TZ Theater: The Cows Come Home				
	Jim Ryan	cs	TZM Aug,85	90
The Mighty Casey	Rod Serling	pl	CBS Jun 17,60	93

*Rod Serling's The Twilight Zone Magazine [v.5 #4, October 1985] Michael Blaine, ed. (TZ Publications, 10/85 [08/85], $2.50, 102pp, pb)
Contents:

				Page
Secrets	Michael Blaine	ed	TZM Oct,85	6
Books	D.W. "Doc" Kennedy	br	TZM	10
TZ Tech	Al Talero & Irma Rubin	ar	TZM	14
TZ Illuminations	Peter Rondinone	ar	TZM	16
The Vampire Lestat	Anne Rice	ex	TZM Oct,85	18
The Love Pet	Ted Hughes	pm	NEW&SEL,82	29
Compensation	John Sherman	vi	TZM Oct,85	32
The Terminator	Donald R. Burleson	ss	TZM Oct,85	32

He and My Shadow	T.M. Swain	ss	TZM Oct,85	34
Post Awful	William John Watkins	ss	TZM Oct,85	40
The Night People	Michael Reaves	ss	TZM Oct,85	44
Explorers	Adam Eisenberg	mr	TZM Oct,85	50
Max's Myth Maker (Interview with George Miller)	Robert Martin	iv	TZM Oct,85	54
Where You Lead... I Will Follow	Robert Grant	ss	TZM Oct,85	56
The Secret of Rowena	Ray Russell	ss	TZM Oct,85	64
Censorship: Another Dimension Behind 'The Twilight Zone'	Hal Erickson	ar	TZM Oct,85	70
A Show-by-Show Guide to Rod Serling's 'Night Gallery', Part 4	J. Michael Straczynski & Kathryn M. Drennan	bi	TZM Oct,85	74
The Purple Testament	Rod Serling	pl	CBS Feb 12,60	82
My Darkest Fantasy	John M. Skipp	ms	TZM Oct,85	92
TZ Screen	Gahan Wilson	mr	TZM	96

*Rod Serling's The Twilight Zone Magazine [v.5 #5, December 1985]
Michael Blaine, ed. (TZ Publications, 12/85 [10/85], $2.95, 114pp, pb)
Contents: Page

In the Twilight Zone: Hype Warp	Michael Blaine	ed	TZM Dec,85	6
Books	D.W. "Doc" Kennedy	br	TZM	8
TZ Illuminations	Peter Rondinone	ar	TZM	12
TZ Tech	Robert Edelstein	ar	TZM	14
The Vampire Lestat	Anne Rice	ex	TZM Dec,85	18
Fade to Black	A.M. Ronning	ss	TZM Dec,85	28
I Don't Know Why She Swallowed the Fly	Jon Cohen	ss	TZM Dec,85	32
Why the Stranger Dreams	Randall Silvis	ss	TZM Dec,85	36
Paladin of the Lost Hour	Harlan Ellison	nv	UNI #15,85	42
Starbursts on the Twilight Zone [very short interviews with Robert Klein, Elliott Gould, Carolyn Seymour and Annie Potts]	Peter Rondinone	iv	TZM Dec,85	4A
New Adventures in the Scream Trade [interview with Stephen King]	Ben Herndon	iv	TZM Dec,85	6A
Real Tube Terror	Ben Herndon	ar	TZM Dec,85	10A
Ellison's Rules	Ben Herndon	iv	TZM Dec,85	12A
Talking Twilight Zone [interview with Phil DeGuere]	Carol Serling	iv	TZM Dec,85	13A
Dwindling	Annette Hard	ss	TZM Dec,85	68
Give Us a Big Smile	Charles L. Grant	ss	TZM Dec,85	76
The Doctor & the Devils	James Verniere	ar	TZM Dec,85	80
A Show-by-Show Guide to Rod Serling's 'Night Gallery', Part 5	Kathryn M. Drennan & J. Michael Straczynski	bi	TZM Dec,85	82
Thing About Machines	Rod Serling	pl	CBS Oct 28,60	90
TZ Video	Welch D. Everman	ar	TZM	103
TZ Screen	Gahan Wilson	mr	TZM	106
TZ Terror	F. Paul Wilson	ar	TZM	112
TZ Dataline	Michael Blaine	ar	TZM	114

*Rod Serling's The Twilight Zone Magazine [v.5 #6, February 1986]
Michael Blaine, ed. (TZ Publications, 02/86 [11/85], $2.50, 102pp, pb)
Contents: Page

In the Twilight Zone	Michael Blaine	ed	TZM Feb,86	6
TZ Illuminations	Peter Rondinone	ar	TZM	10
TZ Tech	Robert Edelstein	ar	TZM	12
Books	D.W. "Doc" Kennedy	br	TZM	14
Talking Terror with Stephen King [extract]	Douglas E. Winter	iv	FACESFR,85	16
The Fifth Quarter	Stephen King	ss	TZM Feb,86	24
King Goes into Overdrive	Tyson Blue	ar	TZM Feb,86	30
Collecting King	Douglas E. Winter	ar	TZM Feb,86	32
The Last One Mo' Once Golden Oldies Revival	F. Paul Wilson	ss	WHA # 5,85	34
The Age of Fish	Patricia Stoll	ss	TZM Feb,86	40
Ska...Zik!	Jeffrey Whitmore	ss	TZM Feb,86	46
F/X Movie Preview	Michael Blaine	ar	TZM Feb,86	50
The Tube Fantastic	Robin Bromley	ar	TZM Feb,86	54
The Crossing	Peter Heyrman	ss	TZM Feb,86	56
The Gift	Richard Partlow	ss	TZM Feb,86	60
Pillaging Poe	A.R. Morlan	ss	TZM Feb,86	64
Televisionaries	Larry Tritten	ss	TZM Feb,86	68
A Show-by-Show Guide to Rod Serling's 'Night Gallery', Part 6	J. Michael Straczynski & Kathryn M. Drennan	bi	TZM Feb,86	72
Will the Real Martian Please Stand Up	Rod Serling	pl	CBS May 26,61	76
TZ Screen	Gahan Wilson	mr	TZM	84
TZ Video	Welch D. Everman	ar	TZM	88
TZ Video List	Alan Rodgers	bi	TZM	92
TZ Film Futures: Psycho III	Richard Partlow	ar	TZM Feb,86	99
TZ Film Futures: The Manhattan Project	Michael Blaine	ar	TZM Feb,86	99
TZ Dataline	Michael Blaine	ar	TZM	102

Rohmer, Sax THE DRUMS OF FU MANCHU (Zebra 0-8217-1617-4, 06/85 [05/85], $3.50, 348pp, pb) Reprint (Doubleday 1939) sf novel, 6th in the "Fu Manchu" series.

Rohmer, Sax THE INSIDIOUS DR. FU MANCHU (Zebra 0-8217-1668-9, 10/85 [10/85], $3.50, 331pp, pb) Reprint (McBride 1913) sf novel, first in the series.

Rohmer, Sax THE TRAIL OF FU MANCHU (Zebra 0-8217-1619-0, 06/85 [05/85], $3.50, 348pp, pb) Reprint (Doubleday 1934) sf novel, 10th in the series.

+**Ronson, Mark, Judy Gardiner & Stella Whitelaw** GRIMALKIN'S TALES Main listing under Stella Whitelaw.

***Rosenberg, Joel** EMILE AND THE DUTCHMAN (NAL/Signet 0-451-14016-8, 01/86 [12/85], $2.95, 254pp, pb) Sf novel. "The galaxy-spanning tale of the two toughest, cleverist mavericks in outer space." Parts are significantly revised versions of earlier printed stories.

***Rosenberg, Joel** GUARDIANS OF THE FLAME: THE WARRIORS (SFBC #02410, 09/85 [08/85], $8.50, 722pp, hc) Omnibus edition of a fantasy trilogy.
Contents: Page

THE SLEEPING DRAGON	Joel Rosenberg	n.	SIG 1983
THE SWORD AND THE CHAIN	Joel Rosenberg	n.	SIG 1984
THE SILVER CROWN	Joel Rosenberg	n.	SIG 1985

***Rosenberg, Joel** THE SILVER CROWN (NAL/Signet 0-451-13531-8, 04/85 [03/85], $2.95, 302pp, pb) Fantasy novel, Book 3 of "Guardians of the Flame".

***Rosinsky, Natalie M.** FEMINIST FUTURES: CONTEMPORARY WOMEN'S SPECULATIVE FICTION (UMI 0-8357-1578-7, 1984 [05/85], $24.95 + postage, 147pp, hc) Non-fiction, literary criticism. This revision of a thesis appeared in 1984, but we didn't see it until 1985.

***Rossi, Leo D.** THE POLITICS OF FANTASY: C.S. LEWIS AND J.R.R. TOLKIEN (UMI 0-8357-1597-3, 1984 [05/85], $24.95 + postage, 143pp, hc) Non-fiction, literary criticsm. This revision of a thesis first appeared in 1984, but we didn't see it until 1985.

***Roszak, Theodore** DREAMWATCHER (Doubleday 0-385-18894-3, 02/85 [01/85], $15.95, 287pp, hc) Fantasy novel of a woman who can see dreams. It's billed as a "psychosexual thriller."

***Rothman, Chuck** STAROAMER'S FATE (Popular Library/Questar 0-445-20102-9, 01/86 [12/85], $3.50, 213pp, pb) Sf novel, a first novel.

Rotsler, William & Gregory Benford SHIVA DESCENDING Main listing under Gregory Benford.

***Rouch, James** THE ZONE #3: HUNTER KILLER (Zebra 0-8217-1662-X, 09/85 [08/85], $2.50, 206pp, pb) Post-holocaust sf adventure novel.

***Rovin, Jeff** THE ENCYCLOPEDIA OF SUPERHEROES (Facts on File 0-8160-1168-0, 11/85 [11/85], $29.95, 443pp, hc) Non-fiction, reference book listing mostly comic superheroes but also some pulp characters, etc.

***Rowley, Christopher** THE BLACK SHIP (Ballantine/Del Rey 0-345-31489-1, 07/85 [06/85], $2.95, 310pp, pb) Sf novel, sequel to THE WAR FOR ETERNITY.

Rucker, Rudy THE FOURTH DIMENSION: A GUIDED TOUR OF HIGHER UNIVERSES (Houghton Mifflin 0-395-39388-4, 09/85 [08/85], $8.95, 228pp, pb) Reprint (Houghton Mifflin 1984), non-fiction; associational. Fittingly described as a "combination of math, philosophy, and fantasy," this book uses some of the techniques of Rucker the sf writer in the cause of Rucker the scientist.

***Rucker, Rudy** MASTER OF SPACE AND TIME (Bluejay 0-312-94297-4, 02/85 [01/85], $14.95, 229pp, hc) Sf novel. The two zaniest inventors since Kuttner's "Gallagher" stories. Very amusing. (DLN)

Rucker, Rudy MASTER OF SPACE AND TIME (Baen 0-671-55997-4, 12/85 [11/85], $2.95, 229pp, pb) Reprint (Bluejay 1985) sf novel.

***Rucker, Rudy** THE SECRET OF LIFE (Bluejay 0-312-94398-9, 06/85 [05/85], $14.95, 246pp, hc) Sf novel, '60s setting, flying saucers, dope and campus revolution.

Russ, Joanna THE ADVENTURES OF ALYX (Women's Press 0-7043-3972-2, 09/85 [10/85], £1.95, 192pp, pb) Reprint (Gregg 1976 as ALYX) collection of five tales featuring the fantasy/sf heroine, including the novel PICNIC ON PARADISE (1968). First British edition. (The dates on the copyright page are wrong.)

Russ, Joanna EXTRA(ORDINARY) PEOPLE (St. Martin's 0-312-27807-1, 01/85 [12/84], $4.95, 160pp, pb) Reprint (St. Martin's 1984) collection. Recommended. (FCM)

***Russ, Joanna** MAGIC MOMMAS, TREMBLING SISTERS, PURITANS AND PERVERTS (Crossing Press 0-89594-163-5, 07/85 [06/85], $6.95, 119pp, pb) Non-sf/fantasy, listed for Russ fans. A collection of feminist essays on sex and pornography. Includes an essay on Kirk/Spock pornography. Recommended. (DLN)

***Russ, Joanna** MAGIC MOMMAS, TREMBLING SISTERS, PURITANS AND PERVERTS (Crossing Press 0-89594-164-3, 07/85 [06/85], $14.95, 119pp, hc) Hardcover version of the above.

Russell, Eric Frank SINISTER BARRIER (Ballantine/Del Rey 0-345-32760-8, 01/86 [12/85], $2.95, 230pp, pb) Reprint (Fantasy Press 1948) sf novel. This is the revised, expanded version of an earlier book (World's Work 1943). This edition has a new introduction by Jack Chalker.

*Russell, Ray HAUNTED CASTLES: THE COMPLETE GOTHIC TALES OF RAY RUSSELL (Maclay 0-940776-20-0, 11/85 [09/85], $12.95, 187pp, hc) Collection of 7 stories, one apparently published here for the first time. Several others have been revised. Horror in the grand old style, with some modern psychological twists. (FCM)
Contents:

				Page
Sardonicus	Ray Russell		nv PBY Jan,61	9
Sagittarius	Ray Russell		nv PBY Mar,62	49
Sanguinarius	Ray Russell		nv HNTDCST,85	89
Comet Wine	Ray Russell		nv PBY Mar,67	127
The Runaway Lovers	Ray Russell		ss 1967	151
The Vendetta [The Man Who Spoke in Rhyme]				
	Ray Russell		ss EQM Nov,69	165
The Cage	Ray Russell		ss 1959	179

Ryan, Thomas J. THE ADOLESCENCE OF P-1 (Baen 0-671-55970-2, 07/85 [06/85], $2.95, 287pp, pb) Reprint (Macmillan 1977) sf novel. An early sentient computer book.

*Ryman, Geoff THE WARRIOR WHO CARRIED LIFE (Allen & Unwin 0-04-823294-7, 05/85 [04/85], £8.95, 173pp, hc) Fantasy novel, a first novel by a recent British award-winner for shorter fiction. Extremely potent and disturbing images; recommended, but not for those with weak stomachs. (DLN)

*Saberhagen, Fred THE BERSERKER THRONE (Simon & Schuster 0-671-55836-6, 06/85 [05/85], $14.95, 319pp, hc) Sf novel in the "Berserker" series.

*Saberhagen, Fred THE BERSERKER THRONE (Simon & Schuster/Fireside 0-671-50387-1, 06/85 [05/85], $6.95, 319pp, pb) Paperback edition of the above.

Saberhagen, Fred THE BERSERKER WARS (Tor 0-812-55320-9, 09/85 [08/85], $2.95, 399pp, pb) Reissue (Tor 1981) collection. The stories are from earlier collections, and this is partially a reprint of BERSERKER (Ballantine 1970). 4th Tor printing.

Saberhagen, Fred BERSERKER'S PLANET (Ace 0-441-05507-9, 01/86 [12/85], $2.95, 233pp, pb) Reissue (DAW 1975) sf novel in the "Berserker" series. 7th Ace printing.

*Saberhagen, Fred BERSERKER: BLUE DEATH (Tor 0-812-55322-5, 11/85 [10/85], $6.95, 282pp, pb) Sf novel in the "Berserker" series. This one seems to be Saberhagen's version of MOBY DICK.

*Saberhagen, Fred THE COMPLETE BOOK OF SWORDS (SFBC #1457, 01/85 [02/85], $7.50, 626pp, hc) Omnibus edition of a fantasy trilogy. It isn't really complete, since Saberhagen signed a contract to write 6 more.
Contents:

			Page
THE FIRST BOOK OF SWORDS	Fred Saberhagen	n. TOR 1983	
THE SECOND BOOK OF SWORDS			
	Fred Saberhagen	n. TOR 1983	
THE THIRD BOOK OF SWORDS	Fred Saberhagen	n. TOR 1984	

Saberhagen, Fred THE DRACULA TAPE (Ace 0-441-11601-6, 06/85 [05/85], $2.95, 281pp, pb) Reissue (Warner 1975) fantasy novel, part of a series. 4th Ace printing. The "true" story of Dracula, told from his point of view.

*Saberhagen, Fred LOVE CONQUERS ALL (Baen 0-671-55953-2, 04/85 [03/85], $2.95, 275pp, pb) A revised version of an earlier (Ace 1979) sf novel.

Saberhagen, Fred THE SECOND BOOK OF SWORDS (Tor 0-812-55305-5, 02/85 [01/85], $2.95, 313pp, pb) Reprint (Tor 1983), first mass market paperback. Second novel in a fantasy series.

Saberhagen, Fred THE THIRD BOOK OF SWORDS (Tor 0-812-55307-1, 08/85 [07/85], $2.95, 320pp, pb) Reprint (Tor 1984) fantasy novel, third in a trilogy.

*Saberhagen, Fred THE VEILS OF AZLAROC (Tor/Otherworlds Club no ISBN, 04/85 [03/85], no price given, 216pp, pb) Reprint (Ace 1978) sf novel. This is a freebie given away by Waldenbooks to buyers of BERSERKER BASE. There were 15,000 copies printed by Tor for the club. Listed for Saberhagen completists and collectors of oddities.

Saberhagen, Fred THE WATER OF THOUGHT (Tor 0-812-55290-3, 04/85 [03/85], $2.95, 251pp, pb) Reissue (Tor 1981) sf novel. This was an expanded version of an earlier book (Ace 1965).

*Saberhagen, Fred, ed. BERSERKER BASE (Tor 0-812-55316-0, 03/85 [02/85], $6.95, 316pp, pb) Collection of stories by 7 authors, including connecting material by Saberhagen, originator of the "Berserker" series. Author credits appear only in the acknowledgements, not on the contents page, making it look like a novel.
Contents:

				Page
Prisoner's Base	Fred Saberhagen	pr	BSRKRBS,85	9
What Makes Us Human	Stephen R. Donaldson	nv	FSF Aug,84	27
Friends Together	Fred Saberhagen	ms	BSRKRBS,85	73
With Friends Like These	Connie Willis	nv	FSF Feb,85	79
The Founts of Sorrow	Fred Saberhagen	ms	BSRKRBS,85	123
Itself Surprised	Roger Zelazny	nv	OMN Aug,84	129
The Great Secret	Fred Saberhagen	ms	BSRKRBS,85	161
Deathwomb	Poul Anderson	nv	ASF Nov,84	165
Dangerous Dreams	Fred Saberhagen	ms	BSRKRBS,85	213
Pilots of the Twilight	Edward Bryant	na	IAS Dec md,84	217
Crossing the Bar	Fred Saberhagen	ms	BSRKRBS,85	287
A Teardrop Falls	Larry Niven	ss	OMN Jun,83	299

Berserker Base	Fred Saberhagen	ms BSRKRBS,85	313

Saberhagen, Fred, ed. BERSERKER BASE (SFBC #4655, 06/85 [07/85], $4.98, 218pp, hc) Reprint (Tor 1985) anthology of "Berserker" stories. This edition doesn't pretend to be a novel, but the authors' names only appear on the copyright page, not on the contents page. This is the first hardcover edition.

*Sadler, Barry CASCA: THE ASSASSIN (Ace/Charter 0-441-09327-2, 03/85 [02/85], $2.75, 183pp, pb) Fantasy novel, #13 in the "Eternal Mercenary" series.

*Sadler, Barry CASCA: THE PHOENIX (Charter 0-441-09329-9, 08/85 [07/85], $2.95, 188pp, pb) Fantasy novel, "The Eternal Mercenary" #14.

*Sadler, Barry CASCA: THE PIRATE (Ace/Charter 0-441-09331-0, 12/85 [11/85], $2.95, 167pp, pb) Fantasy novel, "The Eternal Mercenary" #15.

*Sadler, Frank THE UNIFIED RING: NARRATIVE ART AND THE SCIENCE-FICTION NOVEL (UMI 0-8357-1598-1, 1984 [05/85], $24.95 + postage, 117pp, hc) Non-fiction, literary criticism. This revision of a doctoral thesis appeared in 1984, but we didn't see it until 1985.

*Sagan, Carl CONTACT (Simon & Schuster 0-671-43400-4, 10/85 [09/85], $18.95, 432pp, hc) According to the publisher, this novel about man's first contact with intelligent life beyond earth "is not science fiction." It is, however, fiction about science and the future. A first novel.

*Saha, Arthur W., ed. THE YEAR'S BEST FANTASY STORIES: 11 (DAW 0-88677-097-1, 11/85 [10/85], $2.95, 238pp, pb) Anthology of 1984 fantasy stories.
Contents:

				Page
Introduction	Arthur W. Saha		in	9
Draco, Draco	Tanith Lee	nv	BYNDLND,84	11
The Harvest Child	Steve Rasnic Tem	ss	ELW # 3,84	38
Love Among the Xoids	John Sladek	ss	DRM #15,84	56
Stoneskin	John Morressy	nv	FSF Jun,84	71
Unmistakably the Finest	Scott Bradfield	nv	INZ # 8,84	94
The Foxwife	Jane Yolen	ss	WFC #10,84	119
Golden Apples of the Sun [expanded from Virgin Territory]				
	Gardner Dozois, Jack Dann & Michael Swanwick	nv	PNT Mar,84	127
My Rose and My Glove	Harvey Jacobs	ss	OMN May,84	149
Strange Shadows	Clark Ashton Smith	ss	CRP #25,84	161
A Little Two-Chair Barber Shop on Phillips Street				
	Donald R. Burleson	ss	TZM Apr,84	179
Taking Heart	Stephen L. Burns	ss	S&S # 1,84	186
The Storm	David Morrell	ss	SDW # 7,84	204
A Cabin on the Coast	Gene Wolfe	ss	FSF Feb,84	224

Saha, Arthur W. & Donald A. Wollheim, eds. WOLLHEIM'S WORLD'S BEST SF: SERIES 9 Main listing under Donald A. Wollheim.

*Salmonson, Jessica Amanda OU LU KHEN AND THE BEAUTIFUL MADWOMAN (Ace 0-441-63500-8, 07/85 [06/85], $2.75, 243pp, pb) Oriental fantasy novel.

Salmonson, Jessica Amanda, ed. TALES BY MOONLIGHT (Tor 0-812-52552-3, 01/85 [12/84], $2.95, 286pp, pb) Reprint (Robert T. Garcia 1983) original anthology of dark fantasy stories. First mass market edition.

*Salomoni, Tito THE SURREALISTIC WORLD OF TITO SALOMONI (Prestige Art Galleries no ISBN, 04/85 [03/85], $10.00 + $1.00 postage, 32 plates + text, pb) Non-fiction, art. A privately printed collection of surrealistic paintings by a fine new artist. Some of these have appeared as sf covers, but not too many.

*Salsitz, R.A.V. WHERE DRAGONS LIE (NAL/Signet 0-451-14055-9, 12/85 [11/85], $2.95, 255pp, pb) Fantasy novel.

*Sanders, Scott Russell TERRARIUM (Tor 0-812-55380-2, 09/85 [08/85], $2.95, 276pp, pb) Sf novel.

*Saperstein, David COCOON (Jove 0-515-08400-X, 07/85 [06/85], $3.50, 248pp, pb) Novelization of the film.

*Saralegui, Jorge LAST RITES (Charter 0-441-47185-4, 11/85 [10/85], $3.95, 279pp, pb) Horror/dark fantasy novel of vampires in an old San Francisco hotel.

Sargent, Pamela THE ALIEN UPSTAIRS (Bantam 0-553-24857-X, 02/85 [01/85], $2.75, 165pp, pb) Reprint (Doubleday 1983) sf novel.

*Sargent, Pamela HOMESMIND (Harper & Row 0-06-025198-0, 01/85 [12/84], $7.95, 278pp, pb) Young-adult sf novel. A hardcover library edition was also announced, but not seen.

*Sarrantonio, Al CAMPBELL WOOD (Doubleday 0-385-19458-7, 01/86 [12/85], $12.95, 180pp, hc) Fantasy/horror novel.

*Sarrantonio, Al TOTENTANZ (Tor 0-812-52558-2, 12/85 [11/85], $3.50, 285pp, pb) Horror novel of an evil carnival.

*Sarrantonio, Al THE WORMS (Doubleday 0-385-19030-1, 01/85 [12/84], $11.95, 179pp, hc) Fantasy/horror novel of terror in a New England town. A first novel.

*Saul, John   BRAINCHILD (Bantam 0-553-24975-4, 08/85 [07/85], $3.95, 342pp, pb) Sf/horror novel.

Saul, John   NATHANIEL (Gregg 0-8398-2891-8, 12/85 [12/85], $14.95, 343pp, hc) Reprint (Bantam 1984) fantasy/horror novel. First hardcover edition, offset from the paperback original.

*Saunders, Charles R.   IMARO III: THE TRAIL OF BOHU (DAW 0-88677-087-4, 10/85 [09/85], $2.95, 222pp, pb) Heroic fantasy novel, third in a series set in Africa.

*Sawde, Derek   SCEPTRE MORTAL (Oriflamme 0-948093-00-5, 1985 [12/85], £2.95, 294pp, pb) Fantasy novel a la Tolkien, the first to appear from this new British publisher.

*Saxton, Josephine   THE POWER OF TIME (Chatto & Windus 0-7011-2955-7, 08/85 [10/85], £9.95, 222pp, hc) Collection of 14 stories.
Contents:

			Page
The Power of Time	Josephine Saxton	ss NDM # 1,70	9
Lover from Beyond the Dawn of Time			
	Josephine Saxton	ss PWRTIME,85	25
Food and Love	Josephine Saxton	ss CMP 1975	40
Silence in Having Words: Purple			
New Aesthetics	Josephine Saxton	nv PWRTIME,85	47
The Triumphant Head	Josephine Saxton	ss PWRTIME,85	75
To Market, To Market	Josephine Saxton	ss ALCHEMY,70	90
The Wall	Josephine Saxton	ss WMNSPCE,81	95
Dormant Soul	Josephine Saxton	ss SCF Nov,66	97
Elouise and the Doctors of the Planet Pergamon	Josephine Saxton	ss FSF Feb,69	105
	Josephine Saxton	ss AGNDNGR,72	125
The Snake who had Read Chomsky			
	Josephine Saxton	nv UNI #11,81	142
No Coward Soul	Josephine Saxton	ss INZ # 3,82	165
Black Sabbatical	Josephine Saxton	ss FSF Dec,71	183
Living Wild	Josephine Saxton	nv FSF Oct,71	201

*Saxton, Josephine   THE POWER OF TIME (Chatto & Windus 0-7011-2956-5, 08/85 [10/85], £3.95, 222pp, pb) Paperback edition of the above.

*Scarborough, Elizabeth   THE CHRISTENING QUEST (Bantam 0-553-25122-8, 08/85 [07/85], $2.95, 231pp, pb) Fantasy novel, sequel to BRONWYN'S BANE.

*Schiff, Stuart David, ed.   WHISPERS V (Doubleday 0-385-18944-3, 02/15/85 [02/85], $11.95, 208pp, hc) Anthology of 14 stories of horror/fantasy; most are originals.
Contents:

			Page
Preface	Stuart David Schiff	pr	ix
Substitution Trick	Connie Willis	ss WHA # 5,85	1
Dreams in Amber	David A. Drake	ss WHA # 5,85	10
Footprints in Perdu	Hugh B. Cave	ss WHA # 5,85	23
The Last One Mo' Once Golden Oldies Revival			
	F. Paul Wilson	ss WHA # 5,85	34
A Country Home	Wade Kenny	ss WHA # 5,85	48
Of Time and Kathy Benedict			
	William F. Nolan	nv FTL V7 #13,84	51
Deadspace	Dennis Etchison	nv WHA # 5,85	73
Cabin Number Six	Jerry Sohl	ss WHA # 5,85	95
Father's Day	Steve Rasnic Tem	ss WHA # 5,85	107
The East Beaverton Monster			
	Alan Ryan	ss WHA # 5,85	117
The Horse	Libby Tinker	ss WHA # 5,85	133
Return of the Dust Vampires			
	Sharon N. Farber	ss WHA # 5,85	139
For These and All My Sins			
	David Morrell	ss WHS Dec,84	151
Beyond Any Measure	Karl Edward Wagner	nv WHS Mar,82	164

*Schmidt, Dennis   TWILIGHT OF THE GODS: THE FIRST NAME (Ace 0-441-23929-3, 02/85 [01/85], $2.95, 307pp, pb) Fantasy novel, beginning of "the savage epic of ancient Yggdrasil."

*Schmidt, Dennis   WANDERER (Ace 0-441-87160-7, 11/85 [10/85], $2.95, 202pp, pb) Sf novel, conclusion of the "Kensho" tetralogy. Zen and martial arts in space.

Schmidt, Dennis   WAY-FARER (Ace 0-441-87421-5, 01/86 [12/85], $2.95, 277pp, pb) Reissue (Ace 1978) sf novel, first in the "Kensho" series. 3rd printing.

Schmitz, James H.   THE LION GAME (Ace 0-441-48434-4, 01/85 [12/84], $2.75, 196pp, pb) Reissue (DAW 1973) sf novel, the third book featuring Telzey Amberdon.

*Scholz, Carter   CUTS (Drumm no ISBN, 10/85 [10/85], $6.00, 56pp, pb) Collection of ten new stories and one reprint. This is the limited edition version, 126 signed/numbered copies with a stiff cover and an inset Scholz checklist and poem. The regular edition price is $2.50. Drumm Booklet #20.
Contents:

			Page
Introduction	Carter Scholz	in	4
Recursion	Carter Scholz	ss CUTS ,85	5
s=1/2at2 [The Last Concert of Pierre Valdemar]			
	Carter Scholz	ss NDM #12,81	9
How Should We Celebrate the Bicentennial?			
	Carter Scholz	ss CUTS ,85	11
Why We Have Technology	Carter Scholz	ss CUTS ,85	16
Players, or Some Problems of Form in New York			
	Carter Scholz	ss CUTS ,85	19
The Sickness	Carter Scholz	ss CUTS ,85	23
The Translator	Carter Scholz	vi CUTS ,85	27
Lineage	Carter Scholz	ss CUTS ,85	29
The Sky In Winter	Carter Scholz	vi CUTS ,85	24
Cuts	Carter Scholz	ss CUTS ,85	36
A Grim Tale for Moderns [section cut from PALIMPSESTS]			
	Carter Scholz	ss CUTS ,85	49
A Carter Scholz Checklist			
	Carter Scholz	bi CUTS ,85	ins.
In the blue house	Carter Scholz	pm CUTS ,85	ins.

*Schwartz, Betty Ann, ed.   GREAT GHOST STORIES (S&S/Little Simon 0-671-60179-2, 1985 [12/85], $6.95, 177pp, hc) Anthology of 15 eerie tales, illustrated by Paul Geiger.
Contents:

			Page
Introduction	Betty Ann Schwartz	in	xi
The Tell-Tale Heart	Edgar Allan Poe	ss PIO Jan,1843	3
A Ghost Story	Mark Twain	ss	11
The Secret of the Growing Gold			
	Bram Stoker	ss DRCLGST,14	21
The Open Window	Saki	ss BST&SUP,12	39
Captain Murderer and the Devil's Bargain			
	Charles Dickens	ss	45
The Boy Who Drew Cats	Lafcadio Hearn	ss	61
The Red Room	H.G. Wells	ss IDL Mar,1896	67
Yesterday's Witch	Gahan Wilson	ss WTS Win,73	81
The Adventure of the German Student			
	Washington Irving	ss TLSTRVL,1824	93
The Haunted Trailer	Robert Arthur	nv WRT 1953	103
The Boarded Window	Ambrose Bierce	ss INMIDST,1891	127
In a Dim Room	Lord Dunsany	ss	135
The Waxwork [as Ex-Private X]			
	A.M. Burrage	ss SMNINRM,31	141
The Haunting of Y-12	Al Sarrantonio	ss 1981	159
Count Dracula	Woody Allen	ss GTNGEVN,71	171

*Schweitzer, Darrell   TOM O'BEDLAM'S NIGHT OUT, AND OTHER STRANGE EXCURSIONS (W. Paul Ganley 0-932445-14-4, 11/85 [11/85], $7.50, 191pp, pb) Collection of 18 stories and a poem, with illustrations by Stephen E. Fabian. This has also been announced in hc for $20.00 and a "very limited" signed, numbered slipcased edition for $35; we have seen neither.
Contents:

			Page
Tom O'Bedlam's Night Out	Darrell Schweitzer	ss FAN Sep,77	9
Raving Lunacy	Darrell Schweitzer	ss AMZ Jul,81	18
Continued Lunacy	Darrell Schweitzer	ss AMZ Mar,83	32
The Story of a Dadar	Darrell Schweitzer	ss AMZ Jun,82	47
A Lantern Maker of Ai Hanlo			
	Darrell Schweitzer	ss AMZ Jul,84	67
The Story of Obbok	Darrell Schweitzer	ss WHS Dec,73	77
The Outcast	Darrell Schweitzer	pm TOMOBED,85	83
The Pretenses of Hinyar	Darrell Schweitzer	ss ARA #69,81	85
The Story of the Brown Man			
	Darrell Schweitzer	ss FCR Jan,77	93
The Last of the Shadow Titans			
	Darrell Schweitzer	ss AMZ Jul,85	101
The Stranger from Baal-ad-Theon			
	Darrell Schweitzer	ss TOMOBED,85	119
The Bermuda Triangle Explained			
	Darrell Schweitzer	ss TOMOBED,85	129
The Adventure in the House of Phaon			
	Darrell Schweitzer	ss TOMOBED,85	139
The Last Child of Masferigon			
	Darrell Schweitzer & John Gregory Betancourt	ss TOMOBED,85	153
A Vision of Rembathene	Darrell Schweitzer	ss FCR Mar,77	159
Jungle Eyes	Darrell Schweitzer	ss TZM Jun,85	167
Sunrise	Darrell Schweitzer	ss PLP Win,83	173
The Game of Sand and Fire [revised from A Part of the Game]			
	Darrell Schweitzer	ss DRG #51,81	179
The Wings of the White Bird [revised]			
	Darrell Schweitzer	ss MYR # 4,78	186

*Schweitzer, Darrell, ed.   DISCOVERING MODERN HORROR FICTION I (Starmont 0-916732-93-2, 09/85 [08/85], $9.95, 156pp, pb) Non-fiction, anthology of critical essays on 12 horror writers (Russell Kirk, Stephen King, T.E.D. Klein, and others), plus a selected, annotated bibliography of critical studies in horror. This is also available in hardcover.

*Schweitzer, Darrell, ed.   DISCOVERING STEPHEN KING (Starmont 0-930261-06-2, 09/85 [08/85], $9.95, 219pp, pb) Non-fiction, anthology of critical essays on King and his works, plus synopses and a bibliography. Also available in hardcover (-07-0, $17.95).

*Schweitzer, Darrell, ed.   EXPLORING FANTASY WORLDS (Borgo 0-89370-262-5, 08/85 [07/85], $6.95, 112pp, pb) Non-fiction; criticism. Essays by Moorcock, de Camp, Leiber, and others, some original while others first appeared in magazines. A hardcover version is also available for $14.95.

*Scliar, Moacyr   THE CENTAUR IN THE GARDEN (Ballantine/Available Press 0-345-31669-X, 05/85 [04/85], $5.95, 215pp, pb) The first English-language edition (translated by Margaret A. Neves) of O CENTAURO NO JARDIN (Editoria Nova Fronteira S.A. 1980). Fantasy novel about a Brazilian Jewish centaur. As the hero gradually leaves centaur-hood behind him, it becomes more and more mainstream. The *New York Times* review aptly labeled it "Yuppies with fetlocks." Offbeat, but pretty lightweight. (FCM)

*Scott, Melissa FIVE TWELFTHS OF HEAVEN (Baen 0-671-55952-4, 04/85 [03/85], $2.95, 339pp, pb) Sf novel. Good combination of science and quasi-magic keeps this space opera entertaining despite some clichés of character. Recommended. (DLN)

*Service, Pamela WINTER OF MAGIC'S RETURN (Atheneum 0-689-31130-3, 09/85 [08/85], $14.95, 192pp, hc) Young-adult fantasy novel: Merlin reborn in a post-holocaust world of magic. It may be a first novel.

+Shaw, Bob ORBITSVILLE DEPARTURE (DAW 0-88677-030-0, 04/85 [03/85], $2.95, 252pp, pb) Reprint (Gollancz 1983) sf novel, sequel to ORBITSVILLE.

*Shaw, Bob THE PEACE MACHINE (Gollancz 0-575-03582-X, 05/85 [04/85], £7.95, 160pp, hc) Revised, updated version of the sf novel GROUND ZERO MAN (Avon 1971).

*Shayol [v.3 #1, Whole No. 7] Arnie Fenner & Pat Cadigan, eds. (Flight Unlimited, Inc., 11/85 [11/85], $4.50, 48pp, pb)
Contents: Page
Contributors   [Misc. Material]   bg   2
Editor's Notes   Arnie Fenner   ed SHY # 7,85   3
What Makes Heironymous Run?
                             Howard Waldrop   ss SHY # 7,85   4
Castoff   Janet Gluckman   ss SHY # 7,85   9
A Spy in the Domain of Arnheim
                             Michael Bishop   ss SHY # 7,85   11
Thomas Blackshear   Hank Jankus   iv SHY # 7,85   16
The Window Jesus   Leigh Kennedy   ss SHY # 7,85   20
King of the North   Donald M. Grant   fa SHY # 7,85   23
Roger Stine   Arnie Fenner   bg SHY # 7,85   24
The Overly Familiar   Edward Bryant   ss SHY # 7,85   32
Fantasy Portfolio   Various Hands   il SHY # 7,85   37
Stompin' at the Savoy   Lewis Shiner   ss SHY # 7,85   43
Creatures of Habit   Steven Utley   ss SHY # 7,85   46

*Shea, Michael IN YANA, THE TOUCH OF UNDYING (DAW 0-88677-080-7, 12/85 [11/85], $3.50, 318pp, pb) Fantasy novel in the Vancian mode, with more than a touch of horror.

Sheckley, Robert DIMENSION OF MIRACLES (Gollancz 0-575-03706-7, 09/85 [08/85], £8.95, 190pp, hc) Reissue (Dell 1968) humorous sf novel.

Sheckley, Robert JOURNEY BEYOND TOMORROW (Gollancz 0-575-03707-5, 09/85 [08/85], £8.95, 189pp, hc) Reissue (NAL/Signet 1962) humorous sf novel, third Gollancz printing.

Sheckley, Robert MINDSWAP (Gollancz 0-575-03705-9, 09/85 [08/85], £8.95, 216pp, hc) Reissue (Delacorte 1966) humorous sf novel.

*Sheffield, Charles BETWEEN THE STROKES OF NIGHT (Baen 0-671-55977-X, 07/85 [06/85], $3.50, 346pp, pb) Sf novel. Sheffield's best hard science novel so far. Recommended. (CNB)

*Shepard, Leslie A., ed. ENCYCLOPEDIA OF OCCULTISM AND PARAPSY-CHOLOGY, Second Edition (Gale 0-8103-0196-2, 08/85? [10/85], $245.00, 3 vols., 1,617pp, hc) Non-fiction, reference book of interest as a tool for writers. Revised, updated edition of "a compendium of information on the occult sciences, magic, demonology, superstitions, spiritism, mysticism, metaphysics, psychical science, and parapsychology."

*Sherred, T.L. & Lloyd Biggle, Jr. ALIEN MAIN Main listing under Lloyd Biggle, Jr.

*Shetterly, Will CATS HAVE NO LORD (Ace 0-441-09493-7, 04/85 [03/85], $2.75, 224pp, pb) Fantasy novel; a first novel.

*Shetterly, Will & Emma Bull, eds. LIAVEK (Ace 0-441-48180-9, 07/85 [06/85], $2.95, 274pp, pb) Original anthology set in the fantasy city Liavek. Another "Thieves' World" clone. The background is more interesting than the essentially one-note stories, though the Wolfe does stand out. (FCM)
Contents: Page
Badu's Luck   Emma Bull   nv LIAVEK ,85   1
The Green Rabbit from S'Rian
                             Gene Wolfe   ss LIAVEK ,85   28
Ancient Curses   Patricia C. Wrede   ss LIAVEK ,85   47
Birth Luck   Nancy Kress   ss LIAVEK ,85   67
An Act of Contrition   Steven Brust   ss LIAVEK ,85   86
The Inn of the Demon Camel
                             Jane Yolen   ss LIAVEK ,85 105
The Hands of the Artist   Kara Dalkey   ss LIAVEK ,85 111
The Green Cat   Pamela Dean   nv LIAVEK ,85 125
A Coincidence of Birth   Megan Lindholm   nv LIAVEK ,85 160
Bound Things   Will Shetterly   ss LIAVEK ,85 181
The Fortune Maker   Barry B. Longyear   na LIAVEK ,85 195
Appendix One: A Tourist's Guide to Liavek in the Year 3317
                             [Misc. Material]   ms LIAVEK ,85 256
Appendix Two: A Magician's Primer
                             [Misc. Material]   ms LIAVEK ,85 269
Appendix Three: Liavek: A Creation Myth
                             [Misc. Material]   ms LIAVEK ,85 272

*Shirley, John ECLIPSE (Bluejay 0-312-94130-7, 10/85 [09/85], $8.95, 339pp, pb) Sf novel, first volume in the "Punk saga" of "A Song Called Youth".

*Shupp, Mike WITH FATE CONSPIRE (Ballantine/Del Rey 0-345-32549-4, 12/85 [11/85], $2.95, 306pp, pb) Sf novel, Book One of "The Destiny Makers", a time war series. A first novel.

*Shwartz, Susan M., ed. MOONSINGER'S FRIENDS (Bluejay 0-312-94325-3, 06/85 [07/85], $16.95, 342pp, hc) Original anthology of fantasy stories dedicated to Andre Norton.
Contents: Page
Andre Norton: Beyond the Siege Perilous
                             Susan M. Shwartz   in   1
Sea Wrack   Marion Zimmer Bradley nv MNSNGRF,85 16
Lior and the Sea   Diane Duane   nv MNSNGRF,85   42
The Pale Girl, the Dark Mage, and the Green Sea
                             Tanith Lee   ss MNSNGRF,85   74
The Forest   Poul Anderson   nv MNSNGRF,85   80
The Shadow Hart   Sandra Miesel   ss MNSNGRF,85 112
The Woman Who Loved Raindeer
                             Meredith Ann Pierce nv MNSNGRF,85 122
The Prince of Lightning   Jayge Carr   nv MNSNGRF,85 157
Bright-Eyed Black Pony   Nancy Springer   ss MNSNGRF,85 183
A Flock of Geese   Anne McCaffrey   ss MNSNGRF,85 201
Of Law and Magic   C.J. Cherryh   nv MNSNGRF,85 217
Team Venture   Jo Clayton   nv MNSNGRF,85 246
Sky Sister   Diana L. Paxson   ss MNSNGRF,85 278
Defender of the Faith   Judith Tarr   ss MNSNGRF,85 298
Catalyst   Katherine Kurtz   ss MNSNGRF,85 314
The Foxwife   Jane Yolen   ss WFC #10,84 327
An Open Letter to Andre Norton
                             Joan D. Vinge   ms MNSNGRF,85 336

*Shwartz, Susan M., ed. MOONSINGER'S FRIENDS (Bluejay 0-312-94326-1, 08/85 [07/85], $8.95, 342pp, pb) Paperback edition of the above.

Siegel, Robert WHALESONG (Berkley 0-425-08272-5, 11/85 [10/85], $2.75, 143pp, pb) Reprint (Crossway 1981) fantasy novel.

*Sievert, John C.A.D.S. (Zebra 0-8217-1641-7, 11/85 [11/85], $3.50, 398pp, pb) Sf war novel of the "Computerized Attack/Defense System". They are the "high-tech soldiers of tomorrow, fighting for America's survival."

Silverberg, Robert THE CONGLOMEROID COCKTAIL PARTY (Gollancz 0-575-03544-7, 02/85 [01/85], £8.95, 284pp, hc) Reprint (Arbor House 1984) collection. First British edition.

Silverberg, Robert THE CONGLOMEROID COCKTAIL PARTY (Bantam Spectra 0-553-25077-9, 07/85 [06/85], $2.95, 317pp, pb) Reprint (Arbor House 1984) collection of the 16 short stories Silverberg wrote between 1980 and 1982. Recommended. (CNB)

Silverberg, Robert GILGAMESH THE KING (Bantam Spectra 0-553-25250-X, 11/85 [09/85], $3.95, 306pp, pb) Reprint (Arbor House 1984) historical novel with elements of fantasy.

+Silverberg, Robert NEEDLE IN A TIMESTACK (Ace 0-441-56872-6, 11/85 [10/85], $2.95, 180pp, pb) Reprint (Sphere 1979) collection, following the revised Sphere edition. The original version appeared from Ballantine in 1966, but about half the stories are different here. This is the first American edition of the revision.
Contents: Page
Preface to the Second Edition
                             Robert Silverberg   pr 1977
The Iron Chancellor   Robert Silverberg   nv GAL May,58   1
The Reality Trip   Robert Silverberg   nv IFS May,70   29
The Shrines of Earth   Robert Silverberg   ss ASF Nov,57   53
Black is Beautiful   Robert Silverberg   ss YR2000 ,70   69
Ringing the Changes   Robert Silverberg   ss ALCHEMY,70   87
Translation Error   Robert Silverberg   nv ASF Mar,59 101
The Shadow of Wings   Robert Silverberg   ss IFS Jul,63 125
Absolutely Inflexible   Robert Silverberg   ss FUN Jul,56 141
His Brother's Weeper   Robert Silverberg   nv FUN Mar,59 157

Silverberg, Robert NEXT STOP THE STARS (Tor 0-812-55462-0, 01/86 [12/85], $2.95, 213pp, pb) Reprint (Ace 1962) collection of 5 stories. As a "bonus," to fill up the short book, there is also the first three chapters of MASTER OF LIFE AND DEATH, coming soon from Tor.

*Silverberg, Robert NIGHTWINGS See listing under Cary Bates, Gene Colan & Neal McPheeters.

*Silverberg, Robert SAILING TO BYZANTIUM (Underwood-Miller 0-88733-007-X, 06/85 [05/85], $35.00, 114pp, hc) 250-copy signed/numbered/boxed edition. The first book version of a novella. The trade edition (-008-8) is available for $12.95.

Silverberg, Robert SHADRACH IN THE FURNACE (Baen 0-671-55956-7, 07/85 [06/85], $2.95, 286pp, pb) Reprint (Bobbs-Merrill 1976) sf novel, one of his best books. Recommended. (CNB)

*Silverberg, Robert THE SILENT INVADERS (Tor 0-812-55460-4, 10/85 [09/85], $2.95, 216pp, pb) Although the title only mentions THE SILENT INVADERS (Ace 1963), this is actually an omnibus which also contains the 1957 novella "Valley Beyond Time" (not to be confused with the collection of the same name).
Contents: Page
THE SILENT INVADERS [expanded from "The Silent Invaders" by Calvin M. Knox, sn INF Oct,58]
                             Robert Silverberg   n. ACE 1963   3
Valley Beyond Time   Robert Silverberg   na SFA Dec,57 149

*Silverberg, Robert <u>TOM O'BEDLAM</u> (Fine 0-917657-31-4, 06/85 [05/85], $16.95, 320pp, hc) Sf novel set in a near-future fragmented U.S.A.

Silverberg, Robert <u>TOM O'BEDLAM</u> (QPB/Donald I. Fine no ISBN, 11/85 [12/85], $8.95, 320pp, pb) Reprint (Fine 1985) sf novel, identical to the hardcover except for the jacket printed as the paperback cover.

Silverberg, Robert <u>UP THE LINE</u> (Ballantine/Del Rey 0-345-32585-0, 10/85 [09/85], $2.95, 250pp, pb) Reissue (Ballantine 1969) sf novel. Sixth printing; there are 239,000 in print.

*Silverberg, Robert & Martin H. Greenberg, eds. <u>THE TIME TRAVELERS: A SCIENCE FICTION QUARTET</u> (Fine 0-917657-34-9, 04/85 [03/85], $16.95, 284pp, hc) Anthology of four novellas.

Contents:

			Page
Introduction	Robert Silverberg	in	7
The Ugly Little Boy [Lastborn]			
	Isaac Asimov	na GAL Sep,58	11
Sidewise in Time	Murray Leinster	na ASF Jun,34	67
Consider Her Ways	John Wyndham	na SMTMNVR,56	143
Vintage Season [as Lawrence O'Donnell]			
	Henry Kuttner & C.L. Moore		
		na ASF Sep,46	223

Simak, Clifford D. <u>WAY STATION</u> (SFBC #5710, 11/85 [11/85], $4.98, 182pp, hc) Reprint (Doubleday 1963) sf novel. This one was a Hugo winner.

*Simmons, Dan <u>SONG OF KALI</u> (Bluejay 0-312-94408-X, 11/85 [12/85], $15.95, 311pp, hc) Dark fantasy novel set in Calcutta. A first novel. Recommended. (FCM)

*Singer, Marilyn <u>HORSEMASTER</u> (Atheneum/Argo 0-689-31102-8, 03/85 [02/85], $13.95, 179pp, hc) Young-adult fantasy novel.

Siodmak, Curt <u>DONOVAN'S BRAIN</u> (Carroll & Graf 0-88184-154-4, 07/85 [06/85], $3.50, 160pp, pb) Reprint (Knopf 1942) sf novel.

*Skerl, Jennie <u>WILLIAM S. BURROUGHS</u> (Twayne 0-8057-7438-6, 1985 [12/85], $15.95, 127pp, hc) Non-fiction, critical study.

*Skipp, John M. & Craig Spector <u>FRIGHT NIGHT</u> (Tor 0-812-52564-7, 09/85 [08/85], $2.95, 250pp, pb) Novelization of a horror movie script by Tom Holland.

Sky, Kathleen <u>DEATH'S ANGEL</u> (Bantam Spectra 0-553-24983-5, 07/85 [06/85], $2.95, 213pp, pb) Reissue (Bantam 1981) Star Trek novel. 4th printing.

Sky, Kathleen <u>VULCAN!</u> (Bantam Spectra 0-553-24633-X, 06/85 [05/85], $2.95, 175pp, pb) Reissue (Bantam 1978) Star Trek novel. 5th printing.

*Sky, Kathleen <u>WITCHDAME</u> (Berkley 0-425-07449-8, 01/85 [12/84], $2.95, 323pp, pb) Fantasy novel, first of a series.

+Sladek, John <u>TIK-TOK</u> (DAW 0-88677-048-3, 06/85 [05/85], $2.95, 254pp, pb) Reprint (Gollancz 1983) sf novel, first U.S. edition. This novel of a robot whose "Asimov circuit" goes wild won the 1984 British SF Award.

Sleator, William <u>FINGERS</u> (Bantam/Starfire 0-553-25004-3, 05/85 [04/85], $2.50, 197pp, pb) Reprint (Atheneum 1983) young-adult sf novel.

*Sleator, William <u>SINGULARITY</u> (Dutton 0-525-44161-1, 05/85 [04/85], $12.95, 170pp, hc) Young-adult sf novel.

*Slote, Alfred <u>THE TROUBLE ON JANUS</u> (Lippincott 0-397-32158-9, 10/85 [10/85], $11.50, 121pp, hc) Young-adult sf novel in the series about Jack Jameson and his robot buddy Danny One. Illustrations by James Watts.

*Slusser, George E. & Eric S. Rabkin, eds. <u>SHADOWS OF THE MAGIC LAMP: FANTASY AND SCIENCE FICTION IN FILM</u> (S. Illinois Univ. Press 0-8093-1150-X, 09/85 [08/85], $19.95, 259pp, hc) 14 essays presented at the 4th Eaton Conference, covering sf, fantasy, and the cinema.

*Smeds, Dave <u>THE SORCERY WITHIN</u> (Ace 0-441-77557-8, 08/85 [07/85], $2.95, 295pp, pb) Fantasy novel, a first novel.

Smith, Cordwainer <u>THE BEST OF CORDWAINER SMITH</u> (Ballantine/Del Rey 0-345-32302-5, 07/85 [06/85], $3.50, 377pp, pb) Reissue (SFBC 1975) collection edited by J.J. Pierce. The one Smith book to read if you haven't read any. Recommended. (CNB) 3rd Del Rey printing.

Smith, Cordwainer <u>THE INSTRUMENTALITY OF MANKIND</u> (Ballantine/Del Rey 0-345-32301-7, 07/85 [06/85], $2.95, 238pp, pb) Reissue (Del Rey 1979) collection. 2nd Del Rey printing.

Smith, Cordwainer <u>NORSTRILIA</u> (Ballantine/Del Rey 0-345-32300-9, 07/85 [06/85], $2.95, 277pp, pb) Reissue (Del Rey 1975) omnibus sf novel. Contains the complete text of the connected novels THE PLANET BUYER (1964) and THE UNDERPEOPLE (1968). The only novel (under this name) by one of the most individual writers in the field. Recommended. (CNB)

Smith, E.E. "Doc" <u>THE SKYLARK OF SPACE</u> (Berkley 0-425-08636-4, 12/85 [11/85], $2.75, 159pp, pb) Reissue (Buffalo Book Co 1946) sf novel, first in the "Skylark" series. 5th Berkley printing.

*Smith, E.E. "Doc" & Stephen Goldin <u>REVOLT OF THE GALAXY</u> (Berkley 0-425-07675-X, 05/85 [04/85], $2.75, 186pp, pb) Sf novel, #10 in the "Family d'Alembert" series, based on work by "Doc" Smith, written by Goldin.

*Smith, Evelyn E. <u>THE COPY SHOP</u> (Doubleday 0-385-03822-4, 06/85 [05/85], $12.95, 178pp, hc) Sf novel. Aliens land in New York and nobody notices.

*Smith, L. Neil <u>THE GALLATIN DIVERGENCE</u> (Ballantine/Del Rey 0-345-30383-0, 09/85 [08/85], $2.95, 223pp, pb) Sf novel, part of a parallel-world series about the North American Confederacy.

*Smith, R. Dixon <u>LOST IN THE RENTHARPIAN HILLS: SPANNING THE DECADES WITH CARL JACOBI</u> (Bowling Green Popular Press 0-87972-288-6, 09/85 [10/85], $8.95, 146pp, pb) Non-fiction, biography and bibliography of a *Weird Tales* writer, illustrated with photos and magazine artwork.

*Smith, R. Dixon <u>LOST IN THE RENTHARPIAN HILLS: SPANNING THE DECADES WITH CARL JACOBI</u> (Bowling Green Popular Press 0-87972-287-7, 09/85 [10/85], $17.95, 146pp, hc) Hardcover version of the above.

*Smith, Stephanie <u>SNOW-EYES</u> (Atheneum/Argo 0-689-31129-X, 09/85 [09/85], $13.95, 185pp, hc) Young-adult fantasy novel, a first novel. Well-written with haunting atmosphere, but the plot is weak. Keep an eye out for Smith's next book. (DLN)

*Snyder, Gene <u>TOMB SEVEN</u> (Charter 0-441-81643-6, 10/85 [09/85], $3.50, 279pp, pb) Adventure/horror/fantasy novel.

Snyder, Zilpha Keatley <u>AND ALL BETWEEN</u> (Tor 0-812-55478-7, 08/85 [07/85], $2.95, 252pp, pb) Reprint (Atheneum 1976) sf novel, second in the "Green Sky" trilogy.

Snyder, Zilpha Keatley <u>BELOW THE ROOT</u> (Tor 0-812-55476-0, 04/85 [03/85], $2.95, 253pp, pb) Reprint (Atheneum 1975) sf novel, first book of the "Green-Sky" trilogy.

Snyder, Zilpha Keatley <u>THE HEADLESS CUPID</u> (Dell Yearling 0-440-43507-2, 10/85 [09/85], $3.25, 203pp, pb) Reprint (Atheneum 1971) young-adult novel, a ghost story about a poltergeist; a Newbery Honor Book.

Snyder, Zilpha Keatley <u>UNTIL THE CELEBRATION</u> (Tor 0-812-55480-9, 11/85 [10/85], $2.95, 254pp, pb) Reprint (Atheneum 1977) sf novel, the Third Book of Green Sky.

Somtow, S.P. <u>VAMPIRE JUNCTION</u> (Berkley 0-425-07746-2, 08/85 [07/85], $3.50, 362pp, pb) Reprint (Donning 1984) horror/fantasy novel. The author is Somtow Sucharitkul.

*<u>Space and Time [#69, Winter 1986]</u> Gordon Linzner, ed. (Space and Time, 12/85 [12/85], $4.00, 118pp, pb)

Contents:

			Page
Editor's Page	Gordon Linzner	ed S&T #69,85	2
Journey from Darchos	Karen Shapiro	ss S&T #69,85	4
Looking at the Cover Illustrations of Science Fiction Novels			
	James L. Dalton	pm S&T #69,85	18
The Apprenticeship of Alan Patch			
	R.E. Klein	ss S&T #69,85	19
Moonborne	Peter Larson	pm S&T #69,85	30
The Champion of Night	John Salonia & Traci Salonia		
		ss S&T #69,85	32
The Entombment	Jean Poynter	pm S&T #69,85	48
Cindy, Grounded	Steve Eng	pm S&T #69,85	48
The Thing in the Icebox	A.K. Molnar	vi S&T #69,85	49
Blue Star	Chris Hayes	ss S&T #69,85	51
Hanging Town	Steve Sneyd	pm S&T #69,85	56
The Return to Hell	David C. Smith	ss S&T #69,85	58
The Two Dimensional Man and What to Do About Him			
	Marion Cohen	pm S&T #69,85	71
The Complex	Richard Singer	ss S&T #69,85	74
The Secret Lives of Drones			
	Robert Frazier	pm S&T #69,85	83
The Host	Sheldon R. Jaffery	ss S&T #69,85	84
Stones	Robert F. Whisler	pm S&T #69,85	88
Bad Chance	John Moore	vi S&T #69,85	89
The Shanahy's Treasure	Cooper McLaughlin	ss S&T #69,85	91

*Spector, Craig & John M. Skipp <u>FRIGHT NIGHT</u> Main listing under John M. Skipp.

*Spinrad, Norman <u>CHILD OF FORTUNE</u> (Bantam Spectra 0-553-5089-3, 07/85 [06/85], $16.95, 483pp, hc) Sf novel. A companion volume (but not a sequel) to THE VOID CAPTAIN'S TALE.

Spinrad, Norman <u>CHILD OF FORTUNE</u> (SFBC #6291, 10/85 [11/85], $6.50, 467pp, hc) Reprint (Bantam Spectra 1985) sf novel. A companion volume to THE VOID CAPTAIN'S TALE.

Spinrad, Norman <u>THE MIND GAME</u> (Bantam Spectra 0-553-25061-2, 08/85 [07/85], $3.50, 342pp, pb) Reprint (Jove 1980) novel. Non-sf, set in Hollywood, listed for Spinrad completists only.

Spinrad, Norman SONGS FROM THE STARS (Bantam Spectra 0-553-24879-0, 07/85 [06/85], $2.95, 275pp, pb) Reprint (Simon & Schuster 1980) sf novel about hippies and '60s values in the future.

Springer, Nancy THE BLACK BEAST (Corgi 0-552-12428-1, 1985 [09/85], £1.75, 207pp, pb) Reprint (Timescape 1982) fantasy novel.

Springer, Nancy THE SABLE MOON (Corgi 0-552-12427-3, 07/85 [06/85], £1.95, 264pp, pb) Reprint (Pocket 1981) fantasy novel, conclusion of the "Book of the Isle" trilogy. First British edition.

Springer, Nancy THE SILVER SUN (Pocket 0-671-61117-8, 12/85 [12/85], $3.50, 292pp, pb) Reissue (Pocket 1980) fantasy novel, Vol. II of "Book of the Isles". This is a revised version of THE BOOK OF SUNS (Pocket 1977).

Springer, Nancy THE WHITE HART (Pocket 0-671-60683-2, 10/85 [09/85], $3.50, 222pp, pb) Reissue (Pocket 1979) fantasy novel.

*__Springer, Nancy__ WINGS OF FLAME (Tor 0-312-93932-9, 05/85 [04/85], $13.95, 252pp, hc) Fantasy quest novel.

Spruill, Steven THE IMPERATOR PLOT (Tor 0-812-55488-4, 06/85 [05/85], $2.95, 283pp, pb) Reprint (Doubleday 1983) sf novel.

*__St. Clair, Margaret__ THE BEST OF MARGARET ST. CLAIR (Academy Chicago 0-89733-164-8, 1985 [11/85], $4.95, 271pp, pb) Collection of 20 stories plus a new introduction by the author, edited by Martin H. Greenberg.
Contents: Page
Introduction   Margaret St. Clair   in   v
Idris' Pig [The Sacred Martian Pig]
                          Margaret St. Clair   nv STS Jul,49   1
The Gardener   Margaret St. Clair   ss TWS Oct,49   40
Child of Void   Margaret St. Clair   ss SSS Nov,49   53
Hathor's Pets   Margaret St. Clair   ss STS Jan,50   70
The Pillows   Margaret St. Clair   ss TWS Jun,50   84
The Listening Child   Margaret St. Clair   ss FSF Dec,50   98
Brightness Falls from the Air
                          Margaret St. Clair   ss FSF Apr,51 109
The Man Who Sold Rope to the Gnoles [as Idris Seabright]
                          Margaret St. Clair   ss FSF Oct,51 117
The Causes [as Idris Seabright]
                          Margaret St. Clair   ss FSF Jun,52 122
An Egg a Month from All Over [as Idris Seabright]
                          Margaret St. Clair   ss FSF Oct,52 135
Prott   Margaret St. Clair   ss GAL Jan,53 143
New Ritual [as Idris Seabright]
                          Margaret St. Clair   ss FSF Jan,53 159
Brenda   Margaret St. Clair   ss WRT Mar,54 168
Short in the Chest [as Idris Seabright]
                          Margaret St. Clair   ss FUN Jul,54 180
Horrer Howce   Margaret St. Clair   ss GAL Jul,56 190
The Wines of Earth [as Idris Seabright]
                          Margaret St. Clair   ss FSF Sep,57 203
The Invested Libido   Margaret St. Clair   ss SAT Aug,58 211
The Nuse Man   Margaret St. Clair   ss GAL Feb,60 220
An Old-Fashioned Bird Christmas
                          Margaret St. Clair   nv GAL Dec,61 232
Wryneck, Draw Me   Margaret St. Clair   ss CRY # 8,80 255

*__Stableford, Brian__ THE COSMIC PERSPECTIVE/CUSTER'S LAST STAND (Drumm no ISBN, 10/85 [10/85], $5.00, 19+25pp, pb) Collection of two new stories printed back-to-back, Ace Double style. This is the limited edition version, signed/numbered with variant cover stock and paper. The regular edition price is $2.00. Drumm Booklet #21.
Contents: Page
Introduction to "The Cosmic Perspective"
                          Brian Stableford   in CSMCPRS,85   3
The Cosmic Perspective   Brian Stableford   ss CSMCPRS,85   5
Introduction to "Custer's Last Stand"
                          Brian Stableford   in CSMCPRS,85   3
Custer's Last Stand   Brian Stableford   ss CSMCPRS,85   5

+__Stableford, Brian__ THE LAST DAYS OF THE EDGE OF THE WORLD (Ace 0-441-47077-7, 09/85 [08/85], $2.75, 167pp, pb) Reprint (Hutchinson 1978) juvenile fantasy novel. First U.S. edition.

*__Stableford, Brian__ SCIENTIFIC ROMANCE IN BRITAIN, 1890-1950 (Fourth Estate 0-947795-85-5, 1985 [10/85], £19.50, 372pp, hc) Non-fiction, critical study of the history, themes, and major writers of these 60 years, including Wells, Hodgson, Doyle, Stapledon, and Shiel.

+__Stableford, Brian & David Langford__ THE THIRD MILLENNIUM: A HISTORY OF THE WORLD: AD 2000-3000 (Knopf 0-394-53980-X, 08/85 [07/85], $20.00, 224pp, hc) Reprint (U.K. 1985), first U.S. edition. Scenario futurology by two sf and science writers. Half way between speculation and fiction.

+__Stableford, Brian & David Langford__ THE THIRD MILLENNIUM: A HISTORY OF THE WORLD: AD 2000-3000 (Knopf 0-394-74151-X, 08/85 [07/85], $13.95, 224pp, pb) Paperback edition of the above.

*__Stacy, Ryder__ DOOMSDAY WARRIOR #4: BLOODY AMERICA (Zebra 0-8217-1556-9, 03/85 [02/85], $2.50, 250pp, pb) Sf survivalist novel.

*__Stacy, Ryder__ DOOMSDAY WARRIOR #5: AMERICA'S LAST DECLARATION (Zebra 0-8217-1608-5, 06/85 [05/85], $2.50, 256pp, pb) Post-catastrophe survivalist novel.

*__Stacy, Ryder__ DOOMSDAY WARRIOR #6: AMERICAN REBELLION (Zebra 0-8217-1659-X, 09/85 [08/85], $2.50, 255pp, pb) Post-holocaust adventure novel.

*__Stardate__ [v.1 # 8, October 1985] Ted White & David F. Bischoff, eds. (Associates International, Inc., 10/85 [09/85], $2.00, 48pp, pb)
Contents: Page
Editorial   David F. Bischoff & Ted White
                                                ed SDA Oct,85   3
Each Prisoner Pent   Damon Knight   ss SDA Oct,85   6
The Other Frank Herbert   Charles Platt   iv SDA Oct,85   9
Operation Shadowfall--a Star Trek Role-playing Scenario
                          Blaine Pardoe & Dale L. Kemper
                                                gr SDA Oct,85   10
The Truce   Thomas Sullivan   ss SDA Oct,85   18
Jaynz Ships of the Galaxy--Wizard Class Ships
                          David Miles & Dale L. Kemper
                                                gr SDA Oct,85   20
Midnight Pearls Blue   William F. Wu   vi SDA Oct,85   26
On the Brightside   Steve Stiles   cs SDA   28
Nahallywood: 'George Romero and the Day of the Dead'
                          Ed Naha   mr SDA Oct,85   28
Nahallywood: Coming Attractions
                          Ed Naha   mr SDA   30
Star Bases: The Federation's Handmaiden
                          Pete Rogan   gr SDA Oct,85   32
Roller Derby   Grant Canfield   cs SDA   34
Some Star Bases: A Profile
                          Pete Rogan   gr SDA Oct,85   39
The Rosey-Cheeked Girl Who Danced on the Deck of the Titanic
                          Jack C. Haldeman, II vi SDA Oct,85   44

*__Stardate__ [v.1 # 9, December 1985] Ted White & David F. Bischoff, eds. (Associates International, Inc., 12/85 [12/85], $2.00, 54pp, pb)
Contents: Page
Doctor Who: The Role-Playing Game from FASA (Part One)
                          David F. Bischoff   gr SDA Dec,85   4
Editorial   Ted White   ed SDA Dec,85   6
Cycles   James Stevens   ss SDA Dec,85   10
Science Fiction Cinema   Charles Platt   ar SDA Dec,85   12
Jaynz Ships of the Galaxy: Aral (OSB-0762) Orion Blockade
  Runner   David Miles & Dale L. Kemper
                                                gr SDA Dec,85   16
Jaynz Ships of the Galaxy: Ticonderoga-class Light Cruiser
                          David Miles & Dale L. Kemper
                                                gr SDA Dec,85   18
Nahallywood: Invasion of the Teenagers from Mars
                          Ed Naha   ar SDA Dec,85   20
Nahallywood: Coming Attractions
                          Ed Naha   mr SDA   22
Bye, Bye Lullabies   Charles Sheffield   ss SDA Dec,85   24
The Barrier of Essai   Michael A. DeLuca, II gr SDA Dec,85   26
On the Brightside   Steve Stiles   cs SDA   28
Sensor Readings   G.D. Swick & David F. Bischoff
                                                ar SDA Dec,85   34
Dr. Sharon N. Farber's Science Fiction Weight Loss Diet
                          Sharon N. Farber   ms SDA Dec,85   38
Group Phenomena   Thomas F. Monteleone ss SDA Dec,85   40
Roller Derby   Grant Canfield   cs SDA   42
Dear Ybba   Larry Tritten   ss SDA Dec,85   48
Quartermaster Corps   Pete Rogan   gr SDA Dec,85   50

*__Stasheff, Christopher__ THE WARLOCK ENRAGED (Ace 0-441-87340-5, 12/85 [11/85], $2.95, 251pp, pb) Sf novel, fifth in the "Warlock" series.

*__Steele, Linda__ IBIS (DAW 0-88677-077-7, 09/85 [08/85], $2.95, 221pp, pb) Sf novel, a first novel.

**Steele, Mary Q.__ THE FIRST OF THE PENGUINS (Greenwillow 0-688-04801-3, 07/85 [06/85], $10.25, 152pp, hc) Reprint (Macmillan 1973) young-adult fantasy time travel novel.

*__Sterling, Bruce__ SCHISMATRIX (Arbor House 0-87795-645-6, 06/85 [05/85], $15.95, 288pp, hc) Sf novel set in Sterling's Shaper/Mech universe. A remarkable, intricate vision of the future. Recommended. (FCM)

**Stevens, Francis__ CLAIMED (Carroll & Graf 0-88184-155-2, 07/85 [06/85], $3.95, 192pp, pb) Reprint (Avalon 1966) fantasy novel. The author, Gertrude Bennett (1884-1939?), one of the earliest woman fantasy writers, wrote this dark fantasy in 1920.

**Stewart, Fred Mustard__ THE METHUSELAH ENZYME (Pocket 0-671-54359-8, 12/85 [12/85], $3.95, 307pp, pb) Reprint (Arbor House 1970) sf/medical novel about a rejuvenation drug.

*__Stirling, S.M.__ SNOWBROTHER (NAL/Signet 0-451-13490-7, 03/85 [02/85], $2.95, 251pp, pb) Fantasy novel.

*__Stith, John E.__ MEMORY BLANK (Ace 0-441-52417-6, 01/86 [12/85], $2.95, 230pp, pb) Sf mystery novel set on an orbiting colony.

Stoker, Bram DRACULA (Unicorn 0-88101-020-0, 10/85 [12/85], $14.95, 263pp, hc) Reprint (Constable 1897) classic horror novel, a new illustrated version with art by Greg Hildebrandt. The text follows the first edition. The book is oversize with big print and full-color illustrations. It harks back to the illustrated books of the early 20th century.

*Stout, Rex UNDER THE ANDES (Penzler 0-89296-119-8, 08/85 [07/85], $15.95, 286pp, hc) First book publication of an early, really bad novel which originally appeared in *All-Story Magazine* in 1914 -- adventures with a lost race of Incas. (CNB)

*Straub, Peter BLUE ROSE (Underwood-Miller 0-88733-005-3, 09/85 [09/85], $35.00, 92pp, hc) Novelette of horror/dark fantasy. Signed, slipcased, limited edition of 600 numbered copies.

Straub, Peter FLOATING DRAGON (Berkley 0-425-08206-7, 11/85 [10/85], $4.50, 595pp, pb) Reissue (Putnam 1983) horror/dark fantasy novel of man-made and supernatural evils besetting a suburban town; 6th Berkley printing.

Straub, Peter GHOST STORY (Hill House 0-931771-00-5, 03/85 [02/85], $50.00 + $1.75 postage, 483pp, hc) Reprint (Coward McCann 1979) fantasy novel, in a boxed, signed, numbered edition of 400 copies. There are excellent illustrations by Stephen Gervais. This is the first book from a new limited editions publisher.

Straub, Peter IF YOU COULD SEE ME NOW (Pocket 0-671-50633-1, 01/86 [12/85], $3.95, 328pp, pb) Reissue (Cape 1977) horror novel, 7th printing.

Straub, Peter SHADOWLAND (Berkley 0-425-08207-5, 11/85 [10/85], $4.50, 468pp, pb) Reissue (Coward, McCann 1980) horror/dark fantasy novel of a magician's apprentices in an old house in Vermont; 13th Berkley printing.

Straub, Peter UNDER VENUS (Berkley 0-425-07033-6, 02/85 [01/85], $3.95, 289pp, pb) Reprint from the omnibus volume WILD ANIMALS (Putnam 1984). Associational -- non-fantasy. This is Straub's previously unpublished second novel. This edition is the first separate one.

Straub, Peter WILD ANIMALS (Quality Paperback Book Club/Putnam no ISBN, 1985 [10/85], no price given, 591pp, pb) Reprint (Putnam 1984) omnibus edition of JULIA (1975), IF YOU COULD SEE ME NOW (1978), and his previously unpublished second novel UNDER VENUS. Hardcover printing with trade paperback binding; available only to book club members.

Straub, Peter & Stephen King THE TALISMAN Main listing under Stephen King.

*Streiber, Whitley WOLF OF SHADOWS (Sierra Club/Knopf 0-394-87224-X, 09/85 [09/85], $9.95, 105pp, hc) Young-adult sf novella of a wolf pack during a nuclear winter.

Streiber, Whitley & James Kunetka WAR DAY (Warner 0-446-32630-5, 04/85 [03/85], $4.50, 515pp, pb) Reprint (Holt 1984) post-holocaust sf novel, with a 1,400,000 first printing.

*Stryker, Hal NYPD 2025 (Pinnacle 0-523-42514-7, 06/85 [05/85], $2.95, 185pp, pb) Sf novel; near-future police adventure, first of a new series.

Sturgeon, Theodore THE DREAMING JEWELS (Bluejay 0-312-94118-8, 04/85 [03/85], $7.95, 186pp, pb) Reprint (Greenberg 1950) sf novel, with new b&w illustrations by Rowena Morrill. Despite the jacket blurb, this book did not win the International Fantasy Award. It's Sturgeon's first novel and quite good. (CNB)

Sturgeon, Theodore THE GOLDEN HELIX (Bluejay 0-312-94186-2, 05/85 [04/85], $7.95, 335pp, pb) Reprint (SFBC 1979) collection.

*Sucharitkul, Somtow THE DARKLING WIND (Bantam Spectra 0-553-24982-7, 07/85 [06/85], $3.50, 384pp, pb) Sf novel, conclusion of the "Inquestor" series.

*Sucharitkul, Somtow V: THE ALIEN SWORDMASTER (Pinnacle 0-523-42441-8, 04/85 [03/85], $2.95, 185pp, pb) Sf novel based on the tv series.

*Sullivan, Faith MRS. DEMMING AND THE MYTHICAL BEAST (Macmillan 0-02-527320-5, 11/85 [12/85], $16.95FPT, 341pp, hc) A housewife encounters the god Pan in this literary fantasy novel.

*Sullivan, Timothy V: THE FLORIDA PROJECT (Pinnacle 0-523-43418-9, 03/85 [02/85], $2.95, 178pp, pb) Novelization based on the tv series. Fifth book in the series.

*Sullivan, Timothy V: THE NEW ENGLAND RESISTANCE (Pinnacle 0-523-42467-1, 07/85 [06/85], $2.95, 180pp, pb) Media tie-in sf novel.

*Sussex, Lucy, Jenny Blackford, Russell Blackford & Norman Talbot, eds. CONTRARY MODES Main listing under Jenny Blackford.

*Suyin, Han THE ENCHANTRESS (Bantam 0-553-05071-0, 02/85 [01/85], $16.95, 345pp, hc) Historical novel with elements of fantasy set in medieval China and Siam. Recommended. (CNB)

Suyin, Han THE ENCHANTRESS (Bantam 0-553-25151-1, 01/86 [12/85], $3.95, 375pp, pb) Reprint (Bantam hc 1985) historical novel with elements of fantasy.

*Swanwick, Michael IN THE DRIFT (Ace 0-441-35869-1, 02/85 [01/85], $2.95, 195pp, pb) Ace SF Special, a first novel. Although this has flashes of Swanwick's fine writing, it's extremely uneven. (DLN)

*Swycaffer, Jefferson P. BECOME THE HUNTED (Avon 0-380-89608-7, 07/85 [06/85], $2.95, 160pp, pb) Sf novel; a prequel to his first novel, NOT IN OUR STARS.

*Swycaffer, Jefferson P. THE PRAESIDIUM OF ARCHIVE (Avon 0-380-89663-X, 01/86 [12/85], $2.95, 197pp, pb) Collection of 6 connected sf stories. They all seem to be originals. This is the fourth book set in the "Concordat" universe.
Contents:

			Page
Upon the Eve of the Last of Days	Jefferson P. Swycaffer	pr PRSDMAR,86	1
Case and Cause	Jefferson P. Swycaffer	nv PRSDMAR,86	5
The Damnable Price	Jefferson P. Swycaffer	nv PRSDMAR,86	41
Escalation	Jefferson P. Swycaffer	nv PRSDMAR,86	86
A Precise Young Death	Jefferson P. Swycaffer	nv PRSDMAR,86	133
To Live; To Learn	Jefferson P. Swycaffer	nv PRSDMAR,86	154
Archive Midwinter	Jefferson P. Swycaffer	nv PRSDMAR,86	175

*Swycaffer, Jefferson P. THE UNIVERSAL PREY (Avon 0-380-89662-1, 10/85 [09/85], $2.95, 191pp, pb) Sf novel. "He's an assassin without fear...on a deadly mission that could blow the Concordat apart." Third book of a series.

+Synge, Ursula SWAN'S WING (Ace 0-441-79094-1, 04/85 [03/85], $2.95, 152pp, pb) Reprint (Bodley Head 1981) fantasy novel. First U.S. edition.

Takei, George & Robert Lynn Asprin MIRROR FRIEND, MIRROR FOE Main listing under Robert Lynn Asprin.

*Talbot, Norman, Jenny Blackford, Russell Blackford & Lucy Sussex, eds. CONTRARY MODES Main listing under Jenny Blackford.

*Tarr, Judith THE GOLDEN HORN (Bluejay 0-312-94190-0, 09/85 [08/85], $14.95, 262pp, hc) Fantasy novel, second in "The Hound and the Falcon" trilogy. It's set in Byzantium at the time of the Crusaders' invasion and has more of the historical and less of the fantastic than the first book; Brother Alf's powers and problems seem less compelling this time, but the writing is still good. (FCM)

*Tarr, Judith THE ISLE OF GLASS (Bluejay 0-312-94237-0, 03/85 [02/85], $14.95, 276pp, hc) Fantasy novel, a first novel and the first book in a trilogy. Recommended. (FCM)

*Teague, Robert & Michael Goodwin A GUIDE TO THE COMMONWEALTH: THE OFFICIAL GUIDE TO ALAN DEAN FOSTER'S HUMANX COMMONWEALTH UNIVERSE (Galagraphics no ISBN, 09/85 [09/85], price unknown, 70pp, pb) Non-fiction guide to Foster's fictional worlds, with maps, sections on natural history and technology, etc.; there's an introduction by Foster. For further information, write to Michael C. Goodwin, 4987 S. 2700 West, Roy UT 84067.

*Tepper, Sheri S. BLOOD HERITAGE (Tor 0-812-526233-6, 01/86 [12/85], $3.50, 287pp, pb) Horror novel.

*Tepper, Sheri S. THE FLIGHT OF MAVIN MANYSHAPED (Ace 0-441-24092-5, 06/85 [05/85], $2.75, 186pp, pb) Fantasy novel, book 2 in the "Mavin" series.

*Tepper, Sheri S. JINIAN FOOTSEER (Tor 0-812-55610-0, 09/85 [08/85], $2.95, 284pp, pb) Fantasy novel set in the "Land of the True Game", first of a new series.

*Tepper, Sheri S. MARIANNE, THE MAGUS, AND THE MANTICORE (Ace 0-441-51944-X, 12/85 [11/85], $2.75, 185pp, pb) Fantasy novel set in the modern world but featuring legendary creatures in a quasi-Turkish country and another world.

*Tepper, Sheri S. THE SEARCH OF MAVIN MANYSHAPED (Ace 0-441-75712-X, 09/85 [08/85], $2.75, 168pp, pb) Fantasy novel, book 3 in the "Mavin" series.

*Tepper, Sheri S. THE SONG OF MAVIN MANYSHAPED (Ace 0-441-77523-3, 03/85 [02/85], $2.75, 183pp, pb) Fantasy novel, book 1 in the "Mavin" series.

*Tepper, Sheri S. THE TRUE GAME (Corgi 0-552-12620-9, 08/85 [10/85], £4.95, 543pp, pb) Omnibus edition of a fantasy trilogy set in the land of the True Game.
Contents:

			Page
KING'S BLOOD FOUR	Sheri S. Tepper	n. ACE	1983
NECROMANCER NINE	Sheri S. Tepper	n. ACE	1983
WIZARD'S ELEVEN	Sheri S. Tepper	n. ACE	1984

+Tepper, Sheri S. THE TRUE GAME (SFBC #6319, 10/85 [11/85], $7.98, 470pp, hc) Omnibus edition of KING'S BLOOD FOUR (Berkley 1983), NECROMANCER NINE (Berkley 1983), and WIZARD'S ELEVEN (Berkley 1984) plus some maps and notes. An earlier version appeared in England (Corgi 1985).

Tessier, Thomas PHANTOM (Berkley 0-425-08027-7, 06/85 [05/85], $2.95, 228pp, pb) Reprint (Atheneum 1982) dark fantasy/horror novel.

Tevis, Walter MOCKINGBIRD (Bantam 0-553-14144-9, 02/85 [01/85], $2.95, 276pp, pb) Reissue (Doubleday 1980) sf novel, a Nebula Award finalist. 2nd printing.

Tevis, Walter THE STEPS OF THE SUN (Berkley 0-425-07645-8, 04/85 [03/85], $2.95, 259pp, pb) Reprint (Doubleday 1983) sf novel.

Tevis, Walter THE STEPS OF THE SUN (Corgi 0-552-12496-6, 07/85 [06/85], £2.95, 253pp, pb) Reprint (Doubleday 1983) sf novel. First British paperback.

+Thomas, Gwyn & Kevin Crossley-Holland, trans. TALES FROM THE MABINOGION Main listing under Kevin Crossley-Holland.

*Thompson, Raymond H. THE RETURN FROM AVALON: A STUDY OF THE ARTHURIAN LEGEND IN MODERN FICTION (Greenwood 0-313-23291-1, 02/85 [08/85], $29.95, 206pp, hc) Non-fiction, critical study covering Arthurian themes in realistic fiction, historical fiction, and fantasy/sf.

Thompson, Ruth Plumly THE COWARDLY LION OF OZ (Ballantine/Del Rey 0-345-31586-3, 07/85 [06/85], $5.95, 252pp, pb) Reprint (Reilly & Lee 1923) juvenile fantasy novel, "Oz" #17, with the original Neill illustrations.

Thompson, Ruth Plumly THE GIANT HORSE OF OZ (Ballantine/Del Rey 0-345-32359-9, 10/85 [09/85], $5.95, 238pp, pb) Reprint (Reilly & Lee 1928) juvenile fantasy novel, "Oz" #22, with the original Neill illustrations.

Thompson, Ruth Plumly THE GNOME KING OF OZ (Ballantine/Del Rey 0-345-32358-0, 10/85 [09/85], $5.95, 237pp, pb) Reprint (Reilly & Lee 1927) juvenile fantasy novel, "Oz" #21, with the original Neill illustrations.

Thompson, Ruth Plumly GRAMPA IN OZ (Ballantine/Del Rey 0-345-31587-1, 07/85 [06/85], $5.95, 227pp, pb) Reprint (Reilly & Lee 1924) juvenile fantasy novel, "Oz" #18, with the original Neill illustrations.

Thompson, Ruth Plumly THE HUNGRY TIGER OF OZ (Ballantine/Del Rey 0-345-31589-8, 07/85 [06/85], $5.95, 214pp, pb) Reprint (Reilly & Lee 1926) juvenile fantasy novel, "Oz" #20, with the original Neill illustrations.

Thompson, Ruth Plumly JACK PUMPKINHEAD OF OZ (Ballantine/Del Rey 0-345-32360-2, 10/85 [09/85], $5.95, 222pp, pb) Reprint (Reilly & Lee 1929) juvenile fantasy novel, "Oz" #23, with the original Neill illustrations.

Thompson, Ruth Plumly KABUMPO IN OZ (Ballantine/Del Rey 0-345-31585-5, 07/85 [06/85], $5.95, 259pp, pb) Reprint (Reilly & Lee 1922) juvenile fantasy novel, "Oz" #16, with the original Neill illustrations.

Thompson, Ruth Plumly THE LOST KING OF OZ (Ballantine/Del Rey 0-345-31588-X, 07/85 [06/85], $5.95, 236pp, pb) Reprint (Reilly & Lee 1925) juvenile fantasy novel, "Oz" #19, with the original Neill illustrations.

Thompson, Ruth Plumly THE ROYAL BOOK OF OZ (Ballantine/Del Rey 0-345-31584-7, 07/85 [06/85], $5.95, 263pp, pb) Reprint (Reilly & Lee 1921) juvenile fantasy novel, "Oz" #15. This whole series is a strange size -- the height of a trade paperback, but the width of a mass market book. The original John R. Neill illustrations are included.

*Thompson, William Irwin ISLANDS OUT OF TIME: A MEMOIR OF THE LAST DAYS OF ATLANTIS (Dial/Doubleday 0-385-19571-0, 09/85 [08/85], $16.95, 222pp, hc) Fantasy novel of Atlantis doomed by technology. It's billed as "metafiction."

*Thurston, Robert Q COLONY (Ace 0-441-69660-0, 02/85 [01/85], $2.75, 218pp, pb) Sf novel.

*Thurston, Robert & Glen S. Larson BATTLESTAR GALACTICA 11: THE NIGHTMARE MACHINE Main listing under Glen S. Larson.

Tilley, Patrick THE AMTRAK WARS, BOOK TWO: FIRST FAMILY (Severn House 0-7278-1226-2, 11/85 [10/85], £8.95, 344pp, hc) Reprint (Sphere 1985) Sf novel of a post-holocaust Federation vs. mutants; second in the series. This is the first hardcover edition.

Tilley, Patrick CLOUD WARRIOR (Baen 0-671-55972-9, 08/85 [07/85], $3.50, 222pp, pb) Reprint (Sphere 1983 as THE AMTRAK WARS PART 1, CLOUD WARRIOR) sf novel, first in "The Amtrak Wars" series, set in a post-holocaust world.

*Tiptree, James, Jr. BRIGHTNESS FALLS FROM THE AIR (Tor 0-312-93097-6, 03/85 [02/85], $14.95, 382pp, hc) Sf novel. A near perfect blend of science fiction, mystery and romance, paced too well to put down at all. One of the year's best books. (DLN)

Tiptree, James, Jr. BRIGHTNESS FALLS FROM THE AIR (SFBC #6341, 05/85 [04/85], $4.98, 270pp, hc) Reprint (Tor 1985) sf novel.

*Tiptree, James, Jr. BYTE BEAUTIFUL: EIGHT SCIENCE FICTION STORIES (Doubleday 0-385-19653-9, 11/85 [11/85], $12.95, 177pp, hc) Collection of eight stories with an introduction by Michael Bishop. The stories are partly from earlier collections and are gathered as a "best of."
Contents: Page
Introduction: Bringing It All Back Home
                           Michael Bishop   in   ix
With Delicate Mad Hands   James Tiptree, Jr.   na OUTEVRY,81 1
Beam Us Home   James Tiptree, Jr.   ss GAL Apr,69 54
Love Is the Plan the Plan Is Death
                           James Tiptree, Jr.   ss ALNCNDT,73 66
The Man Who Walked Home   James Tiptree, Jr.   ss AMZ May,72 82
Your Faces, O My Sisters! Your Faces Filled of Light! [as
Raccoona Sheldon]   James Tiptree, Jr.   ss AURORA ,76 97
The Peacefulness of Vivyan
                           James Tiptree, Jr.   ss AMZ Jul,71 113
Excursion Fare   James Tiptree, Jr.   nv STL # 7,81 127
I'll Be Waiting for You When the Swimming Pool Is Empty
                           James Tiptree, Jr.   ss PROTOST,71 166

Tolkien, J.R.R. THE BOOK OF LOST TALES 1 (Allen & Unwin/Unicorn 0-04-823281-5, 04/85 [03/85], £2.95, 297pp, pb) Reprint (Allen & Unwin 1983) of the first part of an early history of Middle Earth which preceded THE SILMARILLION.

*Tolkien, J.R.R. THE LAYS OF BELERIAND: THE HISTORY OF MIDDLE-EARTH, VOL. III (Allen & Unwin 0-04-82377-7, 08/85 [10/85], £14.95, 393pp, hc) Third book in the edition of previously unpublished materials from Tolkien's writings on Middle Earth. This volume has two long poems plus exhaustive comments by the editor, Tolkien's son, Christopher.
Contents: Page
Preface   Christopher Tolkien   pr   1
The Lay of the Children of Hurin
                           J.R.R. Tolkien   pm   3
Poems Early Abandoned   J.R.R. Tolkien   pm   131
The Lay of Leithian   J.R.R. Tolkien   pm   150
Commentary   C.S. Lewis   ms   315
The Lay of Leithian Recommenced
                           J.R.R. Tolkien   pm   330
Note on the original submission on the Lay of Leithian and
The Silmarillion in 1937
                           Christopher Tolkien   ar   364
Glossary of Obsolete, Archaic, and Rare Words and Meanings
                           [Misc. Material]   ms   368
Index   [Misc. Material]   ix   373

+Tolkien, J.R.R. THE LAYS OF BELERIAND: THE HISTORY OF MIDDLE-EARTH, VOL. III (Houghton Mifflin 0-395-39429-5, 11/85 [10/85], $16.95, 393pp, hc) Reprint (Allen & Unwin 1985) first U.S. edition of this third book of previously-unpublished Tolkien manuscripts, with two long poems and a critique by C.S. Lewis.

*Touponce, William F. RAY BRADBURY AND THE POETICS OF REVERIE: FANTASY, SCIENCE FICTION, AND THE READER (UMI 0-8357-1569-8, 1984 [05/85], $24.95 + postage, 131pp, hc) Non-fiction, literary criticism. This revision of a thesis appeared in 1984, but we didn't see it until 1985.

*Tubb, E.C. THE TEMPLE OF TRUTH (DAW 0-88677-059-9, 07/85 [06/85], $2.95, 222pp, pb) Sf novel, "Dumarest of Terra" #31. He's still searching for lost Earth after 31 disappointments.

Tulloch, John & Manuel Alvarado DOCTOR WHO: THE UNFOLDING TEXT (St. Martin's 0-312-21480-4, 01/85 [12/84], $9.95, 342pp, pb) Reprint (U.K. 1983), scholarly critical study of the popular tv series and films.

*Turner, Frederick THE NEW WORLD: AN EPIC POEM (Princeton Univ. Press 0-691-06641-8, 09/85 [10/85], $26.00, 182pp, hc) A narrative poem set in 2376. Flawed, but sometimes astonishingly beautiful. (FCM)

*Turner, Frederick THE NEW WORLD: AN EPIC POEM (Princeton Univ. Press 0-691-01420-5, 09/85 [10/85], $9.95, 182pp, pb) Paperback edition of the above.

Tuttle, Lisa & George R.R. Martin WINDHAVEN Main listing under George R.R. Martin.

*Twain, Mark THE SCIENCE FICTION OF MARK TWAIN (Shoe String/Archon 0-208-02036-5, 10/84 [12/84], $27.50, xxxiii + 305pp, hc) Collection edited by David Ketterer, with introduction and bibliography.
Contents: Page
Texts and Acknowledgments
                           David Ketterer   bi   ix
Introduction   David Ketterer   in xiii
Petrified Man   Mark Twain   vi TRE Oct 4,1862   3
Earthquake Almanac   Mark Twain   vi DRC Oct 17,1865 4
A Curious Pleasure Excursion
                           Mark Twain   ss NYH Jul 6,1874   6
The Curious Republic of Gondour [as Anonymous]
                           Mark Twain   ss ATL Oct,1875   10
Captain Stormfield's Visit to Heaven [Extracts from Captain
Stormfield's Visit to Heaven]
                           Mark Twain   nv HRP Dec +1,07   14

```
        Most complete version, this copy text from part 1:
                                            MTQRHVN,70
The Loves of Alonzo Fitz Clarence and Rosannah Ethelton
                        Mark Twain          ss ATL Mar,1878    61
Time Travel Contexts from A CONNECTICUT YANKEE IN KING
  ARTHUR'S COURT     Mark Twain      ex WEB Dec 10,1889    77
Mental Telegraphy       Mark Twain          ss HRP Dec,1891    96
Mental Telegraphy Again  Mark Twain         ss HRP Sep,1895   112
My Platonic Sweetheart  [originally entitled The Lost
  Sweetheart, written Jul-Aug 1898]
                        Mark Twain          ss HRP Dec,12    117
From the "London Times" of 1904
                        Mark Twain          ss CNY Nov,1898   127
"The Great Dark"  [written Aug-Sep 1898]
                        Mark Twain          nv LTRSERT,62    139
The Secret History of Eddypus, the World-Empire  [written
  Feb-Mar 1901 and Feb-Mar 1902]
                        Mark Twain          nv MTFBLMN,72    176
Sold to Satan  [written Jan 1904]
                        Mark Twain          ss EUR&ELW,23    226
3,000 Years Among the Microbes  [written May-Jun 1905]
                        Mark Twain          na MTWHDRM,67    233
"The Mysterious Balloonist"  [written July 1868]
                        Mark Twain          uw MTNTEBK,35    327
    Full version and this copy text:      MTN V 1,75
Synopsis of "A Murder, a Mystery, and a Marriage"  [written
  in 1876]     Mark Twain          ex MSH 1945   331
"The Generation Iceberg"  [written in 1884]
                        Mark Twain          uw MTNTEBK,35    334
    This copy text:                   MTN V 3,79
Shackleford's Ghost  [probably written in 1897 or 1898]
                        Mark Twain          ss SFMRKTW,84    335
"History 1,000 Years from Now"  [probably written Jan 1901]
                        Mark Twain          nv MTFBLMN,72    338
Explanatory Notes       David Ketterer          ms    341
Selected Bibliography   David Ketterer          bi    381
```

*Tymn, Marshall B. THE YEAR'S SCHOLARSHIP IN SCIENCE FICTION, FANTASY AND HORROR LITERATURE (Kent State Univ. Press 0-87338-302-8, 06/85 [05/85], $7.50, 107pp, pb) Non-fiction, reference. An annotated list of 1982 articles and books on sf, broken down by 10 subjects.

Underwood, Tim & Chuck Miller, eds. FEAR ITSELF: THE HORROR FICTION OF STEPHEN KING (NAL/Signet 0-451-13859-7, 10/85 [09/85], $3.95, 286pp, pb) Reprint (Underwood-Miller 1982) group of non-fiction, critical essays on King and his works.

Updike, John THE WITCHES OF EASTWICK (Fawcett/Crest 0-449-20647-5, 07/85 [06/85], $4.50, 343pp, pb) Reprint (Knopf 1984) fantasy novel by a literary author.

Uttley, Alison A TRAVELLER IN TIME (Ace 0-441-82213-4, 01/86 [12/85], $2.95, 197pp, pb) Reprint (Faber & Faber 1939) fantasy novel of time travel to the era of Mary Stuart.

+Vallejo, Boris BORIS VALLEJO'S FANTASY ART TECHNIQUES (Arco/Simon & Schuster 0-668-06234-7, 12/85 [12/85], $19.95, 127pp, hc) Art book in full color, with sketches and technical explanations as well as final versions. This may or may not be simultaneous with the British edition from Dragon's World. First American edition.

*Van Allsburg, Chris THE POLAR EXPRESS (Houghton Mifflin 0-395-38949-6, 10/85 [11/85], $15.95FPT, unpaginated, hc) A Christmas fantasy tale written and illustrated by Van Allsburg. Art book. Winner of the Caldecott Medal.

*Van Hise, Della STAR TREK #24: KILLING TIME (Pocket 0-671-52488-7, 07/85 [06/85], $3.50, 311pp, pb) Star Trek novel, a first novel. This was revised part way into the print run so there are apparently two versions, the first has an embossed cover.

*Van Scyoc, Sydney J. DAUGHTERS OF THE SUNSTONE (SFBC #04729, 09/85 [08/85], $8.50, 697pp, hc) Omnibus edition of a sf trilogy.
Contents: Page
DARKCHILD   Sydney J. Van Scyoc   n. BRK 1982
BLUESONG   Sydney J. Van Scyoc   n. BRK 1982
STARSILK   Sydney J. Van Scyoc   n. BRK 1982

Van Scyoc, Sydney J. STARSILK (Berkley 0-425-08077-3, 09/85 [08/85], $2.95, 248pp, pb) Reprint (Berkley 1984) sf novel, conclusion of the "Darkchild" trilogy.

van Vogt, A.E. COMPUTER EYE (DAW 0-88677-063-7, 07/85 [06/85], $2.95, 203pp, pb) Reissue (DAW 1983 as COMPUTERWORLD) sf novel.

van Vogt, A.E. NULL A-3 (Morrison, Raven Hill no ISBN, 09/85 [09/85], $29.95, 213pp, hc) Reprint (Sphere 1985) sf novel in limited, slipcased edition of 750 copies, numbered, signed and with a selection of the original typed manuscript included. The copyright date inside is 1984 and it states "first edition." Neither is true, but this is the only hardcover.

*van Vogt, A.E. NULL-A THREE (Sphere 0-7221-8841-2, 06/85 [05/85], £1.95, 215pp, pb) Sf novel, the third in a series. This is the first English-language edition, following French and Dutch ones. Van Vogt has written a summary of the first two books by way of introduction.

+van Vogt, A.E. NULL-A THREE (DAW 0-88677-056-4, 07/85 [06/85], $3.50, 254pp, pb) Reprint (Sphere 1985) sf novel, conclusion of the "Null-A" trilogy. The actual first edition was in French in 1984. Once more, Gilbert Gosseyn, the man with the extra brain, has to save the universe. This is the first American edition.

van Vogt, A.E. ROGUE SHIP (DAW 0-88677-061-0, 07/85 [06/85], $2.95, 172pp, pb) Reissue (Doubleday 1965) sf novel.

van Vogt, A.E. THE SILKIE (DAW 0-88677-062-9, 07/85 [06/85], $2.95, 160pp, pb) Reissue (Ace 1969) sf novel.

van Vogt, A.E. & E. Mayne Hull THE WINGED MAN (DAW 0-88677-060-2, 07/85 [06/85], $2.95, 158pp, pb) Reissue (Doubleday 1966) sf novel. Van Vogt expanded the 1944 serial written by his first wife.

*Vance, Jack THE COMPLETE MAGNUS RIDOLPH (Underwood-Miller 0-934438-98-6, 01/85 [12/84], $30.00 signed/numbered edition of 200; $15.95 trade edition of 500, 204pp, hc) Collection, the first to include all 10 of Vance's sf stories of Ridolph.
Contents: Page
The Kokod Warriors   Jack Vance   nv TWS Oct,52   7
The Unspeakable McInch   Jack Vance   nv STS Nov,48   39
The Howling Bounders   Jack Vance   nv STS Mar,49   56
The King of Thieves   Jack Vance   nv STS Nov,49   74
The Spa of the Stars   Jack Vance   nv STS Jul,50   92
Coup de Grace [Worlds of Origin]
                          Jack Vance   nv SUP Feb,58   111
The Sub-standard Sardines
                          Jack Vance   ss STS Jan,49   132
To B or Not to C or to D [Cosmic Hotfoot]
                          Jack Vance   nv STS Sep,50   154
Hard-Luck Diggings   Jack Vance   ss STS Jul,48   177
Sanatoris Short-cut   Jack Vance   ss STS Sep,48   189

Vance, Jack THE DRAGON MASTERS (Berkley 0-425-08274-1, 11/85 [10/85], $2.75, 137pp, pb) Reprint (Ace 1963) sf short novel. It won a 1962 Hugo as a novella.

Vance, Jack THE LAST CASTLE (Berkley 0-425-08478-7, 01/86 [12/85], $2.75, 113pp, pb) Reprint (Ace 1966) sf novella. It won both Hugo and Nebula when it first appeared. Recommended. (CNB)

*Vance, Jack LIGHT FROM A LONE STAR (NESFA Press 0-915368-31-5, 08/85 [09/85], $13.00, 125pp, hc) Guest of Honor publication for the 1985 NASFiC in Austin TX. It includes reprinted stories (one original), an interview, and an introduction to Vance's work. A smaller signed edition sold out at Austin.
Contents: Page
Introduction   Russell Letson   in   v
The Men Return   Jack Vance   ss INF Jul,57   3
Hard-Luck Diggings   Jack Vance   ss STS Jul,48   15
First Star I See Tonight Jack Vance   ss MMM Mar,54   33
The Potters of Firsk   Jack Vance   nv ASF May,50   53
Noise   Jack Vance   ss STS Aug,52   77
Cat Island   Jack Vance   ss LGTLNST,85   93
A Talk with Jack Vance   Tim Underwood   iv LGTLNST,85   99
A Vance Encyclopedia   Jack Vance   ms LGTLNST,85   105

*Vance, Jack LYONESSE II: THE GREEN PEARL (Underwood-Miller 0-88733-010-X, 06/85 [05/85], $60.00 500-copy signed/numbered/boxed edition, 360pp, hc) Fantasy novel, sequel to LYONESSE (SULDRUN'S GARDEN). A major book; highly recommended. (CNB)

Vance, Jack RHIALTO THE MARVELLOUS (Baen 0-671-55991-5, 11/85 [10/85], $3.50, 219pp, pb) Reprint (Underwood-Miller 1984) fantasy collection of 3 novellas billed as a novel. Bound in at the end of it is a story "Basileus" by C.J. Cherryh and Janet Morris, excerpted from the forthcoming original anthology HEROES IN HELL -- another headache for short-fiction bibliographers.
Contents: Page
Basileus   C.J. Cherryh & Janet Morris
                                            nv RHIALTO,85   223

*Vance, Jack STRANGE NOTIONS & THE DARK OCEAN (Underwood-Miller 0-88733-015-0 & -016-9, 1985 [12/85], $60.00, 2 vols. in slipcase, signed limited edition of 500, 154 + 180pp, hc) Non-sf/fantasy, associational. The first publication of two mystery/suspense novels Vance wrote in the early '60s.

*Vande Velde, Vivian A HIDDEN MAGIC (Crown 0-517-55534-4, 11/85 [11/85], $8.95, 117pp, hc) Juvenile fantasy, illustrated by Trina Schart Hyman. Princess seeks help from young sorcerer in battling evil witch.

*Vardeman, Robert E. THE FROZEN WAVES (Avon 0-380-89799-7, 05/85 [04/85], $2.95, 204pp, pb) Fantasy novel, #2 in the "Jade Demons" series.

*Vardeman, Robert E. THE JADE DEMONS #3: THE CRYSTAL CLOUDS (Avon 0-380-89800-4, 09/85 [08/85], $2.95, 222pp, pb) Fantasy novel, third in a series.

*Vardeman, Robert E. THE QUAKING LANDS (Avon 0-380-89518-8, 01/85 [12/84], $2.95, 206pp, pb) Fantasy novel. "Jade Demons" #1, start of a new series.

*Vardeman, Robert E. THE WHITE FIRE (Avon 0-380-89801-2, 01/86 [12/85], $2.95, 199pp, pb) Fantasy novel, "Jade Demons" #4.

VARDEMAN, ROBERT E. & VICTOR MILAN   **WAGNER, KARL EDWARD & DAVID A. DRAKE**

Vardeman, Robert E. & Victor Milan THE CITY IN THE GLACIER (Ace 0-441-10633-1, 10/85 [09/85], $2.75, 224pp, pb) Reprint (Playboy 1980) fantasy novel, #2 in the six-book "War Of Powers" series.

Vardeman, Robert E. & Victor Milan THE DESTINY STONE (Ace 0-441-14308-3, 12/85 [11/85], $2.75, 221pp, pb) Reprint (Playboy 1980) fantasy novel, "War of Powers" #3.

Vardeman, Robert E. & Victor Milan THE FALLEN ONES (Ace 0-441-22612-4, 01/86 [12/85], $2.95, 222pp, pb) Reissue (Playboy 1982) fantasy novel, "The War of Powers" #4.

Vardeman, Robert E. & Victor Milan THE SUNDERED REALM (Ace 0-441-79091-7, 08/85 [07/85], $2.75, 222pp, pb) Reprint (Playboy 1980) fantasy novel, "The War of Powers: Book One," first of a sextology.

*Vardeman, Robert E. & George W. Proctor BLOOD FOUNTAIN (Ace 0-441-06778-6, 11/85 [10/85], $2.75, 184pp, pb) Fantasy novel, "Swords of Raemllyn" #3. Heroes vs. an evil sorcerer.

*Vardeman, Robert E. & George W. Proctor TO DEMONS BOUND (Ace 0-441-81464-6, 03/85 [02/85], $2.75, 215pp, pb) Start of a new fantasy series, "Swords of Raemllyn" #1.

*Vardeman, Robert E. & George W. Proctor A YOKE OF MAGIC (Ace 0-441-94840-5, 07/85 [06/85], $2.75, 195pp, pb) Fantasy novel, "Swords of Raemllyn" #2.

Varley, John DEMON (Berkley 0-425-08271-7, 11/85 [10/85], $3.50, 464pp, pb) Reprint (Berkley 1984) sf novel, 3rd in the "Titan" trilogy.

Varley, John MILLENNIUM (Berkley 0-425-07674-1, 05/85 [04/85], $2.95, 247pp, pb) Reprint (Berkley 1983) sf novel. First mass market edition.

Varley, John TITAN (Berkley 0-425-08670-4, 11/85 [10/85], $3.50, 309pp, pb) Reissue (Berkley-Putnam 1979) sf novel, first in a trilogy; 10th printing.

Varley, John WIZARD (Berkley 0-425-08166-4, 11/85 [10/85], $3.50, 372pp, pb) Reissue (Berkley/Putnam 1980) sf novel, second in the "Titan" trilogy; 9th printing.

*Vasbinder, Samuel Holmes SCIENTIFIC ATTITUDES IN MARY SHELLEY'S FRANKENSTEIN (UMI 0-8357-1580-9, 1984 [05/85], $24.95 + postage, 111pp, hc) Non-fiction, literary criticism. This revision of a thesis appeared in 1984, but we didn't see it until 1985.

Verne, Jules JOURNEY TO THE CENTER OF THE EARTH (NAL/Signet 0-451-51982-5, 01/86 [12/85], $2.75, 304pp, pb) Reissue (Griffith 1872) sf novel, with an afterword by Carl Beale.

*Vernon, William, David Carson & Daryl Lane THE SOUND OF WONDER: INTERVIEWS FROM "THE SCIENCE FICTION RADIO SHOW", Main listing under Daryl Lane.

*Vernon, William, David Carson & Daryl Lane THE SOUND OF WONDER: INTERVIEWS FROM "THE SCIENCE FICTION RADIO SHOW", VOL. 2 Main listing under Daryl Lane.

*Vinge, Joan D. LADYHAWKE (NAL/Signet 0-451-13321-8, 03/85 [02/85], $3.50, 252pp, pb) Novelization of a fantasy film; movie tie-in edition, with stills.

*Vinge, Joan D. MAD MAX III: BEYOND THUNDERDOME (Warner 0-446-32951-7, 07/85 [06/85], $2.95, 219pp, pb) Novelization of the third film in the series, based on a screenplay by Terry Hayes & George Miller.

Vinge, Joan D. THE OUTCASTS OF HEAVEN BELT (NAL/Signet 0-451-11653-4, 03/85 [02/85], $2.50, 198pp, pb) Reissue (NAL 1978) sf novel.

*Vinge, Joan D. PHOENIX IN THE ASHES (Bluejay 0-312-94364-4, 01/85 [01/85], $14.95, 230pp, hc) Collection of 6 stories with new afterwords for each. There are some awful illustrations by Susan Collins and there is no contents page or previous publication acknowledgements. (CNB)
Contents: Page
Phoenix in the Ashes   Joan D. Vinge   nv MLNLWMN,78   1
Voices from the Dust   Joan D. Vinge   ss DST V2 #2,80 37
The Storm King   Joan D. Vinge   nv IAS Apr,80   57
The Peddler's Apprentice Joan D. Vinge & Vernor Vinge
                                               nv ASF Aug,75   86
Psiren   Joan D. Vinge   nv NWV # 4,81   123
Mother & Child   Joan D. Vinge   na ORB #16,75   170

Vinge, Joan D. PSION (Dell/Laurel Leaf 0-440-97192-6, 02/85 [01/85], $2.95, 346pp, pb) Reprint (Delacorte 1982) young-adult sf novel.

*Vinge, Joan D. RETURN TO OZ (Ballantine/Del Rey 0-345-32207-X, 06/85 [05/85], $2.95, 214pp, pb) Movie novelization based on the screenplay by Walter Murch and Gill Dennis, with color stills from the film.

*Vinge, Joan D. THE SANTA CLAUS STORYBOOK (Grosset & Dunlap 0-448-10281-1, 10/85 [09/85], $6.95, unpaginated, hc) Juvenile adaptation of the movie screenplay by David & Leslie Newman, illustrated with color stills from the film. Listed for Vinge completists.

*Vinge, Joan D. SANTA CLAUS: THE MOVIE (Berkley 0-425-08385-3, 12/85 [11/85], $3.50, 244pp, pb) Novelization of a story and film script by David & Leslie Newman.

Vinge, Vernor THE PEACE WAR (Baen 0-671-55965-6, 06/85 [05/85], $3.50, 378pp, pb) Reprint (Bluejay 1984) sf novel.

Vinge, Vernor TRUE NAMES (Bluejay 0-312-94444-6, 02/85 [01/85], $6.95, 153pp, pb) Reprint (part of BINARY STARS 5, Dell 1981) short sf novel. Illustrations by Bob Walters. There is no copyright notice of earlier publication.

*Voigt, Cynthia JACKAROO (Atheneum/Argo 0-689-31123-0, 09/85 [10/85], $14.95, 291pp, hc) Young-adult adventure novel set in a mythical medieval land; marginally fantasy.

von Niebelschutz, Wolf THE BADGER OF GHISSI (Allen & Unwin/Unicorn 0-04-82372-6, 09/85 [10/85], £2.95, 262pp, pb) Reprint (Allen & Unwin 1963) fantasy novel, translated by Barrows Mussey from the first part of DIE KINDER DER FINSTERNIS (Eugen Diederichs Verlag, Dusseldorf-Koln 1959).

Vonnegut, Kurt DEAD-EYE DICK (Dell 0-440-11765-8, 1985 [10/85], $3.95, 240pp, pb) Reprint (Delacorte 1982) sf novel.

*Vonnegut, Kurt GALAPAGOS (Delacorte 0-385-29416-6, 10/85 [09/85], $16.95, 295pp, hc) Sf novel partly set a million years in the future, where a group of stranded tourists in the Galapagos have sired the only human survivors. There is also a signed limited edition.

Vonnegut, Kurt HAPPY BIRTHDAY, WANDA JUNE (Dell/Delta 0-385-28386-5, 10/85 [10/85], $9.95, 199pp, pb) Reissue (Delacorte 1971) fantasy play.

Vonnegut, Kurt THE SIRENS OF TITAN (Dell/Delta 0-385-29421-2, 10/85 [10/85], $9.95, 319pp, pb) Reissue (Dell 1959) sf novel.

Vonnegut, Kurt SLAUGHTERHOUSE FIVE: OR THE CHILDREN'S CRUSADE (Dell/Delta 0-385-28940-5, 10/85 [10/85], $9.95, 186pp, pb) Reprint (Delacorte 1969) sf novel.

Vonnegut, Kurt WAMPETERS, FOMA & GRANFALLOONS (Dell/Delta 0-385-29422-0, 10/85 [10/85], $9.95, 285pp, pb) Reissue (Delacorte 1974); non-fiction, associational. Collection of essays, reviews, etc., with sf as one of the topics.

Vonnegut, Kurt WELCOME TO THE MONKEY HOUSE (Dell/Delta 0-385-29127-2, 10/85 [10/85], $9.95, 298pp, pb) Reissue (Delacorte 1968) collection of stories and essays.

*Wagner, Karl Edward THE BOOK OF KANE (Donald M. Grant 0-937986-72-0, 10/85 [11/85], $40.00 deluxe, signed edition, 224pp, hc) [trade edition -73-9, $20.00] Collection of 5 stories featuring fantasy anti-hero Kane, with color illustrations by Jeff Jones. These stories are mostly from semi-pro sources.
Contents: Page
Reflections for the Winter of My Soul
                          Karl Edward Wagner   na DTHANGL,73   11
Misericorde   Karl Edward Wagner   nv SAP #17,83   91
The Other One   Karl Edward Wagner   ss ESP # 1,77   121
Sing a Last Song of Valdese
                          Karl Edward Wagner   nv CHA # 1,76   135
Raven's Eyrie   Karl Edward Wagner   na CHA # 2,77   157

*Wagner, Karl Edward, ed. THE YEAR'S BEST HORROR STORIES: SERIES XIII (DAW 0-88677-086-6, 10/85 [09/85], $2.95, 251pp, pb) Anthology of 18 horror and fantasy stories from 1984. Wagner searches out some totally obscure sources.
Contents: Page
Introduction: 13 Is a Lucky Number
                          Karl Edward Wagner   in   11
Mrs. Todd's Shortcut   Stephen King   nv RBK May,84   13
Are You Afraid of the Dark?
                          Charles L. Grant   ss FYC # 9,84   41
Catch Your Death   John Gordon   ss CTCHDTH,84   59
Dinner Party   Gardner Dozois   ss LGTYR&D,84   72
Tiger in the Snow   Daniel Wynn Barber   ss HSH F11,84   88
Watch the Birdie   Ramsey Campbell   ss WTCHBRD,84   94
Coming Soon to a Theatre Near You [as Oliver Lowenbruck]
                          David J. Schow   ss TZM Apr,84   101
Hands with Long Fingers   Leslie Halliwell   ss GHSTSHR,84   121
Weird Tales   Fred Chappell   ss TXR Spr,84   133
The Wardrobe   Jovan Panich   ss PBM # 7,84   145
Angst for the Memories   Vincent McHardy   ss DAMNTNS,84   161
The Thing in the Bedroom David Langford   ss KNB Nov,84   170
Borderland   John Brizzolara   ss TZM Dec,84   181
The Scarecrow   Roger Johnson   ss G&S # 6,84   191
The End of the World   James B. Hemesath ss WDL V14 #51,84   204
Never Grow Up   John Gordon   ss CTCHDTH,84   217
Deadlights   Charles Wagner   ss TWT # 9,84   224
Talking in the Dark   Dennis Etchison   ss SDW # 7,84   233

*Wagner, Karl Edward & David A. Drake KILLER Main listing under David A. Drake.

*Walters, Ray PAPERBACK TALK (Academy Chicago 0-89733-108-7, 11/85 [10/85], $19.95, 329pp, hc) Non-fiction, of associational interest. A survey of paperback publishing in the U.S., based on Walters' *New York Times* book review column and other articles which have appeared over the past 25 years. It's a compendium of short pieces, rather than a history and has sections on sf, fantasy, and horror; it even mentions sf conventions. The introduction is by the Ballantines, and the new "Future of Publishing" essay is of particular interest. Recommended. (CNB)

+Walther, Daniel SHAI'S DESTINY (DAW 0-88677-033-5, 04/85 [03/85], $2.75, 221pp, pb) Fantasy novel, the second book of Shai. This French novel has been translated by C.J. Cherryh.

*Wangerin, Walter THE BOOK OF SORROWS (Harper & Row 0-06-2500929-2, 06/85 [05/85], $14.95, 338pp, hc) Fantasy novel, sequel to THE BOOK OF THE DUN COW.

*Watkins, William John THE CENTRIFUGAL RICKSHAW DANCER (Popular Library/Questar 0-445-20131-2, 11/85 [10/85], $2.95, 233pp, pb) Sf novel.

*Watson, Ian THE BOOK OF BEING (Gollancz 0-575-03596-X, 06/85 [05/85], £8.95, 184pp, hc) Sf novel, conclusion of the "Book of the River" trilogy.

*Watson, Ian THE BOOK OF IAN WATSON (Ziesing 0-9612970-4-2, 09/85 [08/85], $35.00 signed, 366pp, hc) Collection of fiction and essays, mostly culled from a wide variety of magazines, put together as a sort of autobiography.

*Watson, Ian THE BOOK OF IAN WATSON (Ziesing 0-9612970-3-4, 09/85 [08/85], $18.50, 366pp, hc) Trade edition of the above.

+Watson, Ian THE BOOK OF THE RIVER (DAW 0-88677-104-8, 01/86 [12/85], $3.50, 256pp, pb) Reprint (Gollancz 1984) sf quasi-novel (the four parts appeared earlier in magazines), first U.S. edition. The first of a trilogy.

+Watson, Ian CONVERTS (St. Martin's 0-312-16945-0, 03/85 [02/85], $11.95, 191pp, hc) Sf novel; first American edition (Panther 1984) and first hardcover edition.

*Watson, Ian SLOW BIRDS AND OTHER STORIES (Gollancz 0-575-03675-3, 10/85 [10/85], £8.95, 190pp, hc) Collection of 11 stories. Recommended. (FCM)

Cruising	Ian Watson	ss IAS Dec md,83	120
Universe on the Turn	Ian Watson	ss LWV 1984	127
The Flesh of Her Hair	Ian Watson	ss FSF Oct,84	142
The Mystic Marriage of Salome			
	Ian Watson	ss PCTEXHB,81	159
The Bloomsday Revolution	Ian Watson	ss LGTYR&D,84	172

*Watt-Evans, Lawrence THE MISENCHANTED SWORD (Ballantine/Del Rey 0-345-31822-6, 09/85 [08/85], $2.95, 292pp, pb) Fantasy novel.

*Waugh, Charles G., Robert Adams & Martin H. Greenberg, eds. BARBARIANS Main listing under Robert Adams.

*Waugh, Charles G., Poul Anderson & Martin H. Greenberg, eds. MERCENARIES OF TOMORROW Main listing under Poul Anderson.

*Waugh, Charles G., Poul Anderson & Martin H. Greenberg, eds. TERRORISTS OF TOMORROW Main listing under Poul Anderson.

*Waugh, Charles G., Isaac Asimov & Martin H. Greenberg, eds. BAKER'S DOZEN: 13 SHORT SCIENCE FICTION NOVELS Main listing under Isaac Asimov.

*Waugh, Charles G., Isaac Asimov & Martin H. Greenberg, eds. GREAT SCIENCE FICTION BY THE WORLD'S GREAT SCIENTISTS Main listing under Isaac Asimov.

*Waugh, Charles G., Isaac Asimov & Martin H. Greenberg, eds. ISAAC ASIMOV'S MAGICAL WORLDS OF FANTASY #3: COSMIC KNIGHTS Main listing under Isaac Asimov.

*Waugh, Charles G., Isaac Asimov & Martin H. Greenberg, eds. ISAAC ASIMOV'S MAGICAL WORLDS OF FANTASY #4: SPELLS Main listing under Isaac Asimov.

*Waugh, Charles G., Isaac Asimov & Martin H. Greenberg, eds. ISAAC ASIMOV'S MAGICAL WORLDS OF FANTASY #5: GIANTS Main listing under Isaac Asimov.

*Waugh, Charles G., Isaac Asimov & Martin H. Greenberg, eds. ISAAC ASIMOV'S MAGICAL WORLDS OF FANTASY: WITCHES & WIZARDS Main listing under Isaac Asimov.

Waugh, Charles G., Isaac Asimov & Martin H. Greenberg, eds. THE LAST MAN ON EARTH Main listing under Isaac Asimov.

*Waugh, Charles G., Isaac Asimov & Martin H. Greenberg, eds. YOUNG GHOSTS Main listing under Isaac Asimov.

*Waugh, Charles G., Isaac Asimov & Martin H. Greenberg, eds. YOUNG MONSTERS Main listing under Isaac Asimov.

*Waugh, Charles G., Martin H. Greenberg & Richard Matheson, eds. THE TWILIGHT ZONE: THE ORIGINAL STORIES Main listing under Martin H. Greenberg.

*Weaver, Lydia SPLASHMAN (NAL/Signet Vista 0-451-14020-6, 12/85 [11/85], $2.50, 190pp, pb) Young-adult fantasy novel of a teen-age merman. "Is Jane's crush on a teenage merman leading her into deep water?"

*Webb, Sharon THE ADVENTURES OF TERRA TARKINGTON, R.N. (Bantam 0-553-24862-6, 03/85 [02/85], $2.95, 203pp, pb) Episodic sf novel; the adventures of an interstellar nurse. The listed pieces appeared previously. Somewhat tongue-in-cheek.

Webb, Sharon RAM SONG (Bantam Spectra 0-553-25168-6, 10/85 [09/85], $2.95, 220pp, pb) Reprint (Atheneum 1984) sf novel, conclusion of a trilogy.

*Weinstein, Howard V: PRISONERS AND PAWNS (Pinnacle 0-523-42439-6, 03/85 [02/85], $2.95, 181pp, pb) Sf novelization based on the continuing tv series. Sixth book in the series.

Weinstein, Howard & A.C. Crispin V: EAST COAST CRISIS (Gregg 0-8398-2841-1, 01/85 [12/84], $12.95, 305pp, hc) Reprint (Pinnacle 1984) sf novel based on the tv series. First hardcover edition.

*Weirdbook 20 [Spring 1985] W. Paul Ganley, ed. (W. Paul Ganley, 01/85 [01/85], $5.00 + $.75 p&h, 62pp, pb)

Not a Creature Was Stirring
	John Alfred Taylor	ss WDB #20,85	46
Araunah	Susannah Bates	ss WDB #20,85	49
The Unforgiven	John Maclay	pm WDB #20,85	51
The Fallen	Morris Liebson	pm WDB #20,85	51
After Dowson, After Paul Verlain			
	Steve Troyanovich	pm WDB #20,85	51
Aisling	Peter Tremayne	ss WDB #20,85	52
The Serpents' Shrine	Charles Denton	pm WDB #20,85	62

*Weis, Margaret & Tracy Hickman DRAGONLANCE CHRONICLES, VOL. 2: DRAGONS OF WINTER NIGHT (TSR 0-88038-174-4, 06/85 [05/85], $3.50, 399pp, pb) Fantasy novel based on a role-playing game.

*Weis, Margaret & Tracy Hickman DRAGONLANCE CHRONICLES, VOL. 3: DRAGONS OF SPRING DAWNING (TSR 0-394-74183-8, 09/85 [09/85], $3.50, 380pp, pb) Gaming-influenced fantasy novel, conclusion of a trilogy.

+Welfare, Simon & John Fairley ARTHUR C. CLARKE'S WORLD OF STRANGE POWERS Main listing under John Fairley.

*Weller, Tom SCIENCE MADE STUPID (Houghton Mifflin 0-395-36646-1, 02/85 [01/85], $6.95, 80pp, pb) Non-sf, associational. Written and illustrated by Weller, this humor book does for science what AIRPLANE did for plane-in-distress movies. It's utterly silly, and hilarious. Don't miss the typographical credits and the ads at the back. (FCM)

*Wellman, Manly Wade THE SCHOOL OF DARKNESS (Doubleday 0-385-19065-4, 12/85 [11/85], $12.95, 182pp, hc) Fantasy novel featuring John Thunstone, psychic investigator.

*Wellman, Manly Wade THE VOICE OF THE MOUNTAIN (Doubleday 0-385-18397-6, 01/85 [12/84], $11.95, 178pp, hc) Fantasy novel of "Silver John."

Wells, H.G. IN THE DAYS OF THE COMET (Hogarth 0-7012-0580-6, 09/85 [10/85], £3.95, 249pp, pb) Reprint (Macmillan U.K. 1906) visonary sf novel of England transformed by a comet into a Utopia. Introduction by Brian Aldiss.

*Wendland, Albert SCIENCE, MYTH, AND THE FICTIONAL CREATION OF ALIEN WORLDS (UMI 0-8357-1608-2, 06/85 [05/85], $24.95 + postage, 200pp, hc) Non-fiction, literary criticism. This is a revision of a thesis.

West, Anthony H.G. WELLS: ASPECTS OF A LIFE (NAL/Meridian 0-452-00735-6, 07/85 [06/85], $10.95, 405pp, pb) Reprint (Random House 1984) biography by the author's son. Non-fiction, associational.

Westall, Robert THE DEVIL ON THE ROAD (Ace 0-441-14290-7, 11/85 [10/85], $2.75, 200pp, pb) Reprint (Greenwillow 1978) fantasy novel of time travel into the 17th century, where the hero meets a witch. A less-than-traditional hero, a time-traveling cat, and an excellent sense of place combine to make this a well-above-average fantasy for all ages. Recommended. (DLN)

*Weston, Susan CHILDREN OF THE LIGHT (St. Martin's 0-312-13236-0, 12/85 [11/85], $15.95, 262pp, hc) Post holocaust sf novel, a first novel. It's beautifully written, avoiding despair as well as pulpish adventure to focus on the continuing richness of human nature. Highly recommended. (FCM)

Wharton, Edith THE GHOST STORIES OF EDITH WHARTON (Scribner's 0-684-18582-X, 04/85 [03/85], $8.95, 276pp, pb) Reissue (Scribner's 1973) collection of 11 stories. Also available (-14829-3) in a library hc edition.

*Whispers [v.6 #1-2, December 1984] Stuart David Schiff, ed. (Stuart David Schiff, 01/85 [01/85], $6.00, 176pp, pb)
Contents:
			Page
Editorial	Stuart David Schiff	ed WHS Dec,84	2
News	Stuart David Schiff	ar WHS Dec,84	3
The Bones Wizard	Alan Ryan	ss WHS Dec,84	14
The Right Thing	Jean Darling	ss WHS Dec,84	22
The Yazata	Gregory Frost	ss WHS Dec,84	31
The Abomination	John Brizzolara	ss WHS Dec,84	38
Pinewood	Tanith Lee	ss WHS Dec,84	48
Shadowman	Susan Casper	ss WHS Dec,84	53
Bundoran, Co. Donegal	Alan Ryan	ss WHS Dec,84	60
Space Trip	Margo Skinner	ss WHS Dec,84	71
Small Gift from Home	J.N. Williamson	ss WHS Dec,84	77
The Ones Who Never Talk	Peter D. Pautz	ss WHS Dec,84	80
Damballa's Slough	Hugh B. Cave	ss WHS Dec,84	89
Books	Chris Henderson	br WHS Dec,84	99
The Blueberry Witch	Margaret Coleman	ss WHS Dec,84	111
Mr. Right	Richard Christian Matheson		
		vi WHS Dec,84	115
The Woman in Black	Dennis Etchison	ss WHS Dec,84	118
Help! The Paranoids Are After Me			
	Charles E. Fritch	ss WHS Dec,84	129
Barelli's Demon	Ken Wisman	ss WHS Dec,84	135
Black Has Its Charms	Fritz Leiber	ss WHS Dec,84	149
The Corn Dolly	Al Sarrantonio	ss WHS Dec,84	157
For These and All My Sins			
	David Morrell	ss WHS Dec,84	166

*White, Edmund CARACOLE (Dutton 0-525-24281-3, 09/85 [09/85], $17.95, 342pp, hc) This is billed as an erotic "epic fantasy novel." It's set in an imagined world which "recalls Paris under the Nazis, Venice under the Austrians, or Rio under the Portuguese."

White, James HOSPITAL STATION (Ballantine/Del Rey 0-345-32068-9, 01/85 [12/84], $2.50, 191pp, pb) Reissue (Ballantine 1962) sf novel. Fifth printing. First in the "Sector General" series.

*White, James STAR HEALER (Ballantine/Del Rey 0-345-32089-1, 01/85 [12/84], $2.75, 217pp, pb) Sf novel, part of the "Sector General" series.

White, Ted & David F. Bischoff FORBIDDEN WORLD (Popular Library/Questar 0-445-20017-0, 05/85 [04/85], $2.95, 224pp, pb) Reprint (Fawcett/Popular Library 1978) sf novel. Since this was originally a Fawcett/Popular Library book and is now Warner/Popular Library/Questar, it's hard to decide if we should call it a reprint or a reissue....

+Whiteford, Wynne BREATHING SPACE ONLY (Ace 0-441-07288-7, 01/86 [12/85], $2.75, 152pp, pb) Reprint (Cory & Collins 1980) sf novel, first U.S. edition.

+Whiteford, Wynne THOR'S HAMMER (Ace 0-441-80755-0, 11/85 [10/85], $2.75, 138pp, pb) Reprint (Cory & Collins 1983), first U.S. edition; short sf novel about troubleshooters vs. a rebellious asteroid miner.

+Whitelaw, Stella, Judy Gardiner & Mark Ronson GRIMALKIN'S TALES (St. Martin's 0-312-35057-0, 09/85 [09/85], $10.95, 160pp, hc) Reprint (U.K. 1983) original anthology of 12 stories, 4 by each author, dealing with cats; the tales include sf and fantasy.
Contents:
			Page
The Cat That Could Fly	Stella Whitelaw	ss GRMLKNS,83	7
In My Grandmother's House			
	Judy Gardiner	ss GRMLKNS,83	19
Strauss	Mark Ronson	ss GRMLKNS,83	34
Nine Lives	Stella Whitelaw	ss GRMLKNS,83	49
The Bad Luck Cat	Judy Gardiner	ss GRMLKNS,83	58
Tico	Mark Ronson	ss GRMLKNS,83	70
Arbuthnot Road	Stella Whitelaw	ss GRMLKNS,83	86
Gershwin	Judy Gardiner	ss GRMLKNS,83	102
Smokey	Mark Ronson	ss GRMLKNS,83	115
The Great God Mau	Stella Whitelaw	ss GRMLKNS,83	128
Cats Do Make a Home, Don't They?			
	Judy Gardiner	ss GRMLKNS,83	138
Samkin	Mark Ronson	ss GRMLKNS,83	147

Wilder, Cherry A PRINCESS OF THE CHAMELN (Baen 0-671-55966-4, 07/85 [06/85], $2.95, 345pp, pb) Reprint (Atheneum 1984) fantasy novel, first of a trilogy.

Wilder, Cherry YORATH THE WOLF (Baen 0-671-55987-7, 10/85 [09/85], $2.95, 246pp, pb) Reprint (Atheneum 1984) fantasy novel, #2 in "The Rulers of Hylor".

*Wilder, Joan THE JEWEL OF THE NILE (Avon 0-380-89984-1, 11/85 [11/85], $3.50, 281pp, pb) Novelization of the romantic fantasy sequel to ROMANCING THE STONE. The author is given as "Catherine Lanigan writing as Joan Wilder;" based on a screenplay by Mark Rosenthal and Lawrence Konner.

Wilhelm, Kate WELCOME, CHAOS (Berkley 0-425-07585-0, 03/85 [02/85], $2.95, 297pp, pb) Reprint (Houghton Mifflin 1983) sf novel. Recommended. (CNB)

Wilkes, Marilyn Z. C.L.U.T.Z. AND THE FIZZION FORMULA (Gollancz 0-575-03692-3, 08/85 [07/85], £6.50, 136pp, hc) Reprint (Dial 1985) juvenile sf novel. We have not seen the Dial edition and it may not exist, in which case this would be the first edition.

*Willard, Nancy THINGS INVISIBLE TO SEE (Knopf 0-394-54058-1, 02/85 [01/85], $14.95 FPT, 263pp, hc) A delightful literary fantasy of metaphysics, baseball, and nostalgia. Recommended. (FCM)

Willard, Nancy THINGS INVISIBLE TO SEE (Bantam Spectra 0-553-25563-0, 01/86 [12/85], $3.50, 262pp, pb) Reprint (Knopf 1985) fantasy novel of baseball, love, and World War II.

*Williams, Paul O. THE SWORD OF FORBEARANCE (Ballantine/Del Rey 0-345-32504-4, 10/85 [09/85], $2.95, 245pp, pb) Sf novel, conclusion of the "Pelbar Cycle" (Book #7).

*Williams, Tad TAILCHASER'S SONG (DAW 0-8099-0002-5, 11/85 [11/85], $15.95FPT, 333pp, hc) Fantasy novel, a first novel. A feline version of WATERSHIP DOWN.

*Williams, Walter Jon KNIGHT MOVES (Tor 0-812-55794-8, 02/85 [01/85], $2.95, 317pp, pb) Sf novel. Very early Zelazny-esque, but with its own flavor. Recommended. (DLN)

*Williamson, J.N. THE NEW DEVIL'S DICTIONARY: CREEPY CLICHES AND SINISTER SYNONYMS (Ganley 0-932445-13-6, 09/85 [08/85], $15.00, 57pp, hc) Less a dictionary than a compendium of horror clichés, with estimates of the percentage of authors who resort to them. Suitably gruesome illustrations by J.K. Potter. A deluxe signed edition (-20-9, $30.00) is also available.

*Williamson, J.N. THE NEW DEVIL'S DICTIONARY: CREEPY CLICHES AND SINISTER SYNONYMS (Ganley 0-932445-12-8, 09/85 [08/85], $5.00, 57pp, pb) Paperback edition of the above.

Williamson, Jack THE HUMANOID TOUCH (Bantam 0-553-24967-3, 04/85 [03/85], $2.75, 210pp, pb) Reissue (Phantasia 1980) sf novel. Sequel to THE HUMANOIDS. 3rd printing.

Williamson, Jack THE LEGION OF TIME (Bluejay 0-312-94283-4, 11/85 [12/85], $8.95, 247pp, pb) Reprint (Fantasy Press 1952) collection of two short novels, "The Legion of Time" and "After Worlds End", with illustrations by Ilene Meyer.

Williamson, Jack LIFEBURST (Ballantine/Del Rey 0-345-32977-5, 11/85 [10/85], $2.95, 286pp, pb) Reprint (Del Rey 1984) sf novel.

Williamson, Jack WONDER'S CHILD: MY LIFE IN SCIENCE FICTION (Bluejay 0-312-94456-X, 11/85 [12/85], $8.95, 275pp, pb) Reprint (Bluejay 1984), non-fiction, autobiography. This book won the Hugo in 1985.

*Willis, Connie FIRE WATCH (Bluejay 0-312-94162-5, 02/85 [01/85], $14.95, 274pp, hc) Collection of 12 stories by a major new talent. There is one new story, "All My Darling Daughters". Recommended. (CNB)
Contents:

				Page
Fire Watch	Connie Willis	nv	IAS Feb 15,82	2
Service for the Burial of the Dead				
	Connie Willis	nv	FSF Nov,82	47
Lost and Found	Connie Willis	ss	TZM Jan,82	68
All My Darling Daughters	Connie Willis	nv	FIREWTC,85	85
The Father of the Bride	Connie Willis	ss	TZM May,82	110
A Letter from the Clearys				
	Connie Willis	ss	IAS Jul,82	115
And Come from Miles Around				
	Connie Willis	ss	GLL Sep,79	130
The Sidon in the Mirror	Connie Willis	nv	IAS Apr,83	146
Daisy, in the Sun	Connie Willis	nv	GLL Nov,79	182
Mail-Order Clone	Connie Willis	ss	FSF Aug,82	205
Samaritan	Connie Willis	nv	GLL May,79	215
Blued Moon	Connie Willis	nv	IAS Jan,84	236

*Willis, Donald, ed. VARIETY'S COMPLETE SCIENCE FICTION REVIEWS (Garland 0-8240-8712-7, 02/86 [12/85], $17.95, 479pp, pb) Non-fiction, reference book. Photoreproduction of sf/fantasy movie reviews from *Variety* from 1907 through 1984. It was also announced in hardcover, -6263-9, $27.95.

Wilson, Colin LIFEFORCE (Warner 0-446-32611-9, 06/85 [05/85], $2.95, 220pp, pb) Reprint (Random House 1976 as THE SPACE VAMPIRES) sf novel; movie tie-in edition, but there are no stills from the film.

Wilson, F. Paul WHEELS WITHIN WHEELS (Berkley 0-425-07451-X, 01/85 [12/84], $2.75, 186pp, pb) Reprint (Doubleday 1978) sf novel.

*Wilson, Gahan GAHAN WILSON'S AMERICA (Simon & Schuster 0-671-55512-X, 11/85 [11/85], $14.95, 143pp, hc) Gahan Wilson's latest cartoon collection targets the U.S.A.

*Wilson, Robert Anton THE WIDOW'S SON (Bluejay 0-312-94457-8, 1985 [12/85], $9.95, 343pp, pb) Historical novel, Vol. II of the "Historical Illuminatus Chronicles".

*Wilson, Snoo INSIDE BABEL (Chatto & Windus 0-7011-2853-4, 08/85 [10/85], £9.95, 208pp, hc) "Spoof sf" satirical novel -- Chrissie's adventures in a strange future society.

*Windling, Terri, ed. FAERY! (Ace 0-441-22564-0, 01/85 [12/84], $2.95, 308pp, pb) Anthology including both original and reprint material.
Contents:

				Page
A Troll and Two Roses	Patricia A. McKillip	ss	FAERY! ,85	1
The Thirteenth Fey	Jane Yolen	ss	FAERY! ,85	13
Lullaby for a Changeling	Nicholas Stuart Gray	ss	EDGEVNG,76	25
Brat	Theodore Sturgeon	ss	UNK Dec,41	43
Wild Garlic	William F. Wu	ss	FAERY! ,85	61
The Stranger	Shulamith Oppenheim	ss	SHPSHFT,78	79
Spirit Places	Keith Taylor	ss	FAERY! ,85	85
The Box of All Possibility				
	Z. Greenstaff	ss	FAERY! ,85	99
The Seekers of Dreams	Felix Marti-Ibanez	ss	ALLWNDR,63	109
Bridge	Steven R. Boyett	ss	FAERY! ,85	127
Crowley and the Leprechaun				
	Gregory Frost	ss	FAERY! ,85	139
The Antrim Hills	Mildred Downey Broxon	nv	AURORA ,76	151
The Snow Fairy	M. Lucie Chin	nv	FAERY! ,85	173
The Five Black Swans	Sylvia Townsend Warner			
		ss	NYM Jun 23,73	215
Thomas the Rhymer	Traditional Scots Ballad	pm		223
Prince Shadowbow	Sheri S. Tepper	ss	FAERY! ,85	227
The Erlking	Angela Carter	ss	BNA 1979	239
The Elphin Knight	Traditional Scots Ballad	pm		247
Rhian and Garanhir	Grail Undwin	ss	YBF # 5,80	251
The Woodcutter's Daughter				
	Alison Uttley	ss	FBRBKMF,85	257
The Famous Flower of Serving Men				
	Traditional Scots Ballad	pm		271
Touk's House	Robin McKinley	nv	FAERY! ,85	275

The Boy Who Dreamed of Tir na n-Og
Michael M. McNamara   ss FSF Dec,79 299

*Wingrove, David, ed. SCIENCE FICTION FILM SOURCE BOOK (Longman 0-582-89239-2, 11/85 [11/85], price unknown, 312pp, hc) Non-fiction, reference work, with plot outlines, critiques, cast and production details, and articles on literary sources, special effects, etc. This is in the same format as Wingrove's earlier SCIENCE FICTION SOURCE BOOK, with star rating systems. There is a foreword by Brian Aldiss.

*Winter, Douglas E. FACES OF FEAR: ENCOUNTERS WITH THE CREATORS OF MODERN HORROR (Berkley 0-425-07670-9, 11/85 [11/85], $6.95, 277pp, pb) Non-fiction, interviews of 17 horror writers including King, Straub, Barker, and Bloch, plus a horror fiction buying guide and lists of recommended books and films.

*Wiseman, David ADAM'S COMMON (Houghton Mifflin 0-395-35976-7, 01/85 [12/84], $11.95, 175pp, hc) Young-adult fantasy novel about a girl who travels back in time.

*Wisher, Bill & Randal Frakes THE TERMINATOR Main listing under Randal Frakes.

*Wold, Allen V: THE CRIVIT EXPERIMENT (Pinnacle 0-523-42466-3, 07/85 [06/85], $2.95, 181pp, pb) Media tie-in sf novel.

Wold, Allen V: THE PURSUIT OF DIANA (Gregg 0-8398-2868-3, 04/85 [03/85], $12.95, 186pp, hc) Reprint (Pinnacle 1984) sf novel based on the tv show. First hardcover edition.

+Wolfe, Gene FREE LIVE FREE (Gollancz 0-575-03725-3, 09/85 [08/85], £9.95, 399pp, hc) Reprint (Ziesing 1984) sf novel, billed as "a fantasy" but more a mainstream novel of character than anything else. This edition has been slightly revised from the limited edition issued last year. Wolfe's love for his characters infuses this book about the down-and-outs of the world with a very special charm. Recommended. (DLN)

Wolfe, Gene FREE LIVE FREE (Tor 0-312-93248-0, 11/85 [10/85], $16.95, 403pp, hc) Reprint (Ziesing 1984) sf novel. This is a slightly revised edition. It follows the text of the 1985 Gollancz edition.

*Wollheim, Donald A., ed. THE 1985 ANNUAL WORLD'S BEST SF (DAW 0-88677-047-5, 06/85 [05/85], $2.95, 302pp, pb) Sf anthology.
Contents:

				Page
Introduction	Donald A. Wollheim	in		7
The Picture Man	John Dalmas	nv	FSF Aug,84	11
Cash Crop	Connie Willis	nv	MIS V7 #2,84	34
We Remember Babylon	Ian Watson	nv	FSF Aug,84	59
What Makes Us Human	Stephen R. Donaldson	nv	FSF Aug,84	85
Salvador	Lucius Shepard	nv	FSF Apr,84	128
PRESS ENTER ■	John Varley	na	IAS May,84	151
The Aliens Who Knew, I Mean, Everything				
	George Alec Effinger	ss	FSF Oct,84	226
Bloodchild	Octavia E. Butler	nv	IAS Jun,84	246
Coming of the Goonga	Gary W. Shockley	ss	CLRAWDS,84	270
Medra	Tanith Lee	ss	IAS Jun,84	284

Wollheim, Donald A., ed. THE 1985 ANNUAL WORLD'S BEST SF (SFBC #4755, 09/85 [10/85], $4.98, 239pp, hc) Reprint (DAW 1985) anthology, first hardcover edition.

Wollheim, Donald A. & Arthur W. Saha, eds. WOLLHEIM'S WORLD'S BEST SF: SERIES 9 (DAW 0-88677-099-8, 12/85 [11/85], $2.95, 284pp, pb) Reissue (DAW 1980 as THE 1980 ANNUAL WORLD'S BEST SF) anthology. 3rd printing.

*Wrede, Patricia C. THE HARP OF IMACH THYSSEL (Ace 0-441-31756-1, 04/85 [03/85], $2.95, 234pp, pb) Fantasy novel.

*Wrede, Patricia C. TALKING TO DRAGONS (Ace/Tempo 0-441-79591-9, 01/85 [12/84], $2.25, 232pp, pb) Juvenile fantasy novel, the first original novel in Tempo's MagicQuest line. Illustrations by Judy Mitchell.

Wren, M.K. HOUSE OF THE WOLF (Berkley 0-425-08273-3, 11/85 [10/85], $2.95, 310pp, pb) Reissue (Berkley 1981) sf novel, Book Three of "The Phoenix Legacy"; 2nd printing.

Wren, M.K. SHADOW OF THE SWAN (Berkley 0-425-07965-1, 07/85 [06/85], $2.95, 338pp, pb) Reissue (Berkley 1981) sf novel, Book Two of "The Phoenix Legacy". A family saga in outer space. 3rd printing.

Wren, M.K. SWORD OF THE LAMB (Berkley 0-425-07587-7, 03/85 [02/85], $3.50, 436pp, pb) Reissue (Berkley 1981) sf novel, Book One of "The Phoenix Legacy". 3rd printing.

*Wrightson, Patricia NIGHT OUTSIDE (Atheneum 0-689-50363-6, 10/85 [11/85], $11.95, 67pp, hc) Young-adult fantasy novella, illustrated by Beth Peck.

Wyndham, John THE DAY OF THE TRIFFIDS (Ballantine/Del Rey 0-345-32817-5, 01/86 [12/85], $2.95, 191pp, pb) Reprint (Doubleday 1951) sf novel.

*Yarbro, Chelsea Quinn FOUR HORSES FOR TISHTRY (Harper & Row 0-06-026638-4, 05/85 [04/85], $12.50, 224pp, hc) Non-sf/fantasy, associational--listed for Yarbro fans. This a young-adult historical novel set during the Roman Empire.

*Yarbro, Chelsea Quinn A MORTAL GLAMOUR (Bantam 0-553-24587-2, 01/85 [12/84], $3.50, 308pp, pb) Fantasy novel of evil in a 14th-century convent.

*Yarbro, Chelsea Quinn TO THE HIGH REDOUBT (Popular Library/Questar 0-445-20122-3, 10/85 [09/85], $3.50, 370pp, pb) Fantasy novel set in the 16th century and featuring a Polish warrior and a tantric adept. An interesting attempt at bringing together very different historical cultures. (DLN)

*Yates, W.R. DIASPORAH (Baen 0-671-55974-5, 08/85 [07/85], $2.95, 307pp, pb) Sf novel of "New Israel" in space; a first novel.

*Yeager, General Chuck & Leo Janos YEAGER: AN AUTOBIOGRAPHY (Bantam 0-553-05093-1, 07/85 [06/85], $17.95, 342pp, hc) Non-fiction, associational. A marvelous autobiography (including contributions from colleagues and relatives) of a remarkable man -- fascinating for sf fans as well as anyone interested in aviation history and adventure. (FCM)

*Yep, Laurence DRAGON STEEL (Harper & Row 0-06-026748-8, 05/85 [04/85], $12.50, 278pp, hc) Juvenile fantasy novel, sequel to DRAGON OF THE LOST SEA. Recommended. (DLN)

*Yep, Laurence THE SHADOW LORD (Pocket 0-671-47392-1, 03/85 [02/85], $3.50, 280pp, pb) Star Trek novel.

*Yoke, Carl B. & Donald M. Hassler, eds. DEATH AND THE SERPENT: IMMORTALITY IN SCIENCE FICTION (Greenwood 0-313-23289-2, 03/85 [02/85], $35.00, viii + 235pp, hc) Non-fiction, a group of 18 scholarly essays on immortality in sf and fantasy from Tolkien to Heinlein.

Yolen, Jane CARDS OF GRIEF (SFBC #5987, 06/85 [05/85], $4.98, 143pp, hc) Reprint (Ace 1984) sf novel, first hardcover edition.

*Yolen, Jane DRAGONFIELD AND OTHER STORIES (Ace 0-441-16622-9, 09/85 [08/85], $2.95, 241pp, pb) Collection of stories and poems.
Contents:

			Page
Introduction	Patricia A. McKillip	in WFC 1984	xi
Dragonfield	Jane Yolen	nv 1985	1
The Thirteenth Fey	Jane Yolen	ss FAERY! ,85	31
The Storyteller	Jane Yolen	pm NSJ 1984	46
The Five Points of Roguery			
	Jane Yolen	ss FSF Nov,84	49
DREAM WEAVER	Jane Yolen	co DRMWEVR,79	59
Seven stories tied together by narrative.			
Brother Hart	Jane Yolen	ss FSF Nov,78	60
Man of Rock, Man of Stone			
	Jane Yolen	ss DRMWEVR,79	70
The Tree's Wife	Jane Yolen	ss FSF Jun,78	77
The Cat Bride	Jane Yolen	ss DRMWEVR,79	85
The Boy Who Sang for Death			
	Jane Yolen	ss DRMWEVR,79	88
Princess Heart O'Stone	Jane Yolen	ss DRMWEVR,79	97
The Pot Child	Jane Yolen	ss FSF Feb,79	105
The Fates	Jane Yolen	pm S*L 1982	112
Salvage	Jane Yolen	ss IAS May,84	114
The Bull & the Crowth	Jane Yolen	ss WHITEHN,84	121
The River Maid	Jane Yolen	ss FSF Jan,81	125
Caliban	Jane Yolen	pm GRC 1960	132
The Corridors of the Sea	Jane Yolen	nv FSF Sep,81	133
The Girl Who Cried Flowers			
	Jane Yolen	ss GRLWHOC,74	154
Dryad's Lament	Jane Yolen	pm F&T 1984	159
The Inn of the Demon Camel			
	Jane Yolen	ss LIAVEK ,85	160
The Hundredth Dove	Jane Yolen	ss FSF Apr,77	167
The Lady and the Merman	Jane Yolen	ss FSF Sep,76	173
Angelica	Jane Yolen	ss FSF Dec,79	177
The Wild Child	Jane Yolen	pm	182
Happy Dens, or A Day in the Old Wolves Home			
	Jane Yolen	ss ELW V 3,84	184
The Undine	Jane Yolen	ss NPTNRIS,82	199
Undine	Jane Yolen	pm NPTNRIS,82	204
The White Seal Maid	Jane Yolen	ss PRB 1977	206
Once a Good Man	Jane Yolen	ss 100thDV,76	212
The Malaysian Mer	Jane Yolen	ss NPTNRIS,82	216
Into the Wood	Jane Yolen	pm IAS Feb,85	225
The Tower Bird	Jane Yolen	vi ARI # 4,78	227
The Face in the Cloth	Jane Yolen	ss FSF Feb,85	230

*Young, Robert F. THE VIZIER'S SECOND DAUGHTER (DAW 0-88677-004-1, 02/85 [01/85], $2.50, 203pp, pb) Humorous fantasy novel with sf elements. "A timenapper in the Arabian Nights."

*Yourcenar, Marguerite ORIENTAL TALES (Farrar, Straus & Giroux 0-374-22728-4, 08/85 [09/85], $12.95, length not known, hc) Collection of 10 tales, many with elements of fantasy. This is the first English translation of a book that appeared in France in 1938.

Yulsman, Jerry ELLEANDER MORNING (Tor 0-812-59073-2, 05/85 [04/85], $3.95, 382pp, pb) Reprint (St. Martin's 1984) fantasy novel of time travel and parallel worlds. Recommended. (CNB)

*Zahn, Timothy COBRA (Baen 0-671-55960-5, 05/85 [04/85], $2.95, 346pp, pb) Sf novel.

*Zahn, Timothy A COMING OF AGE (Bluejay 0-312-94058-0, 04/85 [03/85], $14.95, 292pp, hc) Sf novel.

*Zahn, Timothy SPINNERET (Bluejay 0-312-94411-X, 11/85 [12/85], $15.95, 339pp, hc) Sf novel.

*Zebrowski, George THE MONADIC UNIVERSE (Ace 0-441-53541-0, 05/85 [04/85], $2.95, 167pp, pb) Revised edition of a 1977 Ace collection, with a new introduction, some alterations, and two additional stories.
Contents:

			Page
Foreword: Ideas that Will Kill Your Grandmother			
	Howard Waldrop	fw	xi
This Is: An Introduction	Thomas N. Scortia	in	xv
First Love, First Fear	George Zebrowski	ss STRNGBD,72	1
Starcrossed	George Zebrowski	ss EROSORB,73	11
Assassins of Air	George Zebrowski	ss FUTCITY,73	18
Parks of Rest and Culture			
	George Zebrowski	ss SVNGWRL,73	27
The Water Sculptor [The Water Sculptor of Station 233]			
	George Zebrowski	ss INY # 1,70	39
Rope of Glass	George Zebrowski	ss TWOVIEW,73	47
Heathen God	George Zebrowski	ss FSF Jan,71	60
Interpose	George Zebrowski	ss INY # 5,73	71
The History Machine	George Zebrowski	ss NWQ # 3,72	79
The Cliometricon	George Zebrowski	ss AMZ May,75	86
Stance of Splendor	George Zebrowski	ss NWQ # 5,73	94
Wayside World	George Zebrowski	nv WRLDCLP,77	100
The Monadic Universe	George Zebrowski	nv INY # 3,72	129
The Word Sweep	George Zebrowski	ss FSF Aug,79	156

*Zebrowski, George THE STARS WILL SPEAK (Harper & Row 0-06-026886-7, 09/85 [09/85], $11.95, 216pp, hc) Young-adult sf novel, sequel to SUNSPACER.

*Zebrowski, George, ed. NEBULA AWARDS 20: SFWA'S CHOICES FOR THE BEST IN SCIENCE FICTION 1984 (Harcourt Brace Jovanovich 0-14-164927-8, 11/85 [12/85], $17.95, 372pp, hc) Anthology featuring winners and runners-up for the 1984 Nebula Awards.
Contents:

			Page
Introduction	George Zebrowski	in	ix
1984 or Against	Algis Budrys	ar 1985	1
Bloodchild	Octavia E. Butler	nv IAS Jun,84	16
The Man Who Painted the Dragon Griaule			
	Lucius Shepard	nv FSF Dec,84	38
PRESS ENTER ■	John Varley	na IAS May,84	69
New Rose Hotel	William Gibson	ss OMN Jul,84	136
The Greening of Bed-Stuy	Frederik Pohl	na FSF Jul,84	149
The Lucky Strike	Kim Stanley Robinson	nv UNI #14,84	213
Morning Child	Gardner Dozois	ss OMN Jan,84	252
The Aliens Who Knew, I Mean, Everything			
	George Alec Effinger	ss FSF Oct,84	260
A Cabin on the Coast	Gene Wolfe	ss FSF Feb,84	278
Dogs' Lives	Michael Bishop	nv MIS V7 #2,84	292
The Eichmann Variations	George Zebrowski	ss LGTYR&D,84	313
Love Song to Lucy	Herman Herlich	pm S83 1983	323
Lucy Answers	Herman Herlich	pm S83 1983	324
Saul's Death: Two Sestinas			
	Joe W. Haldeman	pm WAR V 1,83	325
Science Fiction Films of 1984			
	Bill Warren	ar 1985	328
SFWA, the Guild	Norman Spinrad	ar 1985	355
About the Nebula Award	[Misc. Material]	ar	361
The 1984 Nebula Awards Ballot			
	[Misc. Material]	bi	363
Past Nebula Award Winners			
	[Misc. Material]	ms	366

*Zebrowski, George, ed. NEBULA AWARDS 20: SFWA'S CHOICES FOR THE BEST IN SCIENCE FICTION 1984 (HBJ/Harvest 0-15-665477-6, 11/85 [12/85], $8.95, 372pp, pb) Paperback edition of the above.

Zelazny, Roger ISLE OF THE DEAD (Ace 0-441-37471-9, 02/85 [01/85], $2.75, 190pp, pb) Reissue (Ace 1969) sf novel. 8th Ace printing. One of Zelazny's best. Highly recommended. (CNB)

Zelazny, Roger JACK OF SHADOWS (NAL/Signet 0-451-13576-8, 05/85 [04/85], $2.75, 236pp, pb) Reissue (Walker 1971) fantasy novel.

*Zelazny, Roger TRUMPS OF DOOM (Arbor House 0-87795-718-5, 06/85 [05/85], $14.95, 183pp, hc) Fantasy novel in the "Amber" series. It ends with a cliffhanger.

Zelazny, Roger TRUMPS OF DOOM (Underwood-Miller 0-88733-006-1, 08/85 [07/85], $50.00, 183pp, hc) Reprint (Arbor House 1985) fantasy novel, start of a new "Amber" series. It's a signed, numbered, slipcased limited edition of 500 copies. There's a new three-page prologue.

Zelazny, Roger TRUMPS OF DOOM (SFBC #04714, 09/85 [08/85], $4.98, 183pp, hc) Reprint (Arbor House 1985) fantasy novel in the "Amber" series.

*Ziegfeld, Richard E. STANISLAW LEM (Ungar 0-8044-2994-4, 12/85 [12/85], $14.95, 188pp, hc) Non-fiction, critical study, including a primary and secondary bibliography.

*Ziegfeld, Richard E. STANISLAW LEM (Ungar 0-8044-6992-X, 12/85 [12/85], $8.95, 188pp, pb) Paperback edition of the above.

Sf in Non-Genre Publications

Contents:

TITLE LIST, BOOKS

100 GREAT FANTASY SHORT STORIES
Isaac Asimov, Terry Carr & Martin H.
Greenberg, eds.   an Avon,85
*THE 1985 ANNUAL WORLD'S BEST SF
Donald A. Wollheim, ed.   an DAW,85
THE 1985 ANNUAL WORLD'S BEST SF
Donald A. Wollheim, ed.   an SFBC,85
*THE 1985 RHYSLING ANTHOLOGY
Anonymous
an Science Fiction Poetry Association,85
2010: ODYSSEY TWO   Arthur C. Clarke
n. Quality Paperback Book Club/Del Rey,85
THE 40-MINUTE WAR   Janet Morris & Chris Morris   n. Baen,85
*A. MERRITT: REFLECTIONS IN THE MOON POOL
Sam Moskowitz, ed.   nf Oswald Train,85
ACROSS THE SEA OF SUNS   Gregory Benford   n. SFBC,85
*ACT OF GOD   Eric Kotani & John Maddox Roberts
n. Baen,85
*ACTIVE MEASURES   Janet Morris & David A. Drake n. Baen,85
*ADAM'S COMMON   David Wiseman   n. Houghton Mifflin,85
THE ADOLESCENCE OF P-1   Thomas J. Ryan   n. Baen,85
*ADVENTURES   Mike Resnick   n. NAL/Signet,10
THE ADVENTURES OF ALYX   Joanna Russ   co Women's Press,85
*THE ADVENTURES OF TERRA TARKINGTON, R.N.
Sharon Webb   n. Bantam,85
THE ADVERSARY   Julian May   n. Ballantine/Del Rey,85
*AFTER THE BOMB   Gloria D. Miklowitz
n. Scholastic/Point,85
*AFTER THE FLAMES   Elizabeth Mitchell, ed.   an Baen,85
AFTER THINGS FELL APART   Ron Goulart   n. Berkley,85
*AFTERWAR   Janet Morris, ed.   oa Baen,85
AGE OF MIRACLES   John Brunner   n. DAW,85
*AGE OF WONDERS: EXPLORING THE WORLD OF SCIENCE FICTION
David Hartwell   nf Walker,84
AGE OF WONDERS: EXPLORING THE WORLD OF SCIENCE FICTION
David Hartwell   nf McGraw-Hill,85
AGENT OF THE TERRAN EMPIRE
Poul Anderson   co Ace,85
+ALAN GARNER'S BOOK OF BRITISH FAIRY TALES
Alan Garner   co Delacorte,85
*ALIEN MAIN   Lloyd Biggle, Jr. & T.L. Sherred
n. Doubleday,85
*ALIEN STARS   Elizabeth Mitchell, ed.   oa Baen,85
THE ALIEN UPSTAIRS   Pamela Sargent   n. Bantam,85
ALL THESE EARTHS   F.M. Busby   n. Bantam Spectra,85
*ALLISTAR: JOURNEY THROUGH A MIND
Kurt W. Aigner   n. Vantage,85
*ALONE IN THE ASHES   William W. Johnstone   n. Zebra,85
*THE ALTERNATE ASIMOVS   Isaac Asimov   co Doubleday,86
*ALWAYS COMING HOME   Ursula K. Le Guin   oc Harper & Row,85
*AMAZING STORIES: 60 YEARS OF THE BEST SCIENCE FICTION
Isaac Asimov & Martin H. Greenberg, eds.
an TSR,85
THE AMTRAK WARS, BOOK TWO: FIRST FAMILY
Patrick Tilley   n. Severn House,85
*AMY'S EYES   Richard Kennedy   n. Harper & Row,85
*ANALOG: THE BEST OF SCIENCE FICTION
Anonymous   an A&W/Galahad,85
*ANCIENT OF DAYS   Michael Bishop   n. Arbor House,85
ANCIENT OF DAYS   Michael Bishop   n. SFBC,85
AND ALL BETWEEN   Zilpha Keatley Snyder   n. Tor,85
+AND STILL THE EARTH   Ignacio deLoyola Brandao n. Avon/Bard,85
*ANGEL WITH THE SWORD   C.J. Cherryh   n. DAW,85
ANNA TO THE INFINITE POWER
Mildred Ames   n. Scholastic/Point,85
*THE ANNOTATED GUIDE TO FANTASTIC ADVENTURES
Edward J. Gallagher   nf Starmont,85
*ANTHONOLOGY   Piers Anthony   co Tor,85
THE ANUBIS GATES   Tim Powers   n. Ace,85
THE ANUBIS GATES   Tim Powers   n. Chatto & Windus,85
*APPROACHES TO THE FICTION OF URSULA K. LE GUIN
James Bittner   nf UMI,84
APPROACHING OBLIVION   Harlan Ellison   co Bluejay,85
ARIEL   Jack M. Bickham   n. Tor,85
THE ARMAGEDDON RAG   George R.R. Martin   n. Pocket,85
*THE ART OF SKELETON CREW J.K. Potter   pi Scream/Press,85
+ARTHUR C. CLARKE'S WORLD OF STRANGE POWERS
John Fairley & Simon Welfare
nf Putnam,85
*ARTIFACT   Gregory Benford   n. Tor,85
AS ON A DARKLING PLAIN   Ben Bova   n. Tor,85
ASCENDANCIES   D.G. Compton   n. Ace,85
*THE ASTRAL MIRROR   Ben Bova   co Tor,85
*AT ANY PRICE   David A. Drake   n. Baen,85
AT THE EARTH'S CORE   Edgar Rice Burroughs   n. Ace,85
AT THE MOUNTAINS OF MADNESS
H.P. Lovecraft   co Arkham House,85
ATLAN   Jane Gaskell   n. DAW,85
*ATLAS   Jorge Luis Borges   nf Dutton,85
THE ATLAS OF PERN   Karen Wynn Fonstad   nf SFBC,85
*THE ATLAS OF THE LAND   Karen Wynn Fonstad   nf Ballantine,85
*THE ATLAS OF THE LAND   Karen Wynn Fonstad
nf Ballantine/Del Rey,85
*BAAA   David Macaulay   na Houghton Mifflin,85
*THE BACHMAN BOOKS: FOUR EARLY NOVELS BY STEPHEN KING
Stephen King   om NAL,85
*THE BACHMAN BOOKS: FOUR EARLY NOVELS BY STEPHEN KING
Stephen King   om NAL/Plume,85
*BACK TO THE FUTURE   George Gipe   n. Berkley,85
BACK TO THE STONE AGE   Edgar Rice Burroughs   n. Ace,85
THE BADGER OF GHISSI   Wolf von Niebelschutz
n. Allen & Unwin/Unicorn,85

*A BAIT OF DREAMS   Jo Clayton   n. DAW,85
*BAKER'S DOZEN: 13 SHORT SCIENCE FICTION NOVELS
Isaac Asimov, Martin H. Greenberg &
Charles G. Waugh, eds.   an Bonanza,85
*THE BANTAM SPECTRA SAMPLER
Lou Aronica, ed.   an Bantam Spectra,85
*BARBARIANS   Robert Adams, Martin H. Greenberg &
Charles G. Waugh, eds. an NAL/Signet,86
*BARNABY #1: WANTED: A FAIRY GODFATHER
Crockett Johnson
cs Ballantine/Del Rey,85
*BARNABY #2: MR. O'MALLEY AND THE HAUNTED HOUSE
Crockett Johnson
cs Ballantine/Del Rey,85
*BARNABY #3: JACKEEN J.O. O'MALLEY FOR CONGRESS
Crockett Johnson
cs Ballantine/Del Rey,86
*BATTLESTAR GALACTICA 11: THE NIGHTMARE MACHINE
Glen S. Larson & Robert Thurston
n. Berkley,85
BEARING AN HOURGLASS   Piers Anthony   n. SFBC,85
BEARING AN HOURGLASS   Piers Anthony   n. Ballantine/Del Rey,85
*THE BEAST OF HEAVEN   Victor Kelleher
n. Univ. of Queensland Press,84
*BEASTMARKS   A.A. Attanasio   oc Ziesing,85
BEASTS OF GOR   John Norman   n. DAW,85
*THE BEASTS OF VALHALLA   George C. Chesbro   n. Atheneum,85
BEAUTY   Robin McKinley   n. Harper & Row,85
*BECOME THE HUNTED   Jefferson P. Swycaffer   n. Avon,85
THE BEGGAR QUEEN   Lloyd Alexander   n. Dell/Laurel Leaf,85
BEHIND THE ATTIC WALL   Sylvia Cassidy   n. Avon/Camelot,85
THE BELGARIAD 1   David Eddings   om Century,85
THE BELGARIAD 2   David Eddings   om Century,85
*THE BELGARIAD: PART ONE   David Eddings   om SFBC,85
*THE BELGARIAD: PART TWO   David Eddings   om SFBC,85
BELOVED EXILE   Parke Godwin   n. Bantam Spectra,85
BELOW THE ROOT   Zilpha Keatley Snyder   n. Tor,85
*BENCHMARKS: GALAXY BOOKSHELF
Algis Budrys
nf S. Illinois Univ. Press,85
*BERSERKER BASE   Fred Saberhagen, ed.   an Tor,85
BERSERKER BASE   Fred Saberhagen, ed.   an SFBC,85
*THE BERSERKER THRONE   Fred Saberhagen   n. Simon & Schuster,85
*THE BERSERKER THRONE   Fred Saberhagen
n. Simon & Schuster/Fireside,85
THE BERSERKER WARS   Fred Saberhagen   co Tor,85
BERSERKER'S PLANET   Fred Saberhagen   n. Ace,86
*BERSERKER: BLUE DEATH   Fred Saberhagen   n. Tor,85
THE BEST OF CORDWAINER SMITH
Cordwainer Smith
co Ballantine/Del Rey,85
*THE BEST OF MARGARET ST. CLAIR
Margaret St. Clair co Academy Chicago,85
*THE BEST OF MARION ZIMMER BRADLEY
Marion Zimmer Bradley
co Academy Chicago,85
*THE BEST OF TREK #8   Walter Irwin & G.B. Love, eds.
nf NAL/Signet,85
*THE BEST OF TREK #9   Walter Irwin & G.B. Love, eds.
nf NAL/Signet,85
BEST SF OF THE YEAR #14   Terry Carr, ed.   an Gollancz,85
THE BEST SHORT STORIES OF J.G. BALLARD
J.G. Ballard
co Pocket/Washington Square Press,85
*BESTIARY MOUNTAIN   John Forrester   n. Bradbury Press,85
*BESTIARY!   Jack Dann & Gardner Dozois, eds.
an Ace,85
*BETWEEN THE STROKES OF NIGHT
Charles Sheffield   n. Baen,85
*BEYOND ARMAGEDDON   Walter M. Miller, Jr. & Martin H.
Greenberg, eds.   an Donald I Fine,85
*BEYOND SANCTUARY   Janet Morris   n. Baen,85
BEYOND SANCTUARY   Janet Morris   n. SFBC,85
BEYOND THE BLUE EVENT HORIZON
Frederik Pohl   n. Ballantine/Del Rey,85
*BEYOND THE DAR AL-HARB   Gordon R. Dickson   co Tor,85
*BEYOND THE VEIL   Janet Morris   n. Baen,86
THE BICENTENNIAL MAN...AND OTHER STORIES
Isaac Asimov   co Ballantine/Del Rey,85
BIO OF A SPACE TYRANT, VOL. I: REFUGEE
Piers Anthony   n. Gregg,85
BIO OF A SPACE TYRANT, VOL. II: MERCENARY
Piers Anthony   n. Gregg,85
*BIO OF A SPACE TYRANT, VOL. III: POLITICIAN
Piers Anthony   n. Avon,85
BIO OF A SPACE TYRANT, VOL. III: POLITICIAN
Piers Anthony   n. Gregg,85
*BIO OF A SPACE TYRANT, VOL. IV: EXECUTIVE
Piers Anthony   n. Avon,85
*BIOBLAST   Raymond Z. Gallun   n. Berkley,85
*BIOLOGICAL THEMES IN MODERN SCIENCE FICTION
Helen N. Parker   nf UMI,84
BIRDS OF PREY   David A. Drake   n. Tor,85
THE BIRTHGRAVE   Tanith Lee   n. DAW,86
THE BISHOP'S HEIR   Katherine Kurtz   n. SFBC,85
THE BISHOP'S HEIR   Katherine Kurtz n. Ballantine/Del Rey,85
THE BLACK BEAST   Nancy Springer   n. Corgi,85
THE BLACK FLAME   Lynn Abbey   n. Ace,85
*THE BLACK SHIP   Christopher Rowley
n. Ballantine/Del Rey,85
*BLACK STAR RISING   Frederik Pohl   n. Ballantine/Del Rey,85
BLACK STAR RISING   Frederik Pohl   n. SFBC,85

*BLACK SUITS FROM OUTER SPACE
        Gene DeWeese   n. Putnam,85
*BLACK VENUS   Angela Carter
        co Chatto & Windus/Hogarth Press,85
*BLOOD AND DREAMS   Richard Monaco   n. Berkley,85
*BLOOD AUTUMN   Kathryn Ptacek   n. Tor,85
*BLOOD FOUNTAIN   Robert E. Vardeman & George W. Proctor
                                                n. Ace,85
*BLOOD HERITAGE   Sheri S. Tepper   n. Tor,86
*BLOOD IN THE ASHES   William W. Johnstone   n. Zebra,85
*BLOOD MUSIC   Greg Bear   n. Arbor House,85
 BLOOD MUSIC   Greg Bear   n. SFBC,85
 THE BLOODY SUN   Marion Zimmer Bradley   co Ace,85
*BLUE ROSE   Peter Straub   nv Underwood-Miller,85
*THE BOOK OF BEING   Ian Watson   n. Gollancz,85
*A BOOK OF DRAGONS   Hosie Baskin & Leonard Baskin
                                             pi Knopf,85
*THE BOOK OF IAN WATSON   Ian Watson   co Ziesing,85
*THE BOOK OF KANE   Karl Edward Wagner co Donald M. Grant,85
*THE BOOK OF KELLS   R.A. MacAvoy   n. Bantam Spectra,85
 THE BOOK OF LOST TALES 1 J.R.R. Tolkien
                     ms Allen & Unwin/Unicorn,85
*THE BOOK OF SORROWS Walter Wangerin   n. Harper & Row,85
+THE BOOK OF THE RIVER   Ian Watson   n. DAW,86
*BOOKS OF BLOOD   Clive Barker   om Scream/Press,85
+BORIS VALLEJO'S FANTASY ART TECHNIQUES
                     Boris Vallejo
                     pi Arco/Simon & Schuster,85
 BORROWED TIME   Alan Hruska   n. Baen,85
 THE BORROWERS AVENGED Mary Norton   n. HBJ/Voyager,85
*A BOX OF NOTHING   Peter Dickinson   n. Gollancz,85
+BOXEN: THE IMAGINARY WORLD OF THE YOUNG C.S. LEWIS
                     C.S. Lewis
                     co Harcourt Brace Jovanovich,85
 BRAIN WAVE   Poul Anderson n. Ballantine/Del Rey,85
*BRAINCHILD   John Saul   n. Bantam,85
*BRAINZ, INC.   Ron Goulart   n. DAW,85
+BREATHING SPACE ONLY Wynne Whiteford   n. Ace,86
 BREED TO COME   Andre Norton   n. Ace,85
*THE BRIDE: A TALE OF LOVE AND DOOM
                     Les Martin   na Random House,85
 BRIDGE OF BIRDS   Barry Hughart n. Ballantine/Del Rey,85
 BRIGHT COMPANION   Edward Llewellyn   n. DAW,85
*BRIGHT SHADOW   Avi   n. Bradbury Press,85
*BRIGHTNESS FALLS FROM THE AIR
                     James Tiptree, Jr.   n. Tor,85
 BRIGHTNESS FALLS FROM THE AIR
                     James Tiptree, Jr.   n. SFBC,85
*BROKEDOWN PALACE   Steven Brust   n. Ace,86
*BROKEN STONE   Richard Monaco   n. Ace,85
*THE BRONZE KING   Suzy McKee Charnas
                                    n. Houghton Mifflin,85
*BROTHER JONATHAN   Crawford Kilian   n. Ace,85
*THE BURNT LANDS   Richard Elliott n. Fawcett/Gold Medal,85
*BYTE BEAUTIFUL: EIGHT SCIENCE FICTION STORIES
                     James Tiptree, Jr.   co Doubleday,85
*C.A.D.S.   John Sievert   n. Zebra,85
 C.L.U.T.Z. AND THE FIZZION FORMULA
                     Marilyn Z. Wilkes   n. Gollancz,85
+C.S. LEWIS AT THE BREAKFAST TABLE, AND OTHER REMINISCENCES
                     James T. Como, ed.   nf Collier,85
*CADRE ONE   Robert O'Riordan   n. Ace,86
*CAMPBELL WOOD   Al Sarrantonio   n. Doubleday,86
*CARACOLE   Edmund White   n. Dutton,85
 CARDS OF GRIEF   Jane Yolen   n. SFBC,85
 THE CARNELIAN THRONE Janet Morris   n. Baen,85
*CASCA: THE ASSASSIN Barry Sadler   n. Ace/Charter,85
*CASCA: THE PHOENIX   Barry Sadler   n. Charter,85
*CASCA: THE PIRATE   Barry Sadler   n. Ace/Charter,85
 CASTAWAYS IN TIME   Robert Adams   n. NAL/Signet,85
*THE CAT WHO WALKS THROUGH WALLS: A COMEDY OF MANNERS
                     Robert A. Heinlein   n. Putnam,85
*CATS HAVE NO LORD   Will Shetterly   n. Ace,85
+THE CAVES OF KLYDOR Douglas Hill   n. Atheneum/Argo,85
*THE CENTAUR IN THE GARDEN
                     Moacyr Scliar
                     n. Ballantine/Available Press,85
 THE CENTAURI DEVICE M. John Harrison   n. Bantam,85
*THE CENTRIFUGAL RICKSHAW DANCER
                     William John Watkins
                     n. Popular Library/Questar,85
 THE CEREMONIES   T.E.D. Klein   n. Bantam,85
 CHAINING THE LADY   Piers Anthony   n. Avon,85
 THE CHAMPION OF GARATHORM
                     Michael Moorcock   n. Berkley,85
 THE CHANGEOVER: A SUPERNATURAL ROMANCE
                     Margaret Mahy   n. Scholastic/Point,85
*CHANGER'S MOON   Jo Clayton   n. DAW,85
*THE CHANGES TRILOGY Peter Dickinson   om Puffin,85
 CHANUR'S VENTURE   C.J. Cherryh   n. DAW,85
 CHANUR'S VENTURE   C.J. Cherryh   n. SFBC,85
*CHAPTER HOUSE DUNE   Frank Herbert   n. Gollancz,85
+CHAPTERHOUSE: DUNE   Frank Herbert   n. Putnam,85
 CHILD OF FORTUNE   Norman Spinrad   n. Bantam Spectra,85
 CHILD OF FORTUNE   Norman Spinrad   n. SFBC,85
*CHILD OF TOMORROW   Barbara Bartholomew n. NAL/Signet,85
*THE CHILDREN OF ANTHI Jay D. Blakeney   n. Ace,85
 CHILDREN OF MORROW   H.M. Hoover   n. Puffin,85
*CHILDREN OF THE DRAGON Rose Estes   n. Random House,85
*CHILDREN OF THE DUST Louise Lawrence   n. Harper & Row,85
*CHILDREN OF THE LIGHT Susan Weston   n. St. Martin's,85
*THE CHRISTENING QUEST Elizabeth Scarborough n. Bantam,85

*THE CHRONICLES OF CASTLE BRASS
                     Michael Moorcock   om Granada,85
*THE CHRONICLES OF THE DERYNI
                     Katherine Kurtz   om SFBC,85
*THE CINGULUM   John Maddox Roberts   n. Tor,85
*CINNABAR   Graham Diamond n. Fawcett Gold Medal,85
 CIRCUMPOLAR!   Richard A. Lupoff   n. Berkley,85
 THE CITY   Jane Gaskell   n. DAW,85
 THE CITY IN THE GLACIER Robert E. Vardeman & Victor Milan
                                                n. Ace,85
*CITY OF A MILLION LEGENDS
                     Jacqueline Lichtenberg   n. Berkley,85
 CITY OF SORCERY   Marion Zimmer Bradley   n. SFBC,85
 CLAIMED   Francis Stevens   n. Carroll & Graf,85
 CLAN OF THE CAVE BEAR Jean Auel   n. Bantam,85
 CLAY'S ARK   Octavia E. Butler   n. Ace,85
 CLIVE BARKER'S BOOKS OF BLOOD, VOL.S ONE, TWO & THREE
                     Clive Barker om Weidenfeld & Nicolson,85
*CLIVE BARKER'S BOOKS OF BLOOD, VOLUME 4
                     Clive Barker   oc Sphere,85
*CLIVE BARKER'S BOOKS OF BLOOD, VOLUME 5
                     Clive Barker   oc Sphere,85
*CLIVE BARKER'S BOOKS OF BLOOD, VOLUME 6
                     Clive Barker   oc Sphere,85
*CLOAK OF ILLUSION   John Maddox Roberts   n. Tor,85
 CLOUD WARRIOR   Patrick Tilley   n. Baen,85
 CLUSTER   Piers Anthony   n. Avon,85
*COBRA   Timothy Zahn   n. Baen,85
*COCOON   David Saperstein   n. Jove,85
*COLD PRINT   Ramsey Campbell   co Scream/Press,85
 COLD WAR IN HELL   Harry Blamires   n. Nelson,85
 COLLECTED STORIES   Gabriel Garcia Marquez
                                    co Perennial Library,85
*THE COLLECTOR'S INDEX TO WEIRD TALES
                     Sheldon R. Jaffery & Fred Cook
                     nf Bowling Green Popular Press,85
 COLOSSUS   D.F. Jones   n. Berkley,85
 THE COLOUR OF MAGIC Terry Pratchett   n. Corgi,85
 THE COLOUR OF MAGIC Terry Pratchett   n. NAL/Signet,85
*COLSEC REBELLION   Douglas Hill   n. Gollancz,85
+COLSEC REBELLION   Douglas Hill   n. Atheneum/Argo,85
*THE COMEDY OF THE FANTASTIC: ECOLOGICAL PERSPECTIVES ON THE
 FANTASY NOVEL   Don D. Elgin   nf Greenwood,85
+THE COMET   Robert Charles   n. Tor,85
*A COMING OF AGE   Timothy Zahn   n. Bluejay,85
*THE COMPLETE BOOK OF SWORDS
                     Fred Saberhagen   om SFBC,85
*THE COMPLETE MAGNUS RIDOLPH
                     Jack Vance   co Underwood-Miller,85
 COMPUTER EYE   A.E. van Vogt   n. DAW,85
 CONAN   Robert E. Howard, Lin Carter & L.
                     Sprague de Camp   co Ace,85
 CONAN OF CIMMERIA   Robert E. Howard, Lin Carter & L.
                     Sprague de Camp   co Ace,85
 CONAN THE FREEBOOTER Robert E. Howard & L. Sprague de Camp
                                              co Ace,86
 CONAN THE TRIUMPHANT Robert Jordan   n. Tor,85
*CONAN THE VALOROUS   John Maddox Roberts   n. Tor,85
 CONAN THE VICTORIOUS Robert Jordan   n. Tor,85
 CONAN THE WANDERER   Robert E. Howard, Lin Carter & L.
                     Sprague de Camp   co Ace,86
 CONAN: THE FLAME KNIFE Robert E. Howard & L. Sprague de Camp
                                                n. Ace,85
 CONAN: THE TREASURE OF TRANICOS
                     Robert E. Howard   n. Ace,85
 CONCRETE ISLAND   J.G. Ballard   n. Vintage,85
 THE CONGLOMEROID COCKTAIL PARTY
                     Robert Silverberg   co Gollancz,85
 THE CONGLOMEROID COCKTAIL PARTY
                     Robert Silverberg   co Bantam Spectra,85
*CONTACT   Carl Sagan   n. Simon & Schuster,85
 THE CONTINENT OF LIES James Morrow   n. Gollancz,85
 THE CONTINENT OF LIES James Morrow   n. Baen,85
*CONTRARY MODES   Jenny Blackford, Russell Blackford, Lucy
                     Sussex & Norman Talbot, eds.
                     nf Ebony Books,85
+CONVERTS   Ian Watson   n. St. Martin's,85
*THE COPPER CROWN   Patricia Kennealy   n. Bluejay,85
*THE COPY SHOP   Evelyn E. Smith   n. Doubleday,85
*THE COSMIC PERSPECTIVE/CUSTER'S LAST STAND
                     Brian Stableford   oc Drumm,85
 COUNT BRASS   Michael Moorcock   n. Berkley,85
*COURT OF A THOUSAND SUNS Allan Cole & Chris Bunch
                     n. Ballantine/Del Rey,86
 THE COWARDLY LION OF OZ Ruth Plumly Thompson
                     n. Ballantine/Del Rey,85
 CRASH   J.G. Ballard   n. Vintage,85
 CREATOR   Jeremy Levin   n. Pocket,85
*A CREED FOR THE THIRD MILLENNIUM
                     Colleen McCullough n. Harper & Row,85
*CREWEL LYE   Piers Anthony n. Ballantine/Del Rey,85
 CREWEL LYE   Piers Anthony   n. SFBC,85
*CROSS-CURRENTS   Robert Lynn Asprin & Lynn Abbey, eds.
                                             om SFBC,84
 THE CROSSROADS OF TIME Andre Norton   n. Ace,85
*THE CRYSTAL CITY   Nancy Etchemendy   n. Avon/Camelot,85
 THE CRYSTAL GRYPHON Andre Norton   n. Tor,85
 CRYSTAL SINGER   Anne McCaffrey n. Ballantine/Del Rey,85
*CUCKOO'S EGG   C.J. Cherryh   n. Phantasia,85
 CUCKOO'S EGG   C.J. Cherryh   n. DAW,85
 CUCKOO'S EGG   C.J. Cherryh   n. SFBC,85

THE HAMMER OF DARKNESS   KROZAIR OF KREGEN

*WAR WITH THE NEWTS	Karel Capek	n. Allen & Unwin/Unicorn,85
*WARLOCK	Glen Cook	n. Popular Library/Questar,85
+WARLOCK AT THE WHEEL AND OTHER STORIES		
	Diana Wynne Jones	co Greenwillow,85
*THE WARLOCK ENRAGED	Christopher Stasheff	n. Ace,85
*THE WARLOCK OF RHADA	Robert Cham Gilman	n. Ace,85
*THE WARLORD #5: TERMINAL ISLAND		
	Jason Frost	n. Zebra,85
THE WARLORDS OF NIN	Stephen Lawhead	n. Crossway,85
*THE WARRIOR WHO CARRIED LIFE		
	Geoff Ryman	n. Allen & Unwin,85
*WARRIOR WITCH OF HEL	Asa Drake	n. Popular Library/Questar,85
*WARRIOR WOMAN	Marion Zimmer Bradley	n. DAW,85
THE WARRIORS OF DAWN	M.A. Foster	n. DAW,84
THE WATCHERS OF SPACE	Nancy Etchemendy	n. Avon/Camelot,85
THE WATER OF THOUGHT	Fred Saberhagen	n. Tor,85
WATERSHIP DOWN	Richard Adams	n. Avon,86
WAY STATION	Clifford D. Simak	n. SFBC,85
WAY-FARER	Dennis Schmidt	n. Ace,86
*WEB OF DARKNESS	Marion Zimmer Bradley	om Richard Drew,85
WELCOME TO THE MONKEY HOUSE		
	Kurt Vonnegut	co Dell/Delta,85
WELCOME, CHAOS	Kate Wilhelm	n. Berkley,85
THE WELL-WISHERS	Edward Eager	n. HBJ/Voyager,85
*WEREWOLVES OF KREGEN	Dray Prescot	n. DAW,85
WEST OF EDEN	Harry Harrison	n. SFBC,85
WEST OF EDEN	Harry Harrison	n. Bantam Spectra,85
WHALESONG	Robert Siegel	n. Berkley,85
+WHAT'S BRED IN THE BONE	Robertson Davies	n. Viking,85
WHEELS WITHIN WHEELS	F. Paul Wilson	n. Berkley,85
*WHEN DREAMERS CEASE TO DREAM		
	Barbara Bartholomew	
		n. NAL/Signet/Vista,85
*WHERE DRAGONS LIE	R.A.V. Salsitz	n. NAL/Signet,85
*WHISPERS V	Stuart David Schiff, ed.	oa Doubleday,85
*THE WHITE FIRE	Robert E. Vardeman	n. Avon,86
THE WHITE HART	Nancy Springer	n. Pocket,85
*THE WHITE PIPES	Nancy Kress	n. Bluejay,85
*THE WHITE ROSE	Glen Cook	n. Tor,85
*WHITE WING	Gordon Kendall	n. Tor,85
*WHO SAYS PARANOIA ISN'T "IN" ANY MORE?		
	Alexis Gilliland	
		ct Loompanics Unlimited,85
*THE WIDOW'S SON	Robert Anton Wilson	n. Bluejay,85
WILD ANIMALS	Peter Straub	
		om Quality Paperback Book Club/Putnam,85
*WILD COUNTRY	Dean Ing	n. Tor,85
+THE WILD ONES	A. Bertram Chandler	n. DAW,85
WILDRAITH'S LAST BATTLE	Phyllis Ann Karr	n. Berkley,85
*THE WILL OF THE GODS	Sharon Green	n. DAW,85
*WILLIAM S. BURROUGHS	Jennie Skerl	nf Twayne,85
WIND DANCERS	R.M. Meluch	n. NAL/Signet,86
WIND FROM THE ABYSS	Janet Morris	n. Baen,85
WINDHAVEN	George R.R. Martin & Lisa Tuttle	
		n. Pocket,85
*THE WINDRIDER	Stephanie T. Hoppe	n. DAW,85
THE WINDS OF DARKOVER	Marion Zimmer Bradley	n. Ace,85
THE WINGED MAN	A.E. van Vogt & E. Mayne Hull	n. DAW,85
*WINGS OF FLAME	Nancy Springer	n. Tor,85
WINGS OF OMEN	Robert Lynn Asprin & Lynn Abbey, eds.	
		oa Ace,85
*WINTER OF MAGIC'S RETURN	Pamela Service	n. Atheneum,85
*WINTERKING	Paul Hazel	n. Atlantic Monthly,85
*THE WISHSONG OF SHANNARA	Terry Brooks	n. Ballantine/Del Rey,85
THE WISHSONG OF SHANNARA	Terry Brooks	n. SFBC,85
WITCH WORLD	Andre Norton	n. Ace,86
*WITCHDAME	Kathleen Sky	n. Berkley,85
THE WITCHES OF EASTWICK	John Updike	n. Fawcett/Crest,85
*WITCHES OF KREGEN	Dray Prescot	n. DAW,85
*WITH A TANGLED SKEIN	Piers Anthony	n. Ballantine/Del Rey,85

*WITH FATE CONSPIRE	Mike Shupp	n. Ballantine/Del Rey,85
*WITH MAGICAL HORSES TO RIDE		
	Winifred Morris	n. Atheneum,85
*WITH MERCY TOWARD NONE	Glen Cook	n. Baen,85
WIZARD	John Varley	n. Berkley,85
THE WIZARD OF OZ	L. Frank Baum	n. Unicorn,85
*WIZARD OF THE PIGEONS	Megan Lindholm	n. Ace,86
*WOLF OF SHADOWS	Whitley Streiber	na Sierra Club/Knopf,85
WOLFLING	Gordon R. Dickson	n. Baen,85
WOLLHEIM'S WORLD'S BEST SF: SERIES 9		
	Donald A. Wollheim & Arthur W. Saha, eds.	an DAW,85
*THE WOMAN WHO LOVED REINDEER		
	Meredith Ann Pierce	
		n. Atlantic Monthly,85
WONDER'S CHILD: MY LIFE IN SCIENCE FICTION		
	Jack Williamson	nf Bluejay,85
WORDCHANGER	Mary Haynes	n. Dell/Laurel Leaf,85
*THE WORK OF JEFFREY M. ELLIOT: AN ANNOTATED BIBLIOGRAPHY AND GUIDE		
	Boden Clarke	nf Borgo,85
*THE WORK OF JULIAN MAY: AN ANNOTATED BIBLIOGRAPHY & GUIDE		
	Thaddeus Dikty, & R. Reginald	nf Borgo,85
*THE WORK OF R. REGINALD: AN ANNOTATED BIBLIOGRAPHY AND GUIDE		
	Michael Burgess & Jeffrey M. Elliot	nf Borgo,85
*THE WORLD ENDS IN HICKORY HOLLOW		
	Ardath Mayhar	n. Doubleday,85
WORLD ENOUGH AND TIME	James Kahn	n. Ballantine/Del Rey,85
*A WORLD IN AMBER	A. Orr	n. Bluejay,85
+THE WORLD OF FANTASTIC FILMS: AN ILLUSTRATED SURVEY		
	Peter Nicholls	nf Dodd Mead,85
+THE WORLD OF OZ: A FANTASTIC EXPEDITION OVER THE RAINBOW		
	Allen Eyles	nf HP Books,85
*WORLD TALES	G. Randal Rau, ed.	
		oa 1985 World Fantasy Convention,85
WORLD WITHOUT END	Joe W. Haldeman	n. Bantam,85
THE WORLD WRECKERS	Marion Zimmer Bradley	n. Ace,85
*WORLDMAKER	A.C. Ellis	n. Ace,85
WORLDS OF THE IMPERIUM	Keith Laumer	co Tor,86
*THE WORMS	Al Sarrantonio	n. Doubleday,85
*WRAITH BOARD	David F. Bischoff	n. NAL/Signet,85
*YEAGER: AN AUTOBIOGRAPHY	General Chuck Yeager & Leo Janos	
		nf Bantam,85
*THE YEAR'S BEST FANTASY STORIES: 11		
	Arthur W. Saha, ed.	an DAW,85
*THE YEAR'S BEST HORROR STORIES: SERIES XIII		
	Karl Edward Wagner, ed.	an DAW,85
*THE YEAR'S BEST SCIENCE FICTION, SECOND ANNUAL COLLECTION		
	Gardner Dozois, ed.	an Bluejay,85
*THE YEAR'S SCHOLARSHIP IN SCIENCE FICTION, FANTASY AND HORROR LITERATURE	Marshall B. Tymn	
		nf Kent State Univ. Press,85
THE YEARS OF THE CITY	Frederik Pohl	co Pocket,85
*A YOKE OF MAGIC	Robert E. Vardeman & George W. Proctor	
		n. Ace,85
YORATH THE WOLF	Cherry Wilder	n. Baen,85
*YOUNG ADULTS	Daniel M. Pinkwater	co Tor,85
*YOUNG GHOSTS	Isaac Asimov, Martin H. Greenberg & Charles G. Waugh, eds.	
		an Harper & Row,85
*YOUNG MONSTERS	Isaac Asimov, Martin H. Greenberg & Charles G. Waugh, eds.	
		an Harper & Row,85
YURTH BURDEN	Andre Norton	n. DAW,85
THE ZAP GUN	Philip K. Dick	n. Bluejay,85
THE ZERO STONE	Andre Norton	n. Ace,85
*THE ZONE #3: HUNTER KILLER		
	James Rouch	n. Zebra,85

1985 ORIGINAL PUBLICATIONS

Aaron, Chester
OUT OF SIGHT, OUT OF MIND   n. Lippincott,85

Abbey, Lynn
Children of All Ages   nv SOULCTY,86
The God-Chosen   nv DEADWIN,85
The Small Powers that Endure   nv SOULCTY,86

Abbey, Lynn & Robert Lynn Asprin, eds.
THIEVES' WORLD, BOOK 7: THE DEAD OF WINTER   oa Ace,85
THIEVES' WORLD, BOOK 8: SOUL OF THE CITY   oa Ace,86

Abrams, R. Vaughan
PARA   n. Seven Suns,86

Adams, Douglas
THE ORIGINAL HITCHHIKER RADIO SCRIPTS   co Crown/Harmony,85

Adams, Richard
MAIA   n. Knopf,85

Adams, Robert
Battle at Kahlkhopolis   nv WAR V 4,85
HORSES OF THE NORTH   n. NAL/Signet,85
THE SEVEN MAGICAL JEWELS OF IRELAND   n. NAL/Signet,85
TALES OF THE HORSECLANS   om NAL/Plume,85

Adams, Robert, Martin H. Greenberg & Charles G. Waugh, eds.
BARBARIANS   an NAL/Signet,86

Adams, Robert & Andre Norton, eds.
MAGIC IN ITHKAR   oa Tor,85
MAGIC IN ITHKAR 2   oa Tor,85

Adkins, Lee
The Vixen   pm FBM Sep,85

Ahern, Jerry
THE SURVIVALIST #12: THE REBELLION   n. Zebra,85

Aickman, Robert
NIGHT VOICES: STRANGE STORIES   co Gollancz,85
Rosamund's Bower   nv NTVOICE,85

Aigner, Kurt W.
ALLISTAR: JOURNEY THROUGH A MIND   n. Vantage,85

Aiken, Joan
UP THE CHIMNEY DOWN AND OTHER STORIES   oc Harper & Row,85

Aikin, Jim
My Life in the Jungle   ss FSF Feb,85
WALK THE MOONS ROAD   n. Ballantine/Del Rey,85

Aldiss, Brian W.
THE HELLICONIA TRILOGY   om Atheneum,85
HELLICONIA WINTER   n. Atheneum,85
HELLICONIA WINTER   n. Jonathan Cape,85
THE HORATIO STUBBS SAGA   om Granada/Panther,85
THE PALE SHADOW OF SCIENCE   nf Serconia,85
Theodore Sturgeon: 1918-1985   bg BSG 166,85
You Never Asked My Name   ss FSF Nov,85

Alexander, Gary
Buddies   ss IAS Sep,85

Allen, Lori
Family Obligations   ss TZM Feb,85

Allen, Roger Macbride
THE TORCH OF HONOR   n. Baen,85

Allison, Susan, ed.
THE FANTASY SAMPLER   an Berkley/Ace,85

Anderson, Craig
SCIENCE FICTION FILMS OF THE SEVENTIES   nf McFarland,85

Anderson, Kevin J.
Final Performance   ss FSF Jan,85

Anderson, Poul
DIALOGUE WITH DARKNESS   co Tor,85
The Forest   nv MNSNGRF,85
THE GAME OF EMPIRE   n. Baen,85
Pride   nv FFR V 1,85
Star Peace?   ar IAS Sep,85

Anderson, Poul, Martin H. Greenberg & Charles G. Waugh, eds.
MERCENARIES OF TOMORROW   an Critic's Choice,85
TERRORISTS OF TOMORROW   an Critic's Choice,86

Angelo, Ivan
Conquest   nv TWRGLSS,86
Friday Night/Saturday Morning   nv TWRGLSS,86
Lost & Found   nv TWRGLSS,86
The Real True Son of the Bitch   nv TWRGLSS,86
THE TOWER OF GLASS   co Avon/Bard,86
The Tower of Glass   nv TWRGLSS,86

Anonymous
THE 1985 RHYSLING ANTHOLOGY   an Science Fiction Poetry Association,85
ANALOG: THE BEST OF SCIENCE FICTION   an A&W/Galahad,85

Anthony, Piers
ANTHONOLOGY   co Tor,85
BIO OF A SPACE TYRANT, VOL. III: POLITICIAN   n. Avon,85
BIO OF A SPACE TYRANT, VOL. IV: EXECUTIVE   n. Avon,85
CREWEL LYE   n. Ballantine/Del Rey,85
Gone to the Dogs   ss ANTHNGY,85
STEPPE   n. Tor,85
The Toaster   ss ANTHNGY,85
WITH A TANGLED SKEIN   n. Ballantine/Del Rey,85

Antieau, Kim
Cycles   ss SDW # 8,85
Hauntings   ss IAS Feb,85

Aquino, John T.
The Sad Wizard   nv FBM Dec,85

Arbur, Rosemarie
MARION ZIMMER BRADLEY   nf Starmont,85

Armistead, Barbara
On the Trail   ss FRAMZDK,85

Armstrong, Michael
Going After Arviq   nv AFTRWAR,85

Aronica, Lou, ed.
THE BANTAM SPECTRA SAMPLER   an Bantam Spectra,85

Arscott, David & David Marl
A FLIGHT OF BRIGHT BIRDS   n. Allen & Unwin,85

Arthurs, Bruce D.
Unicorn's Blood   nv S&S # 2,85

Ashe, Geoffrey
THE DISCOVERY OF KING ARTHUR   nf Doubleday/Anchor,85

Ashley, Mike
Algernon Blackwood: The Ghostly Tale's Great Visionary   iv TZM Jun,85

Ashley, Mike & Frank H. Parnell
MONTHLY TERRORS: AN INDEX TO THE WEIRD FANTASY MAGAZINES
   PUBLISHED IN THE UNITED STATES AND GREAT BRITAIN   nf Greenwood,85

Ashley, Steven
LOVE OUT OF TIME   n. Berkley,85

Asimov, Isaac
THE ALTERNATE ASIMOVS   co Doubleday,86
Belief [first version]   nv ALTASMV,86
Civil War   ed IAS Dec,85
Dialog   ed IAS Apr,85
THE EDGE OF TOMORROW   co Tor,85
Editors   ed IAS Nov,85
THE END OF ETERNITY [written in winter of 1953-1954]   n. ALTASMV,86
The Eye of the Beholder   ss IAS Jan,86
Fairy Tales   ed IAS Oct,85
GROW OLD ALONG WITH ME [written in summer of 1947]   n. ALTASMV,86
He Travels the Fastest   ss IAS Nov,85
Irritations   ed IAS Dec md,85
The Little Tin God of Characterization   ar IAS May,85
Logic is Logic   ss IAS Aug,85
Magic   ed IAS Mar,85
Moonshine   ed IAS May,85
Old Hundredth   ed IAS Jan,86
OPUS 300   nf Houghton Mifflin,85
Plagiarism   ed IAS Aug,85
ROBOTS AND EMPIRE   n. Doubleday,85
ROBOTS AND EMPIRE   n. Phantasia,85
Science: A Little Leaven   ar FSF Oct,85
Science: Arise, Fair Sun!   ar FSF May,85
Science: Chemistry of the Void   ar FSF Jan,86
Science: Current Affairs   ar FSF Mar,85
Science: Far, Far Below   ar FSF Jan,85
Science: Forcing the Lines   ar FSF Apr,85
Science: Poison in the Negative   ar FSF Jul,85
Science: Salt and Battery   ar FSF Feb,85
Science: The Biochemical Knife Blade   ar FSF Nov,85
Science: The Discovery of the Void   ar FSF Dec,85
Science: The Goblin Element   ar FSF Sep,85
Science: The Rule of Numerous Small   ar FSF Jun,85
Science: Tracing the Traces   ar FSF Aug,85
Slush   ed IAS Feb,85
Star Wars!   ed IAS Sep,85
Superstupidity   ed IAS Jul,85
Sword and Sorcery   ed IAS Jan,85
Symbolism   ed IAS Jun,85
Theodore Sturgeon: 1918-1985   bg IAS Jan,86
Unique Is Where You Find It   ss EDGTMRW,85
Writing of Two Sorts   ar PLANETS,85

Benford, Gregory (continued)
  The Future of the Jovian System   ss PLANETS,85
  Immortal Night   ss OMN Apr,85
  Newton Sleep   nv FSF Jan,86
  Reactionary Utopias   ar FFR V 4,86
  Time's Rub   ss IAS Apr,85
  To the Storming Gulf   na FSF Apr,85

Benford, James
  Star Wars is Not MAD   ar FFR V 4,86

Benni, Stefano
  TERRA!   n. Pantheon,85

Benoit, Hendra
  PSI PATROL: HENDRA'S BOOK   n. Scholastic/Point,85

Benson, Michael
  VINTAGE SCIENCE FICTION FILMS, 1896-1949   nf McFarland,85

Betancourt, John Gregory
  Faramigon's Eye   nv FBM Dec,85
  Memo from a Savage   pm AMZ Nov,85
  Memo to an Asteroid Miner   pm AMZ Jul,85
  The Weird of Mazal   ss FBM Sep,85

Betancourt, John Gregory & Darrell Schweitzer
  The Last Child of Masferigon   ss TOMOBED,85

Bickel, Bill
  Aftermath   ss IAS Dec md,85

Bigelow, Jane M.H.
  Tactics   ss FRAMZDK,85

Biggle, Lloyd, Jr. & T.L. Sherred
  ALIEN MAIN   n. Doubleday,85

Bird, Carmel
  Cave Amantem   ss STRGATR,85

Bischoff, David F.
  THE DESTINY DICE   n. NAL/Signet,85
  Doctor Who: The Role-Playing Game from FASA (Part One)
                                           gr SDA Dec,85
  GALACTIC WARRIORS   n. Ace,85
  STAR HOUNDS, BOOK ONE: THE INFINITE BATTLE   n. Ace,85
  WRAITH BOARD   n. NAL/Signet,85

Bischoff, David F., Rich Brown & Linda Richardson
  A PERSONAL DEMON   n. NAL/Signet,85

Bischoff, David F. & Thomas F. Monteleone
  NIGHT OF THE DRAGONSTAR   n. Berkley,85

Bischoff, David F. & G.D. Swick
  Sensor Readings   ar SDA Dec,85

Bischoff, David F. & Ted White
  Editorial   ed SDA Oct,85

Bischoff, David F. & Ted White, eds.
  Stardate [v.1 # 8, October 1985]
                      mg Associates International, Inc.,85
  Stardate [v.1 # 9, December 1985]
                      mg Associates International, Inc.,85

Bishop, Michael
  ANCIENT OF DAYS   n. Arbor House,85
  The Bob Dylan Tambourine Software & Satori Support Services
    Consortium Ltd.   ss INZ #12,85
  A Gift from the Graylanders   nv IAS Sep,85
  A Spy in the Domain of Arnheim   ss SHY # 7,85
  To a Chimp Held Captive for Purposes of Research   pm IAS Jan,85

Blackford, Jenny, Russell Blackford, Lucy Sussex & Norman Talbot,
  eds.
  CONTRARY MODES   nf Ebony Books,85

Blackford, Russell
  Glass Reptile Breakout   ss STRGATR,85

Blackford, Russell, Jenny Blackford, Lucy Sussex & Norman Talbot,
  eds.
  CONTRARY MODES   nf Ebony Books,85

Blackford, Russell & David King, eds.
  URBAN FANTASIES   oa Ebony Books,85

Blaine, Michael
  F/X Movie Preview   ar TZM Feb,86
  In the Twilight Zone   ed TZM Feb,86
  In the Twilight Zone: Hype Warp   ed TZM Dec,85
  The Screening   ss TZM Jun,85
  Secrets   ed TZM Oct,85
  TZ Film Futures: The Manhattan Project   ar TZM Feb,86

Blaine, Michael, ed.
  Rod Serling's The Twilight Zone Magazine [v.5 #4, October 1985]
                                           mg TZ Publications,85
  Rod Serling's The Twilight Zone Magazine [v.5 #5, December
    1985]   mg TZ Publications,85

Blaine, Michael, ed. (continued)
  Rod Serling's The Twilight Zone Magazine [v.5 #6, February
    1986]   mg TZ Publications,86

Blakeney, Jay D.
  THE CHILDREN OF ANTHI   n. Ace,85

Blaylock, James P.
  Lord Kelvin's Machine   nv IAS Dec md,85
  Paper Dragons   nv IMGNLND,85

Bleiler, E.F., ed.
  SUPERNATURAL FICTION WRITERS: FANTASY & HORROR, 2 VOLS.
                                           nf Scribners,85

Bloch, Robert
  Nocturne   ss GRYSTBY,85
  The Yougoslaves   nv NCR V1 #5,86

Blue, Tyson
  King Goes into Overdrive   ar TZM Feb,86

Bobley, Peter A.
  The Dog That Ate the Baby   vi NCR V1 #4,85

Bonanno, Margaret Wander
  DWELLERS IN THE CRUCIBLE   n. Pocket,85

Borges, Jorge Luis
  ATLAS   nf Dutton,85

Boston, Bruce
  The Berserker Enters a Plea on the Death of Greater Los Angeles
                                           pm IAS May,85
  The Evolution of the Death Murals   pm IAS Sep,85
  Roger, Roger   ss CVL Aug,85

Bova, Ben
  Amorality Tale   ss 1985
  THE ASTRAL MIRROR   co Tor,85
  Beisbol   ss ASF Nov,85
  The Jefferson Orbit   ar FFR V 1,85
  Nuclear Autumn   ss FFR V 2,85
  Primary   ss IAS Feb,85
  PRIVATEERS   n. Tor,85
  Robot Welfare   ar 1985
  Science Fiction   ar 1985
  Space Weapons   ar AMZ Jul,85

Boyajian, Jerry & Kenneth R. Johnson
  INDEX TO THE SCIENCE FICTION MAGAZINES 1984   nf Twaci Press,85

Boyd, J.P.
  The Werebear and the Rainbow   ss AMZ May,85

Boyett, Steven R.
  Bridge   ss FAERY! ,85

Boyle, T. Coraghessan
  on for the Long Haul   nv IAS Aug,85

Bracken, Michael
  The Dregs   ss GNC Mar,85
  Microchick   ss OUI Apr,85
  Of Memories Dying   ss MIDNGHT,85

Bradbury, Ray
  DEATH IS A LONELY BUSINESS   n. Knopf,85
  The Love Affair   ss PLANETS,85
  Trapdoor   ss OMN Apr,85

Bradley, Marion Zimmer
  THE BEST OF MARION ZIMMER BRADLEY   co Academy Chicago,85
  Knives   ss FRAMZDK,85
  NIGHT'S DAUGHTER   n. Ballantine/Del Rey,85
  Sea Wrack   nv MNSNGRF,85
  WARRIOR WOMAN   n. DAW,85
  WEB OF DARKNESS   om Richard Drew,85

Bradley, Marion Zimmer, ed.
  SWORD AND SORCERESS II   oa DAW,85

Bradley, Marion Zimmer & The Friends of Darkover
  FREE AMAZONS OF DARKOVER   oa DAW,85

Brandner, Gary
  THE HOWLING III   n. Fawcett/Gold Medal,85

Brantingham, Juleen
  Giraffe Tuesday   ss UNI #15,85
  The Haunting of Goodhope   ss FSF May,85

Braunbeck, Gary A.
  The Eldritch Eye   mr EDT #11,85

Brennan, Joseph Payne
  Canavan Calling   ss NGV # 2,85
  The Haunting at Juniper Hill   nv NGV # 2,85
  A Heritage Upheld   nv GRYSTBY,85
  It Shall Not Lack   pm WDB #20,85
  Oasis of Abomination   nv NGV # 2,85
  Pick-Up   ss NGV # 2,85

Davies, Robertson
  WHAT'S BRED IN THE BONE   n. Viking,85

Davin, Eric L.
  Avenging Angel   ss FFR V 2,85

Davis, Frederick C.
  THE NIGHT NEMESIS: THE COMPLETE ADVENTURES OF THE MOON MAN--VOL.
  ONE   co Purple Prose Press,85

Davis, Grania
  What Happened on Cranberry Road   nv AMZ Mar,85

de Camp, L. Sprague
  THE RELUCTANT KING   om SFBC,85

de Jong, Daphne
  Roimata   nv FSF Mar,85

de Larrabeiti, Michael
  The Curse of Igamor   ss IMGNLND,85

de Lint, Charles
  Cold Blows the Wind   ss S&S # 2,85
  THE HARP OF THE GREY ROSE   n. Donning/Starblaze,85
  MULENGRO   n. Ace,85

Dean, Martyn, ed.
  THE GUIDE TO FANTASY ART TECHNIQUES   nf Arco,85

Dean, Martyn & Roger Dean
  MAGNETIC STORM   nf Harmony,85

Dean, Pamela
  The Green Cat   nv LIAVEK ,85
  THE SECRET COUNTRY   n. Ace,85

Dean, Roger & Martyn Dean
  MAGNETIC STORM   nf Harmony,85

DeGaris, Roger, ed.
  EARTH AND ELSEWHERE   an Macmillan,86

Delaney, Joseph H.
  IN THE FACE OF MY ENEMY   n. Baen,85
  The Neighbors   ss ASF Jan,86
  Painkillers   nv ASF Jan,85

Delany, Samuel R.
  Appendix A: The Tale of Plagues and Carnivals, or, Some Informal
    Remarks toward the Modular Calculus, Part Five   na FLGTNVR,85
  Appendix B: Closures and Openings   nv FLGTNVR,85
  An Appreciation: Theodore Sturgeon   bg NCR V1 #4,85
  FLIGHT FROM NEVERYON   oc Bantam,85
  The Mummer's Tale   nv FLGTNVR,85
  The Tale of Fog and Granite   na FLGTNVR,85

Dell, Timothy
  A Step in Any Direction   ss STRGATR,85

deLoyola Brandao, Ignacio
  AND STILL THE EARTH   n. Avon/Bard,85

DeLuca, Michael A., II
  The Barrier of Essai   gr SDA Dec,85

Denton, Bradley
  Mountain Shadow: Shawnee County, Kansas   pm IAS Aug,85
  The Summer We Saw Diana   nv FSF Aug,85
  Top of the Charts   ss FSF Mar,85

Denton, Charles
  The Serpents' Shrine   pm WDB #20,85

Deppe, Carol
  Everybody Draws Lines   ss AMZ Jan,86

Devin, John
  The Cave of Shadows   pm AMZ Jan,85
  Field Guide   pm AMZ May,85
  For Those Who Love Danger   pm AMZ May,85

DeVore, Howard & Donald Franson
  A HISTORY OF THE HUGO, NEBULA, AND INTERNATIONAL FANTASY AWARDS,
  Updated Edition   nf Misfit,85

Dewdney, Christopher
  Points in Time   pm TESRCTS,85

DeWeese, Gene
  BLACK SUITS FROM OUTER SPACE   n. Putnam,85
  Everything's Going to Bee All Right   ss SDW # 8,85

Dexter, Susan
  THE SWORD OF CALANDRA   n. Ballantine/Del Rey,85

Diamond, Graham
  CINNABAR   n. Fawcett Gold Medal,85

Dick, Philip K.
  How to Build a Universe That Doesn't Fall Apart Two Days Later
                                                  sp IHOPEIS,85

Dick, Philip K. (continued)
  I HOPE I SHALL ARRIVE SOON   co Doubleday,85
  IN MILTON LUMKY TERRITORY   n. Dragon Press,85
  PUTTERING ABOUT IN A SMALL LAND   n. Academy Chicago,85
  RADIO FREE ALBEMUTH   n. Arbor House,85
  Strange Memories of Death   ss IHOPEIS,85
  UBIK: THE SCREENPLAY   pl Corroboree,85

Dickinson, Peter
  A BOX OF NOTHING   n. Gollancz,85
  THE CHANGES TRILOGY   om Puffin,85
  Flight   nv IMGNLND,85
  THE HEALER   n. Delacorte,85

Dickson, Gordon R.
  BEYOND THE DAR AL-HARB   co Tor,85
  Beyond the Dar al-Harb   na BYNDDAR,85
  FORWARD!   co Baen,85
  House of Weapons   na FFR V 2,85
  INVADERS!   co Baen,85
  See Now, a Pilgrim   na ASF Sep,85

DiFilippo, Paul
  Rescuing Andy   ss TZM Jun,85
  Stone Lives   nv FSF Aug,85

Dikty, Thaddeus, & R. Reginald
  THE WORK OF JULIAN MAY: AN ANNOTATED BIBLIOGRAPHY & GUIDE
                                                  nf Borgo,85

Dillard, J.M.
  STAR TREK #27: MINDSHADOW   n. Pocket,86

Disch, Thomas M.
  Dialogue With a Spider   pm AMZ Jul,85
  The Mittens of Ulysses   pm AMZ Mar,85
  Skydiver   pm AMZ Sep,85
  Under the Boughs of Westbrookville   pm AMZ Nov,85

Donaldson, Stephanie
  Stephen R. Donaldson: Six Appreciations   in WRLDTLS,85

Donaldson, Stephen R.
  The Djinn Who Watches Over the Accursed   ss WRLDTLS,85
  The Resume of Stephen R. Donaldson   bg WRLDTLS,85

Donaldson, Thomas
  How to Go Faster than Light   ar ASF Jun,85

Dorsey, Candas Jane
  Johnny Appleseed and the New World   ss TESRCTS,85

Douglas, Carole Nelson
  PROBE   n. Tor,85

Dowling, Terry
  The Bullet that Grows in the Gun   ss URBANFN,85

Doxey, W.S.
  The Armistead House   ss FSF Sep,85

Dozois, Gardner, ed.
  Isaac Asimov's Science Fiction Magazine [v.10 # 1, January
  1986]   mg Davis,86
  THE YEAR'S BEST SCIENCE FICTION, SECOND ANNUAL COLLECTION
                                                  an Bluejay,85

Dozois, Gardner & Susan Casper
  Send No Money   ss IAS Dec md,85

Dozois, Gardner, Susan Casper & Jack Dann
  The Clowns   ss PBY Aug,85

Dozois, Gardner & Jack Dann, eds.
  BESTIARY!   an Ace,85
  MERMAIDS!   an Ace,86

Dozois, Gardner, Jack Dann & Michael Swanwick
  The Gods of Mars   ss OMN Mar,85

Drake, Asa
  WARRIOR WITCH OF HEL   n. Popular Library/Questar,85

Drake, David A.
  AT ANY PRICE   r. Baen,85
  The Bond   ss FFR V 3,85
  Dreams in Amber   ss WHA # 5,85
  The Guardroom   nv AFTRWAR,85

Drake, David A. & Janet Morris
  ACTIVE MEASURES   r. Baen,85

Drake, David A. & Karl Edward Wagner
  KILLER   n. Baen,85

Drennan, Kathryn M. & J. Michael Straczynski
  Rod Serling's 'Night Gallery' [Part 1]   ar TZM Apr,85
  Rod Serling's 'Night Gallery' [Part 2]   ar TZM Jun,85
  Rod Serling's 'Night Gallery' [Part 3]   ar TZM Aug,85
  A Show-by-Show Guide to Rod Serling's 'Night Gallery', Part 1
                                                  bi TZM Apr,85

FERGUSON, NEIL

Ferguson, Neil
  Randy and Alexei Go Jaw Jaw   ss INZ #13,85

Fergusson, P.M.
  Art Appreciation   ss ASF Mar,85
  Body Language   ss ASF Jul,85
  The Darkling Plain   nv ASF Nov,85
  Gertrude   ss ASF May,85
  Snapshot of the Soul   ss ASF Dec md,85

Ferman, Edward L., ed.
  The Magazine of Fantasy & Science Fiction [v.68 #1, January
  1985]   mg Mercury Press,85
  The Magazine of Fantasy & Science Fiction [v.68 #2, February
  1985]   mg Mercury Press,85
  The Magazine of Fantasy & Science Fiction [v.68 #3, March 1985]
                                              mg Mercury Press,85
  The Magazine of Fantasy & Science Fiction [v.68 #4, April 1985]
                                              mg Mercury Press,85
  The Magazine of Fantasy & Science Fiction [v.68 #5, May 1985]
                                              mg Mercury Press,85
  The Magazine of Fantasy & Science Fiction [v.68 #6, June 1985]
                                              mg Mercury Press,85
  The Magazine of Fantasy & Science Fiction [v.69 #1, July 1985]
                                              mg Mercury Press,85
  The Magazine of Fantasy & Science Fiction [v.69 #2, August
  1985]   mg Mercury Press,85
  The Magazine of Fantasy & Science Fiction [v.69 #3, September
  1985]   mg Mercury Press,85
  The Magazine of Fantasy & Science Fiction [v.69 #4, October
  1985]   mg Mercury Press,85
  The Magazine of Fantasy & Science Fiction [v.69 #5, November
  1985]   mg Mercury Press,85
  The Magazine of Fantasy & Science Fiction [v.69 #6, December
  1985]   mg Mercury Press,85
  The Magazine of Fantasy & Science Fiction [v.70 #1, January
  1986]   mg Mercury Press,86

Ferrell, Keith
  GEORGE ORWELL: THE POLITICAL PEN   nf Evans,85

Finch, Sheila
  INFINITY'S WEB   n. Bantam Spectra,85

Finch-Rayner, Sheila
  The Seventh Dragon   ss FBM Jun,85

Findley, Timothy
  NOT WANTED ON THE VOYAGE   n. Delacorte,85

Fisher, Walter L.
  Trading Run   nv ASF Jun,85

Fitzpatrick, Jim
  ERINSAGA: THE MYTHOLOGICAL PAINTINGS OF JIM FITZPATRICK
                                              pi De Danann,85

Fleming, Robert Loren & Keith Giffen
  HELL ON EARTH   pi DC Comics,85

Fletcher, Jo & Stephen Jones, eds.
  Fantasycon X Programme Booklet   oa Fantasycon X,85

Flinn, M.
  Cartoon   ct TZM Apr,85

Flint, Kenneth C.
  MASTER OF THE SIDHE   n. Bantam Spectra,85

Flynn, John L.
  FUTURE THREADS: COSTUME DESIGN FOR THE SCIENCE FICTION WORLD
                                              nf New Media,85

Flynn, Michael F.
  A Medieval Management Report   ms ASF Sep,85

Foglio, Phil & Robert Lynn Asprin
  MYTH ADVENTURES ONE   pi Donning/Starblaze,85

Fonstad, Karen Wynn
  THE ATLAS OF THE LAND   nf Ballantine,85
  THE ATLAS OF THE LAND   nf Ballantine/Del Rey,85

Forbes, Caroline
  The Comet's Tail   na NEDLFUL,85
  Equal Rights   ss NEDLFUL,85
  London Fields   na NEDLFUL,85
  THE NEEDLE ON FULL: LESBIAN FEMINIST SCIENCE FICTION
                                              co Onlywomen,85
  Night Life   ss NEDLFUL,85
  The Visitors   ss NEDLFUL,85

Ford, John M.
  Scrabble with God   vi IAS Oct,85
  SF Cliches III: Time Machines   pm AMZ Jan,85

Forrester, John
  BESTIARY MOUNTAIN   n. Bradbury Press,85

Forstchen, William R.
  A DARKNESS UPON THE ICE   n. Ballantine/Del Rey,85

Forward, Robert L.
  The Paradox of Interstellar Transport   ar FFR V 1,85
  STARQUAKE   n. Ballantine/Del Rey,85

Foster, Alan Dean
  Batrachian   ss AMZ Sep,85
  Collectible   ss FSF Apr,85
  THE PATHS OF THE PERAMBULATOR   n. Phantasia,85
  SEASON OF THE SPELLSONG   om SFBC,85
  SENTENCED TO PRISM   n. Ballantine/Del Rey,85

Foster, David
  The Elixir Operon   ss STRGATR,85

Foster, M.A.
  The Conversation   na OWLTIME,85
  Leanne   na OWLTIME,85
  The Man Who Loved Owls   na OWLTIME,85
  OWL TIME   oc DAW,85
  PRESERVER   n. DAW,85

Fowler, Karen Joy
  The Lake Was Full of Artificial Things   ss IAS Oct,85
  The Poplar Street Study   ss FSF Jun,85
  Praxis   ss IAS Mar,85
  Recalling Cinderella   nv WRTRFUT,85
  The War of the Roses   nv IAS Dec,85

Fowles, John
  A MAGGOT   n. Little, Brown,85

Fox, Janet
  Christobel   ss BLD V1 #3,85
  Taking Care of Bertie   ss EDT #11,85

Fox-Davis, Susan L.
  Indistinguishable from Magic   vi FBM Mar,85

Frahm, Leanne
  The Visitor   ss MIDNGHT,85

Frakes, Randal & Bill Wisher
  THE TERMINATOR   n. Bantam,85

Franson, Donald & Howard DeVore
  A HISTORY OF THE HUGO, NEBULA, AND INTERNATIONAL FANTASY AWARDS,
  Updated Edition   nf Misfit,85

Frazetta, Frank
  FRANK FRAZETTA: BOOK FIVE   pi Bantam,85

Frazier, Robert
  Doppler Effects   pm IAS Feb,85
  Ed White, Spacewalking, June 3, 1965   pm IAS May,85
  In the Frozen Zoo for Extinct Beasts   pm FBM Sep,85
  The Mermaid Barnacle   pm FBM Dec,85
  On the Rio Madera   pm BPC #26,85
  Paleontologists Who Live in Backward Time   pm IAS Aug,85
  Perception Barriers   pm IAS Dec,85
  A Quotella for Ted Sturgeon   pm IAS Jan,86
  The Secret Lives of Drones   pm S&T #69,85

Frazier, Robert & Andrew Joron
  The Wake of Gravity   pm IAS Nov,85

Freddi, Cris
  THE ELDER   n. Knopf,85

Freedman, Benjamin
  On the Planet Grafool   ss TESRCTS,85

Frenkel, Karen A. & Isaac Asimov
  ROBOTS: MACHINES IN MAN'S IMAGE   nf Crown/Harmony,85

Frentzen, Jeffrey & David J. Schow
  The Outer Limits Show-by-Show Guide, Part 7   bi TZM Feb,85

Friedman, Michael Jan
  THE HAMMER AND THE HORN   n. Popular Library/Questar,85
  THE SEEKERS AND THE SWORD   n. Popular Library/Questar,85

Friends of Darkover, The & Marion Zimmer Bradley
  FREE AMAZONS OF DARKOVER   oa DAW,85

Friesner, Esther M.
  Billingsgate Molly   nv FBM Dec,85
  Chivalry   pm FBM Sep,85
  The Death of Nimue   ss FBM Jun,85
  Dragonet   ss AMZ Jan,86
  A Friendly Game of Crola   ss AMZ Sep,85
  A Gaming Song   pm AMZ Nov,85
  The Jester's Tale   ss FBM Mar,85
  The Monk's Tale   ss FBM Jun,85
  More SF Clerihews   pm AMZ Jan,86
  MUSTAPHA AND HIS WISE DOG   n. Avon,85
  Primary   ss AFTRWAR,85
  The Sailor's Bride   ss AMZ Nov,85
  A Short Slew of SF Clerihews   pm AMZ Jan,86
  The Vampire of Gretna Green   pm FBM Dec,85
  Yet More SF Clerihews   pm AMZ Jan,86

Hoppe, Stephanie T.
  THE WINDRIDER   n. DAW,85

Horowitz, Anthony
  THE NIGHT OF THE SCORPION   n. Putnam/Pacer,85

Horvitz, Leslie Ann
  Pictures of a Woman Gone   nv MIDNGHT,85

Howard, Robert E.
  Buccaneer Treasure   pm AMZ Jan,85

Howard, Robert E. & Robert M. Price
  Black Eons   nv FBM Jun,85

Hubbard, L. Ron
  MISSION EARTH, VOL. I: THE INVADERS PLAN   n. Bridge,85

Hughes, Edward P.
  A Cure for Croup   nv FFR V 2,85
  THE LONG MYND   n. Baen,85

Hughes, Monica
  DEVIL ON MY BACK   n. Atheneum/Argo,85

Hughes, Robert Don
  THE POWER AND THE PROPHET   n. Ballantine/Del Rey,85

Hurley, Maxwell
  PSI PATROL #3: MAX'S BOOK   n. Scholastic/Point,85

Hutman, Norma
  The Land of the Leaves   ss WRTRFUT,85

Hyams, Peter & Arthur C. Clarke
  THE ODYSSEY FILE   nf Ballantine/Del Rey,85

Hyman, Jackie
  The 9 to 5 Wizard   vi AMZ Nov,85

Indick, Ben P.
  Quiz: Break a Leg!   pz TZM Aug,85

Ing, Dean
  Evileye   ss FFR V 2,85
  Lost in Translation   ss FFR V 1,85
  Sam and the Banzi Runner   ss OMN Jan,86
  WILD COUNTRY   n. Tor,85

Ing, Dean & Mack Reynolds
  TROJAN ORBIT   n. Baen,85

Ireland, Beverley
  Long Shift   ss DSPTCHS,85

Irwin, Walter & G.B. Love, eds.
  THE BEST OF TREK #8   nf NAL/Signet,85
  THE BEST OF TREK #9   nf NAL/Signet,85

Iverson, Eric G.
  Bluff   nv ASF Feb,85
  Les Mortes D'Arthur   nv ASF Aug,85
  Noninterference   ss ASF Jul,85
  The R Strain   ss ASF Jun,85
  Unholy Trinity   nv AMZ Jul,85
  Vilest Beast   nv ASF Sep,85

Jablokov, Alexander
  Beneath the Shadow of Her Smile   nv IAS Apr,85
  A Wink in the Eye of the Wolf   nv FFR V 3,85

Jacobs, Harvey
  Seymourlama   ss FSF Jan,86

Jacobs, M.G.
  Minor Surgery and a Poker Game   ss OMN Mar,85

Jacobs, Rivka
  The Boys from the Moon   nv FFR V 1,85
  The Milk of Paradise   ss FSF Jan,85
  Morning on Venus   nv FFR V 3,85

Jaffery, Sheldon R.
  The Host   ss S&T #69,85

Jaffery, Sheldon R., ed.
  SENSUOUS SCIENCE FICTION FROM THE WEIRD AND SPICY PULPS
                          an Bowling Green Popular Press,85

Jaffery, Sheldon R. & Fred Cook
  THE COLLECTOR'S INDEX TO WEIRD TALES
                          nf Bowling Green Popular Press,85

Janifer, Laurence M.
  Fractured Skill   ss ASF Dec md,85

Jankus, Hank
  Thomas Blackshear   iv SHY # 7,85

Janos, Leo & General Chuck Yeager
  YEAGER: AN AUTOBIOGRAPHY   nf Bantam,85

Janson, Klaus
  FROST AND FIRE   pi DC Comics,85

Jeffers, Alex M.
  Brake   pm IAS Apr,85

Jennings, Jor
  Tiger Hunt   nv WRTRFUT,85

Jeppson, J.O.
  The Amulet of the Firegod   ss AMZ Sep,85
  August Angst   ss MYSCURE,85
  THE MYSTERIOUS CURE AND OTHER STORIES OF PSHRINKS ANONYMOUS
                                               co Doubleday,85
  The Noodge Factor   ss MYSCURE,85

Jeschke, Wolfgang
  The Land of Osiris   na IAS Mar,85

Jeter, K.W.
  THE GLASS HAMMER   n. Bluejay,85

Joels, Kerry Mark
  THE MARS ONE CREW MANUAL   ms Ballantine/Del Rey,85

Johnson, Anabelle & Edgar Johnson
  PRISONERS OF PSI   n. Atheneum/Argo,85

Johnson, Bill
  Respect   ss ASF Jun,85

Johnson, Crockett
  BARNABY #1: WANTED: A FAIRY GODFATHER   cs Ballantine/Del Rey,85
  BARNABY #2: MR. O'MALLEY AND THE HAUNTED HOUSE
                                          cs Ballantine/Del Rey,85
  BARNABY #3: JACKEEN J.O. O'MALLEY FOR CONGRESS
                                          cs Ballantine/Del Rey,86

Johnson, Denis
  FISKADORO   n. Knopf,85

Johnson, Edgar & Anabelle Johnson
  PRISONERS OF PSI   n. Atheneum/Argo,85

Johnson, Kenneth R. & Jerry Boyajian
  INDEX TO THE SCIENCE FICTION MAGAZINES 1984   nf Twaci Press,85

Johnson, Will
  Innocents   pm EDT #11,85

Johnstone, William W.
  ALONE IN THE ASHES   n. Zebra,85
  BLOOD IN THE ASHES   n. Zebra,85

Jones, Diana Wynne
  WARLOCK AT THE WHEEL AND OTHER STORIES   co Greenwillow,85

Jones, Gwyneth
  The Intersection   ss DSPTCHS,85

Jones, Stephen, ed.
  Fantasy Tales [v.7 #14, Summer 1985]   mg Stephen Jones,85

Jones, Stephen & Jo Fletcher, eds.
  Fantasycon X Programme Booklet   oa Fantasycon X,85

Joron, Andrew
  Shipwrecked on Destiny Five   pm IAS May,85

Joron, Andrew & Robert Frazier
  The Wake of Gravity   pm IAS Nov,85

Kadrey, Richard
  The Fire Catcher   ss IMZ #12,85

Kagan, Janet
  UHURA'S SONG   n. Pocket,85

Karl, Jean E.
  STRANGE TOMORROW   n. Dutton,85

Karr, Phyllis Ann
  A Night at Two Inns   nv S&S # 2,85

Kathenor, Sansoucy
  Captain Omra and the Cats   ss YAM May,85
  A Spell in Time   nv FBM Dec,85

Kaveney, Roz
  Editorial   ed IMZ #11,85

Kay, Guy Gavriel
  THE SUMMER TREE   n. Arbor House,85

Kaye, Marvin, ed.
  MASTERPIECES OF TERROR AND THE SUPERNATURAL   an SFBC,85

Keillor, Garrison
  What Did We Do Wrong?   ss NYM Sep 16,85

Kelley, James Patrick
  The Last   ss FSF Jun,85

Pattrick, William, ed.
MYSTERIOUS SEA STORIES   an Salem House,85

Paxson, Diana L.
  The Color of Magic   nv DEADWIN,85
  The Mother Quest   nv FRAMZDK,85
  The Phoenix Garden   nv AFTRWAR,85
  The Servant of Saibel   ss AMZ Jan,85
  Shadow Wood   nv S&S # 2,85
  The Shaper of Butterflies   nv FBM Dec,85
  Sky Sister   ss MNSNGRF,85

Payack, Peter
  Interstellar Dust   pm IAS Jan,86
  Moonburn   pm IAS Jan,86
  A Trivial Matter   pm IAS Jan,86
  Why There Is Now (and Most Probably Always Will Be) a Shortage
    of Subatomic Physicists   ms IAS Jan,86

Peacey, Anthony
  Jagging   nv STRGATR,85
  Time and Flowers   ss STRGATR,85

Pearce, Howard D. & Robert A. Collins, eds.
  THE SCOPE OF THE FANTASTIC: CULTURE, BIOGRAPHY, THEMES,
    CHILDREN'S LITERATURE   nf Greenwood,85
  THE SCOPE OF THE FANTASTIC: THEORY, TECHNIQUE, MAJOR AUTHORS
                                                    nf Greenwood,85

Peck, Claudia
  The Lingering Chill   ss EDT #11,85

Peja, Edward R.
  Inertial God   ss PGP Oct,85

Pelham, David & Heather Couper
  UNIVERSE   pi Random House,85

Pellegrino, Charles R.
  The Ultimate Whodunit   ar FFR V 3,85

Perry, Steve
  THE MAN WHO NEVER MISSED   n. Ace,85

Pierce, Meredith Ann
  The Woman Who Loved Raindeer   nv MNSNGRF,85
  THE WOMAN WHO LOVED REINDEER   n. Atlantic Monthly,85

Pimple, Dennis J.
  Arcadus Arcane   ss WRTRFUT,85

Pinckard, Terri E.
  The Rape   vi FBM Dec,85

Pinkwater, Daniel M.
  The Buttonaid (Buttons Through the Ages)   cs YNGADLT,85
  Confessions of Pinkwater by Ken Kelman   ss YNGADLT,85
  The Dada Boys in Collitch (The First Chapter)   ex YNGADLT,85
  Dead End Dada   nv YNGADLT,85
  Pigamorphosis   cs YNGADLT,85
  W.A. Mozart, Superhero I   cs YNGADLT,85
  W.A. Mozart, Superhero II   cs YNGADLT,85
  YOUNG ADULTS   co Tor,85

Platt, Charles
  The Other Frank Herbert   iv SDA Oct,85
  Science Fiction Cinema   ar SDA Dec,85

Playford, John
  The Sanctuary Tree   ss STRGATR,85

Pohl, Frederik
  BLACK STAR RISING   n. Ballantine/Del Rey,85
  The Coming of the Quantum Cats [Part 1 of 4]   sl ASF Jan,86
  Fermi and Frost   ss IAS Jan,85
  The Things That Happen   nv IAS Oct,85

Pohl, Frederik & C.M. Kornbluth
  SEARCH THE SKY   n. Baen,85
  VENUS, INC.   om SFBC,85

Polikarpus, Viido & Tappan King
  DOWNTOWN   n. Arbor House,85

Pollack, Rachel
  The Red Guild   nv S&S # 2,85

Popkes, Steven
  Deathwitch   ss IAS Feb,85
  Hellcatcher   ss NCR V1 #5,86
  Tip of the Scorpion   ss TZM Aug,85

Potter, J.K.
  THE ART OF SKELETON CREW   pi Scream/Press,85

Pournelle, Jerry E.
  Editor's Afterword to: John Brunner's "A Way Out Maybe."
                                                    aw WAR V 4,85
  Editors Introduction to: A Step Further Out   in FFR V 1,85
  A Step Further Out   ar FFR V 3,85
  A Step Further Out: "A Few Good Books..."   ar FFR V 2,85

Pournelle, Jerry E. (continued)
  A Step Further Out: "The Association for the Abolition of
    Science"   ar FFR V 1,85

Pournelle, Jerry E., ed.
  THERE WILL BE WAR, VOL. IV: DAY OF THE TYRANT   an Tor,85

Pournelle, Jerry E. & Jim Baen, eds.
  FAR FRONTIERS   oa Baen,85
  FAR FRONTIERS VOL. II/SUMMER 1985   oa Baen,85
  FAR FRONTIERS VOL. III/FALL 1985   oa Baen,85
  FAR FRONTIERS VOL. IV/WINTER 1985   oa Baen,86

Pournelle, Jerry E., Jim Baen & John F. Carr, eds.
  THE SCIENCE FICTION YEARBOOK   an Baen,85

Pournelle, Jerry E. & Larry Niven
  FOOTFALL   n. Ballantine/Del Rey,85

Powell, Larry
  Siblings   ss ASF Nov,85

Powys, John Cowper
  THREE FANTASIES   co Carcanet,85

Poynter, Jean
  The Entombment   pm S&T #69,85

Poyser, Victoria
  The Works of Victoria Poyser   bi WRLDTLS,85

Preiss, Byron, ed.
  THE PLANETS   oa Bantam,85

Prescot, Dray
  OMENS OF KREGEN   n. DAW,85
  STORM OVER VALHALLA   n. DAW,85
  WEREWOLVES OF KREGEN   n. DAW,85
  WITCHES OF KREGEN   n. DAW,85

Preuss, Paul
  HUMAN ERROR   n. Tor,85
  Small Bodies   ss PLANETS,85

Price, D.M.
  Future City   pm TESRCTS,85
  The Last Will and Testament of the Unknown Earthman Lost in the
    Second Vegan Campaign   pm TESRCTS,85

Price, E. Hoffmann
  OPERATION EXILE   n. Ballantine/Del Rey,86

Price, Patrick L. & George H. Scithers
  The Observatory   ed AMZ Sep,85

Price, Robert M. & Robert E. Howard
  Black Eons   nv FBM Jun,85

Priest, Christopher
  THE GLAMOUR   n. Doubleday,85

Pringle, David
  SCIENCE FICTION: THE 100 BEST NOVELS   nf Xanadu,85

Pringle, David, John Clute & Colin Greenland, eds.
  INTERZONE: THE 1ST ANTHOLOGY   an Dent/Everyman,85

Pringle, David, Colin Greenland & Simon Ounsley, eds.
  Interzone [#11, Spring 1985]   mg Interzone,85
  Interzone [#12, Summer 1985]   mg Interzone,85

Pringle, David & Simon Ounsley
  Editorial   ed INZ #12,85

Pringle, David & Simon Ounsley, eds.
  Interzone [#13, Autumn 1985]   mg Interzone,85
  Interzone [#14, Winter 1985/86]   mg Interzone,85

Proctor, George W.
  V: THE CHICAGO CONVERSION   n. Pinnacle,85
  V: THE TEXAS RUN   n. Pinnacle,85

Proctor, George W. & Robert E. Vardeman
  BLOOD FOUNTAIN   n. Ace,85
  TO DEMONS BOUND   n. Ace,85
  A YOKE OF MAGIC   n. Ace,85

Pronzini, Bill
  Toy   ss SDW # 8,85

Ptacek, Kathryn
  BLOOD AUTUMN   n. Tor,85
  Power   nv GRYSTBY,85

Purdom, Tom
  Eyes   ss ASF Jul,85

Purtill, Richard L.
  Gorgonissa   ss IAS Jan,85
  J.R.R. TOLKIEN: MYTH, MORALITY, AND RELIGION   nf Harper & Row,85

QUAGMIRE, JOSHUA

SHETTERLY, WILL

Shetterly, Will
  Bound Things   ss LIAVEK ,85
  CATS HAVE NO LORD   n. Ace,85

Shetterly, Will & Emma Bull, eds.
  LIAVEK   oa Ace,85

Shiner, Lewis
  Jeff Beck   ss IAS Jan,86
  Stompin' at the Savoy   ss SHY # 7,85
  The War At Home   ss IAS May,85

Shiner, Lewis & Bruce Sterling
  Mozart in Mirrorshades   ss OMN Sep,85

Shirley, John
  ECLIPSE   n. Bluejay,85
  The Incorporated   ss IAS Jul,85

Shirley, John & Bruce Sterling
  The Unfolding   ss INZ #11,85

Shirvanian, Vahan
  The Big Bang Theory of Creation   ct TZM Apr,85

Shupp, Mike
  WITH FATE CONSPIRE   n. Ballantine/Del Rey,85

Shwartz, Susan M.
  Growing Pains   ss FRAMZDK,85
  Homecoming   nv MGI # 1,85

Shwartz, Susan M., ed.
  MOONSINGER'S FRIENDS   oa Bluejay,85

Sievert, John
  C.A.D.S.   n. Zebra,85

Silverberg, Robert
  NEEDLE IN A TIMESTACK   co Ace,85
  Pluto: Outermost   ar PLANETS,85
  SAILING TO BYZANTIUM   n. Underwood-Miller,85
  Sailing to Byzantium   na IAS Feb,85
  THE SILENT INVADERS   om Tor,85
  Sunrise on Pluto   ss PLANETS,85
  Symbiont   ss PBY Jun,85
  TOM O'BEDLAM   n. Fine,85
  A Writer's Beginnings   ar WRTRFUT,85

Silverberg, Robert & Martin H. Greenberg, eds.
  THE TIME TRAVELERS: A SCIENCE FICTION QUARTET   an Fine,85

Silvestri, Margaret
  Cast Off Your Chains   ss FRAMZDK,85

Silvis, Randall
  Why the Stranger Dreams   ss TZM Dec,85

Simmons, Dan
  SONG OF KALI   n. Bluejay,85

Singer, Marilyn
  HORSEMASTER   n. Atheneum/Argo,85

Singer, Richard
  The Complex   ss S&T #69,85

Skerl, Jennie
  WILLIAM S. BURROUGHS   nf Twayne,85

Skipp, John M.
  My Darkest Fantasy   ms TZM Oct,85
  The Spirit of Things   ss BLD V1 #3,85

Skipp, John M. & Craig Spector
  FRIGHT NIGHT   n. Tor,85
  The Light at the End   ex BAN 1986

Sky, Kathleen
  WITCHDAME   n. Berkley,85

Sladek, John
  TIK-TOK   n. DAW,85

Sleator, William
  SINGULARITY   n. Dutton,85

Slote, Alfred
  THE TROUBLE ON JANUS   n. Lippincott,85

Slusser, George E. & Eric S. Rabkin, eds.
  SHADOWS OF THE MAGIC LAMP: FANTASY AND SCIENCE FICTION IN FILM
                      nf S. Illinois Univ. Press,85

Smeds, Dave
  New Breed   ss IKR Sep,85
  THE SORCERY WITHIN   n. Ace,85

Smith, David C.
  The Return to Hell   ss S&T #69,85

Smith, Dean Wesley
  Adrift in the Erotic Zone   ss GEM Jan,85
  One Last Dance   ss WRTRFUT,85
  The Sexual Voyage of the Starship Shirley   ss OUI Sep,85

Smith, E.E. "Doc" & Stephen Goldin
  REVOLT OF THE GALAXY   n. Berkley,85

Smith, Evelyn E.
  THE COPY SHOP   n. Doubleday,85

Smith, L. Neil
  THE GALLATIN DIVERGENCE   n. Ballantine/Del Rey,85

Smith, Nick
  Editorial   ed FBM Dec,85

Smith, Nick & Dennis Mallonee, eds.
  Fantasy Book   [v.4 #1, March 1985]
                mg Fantasy Book Enterprises,85
  Fantasy Book   [v.4 #2, June 1985] mg Fantasy Book Enterprises,85
  Fantasy Book   [v.4 #3, September 1985]
                mg Fantasy Book Enterprises,85
  Fantasy Book   [v.4 #4, December 1985]
                mg Fantasy Book Enterprises,85

Smith, R. Dixon
  LOST IN THE RENTHARPIAN HILLS: SPANNING THE DECADES WITH CARL
  JACOBI   nf Bowling Green Popular Press,85

Smith, Stephanie
  SNOW-EYES   n. Atheneum/Argo,85

Smith, Tom
  M'butu's God   nv FBM Jun,85

Sneyd, Steve
  Hanging Town   pm S&T #69,85

Snyder, Gene
  TOMB SEVEN   n. Charter,85

Sohl, Jerry
  Cabin Number Six   ss WHA # 5,85

Spector, Craig & John M. Skipp
  FRIGHT NIGHT   n. Tor,85
  The Light at the End   ex BAN 1986

Spinrad, Norman
  Alternate Viewpoint   ar IAS Jun,85
  Brain Salad   ss FFR V 1,85
  Child of Fortune   ex BAN Jul,85
  CHILD OF FORTUNE   n. Bantam Spectra,85
  On Books: Books into Movies   br IAS Nov,85
  On Books: Inside, Outside   br IAS Jul,85
  On Books: Must There Be War?   br IAS Jan,86
  On Books: Transatlantic Science Fiction   br IAS Mar,85
  SFWA, the Guild   ar 1985
  World War Last   na IAS Aug,85

Springer, Nancy
  Bright-Eyed Black Pony   ss MNSNGRF,85
  The Prince Out of the Past   ss MGI # 1,85
  WINGS OF FLAME   n. Tor,85

St. Clair, Margaret
  THE BEST OF MARGARET ST. CLAIR   co Academy Chicago,85

Stableford, Brian
  The Cosmic Perspective   ss CSMCPRS,85
  THE COSMIC PERSPECTIVE/CUSTER'S LAST STAND   oc Drumm,85
  Custer's Last Stand   ss CSMCPRS,85
  Introduction to "Custer's Last Stand"   in CSMCPRS,85
  Introduction to "The Cosmic Perspective"   in CSMCPRS,85
  THE LAST DAYS OF THE EDGE OF THE WORLD   n. Ace,85
  SCIENTIFIC ROMANCE IN BRITAIN, 1890-1950   nf Fourth Estate,85

Stableford, Brian & David Langford
  THE THIRD MILLENNIUM: A HISTORY OF THE WORLD: AD 2000-3000
                            ms Knopf,85

Stacy, Ryder
  DOOMSDAY WARRIOR #4: BLOODY AMERICA   n. Zebra,85
  DOOMSDAY WARRIOR #5: AMERICA'S LAST DECLARATION   n. Zebra,85
  DOOMSDAY WARRIOR #6: AMERICAN REBELLION   n. Zebra,85

Stasheff, Christopher
  THE WARLOCK ENRAGED   n. Ace,85

Stauffer, Charles
  October   pm WDB #20,85

Steele, Linda
  IBIS   n. DAW,85

Steinbach, Victor
  Aliens in Hollywood   ar TZM Apr,85

Sterling, Bruce
  The Compassionate, the Digital   ss INZ #14,85
  Dinner in Audoghast   ss IAS May,85

YOKE, CARL B.

Yoke, Carl B. & Donald M. Hassler, eds.
  DEATH AND THE SERPENT: IMMORTALITY IN SCIENCE FICTION
                                              nf Greenwood,85

Yolen, Jane
  The Dragon's Boy   nv FSF Sep,85
  Dragonfield   nv 1985
  DRAGONFIELD AND OTHER STORIES   co Ace,85
  Evian Steel   nv IMGNLND,85
  The Face in the Cloth   ss FSF Feb,85
  An Infestation of Angels   ss IAS Nov,85
  The Inn of the Demon Camel   ss LIAVEK ,85
  Into the Wood   pm IAS Feb,85
  The Sword and the Stone   nv FSF Dec,85
  The Thirteenth Fey   ss FAERY! ,85

Young, Robert F.
  Mars Child   ss AMZ Jan,85
  O Little Town of Bethlehem II   ss IAS Dec,85
  Three-Mile Syndrome   ss FSF Aug,85
  THE VIZIER'S SECOND DAUGHTER   n. DAW,85

Yourcenar, Marguerite
  ORIENTAL TALES   co Farrar, Straus & Giroux,85

Yurk, Klaus Dieter
  The Devil in the Deep   ss EDT #11,85

Zahn, Timothy
  COBRA   n. Baen,85
  A COMING OF AGE   n. Bluejay,85
  Cordon Sanitaire   na ALIENST,85
  Music Hath Charms   ss ASF Apr,85
  SPINNERET   n. Bluejay,85
  Spinneret   [Part 1 of 4]   sl ASF Jul,85
  Spinneret   [Part 2 of 4]   sl ASF Aug,85
  Spinneret   [Part 3 of 4]   sl ASF Sep,85
  Spinneret   [Part 4 of 4]   sl ASF Oct,85

Zahorski, Kenneth
  Evangeline Walton Ensley: An Appreciation bg WRLDTLS,85

Zambreno, Mary Frances
  A Way Out   ss WRTRFUT,85

Zebrowski, George
  Gödel's Doom   ss PCM Feb,85
  THE MONADIC UNIVERSE   co Ace,85
  THE STARS WILL SPEAK   n. Harper & Row,85

Zebrowski, George, ed.
  NEBULA AWARDS 20: SFWA'S CHOICES FOR THE BEST IN SCIENCE FICTION
  1984   an Harcourt Brace Jovanovich,85
  NEBULA AWARDS 20: SFWA'S CHOICES FOR THE BEST IN SCIENCE FICTION
  1984   an HBJ/Harvest,85

Zelazny, Roger
  24 Views of Mt. Fuji, by Hokusai   na IAS Jul,85
  Dayblood   ss TZM Jun,85
  Dreadsong   ss PLANETS,85
  TRUMPS OF DOOM   n. Arbor House,85
  The Writer's Life and Uniqueness   ar WRTRFUT,85

Zend, Robert
  An Adventure in Miracle-Land   pm TESRCTS,85
  A Strange Visitor   pm TESRCTS,85

Ziegfeld, Richard E.
  STANISLAW LEM   nf Ungar,85

Zindell, David
  Caverns   ss INZ #14,85
  Shanidar   nv WRTRFUT,85

Zoline, Pamela
  Instructions for Exiting This Building in Case of Fire
                                             ss INZ #12,85

[Misc. Material]
  About the Artists   bg WRTRFUT,85
  About the Contest   ms WRTRFUT,85
  The Analytical Laboratory   ms ASF Jun,85
  Appendix One: A Tourist's Guide to Liavek in the Year 3317
                                            ms LIAVEK ,85
  Appendix Three: Liavek: A Creation Myth   ms LIAVEK ,85
  Appendix Two: A Magician's Primer   ms LIAVEK ,85
  British Fantasy Awards-1984 [nominees]   ms FYC #10,85
  F&SF Competition: Report on Competition 36 ms FSF Jan,85
  F&SF Competition: Report on Competition 37 ms FSF Jun,85
  F&SF Competition: Report on Competition 38 ms FSF Nov,85
  Fantasy Book Index, Volume 3   ix FBM Mar,85
  Guest Notes   bg FYC #10,85
  Index to 1984   ix ASF Jan,85
  Index to 1984   ix IAS Jan,85
  Index to 1985   ix ASF Jan,86
  Index to 1985   ix IAS Jan,86
  Index to Volume 68   ix FSF Jun,85
  Index to Volume 69   ix FSF Dec,85

SUBJECT LIST, NEW BOOKS

SCIENCE FICTION NOVELS

SCIENCE FICTION NOVELS

Adams, Robert
HORSES OF THE NORTH — n.
THE SEVEN MAGICAL JEWELS OF IRELAND — n.

Ahern, Jerry
THE SURVIVALIST #12: THE REBELLION — n.

Aikin, Jim
WALK THE MOONS ROAD — n.

Aldiss, Brian W.
HELLICONIA WINTER — n.

Allen, Roger Macbride
THE TORCH OF HONOR — n.

Anderson, Poul
THE GAME OF EMPIRE — n.

Anthony, Piers
BIO OF A SPACE TYRANT, VOL. III: POLITICIAN — n.
BIO OF A SPACE TYRANT, VOL. IV: EXECUTIVE — n.
STEPPE — n.

Ashley, Steven
LOVE OUT OF TIME — n.

Asimov, Isaac
ROBOTS AND EMPIRE — n.

Auel, Jean
THE MAMMOTH HUNTERS — n.

Austin, Richard
THE GUARDIANS — n.
THE GUARDIANS #2: TRIAL BY FIRE — n.
THE GUARDIANS: NIGHT OF THE PHOENIX — n.
THE GUARDIANS: THUNDER OF HELL — n.

Baldwin, Merl
THE HELMSMAN — n.

Bartholomew, Barbara
CHILD OF TOMORROW — n.
THE TIME KEEPER — n.
WHEN DREAMERS CEASE TO DREAM — n.

Bayley, Barrington J.
THE ROD OF LIGHT — n.

Bear, Greg
BLOOD MUSIC — n.
EON — n.

Beere, Peter
TRAUMA 2020 #3: SILENT SLAUGHTER — n.

Benford, Gregory
ARTIFACT — n.

Benni, Stefano
TERRA! — n.

Biggle, Lloyd, Jr. & T.L. Sherred
ALIEN MAIN — n.

Bischoff, David F.
GALACTIC WARRIORS — n.
STAR HOUNDS, BOOK ONE: THE INFINITE BATTLE — n.

Bischoff, David F. & Thomas F. Monteleone
NIGHT OF THE DRAGONSTAR — n.

Bishop, Michael
ANCIENT OF DAYS — n.

Blakeney, Jay D.
THE CHILDREN OF ANTHI — n.

Bonanno, Margaret Wander
DWELLERS IN THE CRUCIBLE — n.

Bova, Ben
PRIVATEERS — n.

Brin, David
THE POSTMAN — n.

Brown, Jerry Earl
DARKHOLD — n.

Burdekin, Katharine
SWASTIKA NIGHT — n.

Busby, F.M.
REBEL'S QUEST — n.

Byers, Edward A.
THE LONG FORGETTING — n.

Caidin, Martin
KILLER STATION — n.

Callin, Grant
SATURNALIA — n.

Capek, Karel
WAR WITH THE NEWTS — n.

Card, Orson Scott
ENDER'S GAME — n.

Carr, Jayge
THE TREASURE IN THE HEART OF THE MAZE — n.

Chalker, Jack L.
DOWNTIMING THE NIGHT SIDE — n.
THE MESSIAH CHOICE — n.
SOUL RIDER, BOOK FOUR: THE BIRTH OF FLUX & ANCHOR — n.
SOUL RIDER, BOOK THREE: MASTERS OF FLUX & ANCHOR — n.

Chandler, A. Bertram
KELLY COUNTRY — n.
THE WILD ONES — n.

Charles, Robert
THE COMET — n.

Cherryh, C.J.
ANGEL WITH THE SWORD — n.
CUCKOO'S EGG — n.
THE KIF STRIKE BACK — n.

Chesbro, George C.
THE BEASTS OF VALHALLA — n.

Cleve, John
SPACEWAYS #19: KING OF THE SLAVERS — n.

Cole, Allan & Chris Bunch
COURT OF A THOUSAND SUNS — n.

Cook, Glen
A MATTER OF TIME — n.
PASSAGE AT ARMS — n.

Cook, Paul
DUENDE MEADOW — n.

Cooper, Clare
EARTHCHANGE — n.

Crispin, A.C. & Deborah A. Marshall
V: DEATH TIDE — n.

Daley, Brian
JINX ON A TERRAN INHERITANCE — n.
REQUIEM FOR A RULER OF WORLDS — n.

Dalmas, John
FANGLITH — n.
THE SCROLL OF MAN — n.

Dann, Jack
THE MAN WHO MELTED — n.

Delaney, Joseph H.
IN THE FACE OF MY ENEMY — n.

deLoyola Brandao, Ignacio
AND STILL THE EARTH — n.

DeWeese, Gene
BLACK SUITS FROM OUTER SPACE — n.

Dick, Philip K.
RADIO FREE ALBEMUTH — n.

Dickinson, Peter
THE HEALER — n.

Dillard, J.M.
STAR TREK #27: MINDSHADOW — n.

Douglas, Carole Nelson
PROBE — n.

Drake, David A.
AT ANY PRICE — n.

Drake, David A. & Karl Edward Wagner
KILLER — n.

Drew, Wayland
THE GAIAN EXPEDIENT — n.

Drumm, D.B.
TRAVELER #5: ROAD WAR — n.
TRAVELER #6: BORDER WAR — n.
TRAVELER #7: THE ROAD GHOST — n.

Effinger, George Alec
  THE NICK OF TIME — n.

Elliott, Richard
  THE BURNT LANDS — n.

Ellis, A.C.
  WORLDMAKER — n.

Erickson, Steve
  DAYS BETWEEN STATIONS — n.

Etchemendy, Nancy
  THE CRYSTAL CITY — n.

Farmer, Philip José
  DAYWORLD — n.

Farren, Mick
  PROTECTORATE — n.

Felice, Cynthia
  DOWNTIME — n.

Finch, Sheila
  INFINITY'S WEB — n.

Forrester, John
  BESTIARY MOUNTAIN — n.

Forstchen, William R.
  A DARKNESS UPON THE ICE — n.

Forward, Robert L.
  STARQUAKE — n.

Foster, Alan Dean
  SENTENCED TO PRISM — n.

Foster, M.A.
  PRESERVER — n.

Fowles, John
  A MAGGOT — n.

Frakes, Randal & Bill Wisher
  THE TERMINATOR — n.

Freddi, Cris
  THE ELDER — n.

Frost, Jason
  THE WARLORD #5: TERMINAL ISLAND — n.

Gallun, Raymond Z.
  BIOBLAST — n.

Gilman, Robert Cham
  THE WARLOCK OF RHADA — n.

Gipe, George
  BACK TO THE FUTURE — n.

Gotlieb, Phyllis
  THE KINGDOM OF CATS — n.

Goulart, Ron
  BRAINZ, INC. — n.
  SUICIDE, INC. — n.

Grant, Richard
  SARABAND OF LOST TIME — n.

Green, Roland
  PEACE COMPANY — n.

Green, Roland & John F. Carr
  GREAT KING'S WAR — n.

Green, Sharon
  GATEWAY TO XANADU — n.

Griffin, Russell M.
  THE TIME-SERVERS — n.

Haiblum, Isidore
  THE HAND OF GANZ — n.

Haldeman, Jack C., II
  THE FALL OF WINTER — n.

Hambly, Barbara
  ISHMAEL — n.

Hansen, Karl
  DREAM GAMES — n.

Harding, Richard
  THE OUTRIDER #5: BUILT TO KILL — n.

Harrison, Harry
  A STAINLESS STEEL RAT IS BORN — n.

Hawke, Simon
  THE NAUTILUS SANCTION — n.
  TIMEWARS #4: THE ZENDA VENDETTA — n.

Hawkins, Ward
  RED FLAME BURNING — n.
  SWORD OF FIRE — n.

Heinlein, Robert A.
  THE CAT WHO WALKS THROUGH WALLS: A COMEDY OF MANNERS — n.

Herbert, Brian
  THE GARBAGE CHRONICLES — n.
  SUDANNA, SUDANNA — n.

Herbert, Frank
  CHAPTER HOUSE DUNE — n.
  CHAPTERHOUSE: DUNE — n.

Herbert, James
  DOMAIN — n.

Hill, Carol
  THE ELEVEN MILLION MILE HIGH DANCER — n.

Hill, Douglas
  THE CAVES OF KLYDOR — n.
  COLSEC REBELLION — n.

Hogan, James P.
  THE PROTEUS OPERATION — n.

Hoyle, Trevor
  VAIL — n.

Hubbard, L. Ron
  MISSION EARTH, VOL. I: THE INVADERS PLAN — n.

Hughes, Edward P.
  THE LONG MYND — n.

Hughes, Monica
  DEVIL ON MY BACK — n.

Ing, Dean
  WILD COUNTRY — n.

Jeter, K.W.
  THE GLASS HAMMER — n.

Johnson, Anabelle & Edgar Johnson
  PRISONERS OF PSI — n.

Johnson, Denis
  FISKADORO — n.

Johnstone, William W.
  ALONE IN THE ASHES — n.
  BLOOD IN THE ASHES — n.

Kagan, Janet
  UHURA'S SONG — n.

Karl, Jean E.
  STRANGE TOMORROW — n.

Kelleher, Victor
  THE BEAST OF HEAVEN — n.

Kelly, James Patrick & John Kessel
  FREEDOM BEACH — n.

Kendall, Gordon
  WHITE WING — n.

Kidd, Ronald
  THE GLITCH — n.

Kilian, Crawford
  BROTHER JONATHAN — n.

Killough, Lee
  LIBERTY'S WORLD — n.

Killus, James
  SUNSMOKE — n.

Knight, Damon
  CV — n.

Kotani, Eric & John Maddox Roberts
  ACT OF GOD — n.

Kotzwinkle, William
  E.T.: THE BOOK OF THE GREEN PLANET — n.

Kube-McDowell, Michael P.
  EMPRISE — n.

Lance, Kathryn
  PANDORA'S GENES — n.

SCIENCE FICTION NOVELS

Larson, Glen S. & Robert Thurston
BATTLESTAR GALACTICA 11: THE NIGHTMARE MACHINE   n.

Larson, Majliss
STAR TREK #26: PAWNS AND SYMBOLS   n.

Laumer, Keith
END AS A HERO   n.

Lawhead, Stephen
EMPHYRION: THE SEARCH FOR FIERRA   n.

Lawrence, Louise
CHILDREN OF THE DUST   n.

Lee, Tanith
DAYS OF GRASS   n.

Leroe, Ellen W.
ROBOT ROMANCE   n.

Lichtenberg, Jacqueline
CITY OF A MILLION LEGENDS   n.
DUSHAU   n.
FARFETCH   n.
OUTREACH   n.

Llewellyn, Edward
FUGITIVE IN TRANSIT   n.

Longyear, Barry B. & David Gerrold
ENEMY MINE   n.

Lovejoy, Jack
A VISION OF BEASTS 3: THE BROTHERHOOD OF DIABLO   n.

Lumley, Brian
PSYCHAMOK   n.

Mace, David
DEMON-4   n.
NIGHTRIDER   n.

Malzberg, Barry N.
THE REMAKING OF SIGMUND FREUD   n.

Mayhar, Ardath
THE WORLD ENDS IN HICKORY HOLLOW   n.

McCaffrey, Anne
KILLASHANDRA   n.

McCollum, Michael
PROCYON'S PROMISE   n.

McCullough, Colleen
A CREED FOR THE THIRD MILLENNIUM   n.

McEnroe, Richard S.
SKINNER   n.
NOT QUITE HUMAN #1: BATTERIES NOT INCLUDED   n.
NOT QUITE HUMAN #2: ALL GEARED UP   n.
NOT QUITE HUMAN #3: A BUG IN THE SYSTEM   n.

McKillip, Patricia A.
THE MOON AND THE FACE   n.

McQuay, Mike
MOTHER EARTH   n.
MY SCIENCE PROJECT   n.
PURE BLOOD   n.

Meluch, R.M.
JERUSALEM FIRE   n.

Meyers, Richard S.
RETURN TO DOOMSTAR   n.

Michaels, Melisa C.
FIRST BATTLE   n.
SKYRIDER I: SKIRMISH   n.

Miklowitz, Gloria D.
AFTER THE BOMB   n.

Milan, Victor
THE CYBERNETIC SAMURAI   n.

Modesitt, L.E., Jr.
THE HAMMER OF DARKNESS   n.

Morris, Janet & David A. Drake
ACTIVE MEASURES   n.

Murnane, Gerald
THE PLAINS   n.

Nelson, Ray Faraday
TIMEQUEST   n.

Niven, Larry & Jerry E. Pournelle
FOOTFALL   n.

Nolan, William F.
LOOK OUT FOR SPACE   n.

Norman, John
DANCER OF GOR   n.
MERCENARIES OF GOR   n.

Norton, Andre
FORERUNNER: THE SECOND VENTURE   n.

Norwood, Warren
POLAR FLEET   n.

O'Riordan, Robert
CADRE ONE   n.

Palmer, David R.
THRESHOLD   n.

Palmer, Jane
THE PLANET DWELLER   n.

Parvin, Brian
THE SINGING TREE   n.

Perry, Steve
THE MAN WHO NEVER MISSED   n.

Pohl, Frederik
BLACK STAR RISING   n.

Pohl, Frederik & C.M. Kornbluth
SEARCH THE SKY   n.

Powers, Tim
DINNER AT DEVIANT'S PALACE   n.

Preuss, Paul
HUMAN ERROR   n.

Price, E. Hoffmann
OPERATION EXILE   n.

Proctor, George W.
V: THE CHICAGO CONVERSION   n.
V: THE TEXAS RUN   n.

Reed, Kit
FORT PRIVILEGE   n.

Resnick, Mike
TALES OF THE VELVET COMET #3: EROS DESCENDING   n.

Reynolds, Alfred
KITEMAN OF KARANGA   n.

Reynolds, Mack & Dean Ing
TROJAN ORBIT   n.

Roberts, John Maddox
THE CINGULUM   n.
CLOAK OF ILLUSION   n.

Roberts, Keith
KITEWORLD   n.

Robinson, Kim Stanley
THE MEMORY OF WHITENESS   n.

Robinson, Spider
NIGHT OF POWER   n.

Rosenberg, Joel
EMILE AND THE DUTCHMAN   n.

Rothman, Chuck
STAROAMER'S FATE   n.

Rouch, James
THE ZONE #3: HUNTER KILLER   n.

Rowley, Christopher
THE BLACK SHIP   n.

Rucker, Rudy
MASTER OF SPACE AND TIME   n.
THE SECRET OF LIFE   n.

Saberhagen, Fred
THE BERSERKER THRONE   n.
BERSERKER: BLUE DEATH   n.
LOVE CONQUERS ALL   n.

Sagan, Carl
CONTACT   n.

Sanders, Scott Russell
TERRARIUM   n.

SCIENCE FICTION NOVELS

Saperstein, David
COCOON — n.

Sargent, Pamela
HOMESMIND — n.

Saul, John
BRAINCHILD — n.

Schmidt, Dennis
WANDERER — n.

Scott, Melissa
FIVE TWELFTHS OF HEAVEN — n.

Shaw, Bob
ORBITSVILLE DEPARTURE — n.
THE PEACE MACHINE — n.

Sheffield, Charles
BETWEEN THE STROKES OF NIGHT — n.

Shirley, John
ECLIPSE — n.

Shupp, Mike
WITH FATE CONSPIRE — n.

Sievert, John
C.A.D.S. — n.

Silverberg, Robert
TOM O'BEDLAM — n.

Sladek, John
TIK-TOK — n.

Sleator, William
SINGULARITY — n.

Slote, Alfred
THE TROUBLE ON JANUS — n.

Smith, E.E. "Doc" & Stephen Goldin
REVOLT OF THE GALAXY — n.

Smith, Evelyn E.
THE COPY SHOP — n.

Smith, L. Neil
THE GALLATIN DIVERGENCE — n.

Spinrad, Norman
CHILD OF FORTUNE — n.

Stacy, Ryder
DOOMSDAY WARRIOR #4: BLOODY AMERICA — n.
DOOMSDAY WARRIOR #5: AMERICA'S LAST DECLARATION — n.
DOOMSDAY WARRIOR #6: AMERICAN REBELLION — n.

Stasheff, Christopher
THE WARLOCK ENRAGED — n.

Steele, Linda
IBIS — n.

Sterling, Bruce
SCHISMATRIX — n.

Stith, John E.
MEMORY BLANK — n.

Stout, Rex
UNDER THE ANDES — n.

Stryker, Hal
NYPD 2025 — n.

Sucharitkul, Somtow
THE DARKLING WIND — n.
V: THE ALIEN SWORDMASTER — n.

Sullivan, Timothy
V: THE FLORIDA PROJECT — n.
V: THE NEW ENGLAND RESISTANCE — n.

Swanwick, Michael
IN THE DRIFT — n.

Swycaffer, Jefferson P.
BECOME THE HUNTED — n.
THE UNIVERSAL PREY — n.

Thurston, Robert
Q COLONY — n.

Tiptree, James, Jr.
BRIGHTNESS FALLS FROM THE AIR — n.

Tubb, E.C.
THE TEMPLE OF TRUTH — n.

Van Hise, Della
STAR TREK #24: KILLING TIME — n.

van Vogt, A.E.
NULL-A THREE — n.

Vinge, Joan D.
MAD MAX III: BEYOND THUNDERDOME — n.

Vonnegut, Kurt
GALÁPAGOS — n.

Watkins, William John
THE CENTRIFUGAL RICKSHAW DANCER — n.

Watson, Ian
THE BOOK OF BEING — n.
THE BOOK OF THE RIVER — n.
CONVERTS — n.

Webb, Sharon
THE ADVENTURES OF TERRA TARKINGTON, R.N. — n.

Weinstein, Howard
V: PRISONERS AND PAWNS — n.

Weston, Susan
CHILDREN OF THE LIGHT — n.

White, James
STAR HEALER — n.

Whiteford, Wynne
BREATHING SPACE ONLY — n.
THOR'S HAMMER — n.

Williams, Paul O.
THE SWORD OF FORBEARANCE — n.

Williams, Walter Jon
KNIGHT MOVES — n.

Wilson, Snoo
INSIDE BABEL — n.

Wold, Allen
V: THE CRIVIT EXPERIMENT — n.

Wolfe, Gene
FREE LIVE FREE — n.

Yates, W.R.
DIASPORAH — n.

Yep, Laurence
THE SHADOW LORD — n.

Zahn, Timothy
COBRA — n.
A COMING OF AGE — n.
SPINNERET — n.

Zebrowski, George
THE STARS WILL SPEAK — n.

FANTASY NOVELS

Aaron, Chester
OUT OF SIGHT, OUT OF MIND — n.

Abrams, R. Vaughan
PARA — n.

Adams, Richard
MAIA — n.

Aigner, Kurt W.
ALLISTAR: JOURNEY THROUGH A MIND — n.

Anthony, Piers
CREWEL LYE — n.
WITH A TANGLED SKEIN — n.

Arscott, David & David Marl
A FLIGHT OF BRIGHT BIRDS — n.

Asprin, Robert Lynn
LITTLE MYTH MARKER — n.
MYTH-ING PERSONS — n.

Avi
BRIGHT SHADOW — n.

Bailey, Robin W.
SKULL GATE — n.

Barker, Clive
THE DAMNATION GAME — n.

Barker, M.A.R.
FLAMESONG — n.

FANTASY NOVELS

Barrie, Monica
QUEEN OF KNIGHTS — n.

Bayley, Barrington J.
THE FOREST OF PELDAIN — n.

Bellairs, John
THE REVENGE OF THE WIZARD'S GHOST — n.

Benoit, Hendra
PSI PATROL: HENDRA'S BOOK — n.

Bischoff, David F.
THE DESTINY DICE — n.
WRAITH BOARD — n.

Bischoff, David F., Rich Brown & Linda Richardson
A PERSONAL DEMON — n.

Bradley, Marion Zimmer
NIGHT'S DAUGHTER — n.
WARRIOR WOMAN — n.

Brandner, Gary
THE HOWLING III — n.

Brindel, June Rachny
PHAEDRA — n.

Brooks, Terry
THE WISHSONG OF SHANNARA — n.

Brust, Steven
BROKEDOWN PALACE — n.

Campbell, Ramsey
OBSESSION — n.

Carl, Lillian Stewart
SABAZEL — n.

Carter, Angela
NIGHTS AT THE CIRCUS — n.

Carter, Lin
FOUND WANTING — n.

Chalker, Jack L.
VENGEANCE OF THE DANCING GODS — n.

Charnas, Suzy McKee
THE BRONZE KING — n.

Chetwin, Grace
OUT OF THE DARK WORLD — n.

Clayton, Jo
A BAIT OF DREAMS — n.
CHANGER'S MOON — n.

Clough, B.W.
THE DRAGON OF MISHBIL — n.

Coffey, Frank
NIGHT PRAYERS — n.

Cook, Glen
DARKWAR TRILOGY 1: DOOMSTALKER — n.
WARLOCK — n.
THE WHITE ROSE — n.
WITH MERCY TOWARD NONE — n.

Cooke, Catherine
MASK OF THE WIZARD — n.

Cooper, Louise
THE INITIATE — n.

Cunningham, Jere
LOVE OBJECT — n.

Davies, Robertson
WHAT'S BRED IN THE BONE — n.

de Lint, Charles
THE HARP OF THE GREY ROSE — n.
MULENGRO — n.

Dean, Pamela
THE SECRET COUNTRY — n.

Dexter, Susan
THE SWORD OF CALANDRA — n.

Diamond, Graham
CINNABAR — n.

Dickinson, Peter
A BOX OF NOTHING — n.

Drake, Asa
WARRIOR WITCH OF HEL — n.

Duane, Diane
DEEP WIZARDRY — n.

Easton, M. Coleman
MASTERS OF GLASS — n.

Emerson, Ru
THE PRINCESS OF FLAMES — n.

Ende, Michael
MOMO — n.

Estes, Rose
CHILDREN OF THE DRAGON — n.

Feist, Raymond E.
SILVERTHORN — n.

Findley, Timothy
NOT WANTED ON THE VOYAGE — n.

Flint, Kenneth C.
MASTER OF THE SIDHE — n.

Foster, Alan Dean
THE PATHS OF THE PERAMBULATOR — n.

Friedman, Michael Jan
THE HAMMER AND THE HORN — n.
THE SEEKERS AND THE SWORD — n.

Friesner, Esther M.
MUSTAPHA AND HIS WISE DOG — n.

Garrett, Randall & Vicki Ann Heydron
RETURN TO EDDARTA — n.

Gemmell, David
THE KING BEYOND THE GATE — n.

Gentle, Mary
A HAWK IN SILVER — n.

Gilmour, William
THE UNDYING LAND — n.

Giroux, Leo, Jr.
THE RISHI — n.

Godwin, Parke
THE LAST RAINBOW — n.

Goldstein, Lisa
THE DREAM YEARS — n.

Grant, Charles L.
THE TEA PARTY — n.

Green, Roland & Frieda Murray
THE THRONE OF SHERRAN, VOL. I: THE BOOK OF KANTELA — n.

Green, Sharon
THE WILL OF THE GODS — n.

Guigonnat, Henri
DAEMON IN LITHUANIA — n.

Hailey, Johanna
ENCHANTED PARADISE — n.

Hambly, Barbara
DRAGONSBANE — n.

Hancock, Niel
THE FIRES OF WINDAMEIR — n.

Harpur, Patrick
THE SERPENT'S CIRCLE — n.

Hawdon, Robin
A RUSTLE IN THE GRASS — n.

Hazel, Paul
WINTERKING — n.

Hildebrandt, Rita & Tim Hildebrandt
MERLIN AND THE DRAGONS OF ATLANTIS — n.

Hodgell, P.C.
DARK OF THE MOON — n.

Holdstock, Robert
MYTHAGO WOOD — n.

Hoppe, Stephanie T.
THE WINDRIDER — n.

Horowitz, Anthony
THE NIGHT OF THE SCORPION — n.

Hughes, Robert Don
THE POWER AND THE PROPHET — n.

FANTASY NOVELS

Hurley, Maxwell
  PSI PATROL #3: MAX'S BOOK   n.

Kay, Guy Gavriel
  THE SUMMER TREE   n.

Kennealy, Patricia
  THE COPPER CROWN   n.

Kennedy, Richard
  AMY'S EYES   n.

King, Bernard
  STARKADDER   n.

King, Stephen
  THE EYES OF THE DRAGON   n.

King, Tappan & Viido Polikarpus
  DOWNTOWN   n.

Koontz, Dean R.
  TWILIGHT EYES   n.

Kress, Nancy
  THE WHITE PIPES   n.

Kurtz, Katherine
  THE KING'S JUSTICE   n.

Laws, Stephen
  GHOST TRAIN   n.

Leiber, Justin
  THE SWORD AND THE EYE   n.
  THE SWORD AND THE TOWER   n.

Lindholm, Megan
  WIZARD OF THE PIGEONS   n.

Linzner, Gordon
  THE SPY WHO DRANK BLOOD   n.

Liquori, Sal
  PSI PATROL: SAL'S BOOK   n.

Lupoff, Richard A.
  LOVECRAFT'S BOOK   n.

MacAvoy, R.A.
  THE BOOK OF KELLS   n.

MacLeod, Charlotte
  THE CURSE OF THE GIANT HOGWEED   n.

Mayhar, Ardath
  THE SAGA OF GRITTEL SUNDOTHA   n.

McDowell, Michael
  JACK AND SUSAN IN 1953   n.
  TOPLIN   n.

Meaney, Dee Morrison
  ISEULT   n.

Millhiser, Marlys
  THE THRESHOLD   n.

Monaco, Richard
  BLOOD AND DREAMS   n.
  BROKEN STONE   n.
  JOURNEY TO THE FLAME   n.

Morressy, John
  THE TIME OF THE ANNIHILATOR   n.

Morris, Janet
  BEYOND SANCTUARY   n.
  BEYOND THE VEIL   n.

Morris, Winifred
  WITH MAGICAL HORSES TO RIDE   n.

Mueller, Richard
  GHOSTBUSTERS: THE SUPERNATURAL SPECTACULAR   n.

Murphy, Shirley Rousseau
  NIGHTPOOL   n.

Newman, Sharan
  GUINEVERE EVERMORE   n.

Orr, A.
  A WORLD IN AMBER   n.

Phillips, Ann
  THE OAK KING & THE ASH QUEEN   n.

Pierce, Meredith Ann
  THE WOMAN WHO LOVED REINDEER   n.

FANTASY NOVELS

Prescot, Dray
  OMENS OF KREGEN   n.
  STORM OVER VALHALLA   n.
  WEREWOLVES OF KREGEN   n.
  WITCHES OF KREGEN   n.

Priest, Christopher
  THE GLAMOUR   n.

Ptacek, Kathryn
  BLOOD AUTUMN   n.

Reinius, Trish
  POWER OF THE WHITE WOLF   n.

Resnick, Mike
  ADVENTURES   n.

Rice, Anne
  THE VAMPIRE LESTAT   n.

Roberson, Jennifer
  THE SONG OF HOMANA   n.

Roberts, John Maddox
  CONAN THE VALOROUS   n.

Rosenberg, Joel
  THE SILVER CROWN   n.

Roszak, Theodore
  DREAMWATCHER   n.

Ryman, Geoff
  THE WARRIOR WHO CARRIED LIFE   n.

Sadler, Barry
  CASCA: THE ASSASSIN   n.
  CASCA: THE PHOENIX   n.
  CASCA: THE PIRATE   n.

Salmonson, Jessica Amanda
  OU LU KHEN AND THE BEAUTIFUL MADWOMAN   n.

Salsitz, R.A.V.
  WHERE DRAGONS LIE   n.

Saralegui, Jorge
  LAST RITES   n.

Sarrantonio, Al
  CAMPBELL WOOD   n.
  TOTENTANZ   n.
  THE WORMS   n.

Saunders, Charles R.
  IMARO III: THE TRAIL OF BOHU   n.

Sawde, Derek
  SCEPTRE MORTAL   n.

Scarborough, Elizabeth
  THE CHRISTENING QUEST   n.

Schmidt, Dennis
  TWILIGHT OF THE GODS: THE FIRST NAME   n.

Scliar, Moacyr
  THE CENTAUR IN THE GARDEN   n.

Service, Pamela
  WINTER OF MAGIC'S RETURN   n.

Shea, Michael
  IN YANA, THE TOUCH OF UNDYING   n.

Shetterly, Will
  CATS HAVE NO LORD   n.

Silverberg, Robert
  SAILING TO BYZANTIUM   n.

Simmons, Dan
  SONG OF KALI   n.

Singer, Marilyn
  HORSEMASTER   n.

Sky, Kathleen
  WITCHDAME   n.

Smeds, Dave
  THE SORCERY WITHIN   n.

Smith, Stephanie
  SNOW-EYES   n.

Snyder, Gene
  TOMB SEVEN   n.

Springer, Nancy
  WINGS OF FLAME   n.

FANTASY NOVELS

Stableford, Brian
THE LAST DAYS OF THE EDGE OF THE WORLD   n.

Stirling, S.M.
SNOWBROTHER   n.

Sullivan, Faith
MRS. DEMMING AND THE MYTHICAL BEAST   n.

Suyin, Han
THE ENCHANTRESS   n.

Synge, Ursula
SWAN'S WING   n.

Tarr, Judith
THE GOLDEN HORN   n.
THE ISLE OF GLASS   n.

Tepper, Sheri S.
BLOOD HERITAGE   n.
THE FLIGHT OF MAVIN MANYSHAPED   n.
JINIAN FOOTSEER   n.
MARIANNE, THE MAGUS, AND THE MANTICORE   n.
THE SEARCH OF MAVIN MANYSHAPED   n.
THE SONG OF MAVIN MANYSHAPED   n.

Thompson, William Irwin
ISLANDS OUT OF TIME: A MEMOIR OF THE LAST DAYS OF ATLANTIS   n.

Vance, Jack
LYONESSE II: THE GREEN PEARL   n.

Vande Velde, Vivian
A HIDDEN MAGIC   n.

Vardeman, Robert E.
THE FROZEN WAVES   n.
THE JADE DEMONS #3: THE CRYSTAL CLOUDS   n.
THE QUAKING LANDS   n.
THE WHITE FIRE   n.

Vardeman, Robert E. & George W. Proctor
BLOOD FOUNTAIN   n.
TO DEMONS BOUND   n.
A YOKE OF MAGIC   n.

Vinge, Joan D.
LADYHAWKE   n.
RETURN TO OZ   n.
THE SANTA CLAUS STORYBOOK   n.
SANTA CLAUS: THE MOVIE   n.

Voigt, Cynthia
JACKAROO   n.

Walther, Daniel
SHAI'S DESTINY   n.

Wangerin, Walter
THE BOOK OF SORROWS   n.

Watt-Evans, Lawrence
THE MISENCHANTED SWORD   n.

Weaver, Lydia
SPLASHMAN   n.

Weis, Margaret & Tracy Hickman
DRAGONLANCE CHRONICLES, VOL. 2: DRAGONS OF WINTER NIGHT   n.
DRAGONLANCE CHRONICLES, VOL. 3: DRAGONS OF SPRING DAWNING   n.

Wellman, Manly Wade
THE SCHOOL OF DARKNESS   n.
THE VOICE OF THE MOUNTAIN   n.

White, Edmund
CARACOLE   n.

Wilder, Joan
THE JEWEL OF THE NILE   n.

Willard, Nancy
THINGS INVISIBLE TO SEE   n.

Williams, Tad
TAILCHASER'S SONG   n.

Wiseman, David
ADAM'S COMMON   n.

Wrede, Patricia C.
THE HARP OF IMACH THYSSEL   n.
TALKING TO DRAGONS   n.

Wrightson, Patricia
NIGHT OUTSIDE   n.

Yarbro, Chelsea Quinn
A MORTAL GLAMOUR   n.
TO THE HIGH REDOUBT   n.

Yep, Laurence
DRAGON STEEL   n.

Young, Robert F.
THE VIZIER'S SECOND DAUGHTER   n.

Zelazny, Roger
TRUMPS OF DOOM   n.

NOVELIZATIONS

Bonanno, Margaret Wander
DWELLERS IN THE CRUCIBLE   n.

Crispin, A.C. & Deborah A. Marshall
V: DEATH TIDE   n.

Dillard, J.M.
STAR TREK #27: MINDSHADOW   n.

Frakes, Randal & Bill Wisher
THE TERMINATOR   n.

Gipe, George
BACK TO THE FUTURE   n.

Hambly, Barbara
ISHMAEL   n.

Kagan, Janet
UHURA'S SONG   n.

Kotzwinkle, William
E.T.: THE BOOK OF THE GREEN PLANET   n.
E.T.: THE STORYBOOK OF THE GREEN PLANET   na

Larson, Glen S. & Robert Thurston
BATTLESTAR GALACTICA 11: THE NIGHTMARE MACHINE   n.

Larson, Majliss
STAR TREK #26: PAWNS AND SYMBOLS   n.

Longyear, Barry B. & David Gerrold
ENEMY MINE   n.

Martin, Les
THE BRIDE: A TALE OF LOVE AND DOOM   na

McQuay, Mike
MY SCIENCE PROJECT   n.

Mueller, Richard
GHOSTBUSTERS: THE SUPERNATURAL SPECTACULAR   n.

Proctor, George W.
V: THE CHICAGO CONVERSION   n.
V: THE TEXAS RUN   n.

Roberts, John Maddox
CONAN THE VALOROUS   n.

Saperstein, David
COCOON   n.

Skipp, John M. & Craig Spector
FRIGHT NIGHT   n.

Smith, E.E. "Doc" & Stephen Goldin
REVOLT OF THE GALAXY   n.

Sucharitkul, Somtow
V: THE ALIEN SWORDMASTER   n.

Sullivan, Timothy
V: THE FLORIDA PROJECT   n.
V: THE NEW ENGLAND RESISTANCE   n.

Van Hise, Della
STAR TREK #24: KILLING TIME   n.

Vinge, Joan D.
LADYHAWKE   n.
MAD MAX III: BEYOND THUNDERDOME   n.
RETURN TO OZ   n.
THE SANTA CLAUS STORYBOOK   n.
SANTA CLAUS: THE MOVIE   n.

Weinstein, Howard
V: PRISONERS AND PAWNS   n.

Wilder, Joan
THE JEWEL OF THE NILE   n.

Wold, Allen
V: THE CRIVIT EXPERIMENT   n.

Yep, Laurence
THE SHADOW LORD   n.

OMNIBUS VOLUMES

Adams, Robert
TALES OF THE HORSECLANS — om

Aldiss, Brian W.
THE HELLICONIA TRILOGY — om
THE HORATIO STUBBS SAGA — om

Asimov, Isaac, Martin H. Greenberg & Charles G. Waugh, eds.
ISAAC ASIMOV'S MAGICAL WORLDS OF FANTASY: WITCHES & WIZARDS — om

Asprin, Robert Lynn & Lynn Abbey, eds.
CROSS-CURRENTS — om

Barker, Clive
BOOKS OF BLOOD — om

Bradley, Marion Zimmer
WEB OF DARKNESS — om

de Camp, L. Sprague
THE RELUCTANT KING — om

Dickinson, Peter
THE CHANGES TRILOGY — om

Eddings, David
THE BELGARIAD: PART ONE — om
THE BELGARIAD: PART TWO — om

Foster, Alan Dean
SEASON OF THE SPELLSONG — om

King, Stephen
THE BACHMAN BOOKS: FOUR EARLY NOVELS BY STEPHEN KING — om

Kurtz, Katherine
THE CHRONICLES OF THE DERYNI — om

Le Guin, Ursula K.
FIVE COMPLETE NOVELS — om

Levin, Ira
THREE BY IRA LEVIN: ROSEMARY'S BABY, THIS PERFECT DAY, THE STEPFORD WIVES — om

MacAvoy, R.A.
A TRIO FOR LUTE — om

McCaffrey, Anne
THE IRETA ADVENTURE — om

Moorcock, Michael
THE CHRONICLES OF CASTLE BRASS — om

Pohl, Frederik & C.M. Kornbluth
VENUS, INC. — om

Rosenberg, Joel
GUARDIANS OF THE FLAME: THE WARRIORS — om

Saberhagen, Fred
THE COMPLETE BOOK OF SWORDS — om

Silverberg, Robert
THE SILENT INVADERS — om

Tepper, Sheri S.
THE TRUE GAME — om

Van Scyoc, Sydney J.
DAUGHTERS OF THE SUNSTONE — om

COLLECTIONS

Adams, Douglas
THE ORIGINAL HITCHHIKER RADIO SCRIPTS — co

Aickman, Robert
NIGHT VOICES: STRANGE STORIES — co

Aiken, Joan
UP THE CHIMNEY DOWN AND OTHER STORIES — oc

Anderson, Poul
DIALOGUE WITH DARKNESS — co

Angelo, Ivan
THE TOWER OF GLASS — co

Anthony, Piers
ANTHONOLOGY — co

Asimov, Isaac
THE ALTERNATE ASIMOVS — co
THE EDGE OF TOMORROW — co

Attanasio, A.A.
BEASTMARKS — oc

Barker, Clive
CLIVE BARKER'S BOOKS OF BLOOD, VOLUME 4 — oc
CLIVE BARKER'S BOOKS OF BLOOD, VOLUME 5 — oc
CLIVE BARKER'S BOOKS OF BLOOD, VOLUME 6 — oc

Bova, Ben
THE ASTRAL MIRROR — co

Bradley, Marion Zimmer
THE BEST OF MARION ZIMMER BRADLEY — co

Campbell, Ramsey
COLD PRINT — co

Carter, Angela
BLACK VENUS — co

Davis, Frederick C.
THE NIGHT NEMESIS: THE COMPLETE ADVENTURES OF THE MOON MAN--VOL. ONE — co

Delany, Samuel R.
FLIGHT FROM NEVERYON — oc

Dick, Philip K.
I HOPE I SHALL ARRIVE SOON — co

Dickson, Gordon R.
BEYOND THE DAR AL-HARB — co
FORWARD! — co
INVADERS! — co

Forbes, Caroline
THE NEEDLE ON FULL: LESBIAN FEMINIST SCIENCE FICTION — co

Foster, M.A.
OWL TIME — oc

Garner, Alan
ALAN GARNER'S BOOK OF BRITISH FAIRY TALES — co

Haldeman, Joe W.
DEALING IN FUTURES — co

Hamilton, Virginia
THE PEOPLE COULD FLY: AMERICAN BLACK FOLKTALES — co

Harrison, M. John
VIRICONIUM NIGHTS — co

Herbert, Frank
EYE — co

Jeppson, J.O.
THE MYSTERIOUS CURE AND OTHER STORIES OF PSHRINKS ANONYMOUS — co

Jones, Diana Wynne
WARLOCK AT THE WHEEL AND OTHER STORIES — co

King, Stephen
SILVER BULLET — co
SKELETON CREW — co

Klein, T.E.D.
DARK GODS — co

Knight, Damon
LATE KNIGHT EDITION — co

Kotzwinkle, William
JEWEL OF THE MOON — oc

Kress, Nancy
TRINITY AND OTHER STORIES — co

Lafferty, R.A.
SLIPPERY AND OTHER STORIES — oc

Laumer, Keith
ROGUE BOLO — oc

Le Guin, Ursula K.
ALWAYS COMING HOME — oc

Lee, Tanith
THE GORGON AND OTHER BEASTLY TALES — co

Lewis, C.S.
BOXEN: THE IMAGINARY WORLD OF THE YOUNG C.S. LEWIS — co

Lively, Penelope
UNINVITED GHOSTS — co

Longyear, Barry B.
IT CAME FROM SCHENECTADY — co

Lumley, Brian
THE HOUSE OF CTHULHU AND OTHER TALES OF THE PRIMAL LAND — co

Martin, George R.R.
NIGHTFLYERS — co

ANTHOLOGIES

ANTHOLOGIES

Norton, Andre & Robert Adams, eds.
MAGIC IN ITHKAR — oa
MAGIC IN ITHKAR 2 — oa

Pachter, Josh, ed.
TOP FANTASY — an
TOP SCIENCE FICTION — an

Pattrick, William, ed.
MYSTERIOUS SEA STORIES — an

Pournelle, Jerry E., ed.
THERE WILL BE WAR, VOL. IV: DAY OF THE TYRANT — an

Pournelle, Jerry E. & Jim Baen, eds.
FAR FRONTIERS — oa
FAR FRONTIERS VOL. II/SUMMER 1985 — oa
FAR FRONTIERS VOL. III/FALL 1985 — oa
FAR FRONTIERS VOL. IV/WINTER 1985 — oa

Pournelle, Jerry E., Jim Baen & John F. Carr, eds.
THE SCIENCE FICTION YEARBOOK — an

Preiss, Byron, ed.
THE PLANETS — oa

Rau, G. Randal, ed.
WORLD TALES — oa

Saberhagen, Fred, ed.
BERSERKER BASE — an

Saha, Arthur W., ed.
THE YEAR'S BEST FANTASY STORIES: 11 — an

Schiff, Stuart David, ed.
WHISPERS V — oa

Schwartz, Betty Ann, ed.
GREAT GHOST STORIES — an

Shetterly, Will & Emma Bull, eds.
LIAVEK — oa

Shwartz, Susan M., ed.
MOONSINGER'S FRIENDS — oa

Silverberg, Robert & Martin H. Greenberg, eds.
THE TIME TRAVELERS: A SCIENCE FICTION QUARTET — an

Wagner, Karl Edward, ed.
THE YEAR'S BEST HORROR STORIES: SERIES XIII — an

Whitelaw, Stella, Judy Gardiner & Mark Ronson
GRIMALKIN'S TALES — oa

Windling, Terri, ed.
FAERY! — oa

Wollheim, Donald A., ed.
THE 1985 ANNUAL WORLD'S BEST SF — an

Zebrowski, George, ed.
NEBULA AWARDS 20: SFWA'S CHOICES FOR THE BEST IN SCIENCE FICTION 1984 — an

MAGAZINES

Amazing Science Fiction Stories
v.58 #5, January 1985, George H. Scithers, ed. — mg
v.58 #6, March 1985, George H. Scithers, ed. — mg
v.59 #1, May 1985, George H. Scithers, ed. — mg
v.59 #2, July 1985, George H. Scithers, ed. — mg
v.59 #3, September 1985, George H. Scithers, ed. — mg
v.60 #1, November 1985, George H. Scithers, ed. — mg
v.60 #2, January 1986, George H. Scithers, ed. — mg

Analog Science Fiction/Science Fact
v.105 # 1, January 1985, Stanley Schmidt, ed. — mg
v.105 # 2, February 1985, Stanley Schmidt, ed. — mg
v.105 # 3, March 1985, Stanley Schmidt, ed. — mg
v.105 # 4, April 1985, Stanley Schmidt, ed. — mg
v.105 # 5, May 1985, Stanley Schmidt, ed. — mg
v.105 # 6, June 1985, Stanley Schmidt, ed. — mg
v.105 # 7, July 1985, Stanley Schmidt, ed. — mg
v.105 # 8, August 1985, Stanley Schmidt, ed. — mg
v.105 # 9, September 1985, Stanley Schmidt, ed. — mg
v.105 #10, October 1985, Stanley Schmidt, ed. — mg
v.105 #11, November 1985, Stanley Schmidt, ed. — mg
v.105 #12, December 1985, Stanley Schmidt, ed. — mg
v.105 #13, Mid-December 1985, Stanley Schmidt, ed. — mg
v.106 # 1, January 1986, Stanley Schmidt, ed. — mg

Border Land
v.1 #2, R.S. Hadji, ed. — mg
v.1 #3, R.S. Hadji, ed. — mg

Eldritch Tales No. 11
v.3 #2, Crispin Burnham, ed. — mg

Fantasy Book
v.4 #1, March 1985, Dennis Mallonee & Nick Smith, eds. — mg
v.4 #2, June 1985, Dennis Mallonee & Nick Smith, eds. — mg
v.4 #3, September 1985, Dennis Mallonee & Nick Smith, eds. — mg
v.4 #4, December 1985, Dennis Mallonee & Nick Smith, eds. — mg

Fantasy Tales
v.7 #14, Summer 1985, Stephen Jones, ed. — mg

Interzone
#11, Spring 1985, Colin Greenland, Simon Ounsley & David Pringle, eds. — mg
#12, Summer 1985, Colin Greenland, Simon Ounsley & David Pringle, eds. — mg
#13, Autumn 1985, Simon Ounsley & David Pringle, eds. — mg
#14, Winter 1985/86, Simon Ounsley & David Pringle, eds. — mg

Isaac Asimov's Science Fiction Magazine
v. 9 # 1, January 1985, Shawna McCarthy, ed. — mg
v. 9 # 2, February 1985, Shawna McCarthy, ed. — mg
v. 9 # 3, March 1985, Shawna McCarthy, ed. — mg
v. 9 # 4, April 1985, Shawna McCarthy, ed. — mg
v. 9 # 5, May 1985, Shawna McCarthy, ed. — mg
v. 9 # 6, June 1985, Shawna McCarthy, ed. — mg
v. 9 # 7, July 1985, Shawna McCarthy, ed. — mg
v. 9 # 8, August 1985, Shawna McCarthy, ed. — mg
v. 9 # 9, September 1985, Shawna McCarthy, ed. — mg
v. 9 #10, October 1985, Shawna McCarthy, ed. — mg
v. 9 #11, November 1985, Shawna McCarthy, ed. — mg
v. 9 #12, December 1985, Shawna McCarthy, ed. — mg
v. 9 #13, Mid-December 1985, Shawna McCarthy, ed. — mg
v.10 # 1, January 1986, Gardner Dozois, ed. — mg

The Magazine of Fantasy & Science Fiction
v.68 #1, January 1985, Edward L. Ferman, ed. — mg
v.68 #2, February 1985, Edward L. Ferman, ed. — mg
v.68 #3, March 1985, Edward L. Ferman, ed. — mg
v.68 #4, April 1985, Edward L. Ferman, ed. — mg
v.68 #5, May 1985, Edward L. Ferman, ed. — mg
v.68 #6, June 1985, Edward L. Ferman, ed. — mg
v.69 #1, July 1985, Edward L. Ferman, ed. — mg
v.69 #2, August 1985, Edward L. Ferman, ed. — mg
v.69 #3, September 1985, Edward L. Ferman, ed. — mg
v.69 #4, October 1985, Edward L. Ferman, ed. — mg
v.69 #5, November 1985, Edward L. Ferman, ed. — mg
v.69 #6, December 1985, Edward L. Ferman, ed. — mg
v.70 #1, January 1986, Edward L. Ferman, ed. — mg

Night Cry
v.1 #2, Summer 1985, T.E.D. Klein, ed. — mg
v.1 #3, Fall 1985, T.E.D. Klein, ed. — mg
v.1 #4, Winter 1985, Alan Rodgers, ed. — mg
v.1 #5, Spring 1986, Alan Rodgers, ed. — mg

Rod Serling's The Twilight Zone Magazine
v.4 #6, January/February 1985, T.E.D. Klein, ed. — mg
v.5 #1, March/April 1985, T.E.D. Klein, ed. — mg
v.5 #2, May/June 1985, T.E.D. Klein, ed. — mg
v.5 #3, July/August 1985, T.E.D. Klein, ed. — mg
v.5 #4, October 1985, Michael Blaine, ed. — mg
v.5 #5, December 1985, Michael Blaine, ed. — mg
v.5 #6, February 1986, Michael Blaine, ed. — mg

Shayol
v.3 #1, Whole No. 7, Arnie Fenner & Pat Cadigan, eds. — mg

Space and Time
#69, Winter 1986, Gordon Linzner, ed. — mg

Stardate
v.1 # 8, October 1985, Ted White & David F. Bischoff, eds. — mg
v.1 # 9, December 1985, Ted White & David F. Bischoff, eds. — mg

Weirdbook 20
Spring 1985, W. Paul Ganley, ed. — mg

Whispers
v.6 #1-2, December 1984, Stuart David Schiff, ed. — mg

REFERENCE

Aldiss, Brian W.
THE PALE SHADOW OF SCIENCE — nf

Aldridge, Alexandra
THE SCIENTIFIC WORLD VIEW IN DYSTOPIA — nf

Anderson, Craig
SCIENCE FICTION FILMS OF THE SEVENTIES — nf

Arbur, Rosemarie
MARION ZIMMER BRADLEY — nf

Benson, Michael
VINTAGE SCIENCE FICTION FILMS, 1896-1949 — nf

Bittner, James
APPROACHES TO THE FICTION OF URSULA K. LE GUIN — nf

REFERENCE

Blackford, Jenny, Russell Blackford, Lucy Sussex & Norman Talbot, eds.
CONTRARY MODES — nf

Bleich, David
UTOPIA: THE PSYCHOLOGY OF A CULTURAL FANTASY — nf

Bleiler, E.F., ed.
SUPERNATURAL FICTION WRITERS: FANTASY & HORROR, 2 VOLS. — nf

Boyajian, Jerry & Kenneth R. Johnson
INDEX TO THE SCIENCE FICTION MAGAZINES 1984 — nf

Brigg, Peter
J.G. BALLARD — nf

Budrys, Algis
BENCHMARKS: GALAXY BOOKSHELF — nf

Burgess, Michael & Jeffrey M. Elliot
THE WORK OF R. REGINALD: AN ANNOTATED BIBLIOGRAPHY AND GUIDE — nf

Carpenter, Humphrey
SECRET GARDENS: THE GOLDEN AGE OF CHILDREN'S LITERATURE — nf

Chapman, Edgar L.
THE MAGIC LABYRINTH OF PHILIP JOSÉ FARMER — nf

Clarke, Boden
THE WORK OF JEFFREY M. ELLIOT: AN ANNOTATED BIBLIOGRAPHY AND GUIDE — nf

Cohen, Daniel
THE ENCYCLOPEDIA OF THE STRANGE — nf

Collings, Michael R.
STEPHEN KING AS RICHARD BACHMAN — nf

Collings, Michael R. & David Engebretson
THE SHORTER WORKS OF STEPHEN KING — nf

Collins, Robert A. & Howard D. Pearce, eds.
THE SCOPE OF THE FANTASTIC: CULTURE, BIOGRAPHY, THEMES, CHILDREN'S LITERATURE — nf
THE SCOPE OF THE FANTASTIC: THEORY, TECHNIQUE, MAJOR AUTHORS — nf

Como, James T., ed.
C.S. LEWIS AT THE BREAKFAST TABLE, AND OTHER REMINISCENCES — nf

Dikty, Thaddeus, & R. Reginald
THE WORK OF JULIAN MAY: AN ANNOTATED BIBLIOGRAPHY & GUIDE — nf

Elgin, Don D.
THE COMEDY OF THE FANTASTIC: ECOLOGICAL PERSPECTIVES ON THE FANTASY NOVEL — nf

Etherington, Norman
RIDER HAGGARD — nf

Eyles, Allen
THE WORLD OF OZ: A FANTASTIC EXPEDITION OVER THE RAINBOW — nf

Fonstad, Karen Wynn
THE ATLAS OF THE LAND — nf

Franson, Donald & Howard DeVore
A HISTORY OF THE HUGO, NEBULA, AND INTERNATIONAL FANTASY AWARDS, Updated Edition — nf

Gaiman, Neil & Kim Newman
GHASTLY BEYOND BELIEF — hu

Gallagher, Edward J.
THE ANNOTATED GUIDE TO FANTASTIC ADVENTURES — nf

Hardy, Phil, ed.
SCIENCE FICTION: THE COMPLETE FILM SOURCEBOOK — nf

Hartwell, David
AGE OF WONDERS: EXPLORING THE WORLD OF SCIENCE FICTION — nf

Hassler, Donald M., ed.
PATTERNS OF THE FANTASTIC II — nf

Hopkins, Mariane S., ed.
FANDOM DIRECTORY #7, 1985-1986 EDITION — nf

Irwin, Walter & G.B. Love, eds.
THE BEST OF TREK #8 — nf
THE BEST OF TREK #9 — nf

Jaffery, Sheldon & Fred Cook
THE COLLECTOR'S INDEX TO WEIRD TALES — nf

Lane, Daryl, David Carson & William Vernon
THE SOUND OF WONDER: INTERVIEWS FROM "THE SCIENCE FICTION RADIO SHOW" — nf
THE SOUND OF WONDER: INTERVIEWS FROM "THE SCIENCE FICTION RADIO SHOW", VOL. 2 — nf

Lem, Stanislaw
MICROWORLDS: WRITINGS ON SCIENCE FICTION — nf

Lerner, Frederick Andrew
MODERN SCIENCE FICTION AND THE AMERICAN LITERARY COMMUNITY — nf

Lewis, C.S.
LETTERS TO CHILDREN — nf

McEvoy, Seth
SAMUEL R. DELANY — nf

McGuire, Patrick L.
RED STARS: POLITICAL ASPECTS OF SOVIET SCIENCE FICTION — nf

Menville, Douglas & R. Reginald
FUTURE VISIONS: THE GOLDEN AGE OF THE SCIENCE FICTION FILM — nf

Minsky, Marvin, ed.
ROBOTICS — nf

Moskowitz, Sam, ed.
A. MERRITT: REFLECTIONS IN THE MOON POOL — nf

NESFA Press
THE N.E.S.F.A. INDEX TO THE SCIENCE FICTION MAGAZINES AND ORIGINAL ANTHOLOGIES 1983 — nf

Nicholls, Peter
THE WORLD OF FANTASTIC FILMS: AN ILLUSTRATED SURVEY — nf

Parker, Helen N.
BIOLOGICAL THEMES IN MODERN SCIENCE FICTION — nf

Parnell, Frank H. & Mike Ashley
MONTHLY TERRORS: AN INDEX TO THE WEIRD FANTASY MAGAZINES PUBLISHED IN THE UNITED STATES AND GREAT BRITAIN — nf

Pringle, David
SCIENCE FICTION: THE 100 BEST NOVELS — nf

Purtill, Richard L.
J.R.R. TOLKIEN: MYTH, MORALITY, AND RELIGION — nf

Reilly, Robert, ed.
THE TRANSCENDENT ADVENTURE: STUDIES OF RELIGION IN SCIENCE FICTION/FANTASY — nf

Robinson, Kim Stanley
THE NOVELS OF PHILIP K. DICK — nf

Rosinsky, Natalie M.
FEMINIST FUTURES: CONTEMPORARY WOMEN'S SPECULATIVE FICTION — nf

Rossi, Leo D.
THE POLITICS OF FANTASY: C.S. LEWIS AND J.R.R. TOLKIEN — nf

Rovin, Jeff
THE ENCYCLOPEDIA OF SUPERHEROES — nf

Sadler, Frank
THE UNIFIED RING: NARRATIVE ART AND THE SCIENCE-FICTION NOVEL — nf

Schweitzer, Darrell, ed.
DISCOVERING MODERN HORROR FICTION I — nf
DISCOVERING STEPHEN KING — nf
EXPLORING FANTASY WORLDS — nf

Shepard, Leslie A., ed.
ENCYCLOPEDIA OF OCCULTISM AND PARAPSYCHOLOGY, Second Edition — nf

Skerl, Jennie
WILLIAM S. BURROUGHS — nf

Slusser, George E. & Eric S. Rabkin, eds.
SHADOWS OF THE MAGIC LAMP: FANTASY AND SCIENCE FICTION IN FILM — nf

Smith, R. Dixon
LOST IN THE RENTHARPIAN HILLS: SPANNING THE DECADES WITH CARL JACOBI — nf

Stableford, Brian
SCIENTIFIC ROMANCE IN BRITAIN, 1890-1950 — nf

Teague, Robert & Michael Goodwin
A GUIDE TO THE COMMONWEALTH: THE OFFICIAL GUIDE TO ALAN DEAN FOSTER'S HUMANX COMMONWEALTH UNIVERSE — nf

Thompson, Raymond H.
THE RETURN FROM AVALON: A STUDY OF THE ARTHURIAN LEGEND IN MODERN FICTION — nf

Touponce, William F.
RAY BRADBURY AND THE POETICS OF REVERIE: FANTASY, SCIENCE FICTION, AND THE READER — nf

Tymn, Marshall B.
THE YEAR'S SCHOLARSHIP IN SCIENCE FICTION, FANTASY AND HORROR LITERATURE — nf

Vasbinder, Samuel Holmes
SCIENTIFIC ATTITUDES IN MARY SHELLEY'S FRANKENSTEIN — nf

Wendland, Albert
  SCIENCE, MYTH, AND THE FICTIONAL CREATION OF ALIEN WORLDS   nf

Willis, Donald, ed.
  VARIETY'S COMPLETE SCIENCE FICTION REVIEWS   nf

Wingrove, David, ed.
  SCIENCE FICTION FILM SOURCE BOOK   nf

Winter, Douglas E.
  FACES OF FEAR: ENCOUNTERS WITH THE CREATORS OF MODERN HORROR nf

Yoke, Carl B. & Donald M. Hassler, eds.
  DEATH AND THE SERPENT: IMMORTALITY IN SCIENCE FICTION   nf

Ziegfeld, Richard E.
  STANISLAW LEM   nf

ART BOOKS

Asprin, Robert Lynn & Phil Foglio
  MYTH ADVENTURES ONE   pi

Baskin, Hosie & Leonard Baskin
  A BOOK OF DRAGONS   pi

Bates, Cary, Gene Colan & Neal McPheeters
  NIGHTWINGS   cs

Brown, Ken
  NOTES FROM THE NERVOUS BREAKDOWN LANE   ct

Canty, Thomas
  A MONSTER AT CHRISTMAS   pm

Couper, Heather & David Pelham
  UNIVERSE   pi

Cowley, Stewart
  SPACEBASE 2000   pi

Dean, Martyn, ed.
  THE GUIDE TO FANTASY ART TECHNIQUES   nf

Dean, Roger & Martyn Dean
  MAGNETIC STORM   nf

Fitzpatrick, Jim
  ERINSAGA: THE MYTHOLOGICAL PAINTINGS OF JIM FITZPATRICK   pi

Flynn, John L.
  FUTURE THREADS: COSTUME DESIGN FOR THE SCIENCE FICTION WORLD   nf

Frazetta, Frank
  FRANK FRAZETTA: BOOK FIVE   pi

Giffen, Keith & Robert Loren Fleming
  HELL ON EARTH   pi

Holdstock, Robert & Malcolm Edwards, eds.
  LOST REALMS   nf

Janson, Klaus
  FROST AND FIRE   pi

Johnson, Crockett
  BARNABY #1: WANTED: A FAIRY GODFATHER   cs
  BARNABY #2: MR. O'MALLEY AND THE HAUNTED HOUSE   cs
  BARNABY #3: JACKEEN J.O. O'MALLEY FOR CONGRESS   cs

Macaulay, David
  BAAA   na

Matthews, Rodney
  IN SEARCH OF FOREVER   pi

Perret, Patti
  THE FACES OF SCIENCE FICTION   nf

Potter, J.K.
  THE ART OF SKELETON CREW   pi

Reeder, Dan
  THE SIMPLE SCREAMER   nf

Robbins, Trina
  THE SILVER METAL LOVER   pi

Salomoni, Tito
  THE SURREALISTIC WORLD OF TITO SALOMONI   pi

Vallejo, Boris
  BORIS VALLEJO'S FANTASY ART TECHNIQUES   pi

Van Allsburg, Chris
  THE POLAR EXPRESS   pi

Wilson, Gahan
  GAHAN WILSON'S AMERICA   ct

ASSOCIATIONAL

Aldiss, Brian W.
  THE HORATIO STUBBS SAGA   om

Ashe, Geoffrey
  THE DISCOVERY OF KING ARTHUR   nf

Asimov, Isaac
  OPUS 300   nf

Asimov, Isaac & Karen A. Frenkel
  ROBOTS: MACHINES IN MAN'S IMAGE   nf

Borges, Jorge Luis
  ATLAS   nf

Bradbury, Ray
  DEATH IS A LONELY BUSINESS   n.

Carey, Peter
  ILLYWHACKER   n.

Clarke, Arthur C. & Peter Hyams
  THE ODYSSEY FILE   nf

Cohen, Daniel
  THE ENCYCLOPEDIA OF THE STRANGE   nf

Dick, Philip K.
  IN MILTON LUMKY TERRITORY   n.
  PUTTERING ABOUT IN A SMALL LAND   n.

Drury, Nevill
  DICTIONARY OF MYSTICISM AND THE OCCULT   nf

Ellison, Harlan
  AN EDGE IN MY VOICE   nf

Fairley, John & Simon Welfare
  ARTHUR C. CLARKE'S WORLD OF STRANGE POWERS   nf

Ferrell, Keith
  GEORGE ORWELL: THE POLITICAL PEN   nf

Gilliland, Alexis
  WHO SAYS PARANOIA ISN'T "IN" ANY MORE?   ct

Gray, Alasdair
  THE FALL OF KEVIN WALKER   n.

Hartmann, William K., Pamela Lee & Ron Miller
  OUT OF THE CRADLE: EXPLORING THE FRONTIERS BEYOND EARTH   nf

Herron, Don
  THE LITERARY WORLD OF SAN FRANCISCO & ITS ENVIRONS   nf

Holland, Cecilia
  PILLAR OF THE SKY   n.

Maglio, Mitchell
  THE OFFICIAL STAR TREK QUIZ BOOK   nf

Moorcock, Michael
  THE LAUGHTER OF CARTHAGE   n.

Norton, Andre & Phyllis Miller
  RIDE THE GREEN DRAGON   n.

Rickman, Gregg
  PHILIP K. DICK: THE LAST TESTAMENT   nf

Russ, Joanna
  MAGIC MOMMAS, TREMBLING SISTERS, PURITANS AND PERVERTS   nf

Shepard, Leslie A., ed.
  ENCYCLOPEDIA OF OCCULTISM AND PARAPSYCHOLOGY, Second Edition nf

Stableford, Brian & David Langford
  THE THIRD MILLENNIUM: A HISTORY OF THE WORLD: AD 2000-3000   ms

Vance, Jack
  STRANGE NOTIONS & THE DARK OCEAN   n.

Walters, Ray
  PAPERBACK TALK   nf

Weller, Tom
  SCIENCE MADE STUPID   hu

Williamson, J.N.
  THE NEW DEVIL'S DICTIONARY: CREEPY CLICHES AND SINISTER SYNONYMS
                                                                   nf

Wilson, Robert Anton
  THE WIDOW'S SON   n.

Yarbro, Chelsea Quinn
  FOUR HORSES FOR TISHTRY   n.

Yeager, General Chuck & Leo Janos
  YEAGER: AN AUTOBIOGRAPHY   nf

MISCELLANEOUS

Beattie, Ann
  SPECTACLES   ss

Brennan, Joseph Payne
  SIXTY SELECTED POEMS   pm

Buckley, William F., Jr.
  THE TEMPTATION OF WILFRED MALACHEY   ss

Crossley-Holland, Kevin & Gwyn Thomas, trans.
  TALES FROM THE MABINOGION   ms

Dick, Philip K.
  UBIK: THE SCREENPLAY   pl

Joels, Kerry Mark
  THE MARS ONE CREW MANUAL   ms

Le Guin, Ursula K.
  KING DOG: A SCREENPLAY   pl

Okrand, Marc
  STAR TREK: THE KLINGON DICTIONARY   ms

Straub, Peter
  BLUE ROSE   nv

Streiber, Whitley
  WOLF OF SHADOWS   na

Turner, Frederick
  THE NEW WORLD: AN EPIC POEM   pm

AUTHOR LIST, STORIES

ABBEY, LYNN

ANDERSON, POUL

Abbey, Lynn
  Children of All Ages   nv SOULCTY,86
    THIEVES' WORLD, BOOK 8: SOUL OF THE CITY
           Robert Lynn Asprin+ oa
  The Corners of Memory   nv FACECHS,83
    CROSS-CURRENTS   Robert Lynn Asprin+ om
  Dramatis Personae   pr
    THIEVES' WORLD, BOOK 7: THE DEAD OF WINTER
           Robert Lynn Asprin+ oa
    THIEVES' WORLD, BOOK 8: SOUL OF THE CITY
           Robert Lynn Asprin+ oa
  The God-Chosen   nv DEADWIN,85
    THIEVES' WORLD, BOOK 7: THE DEAD OF WINTER
           Robert Lynn Asprin+ oa
  Gyskouras   nv WNGSOMN,84
    CROSS-CURRENTS   Robert Lynn Asprin+ om
  The Small Powers that Endure   nv SOULCTY,86
    THIEVES' WORLD, BOOK 8: SOUL OF THE CITY
           Robert Lynn Asprin+ oa
  Steel   na STRMSSN,82
    CROSS-CURRENTS   Robert Lynn Asprin+ om

Abbey, Lynn & Robert Lynn Asprin
  A Special Note from the Editors   aw WNGSOMN,84
    CROSS-CURRENTS   Robert Lynn Asprin+ om

Abbey, Lynn & Robert Lynn Asprin, eds.
  THE FACE OF CHAOS   oa ACE Oct,83
    CROSS-CURRENTS   Robert Lynn Asprin+ om
  WINGS OF OMEN   oa ACE Nov,84
    CROSS-CURRENTS   Robert Lynn Asprin+ om

Abernathy, Robert
  Heirs Apparent   nv FSF Jun,54
    BEYOND ARMAGEDDON   Walter M. Miller, Jr.+ an

Adams, Robert
  Battle at Kahlkhopolis   nv WAR V 4,85
    THERE WILL BE WAR, VOL. IV: DAY OF THE TYRANT
           Jerry E. Pournelle an
  THE COMING OF THE HORSECLANS   n. PIN 1975
    TALES OF THE HORSECLANS   Robert Adams om
  Introduction   in
    BARBARIANS   Robert Adams+ an
  Prologue   pr
    MAGIC IN ITHKAR   Andre Norton+ oa
    MAGIC IN ITHKAR 2   Andre Norton+ oa
  REVENGE OF THE HORSECLANS   n. PIN 1977
    TALES OF THE HORSECLANS   Robert Adams om
  SWORDS OF THE HORSECLANS   n. PIN 1977
    TALES OF THE HORSECLANS   Robert Adams om

Adkins, Lee
  The Vixen   pm FBM Sep,85
    Fantasy Book [v.4 #3, September 1985]   Dennis Mallonee+ mg

Aickman, Robert
  The Hospice   nv COLDHND,75
    MASTERPIECES OF TERROR AND THE SUPERNATURAL   Marvin Kaye an
  Just a Song at Twilight   ss GHB # 4
    NIGHT VOICES: STRANGE STORIES   Robert Aickman co
  Laura   ss CLDFEAR,77
    NIGHT VOICES: STRANGE STORIES   Robert Aickman co
  Mark Ingestre: The Customer's Tale   ss DRKFRCS,80
    NIGHT VOICES: STRANGE STORIES   Robert Aickman co
  Rosamund's Bower   nv NTVOICE,85
    NIGHT VOICES: STRANGE STORIES   Robert Aickman co
  The Stains   na NWT # 1,80
    NIGHT VOICES: STRANGE STORIES   Robert Aickman co
  The Trains   nv WEAREFR
    NIGHT VOICES: STRANGE STORIES   Robert Aickman co

Aiken, Joan
  The Blades   nv OUTOFTM,84
    OUT OF TIME   Aidan Chambers oa
  Christmas at Troy   nv UPCHMNY,84
    UP THE CHIMNEY DOWN AND OTHER STORIES   Joan Aiken oc
  The Dog on the Roof   nv UPCHMNY,84
    UP THE CHIMNEY DOWN AND OTHER STORIES   Joan Aiken oc
  The Fire Dogs   ss UPCHMNY,84
    UP THE CHIMNEY DOWN AND OTHER STORIES   Joan Aiken oc
  The Gift Giving   ss SIXTEEN
    UP THE CHIMNEY DOWN AND OTHER STORIES   Joan Aiken oc
  The Happiest Sheep in London   nv UPCHMNY,84
    UP THE CHIMNEY DOWN AND OTHER STORIES   Joan Aiken oc
  The Last Chimney Cuckoo   nv UPCHMNY,84
    UP THE CHIMNEY DOWN AND OTHER STORIES   Joan Aiken oc
  A Leg Full of Rubies   ss SMLPNCH,74
    BESTIARY!   Jack Dann+ an
  The Midnight Rose   ss UPCHMNY,84
    UP THE CHIMNEY DOWN AND OTHER STORIES   Joan Aiken oc
  Miss Hooting's Legacy   nv UPCHMNY,84
    UP THE CHIMNEY DOWN AND OTHER STORIES   Joan Aiken oc
  The Missing Heir   nv UPCHMNY,84
    UP THE CHIMNEY DOWN AND OTHER STORIES   Joan Aiken oc
  Potter's Gray   ss UPCHMNY,84
    UP THE CHIMNEY DOWN AND OTHER STORIES   Joan Aiken oc
  Up the Chimney Down   nv UPCHMNY,84
    UP THE CHIMNEY DOWN AND OTHER STORIES   Joan Aiken oc

Aikin, Jim
  My Life in the Jungle   ss FSF Feb,85
    The Magazine of Fantasy & Science Fiction [v.68 #2, February
    1985]   Edward L. Ferman mg
    BEYOND ARMAGEDDON   Walter M. Miller, Jr.+ an

Aldiss, Brian W.
  All the World's Tears   ss NEB May,57
    TOP SCIENCE FICTION   Josh Pachter an
  The Game of God [Segregation]   na NWS Jul,58
    STARSWARM   Brian W. Aldiss co
  Hearts and Engines [Soldiers Running]   ss NWS Jun,60
    STARSWARM   Brian W. Aldiss co
  Intangibles Inc.   nv SCF Feb,59
    STARSWARM   Brian W. Aldiss co
  A Kind of Artistry   nv FSF Oct,62
    STARSWARM   Brian W. Aldiss co
  Legends of Smith's Burst   nv NEB Jun,59
    STARSWARM   Brian W. Aldiss co
  O Moon of My Delight [Moon of Delight]   nv NWS Mar,61
    STARSWARM   Brian W. Aldiss co
  Old Hundredth   ss NWS Nov,60
    STARSWARM   Brian W. Aldiss co
  Shards   ss FSF Apr,62
    STARSWARM   Brian W. Aldiss co
  Theodore Sturgeon: 1918-1985   bg BSG 166,85
    Isaac Asimov's Science Fiction Magazine [v.10 # 1, January
    1986]   Gardner Dozois mg
  The Underprivileged   ss NWS May,63
    STARSWARM   Brian W. Aldiss co
  You Never Asked My Name   ss FSF Nov,85
    The Magazine of Fantasy & Science Fiction [v.69 #5, November
    1985]   Edward L. Ferman mg

Alexander, Gary
  Buddies   ss IAS Sep,85
    Isaac Asimov's Science Fiction Magazine [v. 9 # 9, September
    1985]   Shawna McCarthy mg

Allen, Lori
  Family Obligations   ss TZM Feb,85
    Rod Serling's The Twilight Zone Magazine [v.4 #6,
    January/February 1985]   T.E.D. Klein mg

Allen, Woody
  Count Dracula   ss GTNGEVN,71
    GREAT GHOST STORIES   Betty Ann Schwartz an

Allison, Susan
  Dear Reader   pr
    THE FANTASY SAMPLER   Susan Allison an

Alterman, Peter S.
  Scenicruiser and the Silver Lady   nv TZM Jun,81
    Night Cry [v.1 #2, Summer 1985]   T.E.D. Klein mg

Anderson, Craig W.
  Food, Gas, Lodging   ss TZM Jul,82
    Night Cry [v.1 #2, Summer 1985]   T.E.D. Klein mg

Anderson, Karen
  Landscape With Sphinxes   ss FSF Nov,62
    BESTIARY!   Jack Dann+ an
  Treaty in Tartessos   ss FSF May,63
    BESTIARY!   Jack Dann+ an

Anderson, Kevin J.
  Final Performance   ss FSF Jan,85
    The Magazine of Fantasy & Science Fiction [v.68 #1, January
    1985]   Edward L. Ferman mg

Anderson, Poul
  A Chapter of Revelation   na DAYSUNS,72
    DIALOGUE WITH DARKNESS   Poul Anderson co
  The Communicators   na INY # 1,70
    DIALOGUE WITH DARKNESS   Poul Anderson co
  Conversation in Arcady   ss ASF Dec,63
    DIALOGUE WITH DARKNESS   Poul Anderson co
  Deathwomb   nv ASF Nov,83
    BERSERKER BASE   Fred Saberhagen an
  Dialogue   nv FSTRLGT,76
    DIALOGUE WITH DARKNESS   Poul Anderson co
  The Forest   nv MNSNGRF,85
    MOONSINGER'S FRIENDS   Susan M. Shwartz oa
  Geology, Meteorology, Oceanography, Geology, Nomenclature,
  Biology   ar
    MEDEA: HARLAN'S WORLD   Harlan Ellison an
  Hunter's Moon   nv ASF Nov,78
    THE HUGO WINNERS, VOLUME 4: 1976-1979   Isaac Asimov an
    MEDEA: HARLAN'S WORLD   Harlan Ellison an
  The Immortal Game   ss FSF Feb,54
    ISAAC ASIMOV'S MAGICAL WORLDS OF FANTASY #3: COSMIC KNIGHTS
           Isaac Asimov+ in
  Introduction   in
    TERRORISTS OF TOMORROW   Poul Anderson+ an
    STEEL BROTHER   Gordon R. Dickson co
  Introduction to Mercenaries of Tomorrow   in
    MERCENARIES OF TOMORROW   Poul Anderson+ an
  The Life of Your Time [as Michael Karageorge]   nv ASF Sep,65
    DIALOGUE WITH DARKNESS   Poul Anderson co
  No Truce With Kings   na FSF Jun,63

Anderson, Poul (continued)
THERE WILL BE WAR, VOL. IV: DAY OF THE TYRANT
Jerry E. Pournelle an
Operation Salamander   nv FSF Jan,57
ISAAC ASIMOV'S MAGICAL WORLDS OF FANTASY: WITCHES & WIZARDS
Isaac Asimov+ om
Pride   nv FFR V 1,85
FAR FRONTIERS   Jerry E. Pournelle+ oa
Sam Hall   nv ASF Aug,53
TERRORISTS OF TOMORROW   Poul Anderson+ an
Sister Planet   na SAT May,59
DIALOGUE WITH DARKNESS   Poul Anderson co
The Soldier From the Stars   nv FUN Jun,55
MERCENARIES OF TOMORROW   Poul Anderson+ an
SOS   nv IFS Mar,70
DIALOGUE WITH DARKNESS   Poul Anderson co
Star Peace?   ar IAS Sep,85
Isaac Asimov's Science Fiction Magazine [v. 9 # 9, September
1985]   Shawna McCarthy mg
Swordsman of Lost Terra   nv PLS Nov,51
BARBARIANS   Robert Adams+ an
Time Heals   nv ASF Oct,49
DIALOGUE WITH DARKNESS   Poul Anderson co
Tomorrow's Children   nv ASF Mar,47
BEYOND ARMAGEDDON   Walter M. Miller, Jr.+ an
The Valor of Cappen Varra   ss FUN Jan,57
BESTIARY!   Jack Dann+ an

Anderson, Poul, Hal Clement, Thomas M. Disch, Larry Niven &
Frederik Pohl
Second Thoughts   ms
MEDEA: HARLAN'S WORLD   Harlan Ellison an

Andreyev, Leonid
Lazarus   ss
MASTERPIECES OF TERROR AND THE SUPERNATURAL   Marvin Kaye an

Angelo, Ivan
Conquest   nv TWRGLSS,86
THE TOWER OF GLASS   Ivan Angelo co
Friday Night/Saturday Morning   nv TWRGLSS,86
THE TOWER OF GLASS   Ivan Angelo co
Lost & Found   nv TWRGLSS,86
THE TOWER OF GLASS   Ivan Angelo co
The Real True Son of the Bitch   nv TWRGLSS,86
THE TOWER OF GLASS   Ivan Angelo co
The Tower of Glass   nv TWRGLSS,86
THE TOWER OF GLASS   Ivan Angelo co

Anonymous
The Planet   ss KNB Jul,1853
Introduction by Darrell Schweitzer.
Fantasy Book [v.4 #2, June 1985]   Dennis Mallonee+ mg
Preface   pr
THE 1985 RHYSLING ANTHOLOGY   Anonymous an

Anthony, Piers
Beak by Beak   ss ASF Dec,67
ANTHONOLOGY   Piers Anthony co
The Bridge   ss WOT #24,70
ANTHONOLOGY   Piers Anthony co
Encounter   ss FAN Oct,64
ANTHONOLOGY   Piers Anthony co
Getting Through University   nv IFS Aug,68
ANTHONOLOGY   Piers Anthony co
The Ghost Galaxies   nv IFS Sep,66
ANTHONOLOGY   Piers Anthony co
Gone to the Dogs   ss ANTHNGY,85
ANTHONOLOGY   Piers Anthony co
Hard Sell   ss IFS Aug,72
ANTHONOLOGY   Piers Anthony co
Hurdle   nv IFS Dec,72
ANTHONOLOGY   Piers Anthony co
In the Barn   nv AGNDNGR,72
ANTHONOLOGY   Piers Anthony co
In the Jaws of Danger   nv IFS Nov,67
ANTHONOLOGY   Piers Anthony co
The Life of the Stripe   ss FAN Feb,69
ANTHONOLOGY   Piers Anthony co
On the Uses of Torture   nv BKS V 3,81
ANTHONOLOGY   Piers Anthony co
Phog   ss FAN Jun,65
ANTHONOLOGY   Piers Anthony co
Possible to Rue   ss FAN Apr,63
ANTHONOLOGY   Piers Anthony co
Quinquepedalian   ss AMZ Nov,63
ANTHONOLOGY   Piers Anthony co
Small Mouth, Bad Taste   ss SCIAGMN,70
ANTHONOLOGY   Piers Anthony co
The Toaster   ss ANTHNGY,85
ANTHONOLOGY   Piers Anthony co
Up Schist Crick   nv GENERTN,72
ANTHONOLOGY   Piers Anthony co
The Whole Truth   ss NOV # 1,70
ANTHONOLOGY   Piers Anthony co
Within the Cloud   ss GAL Apr,67
ANTHONOLOGY   Piers Anthony co
Wood You?   ss FSF Oct,70
ANTHONOLOGY   Piers Anthony co

Antieau, Kim
Cycles   ss SDW # 8,85
SHADOWS 8   Charles L. Grant oa
Hauntings   ss IAS Feb,85
Isaac Asimov's Science Fiction Magazine [v. 9 # 2, February
1985]   Shawna McCarthy mg

Aquino, John T.
The Sad Wizard   nv FBM Dec,85
Fantasy Book [v.4 #4, December 1985]   Dennis Mallonee+ mg

Armistead, Barbara
On the Trail   ss FRAMZDK,85
FREE AMAZONS OF DARKOVER   Marion Zimmer Bradley+ oa

Armstrong, Michael
Going After Arviq   nv AFTRWAR,85
AFTERWAR   Janet Morris oa

Arnold, H.F.
The Night Wire   ss WRT Sep,26
MASTERPIECES OF TERROR AND THE SUPERNATURAL   Marvin Kaye an

Aronica, Lou
Dear Reader   in
THE BANTAM SPECTRA SAMPLER   Lou Aronica an

Arthur, Robert
The Haunted Trailer   nv WRT 1953
GREAT GHOST STORIES   Betty Ann Schwartz an
Satan and Sam Shay   ss ELK Aug,42
ISAAC ASIMOV'S MAGICAL WORLDS OF FANTASY #4: SPELLS
Isaac Asimov+ an

Arthurs, Bruce D.
Unicorn's Blood   nv S&S # 2,85
SWORD AND SORCERESS II   Marion Zimmer Bradley oa

Ashley, Mike
Algernon Blackwood: The Ghostly Tale's Great Visionary
iv TZM Jun,85
"Posthumous interview" based on Blackwood's letters and other
writings.
Rod Serling's The Twilight Zone Magazine [v.5 #2, May/June
1985]   T.E.D. Klein mg

Asimov, Isaac
Amazing Stories and I   in
AMAZING STORIES: 60 YEARS OF THE BEST SCIENCE FICTION
Isaac Asimov+ an
Belief   nv ASF Oct,53
ANALOG: THE BEST OF SCIENCE FICTION   Anonymous an
THE EDGE OF TOMORROW   Isaac Asimov co
Belief [ending of the published version]   ex ASF Oct,53
THE ALTERNATE ASIMOVS   Isaac Asimov co
Belief [first version]   nv ALTASMV,86
THE ALTERNATE ASIMOVS   Isaac Asimov co
The Bicentennial Man   nv STL # 2,76
THE HUGO WINNERS, VOLUME 4: 1976-1979   Isaac Asimov an
The Billiard Ball   ss IFS Mar,67
THE EDGE OF TOMORROW   Isaac Asimov co
"Breeds There a Man--?"   nv ASF Jun,51
THE EDGE OF TOMORROW   Isaac Asimov co
ISAAC ASIMOV PRESENTS THE GREAT SF STORIES: 13 (1951)
Isaac Asimov+ an
The Bridge of the Gods   ar FSF Mar,75
THE EDGE OF TOMORROW   Isaac Asimov co
Christmas on Ganymede   ss STS Jan,42
SANTA 2000   Michel Parry an
Civil War   ed IAS Dec,85
Isaac Asimov's Science Fiction Magazine [v. 9 #12, December
1985]   Shawna McCarthy mg
The Comet That Wasn't   ar FSF Nov,76
THE EDGE OF TOMORROW   Isaac Asimov co
Curses!   in
ISAAC ASIMOV'S MAGICAL WORLDS OF FANTASY #4: SPELLS
Isaac Asimov+ an
The Dead Past   nv ASF Apr,56
THE EDGE OF TOMORROW   Isaac Asimov co
Dialog   ed IAS Apr,85
Isaac Asimov's Science Fiction Magazine [v. 9 # 4, April
1985]   Shawna McCarthy mg
Dreamworld   vi FSF Nov,55
ISAAC ASIMOV'S MAGICAL WORLDS OF FANTASY #5: GIANTS
Isaac Asimov+ an
Editors   ed IAS Nov,85
Isaac Asimov's Science Fiction Magazine [v. 9 #11, November
1985]   Shawna McCarthy mg
THE END OF ETERNITY [written in winter of 1953-1954]
n. ALTASMV,86
original version of the novel THE END OF ETERNITY
THE ALTERNATE ASIMOVS   Isaac Asimov co
Euclid's Fifth   ar FSF Mar,71
THE EDGE OF TOMORROW   Isaac Asimov co
The Eureka Phenomenon   ar FSF Jun,71
THE EDGE OF TOMORROW   Isaac Asimov co
The Eye of the Beholder   ss IAS Jan,86
Isaac Asimov's Science Fiction Magazine [v.10 # 1, January
1986]   Gardner Dozois mg
Fairy Tales   ed IAS Oct,85
Isaac Asimov's Science Fiction Magazine [v. 9 #10, October
1985]   Shawna McCarthy mg

Asprin, Robert Lynn, ed.
STORM SEASON   oa ACE Oct,82
  CROSS-CURRENTS   Robert Lynn Asprin+ om

Asprin, Robert Lynn & Lynn Abbey
A Special Note from the Editors   aw WNGSOMN,84
  CROSS-CURRENTS   Robert Lynn Asprin+ om

Asprin, Robert Lynn & Lynn Abbey, eds.
THE FACE OF CHAOS   oa ACE Oct,83
  CROSS-CURRENTS   Robert Lynn Asprin+ om
WINGS OF OMEN   oa ACE Nov,84
  CROSS-CURRENTS   Robert Lynn Asprin+ om

Athearn, Hope
About an Old Closet   pm IAS Feb,85
  Isaac Asimov's Science Fiction Magazine [v. 9 # 2, February
  1985]   Shawna McCarthy mg
The Twenty-Fifth   pm IAS Jul,84
  THE 1985 RHYSLING ANTHOLOGY   Anonymous   an

Atherton, Gertrude
The Bell in the Fog   nv BELLFOG,05
  HAUNTED WOMEN: THE BEST SUPERNATURAL TALES BY AMERICAN WOMEN
  WRITERS   Alfred Bendixen an

Attanasio, A.A.
The Answerer of Dreams   nv BEASTMK,85
  BEASTMARKS   A.A. Attanasio oc
The Last Dragon Master   ss BEASTMK,85
  BEASTMARKS   A.A. Attanasio oc
Matter Mutter Mother   ss BEASTMK,85
  BEASTMARKS   A.A. Attanasio oc
Monkey Puzzle   ss BEASTMK,85
  BEASTMARKS   A.A. Attanasio oc
Nuclear Tan   ss BEASTMK,85
  BEASTMARKS   A.A. Attanasio oc
Over the Rainbow   ss BEASTMK,85
  BEASTMARKS   A.A. Attanasio oc
Sherlock Holmes and Basho   ss BEASTMK,85
  BEASTMARKS   A.A. Attanasio oc

Avallone, Michael
The Man Who Walked On Air   ss WRT Sep,53
  TOP FANTASY   Josh Pachter an

Aylward, David
The Revenge of the Past: Part 2   ar BLD V1 #2,85
  Border Land   [v.1 #2]   R.S. Hadji mg

Bachman, Richard
THE LONG WALK   n. SIG 1979
  THE BACHMAN BOOKS: FOUR EARLY NOVELS BY STEPHEN KING
                                             Stephen King om
RAGE   n. SIG 1977
  THE BACHMAN BOOKS: FOUR EARLY NOVELS BY STEPHEN KING
                                             Stephen King om
ROADWORK   n. SIG 1981
  THE BACHMAN BOOKS: FOUR EARLY NOVELS BY STEPHEN KING
                                             Stephen King om
THE RUNNING MAN   n. SIG 1982
  THE BACHMAN BOOKS: FOUR EARLY NOVELS BY STEPHEN KING
                                             Stephen King om

Bailey, Robin W.
Daughter of the Sun   nv WNGSOMN,84
  CROSS-CURRENTS   Robert Lynn Asprin+ om
Keeping Promises   nv DEADWIN,85
  THIEVES' WORLD, BOOK 7: THE DEAD OF WINTER
                                           Robert Lynn Asprin+ oa

Baker, Charles L.
Eldritch Lair - Dungeon Level   ed EDT #11,85
  Eldritch Tales No. 11 [v.3 #2]   Crispin Burnham mg
The Gospel According to...   bi EDT #11,85
  Eldritch Tales No. 11 [v.3 #2]   Crispin Burnham mg
Shadow of the Immortal (1 of 3)   sl EDT #11,85
  Eldritch Tales No. 11 [v.3 #2]   Crispin Burnham mg

Baker, Mark
A Story Whose Name Is Forgot   nv FBM Jun,85
  Fantasy Book [v.4 #2, June 1985]   Dennis Mallonee+ mg

Baker, Scott
The Lurking Duck   nv OMN Dec,83
  THE FOURTH OMNI BOOK OF SCIENCE FICTION   Ellen Datlow an
Still Life with Scorpion   ss IAS May,84
  ISAAC ASIMOV'S FANTASY   Shawna McCarthy an

Baldwin, Dick
Last Respects   ss 1975
  MASTERPIECES OF TERROR AND THE SUPERNATURAL   Marvin Kaye an

Balfour, Bruce J.
Etc.; The Man Who Killed Santa Claus   ar TZM Feb,85
  Rod Serling's The Twilight Zone Magazine [v.4 #6,
  January/February 1985]   T.E.D. Klein mg
Thunder Pigeon   ss FBM Jun,85
  Fantasy Book [v.4 #2, June 1985]   Dennis Mallonee+ mg

Ballard, J.G.
The Man Who Walked on the Moon   ss INZ #13,85
  Interzone [#13, Autumn 1985]   Simon Ounsley+ mg
Object of the Attack   ss INZ # 9,84
  INTERZONE: THE 1ST ANTHOLOGY   John Clute+ an
Report on an Unidentified Space Station   ss LNDSNVR,82
  TOP FANTASY   Josh Pachter an
The Terminal Beach   ss NWS Mar,64
  BEYOND ARMAGEDDON   Walter M. Miller, Jr.+ an

Barber, Daniel Wynn
Tiger in the Snow   ss HSH F11,84
  THE YEAR'S BEST HORROR STORIES: SERIES XIII
                                         Karl Edward Wagner an

Barker, Clive
The Age of Desire   nv CBB V 4,85
  CLIVE BARKER'S BOOKS OF BLOOD, VOLUME 4   Clive Barker oc
Babel's Children   nv CBB V 5,85
  CLIVE BARKER'S BOOKS OF BLOOD, VOLUME 5   Clive Barker oc
The Body Politic   nv CBB V 4,85
  CLIVE BARKER'S BOOKS OF BLOOD, VOLUME 4   Clive Barker oc
The Book of Blood   ss CBB # 1,84
  THE FANTASY SAMPLER   Susan Allison an
  BOOKS OF BLOOD   Clive Barker om
The Book of Blood (a postscript) On Jerusalem Street
                                                   aw CBB V 6,85
  CLIVE BARKER'S BOOKS OF BLOOD, VOLUME 6   Clive Barker oc
CLIVE BARKER'S BOOKS OF BLOOD, VOLUME 1   oc SPH 1984
  BOOKS OF BLOOD   Clive Barker om
CLIVE BARKER'S BOOKS OF BLOOD, VOLUME 2   oc SPH 1984
  BOOKS OF BLOOD   Clive Barker om
CLIVE BARKER'S BOOKS OF BLOOD, VOLUME 3   oc SPH 1984
  BOOKS OF BLOOD   Clive Barker om
Confession of a (Pornographer's) Shroud   nv CBB # 3,84
  BOOKS OF BLOOD   Clive Barker om
Down, Satan!   ss CBB V 4,85
  CLIVE BARKER'S BOOKS OF BLOOD, VOLUME 4   Clive Barker oc
Dread   nv CBB # 2,84
  BOOKS OF BLOOD   Clive Barker om
The Forbidden   nv CBB V 5,85
  CLIVE BARKER'S BOOKS OF BLOOD, VOLUME 5   Clive Barker oc
  Fantasy Tales [v.7 #14, Summer 1985]   Stephen Jones mg
Hell's Event   nv CBB # 2,84
  BOOKS OF BLOOD   Clive Barker om
How Spoilers Bleed   nv CBB V 6,85
  CLIVE BARKER'S BOOKS OF BLOOD, VOLUME 6   Clive Barker oc
Human Remains   nv CBB # 3,84
  BOOKS OF BLOOD   Clive Barker om
In the Flesh   nv CBB V 5,85
  CLIVE BARKER'S BOOKS OF BLOOD, VOLUME 5   Clive Barker oc
In the Hills, the Cities   nv CBB # 1,84
  BOOKS OF BLOOD   Clive Barker om
The Inhuman Condition   nv CBB V 4,85
  CLIVE BARKER'S BOOKS OF BLOOD, VOLUME 4   Clive Barker oc
Interview by Kim Newman   iv INZ #14,85
  Interzone [#14, Winter 1985/86]   Simon Ounsley+ mg
Jacqueline Ess: Her Will and Testament   nv CBB # 2,84
  BOOKS OF BLOOD   Clive Barker om
The Last Illusion   na CBB V 6,85
  CLIVE BARKER'S BOOKS OF BLOOD, VOLUME 6   Clive Barker oc
The Life of Death   nv CBB V 6,85
  CLIVE BARKER'S BOOKS OF BLOOD, VOLUME 6   Clive Barker oc
The Madonna   nv CBB V 5,85
  CLIVE BARKER'S BOOKS OF BLOOD, VOLUME 5   Clive Barker oc
The Midnight Meat Train   nv CBB # 1,84
  BOOKS OF BLOOD   Clive Barker om
New Murders in the Rue Morgue   nv CBB # 2,84
  BOOKS OF BLOOD   Clive Barker om
Pig Blood Blues   nv CBB # 1,84
  BOOKS OF BLOOD   Clive Barker om
Rawhead Rex   nv CBB # 3,84
  BOOKS OF BLOOD   Clive Barker om
Revelations   nv CBB V 4,85
  CLIVE BARKER'S BOOKS OF BLOOD, VOLUME 4   Clive Barker oc
Scapegoats   nv CBB # 3,84
  BOOKS OF BLOOD   Clive Barker om
Sex, Death and Starshine   nv CBB # 1,84
  BOOKS OF BLOOD   Clive Barker om
The Skins of the Fathers   nv CBB # 2,84
  BOOKS OF BLOOD   Clive Barker om
Son of Celluloid   nv CBB # 3,84
  BOOKS OF BLOOD   Clive Barker om
Twilight at the Towers   nv CBB V 6,85
  CLIVE BARKER'S BOOKS OF BLOOD, VOLUME 6   Clive Barker oc
The Yattering and Jack   ss CBB # 1,84
  BOOKS OF BLOOD   Clive Barker om

Barkin, Haskell
Pain Killer   ss FSF Sep,85
  The Magazine of Fantasy & Science Fiction [v.69 #3, September
  1985]   Edward L. Ferman mg

Barlowe, Wayne
Illustration   il PLANETS,85
  THE PLANETS   Byron Preiss oa

Barnes, John
Finalities Besides the Grave   ss AMZ Sep,85
  Amazing Science Fiction Stories [v.59 #3, September 1985]
                                         George H. Scithers mg

BARNES, STEVE

BIGGLE, LLOYD, JR.

Barnes, Steve & Larry Niven
  The Locusts   nv ASF Jun,79
    LIMITS   Larry Niven co

Barwood, Lee
  Wolf Song   nv FBM Sep,85
    Fantasy Book [v.4 #3, September 1985]   Dennis Mallonee+ mg

Bates, Susannah
  Araunah   ss WDB #20,85
    Weirdbook 20 [Spring 1985]   W. Paul Ganley mg

Battley, Lannah
  Cyclops   ss DSPTCHS,85
    DESPATCHES FROM THE FRONTIERS OF THE FEMALE MIND Jen Green+ oa

Baudino, Gael
  The Persistence of Memory   ss FSF Nov,85
    The Magazine of Fantasy & Science Fiction [v.69 #5, November
    1985]   Edward L. Ferman mg
  The Shadow of the Starlight   nv FSF Apr,85
    The Magazine of Fantasy & Science Fiction [v.68 #4, April
    1985]   Edward L. Ferman mg

Baum
  Cartoon   ct TZM Jun,85
    Rod Serling's The Twilight Zone Magazine [v.5 #2, May/June
    1985]   T.E.D. Klein mg

Baxter, Charles
  Through the Safety Net   ss TZM Jun,85
    Rod Serling's The Twilight Zone Magazine [v.5 #2, May/June
    1985]   T.E.D. Klein mg

Baxter, John
  Down from Demolition   ss URBANFN,85
    URBAN FANTASIES   David King+ oa

Bayley, Barrington J.
  Escapist Literature   ss INZ #13,85
    Interzone [#13, Autumn 1985]   Simon Ounsley+ mg
  The Ship of Disaster   ss NWS Jun,65
    TOP FANTASY   Josh Pachter an

Bean, Alan
  Illustration   il PLANETS,85
    THE PLANETS   Byron Preiss oa

Bear, Greg
  Dead Run   ss OMN Apr,85
  Tangents   ss OMN Jan,86
  Through Road No Whither   ss FFR V 1,85
    FAR FRONTIERS   Jerry E. Pournelle+ oa
  The White Horse Child   ss UNI # 9,79
    ISAAC ASIMOV'S MAGICAL WORLDS OF FANTASY: WITCHES & WIZARDS
                                         Isaac Asimov+ om
  The Wind from a Burning Woman   nv ASF Oct,78
    TERRORISTS OF TOMORROW   Poul Anderson+ an

Beaumont, Charles
  The Beautiful People   ss IFS Sep,52
    THE TWILIGHT ZONE: THE ORIGINAL STORIES
                                     Martin H. Greenberg+ an
  The Devil, You Say?   nv AMZ Jan,51
    THE TWILIGHT ZONE: THE ORIGINAL STORIES
                                     Martin H. Greenberg+ an
  Elegy   ss IMG Feb,53
    THE TWILIGHT ZONE: THE ORIGINAL STORIES
                                     Martin H. Greenberg+ an
  Fritzchen   ss OSF # 1,53
    YOUNG MONSTERS   Isaac Asimov+ an
  The Howling Man [as C.B. Lovehill]   ss ROG Nov,59
    THE TWILIGHT ZONE: THE ORIGINAL STORIES
                                     Martin H. Greenberg+ an
  In His Image [The Man Who Made Himself]   nv IMG Feb,57
    THE TWILIGHT ZONE: THE ORIGINAL STORIES
                                     Martin H. Greenberg+ an
  The Jungle   nv IFS Dec,54
    THE TWILIGHT ZONE: THE ORIGINAL STORIES
                                     Martin H. Greenberg+ an
  Perchance to Dream   ss PBY Oct,58
    THE TWILIGHT ZONE: THE ORIGINAL STORIES
                                     Martin H. Greenberg+ an
  Song for a Lady   ss NGTRIDE,60
    THE TWILIGHT ZONE: THE ORIGINAL STORIES
                                     Martin H. Greenberg+ an

Beddoes, Thomas Lovell
  The Oviparous Tailor   pm BLD V1 #2,85
    Border Land [v.1 #2]   R.S. Hadji mg

Bendixen, Alfred
  Introduction   in
    HAUNTED WOMEN: THE BEST SUPERNATURAL TALES BY AMERICAN WOMEN
    WRITERS   Alfred Bendixen an

Benet, Stephen Vincent
  By the Waters of Babylon [The Place of the Gods] ss SEP Jul,37
    BEYOND ARMAGEDDON   Walter M. Miller, Jr.+ an

Benford, Gregory
  The Future of the Jovian System   ss PLANETS,85
    THE PLANETS   Byron Preiss oa
  Hard Science in the Real World   ar 1984
    THE SCIENCE FICTION YEARBOOK   Jerry E. Pournelle+ an
  Immortal Night   ss OMN Apr,85
  Me/Days   ss UNI #14,84
    THE SCIENCE FICTION YEARBOOK   Jerry E. Pournelle+ an
  The Movement   ss FAW Oct,70
    TERRORISTS OF TOMORROW   Poul Anderson+ an
  Newton Sleep   nv FSF Jan,86
    The Magazine of Fantasy & Science Fiction [v.70 #1, January
    1986]   Edward L. Ferman mg
  Reactionary Utopias   ar FFR V 4,86
    FAR FRONTIERS VOL. IV/WINTER 1985 Jerry E. Pournelle+ oa
  Time's Rub   ss IAS Apr,85
    Isaac Asimov's Science Fiction Magazine [v. 9 # 4, April
    1985]   Shawna McCarthy mg
  To the Storming Gulf   na FSF Apr,85
    The Magazine of Fantasy & Science Fiction [v.68 #4, April
    1985]   Edward L. Ferman mg
    AFTERWAR   Janet Morris oa
  White Creatures   ss NDM # 5,75
    GREAT SCIENCE FICTION BY THE WORLD'S GREAT SCIENTISTS
                                         Isaac Asimov+ an

Benford, Gregory & Marc Laidlaw
  A Hiss of Dragon   nv OMN Dec,78
    THE THIRD OMNI BOOK OF SCIENCE FICTION Ellen Datlow an

Benford, James
  Star Wars is Not MAD   ar FFR V 4,86
    FAR FRONTIERS VOL. IV/WINTER 1985 Jerry E. Pournelle+ oa

Bensink, John Robert
  Midtown Bodies   ss TZM Aug,82
    Night Cry [v.1 #4, Winter 1985]   Alan Rodgers mg

Benson, E.F.
  The Man Who Went Too Far   nv RMINTWR,12
    DARK BANQUET: A FEAST OF 12 GREAT GHOST STORIES
                                         Lincoln Child an

Berryman, John
  Berom   nv ASF Jan,51
    ANALOG: THE BEST OF SCIENCE FICTION Anonymous an

Bester, Alfred
  Adam and No Eve   ss ASF Sep,41
    ANALOG: THE BEST OF SCIENCE FICTION Anonymous an
  Galatea Galante   na OMN Apr,79
    THE THIRD OMNI BOOK OF SCIENCE FICTION Ellen Datlow an
  Hobson's Choice   ss FSF Aug,52
    ISAAC ASIMOV PRESENTS THE GREAT SF STORIES: 14 (1952)
                                         Isaac Asimov+ an
  The Men Who Murdered Mohammed   ss FSF Oct,58
    TOP SCIENCE FICTION   Josh Pachter an

Betancourt, John Gregory
  Book Reviews   br AMZ
    Amazing Science Fiction Stories [v.60 #1, November 1985]
                                     George H. Scithers mg
    Amazing Science Fiction Stories [v.60 #2, January 1986]
                                     George H. Scithers mg
  Faramigon's Eye   nv FBM Dec,85
    Fantasy Book [v.4 #4, December 1985] Dennis Mallonee+ mg
  Memo from a Savage   pm AMZ Nov,85
    Amazing Science Fiction Stories [v.60 #1, November 1985]
                                     George H. Scithers mg
  Memo to an Asteroid Miner   pm AMZ Jul,85
    Amazing Science Fiction Stories [v.59 #2, July 1985]
                                     George H. Scithers mg
  The Weird of Mazal   ss FBM Sep,85
    Fantasy Book [v.4 #3, September 1985] Dennis Mallonee+ mg

Betancourt, John Gregory & Darrell Schweitzer
  The Last Child of Masferigon   ss TOMOBED,85
    TOM O'BEDLAM'S NIGHT OUT, AND OTHER STRANGE EXCURSIONS
                                         Darrell Schweitzer co

Bickel, Bill
  Aftermath   ss IAS Dec md,85
    Isaac Asimov's Science Fiction Magazine [v. 9 #13,
    Mid-December 1985]   Shawna McCarthy mg

Bierce, Ambrose
  The Boarded Window   ss INMIDST,1891
    GREAT GHOST STORIES   Betty Ann Schwartz an
  An Occurrence at Owl Creek Bridge   ss INMIDST,1891
    THE TWILIGHT ZONE: THE ORIGINAL STORIES
                                     Martin H. Greenberg+ an
  One Summer Night   vi
    MASTERPIECES OF TERROR AND THE SUPERNATURAL Marvin Kaye an

Bigelow, Jane M.H.
  Tactics   ss FRAMZDK,85
    FREE AMAZONS OF DARKOVER   Marion Zimmer Bradley+ oa

Biggle, Lloyd, Jr.
  Monument   nv ASF Jun,61
    ANALOG: THE BEST OF SCIENCE FICTION Anonymous an

BOVA, BEN

Bunch, David R.
  And Thank You, Tommy Edison   pm IAS Mar,85
    Isaac Asimov's Science Fiction Magazine [v. 9 # 3, March
    1985]   Shawna McCarthy mg
  One Wish!?   pm IAS Oct,85
    Isaac Asimov's Science Fiction Magazine [v. 9 #10, October
    1985]   Shawna McCarthy mg

Burger, Gottfried August
  Lenore   pm Jun,1844
    English adaption by Dante Gabriel Rossetti
    MASTERPIECES OF TERROR AND THE SUPERNATURAL   Marvin Kaye an

Burleson, Donald R.
  A Little Two-Chair Barber Shop on Phillips Street ss TZM Apr,84
    THE YEAR'S BEST FANTASY STORIES: 11   Arthur W. Saha an
  Night Bus   vi EDT #11,85
    Eldritch Tales No. 11 [v.3 #2]   Crispin Burnham mg
  The Terminator   ss TZM Oct,85
    Rod Serling's The Twilight Zone Magazine [v.5 #4, October
    1985]   Michael Blaine mg

Burnham, Crispin
  Book Reviews   br EDT #11,85
    Eldritch Tales No. 11 [v.3 #2]   Crispin Burnham mg
  Eldritch Lair   ed EDT #11,85
    Eldritch Tales No. 11 [v.3 #2]   Crispin Burnham mg

Burns, Christopher
  Fogged Plates   ss INZ #11,85
    Interzone [#11, Spring 1985]   Colin Greenland+ mg

Burns, Jim
  The Road to Dune   pi EYE ,85
    EYE   Frank Herbert co

Burns, Stephen L.
  The Black Tower   ss S&S # 2,85
    SWORD AND SORCERESS II   Marion Zimmer Bradley oa
  The Man of Peace   ss ASF Dec md,85
    Analog Science Fiction/Science Fact [v.105 #13, Mid-December
    1985]   Stanley Schmidt mg
  Taking Heart   ss S&S # 1,84
    THE YEAR'S BEST FANTASY STORIES: 11   Arthur W. Saha an
  A Touch Beyond   ss ASF Jan,85
    Analog Science Fiction/Science Fact [v.105 # 1, January 1985]
                                             Stanley Schmidt mg

Burrage, A.M.
  The Waxwork [as Ex-Private X]   ss SMNINRM,31
    MASTERPIECES OF TERROR AND THE SUPERNATURAL   Marvin Kaye an
    GREAT GHOST STORIES   Betty Ann Schwartz an

Bussard, Dr. Robert W.
  IRAS, Vega, and Intelligent Life in the Universe   ar FFR V 2,85
    FAR FRONTIERS VOL. II/SUMMER 1985   Jerry E. Pournelle+ oa

Butler, Octavia E.
  Bloodchild   nv IAS Jun,84
    TERRY CARR'S BEST SCIENCE FICTION OF THE YEAR #14
                                               Terry Carr an
    THE YEAR'S BEST SCIENCE FICTION, SECOND ANNUAL COLLECTION
                                           Gardner Dozois an
    THE 1985 ANNUAL WORLD'S BEST SF   Donald A. Wollheim an
    NEBULA AWARDS 20: SFWA'S CHOICES FOR THE BEST IN SCIENCE
    FICTION 1984   George Zebrowski an

Byers, Edward A.
  The Vicious Circle   nv ASF Dec md,85
    Analog Science Fiction/Science Fact [v.105 #13, Mid-December
    1985]   Stanley Schmidt mg

Cadigan, Pat
  After the Days of Dead-Eye 'Dee   ss IAS May,85
    Isaac Asimov's Science Fiction Magazine [v. 9 # 5, May 1985]
                                             Shawna McCarthy mg
  Pretty Boy Crossover   ss IAS Jan,86
    Isaac Asimov's Science Fiction Magazine [v.10 # 1, January
    1986]   Gardner Dozois mg
  Roadside Rescue   ss OMN Jul,85
  Rock On   ss LGTYR&D,84
    THE YEAR'S BEST SCIENCE FICTION, SECOND ANNUAL COLLECTION
                                           Gardner Dozois an

Calabro, Joseph
  Does It Make a Sound?   ss TZM Apr,85
    Short story contest 3rd place winner.
    Rod Serling's The Twilight Zone Magazine [v.5 #1, March/April
    1985]   T.E.D. Klein mg

Calcamuggio, Mark
  The Dismal Dismissal   pm EDT #11,85
    Eldritch Tales No. 11 [v.3 #2]   Crispin Burnham mg
  Stillness   pm EDT #11,85
    Eldritch Tales No. 11 [v.3 #2]   Crispin Burnham mg

Caldwell, John
  Cartoon   ct RUNAMCK,78
    Isaac Asimov's Science Fiction Magazine [v. 9 # 1, January
    1985]   Shawna McCarthy mg
    Isaac Asimov's Science Fiction Magazine [v. 9 # 2, February
    1985]   Shawna McCarthy mg

Caldwell, John (continued)
    Isaac Asimov's Science Fiction Magazine [v. 9 # 5, May 1985]
                                             Shawna McCarthy mg
    Isaac Asimov's Science Fiction Magazine [v. 9 #12, December
    1985]   Shawna McCarthy mg

Campbell, John W., Jr.
  Who Goes There? [as Don A. Stuart]   na ASF Aug,38
    BAKER'S DOZEN: 13 SHORT SCIENCE FICTION NOVELS
                                             Isaac Asimov+ an

Campbell, Ramsey
  Among the pictures are these: ss NYC Mar,81
    COLD PRINT   Ramsey Campbell co
  Before the Storm   ss FRC Mar,80
    COLD PRINT   Ramsey Campbell co
  Blacked Out   ss CLDPRNT,85
    COLD PRINT   Ramsey Campbell co
  The Church in High Street   ss DRKMIND,62
    COLD PRINT   Ramsey Campbell co
  Cold Print   ss TLSCTHU,69
    COLD PRINT   Ramsey Campbell co
  The Depths   ss DRKCMPN,82
    TOP FANTASY   Josh Pachter an
  The Faces at Pine Dunes   nv NTLCTHU,80
    COLD PRINT   Ramsey Campbell co
  The Horror from the Bridge   ss INHBLKE,64
    COLD PRINT   Ramsey Campbell co
  Incarnate [deleted chapter from the novel "Incarnate"]
                                               ex WFC 1983
    Fantasycon X Programme Booklet   Stephen Jones+ oa
  The Inhabitant of the Lake   nv INHBLKE,64
    COLD PRINT   Ramsey Campbell co
  The Insects from Shaggai   ss INHBLKE,64
    COLD PRINT   Ramsey Campbell co
  Introduction   in
    BOOKS OF BLOOD   Clive Barker om
    COLD PRINT   Ramsey Campbell co
  The Moon-Lens   ss INHBLKE,64
    COLD PRINT   Ramsey Campbell co
  Old Cloths   ss MIDNGHT,85
    MIDNIGHT   Charles L. Grant oa
  The Render of the Veils   ss INHBLKE,64
    COLD PRINT   Ramsey Campbell co
  The Room in the Castle   ss INHBLKE,64
    COLD PRINT   Ramsey Campbell co
  Run Through   vi SBH # 1,75
    Weirdbook 20 [Spring 1985]   W. Paul Ganley mg
  The Sneering   ss FTL Sum,85
    Fantasy Tales [v.7 #14, Summer 1985]   Stephen Jones an
  The Tugging   nv DSPCTHU,76
    COLD PRINT   Ramsey Campbell co
  Voice of the Beach   nv FTL Sum,82
    COLD PRINT   Ramsey Campbell co
  Watch the Birdie   ss WTCHBRD,84
    THE YEAR'S BEST HORROR STORIES: SERIES XIII
                                           Karl Edward Wagner an
  The Will of Stanley Brooke   ss INHBLKE,64
    COLD PRINT   Ramsey Campbell co

Canfield, Grant
  Roller Derby   cs SDA
    Stardate [v.1 # 8, October 1985]   Ted White+ mg
    Stardate [v.1 # 9, December 1985]   Ted White+ mg

Carcaterra, Lorenzo
  TZ Profile: Charles Martin Smith: Lighting Up 'Starman'
                                               iv TZM Jun,85
    Rod Serling's The Twilight Zone Magazine [v.5 #2, May/June
    1985]   T.E.D. Klein mg
  TZ Profile: Kenneth McMillan: Never Out of Characters
                                               iv TZM Apr,85
    Rod Serling's The Twilight Zone Magazine [v.5 #1, March/April
    1985]   T.E.D. Klein mg

Card, Orson Scott
  Eumenides in the Fourth Floor Lavatory   nv CRY # 4,79
    MASTERPIECES OF TERROR AND THE SUPERNATURAL   Marvin Kaye an
  The Fringe   nv FSF Oct,85
    The Magazine of Fantasy & Science Fiction [v.69 #4, October
    1985]   Edward L. Ferman mg
  Unaccompanied Sonata   ss OMN Mar,79
    THE FOURTH OMNI BOOK OF SCIENCE FICTION   Ellen Datlow an

Carl, Lillian Stewart
  The King Under the Water   ss BLD VI #3,85
    Border Land [v.1 #3]   R.S. Hadji mg
  The Rim of the Wheel   ss IAS Feb,84
    ISAAC ASIMOV'S FANTASY   Shawna McCarthy an
  Upon the Shoal of Time   ss AMZ Mar,85
    Amazing Science Fiction Stories [v.58 #6, March 1985]
                                             George H. Scithers mg
  Where Is Thy Victory?   ss IAS Nov,85
    Isaac Asimov's Science Fiction Magazine [v. 9 #11, November
    1985]   Shawna McCarthy mg

Carpenter, Leonard
  The Ebbing   nv WRTFFUT,85
    L. RON HUBBARD PRESENTS WRITERS OF THE FUTURE Algis Budrys oa

Carr, Jayge
  Catacombs   nv AMZ Jul,85
    Amazing Science Fiction Stories [v.59 #2, July 1985]
                                       George H. Scithers mg
  Drop-Out   ss ASF Jan,86
    Analog Science Fiction/Science Fact [v.106 # 1, January 1986]
                                        Stanley Schmidt mg
  Finnegan's Wake   ss ASF Oct,85
    Analog Science Fiction/Science Fact [v.105 #10, October 1985]
                                        Stanley Schmidt mg
  Immigrant   ss AMZ Nov,85
    Amazing Science Fiction Stories [v.60 #1, November 1985]
                                       George H. Scithers mg
  The Prince of Lightning   nv MNSNGRF,85
    MOONSINGER'S FRIENDS   Susan M. Shwartz oa
  Webrider   ss OBK # 3,85
    THE THIRD OMNI BOOK OF SCIENCE FICTION Ellen Datlow an

Carr, John Dickson
  The House in Goblin Wood [as Carter Dickson]   ss EQM Nov,47
    MASTERPIECES OF TERROR AND THE SUPERNATURAL Marvin Kaye an

Carr, Michael H.
  Mars: The Red Planet   ar PLANETS,85
    THE PLANETS   Byron Preiss oa

Carr, Terry
  Hop-Friend   ss FSF Nov,62
    TOP SCIENCE FICTION   Josh Pachter an
  Introduction   in
    TERRY CARR'S BEST SCIENCE FICTION OF THE YEAR #14
                                            Terry Carr an
  Recommended Reading   bi
    TERRY CARR'S BEST SCIENCE FICTION OF THE YEAR #14
                                            Terry Carr an
  Touchstone   ss FSF May,64
    TOP FANTASY   Josh Pachter an

Carr, Wooda Nick
  Introducing the Moon Man   ar
    THE NIGHT NEMESIS: THE COMPLETE ADVENTURES OF THE MOON
    MAN--VOL. ONE   Frederick C. Davis co

Carroll, L.E.
  Without Wings   ss WRTRFUT,85
    L. RON HUBBARD PRESENTS WRITERS OF THE FUTURE Algis Budrys oa

Carter, Angela
  Black Venus   ss NXTEDIT,80
    BLACK VENUS   Angela Carter co
  The Cabinet of Edgar Allan Poe   ss INZ # 1,82
    BLACK VENUS   Angela Carter co
    INTERZONE: THE 1ST ANTHOLOGY   John Clute+ an
  The Erlking   ss BNA 1979
    FAERY!   Terri Windling oa
  The Fall River Axe Murders [new title]   ss LRB 1981
    BLACK VENUS   Angela Carter co
  The Kiss   ss HRP 1977
    BLACK VENUS   Angela Carter co
  The Kitchen Child   ss VOG 1979
    BLACK VENUS   Angela Carter co
  Our Lady of the Massacre [new title]   ss STYNTRD,79
    BLACK VENUS   Angela Carter co
  Overture and Incidental Music for "A Midsummer Night's Dream"
                                             ss INZ # 3,82
    BLACK VENUS   Angela Carter co
  Peter and the Wolf   ss FIREBDI,82
    BLACK VENUS   Angela Carter co

Carter, Lin
  Geydelle's Protective   ss MGI # 2,85
    MAGIC IN ITHKAR 2   Andre Norton+ oa
  The Goblinry of Ais   ss MGI # 1,85
    MAGIC IN ITHKAR   Andre Norton+ oa
  Vault of Silence   nv SWDAGTM,70
    BARBARIANS   Robert Adams+ an

Carter, Margaret
  Her Own Blood   ss FRAMZDK,85
    FREE AMAZONS OF DARKOVER   Marion Zimmer Bradley+ oa

Carter, Paul A.
  The Constitutional Origins of Westly v. Simmons   sf ASF Oct,85
    Analog Science Fiction/Science Fact [v.105 #10, October 1985]
                                        Stanley Schmidt mg

Carter, Samuel, III
  If the North Had Won the Civil War   ss YNK Apr,85

Casdagli, Penny
  Mab   ss DSPTCHS,85
    DESPATCHES FROM THE FRONTIERS OF THE FEMALE MIND Jen Green+ oa

Casper, Susan
  Shadowman   ss WHS Dec,84
    Whispers [v.6 #1-2, December 1984] Stuart David Schiff mg
  Spring Fever   ss MIDNGHT,85
    MIDNIGHT   Charles L. Grant oa

Casper, Susan, Jack Dann & Gardner Dozois
  The Clowns   ss PBY Aug,85

Casper, Susan & Gardner Dozois
  Send No Money   ss IAS Dec md,85
    Isaac Asimov's Science Fiction Magazine [v. 9 #13,
    Mid-December 1985]   Shawna McCarthy mg

Castell, Daphne
  Close of Night   ss IAS May,84
    ISAAC ASIMOV'S FANTASY   Shawna McCarthy an

Catalano, Frank
  Book Reviews   br AMZ
    Amazing Science Fiction Stories [v.58 #5, January 1985]
                                       George H. Scithers mg
    Amazing Science Fiction Stories [v.58 #6, March 1985]
                                       George H. Scithers mg
    Amazing Science Fiction Stories [v.59 #1, May 1985]
                                       George H. Scithers mg
    Amazing Science Fiction Stories [v.59 #2, July 1985]
                                       George H. Scithers mg
    Amazing Science Fiction Stories [v.59 #3, September 1985]
                                       George H. Scithers mg
    Amazing Science Fiction Stories [v.60 #1, November 1985]
                                       George H. Scithers mg

Cathey, Ann
  Reaper   pm WDB #20,85
    Weirdbook 20 [Spring 1985]   W. Paul Ganley mg

Cavaliero, Glen
  Afterword   aw
    THREE FANTASIES   John Cowper Powys co

Cave, Hugh B.
  Damballa's Slough   ss WHS Dec,84
    Whispers [v.6 #1-2, December 1984] Stuart David Schiff mg
  Footprints in Perdu   ss WHA # 5,85
    WHISPERS V   Stuart David Schiff oa
  Of Time and Space   ss BLD V1 #2,85
    Border Land [v.1 #2]   R.S. Hadji mg

Cedering, Siv
  A Letter from Caroline Herschel   pm S84 Jun,84
    THE 1985 RHYSLING ANTHOLOGY   Anonymous an

Chambers, Robert W.
  The Yellow Sign   nv KINGYLW,1895
    DARK BANQUET: A FEAST OF 12 GREAT GHOST STORIES
                                          Lincoln Child an

Chapman, Clark R.
  Mercury: The Sun's Closest Companion   ar PLANETS,85
    THE PLANETS   Byron Preiss oa

Chapman, Vera
  Crusader Damosel   ss 1978
    ISAAC ASIMOV'S MAGICAL WORLDS OF FANTASY #3: COSMIC KNIGHTS
                                          Isaac Asimov+ an

Chappell, Fred
  Weird Tales   ss TXR Spr,84
    THE YEAR'S BEST HORROR STORIES: SERIES XIII
                                     Karl Edward Wagner an

Charnas, Suzy McKee
  The Ancient Mind at Work   nv OMN Feb,79
    THE FOURTH OMNI BOOK OF SCIENCE FICTION Ellen Datlow an
  Stephen R. Donaldson: An Appreciation   bg WRLDTLS,85
    WORLD TALES   G. Randal Rau oa

Charteris, Leslie
  Fish Story   ss BBM Nov,53
                                             FSF Jun,54
    MERMAIDS!   Jack Dann+ an

Chast, R.
  Cartoon   ct NYM 1984
    The Magazine of Fantasy & Science Fiction [v.68 #2, February
    1985]   Edward L. Ferman mg

Cheney
  Cartoon   ct TZM Jun,85
    Rod Serling's The Twilight Zone Magazine [v.5 #2, May/June
    1985]   T.E.D. Klein mg

Cherry, David
  Stephen R. Donaldson: An Appreciation   bg WRLDTLS,85
    WORLD TALES   G. Randal Rau oa

Cherryh, C.J.
  Armies of the Night   nv DEADWIN,85
    THIEVES' WORLD, BOOK 7: THE DEAD OF WINTER
                                     Robert Lynn Asprin+ oa
  Cassandra   ss FSF Oct,78
    THE HUGO WINNERS, VOLUME 4: 1976-1979 Isaac Asimov an
  Dagger in the Mind   nv SOULCTY,86
    THIEVES' WORLD, BOOK 8: SOUL OF THE CITY
                                     Robert Lynn Asprin+ oa
  Death in the Meadow   nv SOULCTY,86
    THIEVES' WORLD, BOOK 8: SOUL OF THE CITY
                                     Robert Lynn Asprin+ oa
  Downwind   nv STRMSSN,82
    CROSS-CURRENTS   Robert Lynn Asprin+ om

Delany, Samuel R.
  Appendix A: The Tale of Plagues and Carnivals, or, Some Informal
    Remarks toward the Modular Calculus, Part Five   na FLGTNVR,85
    FLIGHT FROM NEVERYON   Samuel R. Delany oc
  Appendix B: Closures and Openings   nv FLGTNVR,85
    FLIGHT FROM NEVERYON   Samuel R. Delany oc
  An Appreciation: Theodore Sturgeon   bg NCR V1 #4,85
    Night Cry [v.1 #4, Winter 1985]   Alan Rodgers mg
  Driftglass   ss IFS Jun,67
    MERMAIDS!   Jack Dann+ an
  The Mummer's Tale   nv FLGTNVR,85
    FLIGHT FROM NEVERYON   Samuel R. Delany oc
  The Tale of Fog and Granite   na FLGTNVR,85
    FLIGHT FROM NEVERYON   Samuel R. Delany oc

Dell, Timothy
  A Step in Any Direction   ss STRGATR,85
    STRANGE ATTRACTORS   Damien Broderick oa

DeLuca, Michael A., II
  The Barrier of Essai   gr SDA Dec,85
    Stardate [v.1 # 9, December 1985]   Ted White+ mg

Denton, Bradley
  Mountain Shadow: Shawnee County, Kansas   pm IAS Aug,85
    Isaac Asimov's Science Fiction Magazine [v. 9 # 8, August
    1985]   Shawna McCarthy mg
  The Summer We Saw Diana   nv FSF Aug,85
    The Magazine of Fantasy & Science Fiction [v.69 #2, August
    1985]   Edward L. Ferman mg
  Top of the Charts   ss FSF Mar,85
    The Magazine of Fantasy & Science Fiction [v.68 #3, March
    1985]   Edward L. Ferman mg

Denton, Charles
  The Serpents' Shrine   pm WDB #20,85
    Weirdbook 20 [Spring 1985]   W. Paul Ganley mg

Deppe, Carol
  Everybody Draws Lines   ss AMZ Jan,86
    Amazing Science Fiction Stories [v.60 #2, January 1986]
                                               George H. Scithers mg

Devin, John
  The Cave of Shadows   pm AMZ Jan,85
    Amazing Science Fiction Stories [v.58 #5, January 1985]
                                               George H. Scithers mg
  Field Guide   pm AMZ May,85
    Amazing Science Fiction Stories [v.59 #1, May 1985]
                                               George H. Scithers mg
  For Those Who Love Danger   pm AMZ May,85
    Amazing Science Fiction Stories [v.59 #1, May 1985]
                                               George H. Scithers mg

Dewdney, A.K.
  2DWORLD [from "The Planiverse"]   ex MLL 1984
    TESSERACTS   Judith Merril oa

Dewdney, Christopher
  Points in Time   pm TESRCTS,85
    TESSERACTS   Judith Merril oa

DeWeese, Gene
  Everything's Going to Bee All Right   ss SDW # 8,85
    SHADOWS 8   Charles L. Grant oa

Dick, Philip K.
  The Alien Mind   ss FSF Oct,81
    I HOPE I SHALL ARRIVE SOON   Philip K. Dick co
  Chains of Air, Web of Aether   nv STL # 5,80
    I HOPE I SHALL ARRIVE SOON   Philip K. Dick co
  The Days of Perky Pat   nv AMZ Dec,63
    AMAZING STORIES: 60 YEARS OF THE BEST SCIENCE FICTION
                                                  Isaac Asimov+ an
  The Exit Door Leads In   nv RCS Fll,79
    I HOPE I SHALL ARRIVE SOON   Philip K. Dick co
  Explorers We   ss FSF Jan,59
    I HOPE I SHALL ARRIVE SOON   Philip K. Dick co
  Holy Quarrel   nv WOT May,66
    I HOPE I SHALL ARRIVE SOON   Philip K. Dick co
  How to Build a Universe That Doesn't Fall Apart Two Days Later
                                                    sp IHOPEIS,85
    I HOPE I SHALL ARRIVE SOON   Philip K. Dick co
  I Hope I Shall Arrive Soon [Frozen Journey]   ss PBY Dec,80
    I HOPE I SHALL ARRIVE SOON   Philip K. Dick co
  Rautavaara's Case   ss OMN Oct,80
    THE THIRD OMNI BOOK OF SCIENCE FICTION   Ellen Datlow an
    I HOPE I SHALL ARRIVE SOON   Philip K. Dick co
  The Short Happy Life of the Brown Oxford   ss FSF Jan,54
    I HOPE I SHALL ARRIVE SOON   Philip K. Dick co
  Strange Memories of Death   ss IHOPEIS,85
    I HOPE I SHALL ARRIVE SOON   Philip K. Dick co
  What'll We Do with Ragland Park?   nv AMZ Nov,63
    I HOPE I SHALL ARRIVE SOON   Philip K. Dick co

Dickens, Charles
  Captain Murderer and the Devil's Bargain   ss
    GREAT GHOST STORIES   Betty Ann Schwartz an
  The Signalman [from "Mugby Junction"]   ss AYR Chr,1866
    DARK BANQUET: A FEAST OF 12 GREAT GHOST STORIES
                                                   Lincoln Child an

Dickinson, Peter
  THE DEVIL'S CHILDREN   n. GOL 1970
    THE CHANGES TRILOGY   Peter Dickinson om
  Flight   nv IMGNLND,85
    IMAGINARY LANDS   Robin McKinley oa
  HEARTSEASE   n. GOL 1969
    THE CHANGES TRILOGY   Peter Dickinson om
  THE WEATHERMONGER   n. GOL 1969
    THE CHANGES TRILOGY   Peter Dickinson om

Dickson, Gordon R.
  Babes in the Woods   ss OWS May,53
    FORWARD!   Gordon R. Dickson co
  Beyond the Dar al-Harb   na BYNDDAR,85
    BEYOND THE DAR AL-HARB   Gordon R. Dickson co
  Brothers   na ASTNDNG,73
    MERCENARIES OF TOMORROW   Poul Anderson+ an
  Building on the Line   nv GAL Nov,68
    FORWARD!   Gordon R. Dickson co
  The Childe Cycle Status Report [updated]   ar SFW Fll,79
    STEEL BROTHER   Gordon R. Dickson co
  The Cloak and the Staff   nv ASF Aug,80
    THERE WILL BE WAR, VOL. IV: DAY OF THE TYRANT
                                                Jerry E. Pournelle an
  The Dreamsman   ss STR # 6,59
    FORWARD!   Gordon R. Dickson co
  The Error of Their Ways   ss ASF Jul,51
    INVADERS!   Gordon R. Dickson co
  Fellow of the Bees   nv OSF # 3,54
    INVADERS!   Gordon R. Dickson co
  The Game of Five   nv FSF Apr,60
    FORWARD!   Gordon R. Dickson co
  Guided Tour   pm FSF Oct,59
    FORWARD!   Gordon R. Dickson co
  The Hard Way   nv ASF Jan,63
    STEEL BROTHER   Gordon R. Dickson co
  House of Weapons   na FFR V 2,85
    FAR FRONTIERS VOL. II/SUMMER 1985   Jerry E. Pournelle+ oa
  The Invaders   na SPS Oct,52
    INVADERS!   Gordon R. Dickson co
  Itco's Strong Right Arm   nv CSM Jul,54
    INVADERS!   Gordon R. Dickson co
  The Law-Twister Shorty   nv MNYWRLD,71
    ISAAC ASIMOV'S MAGICAL WORLDS OF FANTASY #5: GIANTS
                                                  Isaac Asimov+ an
    INVADERS!   Gordon R. Dickson co
  The Man in the Mailbag   nv GAL Apr,59
    STEEL BROTHER   Gordon R. Dickson co
  The Mortal and the Monster   na STLSNOV,76
    BAKER'S DOZEN: 13 SHORT SCIENCE FICTION NOVELS
                                                  Isaac Asimov+ an
  Napoleon's Skullcap   nv FSF May,62
    FORWARD!   Gordon R. Dickson co
  On Messenger Mountain   na WOT Jun,64
    BEYOND THE DAR AL-HARB   Gordon R. Dickson co
  One on Trial   ss FSF Jan,60
    FORWARD!   Gordon R. Dickson co
  An Ounce of Emotion   nv IFS Oct,65
    INVADERS!   Gordon R. Dickson co
  Out of the Darkness   ss EQM Feb,61
    STEEL BROTHER   Gordon R. Dickson co
  Perfectly Adjusted   na SFS Jul,55
    STEEL BROTHER   Gordon R. Dickson co
  The Queer Critter   ss OSF Dec,54
    FORWARD!   Gordon R. Dickson co
  The R of A   ss FSF Jan,59
    FORWARD!   Gordon R. Dickson co
  Rescue Mission   ss FSF Jan,57
    FORWARD!   Gordon R. Dickson co
  Richochet on Miza   ss PLS Mar,52
    INVADERS!   Gordon R. Dickson co
  Robots are Nice?   ss GAL Oct,57
    FORWARD!   Gordon R. Dickson co
  Roofs of Silver   nv FSF Dec,62
    INVADERS!   Gordon R. Dickson co
  See Now, a Pilgrim   na ASF Sep,85
    Analog Science Fiction/Science Fact [v.105 # 9, September
    1985]   Stanley Schmidt mg
  Steel Brother   nv ASF Feb,52
    STEEL BROTHER   Gordon R. Dickson co
  Things Which Are Caesar's   na DAYSUNS,72
    BEYOND THE DAR AL-HARB   Gordon R. Dickson co
  Twig   nv STL # 1,74
    FORWARD!   Gordon R. Dickson co

DiFilippo, Paul
  Rescuing Andy   ss TZM Jun,85
    Rod Serling's The Twilight Zone Magazine [v.5 #2, May/June
    1985]   T.E.D. Klein mg
  Stone Lives   nv FSF Aug,85
    The Magazine of Fantasy & Science Fiction [v.69 #2, August
    1985]   Edward L. Ferman mg

Disch, Thomas M.
  Books   br TZM
    Rod Serling's The Twilight Zone Magazine [v.4 #6,
    January/February 1985]   T.E.D. Klein mg
  Concepts   nv FSF Dec,78
    MEDEA: HARLAN'S WORLD   Harlan Ellison an
  Dialogue With a Spider   pm AMZ Jul,85
    Amazing Science Fiction Stories [v.59 #2, July 1985]
                                               George H. Scithers mg

Disch, Thomas M. (continued)
  Let Us Quickly Hasten to the Gate of Ivory   ss QRK # 1,70
    TOP FANTASY   Josh Pachter   an
  The Mittens of Ulysses   pm AMZ Mar,85
    Amazing Science Fiction Stories [v.58 #6, March 1985]
                                          George H. Scithers   mg
  Ringtime   ss OMN Dec,81
    THE THIRD OMNI BOOK OF SCIENCE FICTION   Ellen Datlow   an
  The Santa Claus Compromise   ss CRW Dec,74
    SANTA 2000   Michel Parry   an
  Skydiver   pm AMZ Sep,85
    Amazing Science Fiction Stories [v.59 #3, September 1985]
                                          George H. Scithers   mg
  Under the Boughs of Westbrookville   pm AMZ Nov,85
    Amazing Science Fiction Stories [v.60 #1, November 1985]
                                          George H. Scithers   mg

Disch, Thomas M., Poul Anderson, Hal Clement, Larry Niven &
 Frederik Pohl
  Second Thoughts   ms
    MEDEA: HARLAN'S WORLD   Harlan Ellison   an

Disch, Thomas M., Harlan Ellison, Frank Herbert, Robert Silverberg
 & Theodore Sturgeon
  The Concept Seminar   ms
    MEDEA: HARLAN'S WORLD   Harlan Ellison   an
  The Extrapolations, the Questions   ms
    MEDEA: HARLAN'S WORLD   Harlan Ellison   an

Donaldson, Stephanie
  Stephen R. Donaldson: Six Appreciations   in WRLDTLS,85
    WORLD TALES   G. Randal Rau   oa

Donaldson, Stephen R.
  The Djinn Who Watches Over the Accursed   ss WRLDTLS,85
    WORLD TALES   G. Randal Rau   oa
  The Resume of Stephen R. Donaldson   bg WRLDTLS,85
    WORLD TALES   G. Randal Rau   oa
  What Makes Us Human   nv FSF Aug,84
    BERSERKER BASE   Fred Saberhagen   an
    THE 1985 ANNUAL WORLD'S BEST SF   Donald A. Wollheim   an

Donaldson, Thomas
  How to Go Faster than Light   ar ASF Jun,85
    Analog Science Fiction/Science Fact [v.105 # 6, June 1985]
                                            Stanley Schmidt   mg

Dorsey, Candas Jane
  Johnny Appleseed and the New World   ss TESRCTS,85
    TESSERACTS   Judith Merril   oa

Dowling, Terry
  The Bullet that Grows in the Gun   ss URBANFN,85
    URBAN FANTASIES   David King+   oa

Doxey, W.S.
  The Armistead House   ss FSF Sep,85
    The Magazine of Fantasy & Science Fiction [v.69 #3, September
    1985]   Edward L. Ferman   mg

Doyle, Arthur Conan
  The Horror of the Heights   ss SND Nov,13
    DARK BANQUET: A FEAST OF 12 GREAT GHOST STORIES
                                              Lincoln Child   an
  J. Habakuk Jephson's Statement   nv CNH Jan,1884
    MYSTERIOUS SEA STORIES   William Pattrick   an
  Lot No. 249   nv HRP Sep,1892
    ISAAC ASIMOV'S MAGICAL WORLDS OF FANTASY #4: SPELLS
                                            Isaac Asimov+   an

Dozois, Gardner
  Dinner Party   ss LGTYR&D,84
    THE YEAR'S BEST HORROR STORIES: SERIES XIII
                                        Karl Edward Wagner   an
  Honorable Mentions: 1984   bi
    THE YEAR'S BEST SCIENCE FICTION, SECOND ANNUAL COLLECTION
                                          Gardner Dozois   an
  Morning Child   ss OMN Jan,84
    TERRY CARR'S BEST SCIENCE FICTION OF THE YEAR #14
                                              Terry Carr   an
    NEBULA AWARDS 20: SFWA'S CHOICES FOR THE BEST IN SCIENCE
    FICTION 1984   George Zebrowski   an
  Summation: 1984   in
    THE YEAR'S BEST SCIENCE FICTION, SECOND ANNUAL COLLECTION
                                          Gardner Dozois   an

Dozois, Gardner & Susan Casper
  Send No Money   ss IAS Dec md,85
    Isaac Asimov's Science Fiction Magazine [v. 9 #13,
    Mid-December 1985]   Shawna McCarthy   mg

Dozois, Gardner, Susan Casper & Jack Dann
  The Clowns   ss PBY Aug,85

Dozois, Gardner & Jack Dann
  Preface   pr
    BESTIARY!   Jack Dann+   an

Dozois, Gardner, Jack Dann & Michael Swanwick
  The Gods of Mars   ss OMN Mar,85
  Golden Apples of the Sun [expanded from Virgin Territory]
                                              nv PNT Mar,84

Dozois, Gardner, Jack Dann & Michael Swanwick (continued)
    THE YEAR'S BEST FANTASY STORIES: 11   Arthur W. Saha   an

Dozois, Gardner & Jack C. Haldeman, II
  Executive Clemency   nv OMN Nov,81
    THE THIRD OMNI BOOK OF SCIENCE FICTION   Ellen Datlow   an

Dozois, Gardner & Michael Swanwick
  Snow Job   ss HGT Apr,82
    Isaac Asimov's Science Fiction Magazine [v. 9 #10, October
    1985]   Shawna McCarthy   mg

Drake, David A.
  The Bond   ss FFR V 3,85
    FAR FRONTIERS VOL. III/FALL 1985   Jerry E. Pournelle+   oa
  But Loyal to His Own   nv GAL Oct,75
    MERCENARIES OF TOMORROW   Poul Anderson+   oa
  Dreams in Amber   ss WHA # 5,85
    WHISPERS V   Stuart David Schiff   oa
  From the Dark Waters   ss 1976
    ISAAC ASIMOV'S MAGICAL WORLDS OF FANTASY #5: GIANTS
                                            Isaac Asimov+   an
  The Guardroom   nv AFTRWAR,85
    AFTERWAR   Janet Morris   oa
  Men Like Us   nv OMN May,80
    THE THIRD OMNI BOOK OF SCIENCE FICTION   Ellen Datlow   an
  Time Safari   na DST V3 #2,81
    BAKER'S DOZEN: 13 SHORT SCIENCE FICTION NOVELS
                                            Isaac Asimov+   an
  Votary   nv FACECHS,83
    CROSS-CURRENTS   Robert Lynn Asprin+   om

Drennan, Kathryn M. & J. Michael Straczynski
  Rod Serling's 'Night Gallery' [Part 1]   ar TZM Apr,85
    Rod Serling's The Twilight Zone Magazine [v.5 #1, March/April
    1985]   T.E.D. Klein   mg
  Rod Serling's 'Night Gallery' [Part 2]   ar TZM Jun,85
    Rod Serling's The Twilight Zone Magazine [v.5 #2, May/June
    1985]   T.E.D. Klein   mg
  Rod Serling's 'Night Gallery' [Part 3]   ar TZM Aug,85
    Rod Serling's The Twilight Zone Magazine [v.5 #3, July/August
    1985]   T.E.D. Klein   mg
  A Show-by-Show Guide to Rod Serling's 'Night Gallery', Part 1
                                                    bi TZM Apr,85
    Rod Serling's The Twilight Zone Magazine [v.5 #1, March/April
    1985]   T.E.D. Klein   mg
  A Show-by-Show Guide to Rod Serling's 'Night Gallery', Part 2
                                                    bi TZM Jun,85
    Rod Serling's The Twilight Zone Magazine [v.5 #2, May/June
    1985]   T.E.D. Klein   mg
  A Show-by-Show Guide to Rod Serling's 'Night Gallery', Part 3
                                                    bi TZM Aug,85
    Rod Serling's The Twilight Zone Magazine [v.5 #3, July/August
    1985]   T.E.D. Klein   mg
  A Show-by-Show Guide to Rod Serling's 'Night Gallery', Part 4
                                                    bi TZM Oct,85
    Rod Serling's The Twilight Zone Magazine [v.5 #4, October
    1985]   Michael Blaine   mg
  A Show-by-Show Guide to Rod Serling's 'Night Gallery', Part 5
                                                    bi TZM Dec,85
    Rod Serling's The Twilight Zone Magazine [v.5 #5, December
    1985]   Michael Blaine   mg
  A Show-by-Show Guide to Rod Serling's 'Night Gallery', Part 6
                                                    bi TZM Feb,86
    Rod Serling's The Twilight Zone Magazine [v.5 #6, February
    1986]   Michael Blaine   mg

Dryer, Stan
  A Day in the Life of a Classics Professor   nv FSF Dec,84
    THE SCIENCE FICTION YEARBOOK   Jerry E. Pournelle+   an
  Our Extraterrestrial Visitors   nv FSF Dec,85
    The Magazine of Fantasy & Science Fiction [v.69 #6, December
    1985]   Edward L. Ferman   mg

Duane, Diane
  Down by the Riverside   nv DEADWIN,85
    THIEVES' WORLD, BOOK 7: THE DEAD OF WINTER
                                        Robert Lynn Asprin+   oa
  The Hand That Feeds You   nv WNGSOMN,84
    CROSS-CURRENTS   Robert Lynn Asprin+   om
  Lior and the Sea   nv MNSNGRF,85
    MOONSINGER'S FRIENDS   Susan M. Shwartz   oa

Dulski, Thomas R.
  The Case of the Gring's Mill Goblin   nv ASF Dec,85
    Analog Science Fiction/Science Fact [v.105 #12, December
    1985]   Stanley Schmidt   mg

Dumars, Denise
  The Bride   ss FBM Dec,85
    Fantasy Book [v.4 #4, December 1985]   Dennis Mallonee+   mg

Dunkley, Roger F.
  Side Tracked   ss TZM Aug,85
    Rod Serling's The Twilight Zone Magazine [v.5 #3, July/August
    1985]   T.E.D. Klein   mg
  Twisted Shadow   ss
    Rod Serling's The Twilight Zone Magazine [v.4 #6,
    January/February 1985]   T.E.D. Klein   mg

Dunn, Marylois
  If There Be Magic   nv MGI # 2,85
    MAGIC IN ITHKAR 2   Andre Norton+ oa

Dunn, Robert
  The Kite Man   ss OMN Aug,85

Dunsany, Lord
  In a Dim Room   ss
    GREAT GHOST STORIES   Betty Ann Schwartz an

Duntemann, Jeff & Nancy Kress
  Borovsky's Hollow Woman   nv OMN Oct,83
    THE THIRD OMNI BOOK OF SCIENCE FICTION   Ellen Datlow an
    TRINITY AND OTHER STORIES   Nancy Kress co

Easton, Tom
  The Reference Library   br ASF
    Analog Science Fiction/Science Fact [v.105 # 1, January 1985]
                                             Stanley Schmidt mg
    Analog Science Fiction/Science Fact [v.105 # 2, February
      1985]   Stanley Schmidt mg
    Analog Science Fiction/Science Fact [v.105 # 3, March 1985]
                                             Stanley Schmidt mg
    Analog Science Fiction/Science Fact [v.105 # 4, April 1985]
                                             Stanley Schmidt mg
    Analog Science Fiction/Science Fact [v.105 # 5, May 1985]
                                             Stanley Schmidt mg
    Analog Science Fiction/Science Fact [v.105 # 6, June 1985]
                                             Stanley Schmidt mg
    Analog Science Fiction/Science Fact [v.105 # 7, July 1985]
                                             Stanley Schmidt mg
    Analog Science Fiction/Science Fact [v.105 # 8, August 1985]
                                             Stanley Schmidt mg
    Analog Science Fiction/Science Fact [v.105 # 9, September
      1985]   Stanley Schmidt mg
    Analog Science Fiction/Science Fact [v.105 #10, October 1985]
                                             Stanley Schmidt mg
    Analog Science Fiction/Science Fact [v.105 #11, November
      1985]   Stanley Schmidt mg
    Analog Science Fiction/Science Fact [v.105 #12, December
      1985]   Stanley Schmidt mg
    Analog Science Fiction/Science Fact [v.105 #13, Mid-December
      1985]   Stanley Schmidt mg
    Analog Science Fiction/Science Fact [v.106 # 1, January 1986]
                                             Stanley Schmidt mg

Eddings, David
  CASTLE OF WIZARDRY   n. BAL 1984
    THE BELGARIAD: PART TWO   David Eddings om
  ENCHANTERS' END GAME   n. BAL 1984
    THE BELGARIAD: PART TWO   David Eddings om
  MAGICIAN'S GAMBIT   n. BAL 1983
    THE BELGARIAD: PART ONE   David Eddings om
  PAWN OF PROPHECY   n. BAL 1983
    THE BELGARIAD: PART ONE   David Eddings om
  QUEEN OF SORCERY   n. BAL 1982
    THE BELGARIAD: PART ONE   David Eddings om

Edelman, Scott
  You Ain't Just Whistlin' Dixie   nv FBM Mar,85
    Fantasy Book [v.4 #1, March 1985]   Dennis Mallonee+ mg

Edelstein, Robert
  TZ Tech   ar TZM
    Rod Serling's The Twilight Zone Magazine [v.5 #5, December
      1985]   Michael Blaine mg
    Rod Serling's The Twilight Zone Magazine [v.5 #6, February
      1986]   Michael Blaine mg

Edwards, Malcolm
  After-Images   ss INZ # 4,82
    INTERZONE: THE 1ST ANTHOLOGY   John Clute+ an

Effinger, George Alec
  The Aliens Who Knew, I Mean, Everything   ss FSF Oct,84
    TERRY CARR'S BEST SCIENCE FICTION OF THE YEAR #14
                                                   Terry Carr an
    THE 1985 ANNUAL WORLD'S BEST SF   Donald A. Wollheim an
    NEBULA AWARDS 20: SFWA'S CHOICES FOR THE BEST IN SCIENCE
      FICTION 1984   George Zebrowski an
  Babes on Bawd Way   nv MGI # 2,85
    MAGIC IN ITHKAR 2   Andre Norton+ oa
  The Beast from One-Quarter Fathom   ss IAS Apr,85
    Isaac Asimov's Science Fiction Magazine [v. 9 # 4, April
      1985]   Shawna McCarthy mg
  The Bird of Time Bears Bitter Fruit   nv FSF Dec,85
    The Magazine of Fantasy & Science Fiction [v.69 #6, December
      1985]   Edward L. Ferman mg
  How F. Scott Fitzgerald Became Beloved in Springfield
                                                      ss IAS Aug,84
    ISAAC ASIMOV'S FANTASY   Shawna McCarthy an
  Maureen Birnbaum, Barbarian Swordsperson   ss FSF Jan,82
    BARBARIANS   Robert Adams+ an
  My First Game as an Immortal   pm FSF Aug,85
    The Magazine of Fantasy & Science Fiction [v.69 #2, August
      1985]   Edward L. Ferman mg
  My Old Man   nv TZM Feb,82
    Night Cry [v.1 #4, Winter 1985]   Alan Rodgers mg
  The Thing from the Slush   ss TZM Apr,82
    Night Cry [v.1 #2, Summer 1985]   T.E.D. Klein mg

Effinger, George Alec (continued)
  Unferno   nv IAS Jul,85
    Isaac Asimov's Science Fiction Magazine [v. 9 # 7, July 1985]
                                             Shawna McCarthy mg

Egan, Greg
  Tangled Up   ss URBANFN,85
    URBAN FANTASIES   David King+ oa
  The Way She Smiles, the Things She Says   ss STRGATR,85
    STRANGE ATTRACTORS   Damien Broderick oa

Egan, Thomas M.
  Book Reviews   br EDT #11,85
    Eldritch Tales No. 11 [v.3 #2]   Crispin Burnham mg

Eggleton, Bob
  Illustration   il PLANETS,85
    THE PLANETS   Byron Preiss oa

Ehrlich, Helen
  For Alfred, Lord Tennyson   pm S*L V7 #2,84
    THE 1985 RHYSLING ANTHOLOGY   Anonymous an

Eikenberry, Gary
  Anthropology 101   ss BBL # 9,83
    TESSERACTS   Judith Merril oa

Eisenberg, Adam
  Explorers   mr TZM Oct,85
    Rod Serling's The Twilight Zone Magazine [v.5 #4, October
      1985]   Michael Blaine mg

Eisenberg, Evan
  Heimlich's Curse   ss TZM Nov,81
    Night Cry [v.1 #4, Winter 1985]   Alan Rodgers mg

Eisenberg, Larry
  Dr. Snow Maiden   ss FSF Aug,75
    GREAT SCIENCE FICTION BY THE WORLD'S GREAT SCIENTISTS
                                             Isaac Asimov+ an

Eisenstein, Phyllis
  Fair Exchange   nv ASF Dec md,85
    Analog Science Fiction/Science Fact [v.105 #13, Mid-December
      1985]   Stanley Schmidt mg
  In the Western Tradition   na FSF Mar,81
    BAKER'S DOZEN: 13 SHORT SCIENCE FICTION NOVELS
                                             Isaac Asimov+ an
  Sense of Duty   ss IAS Mar,85
    Isaac Asimov's Science Fiction Magazine [v. 9 # 3, March
      1985]   Shawna McCarthy mg
  The Snail out of Space   ss FSF Apr,85
    The Magazine of Fantasy & Science Fiction [v.68 #4, April
      1985]   Edward L. Ferman mg

Elflandsson, Galad
  Something in a Song   ss GRYSTBY,85
    GREYSTONE BAY   Charles L. Grant oa

Elgin, Suzette Haden
  Lexical Gap   pm IAS Oct,85
    Isaac Asimov's Science Fiction Magazine [v. 9 #10, October
      1985]   Shawna McCarthy mg
  Modulation in All Things   ss 1980
    GREAT SCIENCE FICTION BY THE WORLD'S GREAT SCIENTISTS
                                             Isaac Asimov+ an
  Presuppositional Ghostbusting   pm IAS Dec,85
    Isaac Asimov's Science Fiction Magazine [v. 9 #12, December
      1985]   Shawna McCarthy mg

Ellin, Stanley
  The Question [The Question My Son Asked]   ss EQM Nov,62
    MASTERPIECES OF TERROR AND THE SUPERNATURAL   Marvin Kaye an

Ellis, G.F.R. & Tony Rothman
  The Garden of Cosmological Delights   ar ASF May,85
    Analog Science Fiction/Science Fact [v.105 # 5, May 1985]
                                             Stanley Schmidt mg
  Hot Rocks and Water   ar ASF Mar,85
    Analog Science Fiction/Science Fact [v.105 # 3, March 1985]
                                             Stanley Schmidt mg

Ellison, Harlan
  A Boy and His Dog   nv NWS Apr,69
    BEYOND ARMAGEDDON   Walter M. Miller, Jr.+ an
  Cosmic Hod-Carriers   in
    MEDEA: HARLAN'S WORLD   Harlan Ellison an
  Harlan Ellison's Watching   mr FSF
    The Magazine of Fantasy & Science Fiction [v.68 #1, January
      1985]   Edward L. Ferman mg
    The Magazine of Fantasy & Science Fiction [v.68 #2, February
      1985]   Edward L. Ferman mg
    The Magazine of Fantasy & Science Fiction [v.68 #3, March
      1985]   Edward L. Ferman mg
    The Magazine of Fantasy & Science Fiction [v.68 #4, April
      1985]   Edward L. Ferman mg
    The Magazine of Fantasy & Science Fiction [v.68 #6, June
      1985]   Edward L. Ferman mg
    The Magazine of Fantasy & Science Fiction [v.69 #2, August
      1985]   Edward L. Ferman mg
    The Magazine of Fantasy & Science Fiction [v.69 #3, September
      1985]   Edward L. Ferman mg

Finney, Jack
  I'm Scared   ss COL Sep 15,51
    ISAAC ASIMOV PRESENTS THE GREAT SF STORIES: 13 (1951)
                                                 Isaac Asimov+ an

Fisher, Walter L.
  Trading Run   nv ASF Jun,85
    Analog Science Fiction/Science Fact [v.105 # 6, June 1985]
                                                 Stanley Schmidt mg

Fletcher, Jo & Stephen Jones
  Introduction   in
    Fantasycon X Programme Booklet   Stephen Jones+ oa

Flinn, M.
  Cartoon   ct TZM Apr,85
    Rod Serling's The Twilight Zone Magazine [v.5 #1, March/April
    1985]   T.E.D. Klein mg

Flynn, Michael F.
  A Medieval Management Report   ms ASF Sep,85
    Analog Science Fiction/Science Fact [v.105 # 9, September
    1985]   Stanley Schmidt mg

Forbes, Caroline
  The Comet's Tail   na NEDLFUL,85
    THE NEEDLE ON FULL: LESBIAN FEMINIST SCIENCE FICTION
                                                 Caroline Forbes co
  Equal Rights   ss NEDLFUL,85
    THE NEEDLE ON FULL: LESBIAN FEMINIST SCIENCE FICTION
                                                 Caroline Forbes co
  London Fields   na NEDLFUL,85
    THE NEEDLE ON FULL: LESBIAN FEMINIST SCIENCE FICTION
                                                 Caroline Forbes co
  Marianna and the Graduation   ss REACH ,84
    THE NEEDLE ON FULL: LESBIAN FEMINIST SCIENCE FICTION
                                                 Caroline Forbes co
  The Needle on Full   nv CYC 1980
    THE NEEDLE ON FULL: LESBIAN FEMINIST SCIENCE FICTION
                                                 Caroline Forbes co
  Night Life   ss NEDLFUL,85
    THE NEEDLE ON FULL: LESBIAN FEMINIST SCIENCE FICTION
                                                 Caroline Forbes co
  Snake   ss SPN V1 #2,80
    THE NEEDLE ON FULL: LESBIAN FEMINIST SCIENCE FICTION
                                                 Caroline Forbes co
  Transplant   vi CYC 1980
    THE NEEDLE ON FULL: LESBIAN FEMINIST SCIENCE FICTION
                                                 Caroline Forbes co
  The Visitors   ss NEDLFUL,85
    THE NEEDLE ON FULL: LESBIAN FEMINIST SCIENCE FICTION
                                                 Caroline Forbes co

Ford, John M.
  Boundary Echoes   ss OMN Sep,83
    THE FOURTH OMNI BOOK OF SCIENCE FICTION   Ellen Datlow an
  Scrabble with God   vi IAS Oct,85
    Isaac Asimov's Science Fiction Magazine [v. 9 #10, October
    1985]   Shawna McCarthy mg
  SF Cliches III: Time Machines   pm AMZ Jan,85
    Amazing Science Fiction Stories [v.58 #5, January 1985]
                                                 George H. Scithers mg

Forester, C.S.
  The Turn of the Tide   ss 1934
    MYSTERIOUS SEA STORIES   William Pattrick an

Forward, Robert L.
  The Paradox of Interstellar Transport   ar FFR V 1,85
    FAR FRONTIERS   Jerry E. Pournelle+ oa
  The Singing Diamond   ss OMN Feb,79
    GREAT SCIENCE FICTION BY THE WORLD'S GREAT SCIENTISTS
                                                 Isaac Asimov+ an

Foster, Alan Dean
  Batrachian   ss AMZ Sep,85
    Amazing Science Fiction Stories [v.59 #3, September 1985]
                                                 George H. Scithers mg
  Collectible   ss FSF Apr,85
    The Magazine of Fantasy & Science Fiction [v.68 #4, April
    1985]   Edward L. Ferman mg
  THE DAY OF THE DISSONANCE   n. WBK 1984
    SEASON OF THE SPELLSONG   Alan Dean Foster om
  THE HOUR OF THE GATE   n. WBK 1984
    SEASON OF THE SPELLSONG   Alan Dean Foster om
  SPELLSINGER   n. WBK 1983
    SEASON OF THE SPELLSONG   Alan Dean Foster om
  Why Johnny Can't Speed   ss GAL Sep,71
    TOP SCIENCE FICTION   Josh Pachter an

Foster, David
  The Elixir Operon   ss STRGATR,85
    STRANGE ATTRACTORS   Damien Broderick oa

Foster, M.A.
  The Conversation   na OWLTIME,85
    OWL TIME   M.A. Foster oc
  Entertainment   na NWV # 4,81
    OWL TIME   M.A. Foster oc
  Leanne   na OWLTIME,85
    OWL TIME   M.A. Foster oc

Foster, M.A. (continued)
  The Man Who Loved Owls   na OWLTIME,85
    OWL TIME   M.A. Foster oc
  Preface   pr
    OWL TIME   M.A. Foster oc

Fowler, Karen Joy
  The Lake Was Full of Artificial Things   ss IAS Oct,85
    Isaac Asimov's Science Fiction Magazine [v. 9 #10, October
    1985]   Shawna McCarthy mg
  The Poplar Street Study   ss FSF Jun,85
    The Magazine of Fantasy & Science Fiction [v.68 #6, June
    1985]   Edward L. Ferman mg
  Praxis   ss IAS Mar,85
    Isaac Asimov's Science Fiction Magazine [v. 9 # 3, March
    1985]   Shawna McCarthy mg
  Recalling Cinderella   nv WRTRFUT,85
    L. RON HUBBARD PRESENTS WRITERS OF THE FUTURE Algis Budrys oa
  The War of the Roses   nv IAS Dec,85
    Isaac Asimov's Science Fiction Magazine [v. 9 #12, December
    1985]   Shawna McCarthy mg

Fox, Janet
  Christobel   ss BLD V1 #3,85
    Border Land [v.1 #3]   R.S. Hadji mg
  Intimately, With Rain   ss CLG Nov,78
    MIDNIGHT   Charles L. Grant oa
  Taking Care of Bertie   ss EDT #11,85
    Eldritch Tales No. 11 [v.3 #2]   Crispin Burnham mg

Fox-Davis, Susan L.
  Indistinguishable from Magic   vi FBM Mar,85
    Fantasy Book [v.4 #1, March 1985]   Dennis Mallonee+ mg

Frahm, Leanne
  The Visitor   ss MIDNGHT,85
    MIDNIGHT   Charles L. Grant oa

Fraknoi, Andrew
  Selected Reading   bi
    THE PLANETS   Byron Preiss oa
  The Solar System: An Introduction   in
    THE PLANETS   Byron Preiss oa

Frazier, Robert
  Doppler Effects   pm IAS Feb,85
    Isaac Asimov's Science Fiction Magazine [v. 9 # 2, February
    1985]   Shawna McCarthy mg
  Ed White, Spacewalking, June 3, 1965   pm IAS May,85
    Isaac Asimov's Science Fiction Magazine [v. 9 # 5, May 1985]
                                                 Shawna McCarthy mg
  In the Frozen Zoo for Extinct Beasts   pm FBM Sep,85
    Fantasy Book [v.4 #3, September 1985] Dennis Mallonee+ mg
  The Mermaid Barnacle   pm FBM Dec,85
    Fantasy Book [v.4 #4, December 1985] Dennis Mallonee+ mg
  On the Rio Madera   pm BPC #26,85
  Paleontologists Who Live in Backward Time   pm IAS Aug,85
    Isaac Asimov's Science Fiction Magazine [v. 9 # 8, August
    1985]   Shawna McCarthy mg
  Perception Barriers   pm IAS Dec,85
    Isaac Asimov's Science Fiction Magazine [v. 9 #12, December
    1985]   Shawna McCarthy mg
  A Quotella for Ted Sturgeon   pm IAS Jan,86
    Isaac Asimov's Science Fiction Magazine [v.10 # 1, January
    1986]   Gardner Dozois mg
  The Secret Lives of Drones   pm S&T #69,85
    Space and Time [#69, Winter 1986]   Gordon Linzner mg

Frazier, Robert & Andrew Joron
  Hominid Voices   pm URN # 4,84
    THE 1985 RHYSLING ANTHOLOGY   Anonymous an
  The Wake of Gravity   pm IAS Nov,85
    Isaac Asimov's Science Fiction Magazine [v. 9 #11, November
    1985]   Shawna McCarthy mg

Freedman, Benjamin
  On the Planet Grafool   ss TESRCTS,85
    TESSERACTS   Judith Merril oa

Freeman, Mary E. Wilkins
  The Lost Ghost   ss WNDROSE,03
    HAUNTED WOMEN: THE BEST SUPERNATURAL TALES BY AMERICAN WOMEN
    WRITERS   Alfred Bendixen an
  Luella Miller   ss WNDROSE,03
    HAUNTED WOMEN: THE BEST SUPERNATURAL TALES BY AMERICAN WOMEN
    WRITERS   Alfred Bendixen an

Frentzen, Jeffrey & David J. Schow
  The Outer Limits Show-by-Show Guide, Part 7   bi TZM Feb,85
    Rod Serling's The Twilight Zone Magazine [v.4 #6,
    January/February 1985]   T.E.D. Klein mg

Friedlander, Gerald
  The Black Dwarf   nv JWSHFYT,18
    Introduction by Jessica Amanda Salmonson.
    Fantasy Book [v.4 #2, June 1985]   Dennis Mallonee+ mg

Friedman, Bruce Jay
  A Foot in the Door   ss PBY Oct,60
    Rod Serling's The Twilight Zone Magazine [v.5 #3, July/August
    1985]   T.E.D. Klein mg

FRIESNER, ESTHER M.

GEIS, RICHARD E.

Gentle, Mary
　On the Edge　　　　　　　　　　　　　　　　br INZ
　　Interzone [#13, Autumn 1985]　　　Simon Ounsley+ mg
　　Interzone [#14, Winter 1985/86]　　Simon Ounsley+ mg
　A Sun in the Attic　　　　　　　　　　ss DSPTCHS,85
　　DESPATCHES FROM THE FRONTIERS OF THE FEMALE MIND Jen Green+ oa

Gentleman, Dorothy Corbett
　Instinct　　　　　　　　　　　　　　　pm PSP Spr,80
　　TESSERACTS　　　　　　　　　　　　Judith Merril oa

Gibson, V.K.
　American Dream　　　　　　　　　　　ss NCR V1 #5,86
　　Night Cry [v.1 #5, Spring 1986]　　Alan Rodgers mg

Gibson, William
　Count Zero [Part 1 of 3]　　　　　　sl IAS Jan,86
　　Isaac Asimov's Science Fiction Magazine [v.10 # 1, January
　　1986]　　　　　　　　　　　　　Gardner Dozois mg
　Hinterlands　　　　　　　　　　　　　ss OMN Oct,81
　　THE FOURTH OMNI BOOK OF SCIENCE FICTION　Ellen Datlow an
　　TESSERACTS　　　　　　　　　　　　Judith Merril oa
　New Rose Hotel　　　　　　　　　　　ss OMN Jul,84
　　THE YEAR'S BEST SCIENCE FICTION, SECOND ANNUAL COLLECTION
　　　　　　　　　　　　　　　　　Gardner Dozois an
　　THE SCIENCE FICTION YEARBOOK　　Jerry E. Pournelle+ an
　　NEBULA AWARDS 20: SFWA'S CHOICES FOR THE BEST IN SCIENCE
　　FICTION 1984　　　　　　　　　George Zebrowski an
　Winter Market　　　　　　　　　　　ss VNC Nov,85

Gibson, William & Bruce Sterling
　Red Star, Winter Orbit　　　　　　　nv OMN Jul,83
　　THE THIRD OMNI BOOK OF SCIENCE FICTION　Ellen Datlow an

Gibson, William & Michael Swanwick
　Dogfight　　　　　　　　　　　　　ss OMN Jul,85

Gilbert, Christopher
　The Ultimate Diagnostic　　　　　　　ss AMZ Sep,85
　　Amazing Science Fiction Stories [v.59 #3, September 1985]
　　　　　　　　　　　　　　　　　George H. Scithers mg

Gilchrist, Ellen
　The Green Tent　　　　　　　　　　ss FSF Nov,85
　　The Magazine of Fantasy & Science Fiction [v.69 #5, November
　　1985]　　　　　　　　　　　　Edward L. Ferman mg

Gillett, Stephen L., Ph.D.
　The Cambrian Explosion　　　　　　　ar AMZ May,85
　　Amazing Science Fiction Stories [v.59 #1, May 1985]
　　　　　　　　　　　　　　　　　George H. Scithers mg
　The Ozone Rocket　　　　　　　　　ar ASF Aug,85
　　Analog Science Fiction/Science Fact [v.105 # 8, August 1985]
　　　　　　　　　　　　　　　　　Stanley Schmidt mg
　The Postdiluvian World　　　　　　　ar ASF Nov,85
　　Analog Science Fiction/Science Fact [v.105 #11, November
　　1985]　　　　　　　　　　　　Stanley Schmidt mg
　The Scientific Literature　　　　　　ar AMZ Mar,85
　　Amazing Science Fiction Stories [v.58 #6, March 1985]
　　　　　　　　　　　　　　　　　George H. Scithers mg

Gilliland, Alexis
　Cartoon　　　　　　　　　　　　　　ct FSF
　　The Magazine of Fantasy & Science Fiction [v.68 #2, February
　　1985]　　　　　　　　　　　　Edward L. Ferman mg
　　The Magazine of Fantasy & Science Fiction [v.69 #5, November
　　1985]　　　　　　　　　　　　Edward L. Ferman mg

Gilliland, Alexis & William Rotsler
　Cartoon, Cartoon　　　　　　　　　　ct AMZ
　　Amazing Science Fiction Stories [v.58 #5, January 1985]
　　　　　　　　　　　　　　　　　George H. Scithers mg
　　Amazing Science Fiction Stories [v.59 #1, May 1985]
　　　　　　　　　　　　　　　　　George H. Scithers mg
　　Amazing Science Fiction Stories [v.59 #2, July 1985]
　　　　　　　　　　　　　　　　　George H. Scithers mg
　　Amazing Science Fiction Stories [v.60 #1, November 1985]
　　　　　　　　　　　　　　　　　George H. Scithers mg
　　Amazing Science Fiction Stories [v.60 #2, January 1986]
　　　　　　　　　　　　　　　　　George H. Scithers mg

Gilman, Charlotte Perkins
　The Yellow Wallpaper　　　　　　　　ss NEM 1892
　　HAUNTED WOMEN: THE BEST SUPERNATURAL TALES BY AMERICAN WOMEN
　　WRITERS　　　　　　　　　　　　Alfred Bendixen an

Girard, Dian
　Katzenjammer　　　　　　　　　　　ss AMZ Jul,85
　　Amazing Science Fiction Stories [v.59 #2, July 1985]
　　　　　　　　　　　　　　　　　George H. Scithers mg

Girard, Dian & Larry Niven
　Talisman　　　　　　　　　　　　　ss FSF Nov,81
　　LIMITS　　　　　　　　　　　　　Larry Niven co

Glasgow, Ellen
　The Shadowy Third　　　　　　　　　nv SHDW3rd,23
　　YOUNG GHOSTS　　　　　　　　　Isaac Asimov+ an

Gleisser, Benjamin
　The Dark　　　　　　　　　　　　　ss NCR V1 #2,85
　　Night Cry [v.1 #2, Summer 1985]　　T.E.D. Klein mg

Gloss, Molly
　Interlocking Pieces　　　　　　　　　ss UNI #14,84
　　THE YEAR'S BEST SCIENCE FICTION, SECOND ANNUAL COLLECTION
　　　　　　　　　　　　　　　　　Gardner Dozois an

Gluckman, Janet
　Castoff　　　　　　　　　　　　　　ss SHY # 7,85
　　Shayol [v.3 #1, Whole No. 7]　　　Arnie Fenner+ mg

Glyer, Michael
　1984: The Fifty-Candle Blowout　　　ar 1985
　　THE SCIENCE FICTION YEARBOOK　　Jerry E. Pournelle+ an

Goddin, Jeffrey
　House of Ill Repute　　　　　　　　　ss FTL Sum,85
　　Fantasy Tales [v.7 #14, Summer 1985]　Stephen Jones mg

Godwin, Parke
　The Last Rainbow　　　　　　　　　ex BAN Jul,85
　　THE BANTAM SPECTRA SAMPLER　　Lou Aronica an
　Stroke of Mercy　　　　　　　　　　ss TZM Sep,81
　　MASTERPIECES OF TERROR AND THE SUPERNATURAL　Marvin Kaye an

Goethe, Johann Wolfgang Von
　The Erl-King　　　　　　　　　　　　pm
　　English adaption by Marvin Kaye
　　MASTERPIECES OF TERROR AND THE SUPERNATURAL　Marvin Kaye an

Gold, Horace L.
　Inside Man　　　　　　　　　　　　ss GAL Oct,65
　　Fantasy Book [v.4 #3, September 1985]　Dennis Mallonee+ mg
　Trouble with Water　　　　　　　　　ss UNK Mar,39
　　TOP FANTASY　　　　　　　　　　Josh Pachter an

Goldin, Stephen
　The Dungeons of Ravan　　　　　　　nv FBM Mar,85
　　Fantasy Book [v.4 #1, March 1985]　Dennis Mallonee+ mg

Goldsmith, Howard
　The Voices of El Dorado [as Ward Smith]　ss HORRTLS,74
　　YOUNG GHOSTS　　　　　　　　　Isaac Asimov+ an

Goldstein, Lisa
　The Dream Years　　　　　　　　　ex BAN Aug,85
　　THE BANTAM SPECTRA SAMPLER　　Lou Aronica an
　Preliminary Notes on the Jang　　　　ss IAS May,85
　　Isaac Asimov's Science Fiction Magazine [v. 9 # 5, May 1985]
　　　　　　　　　　　　　　　　　Shawna McCarthy mg
　Tourists　　　　　　　　　　　　　ss IAS Feb,85
　　Isaac Asimov's Science Fiction Magazine [v. 9 # 2, February
　　1985]　　　　　　　　　　　　Shawna McCarthy mg

Gordian, Mark
　Notes from the General Secretariat　　ss ASF Aug,85
　　Analog Science Fiction/Science Fact [v.105 # 8, August 1985]
　　　　　　　　　　　　　　　　　Stanley Schmidt mg

Gordon, John
　Catch Your Death　　　　　　　　　ss CTCHDTH,84
　　THE YEAR'S BEST HORROR STORIES: SERIES XIII
　　　　　　　　　　　　　　　　　Karl Edward Wagner an
　Never Grow Up　　　　　　　　　　ss CTCHDTH,84
　　THE YEAR'S BEST HORROR STORIES: SERIES XIII
　　　　　　　　　　　　　　　　　Karl Edward Wagner an

Gotlieb, Phyllis
　Tauf Aleph　　　　　　　　　　　　nv MRWNDRN,81
　　TESSERACTS　　　　　　　　　　Judith Merril oa

Gotschalk, Felix C.
　Vestibular Man　　　　　　　　　　nv FSF Mar,85
　　The Magazine of Fantasy & Science Fiction [v.68 #3, March
　　1985]　　　　　　　　　　　　Edward L. Ferman mg

Goulart, Ron
　Calling Dr. Clockwork　　　　　　　ss AMZ Mar,65
　　AMAZING STORIES: 60 YEARS OF THE BEST SCIENCE FICTION
　　　　　　　　　　　　　　　　　Isaac Asimov+ an
　Nostalgia: Old Dark House for Rent　　ar TZM Feb,85
　　Rod Serling's The Twilight Zone Magazine [v.4 #6,
　　January/February 1985]　　　　　T.E.D. Klein mg
　Please Stand By　　　　　　　　　　nv FSF Jan,62
　　ISAAC ASIMOV'S MAGICAL WORLDS OF FANTASY: WITCHES & WIZARDS
　　　　　　　　　　　　　　　　　Isaac Asimov+ om
　Street Magic　　　　　　　　　　　ss IAS Mar,84
　　ISAAC ASIMOV'S FANTASY　　　　Shawna McCarthy an
　That Wonderful Summer　　　　　　　ss FSF Oct,85
　　The Magazine of Fantasy & Science Fiction [v.69 #4, October
　　1985]　　　　　　　　　　　　Edward L. Ferman mg

Gould, Steven
　Mental Blocks　　　　　　　　　　ss AMZ Jul,85
　　Amazing Science Fiction Stories [v.59 #2, July 1985]
　　　　　　　　　　　　　　　　　George H. Scithers mg

Gracey, Penny
　The Children Open Their Green Flesh　pm BLD V1 #3,85
　　Border Land [v.1 #3]　　　　　　R.S. Hadji mg

Graham, Jefferson
　Special Report: 'The Twilight Zone' Returns　ar TZM Apr,85

HASSE, HENRY   HOOPER, WALTER

Hasse, Henry
  He Who Shrank   na AMZ Aug,36
    ISAAC ASIMOV'S MAGICAL WORLDS OF FANTASY #5: GIANTS
                                                 Isaac Asimov+ an

Haught, Linda
  An Exciting New Technology Comes to Pickerington, Ohio
                                                   vi NCR V1 #4,85
    Night Cry [v.1 #4, Winter 1985]   Alan Rodgers mg

Hawthorne, Nathaniel
  The Christmas Banquet   ss
    MASTERPIECES OF TERROR AND THE SUPERNATURAL   Marvin Kaye an

Hayashi, Kikuo
  Illustration   il PLANETS,85
    THE PLANETS   Byron Preiss oa

Hayes, Chris
  Blue Star   ss S&T #69,85
    Space and Time [#69, Winter 1986]   Gordon Linzner mg

Hearn, Lafcadio
  The Boy Who Drew Cats   ss
    GREAT GHOST STORIES   Betty Ann Schwartz an
  Oshidori   vi KWAIDAN,04
    MASTERPIECES OF TERROR AND THE SUPERNATURAL   Marvin Kaye an

Heath, Phillip C.
  Dead Men's Fingers   nv BLD V1 #2,85
    Border Land [v.1 #2]   R.S. Hadji mg

Hemesath, James B.
  The End of the World   ss WDL V14 #51,84
    THE YEAR'S BEST HORROR STORIES: SERIES XIII
                                           Karl Edward Wagner an

Henderson, Chris
  Books   br WHS Dec,84
    Whispers [v.6 #1-2, December 1984]   Stuart David Schiff mg

Hendrickson, Walter B., Jr.
  Biofeedback in Space   ar ASF Jan,85
    Analog Science Fiction/Science Fact [v.105 # 1, January 1985]
                                            Stanley Schmidt mg

Hensley, Joe L.
  Harpist   ss SPECLTN,82
    TOP FANTASY   Josh Pachter an
  Savant   ss FSF Dec,85
    The Magazine of Fantasy & Science Fiction [v.69 #6, December
    1985]   Edward L. Ferman mg

Herbert, Frank
  By the Book   nv ASF Aug,66
    EYE   Frank Herbert co
  Cease Fire   nv ASF Jan,58
    EYE   Frank Herbert co
  Death of a City   ss FUTCITY,73
    EYE   Frank Herbert co
  Dragon in the Sea [Under Pressure]   ex ASF Nov,55
    EYE   Frank Herbert co
  Frogs and Scientists   vi DST V1 #4,79
    EYE   Frank Herbert co
  Introduction   in
    EYE   Frank Herbert co
  A Matter of Traces   ss FUN Nov,58
    EYE   Frank Herbert co
  Murder Will In   nv FSF May,70
    EYE   Frank Herbert co
  Passage for Piano   nv BKHRBRT,73
    EYE   Frank Herbert co
  Rat Race   nv ASF Jul,55
    EYE   Frank Herbert co
  Seed Stock   ss ASF Apr,70
    EYE   Frank Herbert co
  Songs of a Sentient Flute   nv ASF Feb,79
    MEDEA: HARLAN'S WORLD   Harlan Ellison an
  The Tactful Saboteur   nv GAL Oct,64
    EYE   Frank Herbert co
  Transcript: Mercury Program   ss PLANETS,85
    THE PLANETS   Byron Preiss oa
  Try to Remember   nv AMZ Oct,61
    EYE   Frank Herbert co

Herbert, Frank, Thomas M. Disch, Harlan Ellison, Robert Silverberg
& Theodore Sturgeon
  The Concept Seminar   ms
    MEDEA: HARLAN'S WORLD   Harlan Ellison an
  The Extrapolations, the Questions   ms
    MEDEA: HARLAN'S WORLD   Harlan Ellison an

Herlich, Herman
  Love Song to Lucy   pm S83 1983
    NEBULA AWARDS 20: SFWA'S CHOICES FOR THE BEST IN SCIENCE
    FICTION 1984   George Zebrowski an
  Lucy Answers   pm S83 1983
    NEBULA AWARDS 20: SFWA'S CHOICES FOR THE BEST IN SCIENCE
    FICTION 1984   George Zebrowski an

Herndon, Ben
  Ellison's Rules   iv TZM Dec,85
    Rod Serling's The Twilight Zone Magazine [v.5 #5, December
    1985]   Michael Blaine mg
  New Adventures in the Scream Trade [interview with Stephen
  King]   iv TZM Dec,85
    Rod Serling's The Twilight Zone Magazine [v.5 #5, December
    1985]   Michael Blaine mg
  Real Tube Terror   ar TZM Dec,85
    Rod Serling's The Twilight Zone Magazine [v.5 #5, December
    1985]   Michael Blaine mg

Heyer, Heidi
  Random Sample   ss ASF Nov,85
    Analog Science Fiction/Science Fact [v.105 #11, November
    1985]   Stanley Schmidt mg

Heyrman, Peter
  The Crossing   ss TZM Feb,86
    Rod Serling's The Twilight Zone Magazine [v.5 #6, February
    1986]   Michael Blaine mg
  Snow Blind   ss TZM Aug,85
    Rod Serling's The Twilight Zone Magazine [v.5 #3, July/August
    1985]   T.E.D. Klein mg

Hichens, Robert
  How Love Came to Professor Guildea   nv TNGSCNS,00
    DARK BANQUET: A FEAST OF 12 GREAT GHOST STORIES
                                             Lincoln Child an

Highsmith, Patricia
  The Quest for Blank Claveringi [revised from The Snails]
                                              ss SEP Jun 17,67
    MASTERPIECES OF TERROR AND THE SUPERNATURAL   Marvin Kaye an

Hill, Douglas
  Hally's Paradise   ss OUTOFTM,84
    OUT OF TIME   Aidan Chambers oa

Hill, Hal
  Fear of Flying   ss FSF Dec,85
    The Magazine of Fantasy & Science Fiction [v.69 #6, December
    1985]   Edward L. Ferman mg

Hill, Kenneth
  T.G.I.F.   pm AMZ Sep,85
    Amazing Science Fiction Stories [v.59 #3, September 1985]
                                          George H. Scithers mg

Hjort, James William
  Night Winds and Sepulchral Bells   ss WDB #20,85
    Weirdbook 20 [Spring 1985]   W. Paul Ganley mg

Hoch, Edward D.
  The Faceless Thing   ss MOH Nov,63
    MASTERPIECES OF TERROR AND THE SUPERNATURAL   Marvin Kaye an
  The Witch Is Dead   ss 1956
    ISAAC ASIMOV'S MAGICAL WORLDS OF FANTASY #4: SPELLS
                                             Isaac Asimov+ an

Hochstein, Rolaine
  Neighbors   ss FSF Jul,85
    The Magazine of Fantasy & Science Fiction [v.69 #1, July
    1985]   Edward L. Ferman mg

Hodgell, P.C.
  Stranger Blood   nv IMGNLND,85
    IMAGINARY LANDS   Robin McKinley oa

Hodgson, William Hope
  The Findings of the Graiken   nv
    MYSTERIOUS SEA STORIES   William Pattrick an

Hoffman, Nina Kiriki
  Hiding From the Sun   ss GRYSTBY,85
    GREYSTONE BAY   Charles L. Grant oa
  The Shadow of a Hawk   ss SDW # 8,85
    SHADOWS 8   Charles L. Grant oa
  A Step Into Darkness   nv WRTRFUT,85
    L. RON HUBBARD PRESENTS WRITERS OF THE FUTURE Algis Budrys oa

Hogan, Ernest
  The Yenagloshi Express   ss AMZ Jan,86
    Amazing Science Fiction Stories [v.60 #2, January 1986]
                                          George H. Scithers mg

Holder, Nancy Jones
  Blood Gothic   ss SDW # 8,85
    SHADOWS 8   Charles L. Grant oa

Holdstock, Robert
  The Other Place   ss FYC #10,85
    Fantasycon X Programme Booklet   Stephen Jones+ oa

Holtzer, Susan
  The Camel's Nose   ss FRANZDK,85
    FREE AMAZONS OF DARKOVER   Marion Zimmer Bradley+ oa

Hooper, Walter
  The Boxen Manuscripts   ar 1985
    BOXEN: THE IMAGINARY WORLD OF THE YOUNG C.S. LEWIS
                                             C.S. Lewis co

JANKUS, HANK

KELLEY, JAMES PATRICK

KING, STEPHEN

King, Stephen (continued)
SKELETON CREW [special edition]   Stephen King co
The Reaper's Image   ss STM Spr,69
SKELETON CREW   Stephen King co
SKELETON CREW [special edition]   Stephen King co
Silver Bullet   pl
SILVER BULLET   Stephen King co
Survivor Type   ss TERRORS,82
SKELETON CREW   Stephen King co
SKELETON CREW [special edition]   Stephen King co
Theodore Sturgeon: 1918-1985   bg WPB 1985
Isaac Asimov's Science Fiction Magazine [v.10 # 1, January
1986]   Gardner Dozois mg
Uncle Otto's Truck   ss YNK Oct,83
SKELETON CREW   Stephen King co
SKELETON CREW [special edition]   Stephen King co
The Wedding Gig   ss EQM Dec 1,80
SKELETON CREW   Stephen King co
SKELETON CREW [special edition]   Stephen King co
Why I Was Bachman   fw
THE BACHMAN BOOKS: FOUR EARLY NOVELS BY STEPHEN KING
                                                Stephen King om
Word Processor of the Gods [The Word Processor] ss PBY Jan,83
SKELETON CREW   Stephen King co
SKELETON CREW [special edition]   Stephen King co

Kingsbury, Donald
The Moon Goddess and the Son   na ASF Dec,79
BAKER'S DOZEN: 13 SHORT SCIENCE FICTION NOVELS
                                                Isaac Asimov+ an

Kipling, Rudyard
MacDonough's Song [from As Easy as A.B.C.]   pm LOM Apr,12
THERE WILL BE WAR, VOL. IV: DAY OF THE TYRANT
                                                Jerry E. Pournelle an
A Matter of Fact   ss 1935
MYSTERIOUS SEA STORIES   William Pattrick an
They   nv TRAFFIC,04
DARK BANQUET: A FEAST OF 12 GREAT GHOST STORIES
                                                Lincoln Child an

Kiplinger, Christina
Book Reviews   br EDT #11,85
Eldritch Tales No. 11 [v.3 #2]   Crispin Burnham mg

Kirkpatrick, David
The Effect of Terminal Cancer on Potential Astronauts
                                                nv TESRCTS,85
TESSERACTS   Judith Merril oa

Klass, Morton
In the Beginning   ss ASF Jul,54
GREAT SCIENCE FICTION BY THE WORLD'S GREAT SCIENTISTS
                                                Isaac Asimov+ an

Klein, Jay Kay
Biolog: Don Sakers   bg ASF Jan,85
Analog Science Fiction/Science Fact [v.105 # 1, January 1985]
                                                Stanley Schmidt mg
Biolog: Doug Beekman   bg ASF Jul,85
Analog Science Fiction/Science Fact [v.105 # 7, July 1985]
                                                Stanley Schmidt mg
Biolog: Eric G. Iverson   bg ASF Feb,85
Analog Science Fiction/Science Fact [v.105 # 2, February
1985]   Stanley Schmidt mg
Biolog: J. Brian Clarke   bg ASF May,85
Analog Science Fiction/Science Fact [v.105 # 5, May 1985]
                                                Stanley Schmidt mg
Biolog: Jerry Oltion   bg ASF Apr,85
Analog Science Fiction/Science Fact [v.105 # 4, April 1985]
                                                Stanley Schmidt mg
Biolog: Lester Del Rey   bg ASF Oct,85
Analog Science Fiction/Science Fact [v.105 #10, October 1985]
                                                Stanley Schmidt mg
Biolog: P.M. Fergusson   bg ASF Nov,85
Analog Science Fiction/Science Fact [v.105 #11, November
1985]   Stanley Schmidt mg
Biolog: Robert A. Heinlein   bg ASF Jun,85
Analog Science Fiction/Science Fact [v.105 # 6, June 1985]
                                                Stanley Schmidt mg
Biolog: Tom Ligon   bg ASF Dec md,85
Analog Science Fiction/Science Fact [v.105 #13, Mid-December
1985]   Stanley Schmidt mg
Biolog: W.R. Thompson   bg ASF Aug,85
Analog Science Fiction/Science Fact [v.105 # 8, August 1985]
                                                Stanley Schmidt mg
Biolog: Willey Ley   bg ASF Dec,85
Analog Science Fiction/Science Fact [v.105 #12, December
1985]   Stanley Schmidt mg
Biolog: William F. Wu   bg ASF Sep,85
Analog Science Fiction/Science Fact [v.105 # 9, September
1985]   Stanley Schmidt mg
Mass Communication   vi ASF Aug,85
Analog Science Fiction/Science Fact [v.105 # 8, August 1985]
                                                Stanley Schmidt mg

Klein, R.E.
The Apprenticeship of Alan Patch   ss S&T #69,85
Space and Time [#69, Winter 1986]   Gordon Linzner mg

Klein, T.E.D.
Black Man with a Horn   nv NTLCTHU,80
DARK GODS   T.E.D. Klein co
Bye!   ed TZM Aug,85
Rod Serling's The Twilight Zone Magazine [v.5 #3, July/August
1985]   T.E.D. Klein mg
Children of the Kingdom   na DRKFRCS,80
DARK GODS   T.E.D. Klein co
Fair Warnings   ed TZM Apr,85
Rod Serling's The Twilight Zone Magazine [v.5 #1, March/April
1985]   T.E.D. Klein mg
From the Editor   in
Night Cry [v.1 #2, Summer 1985]   T.E.D. Klein mg
Inspirations   ed TZM Jun,85
Rod Serling's The Twilight Zone Magazine [v.5 #2, May/June
1985]   T.E.D. Klein mg
Nadelman's God   na DRKGODS,85
DARK GODS   T.E.D. Klein co
Petey   na SDW # 2,79
DARK GODS   T.E.D. Klein co
The Story Hour   ed TZM Feb,85
Rod Serling's The Twilight Zone Magazine [v.4 #6,
January/February 1985]   T.E.D. Klein mg

Knight, Damon
Cabin Boy   nv GAL Sep,51
ISAAC ASIMOV'S MAGICAL WORLDS OF FANTASY #5: GIANTS
                                                Isaac Asimov+ an
The Cage   nv LTKNTED,85
LATE KNIGHT EDITION   Damon Knight co
CV (1st of 3 parts)   sl FSF Jan,85
The Magazine of Fantasy & Science Fiction [v.68 #1, January
1985]   Edward L. Ferman mg
CV (2nd of 3 parts)   sl FSF Feb,85
The Magazine of Fantasy & Science Fiction [v.68 #2, February
1985]   Edward L. Ferman mg
CV (3rd of 3 parts)   sl FSF Mar,85
The Magazine of Fantasy & Science Fiction [v.68 #3, March
1985]   Edward L. Ferman mg
Definition   ss STS Feb,53
LATE KNIGHT EDITION   Damon Knight co
Each Prisoner Pent   ss SDA Oct,85
Stardate [v.1 # 8, October 1985]   Ted White+ mg
A Fantasy   vi IAS Jun,85
Isaac Asimov's Science Fiction Magazine [v. 9 # 6, June 1985]
                                                Shawna McCarthy mg
The God Machine   ss FSF Jul,85
The Magazine of Fantasy & Science Fiction [v.69 #1, July
1985]   Edward L. Ferman mg
Good-bye, Henry J. Kostkos, Good-bye   ar CLR # 2,72
LATE KNIGHT EDITION   Damon Knight co
Goodbye, Dr. Ralston   ss FFR V 1,85
FAR FRONTIERS   Jerry E. Pournelle+ oa
I See You   ss FSF Nov,76
LATE KNIGHT EDITION   Damon Knight co
La Ronde   ss FSF Oct,83
LATE KNIGHT EDITION   Damon Knight co
The Man Who Went Back   ss AMZ Nov,85
Amazing Science Fiction Stories [v.60 #1, November 1985]
                                                George H. Scithers mg
Point of View   ss PBY Sep,85
Tarcan of the Hoboes   nv FSF Oct,82
LATE KNIGHT EDITION   Damon Knight co
Theodore Sturgeon: 1918-1985   bg IAS Jan,86
Isaac Asimov's Science Fiction Magazine [v.10 # 1, January
1986]   Gardner Dozois mg
The Third Little Green Man   nv PLS Sum,48
LATE KNIGHT EDITION   Damon Knight co
To Serve Man   ss GAL Nov,50
THE TWILIGHT ZONE: THE ORIGINAL STORIES
                                                Martin H. Greenberg+ an
What Is Science Fiction?   ar TRNGPTS,77
LATE KNIGHT EDITION   Damon Knight co
Who Is Damon Knight?   ar PLS Sum,48
LATE KNIGHT EDITION   Damon Knight co

Knight, Damon & James Blish
Tiger Ride   ss ASF Oct,48
ANALOG: THE BEST OF SCIENCE FICTION   Anonymous an

Koeller, Scott
Ten Common Myths About Ancient Man   pm AMZ Nov,85
Amazing Science Fiction Stories [v.60 #1, November 1985]
                                                George H. Scithers mg

Korabelnikov, Oleg
Tower of Birds   na ERH&ELW,85
EARTH AND ELSEWHERE   Roger DeGaris an

Kornbluth, C.M.
The Altar at Midnight   ss GAL Nov,52
ISAAC ASIMOV PRESENTS THE GREAT SF STORIES: 14 (1952)
                                                Isaac Asimov+ an
The Little Black Bag   nv ASF Jul,50
ANALOG: THE BEST OF SCIENCE FICTION   Anonymous an
The Marching Morons   nv GAL Apr,51
ISAAC ASIMOV PRESENTS THE GREAT SF STORIES: 13 (1951)
                                                Isaac Asimov+ an
That Share of Glory   nv ASF Jan,52
MERCENARIES OF TOMORROW   Poul Anderson+ an
With These Hands   nv GAL Dec,51

LASSWITZ, KURD   **LE GUIN, URSULA K.**

Le Guin, Ursula K. (continued)
A Marriage   pm ALWCMHM,85
  ALWAYS COMING HOME   Ursula K. Le Guin oc
Mazes   ss EPOCH ,75
  TOP SCIENCE FICTION   Josh Pachter an
A Meditation in the Eighth House in Early Spring   pm ALWCMHM,85
  ALWAYS COMING HOME   Ursula K. Le Guin oc
A Meditation on Quail Feather House   pm ALWCMHM,85
  ALWAYS COMING HOME   Ursula K. Le Guin oc
Messages Concerning the Condor   ss ALWCMHM,85
  ALWAYS COMING HOME   Ursula K. Le Guin oc
The Miller   vi ALWCMHM,85
  ALWAYS COMING HOME   Ursula K. Le Guin oc
The Modes of Earth and Sky   ms ALWCMHM,85
  ALWAYS COMING HOME   Ursula K. Le Guin oc
Moon Dance Song   pm ALWCMHM,85
  ALWAYS COMING HOME   Ursula K. Le Guin oc
Moths and Butterflies   pm ALWCMHM,85
  ALWAYS COMING HOME   Ursula K. Le Guin oc
A Note About the Novel   si ALWCMHM,85
  ALWAYS COMING HOME   Ursula K. Le Guin oc
A Note and a Chart Concerning Narrative Modes   ms ALWCMHM,85
  ALWAYS COMING HOME   Ursula K. Le Guin oc
Old Woman Hating   ss ALWCMHM,85
  ALWAYS COMING HOME   Ursula K. Le Guin oc
Old Woman Sings   pm ALWCMHM,85
  ALWAYS COMING HOME   Ursula K. Le Guin oc
On Second Hill   pm ALWCMHM,85
  ALWAYS COMING HOME   Ursula K. Le Guin oc
Owl, Coyote, Soul   vi ALWCMHM,85
  ALWAYS COMING HOME   Ursula K. Le Guin oc
Pandora Converses with the Archivist of the Library of the
  Madrone Lodge at Wakwaha-na   ss ALWCMHM,85
  ALWAYS COMING HOME   Ursula K. Le Guin oc
Pandora Gently to the Gentle Reader   vi ALWCMHM,85
  ALWAYS COMING HOME   Ursula K. Le Guin oc
Pandora No Longer Worrying   ss ALWCMHM,85
  ALWAYS COMING HOME   Ursula K. Le Guin oc
Pandora Sitting by the Creek   vi ALWCMHM,85
  ALWAYS COMING HOME   Ursula K. Le Guin oc
Pandora Worries About What She Is Doing: The Pattern
                                                        vi ALWCMHM,85
  ALWAYS COMING HOME   Ursula K. Le Guin oc
Pandora Worrying About What She Is Doing: She Addresses the
  Reader with Agitation   vi ALWCMHM,85
  ALWAYS COMING HOME   Ursula K. Le Guin oc
Pandora, Worrying About What She Is Doing, Finds a Way into the
  Valley through the Scrub Oak   ss ALWCMHM,85
  ALWAYS COMING HOME   Ursula K. Le Guin oc
Person and Self   vi ALWCMHM,85
  ALWAYS COMING HOME   Ursula K. Le Guin oc
PLANET OF EXILE   n. ACE 1966
  FIVE COMPLETE NOVELS   Ursula K. Le Guin om
Playing   ms ALWCMHM,85
  ALWAYS COMING HOME   Ursula K. Le Guin oc
The Plumed Water   pl ALWCMHM,85
  ALWAYS COMING HOME   Ursula K. Le Guin oc
A Poem Said with the Drum   pm ALWCMHM,85
  ALWAYS COMING HOME   Ursula K. Le Guin oc
Praising the Oaks   vi ALWCMHM,85
  ALWAYS COMING HOME   Ursula K. Le Guin oc
The Priests of This Religion   pm ALWCMHM,85
  ALWAYS COMING HOME   Ursula K. Le Guin oc
Puma Dance   pm ALWCMHM,85
  ALWAYS COMING HOME   Ursula K. Le Guin oc
Quail Rising in Brush   pm ALWCMHM,85
  ALWAYS COMING HOME   Ursula K. Le Guin oc
The Quail Song   pm ALWCMHM,85
  ALWAYS COMING HOME   Ursula K. Le Guin oc
A Response   pm ALWCMHM,85
  ALWAYS COMING HOME   Ursula K. Le Guin oc
ROCANNON'S WORLD   n. ACE 1966
  FIVE COMPLETE NOVELS   Ursula K. Le Guin om
The Rule of Names   ss FAN Apr,64
  BESTIARY!   Jack Dann+ an
Semley's Necklace [The Dowry of Angyar]   ss AMZ Sep,64
  AMAZING STORIES: 60 YEARS OF THE BEST SCIENCE FICTION
                                         Isaac Asimov+ an
  ISAAC ASIMOV'S MAGICAL WORLDS OF FANTASY: WITCHES & WIZARDS
                                         Isaac Asimov+ om
The Serpentine Codex   ss ALWCMHM,85
  ALWAYS COMING HOME   Ursula K. Le Guin oc
Shahugoten   ss ALWCMHM,85
  ALWAYS COMING HOME   Ursula K. Le Guin oc
She Listens   vi ALWCMHM,85
  ALWAYS COMING HOME   Ursula K. Le Guin oc
A Shepherd's Song from Chumo   pm ALWCMHM,85
  ALWAYS COMING HOME   Ursula K. Le Guin oc
The Shouting Man, the Red Woman, and the Bears   pl ALWCMHM,85
  ALWAYS COMING HOME   Ursula K. Le Guin oc
Sinshan   pm ALWCMHM,85
  ALWAYS COMING HOME   Ursula K. Le Guin oc
Sinshan Creek   pm ALWCMHM,85
  ALWAYS COMING HOME   Ursula K. Le Guin oc
Some "Five/Four" Poems from Madidinou   pm ALWCMHM,85
  ALWAYS COMING HOME   Ursula K. Le Guin oc
Some Generative Metaphors   ms ALWCMHM,85
  ALWAYS COMING HOME   Ursula K. Le Guin oc
Some Notes on Medical Practices   ms ALWCMHM,85
  ALWAYS COMING HOME   Ursula K. Le Guin oc
Some of the Other People of the Valley   ms ALWCMHM,85
  ALWAYS COMING HOME   Ursula K. Le Guin oc

Le Guin, Ursula K. (continued)
Some Stories Told Aloud One Evening in the Dry Season at a
  Summer Place Above Sinshan   ss ALWCMHM,85
  ALWAYS COMING HOME   Ursula K. Le Guin oc
A Song to Up the Hill House in Sinshan   pm ALWCMHM,85
  ALWAYS COMING HOME   Ursula K. Le Guin oc
A Song Used in Chumo When Damming a Creek or Diverting Water to
  a Holding Tank for Irrigation   pm WER Jul,85
  ALWAYS COMING HOME   Ursula K. Le Guin oc
Spoken and Written Literature   ms ALWCMHM,85
  ALWAYS COMING HOME   Ursula K. Le Guin oc
Stammersong   pm ALWCMHM,85
  ALWAYS COMING HOME   Ursula K. Le Guin oc
Stone Telling, Part One   nv ALWCMHM,85
  ALWAYS COMING HOME   Ursula K. Le Guin oc
Stone Telling, Part Three   nv ALWCMHM,85
  ALWAYS COMING HOME   Ursula K. Le Guin oc
Stone Telling, Part Two   nv ALWCMHM,85
  ALWAYS COMING HOME   Ursula K. Le Guin oc
The Sun Dance   ms ALWCMHM,85
  ALWAYS COMING HOME   Ursula K. Le Guin oc
The Sun Going South   pm ALWCMHM,85
  ALWAYS COMING HOME   Ursula K. Le Guin oc
Tabetupah   pl ALWCMHM,85
  ALWAYS COMING HOME   Ursula K. Le Guin oc
Teaching Songs: Orders and Dances of the Earth and Sky
                                                           ALWCMHM,85
  ALWAYS COMING HOME   Ursula K. Le Guin oc
Teasing the Kitten   pm ALWCMHM,85
  ALWAYS COMING HOME   Ursula K. Le Guin oc
The Third Child's Story   pm ALWCMHM,85
  ALWAYS COMING HOME   Ursula K. Le Guin oc
This Stone   pm ALWCMHM,85
  ALWAYS COMING HOME   Ursula K. Le Guin oc
Three Poems by Pandora, Written Sideways from the Valley to the
  City of Man   pm ALWCMHM,85
  ALWAYS COMING HOME   Ursula K. Le Guin oc
Three Short Poems   pm ALWCMHM,85
  ALWAYS COMING HOME   Ursula K. Le Guin oc
Time in the Valley   ss HRW V37 #4,85
  ALWAYS COMING HOME   Ursula K. Le Guin oc
To Gahheya   pm ALWCMHM,85
  ALWAYS COMING HOME   Ursula K. Le Guin oc
To the Bullock Roseroot   pm ALWCMHM,85
  ALWAYS COMING HOME   Ursula K. Le Guin oc
To the People on the Hills   pm ALWCMHM,85
  ALWAYS COMING HOME   Ursula K. Le Guin oc
To the Valley Quail   pm ALWCMHM,85
  ALWAYS COMING HOME   Ursula K. Le Guin oc
Towards an Archeology of the Future   in ALWCMHM,85
  ALWAYS COMING HOME   Ursula K. Le Guin oc
The Town of Chumo   vi ALWCMHM,85
  ALWAYS COMING HOME   Ursula K. Le Guin oc
The Train   vi ALWCMHM,85
  ALWAYS COMING HOME   Ursula K. Le Guin oc
The Trampled Spring   pm ALWCMHM,85
  ALWAYS COMING HOME   Ursula K. Le Guin oc
A Treatise on Practices   ms ALWCMHM,85
  ALWAYS COMING HOME   Ursula K. Le Guin oc
The Trouble with the Cotton People   ss MIS V7 #2,84
  THE YEAR'S BEST SCIENCE FICTION, SECOND ANNUAL COLLECTION
                                         Gardner Dozois an
  ALWAYS COMING HOME   Ursula K. Le Guin oc
Under Kaibi   pm ALWCMHM,85
  ALWAYS COMING HOME   Ursula K. Le Guin oc
A Vaunting   pm ALWCMHM,85
  ALWAYS COMING HOME   Ursula K. Le Guin oc
The Visionary: The Life Story of Flicker of the Serpentine of
  Telina-na   nv OMN Oct,84
  ALWAYS COMING HOME   Ursula K. Le Guin oc
A War with the Pig People   ss ALWCMHM,85
  ALWAYS COMING HOME   Ursula K. Le Guin oc
The Wedding Night at Chukulmas   pl ALWCMHM,85
  ALWAYS COMING HOME   Ursula K. Le Guin oc
What They Ate   ms ALWCMHM,85
  ALWAYS COMING HOME   Ursula K. Le Guin oc
What They Wore in the Valley   ms ALWCMHM,85
  ALWAYS COMING HOME   Ursula K. Le Guin oc
Where It Is   ss ALWCMHM,85
  ALWAYS COMING HOME   Ursula K. Le Guin oc
White Tree   ss ALWCMHM,85
  ALWAYS COMING HOME   Ursula K. Le Guin oc
The Wife's Story   ss CMPSRSE,82
  TOP FANTASY   Josh Pachter an
THE WORD FOR WORLD IS FOREST   n. BRK 1976
  FIVE COMPLETE NOVELS   Ursula K. Le Guin om
Words/Birds   vi ALWCMHM,85
  ALWAYS COMING HOME   Ursula K. Le Guin oc
The World Dance   ms ALWCMHM,85
  ALWAYS COMING HOME   Ursula K. Le Guin oc
The Writer to the Morning in Up the Hill House in Sinshan
                                                        pm ALWCMHM,85
  ALWAYS COMING HOME   Ursula K. Le Guin oc
Written Kesh   ms ALWCMHM,85
  ALWAYS COMING HOME   Ursula K. Le Guin oc

Leach, Christopher
In a Ship Called Darkness   ss OUTOFTM,84
  OUT OF TIME   Aidan Chambers oa

Ledbetter, Kenneth W.
  Patera Crossing   ss ASF Mar,85
    Analog Science Fiction/Science Fact [v.105 # 3, March 1985]
                                     Stanley Schmidt mg
Lee, Rand B.
  On Springfield Mountain   nv AMZ Jan,85
    Amazing Science Fiction Stories [v.58 #5, January 1985]
                                     George H. Scithers mg
Lee, Tanith
  After the Guillotine   ss AMZ Jan,85
    Amazing Science Fiction Stories [v.58 #5, January 1985]
                                     George H. Scithers mg
  Anna Medea   ss AMZ Jan,83
    THE GORGON AND OTHER BEASTLY TALES   Tanith Lee co
  Because Our Skins Are Finer   ss TZM Nov,81
    THE GORGON AND OTHER BEASTLY TALES   Tanith Lee co
  Blood-Mantle   ss IAS Nov,85
    Isaac Asimov's Science Fiction Magazine [v. 9 #11, November
    1985]   Shawna McCarthy mg
  Blue Vase of Ghosts   ss DRF # 4,83
    TOP FANTASY   Josh Pachter an
  Chand Veda   ss IAS Oct,83
    ISAAC ASIMOV'S FANTASY   Shawna McCarthy an
  A Day in the Skin (or, The Century We Were Out of Them)
                                              ss HABITAT,84
    TERRY CARR'S BEST SCIENCE FICTION OF THE YEAR #14
                                     Terry Carr an
  Draco, Draco   nv BYNDLND,84
    BESTIARY!   Jack Dann+ an
    THE GORGON AND OTHER BEASTLY TALES   Tanith Lee co
    THE YEAR'S BEST FANTASY STORIES: 11   Arthur W. Saha an
  Foreign Skins   nv TAMASTR,84
    THE YEAR'S BEST SCIENCE FICTION, SECOND ANNUAL COLLECTION
                                     Gardner Dozois an
  The Gorgon   nv SDW # 5,82
    THE GORGON AND OTHER BEASTLY TALES   Tanith Lee co
  The Hunting of Death: The Unicorn   na
    THE GORGON AND OTHER BEASTLY TALES   Tanith Lee co
  La Reine Blanche   ss IAS Jul,83
    THE GORGON AND OTHER BEASTLY TALES   Tanith Lee co
  Love Alters   ss DSPTCHS,85
    DESPATCHES FROM THE FRONTIERS OF THE FEMALE MIND Jen Green+ oa
  Magritte's Secret Agent   nv TZM May,81
    THE GORGON AND OTHER BEASTLY TALES   Tanith Lee co
  Medra   ss IAS Jun,84
    THE 1985 ANNUAL WORLD'S BEST SF Donald A. Wollheim an
  Meow   ss SDW # 4,81
    THE GORGON AND OTHER BEASTLY TALES   Tanith Lee co
  Monkey's Stagger   ss SRCRAPR,79
    THE GORGON AND OTHER BEASTLY TALES   Tanith Lee co
  The Pale Girl, the Dark Mage, and the Green Sea ss MNSNGRF,85
    MOONSINGER'S FRIENDS   Susan M. Shwartz oa
  Pinewood   ss WHS Dec,84
    Whispers [v.6 #1-2, December 1984] Stuart David Schiff mg
  Quatt-Sup   ss
    THE GORGON AND OTHER BEASTLY TALES   Tanith Lee co
  Red as Blood   ss FSF Jul,79
    YOUNG MONSTERS   Isaac Asimov+ an
  Sirriamnis   nv UNSLNGT,81
    THE GORGON AND OTHER BEASTLY TALES   Tanith Lee co
  When the Clock Strikes   ss WTB # 1,81
    MASTERPIECES OF TERROR AND THE SUPERNATURAL   Marvin Kaye an

Lee, William M.
  A Message from Charity   ss FSF Nov,67
    ISAAC ASIMOV'S MAGICAL WORLDS OF FANTASY: WITCHES & WIZARDS
                                     Isaac Asimov+ om

Lefanu, Sarah & Jen Green
  Introduction   in
    DESPATCHES FROM THE FRONTIERS OF THE FEMALE MIND Jen Green+ oa

Leiber, Fritz
  Black Has Its Charms   ss WHS Dec,84
    Whispers [v.6 #1-2, December 1984] Stuart David Schiff mg
  Catch That Zeppelin!   ss FSF Mar,75
    THE HUGO WINNERS, VOLUME 4: 1976-1979   Isaac Asimov an
  Endfray of the Ofay   ss IFS Mar,69
    TOP SCIENCE FICTION   Josh Pachter an
  The Moon is Green   ss GAL May,52
    ISAAC ASIMOV PRESENTS THE GREAT SF STORIES: 14 (1952)
                                     Isaac Asimov+ an
  A Pail of Air   ss GAL Dec,51
    ISAAC ASIMOV PRESENTS THE GREAT SF STORIES: 13 (1951)
                                     Isaac Asimov+ an
  Scylla's Daughter   na FAN May,61
    BARBARIANS   Robert Adams+ an
  The Snow Woman   na FAN Apr,70
    ISAAC ASIMOV'S MAGICAL WORLDS OF FANTASY #4: SPELLS
                                     Isaac Asimov+ an
  Yesterday House   nv GAL Aug,52
    ISAAC ASIMOV PRESENTS THE GREAT SF STORIES: 14 (1952)
                                     Isaac Asimov+ an

Leigh, Stephen
  Flamestones   nv AFTRWAR,85
    AFTERWAR   Janet Morris oa
  Shaping Memory   nv IAS Sep,85
    Isaac Asimov's Science Fiction Magazine [v. 9 # 9, September
    1985]   Shawna McCarthy mg

Leinster, Murray
  Devil's Henchman [as Will F. Jenkins]   ss ARG May,52
    ISAAC ASIMOV'S MAGICAL WORLDS OF FANTASY: WITCHES & WIZARDS
                                     Isaac Asimov+ om
  The Mad Planet   na ARG Jun 12,20
    ISAAC ASIMOV'S MAGICAL WORLDS OF FANTASY #5: GIANTS
                                     Isaac Asimov+ an
  Sidewise in Time   na ASF Jun,34
    THE TIME TRAVELERS: A SCIENCE FICTION QUARTET
                                     Robert Silverberg+ an

Leman, Bob
  Instructions   ss FSF Sep,84
    TERRY CARR'S BEST SCIENCE FICTION OF THE YEAR #14
                                     Terry Carr an

Letson, Russell
  Introduction   in
    LIGHT FROM A LONE STAR   Jack Vance co

Level, Maurice
  Night and Silence   ss WRT Feb,32
    MASTERPIECES OF TERROR AND THE SUPERNATURAL   Marvin Kaye an

Levin, Ira
  ROSEMARY'S BABY   n. RDM 1967
    THREE BY IRA LEVIN: ROSEMARY'S BABY, THIS PERFECT DAY, THE
    STEPFORD WIVES   Ira Levin om
  THE STEPFORD WIVES   n. RDM 1972
    THREE BY IRA LEVIN: ROSEMARY'S BABY, THIS PERFECT DAY, THE
    STEPFORD WIVES   Ira Levin om
  THIS PERFECT DAY   n. RDM 1970
    THREE BY IRA LEVIN: ROSEMARY'S BABY, THIS PERFECT DAY, THE
    STEPFORD WIVES   Ira Levin om

Lewis, Anthony
  The Analog Calendar of Upcoming Events   ms ASF
    Analog Science Fiction/Science Fact [v.105 # 1, January 1985]
                                     Stanley Schmidt mg
    Analog Science Fiction/Science Fact [v.105 # 2, February
    1985]   Stanley Schmidt mg
    Analog Science Fiction/Science Fact [v.105 # 3, March 1985]
                                     Stanley Schmidt mg
    Analog Science Fiction/Science Fact [v.105 # 4, April 1985]
                                     Stanley Schmidt mg
    Analog Science Fiction/Science Fact [v.105 # 5, May 1985]
                                     Stanley Schmidt mg
    Analog Science Fiction/Science Fact [v.105 # 6, June 1985]
                                     Stanley Schmidt mg
    Analog Science Fiction/Science Fact [v.105 # 7, July 1985]
                                     Stanley Schmidt mg
    Analog Science Fiction/Science Fact [v.105 # 8, August 1985]
                                     Stanley Schmidt mg
    Analog Science Fiction/Science Fact [v.105 # 9, September
    1985]   Stanley Schmidt mg
    Analog Science Fiction/Science Fact [v.105 #10, October 1985]
                                     Stanley Schmidt mg
    Analog Science Fiction/Science Fact [v.105 #11, November
    1985]   Stanley Schmidt mg
    Analog Science Fiction/Science Fact [v.105 #12, December
    1985]   Stanley Schmidt mg
    Analog Science Fiction/Science Fact [v.105 #13, Mid-December
    1985]   Stanley Schmidt mg
    Analog Science Fiction/Science Fact [v.106 # 1, January 1986]
                                     Stanley Schmidt mg

Lewis, C.S.
  Boxen: or Scenes from Boxonian City Life   ss BOXEN ,85
    BOXEN: THE IMAGINARY WORLD OF THE YOUNG C.S. LEWIS
                                     C.S. Lewis co
  The Chess Monograph   ss BOXEN ,85
    BOXEN: THE IMAGINARY WORLD OF THE YOUNG C.S. LEWIS
                                     C.S. Lewis co
  Commentary   ms
    THE LAYS OF BELERIAND: THE HISTORY OF MIDDLE-EARTH, VOL. III
                                     J.R.R. Tolkien co
  Encyclopedia Boxoniana   ms BOXEN ,85
    BOXEN: THE IMAGINARY WORLD OF THE YOUNG C.S. LEWIS
                                     C.S. Lewis co
  The Geography of Animal-Land   vi BOXEN ,85
    BOXEN: THE IMAGINARY WORLD OF THE YOUNG C.S. LEWIS
                                     C.S. Lewis co
  History of Animal-Land   ss BOXEN ,85
    BOXEN: THE IMAGINARY WORLD OF THE YOUNG C.S. LEWIS
                                     C.S. Lewis co
  History of Mouse-Land from Stone-Age to Bublish I vi BOXEN ,85
    BOXEN: THE IMAGINARY WORLD OF THE YOUNG C.S. LEWIS
                                     C.S. Lewis co
  The King's Ring   pl BOXEN ,85
    BOXEN: THE IMAGINARY WORLD OF THE YOUNG C.S. LEWIS
                                     C.S. Lewis co
  The Locked Door   nv BOXEN ,85
    BOXEN: THE IMAGINARY WORLD OF THE YOUNG C.S. LEWIS
                                     C.S. Lewis co
  Manx Against Manx   vi BOXEN ,85
    BOXEN: THE IMAGINARY WORLD OF THE YOUNG C.S. LEWIS
                                     C.S. Lewis co
  The Relief of Murry   vi BOXEN ,85
    BOXEN: THE IMAGINARY WORLD OF THE YOUNG C.S. LEWIS
                                     C.S. Lewis co
  The Sailor   nv BOXEN ,85

Lewis, C.S. (continued)
    BOXEN: THE IMAGINARY WORLD OF THE YOUNG C.S. LEWIS
                                            C.S. Lewis co
    Than-Kyu   ss BOXEN ,85
    BOXEN: THE IMAGINARY WORLD OF THE YOUNG C.S. LEWIS
                                            C.S. Lewis co

Lewitt, Shariann
    The Shaman Flute   nv MGI # 2,85
    MAGIC IN ITHKAR 2   Andre Norton+ oa

Liebson, Morris
    The Fallen   pm WDB #20,85
    Weirdbook 20 [Spring 1985]   W. Paul Ganley mg

Ligon, Tom
    A Christmas Adversary   ss ASF Dec md,85
    Analog Science Fiction/Science Fact [v.105 #13, Mid-December
    1985]   Stanley Schmidt mg
    The Devil and the Deep Black Void   nv ASF Jan,86
    Analog Science Fiction/Science Fact [v.106 # 1, January 1986]
                                    Stanley Schmidt mg

Linaweaver, Brad
    Shadow Quest   nv MGI # 2,85
    MAGIC IN ITHKAR 2   Andre Norton+ oa

Lindholm, Megan
    A Coincidence of Birth   nv LIAVEK ,85
    LIAVEK   Will Shetterly+ oa
    Wizard of the Pigeons   ex ACE Jan,86
    THE FANTASY SAMPLER   Susan Allison an

Linzner, Gordon
    Desperate Acts   ss DGM Mar,85
    Editor's Page   ed S&T #69,85
    Space and Time [#69, Winter 1986] Gordon Linzner mg
    The Magistrate's Pillow   ss TZM Apr,85
    Rod Serling's The Twilight Zone Magazine [v.5 #1, March/April
    1985]   T.E.D. Klein mg

Lively, Penelope
    The Disastrous Dog   ss UNVTGST,84
    UNINVITED GHOSTS   Penelope Lively co
    The Dragon Tunnel   ss ALT # 6,74
    UNINVITED GHOSTS   Penelope Lively co
    A Flock of Gryphons   ss UNVTGST,84
    UNINVITED GHOSTS   Penelope Lively co
    The Great Mushroom Mistake   ss UNVTGST,84
    UNINVITED GHOSTS   Penelope Lively co
    A Martian Comes to Stay   ss UNVTGST,84
    UNINVITED GHOSTS   Penelope Lively co
    Princess by Mistake   ss JBLJKNY,77
    UNINVITED GHOSTS   Penelope Lively co
    Time Trouble   ss UNVTGST,84
    UNINVITED GHOSTS   Penelope Lively co
    Uninvited Ghosts   ss BIGDIPR,81
    UNINVITED GHOSTS   Penelope Lively co

Llewellyn, Edward
    The Lords of Creation   ss ASF Mar,85
    Analog Science Fiction/Science Fact [v.105 # 3, March 1985]
                                    Stanley Schmidt mg

Llywelyn, Morgan
    Fletcher Found   ss MGI # 1,85
    MAGIC IN ITHKAR   Andre Norton+ oa

Lofficier, Jean-Marc & Randy Lofficier
    David Lynch: From Art School to Arrakis   iv TZM Feb,85
    Rod Serling's The Twilight Zone Magazine [v.4 #6,
    January/February 1985]   T.E.D. Klein mg

Lofficier, Randy & Jean-Marc Lofficier
    David Lynch: From Art School to Arrakis   iv TZM Feb,85
    Rod Serling's The Twilight Zone Magazine [v.4 #6,
    January/February 1985]   T.E.D. Klein mg

Lombardy, Dana
    Gaming   gr IAS
    Isaac Asimov's Science Fiction Magazine [v. 9 # 1, January
    1985]   Shawna McCarthy mg
    Isaac Asimov's Science Fiction Magazine [v. 9 # 2, February
    1985]   Shawna McCarthy mg
    Isaac Asimov's Science Fiction Magazine [v. 9 # 3, March
    1985]   Shawna McCarthy mg
    Isaac Asimov's Science Fiction Magazine [v. 9 # 4, April
    1985]   Shawna McCarthy mg
    Isaac Asimov's Science Fiction Magazine [v. 9 # 5, May 1985]
                                   Shawna McCarthy mg
    Isaac Asimov's Science Fiction Magazine [v. 9 # 6, June 1985]
                                   Shawna McCarthy mg
    Isaac Asimov's Science Fiction Magazine [v. 9 # 7, July 1985]
                                   Shawna McCarthy mg
    Isaac Asimov's Science Fiction Magazine [v. 9 # 8, August
    1985]   Shawna McCarthy mg
    Isaac Asimov's Science Fiction Magazine [v. 9 # 9, September
    1985]   Shawna McCarthy mg
    Isaac Asimov's Science Fiction Magazine [v. 9 #10, October
    1985]   Shawna McCarthy mg
    Isaac Asimov's Science Fiction Magazine [v. 9 #11, November
    1985]   Shawna McCarthy mg

Lombardy, Dana (continued)
    Isaac Asimov's Science Fiction Magazine [v. 9 #12, December
    1985]   Shawna McCarthy mg
    Isaac Asimov's Science Fiction Magazine [v. 9 #13,
    Mid-December 1985]   Shawna McCarthy mg
    Isaac Asimov's Science Fiction Magazine [v.10 # 1, January
    1986]   Gardner Dozois mg
    On Gaming   gr ASF
    Analog Science Fiction/Science Fact [v.105 # 1, January 1985]
                                    Stanley Schmidt mg
    Analog Science Fiction/Science Fact [v.105 # 2, February
    1985]   Stanley Schmidt mg
    Analog Science Fiction/Science Fact [v.105 # 3, March 1985]
                                    Stanley Schmidt mg
    Analog Science Fiction/Science Fact [v.105 # 4, April 1985]
                                    Stanley Schmidt mg
    Analog Science Fiction/Science Fact [v.105 # 5, May 1985]
                                    Stanley Schmidt mg
    Analog Science Fiction/Science Fact [v.105 # 6, June 1985]
                                    Stanley Schmidt mg
    Analog Science Fiction/Science Fact [v.105 # 7, July 1985]
                                    Stanley Schmidt mg
    Analog Science Fiction/Science Fact [v.105 # 8, August 1985]
                                    Stanley Schmidt mg
    Analog Science Fiction/Science Fact [v.105 # 9, September
    1985]   Stanley Schmidt mg
    Analog Science Fiction/Science Fact [v.105 #10, October 1985]
                                    Stanley Schmidt mg
    Analog Science Fiction/Science Fact [v.105 #11, November
    1985]   Stanley Schmidt mg
    Analog Science Fiction/Science Fact [v.105 #12, December
    1985]   Stanley Schmidt mg
    Analog Science Fiction/Science Fact [v.105 #13, Mid-December
    1985]   Stanley Schmidt mg
    Analog Science Fiction/Science Fact [v.106 # 1, January 1986]
                                    Stanley Schmidt mg

London, Jack
    Make Westing   ss
    MYSTERIOUS SEA STORIES   William Pattrick an
    Moon-Face   ss
    MASTERPIECES OF TERROR AND THE SUPERNATURAL   Marvin Kaye an

Longyear, Barry B.
    Adagio   nv ITCAMEF,84
    IT CAME FROM SCHENECTADY   Barry B. Longyear co
    Catch the Sun   na IAS Nov,80
    IT CAME FROM SCHENECTADY   Barry B. Longyear co
    Collector's Item   ss ASF Apr,81
    IT CAME FROM SCHENECTADY   Barry B. Longyear co
    Dreams   nv IAS Aug,79
    IT CAME FROM SCHENECTADY   Barry B. Longyear co
    Enemy Mine   na IAS Sep,79
    BAKER'S DOZEN: 13 SHORT SCIENCE FICTION NOVELS
                                    Isaac Asimov+ an
    Forepiece   fw
    IT CAME FROM SCHENECTADY   Barry B. Longyear co
    The Fortune Maker   na LIAVEK ,85
    LIAVEK   Will Shetterly+ oa
    The Homecoming   nv IAS Oct,79
    IT CAME FROM SCHENECTADY   Barry B. Longyear co
    The House of If   nv IAS Apr,81
    IT CAME FROM SCHENECTADY   Barry B. Longyear co
    The Initiation [as Mark Ringdahl]   ss IAS Jul,79
    IT CAME FROM SCHENECTADY   Barry B. Longyear co
    The Portrait of Baron Negay   nv IAS Jun,81
    IT CAME FROM SCHENECTADY   Barry B. Longyear co
    Priest of the Baraboo   nv IAS Jul,79
    MERCENARIES OF TOMORROW   Poul Anderson+ an
    SHAWNA, Ltd. [as Frederick Longbeard] ss IAS Sep,79
    IT CAME FROM SCHENECTADY   Barry B. Longyear co
    A Time for Terror [as Frederick Longbeard]   nv IAS Mar,79
    IT CAME FROM SCHENECTADY   Barry B. Longyear co
    Twist Ending   ss IAS Nov,79
    IT CAME FROM SCHENECTADY   Barry B. Longyear co
    Where Do You Get Your Ideas? [as Mark Ringdahl]   vi IAA Fll,79
    IT CAME FROM SCHENECTADY   Barry B. Longyear co

Longyear, Barry B., S.A. Cochran, Jr. & Warren M. Salomon
    A Case of Immunity   ss AMZ Nov,85
    Amazing Science Fiction Stories [v.60 #1, November 1985]
                                    George H. Scithers mg

Lovecraft, H.P.
    The Music of Erich Zann   ss NTA Mar,22
                                            WRT May,25
    MASTERPIECES OF TERROR AND THE SUPERNATURAL   Marvin Kaye an

Lowe, Nick
    Film Reviews   mr INZ #13,85
    Interzone [#13, Autumn 1985]   Simon Ounsley+ mg
    Mutant Popcorn   mr INZ #14,85
    Interzone [#14, Winter 1985/86] Simon Ounsley+ mg

Lowenbruck, Oliver
    Lonesome Coyote Blues   ss TZM Feb,85
    Rod Serling's The Twilight Zone Magazine [v.4 #6,
    January/February 1985]   T.E.D. Klein mg

Lumley, Brian
    Cryptically Yours   ss ESP 1977

LUMLEY, BRIAN

MARTIN, GEORGE R.R.

Lumley, Brian (continued)
                                        SWD # 4,79
    THE HOUSE OF CTHULHU AND OTHER TALES OF THE PRIMAL LAND
                                        Brian Lumley co
  Curse of the Golden Guardians   ss HSCTHLU,84
    THE HOUSE OF CTHULHU AND OTHER TALES OF THE PRIMAL LAND
                                        Brian Lumley co
  The House of Cthulhu   ss WHS V1 #1,73
    THE HOUSE OF CTHULHU AND OTHER TALES OF THE PRIMAL LAND
                                        Brian Lumley co
    TOP FANTASY   Josh Pachter an
  How Kank Thad Returned to Bhur-Esh   nv FAN Jun,77
    THE HOUSE OF CTHULHU AND OTHER TALES OF THE PRIMAL LAND
                                        Brian Lumley co
  Introduction   in 1984
    THE HOUSE OF CTHULHU AND OTHER TALES OF THE PRIMAL LAND
                                        Brian Lumley co
  Isles of the Suhm-Yi   ss HSCTHLU,84
    THE HOUSE OF CTHULHU AND OTHER TALES OF THE PRIMAL LAND
                                        Brian Lumley co
  Kiss of the Lamia   nv WDB #20,85
    Weirdbook 20 [Spring 1985]   W. Paul Ganley mg
  Lords of the Morass   ss HSCTHLU,84
    THE HOUSE OF CTHULHU AND OTHER TALES OF THE PRIMAL LAND
                                        Brian Lumley co
  Mylakhrion the Immortal   ss FTL Sum,77
    THE HOUSE OF CTHULHU AND OTHER TALES OF THE PRIMAL LAND
                                        Brian Lumley co
  Snarker's Son   ss NTLSTRR,80
    Eldritch Tales No. 11 [v.3 #2]   Crispin Burnham mg
  The Sorcerer's Book   ss HSCTHLU,84
    THE HOUSE OF CTHULHU AND OTHER TALES OF THE PRIMAL LAND
                                        Brian Lumley co
  The Sorcerer's Dream   ss WHS V1 #1,79
    THE HOUSE OF CTHULHU AND OTHER TALES OF THE PRIMAL LAND
                                        Brian Lumley co
  Tharquest and the Lamia Orbiquita   nv FAN Nov,76
    THE HOUSE OF CTHULHU AND OTHER TALES OF THE PRIMAL LAND
                                        Brian Lumley co
  The Wine of the Wizard   ss HSCTHLU,84
    THE HOUSE OF CTHULHU AND OTHER TALES OF THE PRIMAL LAND
                                        Brian Lumley co

Lummis, Suzanne
  How It All Began   pm IDIOSYN,84
    THE 1985 RHYSLING ANTHOLOGY   Anonymous an

Lunan, Duncan
  Project Starseed, or, Nuclear Waste Saves the World
                                        ar ASF Feb,85
    Analog Science Fiction/Science Fact [v.105 # 2, February
    1985]   Stanley Schmidt mg

Lunde, David
  The Still Point   pm IAS Apr,84
    THE 1985 RHYSLING ANTHOLOGY   Anonymous an

Lupoff, Richard A.
  Three Centaur Tales   ss FBM Dec,85
    Fantasy Book [v.4 #4, December 1985] Dennis Mallonee+ mg

Lutz, John
  The Real Shape of the Coast   ss EQM Jun,71
    TOP FANTASY   Josh Pachter an

Lynn, Elizabeth A.
  At the Embassy Club   ss OMN Jun,84
    THE YEAR'S BEST SCIENCE FICTION, SECOND ANNUAL COLLECTION
                                        Gardner Dozois an

Lyon, Pete
  Rain, Tunnel and Bombfire   il INZ #11,85
    Interzone [#11, Spring 1985]   Colin Greenland+ mg

MacAvoy, R.A.
  The Book of Kells   ex BAN Aug,85
    THE BANTAM SPECTRA SAMPLER   Lou Aronica an
  DAMIANO   n. BAN 1983
    A TRIO FOR LUTE   R.A. MacAvoy om
  DAMIANO's LUTE   n. BAN 1984
    A TRIO FOR LUTE   R.A. MacAvoy om
  RAPHAEL   n. BAN 1984
    A TRIO FOR LUTE   R.A. MacAvoy om

MacDonald, John D.
  Game for Blondes   ss GAL Oct,52
    ISAAC ASIMOV PRESENTS THE GREAT SF STORIES: 14 (1952)
                                        Isaac Asimov+ an

MacIntyre, F. Gwynplaine
  Improbable Bestiary-- The Empath   pm AMZ Nov,85
    Amazing Science Fiction Stories [v.60 #1, November 1985]
                                        George H. Scithers mg
  Improbable Bestiary-- The Faun   pm AMZ Mar,85
    Amazing Science Fiction Stories [v.58 #6, March 1985]
                                        George H. Scithers mg
  Improbable Bestiary-- The Little Green Men pm AMZ Nov,85
    Amazing Science Fiction Stories [v.60 #1, November 1985]
                                        George H. Scithers mg
  Improbable Bestiary-- The Ogre   pm AMZ Mar,85
    Amazing Science Fiction Stories [v.58 #6, March 1985]
                                        George H. Scithers mg

MacIntyre, F. Gwynplaine (continued)
  The Long-Lost First Draft of Edgar Allan Poe's "The Raven"
                                        pm AMZ Jan,86
    Amazing Science Fiction Stories [v.60 #2, January 1986]
                                        George H. Scithers mg

Mackay, M. Sargent
  Demon Lover   nv FSF Jun,84
    THE SCIENCE FICTION YEARBOOK   Jerry E. Pournelle+ an

MacKenzie, Jonathan Blake
  Thin Edge   ss ASF Dec,63
    ANALOG: THE BEST OF SCIENCE FICTION Anonymous an

Maclay, John
  The Unforgiven   pm WDB #20,85
    Weirdbook 20 [Spring 1985]   W. Paul Ganley mg

MacLean, Katherine
  Incommunicado   nv ASF Jun,50
    ANALOG: THE BEST OF SCIENCE FICTION Anonymous an
  The Missing Man   nv ASF Mar,71
    TERRORISTS OF TOMORROW   Poul Anderson+ an
  Pictures Don't Lie   ss GAL Aug,51
    ISAAC ASIMOV PRESENTS THE GREAT SF STORIES: 13 (1951)
                                        Isaac Asimov+ an
  The Snowball Effect   ss GAL Sep,52
    ISAAC ASIMOV PRESENTS THE GREAT SF STORIES: 14 (1952)
                                        Isaac Asimov+ an

MacLennan, Phyllis
  Good-by, Miss Paterson   ss FSF Jan,72
    YOUNG MONSTERS   Isaac Asimov+ an

Maddern, Philippa C.
  Confusion Day   ss URBANFN,85
    URBAN FANTASIES   David King+ oa

Maddox, Tom
  The Mind Like a Strange Balloon   ss OMN Jun,85

Major, A.R.
  Kissmeowt and the Healing Friar   ss MGI # 2,85
    MAGIC IN ITHKAR 2   Andre Norton+ oa

Mallonee, Dennis
  Editorial   ed FBM Sep,85
    Fantasy Book [v.4 #3, September 1985] Dennis Mallonee+ mg

Malzberg, Barry N.
  1984   vi FSF Feb,85
    The Magazine of Fantasy & Science Fiction [v.68 #2, February
    1985]   Edward L. Ferman mg
  A Galaxy Called Rome   nv FSF Jul,75
    TOP SCIENCE FICTION   Josh Pachter an
  Johann Sebastian Brahms   ss UNI #15,85
    UNIVERSE 15   Terry Carr oa
  Quartermain   ss IAS Jan,85
    Isaac Asimov's Science Fiction Magazine [v. 9 # 1, January
    1985]   Shawna McCarthy mg
  Reason Seven   ss OMN May,85
  Sigmund in Space   ss OMN Jul,80
    THE FOURTH OMNI BOOK OF SCIENCE FICTION Ellen Datlow an
  Spree   ss IAM # 2,84
    ISAAC ASIMOV'S MAGICAL WORLDS OF FANTASY: WITCHES & WIZARDS
                                        Isaac Asimov+ om

Malzberg, Barry N. & Carter Scholz
  The High Purpose   ss FSF Nov,85
    The Magazine of Fantasy & Science Fiction [v.69 #5, November
    1985]   Edward L. Ferman mg

Manners, Margaret
  Squeakie's First Case   nv EQM May,43
    ISAAC ASIMOV'S MAGICAL WORLDS OF FANTASY: WITCHES & WIZARDS
                                        Isaac Asimov+ om

Mark, Jan
  Captain Courage and the Rose Street Gang nv OUTOFTM,84
    OUT OF TIME   Aidan Chambers oa

Markstein, Donald D.
  The Crow's Nest   ms WRLDTLS,85
    WORLD TALES   G. Randal Rau oa
  Production Notes   ms WRLDTLS,85
    WORLD TALES   G. Randal Rau oa

Marryot, Captain Frederick
  The Legend of the Bell Rock   ss
    MYSTERIOUS SEA STORIES   William Pattrick an

Marti-Ibanez, Felix
  The Seekers of Dreams   ss ALLWNDR,63
    FAERY!   Terri Windling oa

Martin, George R.R.
  And Seven Times Never Kill Man   nv ASF Jul,75
    NIGHTFLYERS   George R.R. Martin co
  The Closing Time   ss IAS Nov,82
    ISAAC ASIMOV'S FANTASY   Shawna McCarthy an
  ...for a single yesterday   nv EPOCH ,75
    SONGS THE DEAD MEN SING   George R.R. Martin co

McCammon, Robert R.
  The Red House   nv GRYSTBY,85
    GREYSTONE BAY
                                        Charles L. Grant   oa

McCarthy, Shawna
  Up Front   ms IAS Dec md,85
    Isaac Asimov's Science Fiction Magazine [v. 9 #13,
      Mid-December 1985]
                                        Shawna McCarthy   mg

McConnell, James V.
  Learning Theory   ss IFS Dec,57
    GREAT SCIENCE FICTION BY THE WORLD'S GREAT SCIENTISTS
                                        Isaac Asimov+   an

McCormack, Ken
  Airmail   vi TZM Apr,85
    Rod Serling's The Twilight Zone Magazine [v.5 #1, March/April
      1985]
                                        T.E.D. Klein   mg

McDevitt, Jack
  Promises to Keep   ss IAS Dec,84
    THE YEAR'S BEST SCIENCE FICTION, SECOND ANNUAL COLLECTION
                                        Gardner Dozois   an
  Tidal Effects   ss UNI #15,85
    UNIVERSE 15
                                        Terry Carr   oa

McDonald, Ian
  Empire Dreams   nv IAS Dec,85
    Isaac Asimov's Science Fiction Magazine [v. 9 #12, December
      1985]
                                        Shawna McCarthy   mg
  Scenes from a Shadow Play   ss IAS Jul,85
    Isaac Asimov's Science Fiction Magazine [v. 9 # 7, July 1985]
                                        Shawna McCarthy   mg

McDowell, Ian
  Son of the Morning   ss IAS Dec,83
    ISAAC ASIMOV'S FANTASY
                                        Shawna McCarthy   an

McElroy, Wendy
  Lover as Vampire   pm AMZ Jan,85
    Amazing Science Fiction Stories [v.58 #5, January 1985]
                                        George H. Scithers   mg

McHardy, Vincent
  Angst for the Memories   ss DAMNTNS,84
    THE YEAR'S BEST HORROR STORIES: SERIES XIII
                                        Karl Edward Wagner   an
  Fright Night   ss NCR V1 #3,85
    Night Cry [v.1 #3, Fall 1985]
                                        T.E.D. Klein   mg

McHarris, William C.
  Handedness in Nature   ar ASF Jan,86
    Analog Science Fiction/Science Fact [v.106 # 1, January 1986]
                                        Stanley Schmidt   mg

McKillip, Patricia A.
  Introduction   in WFC 1984
    DRAGONFIELD AND OTHER STORIES
                                        Jane Yolen   co
  The Old Woman and the Storm   ss IMGNLND,85
    IMAGINARY LANDS
                                        Robin McKinley   oa
  A Troll and Two Roses   ss FAERY! ,85
    FAERY!
                                        Terri Windling   oa

McKinley, Robin
  The Stone Fey   nv IMGNLND,85
    IMAGINARY LANDS
                                        Robin McKinley   oa
  Touk's House   nv FAERY! ,85
    FAERY!
                                        Terri Windling   oa

McLaughlin, Cooper
  The Black and Tan Man   nv FSF Nov,85
    The Magazine of Fantasy & Science Fiction [v.69 #5, November
      1985]
                                        Edward L. Ferman   mg
  The Shanahy's Treasure   ss S&T #69,85
    Space and Time [#69, Winter 1986]
                                        Gordon Linzner   mg
  The Shannon Merrow   ss FSF Nov,82
    MERMAIDS!
                                        Jack Dann+   an

McLaughlin, Dean
  The Permanent Implosion   nv ASF Feb,64
    ANALOG: THE BEST OF SCIENCE FICTION
                                        Anonymous   an

McNamara, Michael M.
  The Boy Who Dreamed of Tir na n-Og   ss FSF Dec,79
    FAERY!
                                        Terri Windling   oa

McNeill, Pearlie
  The Awakening   ss DSPTCHS,85
    DESPATCHES FROM THE FRONTIERS OF THE FEMALE MIND Jen Green+ oa

McQuarrie, Ralph
  Illustration   il PLANETS,85
    THE PLANETS
                                        Byron Preiss   oa

Meador, Roger
  Harmony of the Spheres at Spion Kop   pm IAS Jan,86
    Isaac Asimov's Science Fiction Magazine [v.10 # 1, January
      1986]
                                        Gardner Dozois   mg

Medcalf, Robert Randolf, Jr.
  The Spectracycle Cop   pm EDT #11,85
    Eldritch Tales No. 11 [v.3 #2]
                                        Crispin Burnham   mg

Melton, Henry
  Catacomb   ss D&M Feb,85
  Parking Spaces   ss ASF Sep,85
    Analog Science Fiction/Science Fact [v.105 # 9, September
      1985]
                                        Stanley Schmidt   mg

Melville, Herman
  Hoods Isle and the Hermit Oberlus   ss
    MYSTERIOUS SEA STORIES
                                        William Pattrick   an

Merril, Judith
  Afterword: We Have Met the Alien (And It Is Us)   aw
    TESSERACTS   Judith Merril   oa
  Foreword   fw
    TESSERACTS   Judith Merril   oa

Merrill, Lew
  The Robot Awakes   ss SYA Oct,40
    SENSUOUS SCIENCE FICTION FROM THE WEIRD AND SPICY PULPS
                                        Sheldon R. Jaffery   an

Merritt, A.
  A. Merritt's Own Selected Credoes   ar
    A. MERRITT: REFLECTIONS IN THE MOON POOL Sam Moskowitz   nf
  The Autobiography of A. Merritt   bg
    Edited by Walter Wentz
    A. MERRITT: REFLECTIONS IN THE MOON POOL Sam Moskowitz   nf
  Background of Burn, Witch, Burn!   ar
    A. MERRITT: REFLECTIONS IN THE MOON POOL Sam Moskowitz   nf
  Background of Creep, Shadow!   ar
    A. MERRITT: REFLECTIONS IN THE MOON POOL Sam Moskowitz   nf
  Background of Dwellers in the Mirage   ar
    A. MERRITT: REFLECTIONS IN THE MOON POOL Sam Moskowitz   nf
  Bootleg and Witches. A Fragment   ms
    A. MERRITT: REFLECTIONS IN THE MOON POOL Sam Moskowitz   nf
  The Challenge from Beyond [Part 2]   vi FMG Sep,35
    A. MERRITT: REFLECTIONS IN THE MOON POOL Sam Moskowitz   nf
  The Devil in the Heart. An Outline   ms
    A. MERRITT: REFLECTIONS IN THE MOON POOL Sam Moskowitz   nf
  Letters and Correspondence   ms
    A. MERRITT: REFLECTIONS IN THE MOON POOL Sam Moskowitz   nf
  Man and the Universe   ar
    A. MERRITT: REFLECTIONS IN THE MOON POOL Sam Moskowitz   nf
  Pilgrimage, or, Obi Giese   ss
    A. MERRITT: REFLECTIONS IN THE MOON POOL Sam Moskowitz   nf
  The Poems of A. Merritt   pm
    A. MERRITT: REFLECTIONS IN THE MOON POOL Sam Moskowitz   nf
  The Pool of the Stone God   ss AWK Sep 23,23
    MASTERPIECES OF TERROR AND THE SUPERNATURAL Marvin Kaye   an
    A. MERRITT: REFLECTIONS IN THE MOON POOL Sam Moskowitz   nf
  An Unpublished Ending for Dwellers in the Mirage   ms
    A. MERRITT: REFLECTIONS IN THE MOON POOL Sam Moskowitz   nf
  What Is Fantasy?   ar
    A. MERRITT: REFLECTIONS IN THE MOON POOL Sam Moskowitz   nf

Merritt, A. & Jack Chapman Miske
  A. Merritt--His Life and Times   bg
    A. MERRITT: REFLECTIONS IN THE MOON POOL Sam Moskowitz   nf

Meserole, Lynette & Robert Chilson
  The White Box   nv ASF Dec,85
    Analog Science Fiction/Science Fact [v.105 #12, December
      1985]
                                        Stanley Schmidt   mg

Meyer, Frank
  The Promise   vi NCR V1 #5,86
    Night Cry [v.1 #5, Spring 1986]
                                        Alan Rodgers   mg

Michaels, Melisa
  I am Large, I Contain Multitudes   ss BOM # 4,82
    THE FOURTH OMNI BOOK OF SCIENCE FICTION Ellen Datlow   an

Middleton, Richard
  On the Brighton Road   ss GHSTSHP,12
    YOUNG GHOSTS
                                        Isaac Asimov+   an

Miesel, Sandra
  A Conversation With Gordon R. Dickson   iv AGL Spr,78
    STEEL BROTHER
                                        Gordon R. Dickson   co
  Editor's Introduction   in
    FORWARD!
                                        Gordon R. Dickson   co
  Introduction   in
    INVADERS!
                                        Gordon R. Dickson   co
  The Shadow Hart   ss MNSNGRF,85
    MOONSINGER'S FRIENDS
                                        Susan M. Shwartz   oa

Miles, David & Dale L. Kemper
  Jaynz Ships of the Galaxy--Wizard Class Ships gr SDA Oct,85
    Stardate [v.1 # 8, October 1985]
                                        Ted White+   mg
  Jaynz Ships of the Galaxy: Aral (OSB-0762) Orion Blockade Runner
                                                 gr SDA Dec,85
    Stardate [v.1 # 9, December 1985]
                                        Ted White+   mg
  Jaynz Ships of the Galaxy: Ticonderoga-class Light Cruiser
                                                 gr SDA Dec,85
    Stardate [v.1 # 9, December 1985]
                                        Ted White+   mg

Milhaus, Michael F.X.
  In a Pig's Eye   nv FAN May,76
    A PERSONAL DEMON
                                        David F. Bischoff+   no
  A Personal Demon   nv FAN Feb,76
    A PERSONAL DEMON
                                        David F. Bischoff+   no

MUELLER, RICHARD

Mueller, Richard (continued)
The Dark at the End of the Tunnel   nv FBM Sep,85
    Fantasy Book [v.4 #3, September 1985] Dennis Mallonee+ mg
The Day We Really Lost the War   ss IAS Sep,85
    Isaac Asimov's Science Fiction Magazine [v. 9 # 9, September
    1985]   Shawna McCarthy mg
Little Friends   ss FSF Sep,85
    The Magazine of Fantasy & Science Fiction [v.69 #3, September
    1985]   Edward L. Ferman mg
The Nifty Murder Case   ss FSF May,85
    The Magazine of Fantasy & Science Fiction [v.68 #5, May 1985]
                                            Edward L. Ferman mg

Munro, H.H.
The Easter Egg   ss
    MASTERPIECES OF TERROR AND THE SUPERNATURAL   Marvin Kaye an

Munster, William D.
Movie Teaser Quiz   pz TZM Feb,85
    Rod Serling's The Twilight Zone Magazine [v.4 #6,
    January/February 1985]   T.E.D. Klein mg

Murnane, Gerald
The Battle of Acosta Nu   na HLX
    LANDSCAPE WITH LANDSCAPE   Gerald Murnane oc
Charlie Alcock's Cock   nv LANDSCP,85
    LANDSCAPE WITH LANDSCAPE   Gerald Murnane oc
Landscape with Artist   na LANDSCP,85
    LANDSCAPE WITH LANDSCAPE   Gerald Murnane oc
Landscape with Freckled Woman   nv LANDSCP,85
    LANDSCAPE WITH LANDSCAPE   Gerald Murnane oc
Precious Bane   ss STRGATR,85
    STRANGE ATTRACTORS   Damien Broderick oa
A Quieter Place than Clun   nv LANDSCP,85
    LANDSCAPE WITH LANDSCAPE   Gerald Murnane oc
Sipping the Essence   nv LANDSCP,85
    LANDSCAPE WITH LANDSCAPE   Gerald Murnane oc

Murphy, Pat
In the Islands   ss AMZ Mar,83
    AMAZING STORIES: 60 YEARS OF THE BEST SCIENCE FICTION
                                            Isaac Asimov+ an
    MERMAIDS!   Jack Dann+ an
On a Hot Summer Night in a Place Far Away   ss IAS May,85
    Isaac Asimov's Science Fiction Magazine [v. 9 # 5, May 1985]
                                            Shawna McCarthy mg
Sweetly the Waves Call to Me   ss ELW # 1,81
    MERMAIDS!   Jack Dann+ an

Murray, Will
Snail Ghost   ss EDT #11,85
    Eldritch Tales No. 11 [v.3 #2]   Crispin Burnham mg
The Vigilante Era   ar
    THE NIGHT NEMESIS: THE COMPLETE ADVENTURES OF THE MOON
    MAN--VOL. ONE   Frederick C. Davis co

Musgrave, Muff & Real Musgrave
Stephen R. Donaldson: An Appreciation   bg WRLDTLS,85
    WORLD TALES   G. Randal Rau oa

Musgrave, Real & Muff Musgrave
Stephen R. Donaldson: An Appreciation   bg WRLDTLS,85
    WORLD TALES   G. Randal Rau oa

Naegele, Amyas
The Rise and Fall of Father Alex   ss FSF Jan,86
    The Magazine of Fantasy & Science Fiction [v.70 #1, January
    1986]   Edward L. Ferman mg

Naha, Ed
Nahallywood: Coming Attractions   mr SDA
    Stardate [v.1 # 8, October 1985]   Ted White+ mg
    Stardate [v.1 # 9, December 1985]   Ted White+ mg
Nahallywood: Invasion of the Teenagers from Mars   ar SDA Dec,85
    Stardate [v.1 # 9, December 1985]   Ted White+ mg
Nahallywood: 'George Romero and the Day of the Dead'
                                                        mr SDA Oct,85
    Stardate [v.1 # 8, October 1985]   Ted White+ mg

Nahin, Paul J.
The Invitation   ss OBK # 4,85
    THE FOURTH OMNI BOOK OF SCIENCE FICTION Ellen Datlow an
The Man in the Gray Weapons Suit   ss FWR V 1,79
    THERE WILL BE WAR, VOL. IV: DAY OF THE TYRANT
                                            Jerry E. Pournelle an
Publish and Perish   ss ASF Apr,78
    GREAT SCIENCE FICTION BY THE WORLD'S GREAT SCIENTISTS
                                            Isaac Asimov+ an

Nash, Ogden
A Tale of the Thirteenth Floor   pm FSF Jul,55
    MASTERPIECES OF TERROR AND THE SUPERNATURAL   Marvin Kaye an

Naylor, Chris
The Castle at World's End   ss FTL Sum,85
    Fantasy Tales [v.7 #14, Summer 1985]   Stephen Jones mg

Nazarian, Vera
Wound on the Moon   nv S&S # 2,85
    SWORD AND SORCERESS II   Marion Zimmer Bradley oa

Neal, Jim
Incantation   pm FBM Dec,85
    Fantasy Book [v.4 #4, December 1985]   Dennis Mallonee+ mg

Nelson, Harry
Cartoons   ct FBM Mar,85
    Fantasy Book [v.4 #1, March 1985]   Dennis Mallonee+ mg

Nelson, M.L.
Eurydice Back in Hades   pm IAS Jul,85
    Isaac Asimov's Science Fiction Magazine [v. 9 # 7, July 1985]
                                            Shawna McCarthy mg

Newman, Kim
Dreamers   ss INZ # 8,84
    INTERZONE: THE 1ST ANTHOLOGY   John Clute+ an
Film Notes   mr FYC #10,85
    Fantasycon X Programme Booklet   Stephen Jones+ oa
Patricia's Profession   ss INZ #14,85
    Interzone [#14, Winter 1985/86]   Simon Oursley+ mg

Nicholas, Joseph & Judith Hanna
William Gibson   iv INZ #13,85
    Interzone [#13, Autumn 1985]   Simon Oursley+ mg

Nicholson, Sam
What was the Name Again?   ss ASF Jul,85
    Analog Science Fiction/Science Fact [v.105 # 7, July 1985]
                                            Stanley Schmidt mg

Niven, Larry
Biology, Ecology, Xenology   ar
    MEDEA: HARLAN'S WORLD   Harlan Ellison an
The Borderland of Sol   nv ASF Jan,75
    THE HUGO WINNERS, VOLUME 4: 1976-1979   Isaac Asimov an
Flare Time   nv AND # 3,78
    MEDEA: HARLAN'S WORLD   Harlan Ellison an
Flash Crowd   na 3TRPSTM,73
    BAKER'S DOZEN: 13 SHORT SCIENCE FICTION NOVELS
                                            Isaac Asimov+ an
Folk Tale   ss NVNSLWS,84
    LIMITS   Larry Niven co
The Green Marauder   ss DST V2 #1,80
    LIMITS   Larry Niven co
    TOP SCIENCE FICTION   Josh Pachter an
Introduction   in
    LIMITS   Larry Niven co
Limits   ss IAS Sep 28,81
    LIMITS   Larry Niven co
The Lion in His Attic   nv FSF Jul,82
    LIMITS   Larry Niven co
Not Long Before the End   ss FSF Apr,69
    BARBARIANS   Robert Adams+ an
The Real Thing   ss IAS Nov,82
    LIMITS   Larry Niven co
Table Manners   ss FFR V 1,85
    FAR FRONTIERS   Jerry E. Pournelle+ oa
A Teardrop Falls   ss OMN Jun,83
    BERSERKER BASE   Fred Saberhagen an
War Movie   ss ST # 7,81
    LIMITS   Larry Niven co
What Good is a Glass Dagger?   nv FSF Sep,72
    ISAAC ASIMOV'S MAGICAL WORLDS OF FANTASY: WITCHES & WIZARDS
                                            Isaac Asimov+ om
Yet Another Modest Proposal: The Roentgen Standard fa OMN Jul,80
    LIMITS   Larry Niven co

Niven, Larry, Poul Anderson, Hal Clement, Thomas M. Disch &
Frederik Pohl
Second Thoughts   ms
    MEDEA: HARLAN'S WORLD   Harlan Ellison an

Niven, Larry & Steve Barnes
The Locusts   nv ASF Jun,79
    LIMITS   Larry Niven co

Niven, Larry & Dian Girard
Talisman   ss FSF Nov,81
    LIMITS   Larry Niven co

Niven, Larry & Jerry E. Pournelle
Spirals   na DST V1 #3,79
    LIMITS   Larry Niven co

Nolan, William F.
Ceremony   nv MIDNGHT,85
    MIDNIGHT   Charles L. Grant oa
Of Time and Kathy Benedict   nv FTL V7 #13,84
    WHISPERS V   Stuart David Schiff oa
Terror at London Bridge   ar WRLDTLS,85
    WORLD TALES   G. Randal Rau oa

Nordling, Lee & Cheri Lane
Harry Tales   cs FBM Mar,85
    Fantasy Book [v.4 #1, March 1985]   Dennis Mallonee+ mg

Norment, John
Cartoon   ct IAS
    Isaac Asimov's Science Fiction Magazine [v. 9 # 4, April
    1985]   Shawna McCarthy mg
    Isaac Asimov's Science Fiction Magazine [v. 9 # 5, May 1985]
                                            Shawna McCarthy mg

Reaves, Michael
  The Night People   ss TZM Oct,85
    Rod Serling's The Twilight Zone Magazine [v.5 #4, October
    1985]   Michael Blaine mg

Redd, David
  On the Deck of the Flying Bomb   ss INZ # 4,82
    INTERZONE: THE 1ST ANTHOLOGY   John Clute+ an

Reed, Kit
  The Quest   nv FUN Jan,60
    MERCENARIES OF TOMORROW   Poul Anderson+ an

Reinhardt, Hank
  The Age of the Warrior   ss HEROFAN,79
    BARBARIANS   Robert Adams+ an

Resnick, Michael
  Me and My Shadow   ss UNAUTHA,84
    THE SCIENCE FICTION YEARBOOK   Jerry E. Pournelle+ an

Ressmeyer, Roger
  Illustration   il PLANETS,85
    THE PLANETS   Byron Preiss oa

Reyes, Raul
  The Chosen Maiden   ss S&S # 2,85
    SWORD AND SORCERESS II   Marion Zimmer Bradley oa

Reynolds, Mack
  The Business, as Usual   ss FSF Jun,52
    ISAAC ASIMOV PRESENTS THE GREAT SF STORIES: 14 (1952)
                                              Isaac Asimov+ an
  Mercenary   na ASF Apr,62
    MERCENARIES OF TOMORROW   Poul Anderson+ an
  Optical Illusion   ss SST Dec,53
    YOUNG MONSTERS   Isaac Asimov+ an
  Pacifist   ss FSF Jan,64
    TERRORISTS OF TOMORROW   Poul Anderson+ an

Rice, Anne
  The Vampire Lestat   ex TZM Dec,85
    Rod Serling's The Twilight Zone Magazine [v.5 #5, December
    1985]   Michael Blaine mg
  The Vampire Lestat   ex TZM Oct,85
    Rod Serling's The Twilight Zone Magazine [v.5 #4, October
    1985]   Michael Blaine mg

Riggs, P. Alexandra
  To Open a Door   ss FRAMZDK,85
    FREE AMAZONS OF DARKOVER   Marion Zimmer Bradley+ oa

Rizkalla, John
  A Vacancy at the Consulate   ss WDB #20,85
    Weirdbook 20 [Spring 1985]   W. Paul Ganley mg

Robbins, Wayne
  Test-Tube Frankenstein   ss TTL May,40
    SENSUOUS SCIENCE FICTION FROM THE WEIRD AND SPICY PULPS
                                              Sheldon R. Jaffery an

Roberson, Jennifer
  The Lady and the Tiger   ss S&S # 2,85
    SWORD AND SORCERESS II   Marion Zimmer Bradley oa

Roberts, Garyn G. & Gary Hoppenstand
  Black Days and Silver Death: Frederick C. Davis' Moon Man Series
                                              in
    THE NIGHT NEMESIS: THE COMPLETE ADVENTURES OF THE MOON
    MAN--VOL. ONE   Frederick C. Davis co

Roberts, John Maddox
  Joined the Space Force to Wear My Blues   ss WAR V 4,85
    THERE WILL BE WAR, VOL. IV: DAY OF THE TYRANT
                                              Jerry E. Pournelle an

Roberts, Keith
  Kitecadet   ss AMZ May,85
    Amazing Science Fiction Stories [v.59 #1, May 1985]
                                              George H. Scithers mg
    KITEWORLD   Keith Roberts no
  Kitecaptain   na KITEWLD,85
    KITEWORLD   Keith Roberts no
  Kitekillers   ss KITEWLD,85
    KITEWORLD   Keith Roberts no
  Kitemariner   nv KITEWLD,85
    KITEWORLD   Keith Roberts no
  Kitemaster   ss INZ # 1,82
    INTERZONE: THE 1ST ANTHOLOGY   John Clute+ an
    KITEWORLD   Keith Roberts no
  Kitemistress   nv INZ #11,85
    Interzone [#11, Spring 1985]   Colin Greenland+ mg
    KITEWORLD   Keith Roberts no
  Kiteservant   nv KITEWLD,85
    KITEWORLD   Keith Roberts no
  Kitewaif   na KITEWLD,85
    KITEWORLD   Keith Roberts no
  Richenda   nv FSF Sep,85
    The Magazine of Fantasy & Science Fiction [v.69 #3, September
    1985]   Edward L. Ferman mg

Robinette, Stephen
  Number 13   ss OMN Nov,82
    THE THIRD OMNI BOOK OF SCIENCE FICTION   Ellen Datlow an

Robinson, Andrew M.
  Fantasy Game Reviews   gr FBM
    Fantasy Book [v.4 #1, March 1985]   Dennis Mallonee+ mg
    Fantasy Book [v.4 #4, December 1985]   Dennis Mallonee+ mg

Robinson, Frank M.
  The Santa Claus Planet   nv BSFS:51,51
    SANTA 2000   Michel Parry an

Robinson, Jeanne & Spider Robinson
  Stardance   na ASF Mar,77
    THE HUGO WINNERS, VOLUME 4: 1976-1979   Isaac Asimov an

Robinson, Kim Stanley
  Green Mars   na IAS Sep,85
    Isaac Asimov's Science Fiction Magazine [v. 9 # 9, September
    1985]   Shawna McCarthy mg
  The Lucky Strike   nv UNI #14,84
    TERRY CARR'S BEST SCIENCE FICTION OF THE YEAR #14
                                              Terry Carr an
    THE YEAR'S BEST SCIENCE FICTION, SECOND ANNUAL COLLECTION
                                              Gardner Dozois an
    NEBULA AWARDS 20: SFWA'S CHOICES FOR THE BEST IN SCIENCE
    FICTION 1984   George Zebrowski an
  Mercurial   nv UNI #15,85
    UNIVERSE 15   Terry Carr oa

Robinson, Spider
  Antinomy   nv DST V1 #1,78
    MELANCHOLY ELEPHANTS [Canadian edition] Spider Robinson co
    MELANCHOLY ELEPHANTS [U.S. edition]   Spider Robinson co
  The Blacksmith's Tale   na ASF Dec,85
    Analog Science Fiction/Science Fact [v.105 #12, December
    1985]   Stanley Schmidt mg
  By Any Other Name   na ASF Nov,76
    THE HUGO WINNERS, VOLUME 4: 1976-1979   Isaac Asimov an
  Chronic Offender   nv TZM May,81
    MELANCHOLY ELEPHANTS [Canadian edition] Spider Robinson co
    MELANCHOLY ELEPHANTS [U.S. edition]   Spider Robinson co
  Common Sense   ss MLMELPH,85
    MELANCHOLY ELEPHANTS [U.S. edition]   Spider Robinson co
  Concordiat to "Rubber Soul"   aw
    MELANCHOLY ELEPHANTS [U.S. edition]   Spider Robinson co
  Father Paradox   ss MLMELPH,85
    MELANCHOLY ELEPHANTS [U.S. edition]   Spider Robinson co
  God is an Iron   nv OMN May,79
    TESSERACTS   Judith Merril oa
  Half an Oaf   nv ANLGANL,76
    MELANCHOLY ELEPHANTS [Canadian edition] Spider Robinson co
    MELANCHOLY ELEPHANTS [U.S. edition]   Spider Robinson co
  High Infidelity   ss OUI Apr,83
    MELANCHOLY ELEPHANTS [Canadian edition] Spider Robinson co
    MELANCHOLY ELEPHANTS [U.S. edition]   Spider Robinson co
  In the Olden Days   ss MLMELPH,84
    MELANCHOLY ELEPHANTS [Canadian edition] Spider Robinson co
    MELANCHOLY ELEPHANTS [U.S. edition]   Spider Robinson co
  Introduction   in
    MELANCHOLY ELEPHANTS [Canadian edition] Spider Robinson co
  Introductory Note   in
    MELANCHOLY ELEPHANTS [U.S. edition]   Spider Robinson co
  It's a Sunny Day   ss GAL Jan,76
    MELANCHOLY ELEPHANTS [Canadian edition] Spider Robinson co
  Melancholy Elephants   ss ASF Jun,82
    MELANCHOLY ELEPHANTS [Canadian edition] Spider Robinson co
    MELANCHOLY ELEPHANTS [U.S. edition]   Spider Robinson co
  No Renewal   ss GAL Mar,77
    MELANCHOLY ELEPHANTS [Canadian edition] Spider Robinson co
    MELANCHOLY ELEPHANTS [U.S. edition]   Spider Robinson co
  Not Fade Away   ss IAS Aug,82
    MELANCHOLY ELEPHANTS [Canadian edition] Spider Robinson co
    MELANCHOLY ELEPHANTS [U.S. edition]   Spider Robinson co
  Riddle Night at Callahan's Place   pz ASF Nov,85
    Analog Science Fiction/Science Fact [v.105 #11, November
    1985]   Stanley Schmidt mg
  Rubber Soul   ss BOM # 4,82
    MELANCHOLY ELEPHANTS [Canadian edition] Spider Robinson co
    MELANCHOLY ELEPHANTS [U.S. edition]   Spider Robinson co
  Satan's Children   na NWW # 2,79
    MELANCHOLY ELEPHANTS [Canadian edition] Spider Robinson co
    MELANCHOLY ELEPHANTS [U.S. edition]   Spider Robinson co
  Serpent's Teeth   ss OMN Mar,81
    THE FOURTH OMNI BOOK OF SCIENCE FICTION   Ellen Datlow an
  True Minds   nv MLMELPH,84
    MELANCHOLY ELEPHANTS [Canadian edition] Spider Robinson co
    MELANCHOLY ELEPHANTS [U.S. edition]   Spider Robinson co

Robinson, Spider & Jeanne Robinson
  Stardance   na ASF Mar,77
    THE HUGO WINNERS, VOLUME 4: 1976-1979   Isaac Asimov an

Rodgers, Alan
  Terror in the Back Seat   in
    Night Cry [v.1 #3, Fall 1985]   T.E.D. Klein mg
  TZ Video List   bi TZM
    Rod Serling's The Twilight Zone Magazine [v.5 #6, February
    1986]   Michael Blaine mg
  Warning: in NCR V1 #4,85
    Night Cry [v.1 #4, Winter 1985]   Alan Rodgers mg

Rodgers, Alan (continued)
  Welcome to the Magazine of Terror   in NCR V1 #5,86
    Night Cry [v.1 #5, Spring 1986]   Alan Rodgers mg

Rogan, Pete
  Quartermaster Corps   gr SDA Dec,85
    Stardate [v.1 # 9, December 1985]   Ted White+ mg
  Some Star Bases: A Profile   gr SDA Oct,85
    Stardate [v.1 # 8, October 1985]   Ted White+ mg
  Star Bases: The Federation's Handmaiden   gr SDA Oct,85
    Stardate [v.1 # 8, October 1985]   Ted White+ mg

Rolls, Dana Kramer
  Sword of the Mother   ss S&S # 2,85
    SWORD AND SORCERESS II   Marion Zimmer Bradley oa

Rondinone, Peter
  Starbursts on the Twilight Zone [very short interviews with
    Robert Klein, Elliott Gould, Carolyn Seymour and Annie Potts]
         iv TZM Dec,85
    Rod Serling's The Twilight Zone Magazine [v.5 #5, December
    1985]   Michael Blaine mg
  TZ Illuminations   ar TZM
    Rod Serling's The Twilight Zone Magazine [v.5 #4, October
    1985]   Michael Blaine mg
    Rod Serling's The Twilight Zone Magazine [v.5 #5, December
    1985]   Michael Blaine mg
    Rod Serling's The Twilight Zone Magazine [v.5 #6, February
    1986]   Michael Blaine mg

Ronning, A.M.
  Fade to Black   ss TZM Dec,85
    Rod Serling's The Twilight Zone Magazine [v.5 #5, December
    1985]   Michael Blaine mg

Ronson, Mark
  Samkin   ss GRMLKNS,83
    GRIMALKIN'S TALES   Stella Whitelaw+ oa
  Smokey   ss GRMLKNS,83
    GRIMALKIN'S TALES   Stella Whitelaw+ oa
  Strauss   ss GRMLKNS,83
    GRIMALKIN'S TALES   Stella Whitelaw+ oa
  Tico   ss GRMLKNS,83
    GRIMALKIN'S TALES   Stella Whitelaw+ oa

Rose, Rhea
  Chronos' Christmas   ss TESRCTS,85
    TESSERACTS   Judith Merril oa

Rosemund, Victor L.
  The Thing from the Old Seaman's Mouth   ss WRTRFUT,85
    L. RON HUBBARD PRESENTS WRITERS OF THE FUTURE Algis Budrys oa

Rosenberg, Joel
  THE SILVER CROWN   n. SIG 1985
    GUARDIANS OF THE FLAME: THE WARRIORS   Joel Rosenberg om
  THE SLEEPING DRAGON   n. SIG 1983
    GUARDIANS OF THE FLAME: THE WARRIORS   Joel Rosenberg om
  THE SWORD AND THE CHAIN   n. SIG 1984
    GUARDIANS OF THE FLAME: THE WARRIORS   Joel Rosenberg om

Rothman, Tony
  For Tom Rainbow   bg IAS Jan,85
    Isaac Asimov's Science Fiction Magazine [v. 9 # 1, January
    1985]   Shawna McCarthy mg

Rothman, Tony & G.F.R. Ellis
  The Garden of Cosmological Delights   ar ASF May,85
    Analog Science Fiction/Science Fact [v.105 # 5, May 1985]
        Stanley Schmidt mg
  Hot Rocks and Water   ar ASF Mar,85
    Analog Science Fiction/Science Fact [v.105 # 3, March 1985]
        Stanley Schmidt mg

Rotsler, William & Alexis Gilliland
  Cartoon, Cartoon   ct AMZ
    Amazing Science Fiction Stories [v.58 #5, January 1985]
        George H. Scithers mg
    Amazing Science Fiction Stories [v.59 #1, May 1985]
        George H. Scithers mg
    Amazing Science Fiction Stories [v.59 #2, July 1985]
        George H. Scithers mg
    Amazing Science Fiction Stories [v.60 #1, November 1985]
        George H. Scithers mg
    Amazing Science Fiction Stories [v.60 #2, January 1986]
        George H. Scithers mg

Rousseau, Yvonne
  Mr. Lockwood's Narrative   ss STRGATR,85
    STRANGE ATTRACTORS   Damien Broderick oa

Roy, Kenneth, P.E.
  Comment and Discussion on "Elevation of the U.S. Fleet" by
    Captain Richard B. Laning, USN (Ret.)   ar WAR V 4,85
    THERE WILL BE WAR, VOL. IV: DAY OF THE TYRANT
        Jerry E. Pournelle an

Rubin, Irma & Al Talero
  TZ Tech   ar TZM
    Rod Serling's The Twilight Zone Magazine [v.5 #4, October
    1985]   Michael Blaine mg

Rucker, Rudy & Bruce Sterling
  Storming the Cosmos   na IAS Dec md,85
    Isaac Asimov's Science Fiction Magazine [v. 9 #13,
    Mid-December 1985]   Shawna McCarthy mg

Ruffell, Ann
  Pied Piper   ss OUTOFTM,84
    OUT OF TIME   Aidan Chambers oa

Runyon, Damon
  The Informal Execution of Soupbone Pew   ss
    MASTERPIECES OF TERROR AND THE SUPERNATURAL   Marvin Kaye an

Russ, Joanna
  The Cliches from Outer Space   ar WSF V7 #2,84
    DESPATCHES FROM THE FRONTIERS OF THE FEMALE MIND Jen Green+ oa

Russell, Eric Frank
  Fast Falls the Eventide   ss ASF May,52
    ISAAC ASIMOV PRESENTS THE GREAT SF STORIES: 14 (1952)
        Isaac Asimov+ an
  Minor Ingredient   ss ASF Mar,56
    ANALOG: THE BEST OF SCIENCE FICTION   Anonymous an

Russell, Ray
  The Cage   ss 1959
    HAUNTED CASTLES: THE COMPLETE GOTHIC TALES OF RAY RUSSELL
        Ray Russell co
  Comet Wine   nv PBY Mar,67
    HAUNTED CASTLES: THE COMPLETE GOTHIC TALES OF RAY RUSSELL
        Ray Russell co
  The Runaway Lovers   ss 1967
    HAUNTED CASTLES: THE COMPLETE GOTHIC TALES OF RAY RUSSELL
        Ray Russell co
  Sagittarius   nv PBY Mar,62
    HAUNTED CASTLES: THE COMPLETE GOTHIC TALES OF RAY RUSSELL
        Ray Russell co
  Sanguinarius   nv HNTDCST,85
    HAUNTED CASTLES: THE COMPLETE GOTHIC TALES OF RAY RUSSELL
        Ray Russell co
  Sardonicus   nv PBY Jan,61
    MASTERPIECES OF TERROR AND THE SUPERNATURAL   Marvin Kaye an
    HAUNTED CASTLES: THE COMPLETE GOTHIC TALES OF RAY RUSSELL
        Ray Russell co
  The Secret of Rowena   ss TZM Oct,85
    Rod Serling's The Twilight Zone Magazine [v.5 #4, October
    1985]   Michael Blaine mg
  The Vendetta [The Man Who Spoke in Rhyme]   ss EQM Nov,69
    HAUNTED CASTLES: THE COMPLETE GOTHIC TALES OF RAY RUSSELL
        Ray Russell co

Russell, W. Clark
  A Bewitched Ship   ss
    MYSTERIOUS SEA STORIES   William Pattrick an

Ryan, Alan
  The Bones Wizard   ss WHS Dec,84
    Whispers [v.6 #1-2, December 1984]   Stuart David Schiff mg
  Bundoran, Co. Donegal   ss WHS Dec,84
    Whispers [v.6 #1-2, December 1984]   Stuart David Schiff mg
  The East Beaverton Monster   ss WHA # 5,85
    WHISPERS V   Stuart David Schiff oa
  Memory and Desire   nv GRYSTBY,85
    GREYSTONE BAY   Charles L. Grant oa
  Return to the Goblin Tower   pm WDB #20,85
    Weirdbook 20 [Spring 1985]   W. Paul Ganley mg
  Sand   ss SDW # 8,85
    SHADOWS 8   Charles L. Grant oa

Ryan, Jim
  TZ Theater: A Brief Encounter of the Third Kind   cs TZM Apr,85
    Rod Serling's The Twilight Zone Magazine [v.5 #1, March/April
    1985]   T.E.D. Klein mg
  TZ Theater: Shelf Life   cs TZM Feb,85
    Rod Serling's The Twilight Zone Magazine [v.4 #6,
    January/February 1985]   T.E.D. Klein mg
  TZ Theater: The Cows Come Home   cs TZM Aug,85
    Rod Serling's The Twilight Zone Magazine [v.5 #3, July/August
    1985]   T.E.D. Klein mg
  TZ Theater: The Hook   cs TZM Jun,85
    Rod Serling's The Twilight Zone Magazine [v.5 #2, May/June
    1985]   T.E.D. Klein mg

Ryman, Geoff
  O Happy Day!   nv IZA # 1,85
    INTERZONE: THE 1ST ANTHOLOGY   John Clute+ an

Saberhagen, Fred
  Adventure of the Metal Murderer   ss OMN Jan,80
    THE THIRD OMNI BOOK OF SCIENCE FICTION   Ellen Datlow an
  As Duly Authorized   ss FSF Oct,85
    The Magazine of Fantasy & Science Fiction [v.69 #4, October
    1985]   Edward L. Ferman mg
  Berserker Base   ms BSRKRBS,85
    BERSERKER BASE   Fred Saberhagen an
  Crossing the Bar   ms BSRKRBS,85
    BERSERKER BASE   Fred Saberhagen an
  Dangerous Dreams   ms BSRKRBS,85
    BERSERKER BASE   Fred Saberhagen an
  THE FIRST BOOK OF SWORDS   n. TOR 1983
    THE COMPLETE BOOK OF SWORDS   Fred Saberhagen om

Schweitzer, Darrell (continued)
    TOM O'BEDLAM'S NIGHT OUT, AND OTHER STRANGE EXCURSIONS
                                    Darrell Schweitzer co
    The Story of the Brown Man   ss FCR Jan,77
    TOM O'BEDLAM'S NIGHT OUT, AND OTHER STRANGE EXCURSIONS
                                    Darrell Schweitzer co
    The Stranger from Baal-ad-Theon   ss TOMOBED,85
    TOM O'BEDLAM'S NIGHT OUT, AND OTHER STRANGE EXCURSIONS
                                    Darrell Schweitzer co
    Sunrise   ss PLP Win,83
    TOM O'BEDLAM'S NIGHT OUT, AND OTHER STRANGE EXCURSIONS
                                    Darrell Schweitzer co
    Tom O'Bedlam's Night Out   ss FAN Sep,77
    TOM O'BEDLAM'S NIGHT OUT, AND OTHER STRANGE EXCURSIONS
                                    Darrell Schweitzer co
    A Vision of Rembathene   ss FCR Mar,77
    TOM O'BEDLAM'S NIGHT OUT, AND OTHER STRANGE EXCURSIONS
                                    Darrell Schweitzer co
    The Wings of the White Bird [revised] ss MYR # 4,78
    TOM O'BEDLAM'S NIGHT OUT, AND OTHER STRANGE EXCURSIONS
                                    Darrell Schweitzer co

Schweitzer, Darrell & John Gregory Betancourt
    The Last Child of Masferigon   ss TOMOBED,85
    TOM O'BEDLAM'S NIGHT OUT, AND OTHER STRANGE EXCURSIONS
                                    Darrell Schweitzer co

Schweitzer, Darrell & George H. Scithers
    The Observatory   ed AMZ May,85
    Amazing Science Fiction Stories [v.59 #1, May 1985]
                                    George H. Scithers mg

Scithers, George H.
    The Observatory   ed AMZ
    Amazing Science Fiction Stories [v.58 #5, January 1985]
                                    George H. Scithers mg
    Amazing Science Fiction Stories [v.58 #6, March 1985]
                                    George H. Scithers mg
    Amazing Science Fiction Stories [v.59 #2, July 1985]
                                    George H. Scithers mg
    Amazing Science Fiction Stories [v.60 #1, November 1985]
                                    George H. Scithers mg
    Amazing Science Fiction Stories [v.60 #2, January 1986]
                                    George H. Scithers mg

Scithers, George H. & Patrick L. Price
    The Observatory   ed AMZ Sep,85
    Amazing Science Fiction Stories [v.59 #3, September 1985]
                                    George H. Scithers mg

Scithers, George H. & Darrell Schweitzer
    The Observatory   ed AMZ May,85
    Amazing Science Fiction Stories [v.59 #1, May 1985]
                                    George H. Scithers mg

Scortia, Thomas N.
    This Is: An Introduction   in
    THE MONADIC UNIVERSE   George Zebrowski co

Searles, Baird
    On Books   br IAS
    Isaac Asimov's Science Fiction Magazine [v. 9 # 1, January
    1985]   Shawna McCarthy mg
    Isaac Asimov's Science Fiction Magazine [v. 9 # 2, February
    1985]   Shawna McCarthy mg
    Isaac Asimov's Science Fiction Magazine [v. 9 # 3, March
    1985]   Shawna McCarthy mg
    Isaac Asimov's Science Fiction Magazine [v. 9 # 4, April
    1985]   Shawna McCarthy mg
    Isaac Asimov's Science Fiction Magazine [v. 9 # 5, May 1985]
                                    Shawna McCarthy mg
    Isaac Asimov's Science Fiction Magazine [v. 9 # 6, June 1985]
                                    Shawna McCarthy mg
    Isaac Asimov's Science Fiction Magazine [v. 9 # 8, August
    1985]   Shawna McCarthy mg
    Isaac Asimov's Science Fiction Magazine [v. 9 # 9, September
    1985]   Shawna McCarthy mg
    Isaac Asimov's Science Fiction Magazine [v. 9 #10, October
    1985]   Shawna McCarthy mg
    Isaac Asimov's Science Fiction Magazine [v. 9 #12, December
    1985]   Shawna McCarthy mg
    Isaac Asimov's Science Fiction Magazine [v. 9 #13,
    Mid-December 1985]   Shawna McCarthy mg
    Screen Reviews   mr AMZ
    Amazing Science Fiction Stories [v.58 #5, January 1985]
                                    George H. Scithers mg
    Amazing Science Fiction Stories [v.58 #6, March 1985]
                                    George H. Scithers mg
    Amazing Science Fiction Stories [v.59 #1, May 1985]
                                    George H. Scithers mg
    Amazing Science Fiction Stories [v.59 #2, July 1985]
                                    George H. Scithers mg
    Amazing Science Fiction Stories [v.59 #3, September 1985]
                                    George H. Scithers mg
    Amazing Science Fiction Stories [v.60 #1, November 1985]
                                    George H. Scithers mg
    Amazing Science Fiction Stories [v.60 #2, January 1986]
                                    George H. Scithers mg

Serling, Carol
    Preface   pr

Serling, Carol (continued)
    THE TWILIGHT ZONE: THE ORIGINAL STORIES
                                    Martin H. Greenberg+ an
    Talking Twilight Zone [interview with Phil DeGuere]
                                    iv TZM Dec,85
    Rod Serling's The Twilight Zone Magazine [v.5 #5, December
    1985]   Michael Blaine mg
    A Word from the Publisher   fw TZM Apr,85
    Rod Serling's The Twilight Zone Magazine [v.5 #1, March/April
    1985]   T.E.D. Klein mg

Serling, Rod
    And When the Sky Was Opened   pl CBS Dec 11,59
    Based on the story 'Disappearing Act' by Richard Matheson, ss
    FSF Mar,53.
    Rod Serling's The Twilight Zone Magazine [v.5 #2, May/June
    1985]   T.E.D. Klein mg
    The Mighty Casey   pl CBS Jun 17,60
    Rod Serling's The Twilight Zone Magazine [v.5 #3, July/August
    1985]   T.E.D. Klein mg
    The Purple Testament   pl CBS Feb 12,60
    Rod Serling's The Twilight Zone Magazine [v.5 #4, October
    1985]   Michael Blaine mg
    Thing About Machines   pl CBS Oct 28,60
    Rod Serling's The Twilight Zone Magazine [v.5 #5, December
    1985]   Michael Blaine mg
    Where Is Everybody?   pl CBS Oct 2,59
    Rod Serling's The Twilight Zone Magazine [v.5 #1, March/April
    1985]   T.E.D. Klein mg
    Will the Real Martian Please Stand Up   pl CBS May 26,61
    Rod Serling's The Twilight Zone Magazine [v.5 #6, February
    1986]   Michael Blaine mg

Serling-Sutton, Anne
    The Changing of the Guard [by Rod Serling]   sa TZM Feb,85
    YOUNG GHOSTS   Isaac Asimov+ an
    THE TWILIGHT ZONE: THE ORIGINAL STORIES
                                    Martin H. Greenberg+ an
    Rod Serling's The Twilight Zone Magazine [v.4 #6,
    January/February 1985]   T.E.D. Klein mg
    One for the Angels [by Rod Serling]   sa TWLGTZN,85
    THE TWILIGHT ZONE: THE ORIGINAL STORIES
                                    Martin H. Greenberg+ an

Sernine, Daniel
    Stardust Boulevard   ss LVLHMSP,81
    translated by Jane Brierley   TESRCTS,85
    TESSERACTS   Judith Merril oa

Sevigny, Marc
    The Train   ss AURBRL1,83
    translated by Frances Morgan   TESRCTS,85
    TESSERACTS   Judith Merril oa

Shahar, Eluki bes
    Hellflower   nv AMZ Mar,85
    Amazing Science Fiction Stories [v.58 #6, March 1985]
                                    George H. Scithers mg

Shannon, Maureen
    Recruits   ss FRAMZDK,85
    FREE AMAZONS OF DARKOVER   Marion Zimmer Bradley+ oa

Shapiro, Karen
    Journey from Darchos   ss S&T #69,85
    Space and Time [#69, Winter 1986]   Gordon Linzner mg

Shatravka, Alexander
    A Letter from the Soviet Union   ar 1984
    THERE WILL BE WAR, VOL. IV: DAY OF THE TYRANT
                                    Jerry E. Pournelle an

Shaver, Edward F.
    Sport of Kings   nv FSF Nov,85
    The Magazine of Fantasy & Science Fiction [v.69 #5, November
    1985]   Edward L. Ferman mg

Shaw-Mathews, Patricia
    Girls Will Be Girls   ss FRAMZDK,85
    FREE AMAZONS OF DARKOVER   Marion Zimmer Bradley+ oa

Shea, John
    Ah, Whoreson Caterpillars! Bacon-Fed Knaves!   ss TZM Aug,85
    Rod Serling's The Twilight Zone Magazine [v.5 #3, July/August
    1985]   T.E.D. Klein mg

Sheckley, Jay
    Bargain Cinema   ss NCR V1 #4,85
    Night Cry [v.1 #4, Winter 1985]   Alan Rodgers mg

Sheckley, Robert
    Cost of Living   ss GAL Dec,52
    ISAAC ASIMOV PRESENTS THE GREAT SF STORIES: 14 (1952)
                                    Isaac Asimov+ an
    The Impacted Man   ss ASF Dec,52
    ISAAC ASIMOV PRESENTS THE GREAT SF STORIES: 14 (1952)
                                    Isaac Asimov+ an
    The Perfect Woman   ss AMZ Jan,54
    AMAZING STORIES: 60 YEARS OF THE BEST SCIENCE FICTION
                                    Isaac Asimov+ an
    The Store of the Worlds [The World of Heart's Desire]
                                    ss P3Y Sep,59

STOCKTON, FRANK R.   SWANWICK, MICHAEL

Stockton, Frank R. (continued)
  ISAAC ASIMOV'S MAGICAL WORLDS OF FANTASY #4: SPELLS
                                              Isaac Asimov+ an

Stoker, Bram
  Dracula's Guest   ss DRCLGST,14
  MASTERPIECES OF TERROR AND THE SUPERNATURAL   Marvin Kaye an
  The Secret of the Growing Gold   ss DRCLGST,14
  GREAT GHOST STORIES   Betty Ann Schwartz an
  The Squaw   ss
  Night Cry [v.1 #5, Spring 1986]   Alan Rodgers mg

Stoll, Patricia
  The Age of Fish   ss TZM Feb,86
  Rod Serling's The Twilight Zone Magazine [v.5 #6, February
  1986]   Michael Blaine mg

Stowe, Harriet Beecher
  The Ghost in the Cap'n Brown House   ss OLDTOWN,1871
  HAUNTED WOMEN: THE BEST SUPERNATURAL TALES BY AMERICAN WOMEN
  WRITERS   Alfred Bendixen an

Straczynski, J. Michael
  Your Move   ss AMZ Nov,85
  Amazing Science Fiction Stories [v.60 #1, November 1985]
                                            George H. Scithers mg

Straczynski, J. Michael & Kathryn M. Drennan
  Rod Serling's 'Night Gallery' [Part 1]   ar TZM Apr,85
  Rod Serling's The Twilight Zone Magazine [v.5 #1, March/April
  1985]   T.E.D. Klein mg
  Rod Serling's 'Night Gallery' [Part 2]   ar TZM Jun,85
  Rod Serling's The Twilight Zone Magazine [v.5 #2, May/June
  1985]   T.E.D. Klein mg
  Rod Serling's 'Night Gallery' [Part 3]   ar TZM Aug,85
  Rod Serling's The Twilight Zone Magazine [v.5 #3, July/August
  1985]   T.E.D. Klein mg
  A Show-by-Show Guide to Rod Serling's 'Night Gallery', Part 1
                                               bi TZM Apr,85
  Rod Serling's The Twilight Zone Magazine [v.5 #1, March/April
  1985]   T.E.D. Klein mg
  A Show-by-Show Guide to Rod Serling's 'Night Gallery', Part 2
                                               bi TZM Jun,85
  Rod Serling's The Twilight Zone Magazine [v.5 #2, May/June
  1985]   T.E.D. Klein mg
  A Show-by-Show Guide to Rod Serling's 'Night Gallery', Part 3
                                               bi TZM Aug,85
  Rod Serling's The Twilight Zone Magazine [v.5 #3, July/August
  1985]   T.E.D. Klein mg
  A Show-by-Show Guide to Rod Serling's 'Night Gallery', Part 4
                                               bi TZM Oct,85
  Rod Serling's The Twilight Zone Magazine [v.5 #4, October
  1985]   Michael Blaine mg
  A Show-by-Show Guide to Rod Serling's 'Night Gallery', Part 5
                                               bi TZM Dec,85
  Rod Serling's The Twilight Zone Magazine [v.5 #5, December
  1985]   Michael Blaine mg
  A Show-by-Show Guide to Rod Serling's 'Night Gallery', Part 6
                                               bi TZM Feb,86
  Rod Serling's The Twilight Zone Magazine [v.5 #6, February
  1986]   Michael Blaine mg

Strauss, Erwin S.
  SF Conventional Calendar   ms IAS
  Isaac Asimov's Science Fiction Magazine [v. 9 # 1, January
  1985]   Shawna McCarthy mg
  Isaac Asimov's Science Fiction Magazine [v. 9 # 2, February
  1985]   Shawna McCarthy mg
  Isaac Asimov's Science Fiction Magazine [v. 9 # 3, March
  1985]   Shawna McCarthy mg
  Isaac Asimov's Science Fiction Magazine [v. 9 # 4, April
  1985]   Shawna McCarthy mg
  Isaac Asimov's Science Fiction Magazine [v. 9 # 5, May 1985]
                                            Shawna McCarthy mg
  Isaac Asimov's Science Fiction Magazine [v. 9 # 6, June 1985]
                                            Shawna McCarthy mg
  Isaac Asimov's Science Fiction Magazine [v. 9 # 7, July 1985]
                                            Shawna McCarthy mg
  Isaac Asimov's Science Fiction Magazine [v. 9 # 9, September
  1985]   Shawna McCarthy mg
  Isaac Asimov's Science Fiction Magazine [v. 9 #10, October
  1985]   Shawna McCarthy mg
  Isaac Asimov's Science Fiction Magazine [v. 9 #11, November
  1985]   Shawna McCarthy mg
  Isaac Asimov's Science Fiction Magazine [v. 9 #12, December
  1985]   Shawna McCarthy mg
  Isaac Asimov's Science Fiction Magazine [v. 9 #13,
  Mid-December 1985]   Shawna McCarthy mg
  Isaac Asimov's Science Fiction Magazine [v.10 # 1, January
  1986]   Gardner Dozois mg

Streiber, Whitley
  Chelsea Quinn Yarbro: Truth and Fiction   bg WRLDTLS,85
  WORLD TALES   G. Randal Rau oa

Strickland, Brad
  Pira   ss FSF Aug,85
  The Magazine of Fantasy & Science Fiction [v.69 #2, August
  1985]   Edward L. Ferman mg

Strugatsky, Arkady & Boris Strugatsky
  The Way to Amalteia   na ERH&ELW,85
  EARTH AND ELSEWHERE   Roger DeGaris an

Strugatsky, Boris & Arkady Strugatsky
  The Way to Amalteia   na ERH&ELW,85
  EARTH AND ELSEWHERE   Roger DeGaris an

Studach, Stephen
  The Dead Sleep   pm EDT #11,85
  Eldritch Tales No. 11 [v.3 #2]   Crispin Burnham mg

Sturgeon, Theodore
  Brat   ss UNK Dec,41
  FAERY!   Terri Windling oa
  Bright Segment   nv CAVIAR ,55
  Night Cry [v.1 #4, Winter 1985]   Alan Rodgers mg
  The Professor's Teddy Bear   ss WRT Mar,48
  MASTERPIECES OF TERROR AND THE SUPERNATURAL   Marvin Kaye an
  The Riddle of Ragnarok   nv FUN Jun,55
  ISAAC ASIMOV'S MAGICAL WORLDS OF FANTASY #5: GIANTS
                                              Isaac Asimov+ an
  A Touch of Strange   ss FSF Jan,58
  MERMAIDS!   Jack Dann+ an
  What Are You Doing Here?   ar WRTRFUT,85
  L. RON HUBBARD PRESENTS WRITERS OF THE FUTURE Algis Budrys an
  Why Dolphins Don't Bite   nv OMN Feb +2,80
  MEDEA: HARLAN'S WORLD   Harlan Ellison an

Sturgeon, Theodore, Thomas M. Disch, Harlan Ellison, Frank Herbert
  & Robert Silverberg
  The Concept Seminar   ms
  MEDEA: HARLAN'S WORLD   Harlan Ellison an
  The Extrapolations, the Questions   ms
  MEDEA: HARLAN'S WORLD   Harlan Ellison an

Sucharitkul, Somtow
  The Darkling Wind   ex BAN Jul,85
  THE BANTAM SPECTRA SAMPLER   Lou Aronica an
  Theodore Sturgeon: 1918-1985   bg IAS Jan,86
  Isaac Asimov's Science Fiction Magazine [v.10 # 1, January
  1986]   Gardner Dozois mg

Sullivan, Jean
  The Chess Set   ss EDT #11,85
  Eldritch Tales No. 11 [v.3 #2]   Crispin Burnham mg

Sullivan, Thomas
  The Death Runner   ss TZM Apr,81
  Night Cry [v.1 #2, Summer 1985]   T.E.D. Klein mg
  The Extension   ss MIDNGHT,85
  MIDNIGHT   Charles L. Grant oa
  The Mickey Mouse Olympics   ss OMN Jun,79
  THE FOURTH OMNI BOOK OF SCIENCE FICTION   Ellen Datlow an
  A Night at the Head of a Grave   ss SDW # 8,85
  SHADOWS 8   Charles L. Grant oa
  The Truce   ss SDA Oct,85
  Stardate [v.1 # 8, October 1985]   Ted White+ mg

Sullivan, Tim
  Special Education   ss IAS Jan,86
  Isaac Asimov's Science Fiction Magazine [v.10 # 1, January
  1986]   Gardner Dozois mg

Sussex, Lucy
  The Lipton Village Society   ss STRGATR,85
  STRANGE ATTRACTORS   Damien Broderick oa
  Montage   ss URBANFN,85
  URBAN FANTASIES   David King+ oa

Swain, T.M.
  He and My Shadow   ss TZM Oct,85
  Rod Serling's The Twilight Zone Magazine [v.5 #4, October
  1985]   Michael Blaine mg

Swan, Susan
  The Man Doll [revised]   ss DSC F11,82
  TESSERACTS   Judith Merril oa

Swanwick, Michael
  Anyone Here From Utah?   ss IAS May,85
  Isaac Asimov's Science Fiction Magazine [v. 9 # 5, May 1985]
                                            Shawna McCarthy mg
  The Blind Minotaur   ss AMZ Mar,85
  Amazing Science Fiction Stories [v.58 #6, March 1985]
                                            George H. Scithers mg
  BESTIARY!   Jack Dann+ an
  The Feast of Saint Janis   nv NDM #11,80
  BEYOND ARMAGEDDON   Walter M. Miller, Jr.+ an
  The Transmigration of Philip K.   ss IAS Feb,85
  Isaac Asimov's Science Fiction Magazine [v. 9 # 2, February
  1985]   Shawna McCarthy mg
  Trojan Horse   nv OMN Dec,84
  TERRY CARR'S BEST SCIENCE FICTION OF THE YEAR #14
                                              Terry Carr an
  THE YEAR'S BEST SCIENCE FICTION, SECOND ANNUAL COLLECTION
                                            Gardner Dozois an

Swanwick, Michael, Jack Dann & Gardner Dozois
  The Gods of Mars   ss OMN Mar,85
  Golden Apples of the Sun [expanded from Virgin Territory]
                                            nv PNT Mar,84

TIPTREE, JAMES, JR.   TWAIN, MARK

VINGE, VERNOR   WATSON, IAN

YOLEN, JANE   [MISC. MATERIAL]

[MISC. MATERIAL]

[Misc. Material] (continued)
  The Contributors   bg
    MEDEA: HARLAN'S WORLD   Harlan Ellison an
    TESSERACTS   Judith Merril oa
    THE PLANETS   Byron Preiss oa
  F&SF Competition: Report on Competition 36   ms FSF Jan,85
    The Magazine of Fantasy & Science Fiction [v.68 #1, January
    1985]   Edward L. Ferman mg
  F&SF Competition: Report on Competition 37   ms FSF Jun,85
    The Magazine of Fantasy & Science Fiction [v.68 #6, June
    1985]   Edward L. Ferman mg
  F&SF Competition: Report on Competition 38   ms FSF Nov,85
    The Magazine of Fantasy & Science Fiction [v.69 #5, November
    1985]   Edward L. Ferman mg
  Fantasy Book Index, Volume 3   ix FBM Mar,85
    Fantasy Book [v.4 #1, March 1985]   Dennis Mallonee+ mg
  Glossary of Obsolete, Archaic, and Rare Words and Meanings   ms
    THE LAYS OF BELERIAND: THE HISTORY OF MIDDLE-EARTH, VOL. III
                                                 J.R.R. Tolkien co
  Guest Notes   bg FYC #10,85
    Fantasycon X Programme Booklet   Stephen Jones+ oa
  Index   ix
    A. MERRITT: REFLECTIONS IN THE MOON POOL   Sam Moskowitz nf
    THE LAYS OF BELERIAND: THE HISTORY OF MIDDLE-EARTH, VOL. III
                                                 J.R.R. Tolkien co
  Index to 1984   ix ASF Jan,85
    Analog Science Fiction/Science Fact [v.105 # 1, January 1985]
                                                Stanley Schmidt mg
  Index to 1984   ix IAS Jan,85
    Isaac Asimov's Science Fiction Magazine [v. 9 # 1, January
    1985]   Shawna McCarthy mg
  Index to 1985   ix ASF Jan,86
    Analog Science Fiction/Science Fact [v.106 # 1, January 1986]
                                                Stanley Schmidt mg
  Index to 1985   ix IAS Jan,86
    Isaac Asimov's Science Fiction Magazine [v.10 # 1, January
    1986]   Gardner Dozois mg
  Index to Volume 68   ix FSF Jun,85
    The Magazine of Fantasy & Science Fiction [v.68 #6, June
    1985]   Edward L. Ferman mg
  Index to Volume 69   ix FSF Dec,85
    The Magazine of Fantasy & Science Fiction [v.69 #6, December
    1985]   Edward L. Ferman mg
  Notes on Contributors   bg
    STRANGE ATTRACTORS   Damien Broderick oa
    THE NIGHT NEMESIS: THE COMPLETE ADVENTURES OF THE MOON
    MAN--VOL. ONE   Frederick C. Davis co
  Notes on the Authors   bg
    INTERZONE: THE 1ST ANTHOLOGY   John Clute+ an
  Past Nebula Award Winners   ms
    NEBULA AWARDS 20: SFWA'S CHOICES FOR THE BEST IN SCIENCE
    FICTION 1984   George Zebrowski an
  Recommended Reading List   bi
    MERMAIDS!   an
                                               Jack Dann+
  Rhysling Awards--history   bi
    THE 1985 RHYSLING ANTHOLOGY   Anonymous an

TITLE LIST, STORIES

The Crow's Nest	Donald D. Markstein	ms WRLDTLS,85
Crowley and the Leprechaun		
	Gregory Frost	ss FAERY! ,85
Crows, Geese, Rocks	Ursula K. Le Guin	vi ALWCMHM,85
The Crudities of Science Fiction		
	Ian Watson	ar ARN
Cruising	Donald Tyson	ss TZM Sep,82
Cruising	Ian Watson	ss IAS Dec md,83
Crusader Damosel	Vera Chapman	ss 1978
The Crying Hawk at Sinshan		
	Ursula K. Le Guin	pm ALWCMHM,85
Cryptically Yours	Brian Lumley	ss ESP 1977
		SWD # 4,79
The Crystal Spheres	David Brin	nv ASF Jan,84
Cube Root	David Langford	ss INZ #11,85
The Culling	Ian Watson	ss
A Cure for Croup	Edward P. Hughes	nv FFR V 2,85
The Curio Shop	William Kotzwinkle	ss OMN Sep,80
The Curious Consultation	J.O. Jeppson	ss IAS May,82
A Curious Pleasure Excursion		
	Mark Twain	ss NYH Jul 6,1874
The Curious Republic of Gondour [as Anonymous]		
	Mark Twain	ss ATL Oct,1875
Currents	Jo Clayton	na BAITDRM,85
The Curse of Igamor	Michael de Larrabeiti	ss IMGNLND,85
The Curse of Kings	Connie Willis	na IAS Mar,85
Curse of the Golden Guardians		
	Brian Lumley	ss HSCTHLU,84
Curses!	Isaac Asimov	in
Custer's Last Stand	Brian Stableford	ss CSMCPRS,85
Cuts	Carter Scholz	ss CUTS ,85
CV (1st of 3 parts)	Damon Knight	sl FSF Jan,85
CV (2nd of 3 parts)	Damon Knight	sl FSF Feb,85
CV (3rd of 3 parts)	Damon Knight	sl FSF Mar,85
CYCLE OF THE WEREWOLF	Stephen King	n.
Cycles	Kim Antieau	ss SDW # 8,85
Cycles	Don Sakers	ss ASF Jan,85
Cycles	James Stevens	ss SDA Dec,85
Cyclops	Lannah Battley	ss DSPTCHS,85
The Dada Boys in Collitch (The First Chapter)		
	Daniel M. Pinkwater	ex YNGADLT,85
Dagger in the Mind	C.J. Cherryh	nv SOULCTY,86
Daisy, in the Sun	Connie Willis	nv GLL Nov,79
Damballa's Slough	Hugh B. Cave	ss WHS Dec,84
DAMIANO	R.A. MacAvoy	n. BAN 1983
DAMIANO's LUTE	R.A. MacAvoy	n. BAN 1984
The Damnable Price	Jefferson P. Swycaffer	nv PRSDMAR,86
The Dancer from the Dance	M. John Harrison	nv VRCNMNT,85
Dancers in the Time-Flux	Robert Silverberg	ss HEROVIS,83
Dancing the Moon	Ursula K. Le Guin	ss ALWCMHM,85
Dangerous Dreams	Fred Saberhagen	ms BSRKRBS,85
Dangerous People, Chapter Two		
	Ursula K. Le Guin	ss ALWCMHM,85
The Dark	Benjamin Gleisser	ss NCR V1 #2,85
The Dark at the End of the Tunnel		
	Richard Mueller	nv FBM Sep,85
DARKCHILD	Sydney J. Van Scyoc	n. BRK 1982
The Darkling Plain	P.M. Fergusson	nv ASF Nov,85
The Darkling Wind	Somtow Sucharitkul	ex BAN Jul,85
Daughter of the Sun	Robin W. Bailey	nv WNGSOMN,84
David Lynch: From Art School to Arrakis		
	Jean-Marc Lofficier & Randy Lofficier	
		iv TZM Feb,85
Davy Jones' Gift	John Masefield	ss 1907
A Day at the Beach	Carol Emshwiller	ss FSF Aug,59
A Day in the Life of a Classics Professor		
	Stan Dryer	nv FSF Dec,84
A Day in the Skin (or, The Century We Were Out of Them)		
	Tanith Lee	ss HABITAT,84
The Day Is Done	Lester del Rey	ss ASF May,39
Day Million	Frederik Pohl	ss ROG Feb,66
The Day of the Butterflies		
	Marion Zimmer Bradley	ss DAWSFRD,76
THE DAY OF THE DISSONANCE	Alan Dean Foster	n. WBK 1984
The Day Stokowski Saved the World		
	William Kotzwinkle	ss JWLMOON,85
The Day We Really Lost the War		
	Richard Mueller	ss IAS Sep,85
Dayblood	Roger Zelazny	ss TZM Jun,85
The Days of Perky Pat	Philip K. Dick	nv AMZ Dec,63
Dead End Dada	Daniel M. Pinkwater	nv YNGADLT,85
Dead Image	David Morrell	nv NGV # 2,85
Dead in the West (2 of 4)	Joe R. Lansdale	sl EDT #11,85
Dead Men's Fingers	Phillip C. Heath	nv BLD V1 #2,85
The Dead Past	Isaac Asimov	nv ASF Apr,56
Dead Run	Greg Bear	ss OMN Apr,85
The Dead Sleep	Stephen Studach	pm EDT #11,85
Deadlights	Charles Wagner	ss TWT # 9,84
Deadspace	Dennis Etchison	nv WHA # 5,85
Dear Reader	Susan Allison	pr
Dear Reader	Lou Aronica	in
Dear Ybba	Larry Tritten	ss SDA Dec,85
Death Between the Stars	Marion Zimmer Bradley	ss FUN Mar,56
Death in the Meadow	C.J. Cherryh	nv SOULCTY,86
Death in the School-Room	Walt Whitman	ss 1841
Death of a City	Frank Herbert	ss FUTCITY,73
The Death of Nimue	Esther M. Friesner	ss FBM Jun,85
The Death Runner	Thomas Sullivan	ss TZM Apr,81
Death Ship	Richard Matheson	nv FSM Mar,53
Deathglass	Lee Killough	ss IAS Apr,85
Deathwitch	Steven Popkes	ss IAS Feb,85
Deathwomb	Poul Anderson	nv ASF Nov,83

The Deer Dance	Ursula K. Le Guin	pm ALWCMHM,85
Defender of the Faith	Judith Tarr	ss MNSNGRF,85
Definition	Damon Knight	ss STS Feb,53
Delay in Transit	F.L. Wallace	nv GAL Sep,52
A Demon in Rosewood	Sharon Webb	ss SCW # 8,85
Demon Lover	M. Sargent Mackay	nv FSF Jun,84
The Demon of the Gibbet	Fitz-James O'Brien	pm
The Depths	Ramsey Campbell	ss DRKCMPN,82
DERYNI CHECKMATE	Katherine Kurtz	n. BAL 1972
DERYNI RISING	Katherine Kurtz	n. BAL 1970
The Desert of Stolen Dreams		
	Robert Silverberg	na FSF Jun,81
Desertion	Clifford D. Simak	ss ASF Nov,44
Desperate Acts	Gordon Linzner	ss DCM Mar,85
Deus ex Machina	J.V. Brummels	na IAS Nov,85
The Devil and the Deep Black Void		
	Tom Ligon	nv ASF Jan,86
The Devil in the Deep	Klaus Dieter Yurk	ss ECT #11,85
The Devil in the Heart. An Outline		
	A. Merritt	ms
THE DEVIL'S CHILDREN	Peter Dickinson	n. GOL 1970
Devil's Henchman [as Will F. Jenkins]		
	Murray Leinster	ss ARG May,52
The Devil, You Say?	Charles Beaumont	nv AMZ Jan,51
Dialog	Isaac Asimov	ed IAS Apr,85
Dialogue	Poul Anderson	nv FSTRLGT,76
Dialogue With a Spider	Thomas M. Disch	pm AMZ Jul,85
Dies Irae	Charles Sheffield	ss PLANETS,85
A Different Kind of Courage		
	Mercedes Lackey	ss FRAMZDK,85
The Dig	Ardath Mayhar	ss BLD V1 #3,85
Dinner in Audoghast	Bruce Sterling	ss IAS May,85
Dinner Party	Gardner Dozois	ss LGTYR&D,84
DINOSAUR PLANET	Anne McCaffrey	n. FPL 1978
DINOSAUR PLANET SURVIVORS	Anne McCaffrey	n. BAL 1984
Dinosaurs	Geoffrey A. Landis	ss ASF Jun,85
Diplomat-at-Arms	Keith Laumer	nv FAN Jan,60
Dira	Ursula K. Le Guin	ss PRB Win,84
Dirac's Scissors	Martin Gardner	pz IAS Nov,85
Disappearing Act	Richard Matheson	ss FSF Mar,53
The Disastrous Dog	Penelope Lively	ss UNVTGST,84
The Disintegration of Alan		
	Melissa Mia Hall	ss GRYSTBY,85
The Dismal Dismissal	Mark Calcamuggio	pm ECT #11,85
Disturb Not My Slumbering Fair		
	Chelsea Quinn Yarbro	ss CTNYTLS,78
Disturbance Reported on a Pipeline		
	William Kotzwinkle	ss JWLMOON,85
Divers Hands	Darrell Schweitzer	nv YBH # 7,79
Diversity	Byron Preiss	in
Divide and Rule	L. Sprague de Camp	na UNK Apr +1,39
The Djinn Who Watches Over the Accursed		
	Stephen R. Donaldson	ss WRLDTLS,85
Do I Dare to Eat a Peach?	Chelsea Quinn Yarbro	nv SCW # 8,85
"Do It Our Way!"	Stanley Schmidt	ed ASF Dec md,85
The Doctor & the Devils	James Verniere	ar TZM Dec,85
Doctor Who: The Role-Playing Game from FASA (Part One)		
	David F. Bischoff	gr SCA Dec,85
Does It Make a Sound?	Joseph Calabro	ss TZM Apr,85
Short story contest 3rd place winner.		
The Dog at the Door	Ursula K. Le Guin	vi ALWCMHM,85
The Dog on the Roof	Joan Aiken	nv UFCHMNY,84
The Dog That Ate the Baby	Peter A. Bobley	vi NCR V1 #4,85
Dogfight	William Gibson & Michael Swanwick	
		ss OMN Jul,85
Dogs' Lives	Michael Bishop	nv MIS V7 #2,84
Dome of Whispers	Ian Watson	ss IMN
The Dominus Demonstration	Charles Sheffield	nv ASF Apr,84
Don't	J.N. Williamson	vi WDB #20,85
Don't Get Around Much Anymore		
	Ray Brown	nv ASF Mar,85
The Doomsday Device	Dr. John Gribbin	ss ASF Feb,85
Doppler Effects	Robert Frazier	pm IAS Feb,85
Dormant Soul	Josephine Saxton	ss FSF Feb,69
Down by the Riverside	Diane Duane	nv DEADWIN,85
Down from Demolition	John Baxter	ss URBANFN,85
Down the Mine	Ian Watson	ss ARN
Down, Satan!	Clive Barker	ss CBB V 4,85
Downwind	C.J. Cherryh	nv STRMSSN,82
Dr. Sharon N. Farber's Science Fiction Weight Loss Diet		
	Sharon N. Farber	ms SDA Dec,85
Dr. Snow Maiden	Larry Eisenberg	ss FSF Aug,75
Draco, Draco	Tanith Lee	nv BYNDLND,84
Dracula's Guest	Bram Stoker	ss DRCLGST,14
Dragon in the Sea [Under Pressure]		
	Frank Herbert	ex ASF Nov,55
The Dragon Over Hackensack		
	Richard L. Wexelblat	pm 1985
Dragon Reserve, Home Eight		
	Diana Wynne Jones	nv WARLOCK,84
The Dragon Seed	Kate Wilhelm	ss OMN Dec,85
The Dragon Tunnel	Penelope Lively	ss ALT # 6,74
The Dragon's Boy	Jane Yolen	nv FSF Sep,85
Dragon's Horn	J.W. Schutz	nv MGI # 1,85
Dragonet	Esther M. Friesner	ss AMZ Jan,86
Dragonfield	Jane Yolen	nv 1985
Dragonfly Song	Ursula K. Le Guin	pm ALWCMHM,85
Dragons and Dudgeons	Beverly Grant	pm AMZ Jan,85
Dramatic Works	Ursula K. Le Guin	si ALWCMHM,85
Dramatis Personae	Lynn Abbey	pr
Dread	Clive Barker	nv CB3 # 2,84
Dreadsong	Roger Zelazny	ss PLANETS,85

Title	Author	Info
The Girl Who Cried Flowers	Jane Yolen	ss GRLWHOC,74
Girls Will Be Girls	Patricia Shaw-Mathews	ss FRAMZDK,85
Give Us a Big Smile	Charles L. Grant	ss TZM Dec,85
Glass Reptile Breakout	Russell Blackford	ss STRGATR,85
Glossary	Ursula K. Le Guin	ms ALWCMHM,85
Glossary of Obsolete, Archaic, and Rare Words and Meanings	[Misc. Material]	ms
THE GOBLIN TOWER	L. Sprague de Camp	n. PYR 1968
The Goblinry of Ais	Lin Carter	ss MGI # 1,85
God is an Iron	Spider Robinson	nv OMN May,79
The God Machine	Damon Knight	ss FSF Jul,85
God's Hooks	Howard Waldrop	ss UNI #12,82
The God-Chosen	Lynn Abbey	nv DEADWIN,85
Gödel's Doom	George Zebrowski	ss PCM Feb,85
The Gods of Mars	Jack Dann, Gardner Dozois & Michael Swanwick	ss OMN Mar,85
Godson	Andrew J. Offutt	nv STRMSSN,82
Going After Arviq	Michael Armstrong	nv AFTRWAR,85
Going Native	Andrew Weiner	ss NCR V1 #4,85
Going Under	Jack Dann	nv OMN Sep,81
The Gold at the Starbow's End	Frederik Pohl	nv ASF Mar,72
Golden Apples of the Sun [expanded from Virgin Territory]	Jack Dann, Gardner Dozois & Michael Swanwick	nv PNT Mar,84
Golden Dawn	Ronald Anthony Cross	nv FFR V 4,86
The Golden Fleece	Edouard Rene Lefebvre de Laboulaye	nv HRP Apr,1868
Translated by Mary L. Booth, introduction by Jessica Amanda Salmonson.		
Gone to the Dogs	Piers Anthony	ss ANTHNGY,85
Good-by, Miss Paterson	Phyllis MacLennan	ss FSF Jan,72
Good-bye, Henry J. Kostkos, Good-bye	Damon Knight	ar CLR # 2,72
Goodbye, Dr. Ralston	Damon Knight	ss FFR V 1,85
The Gorgon	Tanith Lee	nv SDW # 5,82
The Gorgon Field	Kate Wilhelm	na IAS Aug,85
Gorgonissa	Richard L. Purtill	ss IAS Jan,85
The Gospel According to...	Charles L. Baker	bi EDT #11,85
The Gostak and the Doshes	Miles J. Breuer	ss AMZ Mar,30
The Government in Exile	Paul Collins	vi URBANFN,85
Gramma	Stephen King	nv WDB 1984
Grandma's House	John Edward Damon	pm FBM Mar,85
A Grass Song	Ursula K. Le Guin	pm ALWCMHM,85
The Grass-Green Hound	Josepha Sherman	ss COE Spr,85
Graveyard Shift [The Faces]	Richard Matheson	ss EMB # 1,60
"The Great Dark" [written Aug-Sep 1898]	Mark Twain	nv LTRSERT,62
The Great God Mau	Stella Whitelaw	ss GRMLKNS,83
The Great Mushroom Mistake	Penelope Lively	ss UNVTGST,84
The Great Secret	Fred Saberhagen	ms BSRKRBS,85
The Great Wall	Wayne Wightman	ss FSF Sep,85
Greek	Leigh Kennedy	ss IAS Oct,83
The Green Cat	Pamela Dean	nv LIAVEK ,85
Green Days in Brunei	Bruce Sterling	na IAS Oct,85
Green Hearts	Lee Montgomerie	ss INZ #10,84
The Green Man	Kelvin Jones	ss FTL V7 #12,83
The Green Marauder	Larry Niven	ss DST V2 #1,80
Green Mars	Kim Stanley Robinson	na IAS Sep,85
The Green Rabbit from S'Rian	Gene Wolfe	ss LIAVEK ,85
The Green Tent	Ellen Gilchrist	ss FSF Nov,85
The Greening of Bed-Stuy	Frederik Pohl	na FSF Jul,84
A Grim Tale for Moderns [section cut from PALIMPSESTS]	Carter Scholz	ss CUTS ,85
Group Phenomena	Thomas F. Monteleone	ss SDA Dec,85
GROW OLD ALONG WITH ME [written in summer of 1947]	Isaac Asimov	n. ALTASMV,86
original version of the novel PEBBLE IN THE SKY		
Growing Pains	Susan M. Shwartz	ss FRAMZDK,85
The Guardroom	David A. Drake	nv AFTRWAR,85
Guest Notes	[Misc. Material]	bg FYC #10,85
Guided Tour	Gordon R. Dickson	pm FSF Oct,59
Gyskouras	Lynn Abbey	nv WNGSOMN,84
Half an Oaf	Spider Robinson	nv ANLGANL,76
Halley's Comet	William K. Hartmann	ar PLANETS,85
Hally's Paradise	Douglas Hill	ss OUTOFTM,84
The Hand That Feeds You	Diane Duane	nv WNGSOMN,84
Handedness in Nature	William C. McHarris	ar ASF Jan,86
Handprints on the Moon	William K. Hartmann	ss PLANETS,85
The Hands of the Artist	Kara Dalkey	ss LIAVEK ,85
Hands with Long Fingers	Leslie Halliwell	ss GHSTSHR,84
Hang Head, Vandal!	Mark Clifton	ss AMZ Apr,62
Hanging Town	Steve Sneyd	pm S&T #69,85
The Happiest Sheep in London	Joan Aiken	nv UPCHMNY,84
Happy Dens, or A Day in the Old Wolves Home	Jane Yolen	ss ELW V 3,84
Hard Science in the Real World	Gregory Benford	ar 1984
Hard Sell	Piers Anthony	ss IFS Aug,72
Hard to Credit	John Brunner	ss FSF Oct,85
The Hard Way	Gordon R. Dickson	nv ASF Jan,63
Hard-Luck Diggings	Jack Vance	ss STS Jul,48
The Hardwood Pile	L. Sprague de Camp	nv UNK Sep,40
Harlan Ellison's Watching	Harlan Ellison	mr FSF
Harmony of the Spheres at Spion Kop	Roger Meador	pm IAS Jan,86
Harpist	Joe L. Hensley	ss SPECLTN,82
Harry Tales	Cheri Lane & Lee Nordling	cs FBM Mar,85
The Harvest Child	Steve Rasnic Tem	ss ELW # 3,84
Hatching Season	Harry Turtledove	ss ASF Dec,85
The Haters of Innocence	Carol Ann Cupitt	pm EDT #11,85
Hathor's Pets	Margaret St. Clair	ss STS Jan,50
A Haunted House	Susan Sheppard	pm NCR V1 #4,85
A Haunted Tale of Justice	Jessica Amanda Salmonson	ss FBM Dec,85
The Haunted Trailer	Robert Arthur	nv WRT 1953
The Haunting at Juniper Hill	Joseph Payne Brennan	nv NGV # 2,85
The Haunting of Goodhope	Juleen Brantingham	ss FSF May,85
The Haunting of Y-12	Al Sarrantonio	ss 1981
Hauntings	Kim Antieau	ss IAS Feb,85
He and My Shadow	T.M. Swain	ss TZM Oct,85
He Travels the Fastest	Isaac Asimov	ss IAS Nov,85
He Who Shrank	Henry Hasse	na AMZ Aug,36
Hearts and Engines [Soldiers Running]	Brian W. Aldiss	ss NWS Jun,60
HEARTSEASE	Peter Dickinson	n. GOL 1969
Heathen God	George Zebrowski	ss FSF Jan,71
Heimlich's Curse	Evan Eisenberg	ss TZM Nov,81
Heirs Apparent	Robert Abernathy	nv FSF Nov,54
Heirs of the Perisphere	Howard Waldrop	ss PBY Jul,85
Hell Is Murkey	John Alfred Taylor	nv TZM Nov,82
Hell to Pay	Janet Morris	nv DEADWIN,85
Hell's Event	Clive Barker	nv CBB # 2,84
Hellcatcher	Steven Popkes	ss NCR V1 #5,86
Hellflower	Eluki bes Shahar	nv AMZ Mar,85
Help! The Paranoids Are After Me	Charles E. Fritch	ss WHS Dec,84
Her Letters	Kate Chopin	ss
Her Own Blood	Margaret Carter	ss FRAMZDK,85
Here There Be Tygers	Stephen King	ss UBR Spr,68
A Heritage Upheld	Joseph Payne Brennan	nv GRYSTBY,85
Hero	Joe W. Haldeman	nv ASF Jun,72
The Hero Who Returned	Gerald W. Page	nv HEROFAN,79
Hero's Moon	Marion Zimmer Bradley	nv FSF Oct,76
Hero's Welcome	Janet Morris	ss AFTRWAR,85
Hiding From the Sun	Nina Kiriki Hoffman	ss GRYSTBY,85
HIGH DERYNI	Katherine Kurtz	n. BAL 1973
High Infidelity	Spider Robinson	ss OUI Apr,83
High Moon	Janet Morris	na FACECHS,83
The High Purpose	Barry N. Malzberg & Carter Scholz	ss FSF Nov,85
Hinterlands	William Gibson	ss OMN Oct,81
His Brother's Weeper	Robert Silverberg	nv FUN Mar,59
His Unconquerable Enemy	W.C. Morrow	ss
A Hiss of Dragon	Gregory Benford & Marc Laidlaw	nv OMN Dec,78
"History 1,000 Years from Now" [probably written Jan 1901]	Mark Twain	ss MTFBLMN,72
History Lesson	W.R. Thompson	ss ASF Aug,85
The History Machine	George Zebrowski	ss NWQ # 3,72
History of Animal-Land	C.S. Lewis	ss BOXEN ,85
History of Mouse-Land from Stone-Age to Bublish I	C.S. Lewis	vi BOXEN ,85
Hitch on the Bull Run	Sharon Webb	ss IAS Jun,79
Hitch Your Spaceship to a Star	Donald E. Westlake	ss PBY Dec,85
Hobson's Choice	Alfred Bester	ss FSF Aug,52
A Hole in the Air	Ursula K. Le Guin	ss ALWCMHM,85
The Holiday House	A.R. Morlan	ss NCR V1 #5,86
Holy Quarrel	Philip K. Dick	nv WOT May,66
Home by the Sea	Elisabeth Vonarburg	ss TESRCTS,85
translated by Jane Brierley		
Home Is the Hangman	Roger Zelazny	na ASF Nov,75
Homecoming	Ray Bradbury	ss MAD Oct,46
The Homecoming	Barry B. Longyear	nv IAS Oct,79
Homecoming	Susan M. Shwartz	nv MGI # 1,85
Hominid Voices	Robert Frazier & Andrew Joron	pm URN # 4,84
A Hong's Bluff	William F. Wu	ss OMN Mar,85
Honorable Mentions: 1984	Gardner Dozois	bi
Hoods Isle and the Hermit Oberlus	Herman Melville	ss
Hop-Friend	Terry Carr	ss FSF Nov,62
Hop-Frog	Edgar Allan Poe	ss SLM Apr,1836
The Horn of Elfland	J.O. Jeppson	ss IAS Mar,83
Horrer Howce	Margaret St. Clair	ss GAL Jul,56
The Horror from the Bridge	Ramsey Campbell	ss INHBLKE,64
The Horror of the Heights	Arthur Conan Doyle	ss SND Nov,13
Horrorscope	Ian Watson	ss
The Horse	Libby Tinker	ss WHA # 5,85
The Hospice	Robert Aickman	nv COLDHND,75
The Host	Sheldon R. Jaffery	ss S&T #69,85
Hot Rocks and Water	G.F.R. Ellis & Tony Rothman	ar ASF Mar,85
The Hotter Flash	J.O. Jeppson	ss IAS Apr,81
THE HOUR OF THE GATE	Alan Dean Foster	n. WBK 1984
The House in Goblin Wood [as Carter Dickson]	John Dickson Carr	ss EQM Nov,47
The House of Cthulhu	Brian Lumley	ss WHS V1 #1,73
The House of If	Barry B. Longyear	nv IAS Apr,81
House of Ill Repute	Jeffrey Goddin	ss FTL Sum,85
The House of Sounds	M.P. Shiel	nv PALEAPE,11
The House of the Nightmare	Edward Lucas White	ss TTB Sep,19
House of Weapons	Gordon R. Dickson	na FFR V 2,85
Houston, Houston, Do You Read?	James Tiptree, Jr.	na AURORA ,76

Title	Author	Publication
Nahallywood: Coming Attractions	Ed Naha	mr SDA
Nahallywood: Invasion of the Teenagers from Mars	Ed Naha	ar SDA Dec,85
Nahallywood: 'George Romero and the Day of the Dead'	Ed Naha	mr SDA Oct,85
Napoleon's Skullcap	Gordon R. Dickson	nv FSF May,62
The Nasty Naughty Nazi Ninja Nudnik Elves	Joshua Quagmire	cs FBM Dec,85
The Nebraskan and the Nereid	Gene Wolfe	ss IAS Dec,85
NECROMANCER NINE	Sheri S. Tepper	n. ACE 1983
Necromant	C.J. Cherryh	nv FACECHS,83
Need	James Sallis	ss IAS Jan,85
The Need to Believe	Stanley Schmidt	ed ASF Jun,85
The Needle Men	George R.R. Martin	ss FSF Oct,81
The Needle on Full	Caroline Forbes	nv CYC 1980
The Neighbor's Wife	Susan Palwick	pm AMZ Jul,85
The Neighbors	Joseph H. Delaney	ss ASF Jan,86
Neighbors	Rolaine Hochstein	ss FSF Jul,85
Neptune: Farthest Giant	Dale P. Cruikshank	ar PLANETS,85
Never Grow Up	John Gordon	ss CTCHDTH,84
New Adventures in the Scream Trade [interview with Stephen King]	Ben Herndon	iv TZM Dec,85
New Aesthetics	Josephine Saxton	ss PWRTIME,85
New Breed	Dave Smeds	ss IKR Sep,85
New Man	Barbara Owens	ss TZM Mar,82
New Murders in the Rue Morgue	Clive Barker	nv CBB # 2,84
New Ritual [as Idris Seabright]	Margaret St. Clair	ss FSF Jan,53
New Rose Hotel	William Gibson	ss OMN Jul,84
The New Science Fiction	Vincent Omniaveritas	ar INZ #14,85
New Year's Eve at Tambimatu	Ian Watson	na FSF Dec,83
News	Stuart David Schiff	ar WHS Dec,84
A Newsman's Notebook	Gilbert Brown	ar
Newton Sleep	Gregory Benford	nv FSF Jan,86
The Nifty Murder Case	Richard Mueller	ss FSF May,85
Night and Silence	Maurice Level	ss WRT Feb,32
A Night at the Head of a Grave	Thomas Sullivan	ss SDW # 8,85
A Night at Two Inns	Phyllis Ann Karr	nv S&S # 2,85
Night Bus	Donald R. Burleson	vi EDT #11,85
Night Catch	Chelsea Quinn Yarbro	nv GRYSTBY,85
Night Life	Caroline Forbes	ss NEDLFUL,85
Night Nemesis	Frederick C. Davis	nv TDA Nov,33
Night on the Interchange	James Haralson	ss AMZ May,85
The Night People	Michael Reaves	ss TZM Oct,85
Night Win	Nancy Kress	nv IAS Sep,83
Night Winds and Sepulchral Bells	James William Hjort	ss WDB #20,85
The Night Wire	H.F. Arnold	ss WRT Sep,26
Night-Scape: A Painter's Tale	Morgan Griffith	pm EDT #11,85
Nightfall	Isaac Asimov	nv ASF Sep,41
Nightflyers [expanded from ASF Apr,80]	George R.R. Martin	na BST # 5,81
Nightmare	Larry Brown	vi TZM Feb,85
Nightmare at 20,000 Feet	Richard Matheson	ss ALONEBY,62
Nine Lives	Stella Whitelaw	ss GRMLKNS,83
No Coward Soul	Josephine Saxton	ss INZ # 3,82
No Future in It	Joe W. Haldeman	ss OMN Apr,79
No Life For Me Without You, Vodyanoi	Stephen Gallagher	nv FSF Sep,85
No One	Diana Wynne Jones	nv WARLOCK,84
No Other Gods	Reginald Bretnor	nv MIDNGHT,85
No Regrets	Lisa Tuttle	ss FSF May,85
No Renewal	Spider Robinson	ss GAL Mar,77
No Truce With Kings	Poul Anderson	na FSF Jun,63
No. 252 Rue M. Le Prince	Ralph Adams Cram	ss BLKSPRT,1895
The Nobel Prize That Wasn't	Isaac Asimov	ar FSF Apr,70
Nocturne	Robert Bloch	ss GRYSTBY,85
Noise	Jack Vance	ss STS Aug,52
Nona	Stephen King	nv SDW # 1,78
Noninterference	Eric G. Iverson	ss ASF Jul,85
The Noodge Factor	J.O. Jeppson	ss MYSCURE,85
Nor the Many-Colored Fires of a Star Ring	George R.R. Martin	nv FSTRLGT,76
Nostalgia: Old Dark House for Rent	Ron Goulart	ar TZM Feb,85
Not a Creature Was Stirring	John Alfred Taylor	ss WDB #20,85
Not Fade Away	Spider Robinson	ss IAS Aug,82
Not Long Before the End	Larry Niven	ss FSF Apr,69
A Note About the Novel	Ursula K. Le Guin	si ALWCMHM,85
A Note and a Chart Concerning Narrative Modes	Ursula K. Le Guin	ms ALWCMHM,85
Note on the original submission on the Lay of Leithian and The Silmarillion in 1937	Christopher Tolkien	ar
A Note on the Selections	Lincoln Child	pr
Notes	Stephen King	bi
Notes for a Newer Testament	David Langford	ss AFTRWAR,85
Notes from the General Secretariat	Mark Gordian	ss ASF Aug,85
Notes on Contributors	[Misc. Material]	bg
Notes on the Authors	[Misc. Material]	bg
Nothing in the Rules	L. Sprague de Camp	nv UNK Jul,39
Nuclear Autumn	Ben Bova	ss FFR V 2,85
Nuclear Tan	A.A. Attanasio	ss BEASTMK,85

Title	Author	Publication
Null-P	William Tenn	ss WBY Jan,51
Number 13	Stephen Robinette	ss OMN Nov,82
The Nuse Man	Margaret St. Clair	ss GAL Feb,60
O Happy Day!	Geoff Ryman	nv IZA # 1,85
O Homo, O Femina, O Tempora	Kate Wilhelm	ss OMN May,85
O Little Town of Bethlehem II	Robert F. Young	ss IAS Dec,85
O Lyric Love	Charles L. Harness	ss AMZ May,85
O Moon of My Delight [Moon of Delight]	Brian W. Aldiss	nv NWS Mar,61
Oasis of Abomination	Joseph Payne Brennan	nv NGV # 2,85
The Oath of the Free Amazons	Walter Breen	ms DRKOVRC,79
Oath of the Free Amazons: Terran, Techno Period	Jaida n'ha Sandra	ms FRAMZDK,85
Object of the Attack	J.G. Ballard	ss INZ # 9,84
The Observatory	Patrick L. Price & George H. Scithers	ed AMZ Sep,85
The Observatory	Darrell Schweitzer & George H. Scithers	ed AMZ May,85
The Observatory	George H. Scithers	ed AMZ
The Occupant of the Room	Algernon Blackwood	ss DAY&NGT,17
Occupational Hazard	G.L. Raisor	vi NCR V1 #4,85
An Occurrence at Owl Creek Bridge	Ambrose Bierce	ss INMIDST,1891
October	Charles Stauffer	pm WDB #20,85
Of Law and Magic	C.J. Cherryh	nv MNSNGRF,85
Of Memories Dying	Michael Bracken	ss MIDNGHT,85
Of Time and Kathy Benedict	William F. Nolan	nv FTL V7 #13,84
Of Time and Space	Hugh B. Cave	ss BLD V1 #2,85
Offerings at Medusa	Joel Henry Sherman	ss AMZ May,85
Ogre	Clifford D. Simak	nv ASF Jan,44
Old Acquaintances and New	Jo Clayton	na BAITDRM,85
Old Cloths	Ramsey Campbell	ss MIDNGHT,85
Old Haunts	Richard Matheson	ss FSF Oct,57
Old Hundredth	Brian W. Aldiss	ss NWS Nov,60
Old Hundredth	Isaac Asimov	ed IAS Jan,86
Old Loves	Karl Edward Wagner	ss NGV # 2,85
The Old Man	Henry Slesar	ss DCM 1962
The Old Refrains	Stanley Schmidt	ed ASF Nov,85
The Old Woman and the Storm	Patricia A. McKillip	ss IMGNLND,85
Old Woman Hating	Ursula K. Le Guin	ss ALWCMHM,85
Old Woman Sings	Ursula K. Le Guin	pm ALWCMHM,85
An Old-Fashioned Bird Christmas	Margaret St. Clair	nv GAL Dec,61
On a Hot Summer Night in a Place Far Away	Pat Murphy	ss IAS May,85
On Books	Baird Searles	br IAS
On Books: Books into Movies	Norman Spinrad	br IAS Nov,85
On Books: Inside, Outside	Norman Spinrad	br IAS Jul,85
On Books: Must There Be War?	Norman Spinrad	br IAS Jan,86
On Books: Transatlantic Science Fiction	Norman Spinrad	br IAS Mar,85
On First Looking into Bradley's Guidelines, or Stories I Don't Want to Read Either	Elizabeth Thompson	pm S&S # 2,85
on for the Long Haul	T. Coraghessan Boyle	nv IAS Aug,85
On Gaming	Dana Lombardy	gr ASF
On Messenger Mountain	Gordon R. Dickson	na WOT Jun,64
On Science Fiction	Jack Williamson	ar WRTRFUT,85
On Second Hill	Ursula K. Le Guin	pm ALWCMHM,85
On Shaping Creativity	Algis Budrys	ar WRTRFUT,85
On Springfield Mountain	Rand B. Lee	nv AMZ Jan,85
On the Brighton Road	Richard Middleton	ss GHSTSHP,12
On the Brightside	Steve Stiles	cs SDA
On the Deck of the Flying Bomb	David Redd	ss INZ # 4,82
On the Dream Channel Panel	Ian Watson	ss AMZ Mar,85
On the Edge	Mary Gentle	br INZ
On the Fourth Planet	J.F. Bone	ss GAL Apr,63
On the Nursery Floor	George Turner	nv STRGATR,85
On the Planet Grafool	Benjamin Freedman	ss TESRCTS,85
On the Rio Madera	Robert Frazier	pm BPC #26,85
On the Trail	Barbara Armistead	ss FRAMZDK,85
On the Uses of Torture	Piers Anthony	nv BKS V 3,81
Once a Good Man	Jane Yolen	ss 100thDV,76
One for the Angels [Rod Serling]	Anne Serling-Sutton	sa TWLGTZN,85
One for the Road	Stephen King	ss MNE Mar,77
One Last Dance	Dean Wesley Smith	ss WRTRFUT,85
One on Trial	Gordon R. Dickson	ss FSF Jan,60
One Summer Night	Ambrose Bierce	vi
One Wish!?	David R. Bunch	pm IAS Oct,85
The One-Shoe Blues	Ron Wolfe	ss IAS Nov,85
The Ones Who Never Talk	Peter D. Pautz	ss WHS Dec,84
The Only	Al Sarrantonio	ss GRYSTBY,85
The Only Neat Thing to Do	James Tiptree, Jr.	na FSF Oct,85
The Oogenesis of Bird City	Philip José Farmer	ss AMZ Sep,70
An Open Letter to Andre Norton	Joan D. Vinge	ms MNSNGRF,85
The Open Window	Saki	ss BST&SUP,12
Opening Move on Egil's World	John Dalmas	nv FFR V 4,86
Operation Salamander	Poul Anderson	nv FSF Jan,57

WORD PROCESSOR OF THE GODS [THE WORD PROCESSOR]

APPENDICES

BOOK SUMMARY

It's an old joke among executives that the time to really worry is when things are going too well. They're bound to change quickly, so you'd better have your plans ready when they do.

1985 was a record year in sf in both numbers of books published and books sold. Most publishing executives are worried about 1986 -- with cause.

Those of you who remember 1984 will remember that the year ended with the bestseller lists awash with hardcover science fiction, the movie screens alight with science fiction, and the chain bookstores, Waldenbooks and B. Dalton, posting record sales on sf books.

The publishers responded by putting out more books in 1985 (a record 1332), getting more copies out to the chains, and upping the number of hardcovers. Newer publishers also jumped on the bandwagon. (Despite the various mergers, we listed 122 publishers doing sf last year, up from 111 the year before.) Naturally, there are now too many books, returns are up, and the chains will probably be cutting back on sf because it is no longer expanding as a profit center. Most publishers agree there are too many books, but are afraid to cut back. Income in the publishing industry is the money for present books less the amount for past returns. If you cut your present titles, your income goes way down. The classic way around this is to raise prices and expand into an area which is becoming popular. Indeed, the $2.95 paperback is on its way out and $3.50 will be the common price in 1986. Mystery fiction is enjoying a huge expansion with publishers and bookstores. Unfortunately, the price of paper also went up and returns went way up -- and not only in traditional paperbacks. 1985 saw the mass market hardcover come into its own -- hardcovers which sold in paperback numbers to a normally paperback audience. They were also paperback-style returns for the first time.

The chains also got caught in something new: a price war. Books normally cost 60% of cover price, overhead and cost of money is usually 20%, and gross profit is 20%. If Crown, Waldenbooks, and Dalton discount hardcovers 35%, they've created loss leaders. If they discount 20%, they probably break even.

This Christmas, all the chains discounted THE MAMMOTH HUNTERS by Jean Auel by 38% off and sold record numbers. The earlier two books in the series went back on bestseller lists in hardcover even though the Bantam paperbacks were also available. Bantam, which owns paperback rights, is worried that the million-copy sale in hardcover will come right off the top of the paperback sale.

Two decades ago, discounting forced the record industry to give deeper discounts to stores, and list prices became a fiction. It may happen in the book field. Meanwhile, the chains need 20% to 30% expansion each year. They can partially get it by opening more stores and partially by expanding areas which are undersold right now. Mysteries, video products, and audio products are expanding. The stores are the same size. Therefore, areas such as science fiction will be cut back on even though they're selling better than ever. Now you know why publishers are worried.

Anyway, 1985 was a great year. The total of books, 1332, was up 13% from the year before. What do we count or not count? Our monthly book listing is the basis. Everything counted has appeared there, but not everything appearing there is counted. We exclude British and other foreign books, non-sf books by sf authors, science books, and some non-fiction which has only a passing reference to sf. We also exclude pamphlets and chapbooks. Because the list covers all books seen in 1985, it includes some 1984 titles which either appeared late or were missed. It also includes most publications dated January 1986, and thus differs from other lists. It evens out every year, but *Locus* Award eligibility essentially runs from February to January instead of January to December.

We count first American editions as new books even though we may have mentioned an earlier British one. Omnibus volumes are new even if everything in them has appeared before. A book broken up into more volumes, however, is considered a reprint. If a paperback and hardcover are done nearly simultaneously, the hardcover is considered new and the paperback a reprint. In most cases the paperback is distributed at least a month before the hardcover and is considered the first. We mention it if a publisher says there is a library hardcover available, but don't count it unless we actually get a copy. Our count is definitely under instead of over, because we know some books exist, particularly small press and limited edition, which we did not see and did not count.

Mass market paperbacks are rack-size books available on newsstands as well as in bookstores. Trade paperbacks are usually oversize (and overpriced) but can also be rack-size. They're available only at trade outlets: bookstores, department stores, etc.

Of the 1332 books listed, 715 (54%) were new. The percentage

CHART #1

Sf novels	249	Novelizations	39
Fantasy novels	177	Art	28
Reference	74	Omnibus	20
Anthologies	64	Misc.	17
Collections	48		

CHART 2: ORIGINAL BOOKS

	1985	1984	1983	1982	1981
SF	34.8%	32.4%	32.4%	32.2%	32.3%
Fantasy	24.8%	28.1%	25.4%	22.6%	23.5%
Anthology	9.0%	9.3%	9.2%	11.0%	12.8%
Collection	6.7%	8.8%	7.0%	10.8%	9.7%
Reference	10.3%	10.3%	10.1%	8.4%	6.4%
Nvlization	5.5%	4.9%	6.4%	5.1%	4.5%
Omnibus	2.8%	1.8%	3.1%	3.0%	2.2%
Art	3.9%	3.3%	1.2%	3.1%	1.0%
Misc.	2.2%	1.1%	5.1%	3.8%	7.6%

CHART 3: TOP PUBLISHERS -- TOTAL BOOKS

	1985	1984	1983	1982	1981
Putnam/Ace/Berkley	237	255	222	221	202
Tor	102	55	47	31	19
Bal./Del Rey	100	104	108	92	94
DAW	85	80	69	67	64
Bantam	77	71	58	42	57
SFBC	63	55	61	59	56
Baen	57	28	--	--	--
NAL/Signet	45	28	30	33	25
Bluejay	39	33	--	--	--
S&S/Pocket/etc.	38	59	88	81	79

CHART 4: TOP PUBLISHERS -- ORIGINAL BOOKS

	'85	'84	'83	'82	'81	'80
Ptm./Ace/Berkley	92	84	87	65	84	90
Tor	54	28	29	24	14	--
Bal./Del Rey	41	40	45	43	32	33
DAW	41	39	42	37	39	38
Baen	32	17	--	--	--	--
Bantam	28	30	20	23	26	26
Doubleday	28	30	24	19	32	29
NAL/Signet	24	16	16	20	14	15
Bluejay	23	17	--	--	--	--
S&S/Pocket	20	29	44	45	49	44

CHART 5: RECOMMENDED BOOKS

	1985	1984	1983	1982	1981
Ptm./Berkley/Ace	22	20	17	12	18
Tor	14	1	2	2	-
Bluejay	13	10	-	-	-
Bal./Del Rey	12	12	10	13	9
Bantam	12	6	5	7	7
DAW	9	9	12	9	14
Baen	8	6	-	-	-
Doubleday	7	4	7	7	9
Arbor House	7	3	1	0	2

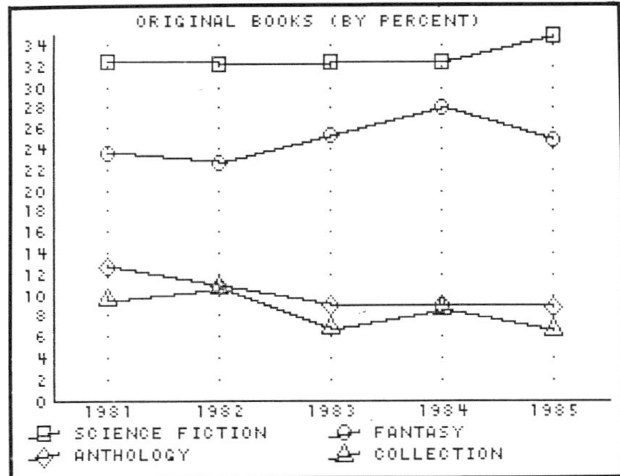

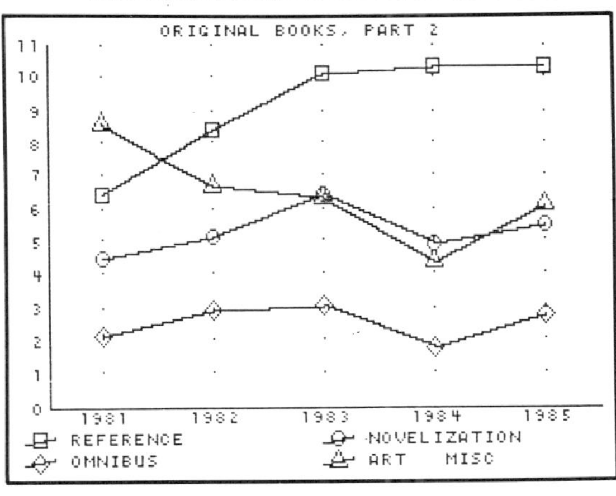

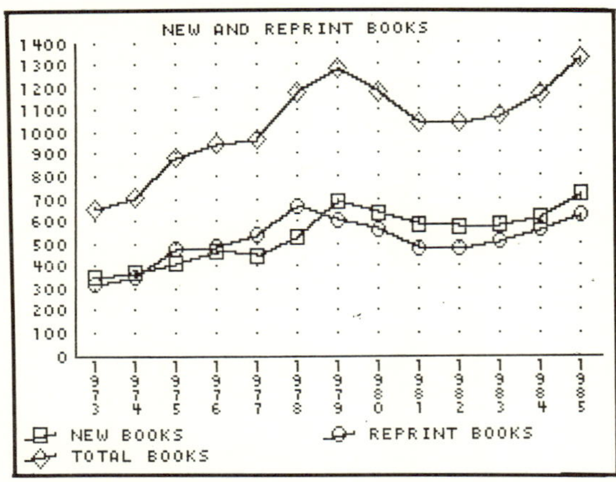

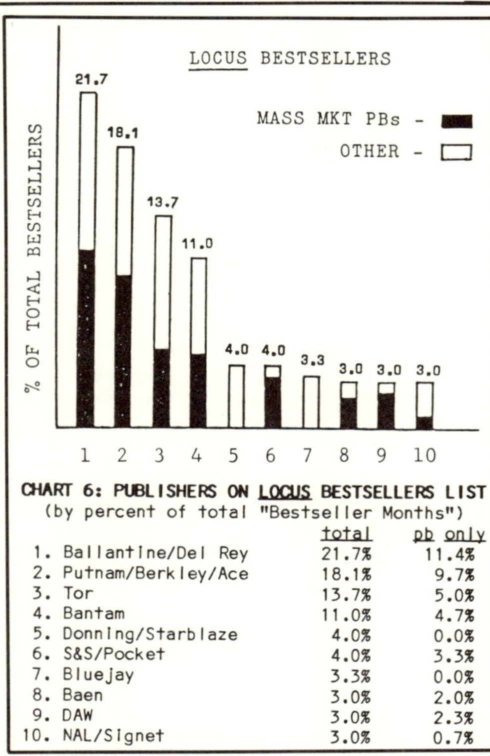

CHART 6: PUBLISHERS ON LOCUS BESTSELLERS LIST
(by percent of total "Bestseller Months")

		total	pb only
1.	Ballantine/Del Rey	21.7%	11.4%
2.	Putnam/Berkley/Ace	18.1%	9.7%
3.	Tor	13.7%	5.0%
4.	Bantam	11.0%	4.7%
5.	Donning/Starblaze	4.0%	0.0%
6.	S&S/Pocket	4.0%	3.3%
7.	Bluejay	3.3%	0.0%
8.	Baen	3.0%	2.0%
9.	DAW	3.0%	2.3%
10.	NAL/Signet	3.0%	0.7%

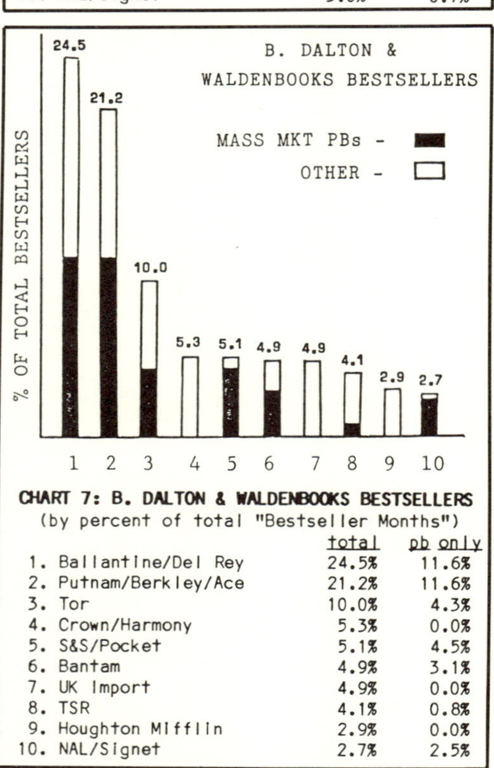

CHART 7: B. DALTON & WALDENBOOKS BESTSELLERS
(by percent of total "Bestseller Months")

		total	pb only
1.	Ballantine/Del Rey	24.5%	11.6%
2.	Putnam/Berkley/Ace	21.2%	11.6%
3.	Tor	10.0%	4.3%
4.	Crown/Harmony	5.3%	0.0%
5.	S&S/Pocket	5.1%	4.5%
6.	Bantam	4.9%	3.1%
7.	UK Import	4.9%	0.0%
8.	TSR	4.1%	0.8%
9.	Houghton Mifflin	2.9%	0.0%
10.	NAL/Signet	2.7%	2.5%

PUBLISHER	HARDCOVER New	Reprint	PAPERBACK New	Reprint	TRADE PB New	Reprint	TOTAL
Putnam/Berkley/Ace/etc.	9	2	81	141	2	2	237
Tor	13	-	34	48	7	-	102
Ballantine/Del Rey/Fawcett	9	-	31	47	1	12	100
DAW	2	-	39	43	-	1	85
Bantam	6	-	19	49	3	-	77
SFBC	14	49	-	-	-	-	63
Baen	4	-	28	25	-	-	57
NAL/Signet	1	-	21	17	2	4	45
Bluejay	19	1	-	-	5	14	39
S&S/Pocket/Arco/Wash. Sq.	7	-	12	14	1	4	38
Avon	-	-	16	16	1	-	33
Doubleday/Dial	28	1	-	-	-	-	29
Warner/Popular Library	-	-	18	11	-	-	29
Harper & Row	15	2	-	-	2	3	22
Random House/Knopf/etc.	13	-	-	-	2	7	22
Dell/Delacorte/Delta	4	-	3	4	-	10	21
Scribners/Atheneum	17	2	-	-	-	1	20
Zebra	-	-	12	4	-	-	16
Harcourt Brace Jovanovich	3	-	-	-	-	10	13
UMI Research	12	-	-	-	-	-	12
Arbor House	10	-	-	-	-	-	10
Crown/Harmony/Bonanza	5	2	-	-	3	-	10
Pinnacle	-	-	9	1	-	-	10
St. Martin's	7	-	-	-	1	1	9
Gregg/G.K. Hall/Twayne	2	6	-	-	-	-	8
Starmont	-	-	-	-	8	-	8
Viking/Penguin	4	-	-	-	-	4	8
Greenwood	7	-	-	-	-	-	7
Houghton Mifflin	5	-	-	-	1	1	7
Macmillan/Bradbury/Collier	6	-	-	-	1	-	7
Dutton	6	-	-	-	-	-	6
Phantasia Press	5	1	-	-	-	-	6
Quality Paperback Book Club	-	-	-	-	-	6	6
Scholastic	-	-	4	2	-	-	6
Scream/Press	4	1	-	-	1	-	6
Borgo	-	-	-	-	5	-	5
Crossway	-	-	-	-	1	4	5
Donald M. Grant	3	2	-	-	-	-	5
Morrow/Greenwillow/Lothrop	3	2	-	-	-	-	5
Ungar	3	-	-	-	-	2	5
82 misc. publishers	59	13	5	5	31	20	133
TOTAL	305	84	332	427	78	106	1332

		HARDBOUND		TRADE PB		MASS MKT PB		ALL BOOKS		% NEW
1972	New	85				140		225		
	Reprint	28				95		123		
	Total	113				235		348		65%
1973	New	155	(+82%)			191	(+36%)	346	(+54%)		
	Reprint	35	(+25%)			280	(+195%)	315	(+156%)		
	Total	190	(+68%)			471	(+100%)	661	(+90%)	52%	
1974	New	172	(+11%)			201	(+ 5%)	373	(+ 8%)		
	Reprint	59	(+69%)			288	(+ 3%)	347	(+10%)		
	Total	231	(+22%)			489	(+ 4%)	720	(+ 9%)	52%	
1975	New	160	(- 7%)			251	(+25%)	411	(+10%)		
	Reprint	149	(+152%)			330	(+15%)	479	(+38%)		
	Total	309	(+34%)			581	(+19%)	890	(+24%)	46%	
1976	New	186	(+16%)			284	(+13%)	470	(+14%)		
	Reprint	160	(+ 7%)			324	(- 2%)	484	(+ 1%)		
	Total	346	(+12%)			608	(+ 5%)	954	(+ 7%)	49%	
1977	New	220	(+18%)			225	(-21%)	445	(- 5%)		
	Reprint	95	(-41%)			441	(+36%)	536	(+11%)		
	Total	315	(- 9%)			666	(+10%)	981	(+ 3%)	45%	
1978	New	239	(+ 9%)			289	(+28%)	528	(+19%)		
	Reprint	173	(+82%)			488	(+11%)	661	(+23%)		
	Total	412	(+31%)			777	(+17%)	1189	(+21%)	44%	
1979	New	320	(+34%)			365	(+26%)	685	(+30%)		
	Reprint	132	(-24%)			471	(- 3%)	603	(- 9%)		
	Total	452	(+10%)			836	(+ 8%)	1288	(+ 8%)	53%	
1980	New	264	(-18%)	43		323		630	(- 8%)		
	Reprint	106	(-20%)	62		386		554	(- 8%)		
	Total	370	(-18%)	105		709		1184	(- 8%)	53%	
1981	New	247	(- 6%)	35	(-19%)	297	(- 8%)	579	(- 8%)		
	Reprint	77	(-27%)	54	(-13%)	343	(-11%)	474	(-14%)		
	Total	324	(-12%)	89	(-15%)	640	(-10%)	1053	(-11%)	55%	
1982	New	246	(--)	49	(+40%)	277	(- 7%)	572	(- 1%)		
	Reprint	70	(- 9%)	61	(+13%)	344	(--)	475	(--)		
	Total	316	(- 2%)	110	(+24%)	621	(- 3%)	1047	(- 1%)	55%	
1983	New	252	(+ 2%)	69	(+41%)	260	(- 6%)	581	(+ 2%)		
	Reprint	80	(+14%)	61	(--)	363	(+ 5%)	504	(+ 6%)		
	Total	332	(+ 5%)	130	(+18%)	623	(--)	1085	(+ 4%)	54%	
1984	New	270	(+ 7%)	69	(--)	274	(+ 5%)	613	(+ 6%)		
	Reprint	92	(+15%)	76	(+25%)	395	(+ 9%)	563	(+12%)		
	Total	362	(+ 9%)	145	(+12%)	669	(+ 7%)	1176	(+ 8%)	52%	
1985	New	305	(+13%)	78	(+13%)	332	(+21%)	715	(+17%)		
	Reprint	84	(- 9%)	106	(+39%)	427	(+ 8%)	617	(+10%)		
	Total	389	(+ 7%)	184	(+27%)	759	(+13%)	1332	(+13%)	54%	

doesn't change much over the years. The interesting statistic was in quality reprints. Hardcovers were down and trade paperbacks were up. Even university presses have switched to trade paperbacks.

For a comparison with past years, we converted figures to percentages (see Chart 2). It's interesting to note that the breakdown changes little from year to year. There may seem to be nothing published but fantasy novels, but it just isn't so.

The 249 sf novels include 24 young-adult or juvenile, 13 literary with sf trappings, 17 survivalist novels, 2 translations, and 20 first novels.

The fantasy novels had 28 YA/juveniles, 20 first novels, 11 horror novels (we only list horror if the fantasy element is central), 9 literary works with fantasy trappings, and 3 translations.

Reference grows every year. This group of 74 had 41 volumes of literary criticism, 11 bibliography, 8 biography, 4 on movies, and 10 miscellaneous.

The rest of the categories are self-explanatory. The anthologies had 26 primarily with original stories and 38 mostly reprint.

The Berkley/Ace group again led the field in total titles published and in number of originals (see Charts 3 and 4), but Tor edged out Del Rey for second place in both categories. Of the leading publishers, only Tor and Baen produced more originals than reprints and reissues.

Berkley/Ace again had the lion's share of our recommended books (see Chart 5), but Tor has jumped to second place. We leave it to the reader to divide recommended books into total new books and discuss the significance of it. There are lots of other figures which can be generated from the ones listed.

Finally, we have a series of bar graphs and charts which show percentage of bestsellers on the *Locus* list and on the combined Waldenbooks/Dalton list. We keep them separate because buying patterns are different. These charts, when you look closely, show not only the dominance of Del Rey and why it's considered the most profitable line -- a larger percentage of its books reach the bestseller lists -- but the hardcover/paperback integration of sf. The separate paperback figures which cover mass market only (trade paperbacks are included with hardcovers) show that no line of just paperbacks can do well enough. Putnam, with only a few sf titles (Herbert, Farmer) has nearly as many bestseller months as Berkley/Ace. Series books help. Pocket's bestsellers are all Star Trek or Douglas Adams. TSR is the "Dragonlance" series only, Crown is Douglas Adams only, and UK imports are all Dr. Who.

The most interesting thing about looking at these figures all at once was that fantasy novels dominated the books which appeared once and then disappeared, while sf was lower down but seemed to last longer. Publishers must agree, because they're still producing more sf than fantasy.

We don't have any financial figures this year on how the companies are doing, but they all say they're doing well despite the significant increase in returns.

For 1986? Probably no decrease in number of books, because paperback schedules are set almost a year in advance. Higher prices on paperbacks of course. If hardcover returns keep up, there may be a shift to trade paperbacks. If trade paperbacks finally sell, mass market editions will be delayed or cancelled. It should be a very interesting year.

--<u>C.N. Brown</u>

CINEMA SUMMARY

1985 was a disappointing year for the film industry, with the collective box-office gross registering an approximate 5% drop from 1984. Sadly, science fiction and horror films were especially hard hit.

Even granting the growing popularity of VCRs, lack of "attractive" (read "commercial") product seemed the more obvious reason for the drop, since the number of big-budget, well-crafted science fiction films with solid story lines, so much in evidence in '84, had diminished drastically in '85.

Of the top ten grossing films, only four could be labeled science fiction (versus six last year). In order: <u>Back to the Future</u>, biggest grosser of the year at $190 million, followed by <u>Cocoon</u> at $76 million, <u>Goonies</u> at $56.8 million, and <u>A View to a Kill</u> at $49.7 million. Of these, <u>Goonies</u> and <u>A View to a Kill</u> were more adventure than pure science fiction, but let's stretch the definition (though not far enough to include <u>Rambo</u> and <u>Rocky IV</u>, flag-waving fantasies of a different kind).

Other respectable grossers during the year were <u>Mad Max Beyond Thunderdome</u> ($33 million); <u>Teen Wolf</u> ($33 million), riding on the popularity of its star, Michael J. Fox, who also starred in <u>Back to the Future</u>; <u>Fright Night</u> ($25 million), a stylish and clever vampire flick; <u>The Black Cauldron</u> ($21 million), the first new Disney animation in years, though it's doubtful it made a profit because of its high cost; and the re-release of <u>E.T.</u> ($33 million).

Almost everything else, depending on negative cost and the price of hype, went in the toilet, including most of the teenage-scientist movies such as <u>D.A.R.Y.L.</u>, <u>My Science Project</u>, <u>Explorers</u> and <u>Weird Science</u>, and the bulk of the horror exploitation flicks (<u>Day of the Dead</u>, <u>Ghoulies</u>, <u>Herbert West: Re-Animator</u>, etc.). Even Stephen King had tough sledding at the box office, both <u>Silver Bullet</u> and <u>Cat's Eye</u> being commercial disappointments.

<u>Enemy Mine</u>, based on a story by Barry Longyear, was one of the better science fiction films of the year and the only "hardcore" sf spectacular in the style of <u>Alien</u>, <u>Star Wars</u> or <u>Blade Runner</u>. Directed by Wolfgang Petersen (director of <u>Das Boot</u>), this end-of-the-year release was savaged by the critics and ignored at the box office. It has its flaws -- too long, a maudlin ending, Louis Gossett Jr.'s far too cutesy mother-to-be -- but it still rates as an Important Film in the science fiction canon and one not to be missed. The $24 million cost of Petersen's version should all be on screen, both Gossett (when he plays the Drac warrior) and Dennis Quaid (his human counterpart) are excellent, the special effects unobtrusive but convincing, the story needed. See it, if only as an antidote to <u>Rambo</u> and <u>Rocky IV</u> and all the science fiction war films (and books) which have been a staple of the field long before the politicians exported "Star Wars" to outer space. Admittedly a movie with a message, <u>Enemy Mine</u> at least carries a far different one than that peddled by the Stallone movies or the paranoid "The Commies are coming! The Commies are coming!" efforts such as <u>Red Dawn</u> and <u>Invasion U.S.A.</u>.

Also worth catching were two other end-of-the-year releases, <u>The Jewel of the Nile</u> (for the appearance of The Flying Karamazov Brothers and Avner, the Eccentric) and <u>Young Sherlock Holmes</u>, which has attractive young performers as Holmes and Watson, some amazing special effects, a convincing London, and the worst story line since <u>Indiana Jones and the Temple of Doom</u>. In fact, at times it looked like the same story line....

More films deserving at least a passing mention: <u>Ladyhawke</u>, an excellent sword-and-sorcery effort, despite the year's most inappropriate sound track ($18 million); <u>The Company of Wolves</u> ($4.2 million), a fascinating Freudian version of "Little Red Riding Hood" starring Angela Lansbury; and <u>The Emerald Forest</u>, a pastoral fantasy supposedly based on a true-life event and featuring the best-looking noble savages we've ever seen in films (more T&A than a porno flick!).

Big studio loser of the year was Disney, which lost a bundle on <u>Return to Oz</u> ($14 million gross), <u>Baby</u> (another $14 million grosser), and <u>The Black Cauldron</u>. All three were critical disappointments as well; <u>The Black Cauldron</u> showed Disney animation at its best but, again, suffered from a weak story line.

Guessing the final gross of <u>Jewel of the Nile</u> at $75 million and <u>Young Sherlock Holmes</u> at $40 million, the top 10 sf releases of 1985 added to a box office total of about $600 million, versus a gross of close to $900 million for the top 10 sf releases of 1984.

Less "attractive" (commercially appealing) product? You bet. Consider the top 10 science fiction releases in 1984: <u>Ghostbusters</u> ($221 million), <u>Indiana Jones and the Temple of Doom</u> ($176 million), <u>Gremlins</u> ($148 million), <u>Star Trek III</u> ($75 million), <u>Romancing the Stone</u> ($75 million), <u>Splash</u> ($62 million), <u>2010</u> ($40 million), <u>Terminator</u> ($38 million), <u>Starman</u> ($28 million) and <u>Dune</u> ($28 million). And closely following these were <u>Greystoke</u>, <u>The Last Starfighter</u>, <u>The Neverending Story</u>, etc.

(The biggest loser in '84 was <u>Dune</u>, in part because it was released too soon. Competition in 1984 was fierce. By comparison, the competition in 1985 was limp. A spring '85 release might have added another $10 to $20 million to its gross.)

All of this year's grosses will be bolstered by subsequent income from overseas release as well as sales to the networks and cable and cassette markets. As a rough rule of thumb, a movie has to gross two-and-a-half times its negative cost to make money. For <u>2010</u>, let's say that was $25 million. That means it would have to gross $62 million to break even. Its domestic gross is $40 million, its overseas take will probably equal that, and then there are the various subsidiary sales. Say its final take is $90 million. Minus the $62 million, that gives you a profit of $28 million -- more than that if you consider how much of the film's cost (advertising, etc.) was contracted out to various divisions of the same company, all of which will show a profit even if the film itself doesn't.

Every film is unique in how much it costs and how much the studio decides to spend in hyping it in the marketplace. Some of the marginal films will yet show a profit. Still, it's doubtful that 1986 will see a flood of science fiction films aimed solely at the pre- or post-adolescent market.

In television, fantasy, horror and science fiction were the staple of three new anthology shows: <u>Amazing Stories</u>, <u>Alfred Hitchcock</u>, and <u>Twilight Zone</u>. All three shows held great promise, but by mid-season they had sunk to the middle of the ratings and were struggling. Local reaction to Spielberg's <u>Amazing Stories</u> was largely negative, with responses slightly more positive when it came to <u>Hitchcock</u>. The best of the three shows was <u>Twilight Zone</u>, but at year's end it had lost creative consultant Harlan Ellison, while there were rumors that Spielberg wanted out of <u>Amazing Stories</u>. Critical summation: <u>Amazing Stories</u> features upbeat 15-minute tales stretched to 30; <u>Hitchcock</u> is a slick rehash of former stories -- if you liked the old versions, you'll probably like the new ones; <u>Twilight Zone</u> (ah, sweet heresy!) is more slickly produced and better written than the original.

Addenda: Time praised the three installments of HBO's <u>Ray Bradbury Theatre</u> (as well as <u>Amazing Stories</u>), reruns of <u>Dr. Who</u> immediately zoomed in popularity when the good Dr. was cancelled, and devotees of the original <u>Star Trek</u> should investigate the episodes now available on videotape and especially video disc: they make the ordinary reruns look washed-out and grey. Some stations, incidentally, are broadcasting new 35mm prints.

The future for films in 1986: watch for <u>Star Trek IV</u>, the long-awaited sequel to <u>Alien</u> (friends who have read the script give it high marks), and <u>Psycho III</u> (directed by and starring Tony Perkins). Hollywood's one-man-band, Steven Spielberg, will also have a few surprises for us.

In 1985, it became apparent that science fiction (including fantasy and horror) is a very large tail when it comes to the hound called Hollywood. If it wags, the rest of the dog is happy. If the collective gross for science fiction films falls, as it did this year, then the gross for the entire industry goes to hell. In short, science fiction films with substantial production values and solid stories are essential to the health of the movie industry -- there is nothing which can replace them. A sizable number of ticket buyers who can be tempted to queue up for a <u>Star Wars</u> or a <u>Trek</u> or an <u>Indiana Jones</u> won't leave the house for anything else.

All of which, I suppose, is stating the obvious.

--Frank M. Robinson

(Acknowledgement: All figures were gleaned from the Associated Press and weekly *Variety* but should be considered approximate.)

MAGAZINE REPORT

It was another mixed year for the magazine field. Baen Books brought out FAR FRONTIERS, a hybrid anthology/magazine in paperback form; *Twilight Zone* added a digest-size companion, *Night Cry*, a pure horror effort; *Stardate*, a hobby magazine, was revamped as a partial fiction magazine. There were also more sf stories in general magazines. On the other hand, overall circulation was down slightly, the much heralded *L. Ron Hubbard's To the Stars* was delayed, *Weird Tales* vanished again, the semi-professional field is in trouble, and the costs of paper, printing, and labor were up.

Amazing Stories

Amazing, the walking corpse of sf magazines, survived another year. Its circulation even went up slightly, but not enough to matter. The magazine dropped Science Fiction from its title to reflect its growing fantasy content and added "Now a TV Series." It didn't seem to help. *Amazing* is an anomaly because it doesn't have a subscription list. It has nearly the same newsstand sale as *Asimov's* but under 20% of *Asimov's* total sale. *Amazing* desperately needs a subscription drive through Publishers Clearing House. It's obviously a money loser, and I can't understand how it keeps going. The magazine published good to excellent work by Eric Iverson/Harry Turtledove, Jayge Carr, Avram Davidson, Keith Roberts, and others.

Analog Science Fiction/Science Fact

Analog held onto its circulation and in the issue nearest to filing (the figures in the charts are the yearly average) went over 100,000. *Analog* has the best circulation and the best newsstand sale of any digest. The conservative hard sf covers and the magazine's image as the bastion of hard sf stories help tremendously. The type is also the most readable of all the magazines. The fiction was quite good and a bit more varied than usual. A good year for *Analog*.

Isaac Asimov's Science Fiction Magazine

Shawna McCarthy resigned as editor in May and Gardner Dozois took over, but the whole year was edited by Shawna. For the second year in a row, *Asimov's* received critical acclaim but suffered a disastrous drop in circulation. *Asimov's* and *Analog* have the same production, distribution, etc., but *Asimov's* circulation is 20% lower. *Asimov's* has more varied covers and more varied fiction. It's the magazine on the cutting edge with the newest ideas and writers. Unfortunately, readers seem to prefer middle-of-the-road material.

Magazine of Fantasy & Science Fiction

F&SF had an average year. Since the magazine is usually enjoyable, there's nothing wrong with this except that sales also went down. I wish the outside package could be redesigned. It might help.

FAR FRONTIERS

This new hybrid paperback anthology/magazine edited by Pournelle and Baen has the reputation of being a right wing, pro space, pro military propaganda magazine. This is partially true. The editors have strong opinions, are willing to state them, and publish articles specifically written to influence as well as inform the readership. All editors, writers, and most other thinking people in the world try to do this, either directly or subtly. On the other hand, the fiction is as varied and interesting as that in other magazines. I can't think of Brunner, Jacobs, Cherryh, Spinrad, or Knight as right wing propagandists. According to the publisher, the print run is 50,000. The way the paperback industry is going, that probably means a circulation of around 25,000. Unfortunately, there are no subscriptions. The magazine is obviously not a money-maker or major income to either editor. Baen has said it will continue through 1986 at least.

The Twilight Zone

TZ changed editors during the year. T.E.D. Klein left and

Michael Blaine took over. Blaine has more eclectic tastes, and plans to get away from the straight horror image the magazine has. He has already done a fine redesign on the inside, although the covers remain about the same. The circulation dropped, but is still higher than most of the fiction magazines. The media tie-ins help.

Night Cry

The first issue of *Night Cry* appeared in late 1984 as an irregular anthology from *Twilight Zone*. It sold well enough to become a quarterly digest magazine in its own right. The editor, Alan Rodgers, is associate editor of *TZ*. *Night Cry* is a straight horror fiction magazine. It has a sale of around 20,000 and does not take subscriptions. It should. It will probably survive as long as *TZ* does. (It's much cheaper to put out two magazines than one.)

Omni

Omni published 27 sf stories -- up from 19 the year before. Lots of them made our recommended short fiction list. The circulation of the magazine is up significantly (its increase is greater than the total copies sold of *F&SF*), even though newsstand sales are dropping. Its sell through (59%) is very good. *Omni* has a circulation more than twice all the other fiction magazines put together.

Locus

We had a good year and a modest increase in circulation. *Locus* went to full color covers every issue and a slightly increased size, but basically the magazine is the same as it was in 1984. 1986 should be pretty much the same as well.

Semi-Professional Magazines

We define semi-professional magazines as fiction magazines which have no national newsstand circulation but are otherwise professional. They must also appear at least quarterly. Anything else is officially considered an irregular serial by the post office, *Publishers Weekly*, and by us.

Interzone is British and couldn't get newsstand circulation anyway, but it's certainly the best of its kind. It had four issues last year and went to full color covers. It's the bastion of experimental fiction and deserves support. See the Magazines Received section for ordering information. It doesn't publish figures, but I would guess the paid circulation at about 5,000.

Fantasy Book put out 4 issues and had a probable paid circulation of about 2,500. The editorial content seemed about the same -- minor work by published writers mixed with amateur work by sometimes talented beginners. Surprisingly, the weakest part of the magazine is the non-fiction, editorials, etc. *Fantasy Book* has very little personality.

Stardate, a gaming magazine, switched to a partial sf magazine during 1985. It produced two mixed issues -- each a third fiction, a third gaming, and a third media-oriented. The circulation is 5,500 through gaming outlets. They hope to add a subscription list and get into bookstores in 1986. The magazine is scheduled to go monthly with the May issue.

Neither *The Last Wave* nor *Weird Tales* appeared in 1985, and they can be considered dead, or maybe just resting. The best of the irregular serials was *Whispers*, which had one issue in 1985 (dated 1984). We've been promised another semi-pro magazine in 1986 -- *Aboriginal SF* -- and one professional one -- *L. Ron Hubbard's To the Stars.*

Conclusions

The circulation graphs pretty much tell it all. There doesn't seem to be any way to reverse the downward trend of newsstand distribution. A digest magazine costs about 25 cents to print. *Asimov's* and *Analog* sell about 25% of the copies they distribute to newsstands. Therefore each sold copy costs $1.00 to print (the returns are destroyed). Since this is more than the distributor

---

CURRENT PUBLICATION DATA FOR ACTIVE MAGAZINES

Amazing Stories--Bimonthly, $1.75 per copy. George Scithers--editor.
    Editorial address -- P.O. Box 110, Lake Geneva WI 53147.
    Subscriptions -- $9 per year (6 issues) in U.S. & Canada; $15 elsewhere.

Analog--13 issues/year, $2.00 per copy. Stanley Schmidt--editor.
    Editorial address -- 380 Lexington Ave., New York NY 10017.
    Subscription address -- P.O. Box 1936, Marion OH 43305.
    Subscriptions -- $19.50 per year in U.S.; $24.20 elsewhere.

Isaac Asimov's SF Magazine--13 issues/year, $2.00 per copy.
    Gardner Dozois--editor.
    Editorial address -- 380 Lexington Ave., New York NY 10017.
    Subscription address -- Box 1933, Marion OH 43305.
    Subscriptions -- $19.50 per year in U.S.; $24.20 elsewhere.

Fantasy & Science Fiction--Monthly, $1.75 per copy.
    Edward L. Ferman--editor.
    Editorial address -- Box 56, Cornwall CT 06753.
    Subscription address -- same.
    Subscriptions -- $19.50 per year in U.S.; $23.50 elsewhere.

Far Frontiers--Quarterly, $2.95 per copy.
    Jerry Pournelle & Jim Baen, eds.

Editorial addresses -- Jim Baen: 260 5th Ave.,
Suite #3S, New York NY 10001.
No subscriptions available.

Locus--Monthly, $2.50 per copy. Charles N. Brown--editor.
    Editorial address -- Box 13305, Oakland CA 94661.
    Subscription address -- same.
    Subscriptions -- $24.00 per year in U.S.; $27.00 elsewhere.

Night Cry--Quarterly, $2.95 per copy. Alan Rodgers--editor.
    Editorial address -- 800 Second Ave., New York NY 10017.
    Subscription address -- P.O. Box 252, Mount Morris IL 61054.
    No subscriptions available.

Omni--Monthly, $2.50 per copy. Ellen Datlow--fiction editor.
    Editorial address -- 1965 Broadway, New York NY 10023.
    Subscription address -- Box 3039, Harlan IA 51537.
    Subscriptions -- $24.00 per year in U.S.; $28.00 elsewhere.

Twilight Zone--Bimonthly, $2.50 per copy. Michael Blaine--editor.
    Editorial address -- 800 Second Ave., New York NY 10017.
    Subscription address -- P.O. Box 252, Mount Morris IL 61054.
    Subscriptions -- $15.50 per year (6 issues) in U.S.; $18.50 elsewhere.

pays the publisher, it's obvious that every newsstand sale is a loss to the publisher. They justify it by counting advertising revenue and talking about point of sale advertising and increment-al costs of copies, but in the end they lose money on every copy sold. Obviously, national distribution should be dropped and the readers who will not subscribe have to be retrained to shop in bookstores, advertising and promotion has to be done, and sub-scriptions have to be easier to make or renew -- credit cards, 800 numbers, electronic checks, etc. Ok, who will be first? Ed Ferman? Joel Davis? TSR? --C.N. Brown

```
                        PROFESSIONAL MAGAZINES
                    ISSUES PUBLISHED (ALL FICTION ONLY)

   Amazing........................6      1983.......5 fiction titles..........50 issues
   Analog Science Fiction/Science Fact........13    1982.......7 fiction titles..........61 issues
   Fantasy & Science Fiction...................12   1981.......8 fiction titles..........59 issues
   Far Frontiers..........................4      1980.......8 fiction titles..........49 issues
   Isaac Asimov's SF Magazine.................13    1979.......9 fiction titles..........57 issues
   Night Cry..........................4      1978......10 fiction titles..........55 issues
   The Twilight Zone.........................6      1977......13 fiction titles..........73 issues
                                     ---      1976......10 fiction titles..........71 issues
                                     58      1975......10 fiction titles..........89 issues
   TOTAL ISSUES                              1974......13 fiction titles.........109 issues
                                             1973......13 fiction titles..........88 issues
   1985.......7 fiction titles..........58 issues   1972......10 fiction titles..........72 issues
   1984.......5 fiction titles..........50 issues   1971......22 fiction titles..........82 issues
```

CIRCULATION FIGURES

Year	Subscriptions	Newsstand Sales	Returns	%Newsstand Sale	Paid Circulation	Paid Circ. Change
			AMAZING			
1977	1,722	23,980	40,960	37%	25,702	+3.6%
1978	1,522	21,262	42,096	34%	22,784	-11.4%
1979	1,397	20,935	43,188	33%	22,332	-1.9%
1980	900	16,439	48,661	25%	17,339	-22.4%
1981	750	17,034	34,489	33%	17,784	+2.5%
1982	900	10,600	31,000	25%	11,500	-35.0%
1983	1,236	10,050	22,913	30%	11,286	-1.8%
1984	1,861	9,069	17,545	34%	10,931	-3.1%
1985	2,252	10,071	16,233	38%	12,323	+12.7%
			ANALOG			
1977	49,833	55,175	66,500	45%	105,008	4.9%
1978	49,820	54,792	66,117	45%	104,612	-3.7%
1979	45,000	45,000	------	---	90,000*	-14.0%
1980	59,000	45,000	------	---	104,000*	+14.1%
1981	53,846	38,548	70,951	35%	92,394	-11.2%
1982	65,171	34,731	61,023	36%	99,902	+8.1%
1983	81,971	27,838	58,583	32%	109,809	+9.9%
1984	74,124	22,613	62,162	27%	96,739	-11.9%
1985	75,967	21,217	60,653	26%	97,184	+0.5%
		ISAAC ASIMOV'S	SF MAGAZINE			
1978	42,095	66,748	83,742	44%	108,843	---
1979	46,330	48,429	93,402	34%	94,759	-12.9%
1980	59,000	30,000	------	---	89,000	-6.1%
1981	79,164	23,905	70,303	25%	103,069	+15.8%
1982	66,445	19,200	48,674	28%	85,645	-16.9%
1983	88,818	16,369	41,191	28%	105,187	+22.8%
1984	83,931	12,105	44,216	21%	96,036	-8.7%
1985	71,915	11,933	37,365	24%	83,848	-12.7%
	THE MAGAZINE OF	FANTASY &	SCIENCE FICTION			
1978	34,676	23,242	44,316	34%	57,900	0
1979	36,775	20,953	45,854	31%	57,728	-3.0%
1980	40,272	21,799	42,382	34%	62,071	+7.5%
1981	41,132	19,101	39,085	33%	60,233	-3.0%
1982	44,865	16,863	32,850	34%	61,721	+2.5%
1983	47,799	14,507	26,103	36%	62,306	+0.9%
1984	44,164	13,819	21,808	39%	57,983	-6.9%
1985	40,072	14,177	21,972	39%	54,249	-6.4%
			LOCUS			
1978	3,235	601	5	99%	3,836	+20.3%
1979	3,480	1,015	7	99%	4,495	+17.2%
1980	3,592	1,336	29	98%	4,928	+9.6%
1981	3,670	1,253	60	95%	4,924	---
1982	3,836	1,292	13	99%	5,128	+4.1%
1983	4,047	1,891	58	97%	5,938	+15.8%
1984	4,319	2,472	64	97%	6,940	+16/9%
1985	4,440	2,820	89	97%	7,260	+4.6%
			OMNI			
1979	89,218	670,630	268,423	71%	759,848	---
1980	172,238	670,801	314,318	68%	843,039	+10.9%
1981	211,755	552,155	426,727	56%	763,910	-9.4%
1982	205,078	548,098	384,100	59%	753,176	-1.4%
1983	318,179	478,908	325,745	60%	797,087	+5.8%
1984	467,971	369,029	371,448	50%	837,000	+5.0%
1985	566,191	337,358	231,116	59%	903,549	+8.0%
			TWILIGHT ZONE			
1981	1,859	52,196	137,423	28%	54,055	---
1982	6,145	46,561	116,141	29%	52,706	-2.5%
1983	25,237	37,168	99,024	27%	62,405	+18.4%
1984	94,317	31,325	83,369	27%	126,111	+102.1%
1985	73,799	26,971	76,555	26%	100,770	-20.1%

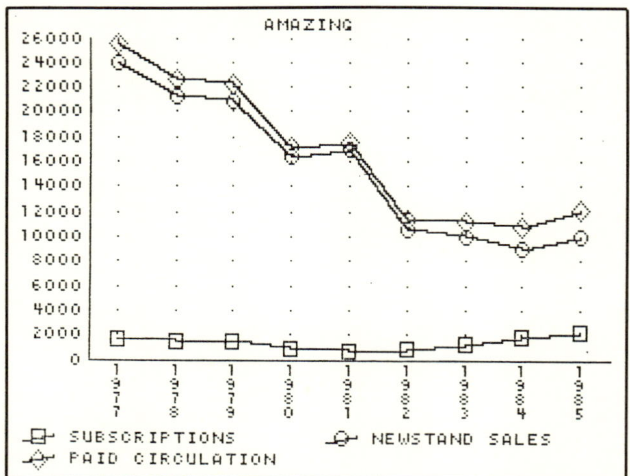
AMAZING
26000
24000
22000
20000
18000
16000
14000
12000
10000
8000
6000
4000
2000
1977 1978 1979 1980 1981 1982 1983 1984 1985
SUBSCRIPTIONS
NEWSSTAND SALES
PAID CIRCULATION

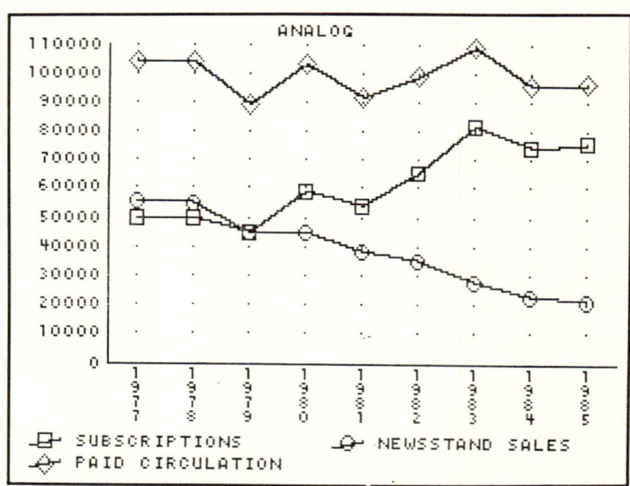
ANALOG
110000
100000
90000
80000
70000
60000
50000
40000
30000
20000
10000
0
1977 1978 1979 1980 1981 1982 1983 1984 1985
SUBSCRIPTIONS
NEWSSTAND SALES
PAID CIRCULATION

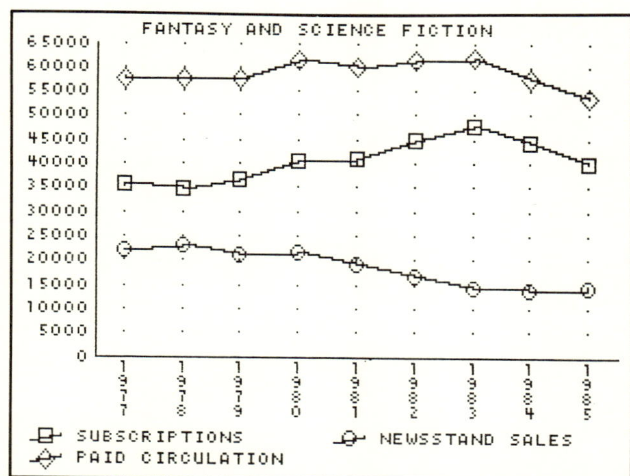
FANTASY AND SCIENCE FICTION
65000
60000
55000
50000
45000
40000
35000
25000
20000
15000
10000
5000
1977 1978 1979 1980 1981 1982 1983 1984 1985
SUBSCRIPTIONS
NEWSSTAND SALES
PAID CIRCULATION

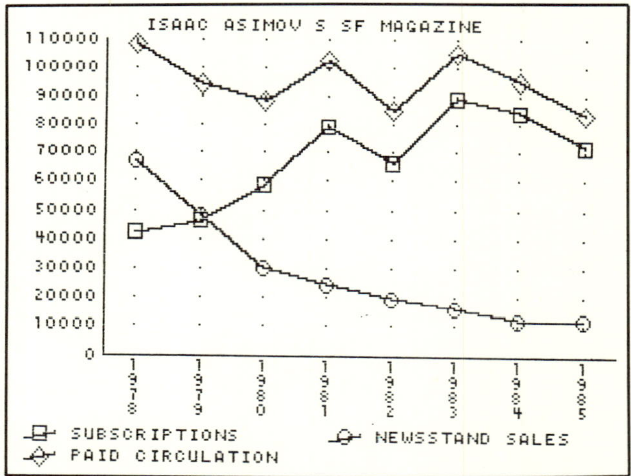
ISAAC ASIMOV'S SF MAGAZINE
110000
100000
90000
80000
70000
60000
50000
40000
30000
20000
10000
0
1978 1979 1980 1981 1982 1983 1984 1985
SUBSCRIPTIONS
NEWSSTAND SALES
PAID CIRCULATION

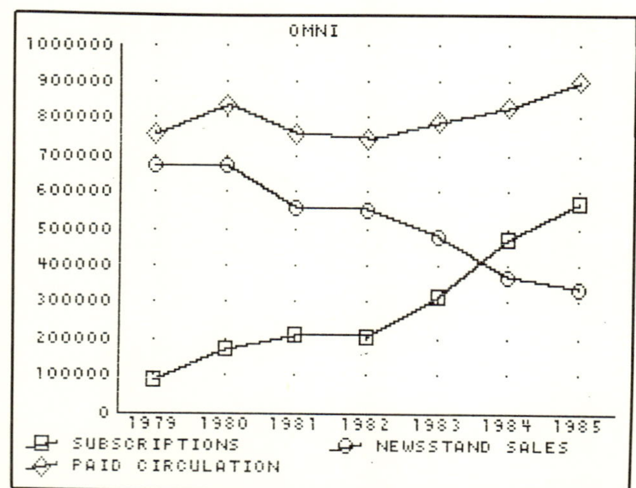
OMNI
1000000
900000
800000
700000
600000
500000
400000
300000
200000
100000
0
1979 1980 1981 1982 1983 1984 1985
SUBSCRIPTIONS
NEWSSTAND SALES
PAID CIRCULATION

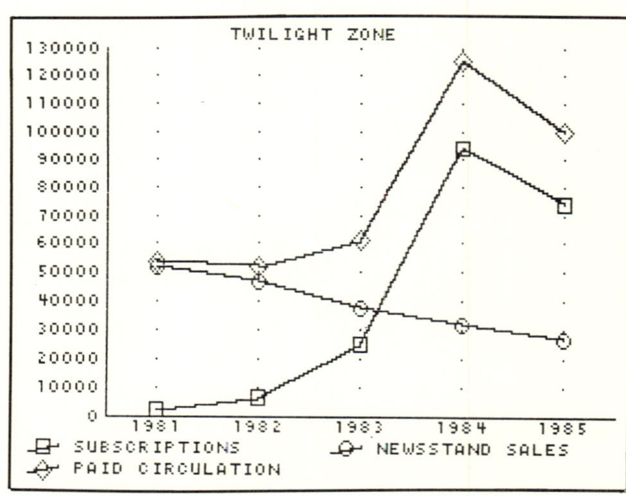
TWILIGHT ZONE
130000
120000
110000
100000
90000
80000
70000
60000
50000
40000
30000
20000
10000
1981 1982 1983 1984 1985
SUBSCRIPTIONS
NEWSSTAND SALES
PAID CIRCULATION

RECOMMENDED READING

Each year *Locus* prints a list of recommended books and stories and each year we start off with the same disclaimer.

This is not a definitive list to be read for Hugo, Nebula, or *Locus* Award voting; nor is it a personal list by the editor. We use lists from about a dozen people, and we check items praised in other review columns. We also include books which are extremely popular. We also use the Nebula recommendations and additions from various Nebula judges.

Eligibility is a bit different for the *Locus* list than for the Hugos and Nebulas. We count books when we see copies, regardless of copyright date. Thus, most books dated January '86 actually appear in 1985 and are 1985 books. Barbara Hambly's DRAGONSBANE is an example. On the other hand, we missed some 1984 books, notably THE SUMMER TREE by Guy Gavriel Kay and THE NOVELS OF PHILIP K. DICK by Kim Stanley Robinson and have recommended them as 1985 books. We're also flexible (or if you wish, capricious). I loved Richard Lupoff's novel featuring H.P. Lovecraft and, even though there is no supernatural element involved, I decided it was an alternate-world fantasy. Some of our recommenders didn't see DINNER AT DEVIANT'S PALACE by Tim Powers or ALIEN STARS edited by Betsy Mitchell until 1985 (they were January 1985 books which we listed in December 1984), so we counted recommendations for them as 1985. The only real headache is FREE LIVE FREE by Gene Wolfe. The limited edition came out in 1984 and we recommended it for that year. The regular trade version (cut and slightly changed) appeared as a trade hardcover in 1985, and the author withdrew it from Nebula voting in favor of the paperback edition which will appear in 1986. The book placed 22nd in last year's *Locus* Awards. I don't think the changes are enough to call the 1985 edition a new book and we don't allow authors to withdraw work unless it's been butchered or re-written by others. We won't recommend it again, but probably will count it if enough people vote for it. I didn't know where to put SCIENCE MADE STUPID even though I knew it belonged somewhere. We added humor to art. The pop-up book THE UNIVERSE also was shoehorned in.

As usual, the short fiction list was the hardest to put together. We got recommendations from Mark Kelly (who did our base list), Terry Carr, Art Saha, Gardner Dozois, Jim Baen, Dave Hartwell, Debbie Notkin, Amy Thomson, Faren Miller, Orson Scott Card, and the Nebula ballot. Any story mentioned by two sources automatically went on the final list, and a few others which the editors felt strongly about also were listed. Our final list has 51 stories from the traditional magazines, 12 from *Omni*, *Playboy*, etc., and 24 from book sources. It adds up to more than the total because several stories appeared in two sources simultaneously. All of the people listed above plus a few others also recommended books. Before we leave 1985, our reviewers should have one more chance to convince you of their good taste.

--C.N. Brown

Science fiction seemed more divided than ever, with styles and subjects as diverse as cyberpunk and hard sf, and writers ranging from the big names (Heinlein, Asimov) to literary authors venturing into the genre for the first time.

Among sf novels where science played a central role, my favorite was Greg Bear's EON, an array of wonders on a grand scale, easily dwarfing its protagonists. Bear's BLOOD MUSIC was also impressive, though its runaway biotechnology finally exploded into surreal and mystical visions. ARTIFACT by Gregory Benford combined physics and anthropology with the trappings of a near-future thriller, for an entertaining adventure with a bonus of ideas.

What might be called humanist sf, attempting to find cultural and philosophical solutions for mankind's deepest ills, produced two notable novels, a Tolstoyan combination of storytelling and polemics in Brian Aldiss's HELLICONIA WINTER, and an elaborate fictional anthropology text in Ursula Le Guin's ALWAYS COMING HOME. Despite some unnecessary pointing the moral, the Aldiss is a fine novel; as for the Le Guin, I'm tempted to vote for it in the Non-Fiction category, since she laid aside many of her novelistic tools for this work, flawlessly imitating a scholarly compendium.

Writers associated in some way with the "new" sf -- cyberpunks, stylists, etc. -- continue to explore areas pioneered by Samuel R. Delany (still ahead of the pack with 1984's STARS IN MY POCKET LIKE GRAINS OF SAND). Though William Gibson didn't have a novel in 1985, high-quality writing and kaleidescopic views of complex cultures were represented by Bruce Sterling's SCHISMATRIX and Kim Stanley Robinson's THE MEMORY OF WHITENESS. This brand of sf still seems to be looking for a center, a depth of plotting to balance the effect of its brilliant surface, yet it continues to create excitement while increasing the sophistication of sf writing.

In a more traditional vein, ENDER'S GAME by Orson Scott Card, CUCKOO'S EGG by C.J. Cherryh, and first novel EMPRISE by Michael P. Kube-McDowell are all excellent works. As for sf with roots in the "literary" mainstream, the outstanding examples were another first novel, Susan B. Weston's CHILDREN OF THE LIGHT, and Denis Johnson's FISKADORO -- both dealing with a fragmented America after a limited but disastrous war.

In fantasy, Guy Gavriel Kay made a superb debut with THE SUMMER TREE, high fantasy with excellent characterization and a deep feeling for myth. THE VAMPIRE LESTAT by Anne Rice offered a fascinating historical perspective plus engaging protagonists. The master of vivid world-making, Jack Vance, returned to the eerie beauty of Lyonesse in THE GREEN PEARL, while Dan Simmons created a hellish setting for a thoughtful horror novel in SONG OF KALI. R.A. MacAvoy and Barbara Hambly developed new twists on old themes in the very enjoyable novels THE BOOK OF KELLS and DRAGONSBANE. Other highlights were Meredith Ann Pierce's THE WOMAN WHO LOVED REINDEER, Megan Lindholm's offbeat WIZARD OF THE PIGEONS, and literary fantasies THINGS INVISIBLE TO SEE by Nancy Willard and Timothy Findley's NOT WANTED ON THE VOYAGE. Not quite fantasy but also worth a mention is Peter Carey's tour de force of Australian tale-spinning, ILLYWHACKER.

The most impressive first novels of the year I've already mentioned in the general SF and Fantasy categories -- THE SUMMER TREE, EMPRISE, and CHILDREN OF THE LIGHT. Aside from these, Richard Grant's SARABAND OF LOST TIME was a delight despite some flaws. I also liked THE ISLE OF GLASS by Judith Ann Tarr, WHITE WING by the pseudonymous Gordon Kendall, and the more modest MASTERS OF GLASS by M. Coleman Easton.

It was a good year for collections, with BEASTMARKS by A.A. Attanasio, CLIVE BARKER'S BOOKS OF BLOOD IV-VI, Angela Carter's BLACK VENUS, Samuel R. Delany's connected stories in FLIGHT FROM NEVERYON, Stephen King's extravagant SKELETON CREW, THE GORGON by Tanith Lee, and Ian Watson's SLOW BIRDS. Among anthologies, THE INTERZONE ANTHOLOGY was particularly impressive. IMAGINARY LANDS, edited by Robin McKinley, was a fine gathering of fantasy.

It was a good year for art books, with a broad range encompassing spectacular pop-up paper engineering in THE UNIVERSE by Couper and Pelham, grotesque humor (and art instruction!) in Dan Reeder's THE SIMPLE SCREAMER, and stylish illustration in Rodney Matthews' long-overdue compendium IN SEARCH OF FOREVER.

As for the other categories, I recommend Aldiss' THE PALE SHADOW OF SCIENCE and Budrys's BENCHMARKS (Non-Fiction), SCIENCE MADE STUPID by Tom Weller and GHASTLY BEYOND BELIEF edited by Gaiman and Newman (Humor), and -- for all its flaws -- THE NEW WORLD by Frederick Turner (Poetry).

--Faren Miller

Although I've heard some people claim otherwise, I think 1985 was a banner year for novels. We have had three very difficult and demanding books which succeeded well-nigh completely, all so different from each other that I'm extremely hard put to pick a favorite. Therefore, I list them here in order of publication: BRIGHTNESS FALLS FROM THE AIR by James Tiptree, Jr., a perfectly structured science fiction mystery with Tiptree's inimitably subtle characterization; THE DREAM YEARS by Lisa Goldstein, an evocative novel of past and future through the eyes of the French surrealist movement; and THE MEMORY OF WHITENESS by Kim Stanley Robinson, a solar-system tour of future civilization seen through its music. Any one would be a more than satisfactory choice for the Nebula and/or the Hugo, and if Goldstein doesn't take home the World Fantasy Award, the judges should have their eyes examined. After those three, the important novels fall into two groups: those successful with straightforward goals and those nearly successful with extremely challenging goals.

In the first group are such diverse books as THE BRONZE KING by Suzy McKee Charnas, a delightful young adult fantasy; MASTER OF SPACE AND TIME by Rudy Rucker, an unabashed romp; DOWNTIME by Cynthia Felice, an old-fashioned science fiction novel with space opera trimmings; and TRUMPS OF DOOM by Roger Zelazny, a prime Amber story with an unforgivable cliffhanger ending.

From the second group, the most provocative book of the year was undoubtedly Ursula Le Guin's ALWAYS COMING HOME. Although I think it has one or two major problems, if you're only going to read one book-length work this year, this should be your choice. It is a pioneer effort in what may become a new genre, has more food for thought and feeling per page than almost any other book I've ever seen, and it will be talked about and responded to for years to come. Geoff Ryman's THE WARRIOR WHO CARRIED LIFE is a singularly graphic and unsettling fantasy, much too strong for most tastes, but well worth reading. Michael Bishop's ANCIENT OF DAYS attempted to take his brilliant novella "Her Habiline Husband" and expand it in directions which don't suit it perfectly, with varying success. Somtow Sucharitkul's THE DARKLING WIND ends the Inquestor trilogy with a lot of exciting flash and dazzle, but isn't quite as strong as the other two books. Paul Preuss' HUMAN ERROR feels just a touch too slick, but offers the extreme satisfaction of an unexpected but perfectly appropriate ending. Tim Powers' DINNER AT DEVIANT'S PALACE represents Powers' first attempt at a darker and less black-humorous tale -- a bit too pulpy, but with lots of memorable material.

P.C. Hodgell's DARK OF THE MOON, a sequel to her delightful GODSTALK, is another very fine book. Full judgment must be reserved until the story is finished, but it could easily be one of the best sword-and-sorcery tales ever. Melissa Scott's FIVE-TWELFTHS OF HEAVEN is also part of a series, but has an excellent blend of magic and science.

Several very encouraging first novels appeared this year as well: WALK THE MOON'S ROAD by Jim Aikin (off-Earth adventure), KNIGHT MOVES by Walter Jon Williams (a Zelaznyesque tale with its own integrity), and THE TORCH OF HONOR by Roger MacBride Allen (a guaranteed pleaser for Heinlein fans) all stand perfectly well against books by more experienced writers. INFINITY'S WEB by Sheila Finch didn't quite live up to its promise, but nonetheless Finch seems to be a welcome addition to the field.

Short fiction is always a slippery category to pin down. Certainly Connie Willis' "All My Darling Daughters" is a story which will outlast all of us. James Tiptree Jr.'s "The Only Neat Thing to Do" should please almost everybody who comes across it. Peter Dickinson's "Flight" is a near-perfect evocation of a civilization through the "dry academic" perspective of one of its archivists (you'll laugh until you cry); Pamela Zoline's "Instructions on Exiting this Building in Case of Fire" simply made me cry. Norman Spinrad's "World War Last" is a guaranteed belly-laugh or three with a wry undertone. Michael Bishop's "The Bob Dylan Tambourine

Satori & Software Support Services Consortium, Ltd." is a spectacular evocation of Dylan as he might become. Geoff Ryman's "O Happy Day" turns at least three sets of tables simultaneously, to chilling effect. Robert Silverberg's "Sailing to Byzantium" describes a truly alien far future (despite the fact that the inhabitants are all human). "With Virgil Oddum at the East Pole" is a rare and satisfying glimpse of Harlan Ellison in quiet, empathic mode. John Crowley's "Snow" is a haunting tale of the near future with a perfectly managed technological metaphor.

And one last note -- my choice for Best Dramatic Presentation won't win because it's too obscure, but if you have a chance to see Lily Tomlin in <u>The Search For Intelligent Life On This Planet</u>, do so.

--<u>Debbie Notkin</u>

1985 will go down in my records as the year that almost was. There were a number of sf novels which made for a superior read, but which fell short by just a little bit of that impossible

1985 LOCUS RECOMMENDED READING LIST

NOVELS—SCIENCE FICTION

HELLICONIA WINTER, Brian Aldiss (Jonathan Cape)
ROBOTS AND EMPIRE, Isaac Asimov (Doubleday)
BLOOD MUSIC, Greg Bear (Arbor House)
EON, Greg Bear (Bluejay)
ARTIFACT, Gregory Benford (Tor)
ANCIENT OF DAYS, Michael Bishop (Arbor House)
THE POSTMAN, David Brin (Bantam Spectra)
ENDER'S GAME, Orson Scott Card (Tor)
CUCKOO'S EGG, C.J. Cherryh (Phantasia)
THE KIF STRIKE BACK, C.J. Cherryh (Phantasia)
DAYWORLD, Philip Jose Farmer (Putnam)
STARQUAKE, Robert L. Forward (Del Rey)
THE CAT WHO WALKS THROUGH WALLS, Robert A. Heinlein (Putnam)
CHAPTERHOUSE: DUNE, Frank Herbert (Putnam)
THE PROTEUS OPERATION, James P. Hogan (Bantam Spectra)
THE GLASS HAMMER, K.W. Jeter (Bluejay)
FISKADORO, Denis Johnson (Knopf)
EMPRISE, Michael P. Kube-McDowell (Del Rey)

ALWAYS COMING HOME, Ursula K. Le Guin (Harper & Row)
THE REMAKING OF SIGMUND FREUD, Barry N. Malzberg (Del Rey)
FOOTFALL, Larry Niven & Jerry Pournelle (Del Rey)
DINNER AT DEVIANT'S PALACE, Tim Powers (Ace)
HUMAN ERROR, Paul Preuss (Tor)
KITEWORLD, Keith Roberts (Gollancz)
THE MEMORY OF WHITENESS, Kim Stanley Robinson (Tor)
MASTER OF SPACE AND TIME, Rudy Rucker (Bluejay)
CONTACT, Carl Sagan (Simon & Schuster)
FIVE-TWELFTHS OF HEAVEN, Melissa Scott (Baen)
BETWEEN THE STROKES OF NIGHT, Charles Sheffield (Baen)
TOM O'BEDLAM, Robert Silverberg (Donald I. Fine)
CHILD OF FORTUNE, Norman Spinrad (Bantam Spectra)
SCHISMATRIX, Bruce Sterling (Arbor House)
THE DARKLING WIND, Somtow Sucharitkul (Bantam Spectra)
BRIGHTNESS FALLS FROM THE AIR, James Tiptree, Jr. (Tor)
KNIGHT MOVES, Walter Jon Williams (Tor)

NOVELS—FANTASY

WITH A TANGLED SKEIN, Piers Anthony (Del Rey)
THE DAMNATION GAME, Clive Barker (Weidenfeld & Nicolson)
THE WISHSONG OF SHANNARA, Terry Brooks (Del Rey)
BROKEDOWN PALACE, Steven Brust (Ace)
THE BRONZE KING, Suzy McKee Charnas (Houghton Mifflin)
MULENGRO, Charles de Lint (Ace)
SILVERTHORN, Raymond E. Feist (Doubleday)
THE LAST RAINBOW, Parke Godwin (Bantam Spectra)
THE DREAM YEARS, Lisa Goldstein (Bantam Spectra)
DRAGONSBANE, Barbara Hambly (Del Rey)
THE FIRES OF WINDAMEIR, Niel Hancock (Warner)
WINTERKING, Paul Hazel (Atlantic Monthly Press)
DARK OF THE MOON, P.C. Hodgell (Atheneum)
THE SUMMER TREE, Guy Gavriel Kay (Arbor House)
THE WHITE PIPES, Nancy Kress (Bluejay)

THE KING'S JUSTICE, Katherine Kurtz (Del Rey)
WIZARD OF THE PIGEONS, Megan Lindholm (Ace)
LOVECRAFT'S BOOK, Richard A. Lupoff (Arkham House)
THE BOOK OF KELLS, R.A. MacAvoy (Bantam Spectra)
THE VAMPIRE LESTAT, Anne Rice (Knopf)
IN YANA, THE TOUCH OF UNDYING, Michael Shea (DAW)
WINGS OF FLAME, Nancy Springer (Tor)
THE ENCHANTRESS, Han Suyin (Bantam)
THE SONG OF MAVIN MANYSHAPED, Sheri S. Tepper (Ace)
MARIANNE, THE MAGUS, AND THE MANTICORE, Sheri S. Tepper (Ace)
LYONESSE: THE GREEN PEARL, Jack Vance (Underwood-Miller)
THINGS INVISIBLE TO SEE, Nancy Willard (Knopf)
TRUMPS OF DOOM, Roger Zelazny (Arbor House)

FIRST NOVELS

WALK THE MOONS ROAD, Jim Aikin (Del Rey)
THE TORCH OF HONOR, Roger MacBride Allen (Baen)
THE LONG FORGETTING, Edward A. Byers (Baen)
SATURNALIA, Grant Callin (Baen)
THE INITIATE, Louise Cooper (Tor)
THE SECRET COUNTRY, Pamela C. Dean (Ace)
MASTERS OF GLASS, M. Coleman Easton (Questar)
PRINCESS OF FLAMES, Ru Emerson (Ace)
INFINITY'S WEB, Sheila Finch (Bantam Spectra)
SARABAND OF LOST TIME, Richard Grant (Avon)
THE SUMMER TREE, Guy Gavriel Kay (Arbor House)
EMPRISE, Michael P. Kube-McDowell (Berkley)
PANDORA'S GENES, Kathryn Lance (Questar)
SKYRIDER 1: SKIRMISH, Melisa C. Michaels (Tor)
A WORLD IN AMBER, A. Orr (Bluejay)

DOWN TOWN, Viido Polikarpus & Tappan King (Arbor House)
STAROAMERS FATE, Chuck Rothman (Popular Library)
THE WARRIOR WHO CARRIED LIFE, Geoff Ryman (Allen & Unwin)
CONTACT, Carl Sagan (Simon & Schuster)
TERRARIUM, Scott Russell Sanders (Tor)
CATS HAVE NO LORD, Will Shetterly (Ace)
WITH FATE CONSPIRE, Mike Shupp (Del Rey)
SONG OF KALI, Dan Simmons (Bluejay)
THE SORCERY WITHIN, Dave Smeds (Ace)
SNOW-EYES, Stephanie A. Smith (Atheneum/Argo)
IBIS, Linda Steele (DAW)
IN THE DRIFT, Michael Swanwick (Ace)
ISLE OF GLASS, Judith Tarr (Bluejay)
CHILDREN OF THE LIGHT, Susan B. Weston (St. Martins)
TAILCHASER'S SONG, Tad Williams (DAW)

SHORT STORY COLLECTIONS

NIGHT VOICES, Robert Aickman (Gollancz)
ANTHONOLOGY, Piers Anthony (Tor)
BEASTMARKS, A.A. Attanasio (Zeising)
CLIVE BARKER'S BOOKS OF BLOOD, VOLS. IV-VI, Clive Barker (Sphere)
THE BEST OF MARION ZIMMER BRADLEY, Marion Zimmer Bradley (Academy Chicago)
FLIGHT FROM NEVERYON, Samuel R. Delany (Bantam)
I HOPE I SHALL ARRIVE SOON, Philip K. Dick (Doubleday)
DEALING IN FUTURES, Joe Haldeman (Viking)
VIRICONIUM NIGHTS, M. John Harrison (Gollancz)
EYE, Frank Herbert (Berkley)
SKELETON CREW, Stephen King (Putnam)

TRINITY AND OTHER STORIES, Nancy Kress (Bluejay)
THE GORGON, Tanith Lee (DAW)
NIGHTFLYERS, George R.R. Martin (Bluejay)
LIMITS, Larry Niven (Del Rey)
MELANCHOLY ELEPHANTS, Spider Robinson (Tor)
THE POWER OF TIME, Josephine Saxton (Chatto & Windus)
BYTE BEAUTIFUL: 8 SCIENCE FICTION STORIES, James Tiptree, Jr. (Doubleday)
PHOENIX IN THE ASHES, Joan D. Vinge (Bluejay)
THE BOOK OF IAN WATSON, Ian Watson (Zeising)
SLOW BIRDS, Ian Watson (Gollancz)
FIRE WATCH, Connie Willis (Bluejay)
DRAGONFIELD AND OTHER STORIES, Jane Yolen (Ace)

REFERENCE

THE PALE SHADOW OF SCIENCE, Brian W. Aldiss (Serconia)
SUPERNATURAL FICTION WRITERS: FANTASY AND HORROR, E.F. Bleiler, ed. (Scribners)
INDEX TO THE SCIENCE FICTION MAGAZINES 1984, Jerry Boyajian & Kenneth R. Johnson (Twaci)
BENCHMARKS: GALAXY BOOKSHELF, Algis Budrys (Southern Illinois University Press)
THE ATLAS OF THE LAND, Karen Wynn Fonstad (Del Rey)
GHASTLY BEYOND BELIEF, Neil Gaiman & Kim Newman (Arrow)
MICROWORLDS, Stanislaw Lem (Harcourt Brace Jovanovich)
RED STARS: POLITICAL ASPECTS OF SOVIET SCIENCE FICTION, Patrick L. McGuire (UMI Research Press)

A. MERRITT: REFLECTIONS IN THE MOON POOL, Sam Moskowitz (Oswald Train)
THE N.E.S.F.A. INDEX TO THE SCIENCE FICTION MAGAZINES AND ORIGINAL ANTHOLOGIES 1983 (NESFA)
MONTHLY TERRORS: AN INDEX TO THE WEIRD FANTASY MAGAZINES PUBLISHED IN THE UNITED STATES AND GREAT BRITAIN, Frank H. Parnell with Mike Ashley (Greenwood)
SCIENCE FICTION: THE 100 BEST NOVELS, David Pringle (Xanadu)
THE NOVELS OF PHILIP K. DICK, Kim Stanley Robinson (UMI Research Press)
FACES OF FEAR: ENCOUNTERS WITH THE CREATORS OF MODERN HORROR, Douglas E. Winter (Berkley)

dream, the perfect novel. Read and contemplate the following: BLOOD MUSIC and EON, both by Greg Bear, HUMAN ERROR by Paul Preuss, CONTACT by Carl Sagan, and BETWEEN THE STROKES OF NIGHT by Charles Sheffield. All are characterized by that quality which makes science fiction so unique and wonderful, a grand unified field theory linking the forces of nature with those that drive humanity. If only Paul Preuss or his editor could have gotten a tiny bit further with HUMAN ERROR, it would unquestionably have been the next FLOWERS FOR ALGERNON. And Sheffield? If only he could smooth the rough edges from his writing and storyline, there would be no hesitation about Arthur C. Clarke's heir apparent. Of all the novels that appeared in 1985, the one the shoe fits the best is Heinlein's THE CAT WHO WALKS THROUGH WALLS. What awful dialogue, what painful writing, what maddening ideas. Yet, it stands out as one of the most significant books of the year, and I keep thinking about it. Only two books struck me as fully realized: HELLICONIA WINTER by Brian Aldiss, and ALWAYS COMING HOME by Ursula K. Le Guin.

1985 LOCUS RECOMMENDED READING LIST

ART BOOKS

A MONSTER AT CHRISTMAS, Thomas Canty; Phil Hale, ill.
  (Grant)
THE UNIVERSE, Heather Couper & David Pelham (Random House)
THE GUIDE TO FANTASY ART TECHNIQUES, Martyn Dean, ed. (Arco)
MAGNETIC STORM, Roger & Martyn Dean (Harmony)
ERINSAGA: THE MYTHOLOGICAL PAINTINGS OF JIM FITZPATRICK,
  Jim Fitzpatrick (De Danann)
FRANK FRAZETTA BOOK FIVE, Betty Ballantine, ed.
  (Peacock/Bantam)

IN SEARCH OF FOREVER, Rodney Matthews (Paper Tiger)
J.K. POTTER'S THE ART OF SKELETON CREW, J.K. Potter
  (Scream/Press)
THE SIMPLE SCREAMER, Dan Reeder (Gibbs M. Smith)
THE SURREALISTIC WORLD OF TITO SALOMONI, Tito Salomoni
  (Prestige Art)
BORIS VALLEJO FANTASY ART TECHNIQUE, Boris Vallejo (Arco)
SCIENCE MADE STUPID, Tom Weller (Houghton Mifflin)

ANTHOLOGIES

THE HUGO WINNERS, VOL. 4: 1976-1979, Isaac Asimov, ed.
  (Doubleday)
ISAAC ASIMOV PRESENTS THE GREAT SF STORIES 13 (1951),
  Isaac Asimov & Martin H. Greenberg, eds. (DAW)
ISAAC ASIMOV PRESENTS THE GREAT SF STORIES 14 (1952),
  Isaac Asimov & Martin H. Greenberg, eds. (DAW)
THIEVES' WORLD #7: THE DEAD OF WINTER, Robert Lynn Asprin &
  Lynn Abbey, eds. (Ace)
L. RON HUBBARD PRESENTS WRITERS OF THE FUTURE,
  Algis Budrys, ed. (Bridge)
TERRY CARR'S BEST SCIENCE FICTION OF THE YEAR,
  Terry Carr, ed. (Tor)
UNIVERSE 15, Terry Carr, ed. (Doubleday)
INTERZONE: THE 1ST ANTHOLOGY, John Clute, Colin Greenland, &
  David Pringle, eds. (Dent)
EARTH AND ELSEWHERE, [Roger de Garis, ed.] (Macmillan)
BESTIARY!, Jack Dann & Gardner Dozois, eds. (Ace)
THE YEAR'S BEST SCIENCE FICTION, SECOND ANNUAL COLLECTION,
  Gardner Dozois, ed. (Bluejay)
THE THIRD OMNI BOOK OF SCIENCE FICTION,
  Ellen Datlow, ed. (Zebra)

MEDEA: HARLAN'S WORLD, Harlan Ellison, ed. (Phantasia)
SHADOWS 8, Charles L. Grant, ed. (Doubleday)
DESPATCHES FROM THE FRONTIERS OF THE FEMALE MIND, Jen Green
  & Sarah Lefanu, eds. (Women's Press)
IMAGINARY LANDS, Robin McKinley, ed. (Ace)
AFTER THE FLAMES, Elizabeth Mitchell, ed. (Baen)
AFTERWAR, Janet Morris, ed. (Baen)
TOP FANTASY, Josh Pachter, ed. (Dent)
THE SCIENCE FICTION YEARBOOK, Jerry Pournelle, Jim Baen, &
  John F. Carr, eds. (Baen)
THE PLANETS, Byron Preiss, ed. (Bantam Spectra)
BERSERKER BASE, Fred Saberhagen et al (Tor)
THE YEAR'S BEST FANTASY STORIES: 11, Arthur W. Saha, ed. (DAW)
WHISPERS 21/22, Stuart David Schiff, ed. (Whispers Press)
LIAVEK, Will Shetterly & Emma Bull, eds. (Bluejay)
THE YEAR'S BEST HORROR STORIES: SERIES XIII,
  Karl Edward Wagner, ed. (DAW)
THE 1985 ANNUAL WORLD'S BEST SF, Donald A. Wollheim, ed. (DAW)
NEBULA AWARDS 20, George Zebrowski, ed.
  (Harcourt Brace Jovanovich)

NOVELLAS

"To the Storming Gulf", Gregory Benford (F&SF 4/85, AFTERWAR)
"Talion", John Brunner (FAR FRONTIERS 2)
"The Scapegoat", C.J. Cherryh (ALIEN STARS 1)
"Duke Pasquale's Ring", Avram Davidson (Amazing 5/85)
"Flight", Peter Dickinson (IMAGINARY LANDS)
"George Washington Slept Here", Charles L. Harness (Analog 7/85)
"When Winter Ends", Michael P. Kube-McDowell (F&SF 7/85)
"Loaves and Fishes", George R.R. Martin (Analog 10/85)
"The Plague Star", George R.R. Martin (Analog 1-2/85)
"Green Mars", Kim Stanley Robinson (IASFM 9/85)

"How the Wind Spoke at Madaket", Lucius Shepard (IASFM 5/85)
"Sailing to Byzantium", Robert Silverberg (SAILING TO BYZANTIUM,
  IASFM 2/85)
"World War Last", Norman Spinrad (IASFM 8/85, AFTER THE FLAMES)
"Green Days in Brunei", Bruce Sterling (IASFM 10/85)
"The Only Neat Thing to Do", James Tiptree, Jr. (F&SF 10/85)
"The Gorgon Field", Kate Wilhelm (IASFM 8/85)
"The Curse of Kings", Connie Willis (IASFM 3/85)
"24 Views of Mt. Fuji, by Hokusai", Roger Zelazny (IASFM 7/85)

NOVELETTES

"A Gift From the GrayLanders", Michael Bishop (IASFM 9/85)
"The Fringe", Orson Scott Card (F&SF 10/85)
"The Slovo Stove", Avram Davidson (UNIVERSE 15)
"Unferno", George Alec Effinger (IASFM 7/85)
"In Media Vita", Gregory Frost (IASFM 1/85)
"Vestibular Man", Felix Gotschalk (F&SF 3/85)
"A Cure for Croup", Edward P. Hughes (FAR FRONTIERS 2)
"Vilest Beast", Eric G. Iverson (Analog 9/85)
"Beneath the Shadow of Her Smile", Alexander Jablokov (IASFM 4/85)
"Solstice", James Patrick Kelley (IASFM 6/85)
"Portraits of His Children", George R.R. Martin (IASFM 11/85)
"Under Siege", George R.R. Martin (Omni 10/85)
"The Things That Happen", Frederik Pohl (IASFM 10/85)
"Kitemistress", Keith Roberts (Interzone Spring 85)

"Mercurial", Kim Stanley Robinson (UNIVERSE 15)
"Storming the Cosmos", Rudy Rucker & Bruce Sterling
  (IASFM mid-Dec 85)
"O Happy Day!", Geoff Ryman (INTERZONE ANTH)
"The End of Life as We Know It", Lucius Shepard (IASFM 1/85)
"The Jaguar Hunter", Lucius Shepard (F&SF 5/85)
"A Spanish Lesson", Lucius Shepard (F&SF 12/85)
"Dogfight", Michael Swanwick & William Gibson (Omni 7/85)
"Rockabye Baby", S.C. Sykes (Analog Mid-Dec 85)
"The Fittest", George Turner (URBAN FANTASIES)
"The Road Not Taken", Harry Turtledove (Analog 11/85)
"Side Effects", Walter Jon Williams (F&SF 6/85)
"All My Darling Daughters", Connie Willis (FIREWATCH)
"Shanidar", David Zindell (WRITERS OF THE FUTURE)

SHORT STORIES

"My Life in the Jungle", Jim Aiken (F&SF 2/85)
"Going After Arvig", Michael Armstrong (AFTERWAR)
"The Last Dragon Master", A.A. Attanasio (BEASTMARKS)
"Time's Rub", Gregory Benford (IASFM 4/85)
"The Bob Dylan Tambourine Software & Satori Support Services
  Consortium Ltd." Michael Bishop (Interzone Summer 85)
"Paper Dragons", James P. Blaylock (IMAGINARY LANDS)
"Roadside Rescue", Pat Cadigan (Omni 7/85)
"Webrider", Jayge Carr (OMNI BOOK OF SF 3)
"Snow", John Crowley (Omni 11/85)
"The Gods of Mars", Gardner Dozois, Jack Dann, & Michael Swanick
  (Omni 3/85)
"With Virgil Oddum at the East Pole", Harlan Ellison
  (Omni 1/85, MEDEA)
"Paladin of the Lost Hour", Harlan Ellison
  (UNIVERSE 15, Twilight Zone 12/85)
"The Lake Was Full of Artificial Things", Karen Joy Fowler
  (IASFM 10/85)
"The Poplar Street Study", Karen Joy Fowler (F&SF 6/85)
"Winter Market", William Gibson (Vancouver 11/85)
"Tourists", Lisa Goldstein (IASFM 2/85)
"The R Strain", Eric Iverson (ANALOG 6)

"Out of All Them Bright Stars", Nancy Kress (F&SF 3/85)
"Fermi and Frost", Frederik Pohl (IASFM 1/85)
"Travels in the Interior", Scott Russell Sanders (Omni 12/85)
"'...How My Heart Breaks When I Sing This Song...'",
  Lucius Shepard (IASFM 12/85)
"Mengele", Lucius Shepard (UNIVERSE 15)
"The War at Home", Lewis Shiner (IASFM 5/85)
"The Incorporated", John Shirley (IASFM 7/85)
"Sunrise on Pluto", Robert Silverberg (THE PLANETS)
"Dinner in Audoghast", Bruce Sterling (IASFM 5/85)
"Mozart in Mirrorshades", Bruce Sterling & Lewis Shiner
  (Omni 9/85)
"The Blind Minotaur", Michael Swanwick (Amazing 3/85, BESTIARY)
"The Transmigration of Philip K.", Michael Swanwick (IASFM 2/85)
"No Regrets", Lisa Tuttle (F&SF 5/85)
"Flying Saucer Rock and Roll", Howard Waldrop (Omni 1/85)
"Heirs of the Perisphere", Howard Waldrop (Playboy 7/85)
"The Great Wall", Wayne Wightman (F&SF 9/85)
"Hong's Bluff", William F. Wu (Omni 3/85)
"Instructions for Exiting this Building in Case of Fire",
  Pamela Zoline (Interzone Summer 85, DESPATCHES FROM THE
  FRONTIERS OF THE FEMALE MIND)

Elsewhere, ROBOTS AND EMPIRE turned out to be one of the best books Isaac Asimov has written in many years. Despite the fact that nothing he has done since quite equals PAVANE, a new Keith Roberts book is always welcome. KITEWORLD is no exception. Of the few first novels I had the opportunity to read, WITH FATE CONSPIRE by Mike Shupp sticks in my mind. I had thought that any book set in an MIT dormitory must be stranger and wilder than any science fiction could be. Yet this one turned out to have resonances of H.G. Wells' THE TIME MACHINE. And while fantasy is not in any way my interest, I could not help but be impressed by Clive Barker's writing in both novel and short story modes. LYONESSE: THE GREEN PEARL was not just another new Vance novel, although that would have been perfectly all right too. Lisa Goldstein continues to greatly impress with THE DREAM YEARS.

For some reason titles in the other categories seemed to be sparse last year, but what did appear is almost enough to form a group that should be called fun: the pop-up book THE UNIVERSE by Couper and Pelham, SCIENCE MADE STUPID by Tom Weller, the British paperback GHASTLY BEYOND BELIEF edited by Gaiman and Newman, and SCIENCE FICTION: THE 100 BEST NOVELS by David Pringle, who was apparently trying to be deadly serious about the whole thing. There was one monumental reference that appeared, to take its place on any serious bibliophile's shelf, SUPERNATURAL WRITERS II: FANTASY AND HORROR edited by the redoubtable E.F. Bleiler.

If there are any of these that you have missed, hurry and read them. The new year is already here, and some important 1986 books have already begun to appear, especially HEART OF THE COMET by Gregory Benford and David Brin.

--<u>Dan Chow</u>

At least 820 works of short fiction were published in 1985, a significant increase over the 650 in 1984. (I said 600 for '84 last year but missed some late magazines and some January '85 anthologies *Locus* considered for that year.) The '85 total breaks down to 480 stories published in genre magazines (including *Whispers* and *Shayol*), 295 in anthologies and single-author collections (by Barker, Attanasio, etc.), and 45 in *Omni* and other sources as listed in *Locus*'s "Outer Limits" section. The genre magazines also published about 70 poems, including one in *Analog*.

The increase over '84 was due to some new magazines (*Night Cry*, FAR FRONTIERS, etc.), and quite a few more anthologies. But more anthologies did not mean more science fiction. Only 4 of the 18 US anthologies of (primarily) original stories were sf: UNIVERSE 15, WRITERS OF THE FUTURE, AFTERWAR, and THE PLANETS. (There were also 2 sf anthologies published in Australia, and 1 in Britain, none of which I've yet seen.) The growth in '85 was of horror/dark fantasy anthologies (5 published) and fantasy anthologies (9). Most of the latter were of the sword-and-sorcery series variety, and though sales must be encouraging them, I confess to little interest in such fiction myself.

Fantasy would seem to be crowding sf out of the magazines too, to read the complaints in the letter columns of *Asimov's* and *Amazing*. Of course, most of the fantasy in these magazines, and

F&SF, is borderline sf/fantasy, not the sword-and-sorcery lately filling anthologies. But it was true that about 1/3 of the stories in *Asimov's*, still the best "sf" magazine for overall quality of fiction, were fantasy this year, even using a liberal definition of sf. Meanwhile, *Analog* remains the one magazine staunchly, strictly sf, though oddly it is almost completely innocent of the most interesting trend in sf lately -- the "cyberpunk" or "neuromantic" movement. Nor does *Analog*'s loyalty to sf make up for the diminishing sf anthology field. I miss the ambitious, unconventional sf that was found in original anthologies a decade ago. Only *Interzone*, with its call for "radical hard sf," is as ambitious these days.

One of the best stories this year was a prime example of "cyberpunk" -- Michael Swanick and William Gibson's "Dogfight" (in the July *Omni*).

Bruce Sterling, another "neuromantic" writer (as shown by his outstanding novel, SCHISMATRIX), published a variety of excellent stories this year, including a near-future third-world novella, "Green Days in Brunei" (*Asimov's* October); a subtle and charming historical fantasy, "Dinner in Audoghast" (*Asimov's* May); and a wild parallel-timeline adventure written with Lewis Shiner, "Mozart in Mirrorshades" (*Omni* September).

Lucius Shepard continued his one-man fusillade in 1985 with another batch of powerful stories, including an exotic fantasy, "The Jaguar Hunter" (*F&SF* May), and a sentimental post-apocalype rock'n'roll story, "'...How My Heart Breaks When I Sing This Song...'" (*Asimov's* December).

Other stories I expecially liked this year are Kim Stanley Robinson's "Green Mars" (*Asimov's* September), Robert Silverberg's "Sailing to Byzantium" (*Asimov's* February), George R.R. Martin's "Under Siege" (*Omni* October), Scott Bradfield's "The Dream of the Wolf" (*Interzone 10*), David Zindell's "Shanidar" (WRITERS OF THE FUTURE), Michael Bishop's "A Gift from the GrayLanders" (*Asimov's* September), Ian McDonald's "Scenes from a Shadowplay" (*Asimov's* July) and Michael Swanick's "The Blind Minotaur" (*Amazing* March, but unexpurgated in BESTIARY!).

The most notable new writer of 1985 was Karen Joy Fowler, who published "The Lake Was Full of Artificial Things" (*Asimov's* October) and numerous others in *F&SF*, *Asimov's*, and WRITERS OF THE FUTURE.

Other impressive debuts included Robert Charles Wilson, for "Boulevard Life" in the December *Asimov's* and a story in *F&SF*; Paul J. McAuley, for "Little Ilya and Spider and Box" in *Interzone 12* and another story in *Interzone 14*; Alexander Jablokov for "Beneath the Shadow of Her Smile" in the April *Asimov's*; Lee Montgomerie, with two stories in *Interzone*, including "Green Hearts" in issue 10; and Paul DiFilippo, with stories in the June *Twilight Zone* and August *F&SF* (his first stories except for one in *UnEarth* in 1977).

New writers with earlier debuts, but who are still eligible for the Campbell New Writer Award, are David Zindell ("Shanidar", and a story in *Interzone 14*) and Ian McDonald (four stories altogether so far, all in *Asimov's*). --<u>Mark R. Kelly</u>

SMALL PRESS PUBLISHER ADDRESSES

Academy Chicago
425 N. Michigan Ave.
Chicago IL 60611

Arco Publishing
215 Park Ave. South
New York NY 10003

Ardis Publishers
2901 Heatherway
Ann Arbor MI 48104

Arkham House
P.O. Box 546
Sauk City WI 53583

Borgo Press
P.O. Box 2845
San Bernardino CA 92406

Bowling Green University Popular Press
Bowling Green OH 43403

Bud Plant, Inc.
Box 1886
Grass Valley CA 95945

Capra Press
Box 2068
Santa Barbara CA 93120

Carcanet Press Ltd.
208-212 Corn Exchange Bldgs.
Manchester M4 3BQ, UK

Citadel Press
120 Enterprise Ave.
Secaucus NJ 07094

Coffee House Press
24 N. Third St.
P.O. Box 10870
Minneapolis MN 55440

Corroboree Press
2729 Bloomington Ave. S.
Minneapolis MN 55407

The Crossing Press
P.O. Box 640
Trumansburg NY 14886

Crossway Books
9825 W. Roosevelt Rd
Westchester IL 60153

Dark Harvest
Box 48134
Niles IL 60648

Dragon Press
P.O. Box 78
Pleasantville NY 10570

Dream/Press
Box 8531
Santa Cruz CA 95061

Ebony Books
GPO Box 1294L
Melbourne, VIC 3001
Australia

M. Evans & Co.
216 East 49th St.
New York NY 10017

Falcon Books, Gibbs M. Smith, Inc.
P.O. Box 667
Layton UT 84041

Fandom Computer Services
P.O. Box 4278
San Bernardino CA 92409

Flatiron Distributors
175 Fifth Ave, Suite 814
New York NY 10010

Fragments West
3908 E. 4th St
Long Beach CA 90814

Gale Research Co.
Book Tower
Detroit MI 48226

W. Paul Ganley
P.O. Box 149, Amherst Branch
Buffalo NY 14226

Garland Publishing
136 Madison Ave.
New York NY 10016

Donald M. Grant
Publisher, Inc.
West Kingston RI 02892

Greenwood Press
88 Post Road West
Box 5007
Westport CT 06881

Gregg Press
70 Lincoln St.
Boston MA 02111

Gryphon Books
P.O. Box 209
Brooklyn NY 11228

Hale & Iremonger Pty Ltd
GPO Box 2552
Sydney NSW
Australia

G.K. Hall & Co.
70 Lincoln St.
Boston MA 02111

Highland Press
P.O. Box 861
Oak Park IL 60303

Hill House
P.O. Box 1783, Grand Central Station
New York NY 10017

Hopkins, Fandom Computer Services
P.O. Box 4278
San Bernardino CA 92409

Indiana University Press
10th & Morton Sts.
Bloomington IN 47405

Inland Book Co.
22 Hemingway Ave.
East Haven CT 06512.

International Polygonics Ltd
Box 1563
New York NY 10159

The Kent State Univ. Press
Kent OH 44242

Land of Enchantment
P.O. Box 5360
Plymouth MI 48170

Loompanics Unlimited
P.O. Box 1197
Port Townsend WA 98368

Maclay & Associates
P.O. Box 16253
Baltimore MD 21210

McFarland & Co., Inc.
Box 611
Jefferson NC 28640

Dennis McMillan Publications
401 N. 6th
Belen NM 87002

Merrimack Publishers' Circle
47 Pelham Rd.
Salem NH 03079

Merrimack Publishers' Circle
c/o Integrated Dist. Services
250 Commercial St.
Manchester NH 03101

Dennis McMillan Publications
401 N 6th
Belen NM 87002

Misfit Press, Howard DeVore
4705 Weddel
Dearborn MI 48125

Morrison, Raven-Hill Publishers
8555 Sunset Blvd.
Los Angeles CA 90069

NESFA Press
Box G, MIT Station
Cambridge MA 02139

The New Establishment Press
447 Roycroft Blvd
Amherst NY 14226

New Media Publishing, Inc.
3530 Mound View Ave.
Studio City CA 91604

Newcastle Publishing Co.
PO Box 7589
Van Nuys CA 91409

Northwestern Univ. Press
1735 Benson Ave.
Evanston IL 60201

Oriflamme Publishing Ltd
60 Charteris Road
London N4 3AB
U.K.

The Oryx Press
2214 N Central at Encanto
Phoenix AZ 85004

Phantasia Press
5536 Crispin Way
West Bloomfield MI 48033

Philtrum Publishing Co.
Box 1186
Bangor ME 04401

Press Porcepic
235-560 Johnson St.
Victoria, BC Canada V8W 3C6

Prestige Art Galleries
3909 West Howard St.
Skokie IL 60076

Princeton Univ. Press
3175 Princeton Pike
Lawrenceville NJ 06848

Purple Prose Press
400 Napoleon Rd #402
Bowling Green OH 43402

Queensland University Press
5 S. Union St.
Lawrence MA 01843

Routledge & Kegan Paul
9 Park St
Boston MA 02108

Scarecrow Press, Inc.
52 Liberty St.
P.O. Box 656
Metuchen NJ 08840

Science Fiction Poetry Association
1819 9th St., #B
Berkelry, CA 94710

Scream/Press
P.O. Box 8531
Santa Cruz CA 95061

The Seal Press
312 S. Washington
Seattle, WA 98104

Serconia Press
P.O. Box 1786
Seattle WA 98111

Seven Suns Publications
Castle Estate, Route 1
Fairfield IA 52556

Shoe String Press
P.O. Box 4327
995 Sherman Ave.
Hamden CT 06514

Southern Illinois Univ. Press
P.O. Box 3697
Carbondale IL 62902

Space & Time
138 W. 70th St., Apt. 4-E
New York NY 10023

Starmont House
P.O. Box 851
Mercer Island WA 98040

Strawberry Hill Press
2594 15th Ave.
San Francisco CA 94127

Tough Dove Books
Box 548
Little River CA 95456

Oswald Train, Publisher
Box 1891
Philadelphia PA 19105

Twaci Press
P.O. Box 87, M.I.T. Branch P.O.
Cambridge MA 02139

UMI Research Press
P.O. Box 1307
Ann Arbor MI 48106

Underwood-Miller
651 Chestnut St
Columbia PA 17512

Unicorn Publishing House
1148 Parsippany Blvd
Parsippany NJ 07054

University of Chicago Press
5801 S. Ellis Ave.
Chicago IL 60637

University of Illinois Press
54 E. Gregory Dr.
Champaign IL 61820

Frederick Ungar Publishing Co.
36 Cooper Sq.
New York NY 10013

Weirdbook Press
Box 149, Amherst Branch
Buffalo, NY 14226-0149

The Women's Press
124 Shoreditch High St.
London E1 6JE
U.K.

World Fantasy Convention
Box 27201
Tempe AZ 85282

Xanadu Publications
5 Uplands Rd
London N8 9NN
U.K.

Mark V. Ziesing
P.O. Box 806
762 Main St. (2nd level)
Willimantic CT 06226

SCIENCE FICTION IN PRINT: 1985 is limited to 500 hardcover copies.

We welcome corrections and additions. Please send them to:

Locus Publications
Box 13305
Oakland CA 94661

We plan to issue correction sheets which will be available free
to buyers of this index. Send name and address on a 3x5 index card
to the above address.

ABBREVIATIONS

ABBREVIATIONS

*	- First Edition
+	- First American Edition
100thDV	- THE HUNDREDTH DOVE, Jane Yolen, co CRO 1976
20HOUSE	- TWENTY HOUSES OF THE ZODIAC, Maxim Jakubowski, oa NEL 1979
2DZDRGN	- TWO DOZEN DRAGON EGGS, Donald A. Wollheim, co POW 1969
334	- 334, Thomas N. Disch, no AVN 1974
3FRTMRW	- THREE FOR TOMORROW, Robert Silverberg, oa MDT 1969
3TRPSTM	- THREE TRIPS IN TIME AND SPACE, Robert Silverberg, oa HAW 1973
73M	- 73 Magazine
9TLSSPC	- 9 TALES OF SPACE AND TIME, Raymond J. Healey, oa HLT 1954
9VISION	- NINE VISIONS, SEA 1983
A&S	- Art & Story
A&U	- George Allen & Unwin (Publishers), Ltd.: London
AAT	- The American Atheist
ABR	- The Adam Bedside Reader
ABS	- Abelard-Schuman: London
ABT	- Ambit
ACC	- Academy Chicago Publishers: Chicago
ACE	- Ace Books: New York
ACH	- Archon Books, The Shoe String Press, Inc.: Hamden, CT
ACP	- Academy Chicago, Publishers: Chicago
ADA	- Ad Astra
ADM&EVE	- ADAM AND EVE AND PINCH ME, A.E. Coppard, co GCP 1921
ADV	- Adventure Magazine
ADVPRPH	- ADVICE TO A PROPHET, Richard Wilbur, co HBJ 1961
ADVSKIN	- ADVENTURES IN THE SKIN TRADE, Dylan Thomas, co NDP 1955
AES	- Ares Magazine
AFTFALL	- AFTER THE FALL, Robert Sheckley, oa ACE 1980
AFTRWAR	- AFTERWAR, Janet Morris, oa BAE 1985
AGL	- Algol, Andrew Porter, ed.
AGN	- The Argonaut
AGNDNGR	- AGAIN, DANGEROUS VISIONS, Harlan Ellison, oa DBL 1972
AHM	- Alfred Hitchcock's Mystery Magazine
AHTMYSP	- THE ARBOR HOUSE TREASURY OF MYSTERY AND SUSPENSE, Bill Pronzine, Barry N. Malzberg & Martin H. Greenberg, an ARH 1981
ALC	- The Alien Critic, Richard E. Geis, ed.
ALCHEMY	- ALCHEMY & ACADEME, Anne McCaffrey, oa DBL 1970
ALIENST	- ALIEN STARS, Elizabeth Mitchell, oa BAE 1985
ALIENWO	- ALIEN WORLDS, Paul Collins, oa VDP 1979
ALL	- W.H. Allen & Co. Ltd.: London
ALLWNDR	- ALL THE WONDERS WE SEEK, Felix Marti-Ibanez, co POT 1963
ALN&LVR	- ALIENS & LOVERS, Millea Kenin, oa UQG 1983
ALNCNDT	- THE ALIEN CONDITION, Stephen Goldin, oa BAL 1973
ALONEBY	- ALONE BY NIGHT, Michael & Don Congdon, an BAL 1962
ALT	- ALLSORTS, Ann Thwaite, oa MTH
ALTASMV	- THE ALTERNATE ASIMOVS, Isaac Asimov, oc DBL 1986
ALWCMHM	- ALWAYS COMING HOME, Ursula K. Le Guin, oc HPR 1985
ALY	- Alyson Publications, Inc.: Boston
AMM	- American Mercury
AMOROTC	- AMOROTICA, Deep River Press 1981
AMPTYAN	- THE AMERICAN POETRY ANTHOLOGY, Daniel Halpern, an WVP 1975
AMZ	- Amazing Science Fiction Stories
an	- anthology
AND	- ANDROMEDA, Peter Weston, oa FPL
ANGELS&	- ANGELS AND SPACESHIPS, Fredric Brown, co DUT 1954
ANLGANL	- ANALOG ANNUAL, Ben Bova, oa PYR 1976
ANS	- Antaeus
ANTHNGY	- ANTHONOLOGY, Piers Anthony, co TOR 1985
ANTICIP	- ANTICIPATIONS, Christopher Priest, oa SCB 1978
APC	- Appleton-Century: New York
APH	- Aphelion, Australia
ar	- article
ARA	- Amra (fanzine)
ARB	- Argosy Magazine, British edition
ARE	- ARIES, John Grant, oa
ARG	- Argosy Magazine
ARH	- Arbor House Publishing Company: New York
ARI	- ARIEL, Thomas Durwood, oa
ARK	- Arkham House Publishers, Inc.: Sauk City, WI
ARN	- The Arena
ASBSPHX	- ASBESTOS PHOINIX, Ramon Guthrie, co FKW 1968
ASF	- Astounding/Analog Science Fiction
ASJ	- Australian Journal
ASN	- Australasian
ASTNDNG	- ASTOUNDING, Harry Harrison, oa RDM 1973
ATA	- Atalanta, British magazine
ATH	- Atheneum Publishers: New York
ATL	- Atlantic Monthly magazine
Aug	- August
AUR	- Aurora Publishers, Inc.
AURBRL1	- AURORES BOREALES 1, an PRM 1983
AURORA	- AURORA: BEYOND EQUALITY, Vonda McIntyre & Susan Anderson, oa FGM 1976
AUT	- Authentic Science Fiction
AVB	- Avenel Books
AVN	- Avon Books: New York
aw	- afterword
AWK	- American Weekly
AWR	- American Whig Review
AYA	- Aya Press: Toronto
AYR	- All the Year Round
AZN	- AMAZONS, Jessica Amanda Salmonson, oa DAW
BAE	- Baen Books: New York
BAITDRM	- A BAIT OF DREAMS, Jo Clayton, no DAW 1985
BAL	- Ballantine Books: New York
BAN	- Bantam Books, Inc.: New York
BAS	- BEST AMERICAN SHORT STORIES

BASILSK	- BASILISK, Ellen Kushner, oa ACE 1980
BAW	- Black and White
BBL	- Bibliofantasiac, Toronto
BBM	- Blue Book Magazine
BCA	- Book Club Associates/Guild Publishing: London
BDL	- The Bodley Head Ltd.: London
BEAMMAL	- BEAM OF MALICE, Alex Hamilton, co 1963
BEASTMK	- BEASTMARKS, A.A. Attanasio, oc ZIE 1985
BEASTWI	- THE BEAST WITH FIVE FINGERS, William F. Harvey, co DNT 1928
BELLFOG	- THE BELL IN THE FOG AND OTHER STORIES, Gertrude Atherton, co HPR 1905
BEU	- Beaufort Books, Inc.: New York
BEY	- Beyond Fantasy Fiction
bg	- biography
BGM	- Burton's Gentleman's Magazine
BGS	- Birmingham Group SF Newsletter
bi	- bibliography
BIGDIPR	- FRANK AND POLLY MUIR'S BIG DIPPER, HEI 1981
BJB	- Bluejay Books, Inc.: New York
BKHRBRT	- THE BOOK OF FRANK HERBERT, Frank Herbert, co DAW 1973
BKM	- Berkley Medallion Books: New York
BKN	- The Broken Shaft, Unwin's Annual
BKS	- THE BERKLEY SHOWCASE, Victoria Schochet & John W. Silbersack, oa BRK
BKW	- A Book of Weird Tales, British
BLD	- Border Land
BLDYSUN	- THE BLOODY SUN, Marion Zimmer Bradley, n. ACE 1964, ACE 1979 edition includes story "To Keep the Oath".
BLF	- Boy's Life
BLKSPRT	- BLACK SPIRITS AND WHITE, Ralph Adams Cram, co 1895
BLODIRN	- BLOOD AND IRON, Jerry E. Pournelle & John F. Carr, an TOR 1984
BLR	- Bloodrake
BLS	- Geoffrey Bles: London
BLT	- The Bulletin, Sydney
BLUECHM	- BLUE CHAMPAGNE, John Varley, co DKH 1986
BNA	- Bananas
BNZ	- Bonanza Books
BOA	- BOAC
BOLO	- BOLO, Keith Laumer, co BKP 1976
BOM	- THE BEST OF OMNI, an
BOP	- Boy's Own Paper, London
BOXEN	- BOXEN, C.S. Lewis, co HBJ 1985
BPC	- Berkeley Poets Cooperative
br	- book review
BRBNSWD	- THE BARBARIAN SWORDSMEN, Sean Richards, an STB 1981
BRG	- Bridge Publications, Inc.: Los Angeles, CA
BRK	- Berkley Books, Berkley Publishing Group: New York
BSF	- Beyond: Science Fiction & Fantasy
BSFS:51	- THE BEST SCIENCE-FICTION STORIES: 1951, Everett F. Bleiler & T.E. Dikty, an FEL 1951
BSFSBAR	- BEST SCIENCE FICTION STORIES OF BRIAN W. ALDISS (REVISED EDITION), Brian W. Aldiss, co FAB 1971
BSL	- Bestsellers
BSP	- Black Sparrow Press: CA
BSRKRBS	- BERSERKER BASE, Fred Saberhagen, an TOR 1985
BST	- BINARY STAR, om DEL
BST&SUP	- BEASTS AND SUPER-BEASTS, Saki, co LNE 1914
BSU	- Ball State University Forum
BSV	- Baltimore Saturday Visitor
BUTFLSR	- BEAUTIFUL LOSERS, Leonard Cohen, co VIK 1966
bx	- boxed set of books
BYNDDAR	- BEYOND THE DAR AL-HARB, Gordon R. Dickson, co Tor 1985
BYNDLND	- BEYOND LANDS OF NEVER, an A&U 1984
C&C	- Cory & Collins: Victoria, Australia
C&W	- Chatto & Windus: London
CANSUCH	- CAN SUCH THINGS BE?, Ambrose Bierce, co 1893
CANYOUF	- CAN YOU FEEL ANYTHING WHEN I DO THIS?, Robert Sheckley, co DBL 1971
CAP	- Jonathan Cape, Ltd.: London
CAS	- Caswell: London
CATFLAP	- THE CAT-FLAP AND THE APPLE PIE, Diana Wynne Jones, co ALL 1979
CAVIAR	- CAVIAR, Theodore Sturgeon, co BAL 1955
CBB	- CLIVE BARKER'S BOOKS OF BLOOD, Clive Barker, oc SPH
CBR	- Corroboree Press: Minneapolis, MN
CBS	- CBS Television System
CCA	- Corio Chronicle and Western Districts Advertiser
CEN	- Computer Entertainment
CHA	- Chacal
CHANGES	- CHANGES, Michael Bishop & Ian Watson, oa ACE 1983
CHL	- Chilton Book Company: London
CHP	- The Coach House Press
CHT	- Charterhouse
CLDFEAR	- COLD FEAR, Hugh Lamb, oa ALL 1977
CLDPRNT	- COLD PRINT, Ramsey Campbell, an S/P 1985
CLG	- Collage
CLL	- Callaloo
CLN	- William Collins Publishers, Inc.
CLR	- CLARION, Robert Scott Wilson, oa SIG
CLRAWDS	- THE CLARION AWARDS, Damon Knight, oa DBL 1984
CLU	- Clues
CMM	- Commentary
CMP	- Cosmopolitan
CMPSRSE	- THE COMPASS ROSE, Ursula K. Le Guin, co HPR 1982
CNH	- Cornhill Magazine: London
CNT	- Coronet Books: London
CNY	- The Century
co	- collection
COE	- The Coe Review
COL	- Colliers

COLDHND - COLD HAND IN MINE, Robert Aickman, co SCB 1975
COLPMRG - COLLECTED POEMS OF ROBERT GRAVES, Robert Graves, co CAS
           1975
COLSSMJ - COLLECTED SHORT STORIES OF M.R. JAMES, M.R. James, co
           1924
COLSTWF - COLLECTED STORIES OF WILLIAM FAULKNER, William Faulkner,
           co 1930
COMBTSF - COMBAT SF, Gordon R. Dickson, an DBL 1975
COSMICO - COSMICOMICS, Italio Calvino, co HBW 1968
CPLSSSA - THE COMPLETE SHORT STORIES OF SAKI, Saki, co 1930
CRC   - Creative Computing Magazine
CRMPR30 - CRIME PREVENTION IN THE 30th CENTURY, Hans Stefan
           Santesson, an WKR 1969
CRN   - Crown Publishers, Inc.: New York
CRO   - Thomas Y. Crowell
CRP   - Crypt of Cthulhu
CRW   - Crawdaddy
CRY   - CHRYSALIS, Roy Torgeson, oa ZEB
cs   - comic strip
CSM   - Cosmos Science Fiction and Fantasy Magazine
CSMCKAL - COSMIC KALEIDOSCOPE, Bob Shaw, co GOL 1976
CSMCPRS - THE COSMIC PERSPECTIVE/CUSTER'S LAST STAND, Brian
           Stableford, oc DRM 1985
CSS   - Cassell: London
CSSNDRA - CASSANDRA RISING, Alice Laurance, oa DBL 1978
ct   - cartoon
CTCHDTH - CATCH YOUR DEATH AND OTHER GHOST STORIES, John Gordon,
           co 1984
CTM   - CONTINUUM, Roger Elwood, oa
CTNYTLS - CAUTIONARY TALES, Chelsea Quinn Yarbro, co DBL 1978
CUP   - College & University Press: New Haven, Conn.
CUTS   - CUTS, Carter Scholz, oc DRM 1985
CVL   - Cavalier
CYC   - Crystal Crone
CYM   - City Miner Magazine
DAMNTNS - DAMNATIONS, R.L. Leming, 1984 [Vincent McHardy]
DAWSFRD - THE DAW SCIENCE FICTION READER, Donald A. Wollheim, oa
           DAW 1976
DAY&NGT - DAY AND NIGHT STORIES, Algernon Blackwood, co CSS 1917
DAYSUNS - THE DAY THE SUN STOOD STILL, Robert Silverberg, oa NEL
           1972
DBL   - Doubleday & Co., Inc.: Garden City, N.Y.
DCH   - The Daily Chronicle
DCM   - The Diners Club Magazine
DCT   - Delacorte Press: New York
DDL   - Dandelion Magazine, Canada
DEADWIN - THE DEAD OF WINTER, Robert Lynn Asprin & Lynn Abbey, oa
           ACE 1985
DEATH   - DEATH, Stuart David Schiff, oa PBP 1982
Dec   - December
DEL   - Dell Publishing Co., Inc.: New York
DFNS83C - Defense '83 Conference in Las Vegas
dg   - digest size magazine
DGC   - Darkover Grand Council Program Book
DGHTRGL - DAUGHTER OF REGALS AND OTHER TALES, Stephen R.
           Donaldson, co BAL 1984
DGM   - Dragon Magazine
DHZ   - Dark Horizons, British Fantasy Society
DKD   - Dark Dreams, c/o Jeff Dempsey, 2 Looe Road, Croxteth,
           Liverpool L11 6LJ, England
DKH   - Dark Harvest: Niles, IL
DMGALHR - THE DODD, MEAD GALLERY OF HORROR, Charles L. Grant, oa
           DOM 1983
DMM   - Dime Mystery Magazine
DMNKIND - DEMON KIND, Roger Elwood, oa AVN 1973
DMR   - Democratic Review
DNGRVIS - DANGEROUS VISIONS, Harlan Ellison, oa DBL 1967
DNN   - The Donning Company/Publishers: Norfolk & Virginia
           Beach, VA
DNSTRRM - THE DOWNSTAIRS ROOM, Kate Wilhelm, co DBL 1968
DNT   - J.M. Dent & Sons Ltd.: London
DOM   - Dodd, Mead: New York
DON   - The Donning Co.: Virginia Beach, VA
DR.OX   - LE DOCTEUR OX, Jules Verne, co 1872
DRC   - The San Francisco Dramatic Chronicle
DRCLGST - DRACULA'S GUEST, Bram Stoker, co 1914
DRD   - Dreadnaught Co-operative
DREAMDY - DREAM DAYS, Kenneth Grahame, co 1899
DRF   - Dragonfields
DRG   - The Dragon
DRG&DRM - DRAGONS & DREAMS, Jane Yolen, Martin H. Greenberg &
           Charles G. Waugh, oa HPR 1986
DRGNDRK - DRAGONS OF DARKNESS, Orson Scott Card, oa ACE 1981
DRGNLGT - DRAGONS OF LIGHT, Orson Scott Card, oa ACE 1980
DRKCMPN - DARK COMPANIONS, Ramsey Campbell, co MAC 1982
DRKFRCS - DARK FORCES, Kirby McCauley, oa VIK 1980
DRKGODS - DARK GODS, T.E.D. Klein, co VIK 1985
DRKIMGN - DARK IMAGININGS, an DEL 1978
DRKMIND - DARK MIND, DARK HEART, August Derleth, oa ARK 1962
DRKMUSC - DARK MUSIC, Jack Snow, co HRL 1947
DRKOVRC - DARKOVER CONCORDANCE, Marion Zimmer Bradley, nf PNP 1979
DRM   - Drumm Booklets, Chris Drumm: Polk City, IA
DRMWEVR - DREAM WEAVER, Jane Yolen, co CLN 1979
DSC   - Descant
DSPCTHU - THE DISCIPLES OF CTHULHU, Edward P. Berglund, oa DAW
           1976
DSPRFUT - THE DISAPPEARING FUTURE, George Hay, oa PTH 1970
DSPTCHS - DESPATCHES FROM THE FRONTIERS OF THE FEMALE MIND, Jen
           Green & Sarah Lefanu, oa WOP 1985
DST   - DESTINIES, James Baen, oa ACE
DTHANGL - DEATH ANGEL'S SHADOW, Karl Edward Wagner, co WBK 1973
DTL   - Detective Tales

DUT   - E.P. Dutton & Co., Inc.: London
DYNGERT - THE DYING EARTH, Jack Vance, oc HIL 1950
DYSTVIS - DYSTOPIAN VISIONS, Roger Elwood, oa PRH 1975
EBN   - Ebony Books: Melbourne
ECO   - Ecco Press: New York
ed   - editorial
EDGEVNG - THE EDGE OF EVENING, Nicholas Stuart Gray, co FAB 1976
EDGTMRW - THE EDGE OF TOMORROW, Isaac Asimov, co TOR 1985
EDT   - Eldritch Tales
ELK   - Elks Magazine
ELW   - ELSEWHERE, Terri Winding & Mark Allan Arnold, oa ACE
EMB   - Ed McBains Mystery Book
ENGNGHT - ENGINES OF THE NIGHT, Barry N. Malzberg, co 1982
EPO   - Epoch
EPOCH   - EPOCH, Roger Elwood & Robert Silverberg, oa BRK 1975
EQM   - Ellery Queen's Mystery Magazine
ERC   - Eerie Country
ERH&ELW - EARTH AND ELSEWHERE, Roger DeGaris, an MAC 1985
EROSORB - EROS IN ORBIT, Joseph Elder, oa TRI 1973
ESC   - Escapade
ESP   - Escape!
ETW   - Etwas, Peggy Rae McKnight, ed.
EUR&ELW - EUROPE AND ELSEWHERE, Mark Twain, ed. Albert Bigelow
           Paine, co HPB 1923
EVTHBLV - EVERYTHING BUT LOVE, an MIR 1973
ex   - extract
EYE   - EYE, Frank Herbert, co BRK 1985
EYR   - Eyre & Spottiswoode: London
F&T   - Fantasy and Terror
fa   - facetious article
FAB   - Faber & Faber, Ltd.: London
FACECHS - THE FACE OF CHAOS, Robert Lynn Asprin & Lynn Abbey, oa
           ACE 1983
FACESFR - FACES OF FEAR, Douglas E. Winter, nf BRK 1985
FAD   - Fantastic Adventures
FAERY!   - FAERY!, Terri Windling, an ACE 1985
FAN   - Fantastic
FARSIDE - THE FAR SIDE OF TIME, Roger Elwood, oa DOM 1974
FATMANI - THE FAT MAN IN HISTORY, Peter Carey, co 1974
FAW   - Fawcett Crest Books
FBK   - Fantasy Book [published by FPCI]
FBM   - Fantasy Book magazine [published by Dennis Mallonee]
FBRBKMF - THE FABER BOOK OF MODERN FAIRY TALES, Sara & Stephen
           Corrin, an FAB 1985
FCR   - Fantasy Crossroads
FEARS   - FEARS, Charles L. Grant, oa BRK 1983
Feb   - February
FEL   - Fredrick Fell, Inc.
FFM   - Famous Fantastic Mysteries magazine
FFR   - FAR FRONTIERS, Jerry Pournelle & Jim Baen, oa BAE
FGM   - Fawcett Gold Medal Books
FIENDIN - THE FIEND IN YOU, Charles Beaumont, an BAL 1962
FIG   - Figaro, Paris
FIGHUMN - FIGURES OF THE HUMAN, David Ignatow, co WUP 1964
FIREBDI - FIREBIRD I, [Angela Carter]
FIREWTC - FIRE WATCH, Connie Willis, co BJB 1985
FKW   - Funk & Wagnalls, Inc.: New York
FLGTNVR - FLIGHT FROM NEVERYON, Samuel R. Delanny, oc BAN 1985
Fll   - Fall
FLLWSHP - FELLOWSHIP OF THE STARS, Terry Carr, oa SAS 1974
FLN   - Flynn's Detective Fiction
FLS   - FLASHING SWORDS, Lin Carter, oa DEL
FLTWYBA - FLEETWAY BOY'S ANNUAL
FMF   - Famous Science Fiction
FMG   - Fantasy Magazine
FNLSTGE - FINAL STAGE, Edward L. Ferman & Barry N. Malzberg, oa
           CHT 1974
FNTRWLD - FRONTIER WORLDS, Paul Collins, oa C&C 1983
FPL   - Futura Publications Limited: London
FRAMZDK - FREE AMAZONS OF DARKOVER, Marion Zimmer Bradley and the
           Friends of Darkover, oa DAW 1985
FRG   - Fantasy Readers Guide
FRGNBDY - FOREIGN BODIES, 1981 [Brian W. Aldiss]
FRIGHTS - FRIGHTS, Kirby McCauley, oa SMP 1976
FRM   - The Forum
FRMOTO1 - FROM ZERO TO ONE, Robert Zend, SNN 1973
FRMHRTD - FROM THE HEART OF DARKNESS, David A. Drake, co TOR 1983
FRYLGND - FAIRY LEGENDS AND TRADITIONS OF THE SOUTH OF IRELAND, T.
           Crofton Croker, co 1825
FSB   - Fantasy, British
FSF   - The Magazine of Fantasy & Science Fiction
FSG   - Farrar, Straus & Giroux, Inc.: New York
FSM   - Fantastic Story Magazine
FSTRLGT - FASTER THAN LIGHT, George Zebrowski & Jack Danr, oa HPR
           1976
FTL   - Fantasy Tales
FUN   - Fantastic Universe Science Fiction
FUT   - Future Science Fiction magazine
FUTCITY - FUTURE CITY, Roger Elwood, oa TRI 1973
FUTPAST - FUTURE PASTIMES, Scott Edelstein, oa AUR 1977
fw   - foreword
FWR   - THE FUTURE AT WAR, Reginald Bretnor, an ACE
FYC   - Fantasycon Programme Booklet
G&S   - GHOSTS & SCHOLARS, Rosemary Pardoe, an
GAL   - Galaxy
GCP   - Golden Cockerell Press: Berkshire
GDY   - Godey's Lady's Book
GEM   - Gem
GENERTN - GENERATION, David Gerrold, oa DEL 1972
GHB   - GHOST BOOK, Aidan Chambers/James Turner, an
GHOSTBK - THE GHOST-BOOK, Cynthia Asquith, an 1926
GHOSTS   - GHOSTS, Edith Wharton, co APC 1937

GHOSTS2 - GHOSTS, Marvin Kaye, an DBL 1981
GHSTANT - GHOST STORIES OF AN ANTIQUARY, M.R. James, co 1904
GHSTLGT - THE GHOST LIGHT, Fritz Leiber, co BRK 1984
GHSTSHP - THE GHOST SHIP, Richard Middleton, co 1912
GHSTSHR - THE GHOST OF SHERLOCK HOLMES, [Leslie Halliwell]
GIRLWTH - THE GIRL WITH THE HUNGRY EYES, Donald A. Wollheim, oa
          AVN 1949
GLDNGTE - GOLDEN GATE AND OTHER STORIES, R.A. Lafferty, co CBR
          1982
GLG   - Graham's Lady's and Gentleman's Magazine
GLL   - Galileo Magazine
GLR   - Gallery Magazine
GLSTBSF - GOLLANCZ - SUNDAY TIMES BEST SF STORIES, oa GOL 1975
GML   - Greystoke Mobray Ltd.
GNC   - Gentleman's Companion
GNL   - W. Paul Ganley: Publisher: Buffalo, NY
gp   - group of related stories
gr   - game review
GRC   - The Grecourt Review
GRL   - Grils, Joyce Fisher, Sue Robinson, and Pam Janisch, eds.
GRLMKNS - GRIMALKIN'S TALES, Stella Whitelaw, Judy Gardiner & Mark
          Rosen, oa 1983
GRLWHOC - THE GIRL WHO CRIED FLOWERS, Jane Yolen, co CRO 1974
GRMLKNS - GRIMALKIN'S TALES, Stella Whitelaw, Judy Gardiner & Mark
          Ronson, oa SMP 1985
GRNGADV - THE GRAND ADVENTURE, Philip José Farmer, co BRK 1984
GRP   - The Graphic
GRUSMBK - THE GRUESOME BOOK, Ramsey Campbell, an PIC 1983
GRYSTBY - GREYSTONE BAY, Charles L. Grant, oa TOR 1985
GTEHELL - THE GATES OF HELL, C.J. Cherryh & Janet Morris, no BAE
          1986
GTH   - Gothism, Robert L. Chomorsky, ed.
GTNGEVN - GETTING EVEN, Woody Allen, co RDM 1971
H&I   - Hale & Ireminger Pty Ltd.: Sydney
HABITAT - HABITATS, Susan Shwartz, oa DAW 1984
HAW   - Hawthorn Books, Inc.
HBC   - Hayden Book Company: Hasbrouck Heights, NJ
HBJ   - Harcourt Brace Jovanovich Inc.: New York
HBW   - Harcourt Brace World Inc.: New York
hc   - hard cover
HECATES - HECATE'S CAULDRON, Susan M. Shwartz, oa DAW 1982
HEI   - William Heinemann Ltd.: London
HEROFAN - HEROIC FANTASY, Gerald W. Page & Hank Reinhardt, oa DAW
          1979
HEROVIS - HEROIC VISIONS, Jessica Amanda Salmonson, oa ACE 1983
HGT   - High Times
HHW   - Household Words
HIL   - Hillman
HKMRLSY - HENRT KUTTNER - A MEMORIAL SYMPOSIUM, Karen Anderson, nf
HLT   - Henry Holt
HLX   - Helix
HMF   - Houghton Mifflin Company: New York
HMS   - Hutchinson's Mystery Story Magazine
HNC   - Hartford Northeast Current
HNDFLDS - A HANDFUL OF DUST, Evelyn Waugh, co 1934
HNDSHLL - THE HOUNDS OF HELL, Michel Parry, an GOL 1974
HNL   - Haunted Library Publications
HNTDCST - HAUNTED CASTLES: THE COMPLETE GOTHIC TALES OF RAY
          RUSSELL, Ray Russell, co 1985
HORRTLS - HORROR TALES, Roger Elwood, oa RAN 1974
HPB   - Harper & Brothers: New York
HPR   - Harper & Row: New York
HRCMLDY - HERE COMES THE LADY, M. P. Shiel, co 1928
HRL   - Herald: New York
HRP   - Harper's Magazine
HRTSTND - HEART OF STONE, DEAR, R.A. Lafferty, co DRM 1984
HRV   - The Hudson Review: A Magazine of Literature and the Arts
HRW   - Holt, Rinehart and Winston: New York
HSCTHLU - THE HOUSE OF CTHULHU AND OTHER TALES OF THE PRIMAL LAND,
          Brian Lumley, co WBP 1984
HSH   - The Horror Show
HSMSHLD - THE HOUSE ON THE MARSHLANDS, Louise Gluck, co ECO 1975
HTS   - Haunts, Nightshade Publications, P.O. Box 3342,
          Providence, RI 02906
HTZ   - J. Hetzel: Paris
hu   - humor
HVNLYHT - HEAVENLY HOST, Isaac Asimov, na
IAA   - Isaac Asimov's SF Adventure Magazine
IAM   - ISAAC ASIMOV'S MAGICAL WORLDS OF FANTASY, Isaac Asimov,
          Martin H. Greenberg & Charles G. Waugh, an SIG
IAS   - Isaac Asimov's Science Fiction Magazine
ibc   - inside back cover
IDIOSYN - IDIOSYNCRACIES, ILP 1984
IDL   - The Idler
IDSTMRW - THE IDES OF TOMORROW, Terry Carr, oa LBR 1976
ifc   - inside front cover
IFS   - If/Worlds of If Science Fiction
IHOPEIS - I HOPE I SHALL ARRIVE SOON, Philip K. Dick, co DBL 1985
IKR   - Inside Karate
il   - illustration
ILP   - Illuminati Press
IMG   - Imagination
IMGNLND - IMAGINARY LANDS, Robin McKinley, oa ACE 1985
IMN   - Imagine
IMP   - (SF) Impulse, formerly Science Fantasy
in   - introduction
INAGLSS - IN A GLASS, DARKLY, Joseph Sheridan Le Fanu, co 1886
INALNFL - IN ALIEN FLESH, Gregory Benford, co TOR 1986
INF   - Infinity Science Fiction
INHBLKE - THE INHABITANT OF THE LAKE, Ramsey Campbell, co ARK 1964
INHSOWN - IN HIS OWN WRITE, John Lennon, co 1964
INMIDST - IN THE MIDST OF LIFE, Ambrose Bierce, co 1891

INR   - Indiana Review
ins   - insert
INTRFCS - INTERFACES, Ursula K. Le Guin & Virginia Kidd, oa ACE
          1980
INY   - INFINITY, Robert Hoskins, oa LAN
INZ   - Interzone
IRV   - The Iowa Review
IS   - Is, Tom Collins, ed.
ISBN   - international standard book number
ISTHATW - IS THAT WHAT PEOPLE DO?, Robert Sheckley, co HRW 1984
ITCAMEF - IT CAME FROM SCHENECTADY, Barry B. Longyear, co BJB 1984
ITM   - International Magazine
iv   - interview
ix   - index
IZA   - INTERZONE ANTHOLOGY, John Clute, Colin Greenland & David
          Pringle, an
Jan   - January
JBLJKNY - JUBILEE JACKANORY, BBC 1977
JDP   - Journal des Debats Politiques et Litteraires
JNK   - Herbert Jenkins: London
JNS   - Janus
Jul   - July
Jun   - June
JWC   - JOHN W. CAMPBELL MEMORIAL AWARDS, George R.R. Martin, oa
          BJB
JWLMOON - JEWEL OF THE MOON, William Kotzwinkle, oc PUT 1985
JWSHFYT - JEWISH FAIRY TALES AND STORIES, Gerald Friedlander, co
          1918
KHT   - Khatru, Jeffrey D. Smith, ed.
KINGYLW - THE KING IN YELLOW, Robert W. Chambers, co NLY 1895
KISSKIS - KISS KISS, Roald Dahl, co 1959
KITEWLD - KITEWORLD, Keith Roberts, no GOL 1985
KLK   - Kalki
KNB   - Knave (U.K. edition)
KNP   - Alfred A. Knopf, Inc.: New York
KPRSPRC - THE KEEPER'S PRICE, Marion Zimmer Bradley, oa DAW 1980
KPS   - Keepsake
KWAIDAN - KWAIDAN, Lafcadio Hearn, co 1904
LAN   - Lancer Books
LANDSCP - LANDSCAPE WITH LANDSCAPE, Gerald Murnane, oc NOR 1985
LAR   - Los Angeles Review
LAS   - Los Alamos Scientific Laboratory News
LAUGHTM - LAUGHING TIME, William Jay Smith, co DCT 1980
LBR   - Little, Brown and Co.
LDYBRGE - THE LADY OF THE BARGE, W.W. Jacobs, co HPR 1902
LGHSTCS - LEGENDS OF HASTUR AND CASSILDA, Marion Zimmer Bradley,
          co THP 1979
LGNDTLS - LEGENDS AND TALES OF THE OLD WEST, co 1962
LGTLNST - LIGHT FROM A LONE STAR, Jack Vance, co NSF 1985
LGTYR&D - LIGHT YEARS AND DARK, Michael Bishop, oa BRK 1984
LIAVEK - LIAVEK, Will Shetterly & Emma Bull, oa ACE 1985
LIP   - J.B. Lippincott Company
LNDLSTC - THE LAND OF LOST CONTENT, Robert Phillips, co 1970
LNDSNVR - LANDS OF NEVER, Maxim Jakubowski, oa A&U 1983
LNE   - John Lane: London
LOM   - London Magazine
lp   - large paperback - 8 1/2 x 11
LRB   - The London Review of Books
LSN   - Literary Storefront Newsletter
LSTBKWN - THE LAST BOOK OF WONDER, Lord Dunsany, co 1916
LTKNTED - LATE KNIGHT EDITION, Damon Knight, co NSF 1985
LTRSERT - LETTERS FROM THE EARTH, Mark Twain, ed. Bernard DeVoto,
          co HPR 1962
LUR   - T. Werner Laurie: London
LVLHMSP - L'VIEIL HOMME ET L'ESPACE, Daniel Sernine, co PRM 1981
LWV   - Last Wave, Scott Edelman, ed.
M&B   - Mills & Boon: London
MAC   - The Macmillan Publishing Co., Inc.: New York & London
MACPRBK - MIDAMERICON PROGRAM BOOK, 1976
MAD   - Mademoiselle
MAM   - Mystery Adventures Magazine
Mar   - March
MAR   - Marvel Science Fiction
May   - May
MCC   - McCalls
MCE   - Macmillan Educational Ltd.: Basingstoke & London
MCHSH10 - THE MACHINE IN SHAFT TEN, M. John Harrison, co PTH 1975
md   - mid, as in mid-December
MDNMASS - MIDNIGHT MASS, Paul Bowles, co BSP 1981
MDS   - Midnight Sun, Gary Hoppenstand, ed.
MDT   - Meredith Press
MENDEEP - MEN OF THE DEEP WATERS, William Hope Hodgson, co 1914
MENOWAR - MEN OF WAR, Jerry E. Pournelle, an TOR 1984
MER   - Magasin d'Education et de Recreation
MERYMEN - THE MERRY MEN AND OTHER TALES AND FABLES, Robert Louis
          Stevenson, co C&W 1887
MFL   - Mayflower Books: London
MFP   - Misfit Press: Dearborn, MI
mg   - magazine
MGB   - Magnum Books: London
MGE   - Mage, c/o The Colgate Science Fiction/Fantasy
          Association, Colgate University Student Association,
          Hamilton NY 13346
MGI   - MAGIC IN ITHCAR, Andre Norton & Robert Adams, oa TOR
          1985
MHT   - Manhunt
MIDNGHT - MIDNIGHT, Charles L. Grant, an TOR 1985
MINEOWN - MINE OWN PEOPLE, Rudyard Kipling, co 1891
MIR   - Mir Publishers: Moscow
MIS   - The Missouri Review
MJS   - Mother Jones
MLL   - McLelland and Stewart

MLNELPH - MELANCHOLY ELEPHANTS, Spider Robinson, co
MLNLWMN - MILLENNIAL WOMEN, Virginia Kidd, oa DCT 1978
MMM   - Malcolm's [Mystery Magazine]
MNE   - Maine Magazine
MNLYMNL - MAINLY IN MOONLIGHT, Nicholas Stuart Grey, co 1965
MNPOLMD - THE MODERN POLISH MIND, Maria Kuncewicz, an LBR 1962
MNSLDMN - THE MAN WHO SOLD THE MOON, Robert A. Heinlein, co SHS
           1950
MNSNGRF - MOONSINGER'S FRIENDS, Susan Shwartz, oa BJB 1985
MNSTRCL - THE MONSTER CLUB
MNWHBKX - THE MAN WHO BROKE OUT OF THE LETTER X, Robert Priest, co
           CHP 1984
MNYWRLD - THE MANY WORLDS OF SCIENCE FICTION, Ben Bova, oa DUT
           1971
MOH   - The Magazine of Horror
MPC   - Montcalm Publishing Corporation: New York
mr   - movie review
MRMAGIC - MORE MAGIC, Larry Niven, oa BRK 1984
MRP   - Moor Park, Miriam Dyches, ed.
MRTLSBW - MORE TALES OF THE BLACK WIDOWERS, Isaac Asimov, co DBL
           1976
MRWNDRN - MORE WANDERING STARS, Jack M. Dann, an DBL 1981
ms   - miscellaneous
MSH   - Manuscript House: New York
MSM   - Mike Shane Mystery Magazine
MSQ   - The Masquerade, Eton
MSRMAUR - MONSIEUR MAURICE, Amelia B. Edwards, co 1873
MSS   - MSS
MSTRFLY - THE MONSTER FLY, Charles A. Piddock, oc XEP 1974
MTFBLMN - MARK TWAIN'S FABLES OF MAN, ed. John S. Tuckey, co UCP
           1972
MTH   - Methuen: London
MTN   - MARK TWAIN'S NOTEBOOKS & JOURNALS, ed. Frederick
           Anderson, et al, co UCP
MTNTEBK - MARK TWAIN'S NOTEBOOK, ed. Albert Bigelow Paine, co HPB
           1935
MTQRHVN - MARK TWAIN'S QUARREL WITH HEAVEN: "CAPTAIN STORMFIELD'S
           VISIT TO HEAVEN" AND OTHER SKETCHES, ed. Ray B. Brown,
           co CUP 1970
MTWHDRM - MARK TWAIN'S WHICH WAS THE DREAM? AND OTHER SYMBOLIC
           WRITINGS OF THE LATER YEARS, ed. John S. Tuckey, co UCP
           1967
MUS   - Muse (Colorado arts newspaper)
MUT   - Mutual Book Co.: Boston
MVS   - Marvel Science Stories
MVT   - Marvel Tales
MYM   - Mystery Monthly Magazine
MYR   - Myrddin
MYSCURE - THE MYSTERIOUS CURE, J.O. Jeppson, co DBL 1985
MYSTHZN - MYSTERIES OF THE HORIZON, Lawrence Raab, co DBL 1972
n.   - novel
na   - novella
NAL   - New American Library: New York
NAR   - North American Review
NAS   - NEBULA AWARD STORIES, an
NCH   - New Classics House, Novel Books Inc.: Chicago
NCR   - Night Cry
NDB   - Nelson Doubleday, Inc.: Garden City, NY. Imprint of the
           Science Fiction Book Club.
NDM   - NEW DIMENSIONS, Robert Silverberg/Marta Randall, oa
NDP   - New Directions Publishing Corporation
NDT   - New Detective Magazine
NEA   - NEA Services, Inc.
NEB   - Nebula Science Fiction
NEDLFUL - THE NEEDLE ON FULL, Caroline Forbes, co OWP 1985
NEL   - Thomas Nelson, Inc.
NEM   - New England Magazine
NEW&SEL - NEW AND SELECTED POEMS, Ted Hughes, co HPR 1982
NEWMIND - THE NEW MIND, Roger Elwood, oa MAC 1973
nf   - non-fiction
NGTCHLS - NIGHT CHILLS, Kirby McCauley, an AVN 1975
NGTRIDE - NIGHT RIDE AND OTHER JOURNEYS, Charles Beaumont, co BAN
           1960
NGTSIDE - NIGHT-SIDE, Joyce Carol Oates, co 1977
NGV   - NIGHT VISIONS, Charles L. Grant, oa
NIE   - Niekas, fanzine published by Ed Meskys
NIVENSL - NIVEN'S LAWS, Larry Niven, co OLS 1984
NLB   - New English Library: London
NLR   - National Review
NLY   - F. Tennyson Neely: New York & Chicago
NOR   - Norstrilia Press: Melbourne, Australia
NOV   - NOVA, Harry Harrison, oa
Nov   - November
NPP   - North Point Press
NPT   - New Pathways into Science Fiction and Fantasy, MGA
           Services, P.O. Box 863994, Plano TX 75086-3994
NPTNRIS - NEPTUNE RISING, Jane Yolen, co PHM 1982
NRV   - New Review
NSA   - The New Satirist
NSF   - NESFA Press: Cambridge, MA
NSJ   - National Storyteller Journal
NSTRTBB - THE NOEL STREATFIELD BIRTHDAY BOOK
NTA   - The National Amateur
NTLCTHU - NEW TALES OF THE CTHULHU MYTHOS, Ramsey Campbell, oc ARK
           1980
NTLSPTM - NEW TALES OF SPACE AND TIME, Raymond J. Healy, oa HLT
           1951
NTLSTRR - NEW TALES OF TERROR, Hugh Lamb, oa MGB 1980
NTSSFWR - NOTES TO A SCIENCE FICTION WRITER, Ben Bova, co SCB 1975
NTVOICE - NIGHT VOICES, Robert Aickman, co GOL 1985
nv   - novelette
NVNSLWS - NIVEN'S LAWS, Larry Niven, co PHS 1984

NVP   - New Victoria Publishers, Inc.: Lebanon, NH
NWA   - New American Review
NWF   - NEW WORLDS OF FANTASY, Terry Carr, an ACE
NWISLND - NEW ISLANDS, Maria Luisa Bombal, co FSG 1982
NWQ   - NEW WORLDS QUARTERLY, Michael Moorcock, oa SPH & BKM
NWR   - NEW WRITINGS IN SF, oa
NWS   - New Worlds, British magazine
NWT   - NEW TERRORS, Ramsey Campbell, oa PAN 1980
NWTSPTM - NEW TALES OF SPACE AND TIME, Raymond J. Healey, oa HLT
           1951
NWV   - NEW VOICES IN SCIENCE FICTION, George R.R. Martin, oa
NXTEDIT - NEXT EDITIONS, 1980 [Angela Carter]
NYC   - Nyctalops
NYH   - The New York Herald
NYM   - New Yorker Magazine
NYR   - The New York Review of Books
oa   - original anthology
OBK   - THE OMNI BOOK OF SCIENCE FICTION, Ellen Datlow, an ZEB
oc   - original collection
Oct   - October
OCT   - Octopus Books Limited: London
ODP   - Odyssey Publications: Melrose Highlands, MA
OLDFIRE - OLD FIRES AND PROFITABLE GHOSTS, Sir Arthur
           Quiller-Couch, co SCB 1900
OLDMNBD - OLD MAN'S BEARD, H. Russell Wakefield, co BLS 1929
OLDTOWN - OLD TOWN FIRESIDE STORIES, Harriet Beecher Stowe, co OSG
           1871
OLS   - Owlswick Press: Philadelphia
om   - omnibus edition
OMEGA   - OMEGA, Roger Elwood, oa WKR 1973
OMN   - Omni
ONCEGNT - ONCE THERE WAS A GIANT, Keith Laumer, co TOR 1984
ORB   - ORBIT, Damon Knight, oa
ORI   - Oriental Stories
ORN   - Orion
OSF   - Orbit Science Fiction
OSG   - James R. Osgood: Boston
OTR   - Outre, J. Vernon Shea, ed.
OUI   - Oui
OUT   - Outworlds, William L. Bowers, ed.
OUTEVRY - OUT OF THE EVERYWHERE, AND OTHER EXTRAORDINARY VISIONS,
           James Tiptree, Jr., co BAL 1981
OUTOFHD - OUT OF MY HEAD, Robert Bloch, co NSF 1986
OUTOFTM - OUT OF TIME, Aidan Chambers, oa BDL 1984
OWF   - Owlflight
OWL   - OTHER WORLDS, Roy Torgesson, oa ZEB
OWLTIME - OWL TIME, M.A. Foster, oc DAW 1985
OWP   - Onlywomen Press: London
OWS   - Other Worlds
PALEAPE - THE PALE APE AND OTHER PULSES, M.P. Shiel, co LUR 1911
PAN   - Pan Books, Ltd.: London
PASTIME - PAST TIMES, Poul Anderson, co TOR 1984
pb   - paperback
PBK   - Paperback Library
PBM   - Potboiler Magazine
PBP   - Playboy Press: New York
PBY   - Playboy magazine
PCB   - Poetry Chapbook, Star/Sword Publications
PCM   - Popular Computing
PCTEXHB - PICTURES AT AN EXHIBITION, Ian Watson, oa GML 1981
PDD   - Pudding Magazine
PDN   - Philadelphia Dollar Newspaper
PEN   - Penguin Books: London
PFP   - Puffin Post
PGP   - Pangloss Papers
PHG   - Phantasmagoria
PHM   - Philomel Books
PHP   - Phantasia Press: West Bloomfield, MI
PHS   - The Philadelphia Science Fiction Society
PHT   - The Phantagraph
pi   - pictorial
PIC   - Piccolo Books, Pan Books Ltd.: London
PIG   - Pig Iron
PIN   - Pinnacle Books: New York
PIO   - The Pioneer
PIT   - Proceedings of the Institute for Twenty-First Century
           Studies
PLANETS - THE PLANETS, Byron Preiss, oa BAN 1985
PLE   - Plant Engineering
PLNTENG - PLAN[E]T ENGINEERING, Gene Wolfe, co NSF 1984
PLP   - Pulpsmith
PLS   - Planet Stories
pm   - poem
PMM   - Pall Mall Magazine
PMSNW&S - POEMS: NEW AND SELECTED (1957-1983), Robert Sward, co
           AYA 1983
PNT   - Pennyfarthing Press: San Francisco, CA
PNT   - Penthouse
POHLSTR - POHLSTARS, Frederik Pohl, co BAL 1984
POT   - Clarkson N. Potter, Publishers: New York
POW   - Powell Publications
pp   - number of pages
PPC   - Press Porcepic: Victoria, BC Canada
pr   - preface
PRB   - Parabola: Myth and the Quest for Meaning
PRH   - Prentice-Hall, Inc.
PRM   - Le Preambule: Longueuil, Quebec
PROTEUS - PROTEUS, Richard S. McEnroe, oa ACE 1981
PROTOST - PROTOSTARS, David Gerrold & Stephen Goldin, ca BAL 1971
PRPTLGT - PERPETUAL LIGHT, Alan Ryan, oa WBK 1982
PRS   - Pearson's Magazine

PRSDMAR - THE PRAESIDIUM OF ARCHIVE, Jefferson P. Swycaffer, oc
           AVN 1986
PSP   - Pierian Spring (Brandon, Manitoba)
PTH   - Panther Books Ltd.: London
PUL   - PULSAR, George Hay, oa PEN
PUN   - Punch
PUR   - Puritan Magazine
PUT   - G.P. Putnam's Sons: New York
PVL   - The Pavlat Report, Larry Shaw, ed.
PWRTIME - THE POWER OF TIME, Josephine Saxton, co C&W 1985
PYR   - Pyramid Books
pz   - puzzle
QDPHBIA - QUADRIPHOBIA, Alan Ryan, oc DBL 1986
qp   - quality paperback
QPB   - Quality Paperback Book Club
QRK   - QUARK, Samuel R. Delany & Marilyn Hacker, oa PBK
QRT   - Quartet Books Limited: London
QRY   - Quarry Magazine
RAN   - Rand, McNally & Company
RBK   - Redbook Magazine
RCR   - Red Clay Reader
RCS   - Rolling Stone College Papers
REACH   - THE REACH AND OTHER STORIES, Lilian Mohin & Sheila
           Shulman, an OWP 1984
REP   - Reporter
RHIALTO - RHIALTO THE MARVELLOUS, Jack Vance, n. Baen 1985 reprint
           contains the short story "Basileus" by C.J. Cherryh and
           Janet Moris, excerpted from a forthcoming original
           anthology HEROES IN HELL.
RIDDLE& - THE RIDDLE AND OTHER STORIES, Walter de la Mare, co S&B
           1923
RIG   - Rigel
RMINTWR - THE ROOM IN THE TOWER AND OTHER STORIES, E.F. Benson, co
           M&B 1912
RMSPRDS - ROOMS OF PARADISE, Lee Harding, oa 1978
RNDMACC - RABDOM ACCESS MESSAGES OF THE COMPUTER AGE, Thomas F.
           Monteleone, an HBC 1984
ROG   - Rogue Magazine
ROGUEBO - ROGUE BOLO, Keith Laumer, oc BAE 1986
RSC   - Rolling Stone College Papers
RST   - Rolling Stone
RTF&PPP - RETIEF AND THE PANGALACTIC PAGEANT OF PULCHRITUDE, Keith
           Laumer, co BAE 1986
RUNAMCK - RUNNING A MUCK, John Caldwell, co WDG 1978
S&B   - Selwyn and Blount: London
S&S   - SWORD AND SORCERESS, Marion Zimmer Bradley, oa DAW
S&T   - Space and Time
S*L   - Star*Line
S.F.B.C. - Science Fiction Book Club: Garden City, NY
S/P   - Scream/Press: Santa Cruz, CA
S83   - Science 83
S84   - Science 84
sa   - story adaptation of a play/screenplay
SADNSPM - SADNESS OF SPACEMEN, Robert Priest, co DRD 1980
SAO   - The South Australian Odd Fellows' Magazine
SAP   - Sorcerer's Apprentice
SAS   - Simon and Schuster, Inc.: New York
SAT   - Satellite Science Fiction
SBH   - STAR BOOK OF HORROR, Hugh Lamb, an STB
SCB   - Charles Scribner's Sons: New York
SCF   - Science Fantasy
SCHLRYM - THE SCHOLARLY MOUSE AND OTHER STORIES, 1957
SCIAGMN - SCIENCE AGAINST MAN, Anthony Cheetham, oa AVN 1970
SCK   - Schocken Books: New York
SCR   - Scribner's Magazine
SDA   - Stardate: The Multi-Media Science Fiction Magazine
SDW   - SHADOWS, Charles L. Grant, oa DBL
SEA   - The Seabury Press: New York
SELPMCS - SELECTED POEMS, Clark Ashton Smith, co ARK 1971
SELWRTC - SELECTED WRITINGS OF TRUMAN CAPOTE, Truman Capote, co
           1947
Sep   - September
SEP   - The Saturday Evening Post
SEV   - Seventeen
sf   - special feature
SF+   - Science Fiction Plus
SFA   - Science Fiction Adventures
SFB   - Science Fiction Adventures, British
SFC   - Scott, Foresman and Company: Glenview, IL
SFMRKTW - THE SCIENCE FICTION OF MARK TWAIN, ed. David Ketterer,
           co ACH 1984
SFQ   - Science Fiction Quarterly
SFS   - (The Original) Science Fiction Stories
SFTALES - SCIENCE FICTION TALES, Roger Elwood, oa RAN 1973
SFW   - SFWA Bulletin
SHDW3rd - THE SHADOWY THIRD AND OTHER STORIES, Ellen Glasgow, co
           DBL 1923
SHOWCSE - SHOWCASE, Roger Elwood, oa HPR 1973
SHPSHFT - SHAPE SHIFTERS, Jane Yolen, an SEA 1978
SHS   - Shasta Publishers
SHY   - Shayol
si   - section introduction
SIG   - Signet Books (NAL): New York
SIXTEEN - SIXTEEN, Donald Gallo, an DCT
SKTNCRW - SKELETON CREW, Stephen King, co PUT 1985
sl   - serial segment
SLIPPRY - SLIPPERY AND OTHER STORIES, R.A. Lafferty, oc DRM 1985
SLM   - Southern Literary Messenger
SLNCAMR - THE SILENCE OF AMOR, Fiona MacLeod, 1896
SLR   - The Seattle Review
SME   - Something Else
SMGSTST - SOME GHOST STORIES, A.M. Burrage, co 1927

SMI   - The Smith
SML   - SPACE MAIL, Isaac Asimov, Martin H. Greenberg, George
           R.R. Martin & Charles G. Waugh, an FAW
SMLPNCH - A SMALL PINCH OF WEATHER, Joan Aiken, co CAP 1974
SMM   - The Saint Mystery Magazine
SMNINRM - SOMEONE IN THE ROOM, Ex-Private X, co 1931
SMP   - St. Martin's Press: New York
SMTMNVR - SOMETIME, NEVER, Anonymous, oa EYR 1956
SMY   - Small Maynard, Publishers: Boston
sn   - short novel
SND   - The Strand Magazine, London
SNN   - Sono Nis: Victoria
SNR   - San Francisco Review
SNT&REL - SAINTS AND RELICS, Rosemary Pardoe
SNV   - SUPERNOVA, Philip Pollock, oa FAB
SOULCTY - SOUL OF THE CITY, Robert Lynn Asprin & Lynn Abbey, oa
           ACE 1986
sp   - speech
SPC   - SPACE, Richard Davis, oa ABS
SPECLTN - SPECULATIONS, Isaac Asimov & Alice Laurance, oa HMF 1982
SPECTER - SPECTER!, Bill Pronzini, an ARH 1982
SPH   - Sphere Books Limited: London
SPINOZA - THE SPINOZA OF MARKET STREET, Isaac Bashevis Singer, co
           FSG 1958
SPL   - The Spirit Lamp, Oxford
SPN   - Spinster
Spr   - Spring
SPS   - Space Stories
SRCRAPR - SORCERER'S APPRENTICE [Tanith Lee]
ss   - short story
SSF   - Space Science Fiction
SSP   - Shoe String Press: Hamden, CT
SSS   - Super Science Stories
SST   - Science Stories
STARSNO - STAR SHORT NOVELS, Frederik Pohl, oa BAL 1954
STB   - Star Books, W.H. Allen & Co. Ltd.: London
STL   - STELLAR, Judy-Lynn del Rey, oa BAL
STLSNOV - STELLAR SHORT NOVELS, Judy-Lynn del Rey, oa BAL 1976
STM   - Startling Mystery Stories
STO   - Story Magazine
STR   - STAR SCIENCE FICTION STORIES, Frederik Pohl, oa BAL
STRGATR - STRANGE ATTRACTIONS, Damien Broderick, oa H&I 1985
STRMSSN - STORM SEASON, Robert Lynn Asprin & Lynn Abbey, oa ACE
           1984
STRNGBD - STRANGE BEDFELLOWS, Thomas N. Scortia, an RDM 1972
STRNGTH - STRANGE THINGS HAPPEN, Robert Randolph Medcalf, Jr.,
           Quixsilver Press 1981
STRYQBC - STORIES FROM QUEBEC, Philip Stratford, an VNR 1974
STS   - Startling Stories
STT   - Strange Tales
STYNTRD - THE SATURDAY NIGHT READER, an [Angela Carter]
Sum   - Summer
SUN   - The Sun newspaper
SUP   - Super Science Fiction
SUPRHOR - SUPERHORROR, Ramsey Campbell, oa ALL 1976
SUPRNRD - THE SUPERNATURAL READER, Groff & Lucy Conklin, an LIP
           1953
SVNGWRL - SAVING WORLDS, Roger Elwood & Virginia Kidd, oa DBL 1973
SVT   - Survival Tomorrow
SVYDRMS - SAVOY DREAMS, 1983
SWC   - Sewickley Magazine
SWD   - SWORDS AGAINST DARKNESS, Andrew J. Offutt, oa ZEB
SWDAGTM - SWORDS AGAINST TOMORROW, Robert Hoskins, an SIG 1970
SWK   - Swank
SWO   - SPWAO Showcase
SYA   - Spicy-Adventure Stories
TABOO   - TABOO, Anonymous, oa NCH 1964
TAMASTR - TAMASTARA, Tanith Lee, DAW 1984
TDA   - Ten Detective Aces
TDW   - Today's Woman
TDY   - Today, The Philadelphia Inquirer Magazine
TERRORS - TERRORS, Charles L. Grant, oa PBP 1982
TESRCTS - TESSERACTS, Judith Merril, oa PPC 1985
THP   - Thendara House Publications: Berkeley, CA
THRUELG - THROUGH ELEGANT EYES, R.A. Lafferty, co CBR 1983
THSKIND - THIS KIND OF WAR, T.R. Fehrenbach, nf 1963
THVSWLD - THIEVES' WORLD, Robert Lynn Asprin, oa ACE 1979
TIG   - Tiger
TKG   - TK Graphics: Baltimore, MD
TLE   - The Leading Edge, 3163 JKHB, Provo UT 84602
TLSCTHU - TALES OF THE CTHULHU MYTHOS, August Derleth, an ARK 1969
TLSFRAM - TALES OF THE FREE AMAZONS, Marion Zimmer Bradley, an THP
           1980
TLSHRSY - TALES OF HEARSAY, Joseph Conrad, co DBL 1925
TLSTRVL - TALES OF A TRAVELLER, Washington Irving, co 1824
TLSWNDR - TALES OF WONDER, Jane Yolen, co SCK 1983
TMP   - Le Temps
TMPTRLM - TIME PATROLMAN, Poul Anderson, oc TOR 1983
TNGFIRE - TONGUES OF FIRE, Algernon Blackwood, co JNK 1924
TNGSCNS - TONGUES OF CONSCIENCE, Robert S. Hichens, co MTH 1900
TOCHPPL - TO THE CHAPEL PERILOUS, Naomi Mitchison, co A&U 1955
TOMOBED - TOM O'BEDLAM'S NIGHT OUT AND OTHER STRANGE EXCURSIONS,
           Darrell Schweitzer, co GNL 1985
TOR   - Tor Books, Tom Doherty Associates: New York
TRAFFIC - TRAFFICS AND DISCOVERIES, Rudyard Kipling, co MAC 1904
TRE   - The Virginia City Territorial Enterprise
TRI   - Trident Press
TRK   - Triskell Press
TRMNLBH - TERMINAL BEACH, J.G. Ballard, co GOL 1964
TRNGPTS - TURNING POINTS: ESSAYS ON THE ART OF SCIENCE FICTION,
           ed. Damon Knight, an 1977
TRNPLCE - THE TURNING PLACE, Jean A. Karl, oc DUT 1976